Get Connected.

FEATURES

LearnSmart™

McGraw-Hill LearnSmart is an adaptive learning program that identifies what an individual student knows and doesn't know. LearnSmart's adaptive learning path helps students learn faster, study more efficiently, and retain more knowledge. Reports available for both students and instructors indicate where students need to study more and assess their success rate in retaining knowledge.

Graphing Tool

The graphing tool within Connect Economics provides opportunities for students to draw, interact with, manipulate, and analyze graphs in their online auto-graded assignments, as they would with pencil and paper. The Connect graphs are identical in presentation to the graphs in the book, so students can easily relate their assignments to their reading material.

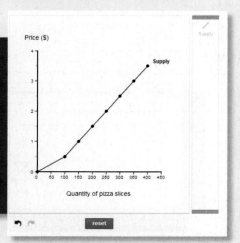

Get Engaged.

eBooks

Connect Plus includes a media-rich eBook that allows you to share your notes with your students. Your students can insert and review their own notes, highlight the text, search for specific information, and interact with media resources. SmartBook is an adaptive eBook that is personalized for each student. Highlighted sections change depending on a student's knowledge, backed by LearnSmart, so students always know what to focus on.

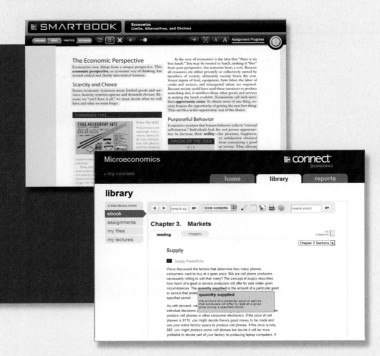

Tegrity Lecture Capture

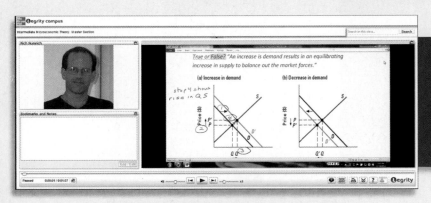

Make your classes available anytime, anywhere with simple, one-click recording. Students can search for a word or phrase and be taken to the exact place in your lecture that they need to review.

MICROECONOMICS

The McGraw-Hill Economics Series

ESSENTIALS OF ECONOMICS

Brue, McConnell, and Flynn
Essentials of Economics
Third Edition

Mandel
Economics: The Basics
Second Edition

Schiller
Essentials of Economics
Eighth Edition

PRINCIPLES OF ECONOMICS

Colander
Economics, Microeconomics, and Macroeconomics
Ninth Edition

Frank and Bernanke
Principles of Economics, Principles of Microeconomics, Principles of Macroeconomics
Fifth Edition

Frank and Bernanke
Brief Editions: Principles of Economics, Principles of Microeconomics, Principles of Macroeconomics
Second Edition

McConnell, Brue, and Flynn
Economics, Microeconomics, Macroeconomics
Nineteenth Edition

McConnell, Brue, and Flynn
Brief Editions: Microeconomics and Macroeconomics
Second Edition

Miller
Principles of Microeconomics
First Edition

Samuelson and Nordhaus
Economics, Microeconomics, and Macroeconomics
Nineteenth Edition

Schiller
The Economy Today, The Micro Economy Today, and The Macro Economy Today
Thirteenth Edition

Slavin
Economics, Microeconomics, and Macroeconomics
Eleventh Edition

ECONOMICS OF SOCIAL ISSUES

Guell
Issues in Economics Today
Sixth Edition

Sharp, Register, and Grimes
Economics of Social Issues
Twentieth Edition

ECONOMETRICS

Gujarati and Porter
Basic Econometrics
Fifth Edition

Gujarati and Porter
Essentials of Econometrics
Fourth Edition

Hilmer and Hilmer
Practical Econometrics
First Edition

MANAGERIAL ECONOMICS

Baye and Prince
Managerial Economics and Business Strategy
Eighth Edition

Brickley, Smith, and Zimmerman
Managerial Economics and Organizational Architecture
Fifth Edition

Thomas and Maurice
Managerial Economics
Eleventh Edition

INTERMEDIATE ECONOMICS

Bernheim and Whinston
Microeconomics
Second Edition

Dornbusch, Fischer, and Startz
Macroeconomics
Twelfth Edition

Frank
Microeconomics and Behavior
Eighth Edition

ADVANCED ECONOMICS

Romer
Advanced Macroeconomics
Fourth Edition

MONEY AND BANKING

Cecchetti and Schoenholtz
Money, Banking, and Financial Markets
Third Edition

URBAN ECONOMICS

O'Sullivan
Urban Economics
Eighth Edition

LABOR ECONOMICS

Borjas
Labor Economics
Sixth Edition

McConnell, Brue, and Macpherson
Contemporary Labor Economics
Tenth Edition

PUBLIC FINANCE

Rosen and Gayer
Public Finance
Tenth Edition

Seidman
Public Finance
First Edition

ENVIRONMENTAL ECONOMICS

Field and Field
Environmental Economics: An Introduction
Sixth Edition

INTERNATIONAL ECONOMICS

Appleyard and Field
International Economics
Eighth Edition

King and King
International Economics, Globalization, and Policy: A Reader
Fifth Edition

Pugel
International Economics
Fifteenth Edition

MICROECONOMICS

Dean Karlan

Yale University and Innovations for Poverty Action

Jonathan Morduch

New York University

With special contribution by

Meredith L. Startz

Yale University and Innovations for Poverty Action

Mc
Graw
Hill
Education

MICROECONOMICS

Published by McGraw-Hill Education, 2 Penn Plaza, New York, NY 10121. Copyright © 2014 by McGraw-Hill Education. All rights reserved. Printed in the United States of America. No part of this publication may be reproduced or distributed in any form or by any means, or stored in a database or retrieval system, without the prior written consent of McGraw-Hill Education, including, but not limited to, in any network or other electronic storage or transmission, or broadcast for distance learning.

Some ancillaries, including electronic and print components, may not be available to customers outside the United States.

This book is printed on acid-free paper.

1 2 3 4 5 6 7 8 9 0 RJC/RJC 1 0 9 8 7 6 5 4 3

ISBN: 978-0-07-733258-7
MHID: 0-07-733258-X

Senior Vice President, Products & Markets: *Kurt L. Strand*
Vice President, Content Production & Technology Services: *Kimberly Meriwether David*
Managing Director: *Douglas Reiner*
Executive Director of Development: *Ann Torbert*
Development Editor: *Alyssa Lincoln*
Director of Digital Content: *Douglas A. Ruby*
Digital Development Editor: *Kevin Shanahan*
Digital Development Editor: *Meg Maloney*
Marketing Manager: *Katie White Hoenicke*
Director, Content Production: *Terri Schiesl*
Content Project Managers: *Marianne L. Musni* and *Lori Koetters*
Senior Buyer: *Debra R. Sylvester*
Senior Designer: *Matt Diamond*
Cover Image: *Roman Samokhin/Shutterstock.com*
Lead Content Licensing Specialist: *Keri Johnson*
Typeface: *10/12 Palatino Roman*
Compositor: *Laserwords Private Limited*
Printer: *R. R. Donnelley*

All credits appearing on page or at the end of the book are considered to be an extension of the copyright page.

Library of Congress Cataloging-in-Publication Data

Karlan, Dean S.
   Microeconomics / Dean Karlan, Yale University and Innovations for Poverty Action; Jonathan Morduch, New York University ; with special contribution by Meredith L. Startz, Yale University and Innovations for Poverty Action.—First edition.
      pages cm.—(the McGraw-Hill series economics)
   Includes index.
   ISBN-13: 978-0-07-733258-7 (alk. paper)
   ISBN-10: 0-07-733258-X (alk. paper)
   1. Microeconomics I. Morduch, Jonathan. II. Title.
HB172.K36 2014
338.5—dc23

                                                                              2013018523

The Internet addresses listed in the text were accurate at the time of publication. The inclusion of a website does not indicate an endorsement by the authors or McGraw-Hill Education, and McGraw-Hill Education does not guarantee the accuracy of the information presented at these sites.

We dedicate this book to our families.

–Dean and Jonathan

dedication

Dean Karlan

Dean Karlan is Professor of Economics at Yale University and President and Founder of Innovations for Poverty Action (IPA). Dean started IPA in 2002, with two aims: to help learn what works and what does not in the fight against poverty and other social problems around the world, and then to implement successful ideas at scale. IPA now works in over 45 countries, with 800 employees around the world. Dean's personal research focuses on using field experiments to learn more about how microfinance works and how to make it work better. His research uses ideas from behavioral economics, and also covers fundraising, voting, health, and education. In recent work, for example, he has studied the impact of microcredit on the lives of the poor, and has worked to create better financial products in the United States to help people manage debt. Dean is also President and cofounder of stickK.com, a start-up that helps people use commitment contracts to achieve personal goals, such as losing weight or completing a problem set on time. Dean is a Sloan Foundation Research Fellow, and in 2007 was awarded a Presidential Early Career Award for Scientists and Engineers. He is coeditor of the *Journal of Development Economics* and on the editorial board of *American Economic Journal: Applied Economics*. He holds a BA from University of Virginia, an MPP and MBA from University of Chicago, and a PhD in Economics from MIT. In 2011, he coauthored *More Than Good Intentions: Improving the Ways the World's Poor Borrow, Save, Farm, Learn, and Stay Healthy.*

Jonathan Morduch

Jonathan Morduch is Professor of Public Policy and Economics at New York University's Wagner Graduate School of Public Service. Jonathan focuses on innovations that expand the frontiers of finance and how financial markets shape economic growth and inequality. Jonathan has lived and worked in Asia, but his newest study follows families in California, Mississippi, Ohio, Kentucky, and New York as they cope with economic ups and downs over a year. The new study jumps off from ideas in *Portfolios of the Poor: How the World's Poor Live on $2 a Day* (Princeton University Press, 2009) which he coauthored and which describes how families in Bangladesh, India, and South Africa devise ways to make it through a year living on $2 a day or less. Jonathan's research on financial markets is collected in *The Economics of Microfinance* and *Banking the World,* both published by MIT Press. At NYU, Jonathan is Executive Director of the Financial Access Initiative, a center that supports research on extending access to finance in low-income communities. Jonathan's ideas have also shaped policy through work with the United Nations, World Bank, and other international organizations. In 2009, the Free University of Brussels awarded Jonathan an honorary doctorate to recognize his work on microfinance. He holds a BA from Brown and a PhD from Harvard, both in Economics.

Karlan and Morduch first met in 2001 and have been friends and colleagues ever since. Before writing this text, they collaborated on research on financial institutions. Together, they've written about new directions in financial access for the middle class and poor, and in Peru they set up a laboratory to study incentives in financial contracts for loans to women to start small enterprises. In 2006, together with Sendhil Mullainathan, they started the Financial Access Initiative, a center dedicated to expanding knowledge about financial solutions for the half of the world's adults who lack access to banks. This text reflects their shared passion for using economics to help solve problems, both in everyday life and in the broader world.

brief contents

ix

We offer this text, *Microeconomics*, as a resource for professors who want to *keep their students engaged* and who have been seeking to *deliver core economic concepts* along with an introduction to *important new ideas* in economic thought. We designed the text to help students see economics as a common thread that enables us to understand, analyze, and solve problems in our local communities and around the world.

Why Do We Teach Economics?

Economics helps us solve problems.

Economic principles can help students understand and respond to everyday situations. Economic ideas are also helping us tackle big challenges, such as fixing our health care system and keeping the government fiscally solvent. We show students how economic ideas are shaping their world, and we provide them with a wide-ranging set of practical insights to help develop their economic intuition.

Engagement with real-world problems is built into the fabric of our chapters, and throughout the text we present economic thinking as a common thread to help solve these. This compelling, problem-solving focus simplifies and streamlines the teaching of basic economic concepts by approaching topics intuitively and in a way that is useful to students. The text imparts to students the *immediacy* of how what they're learning *really matters*. As they read, faculty and students will find content that *breaks down barriers* between what goes on in the classroom and what is going on in our nation and around the world.

By providing a concrete, intuitive approach to introductory concepts, and by keeping the discussion always down-to-earth and lively, we make the learning materials easier to use in the classroom. The chapters are organized around a familiar curriculum while adding empirical context for ideas that students often find overly abstract or too simplified. The innovative, empirical orientation of the book enables us to incorporate intriguing findings from recent studies as well as to address material from such areas as game theory, finance, behavioral economics, and political economy. This approach connects concepts in introductory economics to important new developments in economic research, while placing a premium on *easy-to-understand explanations*.

In every chapter we fulfill three fundamental commitments:

- **To show how economics can solve real-life problems.** This text will engage students by approaching economics as a way of explaining real people and their decisions, and by providing a set of tools that serve to solve many different types of problems. *We show students that economics can make the world a better place*, while challenging them to reach their own conclusions about what "better" really means.
- **To teach principles as analytic tools for dealing with real situations.** The text is centered on examples and issues that resonate with students' experience. Applications come *first*, reinforcing the relevance of the tools that students acquire. Engaging empirical cases are interspersed throughout the content. The applications open up puzzles, anomalies, and possibilities that basic economic principles help explain. The aim is, first and foremost, to ensure that students gain an intuitive grasp of basic ideas.

- **To focus on what matters to students.** Students live in a digital, globalized world. We recognize that they are knowledgeable and care about both local and international issues. *Microeconomics* takes a global perspective, with the United States as a leading example. We remain faithful to the core principles of economics, but we seek to share with students some of the ways that new ideas are expanding the "basics" of economic theory. We recognize and explain the rise of game theory, behavioral economics, and experimental and empirical approaches, in ways that matter to students.

We are excited to offer standalone chapters that dig into some of the new topics in economics, as part of our commitment to teaching economics as a way to help solve important problems. We've watched as topics like political economy, game theory, behavioral economics, and inequality figure more and more prominently in undergraduate curricula with each passing year, and we felt it was important to provide teachers ways to share new ideas and evidence with their students—important concepts that most nonmajors would usually miss. We know how selective teachers must be in choosing which material to cover during the limited time available. In light of this, we've been especially glad to have the guidance we've received from many teachers in finding ways to expose students to some of the newer, and most exciting, parts of economics today.

We promise you will find the discussion and writing style of *Microeconomics* clear, concise, accessible, easy to teach from, and fun to read. We hope that this book will inspire students to continue their studies in economics, and we promise that *Microeconomics* will give them something useful to take away even if they choose other areas of study.

Motivation

Who are we?

Microeconomics draws on our own experiences as academic economists, teachers, and policy advisors. We are based at large research universities, offering advice to NGOs, governments, international agencies, donors, and private firms. Much of our research involves figuring out how to improve the way real markets function. Working with partners in the United States and on six continents, we are involved in testing new economic ideas. *Microeconomics* draws on the spirit of that work, as well as similar research, taking students through the process of engaging with real problems, using analytical tools to devise solutions, and ultimately showing what works and why.

Why have we written this text?

One of the best parts of writing this text has been getting to spend time with instructors across the country. We've been inspired by their creativity and passion and have learned from their pedagogical ideas. One of the questions we often ask is why the instructors originally became interested in economics. A common response, which we share, is an attraction to the logic and power of economics as a social science. We also often hear instructors describe something slightly different: the way that economics appealed to them as a tool for making sense of life's complexities, whether in business, politics, or daily life. We wrote this book to give instructors a way to share with their students both of those ways that economics matters.

Comprehensive and engaging, *Microeconomics* will provide students a solid foundation for considering important issues that they will confront in life. We hope that, in ways small and large, the tools they learn in these pages will help them to think critically about their environment and to live better lives.

Dean Karlan
Yale University

Jonathan Morduch
New York University

economics as a common thread

This text demonstrates how students can use basic economic principles to understand, analyze, and solve problems in their communities and around the world. Several basic pedagogical principles guide the organization of the content and support the implementation of the approach:

- **Concrete teaches abstract.** Interesting questions *motivate the learning of core principles* by showing how they are relevant to students. As often as possible, examples and cases lead into theory.
- **Uses current ideas and media.** The text provides students a view of what is actually going on in the world and in economics *right now*. It is *current in its content, method, and media*.
- **Takes a problem-solving approach.** This text shows economics as a way to explain real people and their decisions, and provides tools that can be used to solve many different types of problems. To complement this problem-solving approach, the authors have taken special care to offer *high-quality end-of-chapter problem sets* that engage students with realistic questions. Smoothly integrated with the chapter text, there are at least two review questions and two problems for each learning objective. Four additional problems for each learning objective also are available in *Connect*.

Four Questions about How Economists Think

The text's discussion is framed by *four questions* that economists ask to break down a new challenge and analyze it methodically. These four questions are explored and then carried throughout *Microeconomics* as a consistent problem-solving approach to a wide variety of examples and case studies so as to demonstrate how they can be used to address real issues. By teaching the *right questions to ask,* the text provides students with a method for working through decisions they'll face as consumers, employees, entrepreneurs, and voters.

Question 1: What are the wants and constraints of those involved? This question introduces the concept of *scarcity*. It asks students to think critically about the preferences and resources driving decision making in a given situation. It links into discussions of utility functions, budget constraints, strategic behavior, and new ideas that expand our thinking about rationality and behavioral economics.

Question 2: What are the trade-offs? This question focuses on *opportunity cost*. It asks students to understand trade-offs when considering any decision, including factors that might go beyond the immediate financial costs and benefits. Consideration of trade-offs takes us to discussions of marginal decision making, sunk costs, nonmonetary costs, and discounting.

Question 3: How will others respond? This question asks students to focus on *incentives*, both their incentives and the incentives of others. Students consider how individual choices aggregate in both expected and unexpected ways, and what happens when incentives change. The question links into understanding supply and demand, elasticity, competition, taxation, game theory, and monetary and fiscal policy.

Question 4: Why isn't everyone already doing it? This question relates to *efficiency*. It asks students to start from an assumption that markets work to provide desired goods and services, and then to think carefully about why something that seems like a good idea isn't already being done. We encourage students to revisit their answers to the previous three questions and see if they missed something about the trade-offs, incentives, or other forces at work, or whether they are looking at a genuine market failure. This question ties in with a range of topics, including public goods, externalities, information gaps, monopoly, arbitrage, and how the economy operates in the long run versus the short run.

Unique Coverage

Microeconomics presents the core principles of economics, but also seeks to share with students some of the ways that new ideas are *expanding* the basics of economic theory. The sequence of chapters follows a fairly traditional route through the core principles. However, the chapters on individual decision making (Part 3) appear before those on firm decisions (Part 4). By thinking first about the choices faced by individuals, students can engage with ideas that more closely relate to their own experiences. In this way, the organization of the text makes core economic ideas more immediately intuitive and better prepares students to eventually understand the choices of firms, groups, and governments. The text proceeds step-by-step from the personal to the public, allowing students to build toward an understanding of aggregate decisions on a solid foundation of individual decision making.

Microeconomics offers several standalone chapters focused on new ideas that are expanding economic theory, which can add nuance and depth to the core principles curriculum:

8	**Behavioral Economics: A Closer Look at Decision Making**	*"I like that [this chapter] is shorter than most chapters so I can cover it in less time. It makes the introduction of this topic, which is super-engaging to students, more flexible for being worked into a class."* — Jennifer Vincent, *Champlain College*
9	**Game Theory and Strategic Thinking**	*"... uses very good examples with which the students are likely to be familiar."* —Greg Salzman, *Albion College*
10	**Information**	*"Excellent introduction to Information Economics—very readable and interesting. The fact that it is presented as an independent chapter is important. [It's] a welcome addition to a principles text."* –Max Grunbaum Nagiel, *Daytona State College*
11	**Time and Uncertainty**	*"This is a topic that trips students up more than other topics, yet it is very important in terms of thinking about business problems and health economics, and . . . is also the foundation for thinking about interest rates. The [chapter] also brings in a lot of 'gee whiz' facts that relate to the concepts and could make for college dinner table discussions."* –Ashley Hodgson, *St. Olaf College*
22	**Political Choices**	*"This is a refreshing chapter not seen in many other introductory level textbooks. The analysis is presented clearly and simply enough that the introductory student can understand it."* –Jason Rudbeck, *University of Georgia*
23	**Public Policy and Choice Architecture**	*"I hope it will intrigue students ... it did me!"* —Karla Lynch, *North Central Texas College*

The text's most important commitment is to make sure that students understand the basic analytical tools of economics. Because students sometimes need reinforcement with the math requirements, *Microeconomics* also contains six unique math appendixes that explain math topics important to understanding economics:

APPENDIX A	Math Essentials: Understanding Graphs and Slope
APPENDIX B	Math Essentials: Working with Linear Equations
APPENDIX C	Math Essentials: Calculating Percentage Change, Slope, and Elasticity
APPENDIX D	Math Essentials: The Area under a Linear Curve
APPENDIX E	Using Indifference Curves
APPENDIX F	Math Essentials: Compounding

McGraw-Hill Create™ enables you to select and arrange the combination of traditional and unique chapters and appendixes that will be perfect for *your* course, at an affordable price for *your* students.

modern teaching approach

In addition to the regular chapter features found in almost every textbook, this text includes several unique features that support a modern teaching approach.

Interesting Examples Open Each Chapter

Interesting examples open each chapter. These chapter-opening stories feature issues that consumers, voters, businesspeople, and family members face, and they are presented in an engaging, journalistic style. The examples then take students through relevant principles that can help frame and solve the economic problem at hand. Here is a sample of the chapter-opening features:

Making an Impact with Small Loans	The Season for Giving
The Origins of a T-Shirt	When Is $20 Not Quite $20?
Mobiles Go Global	Litterbugs Beware
Coffee Becomes Chic	A Solution for Student Loans?
A Broken Laser Pointer Starts an Internet Revolution	Is College Worth It?
	The Fields of California

REAL LIFE
Bazaar competition

Bazaars are often the most vibrant and colorful places in towns and cities around the world. International travelers are sometimes surprised to see massive bazaars that specialize in one very specific type of product, such as fruit, flowers, furniture, or fabric. In many cities, there are huge markets where hundreds and even thousands of vendors all sell exactly the same goods for exactly the same prices.

This tendency may seem perplexing. We sometimes see something similar in the United States: All the auto dealers in town may locate on the same road, for example. This increases the chances of attracting customers who want to test drive next to a ...

WHAT DO YOU THINK?
Is self-sufficiency a virtue?

Why should the United States trade with other countries? If every other country in the world were to disappear tomorrow, the United States would probably manage to fend for itself. It has plenty of fertile land, natural resources, people, and manufacturing capacity. In fact, many observers consider the value Americans place on self-sufficiency to be a cultural trait.

Based on what you now know about specialization and the gains from trade, what do you think about the value of exchange versus the value of self-sufficiency? Economists tend to line up in favor of free international trade; they argue that trade makes both ... ally better ...

What do you think?

1. Do you agree with any of these objections to free trade? Why? When is self-sufficiency more valuable than the gains from trade?
2. Is the choice between trade and self-sufficiency an either/or question? Is there a middle-of-the-road approach that would address concerns on both sides of this issue?

POTENTIALLY CONFUSING
Some books print the negative sign of elasticity estimates; others do not. Another way to think of an elasticity measure is as an absolute value. The *absolute value* of a number is its distance from zero, or its numerical value without regard to its sign. For example, the absolute values of 4 and −4 are both 4. The absolute value of elasticity measures the "size" of the response, while the sign measures its direction. Sometimes only the absolute value will be printed, when it is assumed that you know the direction of the change.

Special Features Build Interest

- **Real Life**—Describes a short case or policy question, findings from history or academic studies, and anecdotes from the field.

- **From Another Angle**—Shows a different way of looking at an economic concept. This feature can be a different way of thinking about a situation, a humorous story, or sometimes just an unusual application of a standard idea.

- **What Do You Think?**—Offers a longer case study, with implications for public policy and student-related issues. This feature offers relevant data or historical evidence and asks students to employ both economic analysis and normative arguments to defend a position. We leave the student with open-ended questions, which professors can assign as homework or use for classroom discussion.

- **Where Can It Take You?**—Directs students to classes, resources, or jobs related to the topic at hand. This feature shows students how they might apply what they learn in careers and as consumers.

- **Potentially Confusing** and **Hints**—Offer additional explanation of a concept or use of terminology that students may find confusing. Rather than smoothing over confusing ideas and language, the text calls attention to common misunderstandings and gives students the support they need to understand economic language and reasoning on a deeper level.

- **Concept Check**—Provides an opportunity at the end of each chapter section for students to quiz themselves on the preceding material before reading on. The Concept Check questions are keyed to related learning objectives, providing students with a built-in review tool and study device.

Strong Materials Support Learning

The chapters contain most of the standard end-of-chapter features to help students solidify and test their understanding of the concepts presented, as well as a few new ideas that expand on those concepts. The authors have taken particular care with student review and instructor materials to guide high-quality homework and test questions.

- **Summary**—Highlights and emphasizes the essential takeaways from the chapter.

- **Key Terms**—Lists the most important terms from the chapter.

- **Review Questions**—Guide students through review and application of the concepts covered in the chapter. The review questions range from straightforward questions about theories or formulas to more open-ended narrative questions.

- **Problems and Applications**—Can be assigned as homework, typically quantitative. All problems and applications are fully integrated with *Connect® Economics*, enabling online assignments and grading.

- **Quick-scan barcodes**—Provide quick, mobile connection to online resources, relevant articles, videos, and other useful student materials. Readers can scan the QR code included at the end of the chapter with their smartphone, or can access the materials via the Online Learning Center at **www.mhhe.com/karlanmorduch** and within *Connect Economics*.

- **Study Econ app**—Provides student study materials on the go. Chapter summaries, key term flashcards, important graphs, math prep, chapter quizzes, and more are available in a convenient app available for both Android and iOS, downloadable in their respective app stores.

- **Online graphing tutorial**—Presents interactive graphing exercises, intended to help students to develop their graphing and math skills in tandem with relevant economic concepts. Simple margin call-outs indicate where tutorial exercises are available to support chapter concepts. These tutorial exercises are located within *Connect Economics*.

> To improve your understanding of consumer, producer, and total surplus, try the online interactive graphing tutorial.

Complete Digital Integration

The Karlan and Morduch product has been built from the ground up in print and digital formats simultaneously, enabling *complete digital integration* of the text and related hands-on learning materials. By authoring content in *Connect* during the "manuscript phase," we have been able to rewrite content in the print version if it doesn't "work" in the digital environment—thus providing users with a **total digital solution.** All digital content is tagged to chapter learning objectives, and all homework and tutorial materials are easily available for download or online access. Further, as the following pages show, this text comes with a robust lineup of learning and teaching products, built for simple and reliable usability. **Read on...**

digital solutions

McGraw-Hill *Connect® Economics*

Less managing. More teaching. Greater learning.

Connect Economics is an online assignment and assessment solution that offers a number of powerful tools and features that make managing assignments easier so faculty can spend more time teaching. With *Connect Economics*, students can engage with their coursework anytime and anywhere, making the learning process more accessible and efficient.

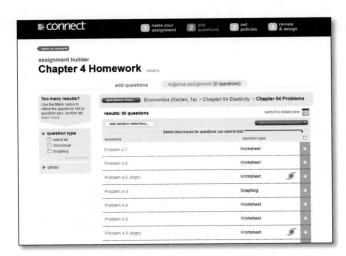

Simple assignment management

With *Connect Economics*, creating assignments is easier than ever, so you can spend more time teaching and less time managing. The assignment management function enables you to:

- Create and deliver assignments easily with selectable end-of-chapter questions and test bank items.
- Streamline lesson planning, student progress reporting, and assignment grading to make classroom management more efficient than ever.
- Go paperless with online submission and grading of student assignments.

Smart grading

Connect Economics helps students learn more efficiently by providing feedback and practice material when they need it, where they need it. The grading function enables instructors to:

- Score assignments automatically, giving students immediate feedback on their work and side-by-side comparisons with correct answers.
- Access and review each response; manually change grades or leave comments for students to review.
- Reinforce classroom concepts with practice tests and instant quizzes.

Instructor library

The *Connect Economics* Instructor Library is your repository for additional resources to improve student engagement in and out of class. You can select and use any asset that enhances your lecture.

Student study center

The *Connect Economics* Student Study Center is the place for students to access additional resources. The Student Study Center offers students quick access to lectures, practice materials, eBooks, study questions, and more.

Student progress tracking

Connect Economics keeps instructors informed about how each student, section, and class is performing, allowing for more productive use of lecture and office hours. The progress-tracking function enables instructors to:

- View scored work immediately and track individual or group performance with assignment and grade reports.
- Access an instant view of student or class performance relative to learning objectives.
- Collect data and generate reports required by many accreditation organizations like AACSB.

McGraw-Hill *Connect® Plus Economics*

McGraw-Hill reinvents the textbook learning experience for the modern student with *Connect Plus Economics*. A seamless integration of an eBook and *Connect Economics, Connect Plus Economics* provides all of the *Connect Economics* features plus the following:

- An integrated eBook, allowing for anytime, anywhere access to the textbook.
- Dynamic links between the problems or questions you assign to your students and the location in the eBook where that problem or question is covered.
- A powerful search function to pinpoint and connect key concepts in a snap.

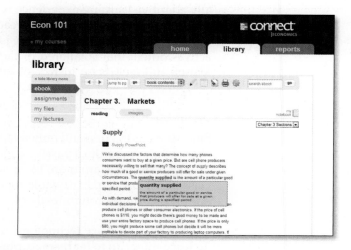

In short, *Connect Plus Economics* and *Connect Economics* offer you and your students powerful tools and features that optimize your time and energies, enabling you to focus on course content, teaching, and student learning. This state-of-the-art, thoroughly tested system supports you in preparing students for the world that awaits.

For more information about *Connect*, go to **www.mcgrawhillconnect.com, or contact your local McGraw-Hill sales representative.**

LearnSmart Advantage

McGraw Hill Education | LEARNSMART®

New from McGraw-Hill Education, LearnSmart Advantage is a series of adaptive learning products fueled by LearnSmart, the most widely used and intelligent adaptive learning resource on the market. Developed to deliver demonstrable results in boosting grades, increasing course retention, and strengthening memory recall, the LearnSmart Advantage series spans the entire learning process, from course preparation to the first adaptive reading experience. A smarter learning experience for students coupled with valuable reporting tools for instructors, LearnSmart Advantage is advancing learning like no other products in higher education today. The LearnSmart Advantage suite available with the Karlan/Morduch product is as follows.

Graphs of a single variable come in three main forms:

Do you know the answer? (Be honest.)

Yes | Probably | Maybe | No—Just guessing

LearnSmart

LearnSmart is one of the most effective and successful adaptive learning resources in the market today, proven to strengthen memory recall, keep students in class, and boost grades. Distinguishing what students know from what they don't, and honing in on concepts they are most likely to forget, LearnSmart continuously adapts to each student's needs by building an individual learning path so students study smarter and retain more knowledge. Reports provide valuable insight to instructors, so precious class time can be spent on higher-level concepts and discussion.

LearnSmart Achieve

LearnSmart Achieve is a revolutionary new learning system that combines a continually adaptive learning experience with necessary course resources to focus students on mastering concepts they don't already know. The program adjusts to each student individually as they progress, creating just-in-time learning experiences by presenting interactive content that is tailored to each student's needs. A convenient time-management feature and reports for instructors also ensure students stay on track.

SmartBook

SmartBook is the first and only adaptive reading experience available today. SmartBook changes reading from a passive and linear experience, to an engaging and dynamic one, in which students are more likely to master and retain important concepts, coming to class better prepared. Valuable reports provide instructors insight as to how students are progressing through textbook content, and are useful for shaping in-class time or assessment.

This revolutionary technology suite is available only from McGraw-Hill Education. To learn more, go to **learnsmart.prod.customer.mcgraw-hill.com** or contact your representative for a demo.

Tegrity Campus: Lectures 24/7

Tegrity Campus is a service that makes class time available 24/7 by automatically capturing every lecture in a searchable format for students to review when they study and complete assignments. With a simple one-click start-and-stop process, you capture all computer screens and corresponding audio. Students can replay any part of any class with easy-to-use browser-based viewing on a PC or Mac.

Educators know that the more students can see, hear, and experience class resources, the better they learn. In fact, studies prove it. With Tegrity Campus, students quickly recall key moments by using Tegrity Campus's unique search feature. This search helps students efficiently find what they need, when they need it, across an entire semester of class recordings. Help turn all your students' study time into learning moments immediately supported by your lecture.

To learn more about Tegrity watch a two-minute Flash demo at **http://tegritycampus .mhhe.com.**

McGraw-Hill Create™

The future of custom publishing is here. McGraw-Hill Create™ is a new, self-service website that allows you to quickly and easily create custom course materials by drawing upon McGraw-Hill's comprehensive, cross-disciplinary content and other third party resources. Creating your own custom book is easy. You, as an instructor, can:

- Select, then arrange the content in a way that makes the most sense for your course.
- Combine material from different sources and even upload your own content.
- Choose the best format for your students—print or eBook.
- Edit and update your course materials as often as you'd like.
- Receive your PDF review copy in minutes or a print review copy in just a few days.

Begin creating now at **www.mcgrawhillcreate.com.**

CourseSmart

CourseSmart is a new way for faculty to find and review eTextbooks. It's also a great option for students who are interested in accessing their course materials digitally. CourseSmart offers thousands of the most commonly adopted textbooks across hundreds of courses from a wide variety of higher education publishers. It is the only place for faculty to review and compare the full text of a textbook online. At CourseSmart, students can save up to 50% off the cost of a print book, reduce their impact on the environment, and gain access to powerful web tools for learning including full text search, notes and highlighting, and email tools for sharing notes between classmates. Complete tech support is also included with each title. Finding your eBook is easy. Visit **www.CourseSmart.com** and search by title, author, or ISBN.

supplements

All supplements have been developed from the ground up to accompany this text in a completely seamless integration. The following ancillaries are available for quick download and convenient access via the Online Learning Center at **www.mhhe.com/karlanmorduch** and within *Connect*. Instructor resources are password protected for security.

For the Student

Online content offers additional topics or more in-depth coverage. Some of the feature boxes, for example, are presented in short, preview form within chapters, with the full-length version presented online. An online *Guide to Data Sources* provides information about sources of economic data, along with brief exercises that give students opportunities to practice finding relevant data.

Multiple-choice quizzes, created by Greg Randolph at Southern New Hampshire University, allow students to test their knowledge on a chapter before attempting high-stakes homework assignments.

Student PowerPoints, created by Gregory Gilpin at Montana State University, provide a review of each chapter's main points and graphs.

Study Econ mobile app and barcodes

 McGraw-Hill is proud to offer a new mobile study app for students learning from Karlan and Morduch's *Microeconomics*. The features of the Study Econ app include flashcards for all key terms, a basic math review, fundamental graphs, customizable self-quizzes, chapter summaries, and common mistakes. Available for the Android and iOS operating systems. For additional information, please refer to the back inside cover of this book. Visit your mobile app stores and download a trial version of the Karlan and Morduch Study Econ app today!

 Further taking advantage of new technologies opening the door for improved pedagogy, scanning barcodes (or QR codes) are located near the end of every chapter. For students using smartphones and tablets, these barcodes provide immediate access to even more resources, such as videos relating to the chapter's discussion or news feeds.

For the Instructor

Test bank

Created by Jennifer Vincent at Champlain College. The test bank contains thousands of quality multiple-choice questions. Each question is tagged with the corresponding learning objective, level of difficulty, economic concept, AACSB learning category, and Bloom's Taxonomy objective. All of the test bank content is available to assign within *Connect*. The test bank is also available in EZ Test, a flexible and easy-to-use electronic testing program. Multiple versions of the test can be created and any test can be exported for use with course management systems such as WebCT, BlackBoard, or Page Out. EZ Test Online is a service that gives you a place to easily administer your EZ Test-created exams and quizzes online. The program is available for Windows and Mac environments.

PowerPoint presentations

Created by Gregory Gilpin at Montana State University. The PowerPoint presentations have been carefully crafted to ensure maximum usefulness in the classroom. Each presentation covers crucial information and supplies animated figures that are identical to those in the book. The presentations also contain sample exercises, instructor notes, and more.

Instructor's manual

Elements include:

- **Learning Objectives:** Lists the learning objectives for each chapter.
- **Chapter Outline:** Shows an outline of the chapter organization for a quick review.
- **Beyond the Lecture:** Presents ideas and activities you can use to start discussion and engage students in class, along with team exercises and assignments you can use outside of class, created by Greg Randolph at Southern New Hampshire University.
- **End-of-Chapter Solutions:** Provides answers to all end-of-chapter questions and problems, written by Diana Beck, New York University; Amanda Freeman, Kansas State University; and Victor Matheson, College of the Holy Cross. All end-of chapter answers and solutions have been accuracy checked by Peggy Dalton, Frostburg State University; Laura Maghoney, Solano Community College; and Daniel Lawson, Oakland Community College.

Assurance of Learning Ready

Many educational institutions today are focused on the notion of *assurance of learning*, an important element of some accreditation standards. Karlan and Morduch's *Microeconomics* is designed specifically to support your assurance of learning initiatives with a simple, yet powerful solution. Each test bank question for *Microeconomics* maps to a specific chapter learning outcome/objective listed in the text. You can use our test bank software, EZ Test and EZ Test Online, or in *Connect® Economics* to easily query for learning outcomes/objectives that directly relate to the learning objectives for your course. You can then use the reporting features of EZ Test to aggregate student results in similar fashion, making the collection and presentation of assurance of learning data simple and easy.

AACSB Statement

McGraw-Hill Education is a proud corporate member of AACSB International. Understanding the importance and value of AACSB accreditation, Karlan and Morduch's *Microeconomics* recognizes the curricula guidelines detailed in the AACSB standards for business accreditation by connecting selected questions in the text and the test bank to the six general knowledge and skill guidelines in the AACSB standards.

The statements contained in *Microeconomics* are provided only as a guide for the users of this textbook. The AACSB leaves content coverage and assessment within the purview of individual schools, the mission of the school, and the faculty. While *Microeconomics* and the teaching package make no claim of any specific AACSB qualification or evaluation, we have within *Microeconomics* labeled selected questions according to the six general knowledge and skills areas.

McGraw-Hill Customer Care Contact Information

At McGraw-Hill, we understand that getting the most from new technology can be challenging. That's why our services don't stop after you purchase our products. You can email our Product Specialists 24 hours a day to get product training online. Or you can search our knowledge bank of Frequently Asked Questions on our support website. For Customer Support, call **800-331-5094**, email **hmsupport@mcgraw-hill.com**, or visit **www.mhhe.com/ support**. One of our Technical Support Analysts will be able to assist you in a timely fashion.

acknowledgments

Many people helped us create this text. It's said that "it takes a village," but it often felt like we had the benefit of an entire town.

We want to give special acknowledgment to Meredith Startz. Meredith has been a partner in the writing process from the very start. Meredith started working on an Innovations for Poverty Action project on microcredit in the Philippines, and we all quickly realized her passion for conveying to introductory audiences ideas about how economics can make the world a better place. So she came back to the United States and joined us in this project. Perhaps because Meredith's own undergraduate training was not far behind her, she helped us make sure that ideas are clear and accessible to students approaching the material for the first time. Meredith's writing is woven throughout the chapters, and we are delighted to recognize her contributions by adding her name to the title page of the text.

The initial inspiration for the project came from Douglas Reiner, Managing Director for Economics, Finance, and the Decision Sciences at McGraw-Hill, who joined us in crafting a vision for teaching economics as a way to solve problems. Douglas urged us to break down the wall between what happens in the classroom and what's happening in our nation and around the world. He gave us the confidence to draw on examples from the news and recent research, both in the United States and globally, and to lead with those examples as we start each chapter. Douglas encouraged us to share with students our own experience as researchers working on practical solutions to everyday problems and society's bigger challenges.

Ann Torbert, Executive Director of Development, McGraw-Hill, has been an exemplary editor. She helped improve the exposition on each page and kept attention on both the big picture and key details. Ann's grace and professionalism made the text much better and the process much easier.

An energetic group of collaborators helped us to shape content in ways that would be relevant and engaging for a student audience. Ted Barnett steered us through the writing of the macro chapters, helping us offer timely treatment of asset price bubbles and global financial crisis—events that were still unfolding when we were writing the text. Kerry Brennan's creativity and attention to detail made her essential throughout the micro chapters. She has a great eye for slightly offbeat, illuminating examples, many of which made their way into the text in chapter-opening stories and From Another Angle boxes. Melanie Morten and John Loser provided invaluable expertise to the macroeconomics section and helped those sections come to life and connect to students' everyday experience. Andrew Hillis brought a recent-student perspective to bear on the whole project and improved the clarity of presentation for figures throughout the text.

Many other talented individuals contributed on and off throughout this project. We thank Yusuf Siddiquee, Selvan Kumar, Hannah Trachtman, Kareem Haggag, Jennifer Severski, Alex Bartik, Martin Rotemberg, and Doug Parkerson in particular, for keeping an eye out for great stories to use to help explain concepts in fun and engaging ways. We appreciate the careful attention that Andrew Wright gave to every chapter.

We thank Diana Beck (New York University), Victor Matheson (College of the Holy Cross), John Kane (State University of New York–Oswego), and Amanda Freeman (Kansas State University) for their many and varied contributions to text and end-of-chapter content, and also for their willingness to provide feedback at a moment's notice. We are very appreciative of the extensive work done by Peggy Dalton (Frostburg State University) in preparing the Connect materials and the work done by Laura Maghoney (Solano Community College) and Daniel Lawson (Oakland Community College) in accuracy-checking it. Special thanks also go to Lisa Gloege (Grand Rapids Community College), David Cusimano (Delgado Community College), Jennifer Pate (Loyola Marymount University), and Amanda Freeman, who helped us accuracy-check the manuscript once it had been typeset. In addition, we thank Peggy Dalton and Russell Kellogg (University of Colorado Denver) for authoring the LearnSmart content, and John Nordstrom (College of Western Idaho) and Christopher Mushrush (Illinois State University) for accuracy-checking it.

We also want to share our appreciation to the following people at McGraw-Hill for the hard work they put into creating the product you see before you: Katie White Hoenicke, Marketing Manager, guided us in communicating the overarching vision, visiting schools, and working with the sales team. Alyssa Lincoln, Development Editor, managed innumerable and indispensable details—reviews, photos, and the many aspects of the digital products and overall package. Lori Koetters, Content Project Manager, performed magic in turning our manuscript into the finished, polished product you see before you. Marianne Musni, Content Project Manager, skillfully guided the digital plan. Thanks, too, to Doug Ruby, Director of Digital Content, Economics, Finance, and ODS; Kevin Shanahan, Digital Development Editor; and Megan Maloney, Digital Development Editor, for their careful shepherding of the digital materials that accompany the text.

Thank You!

This text has gone through a lengthy development process spanning several years, and it wouldn't be the same without the valuable feedback provided by the professors and students who viewed it throughout development. Whether you attended a focus group, a symposium, reviewed the text, or participated in a class test, the authors and McGraw-Hill thank you for sharing your insights and recommendations.

Focus Group Attendees

SPRING 2012

Michael Applegate
Oklahoma State University–Stillwater Campus

Camelia Bouzerdan
Middlesex Community College

Howard Cochran
Belmont University

Marwan El Nasser
State University of New York–Fredonia

Brent Evans
Mississippi State University

Chris Fant
Spartanburg Community College

Tawni Ferrarini
Northern Michigan University

Irene Foster
George Washington University

Bill (Wayne) Goffe
State University of New York–Oswego

Oskar Harmon
University of Connecticut–Stamford

David Hickman
Frederick Community College

Shuyi Jiang
Emmanuel College

Ahmad Kader
University of Nevada–Las Vegas

Joel Kazy
State Fair Community College

Al Mickens
State University of New York–Old Westbury

Nara Mijid
Central Connecticut State University

Rebecca Moryl
Emmanuel College

Emlyn Norman
Texas Southern University

Christian Nsiah
Black Hills State University

Robert Pennington
University of Central Florida–Orlando

Andrew Perumal
University of Massachusetts–Boston

Gregory Pratt
Mesa Community College

Timothy Reynolds
Alvin Community College

Michael Rolleigh
Williams College

Michael Salemi
University of North Carolina–Chapel Hill

Sovathana Sokhom
Loyola Marymount University

Abdulhamid Sukar
Cameron University

Marieta Velikova
Belmont University

Melissa Wiseman
Houston Baptist University

Jeff Woods
University of Indianapolis

FALL 2012

Cindy Clement
University of Maryland–College Park

Chifeng Dai
Southern Illinois University–Carbondale

Eric Eide
Brigham Young University–Provo

John Kane
State University of New York–Oswego

Karla Lynch
North Central Texas College

Martin Milkman
Murray State University

Max Grunbaum Nagiel
Daytona State College–Daytona Beach

Naveen Sarna
Northern Virginia Community College– Alexandria

Marilyn Spencer
Texas A&M University–Corpus Christi

Terry von Ende
Texas Tech University

Part One

The Power of Economics

The two chapters in Part 1 will introduce you to ...

the tools and intuition essential to the study of economics. Chapter 1 presents four questions that introduce the fundamental concepts of economic problem solving. We also describe how economists think about data and analyze policies, typically separating how one *wants* the world to look ("normative" analysis) from how the world *actually* works ("positive" analysis).

Chapter 2 presents the ideas of absolute and comparative advantage to explain how people (and countries) can most effectively use their resources and talents. Should you hire a plumber or fix the pipes yourself? Should you become a pop star or an economist? We develop these ideas to show how trade can make everyone better off, on both a personal and a national level.

This is just a start. Throughout the book, we'll use these tools to gain a deeper understanding of how people interact and manage their resources, which in turn gives insight into tough problems of all sorts. Economic ideas weave a common thread through many subjects, from the purely economic to political, environmental, and cultural issues, as well as personal decisions encountered in everyday life. Economics is much more than just the study of money, and we hope you'll find that what you learn here will shed light far beyond your economics classes.

Economics and Life

LEARNING OBJECTIVES

LO 1.1   Explain the economic concept of scarcity.

LO 1.2   Explain the economic concepts of opportunity cost and marginal decision making.

LO 1.3   Explain the economic concept of incentives.

LO 1.4   Explain the economic concept of efficiency.

LO 1.5   Distinguish between correlation and causation.

LO 1.6   List the characteristics of a good economic model.

LO 1.7   Distinguish between positive and normative analysis.

MAKING AN IMPACT WITH SMALL LOANS

On the morning of October 13, 2006, Bangladeshi economist Muhammad Yunus received an unexpected telephone call from Oslo, Norway. Later that day, the Nobel committee announced that Yunus and the Grameen Bank, which he founded in 1976, would share the 2006 Nobel Peace Prize. Past recipients of the Nobel Peace Prize include Mother Teresa, who spent over 50 years ministering to beggars and lepers; Martin Luther King, Jr., who used peaceful protest to oppose racial segregation; and the Dalai Lama, an exiled Tibetan Buddhist leader who symbolizes the struggle for religious and cultural tolerance. What were an economist and his bank doing in such company?

Grameen is not a typical bank. Yes, it makes loans and offers savings accounts, charging customers for its services, just like other banks. But it serves some of the poorest people in the poorest villages in one of the poorest countries in the world. It makes loans so small that it's hard for people in wealthy countries to imagine what good they can do: The first group of loans Yunus made totaled only $27. Before Grameen came along, other banks had been unwilling to work in these poor communities. They believed it wasn't worth bothering to lend such small amounts; many believed the poor could not be counted on to repay their loans.

Yunus disagreed. He was convinced that even very small loans would allow poor villagers to expand their small businesses—maybe buying a sewing machine, or a cow to produce milk for the local market—and earn more money. As a result, their lives would be more comfortable and secure, and their children would have a better future. Yunus claimed that they would be able to repay the loan, and that his new bank would earn a profit.

Yunus proved the skeptics wrong, and today Grameen Bank serves more than 8 million customers. The bank reports that 98 percent of its loans are repaid—a better rate than

3

some banks in rich countries can claim. Grameen also reports steady profits, which has inspired other banks to start serving poor communities on nearly every continent, including recent start-ups in New York City and Omaha, Nebraska.

Muhammad Yunus was trained as an economist. He earned a PhD at Vanderbilt University in Nashville, and then taught in Tennessee before becoming a professor in Bangladesh. When a devastating famine struck Bangladesh, Yunus became disillusioned with teaching. What did abstract equations and stylized graphs have to do with the suffering he saw all around him?

Ultimately, Yunus realized that economic thinking holds the key to solving hard problems that truly matter. The genius of Grameen Bank is that it is neither a traditional charity nor a traditional bank. Instead, it is a business that harnesses basic economic insights to make the world a better place.[1]

In this book, we'll introduce you to the tools economists are using to tackle some of the world's biggest challenges, from health care reform, to climate change, to lifting people out of poverty. Of course, these tools are not just for taking on causes worthy of Nobel Prizes. Economics can also help you become a savvier consumer, successfully launch a new cell phone app, or simply make smarter decisions about how to spend your time and money. Throughout this book, we promise to ask you not just to memorize theories, but also to apply the ideas you read about to the everyday decisions you face in your own life.

economics the study of how people, individually and collectively, manage resources

microeconomics the study of how individuals and firms manage resources

macroeconomics the study of the economy on a regional, national, or international scale

The Basic Insights of Economics

When people think of economics, they often think of the stock market, the unemployment rate, or media reports saying things like "the Federal Reserve has raised its target for the federal funds rate." Although economics does include these topics, its reach is much broader.

Economics is the study of how people manage resources. Decisions about how to allocate resources can be made by individuals, but also by groups of people in families, firms, governments, and other organizations. In economics, *resources* are not just physical things like cash and gold mines. They are also intangible things, such as time, ideas, technology, job experience, and even personal relationships.

Traditionally, economics has been divided into two broad fields: microeconomics and macroeconomics. **Microeconomics** is the study of how individuals and firms manage resources. **Macroeconomics** is the study of the economy on a regional, national, or international scale. Microeconomics and macroeconomics are highly related and interdependent; we need both to fully understand how economies work.

Economics starts with the idea that people compare the choices available to them and purposefully behave in the way that will best achieve their goals. As human beings, we have ambitions and we make plans to realize them. We strategize. We marshal our resources. When people make choices to achieve their goals in the most effective way possible, economists say they are exhibiting **rational behavior**. This assumption isn't perfect. As we'll see later in the book, people can sometimes be short-sighted or poorly informed about their choices. Nevertheless, the assumption of rational behavior helps to explain a lot about the world.

People use economics every day, from Wall Street to Walmart, from state capitol buildings to Bangladeshi villages. They apply economic ideas to everything from shoe shopping to baseball, from running a hospital to running for political office. What ties these topics together is a common approach to problem solving.

Economists tend to break down problems by asking a set of four questions:

1. What are the wants and constraints of those involved?
2. What are the trade-offs?
3. How will others respond?
4. Why isn't everyone already doing it?

Underneath these questions are some important economics concepts, which we will begin to explore in this chapter. Although the questions, and the underlying concepts, are based on just a few common-sense assumptions about how people behave, they offer a surprising amount of insight into tough problems of all sorts. They are so important to economic problem solving that they will come up again and again in this book. In this chapter we'll take a bird's-eye view of economics, focusing on the fundamental concepts and skimming over the details. Later in the book, we'll return to each question in more depth.

Scarcity

Question 1: What are the wants and constraints of those involved?

LO 1.1 Explain the economic concept of scarcity.

For the most part, most people make decisions that are aimed at getting the things they want. Of course, you can't always get what you want. People want a lot of things, but they are *constrained* by limited resources. Economists define **scarcity** as the condition of wanting more than we can get with available resources. Scarcity is a fact of life. You have only so much time and only so much money. You can arrange your resources in a lot of different ways—studying or watching TV, buying a car or traveling to Las Vegas—but at any given time, you have a fixed range of possibilities. Scarcity also describes the world on a collective level: As a society, we can produce only so many things, and we have to decide how those things are divided among many people.

The first question to ask in untangling a complex economic problem is, "What are the wants and constraints of those involved?" Given both rational behavior and scarcity, we can expect people to work to get what they want, but to be constrained in their choices by the limited resources available to them. Suppose you *want* to spend as much time as possible this summer taking road trips around the country. You are *constrained* by the three months of summer vacation and by your lack of money to pay for gas, food, and places to stay. Behaving rationally, you might choose to work double-shifts for two months to

rational behavior
making choices to achieve goals in the most effective way possible

scarcity the condition of wanting more than we can get with available resources

earn enough to spend one month on the road. Since you are now *constrained* by having only one month to travel, you'll have to prioritize your time, activities, and expenses.

Now put yourself in Muhammad Yunus's shoes, back in 1976. He sees extremely poor but entrepreneurial Bangladeshi villagers and thinks that they could improve their lives with access to loans. Why aren't banks providing financial services for these people? We can apply the first of the economists' questions to start to untangle this puzzle: *What are the wants and constraints of those involved?* In this case, those involved are traditional Bangladeshi banks and poor Bangladeshi villagers.

Let's look at both:

- The banks *want* to make profits by lending money to people who will pay them back with interest. They are *constrained* by having limited funds available to loan or to run branch banks. We can therefore expect banks to prioritize making loans to customers they believe are likely to pay them back. Before 1976, that meant wealthier, urban Bangladeshis, not the very poor in remote rural villages.

- The villagers *want* the chance to increase their incomes. They have energy and business ideas but are *constrained* in their ability to borrow start-up money by the fact that most banks believe they are too poor to repay loans.

Analyzing the wants and constraints of those involved gives us some valuable information about why poor Bangladeshis didn't have access to loans. Banks *wanted* to earn profits and managed their *constrained* funds to prioritize those they thought would be profitable customers. Bangladeshi villagers *wanted* to increase their incomes but couldn't follow up on business opportunities due to *constrained* start-up money. That's good information, but we haven't yet come up with the solution that Dr. Yunus was looking for. To take the next step in solving the puzzle, we turn to another question economists often ask.

Opportunity cost and marginal decision making

Question 2: What are the trade-offs?

LO 1.2 Explain the economic concepts of opportunity cost and marginal decision making.

Every decision in life involves weighing the *trade-off* between costs and benefits. We look at our options and decide whether it is worth giving up one in order to get the other. We choose to do things only when we think that the benefits will be greater than the costs. The potential *benefit* of taking an action is often easy to see: You can have fun road-tripping for a month; bank customers who take out a loan have the opportunity to expand their businesses. The *costs* of a decision, on the other hand, are not always clear.

You might think it *is* clear—that the cost of your road trip is simply the amount of money you spend on gas, hotels, and food. But something is missing from that calculation. The true cost of something is not just the amount you have to pay for it, but also the opportunity you lose to do something else instead. Suppose that if you hadn't gone on your road trip, your second choice would have been to spend that same time and money to buy a big-screen TV and spend a month at home watching movies with friends. The true cost of your road trip is the enjoyment you would have had from owning the TV and hanging out with friends for a month. Behaving rationally, you should go on the road trip only if it will be more valuable to you than the best alternative use for your time and money. This is a matter of personal preference. Because people have different alternatives and place different values on things like a road trip or a TV, they will make different decisions.

Economists call this true cost of your choice the **opportunity cost**, which is equal to the value of what you have to give up in order to get something. Put another way, opportunity cost is the value of your next best alternative—the "opportunity" you have to pass up in order to take your first choice.

opportunity cost
the value of what you have to give up in order to get something; the value of your next-best alternative

Let's return to the road trip. Say you're going with a friend, and her plan B would have been buying a new computer, taking a summer class, and visiting her cousins. The opportunity cost of her vacation is different from yours. For her, the opportunity cost is the pleasure she would have had from a new computer, plus whatever benefits she might have got from the course, plus the fun she would have had with her cousins. If she's behaving rationally, she will go with you on the road trip only if she believes it will be more valuable to her than what she's giving up.

Opportunity cost helps us think more clearly about trade-offs. If someone asked you how much your road trip cost and you responded by adding up the cost of gas, hotels, and food, you would be failing to capture some of the most important and interesting aspects of the trade-offs you made. Opportunity cost helps us to see why, for example, a partner at a law firm and a paralegal at the firm face truly different trade-offs when they contemplate taking the same vacation for the same price. The partner makes a higher salary and therefore forgoes more money when taking unpaid time off from work. The opportunity cost of a vacation for the paralegal is therefore lower than it is for the lawyer, and the decision the paralegal faces is truly different.

Economists often express opportunity cost as a dollar value. Suppose you've been given a gift certificate worth $15 at a restaurant. The restaurant has a short menu: pizza or spaghetti, each of which costs $15. The gift certificate can be used only at this particular restaurant, so the only thing you give up to get pizza is spaghetti, and vice versa. If you didn't have the certificate, you would be willing to pay as much as $15 for the pizza but no more than $10 for the spaghetti.

What is the opportunity cost of choosing the pizza? Even though the price on the menu is $15, the opportunity cost is only $10, because that is the value you place on your best (and only) alternative, the spaghetti. What is the opportunity cost of choosing the spaghetti? It's $15, the value you place on the pizza. Which do you choose? One choice has an opportunity cost of $10, the other $15. Behaving rationally, you should choose the pizza, because it has the lower opportunity cost.

A simpler way of describing this trade-off would be simply to say that you prefer pizza over spaghetti. The opportunity cost of spaghetti is higher because to get it, you have to give up something you like more. But putting it in terms of opportunity cost can be helpful when there are more choices, or more nuances to the choices.

For example, suppose the gift certificate could be used only to buy spaghetti. Now what is the opportunity cost of choosing the spaghetti? It is $0, because you can't do anything else with the gift certificate—your alternative choices are spaghetti or nothing. The opportunity cost of pizza is now $15 because you'd have to pay for it with money you could have spent on $15 worth of other purchases outside the restaurant. So even though you like pizza better, you might now choose the spaghetti because it has a lower opportunity cost in this particular situation.

Once you start to think about opportunity costs, you see them everywhere. For an application of opportunity cost to a serious moral question, read the What Do You Think? box "The opportunity cost of a life."

WHAT DO YOU THINK?
The opportunity cost of a life

Throughout the book, What Do You Think? boxes ask for your opinion about an important policy or life decision. These boxes will present questions that require you to combine facts and economic analysis with values and moral reasoning. They are the sort of tough questions that people face in real life. There are many correct answers, depending on your values and goals.

The philosopher Peter Singer writes that opportunity costs can be a matter of life or death. Imagine you are a salesperson, and on your way to a meeting on a hot summer day, you drive by a lake. Suddenly, you notice that a child who has been swimming in the lake is drowning. No one else is in sight.

You have a choice. If you stop the car and dive into the lake to save the child, you will be late for your meeting, miss out on making a sale, and lose $250. The *opportunity cost* of saving the child's life is $250.

Alternatively, if you continue on to your meeting, you earn the $250 but you lose the opportunity to dive into the lake and save the child's life. The *opportunity cost* of going to the meeting is one child's life.

What would you do? Most people don't hesitate. They immediately say they would stop the car, dive into the lake, and save the drowning child. After all, a child's life is worth more than $250.

Now suppose you're thinking about spending $250 on a new iPod. That $250 could instead have been used for some charitable purpose, such as immunizing children in another country against yellow fever. Suppose that for every $250 donated, an average of one child's life ends up being saved. (In fact, $250 to save one child's life is not far from reality in many cases.) What is the opportunity cost of buying an iPod? According to Peter Singer, it is the same as the opportunity cost of going straight to the meeting: a child's life.

These two situations are not exactly the same, of course, but why does the first choice (jump in the lake) seem so obvious to most people, while the second seems much less obvious?

What do you think?

1. In what ways do the two situations presented by Singer—the sales meeting and the drowning child versus the iPod and the unvaccinated child—differ?
2. Singer argues that even something like buying an iPod is a surprisingly serious moral decision. Do you agree? What sort of opportunity costs do you typically consider when making such a decision?
3. What might be missing from Singer's analysis of the trade-offs people face when making a decision about how to spend money?

marginal decision making comparison of additional benefits of a choice against the additional costs it would bring, without considering related benefits and costs of past choices

Another important principle for understanding trade-offs is the idea that rational people make decisions *at the margin.* **Marginal decision making** describes the idea that rational people compare the *additional* benefits of a choice against the *additional* costs, without considering related benefits and costs of past choices.

For example, suppose an amusement park has a $20 admission price and charges $2 per ride. If you are standing outside the park, the cost of the first ride is $22, because you will have to pay the admission price and buy a ticket to go on the ride. Once you are inside the park, the *marginal* cost of each additional ride is $2. When deciding whether to go on the roller coaster a second or third time, then, you should compare only the benefit or enjoyment you will get from one more ride to the opportunity cost of that additional ride.

This may sound obvious, but in practice, many people don't make decisions on the margin. Suppose you get into the amusement park and start to feel sick shortly thereafter. If doing something else with your $2 and 20 minutes would bring you more enjoyment than another rollercoaster ride while feeling sick, the rational thing to do would be to leave. The relevant trade-off is between the *additional* benefits that going on another ride would bring, versus the additional costs. You cannot get back the $20 admission fee or any of the other money you've already spent on rides. Economists call costs that have already been incurred and cannot be recovered **sunk costs**. Sunk costs should not have any bearing on your *marginal* decision about what to do next. But many people feel the need to go on a few more rides to psychologically justify the $20 admission.

sunk costs costs that have already been incurred and cannot be recovered or refunded

Trade-offs play a crucial role in businesses' decisions about what goods and services to produce. Let's return to the example that started this chapter and apply the idea to a bank in Bangladesh: *What are the trade-offs involved in making a small loan?*

- For traditional banks, the opportunity cost of making small loans to the poor was the money that the bank could have earned by making loans to wealthier clients instead.
- For poor borrowers, the opportunity cost of borrowing was whatever else they would have done with the time they spent traveling to the bank and with the money they would pay in fees and interest on the loan. The benefit, of course, was whatever the loan would enable them to do that they could not have done otherwise, such as starting a small business or buying food or livestock.

Based on this analysis of trade-offs, we can see why traditional banks made few loans to poor Bangladeshis. Because banks perceived the poor to be risky clients, the opportunity cost of making small loans to the poor seemed to outweigh the benefits—unless the banks charged very high fees. From the perspective of poor rural villagers, high fees meant that the opportunity cost of borrowing was higher than the benefits, so they chose not to borrow under the terms offered by banks.

Notice that the answer to this question built off the answer to the first: We had to know the wants and constraints of each party before we could assess the trade-offs they faced. Now that we understand the motivations and the trade-offs that led to the situation Dr. Yunus observed, we can turn to a third question he might have asked himself when considering what would happen when he founded the Grameen Bank.

Incentives

Question 3: How will others respond?

LO 1.3 Explain the economic concept of incentives.

You're in the mood for pizza, so you decide to go back to the restaurant with the short menu. When you get there, you discover that the prices have changed. Pizza now costs $50 instead of $15.

What will you do? Remember that your gift certificate is good for only $15. Unless you can easily afford to shell out $50 for a pizza or just really hate spaghetti, you probably won't be ordering the pizza. We're sure that you can think of ways to spend $35 that are worth more to you than your preference for pizza over spaghetti. But what if the prices had changed less drastically—say, $18 for pizza? That might be a tougher call.

As the trade-offs change, so will the choices people make. When the restaurant owner considers how much to charge for each dish, she must consider *how others will respond* to changing prices. If she knows the pizza is popular, she might be tempted to try charging more to boost her profits. But as she increases the price, fewer diners will decide to order it.

If a trade-off faced by a lot of people changes, even by a small amount, the combined change in behavior by everyone involved can add up to a big shift. The collective reaction to a changing trade-off is a central idea in economics and will come up in almost every chapter of this book. Asking "How will others respond?" to a trade-off that affects a lot of people gives us a complete picture of how a particular decision affects the world. What happens when prices change? What happens when the government implements a new policy? What happens when a company introduces a new product? Answering any of these questions requires us to consider a large-scale reaction, rather than the behavior of just one person, company, or policy-maker.

In answering this question about trade-offs, economists commonly make two assumptions. The first is that people respond to incentives. An **incentive** is something that causes people to behave in a certain way by changing the trade-offs they face. A positive incentive (sometimes just called an *incentive*) makes people *more likely* to do something. A negative incentive (sometimes called a *disincentive*) makes them *less likely* to do it. For example, lowering the price of spaghetti creates a positive incentive for people to order it, because it lowers the opportunity cost—when you pay less for spaghetti, you give up fewer other things you could have spent the money on. Charging people more for pizza is a negative incentive to buy pizza, because they now have to give up more alternative purchases.

incentive
something that causes people to behave in a certain way by changing the trade-offs they face

The second assumption economists make about trade-offs is that nothing happens in a vacuum. That is, you can't change just one thing in the world without eliciting a response from others. If you change your behavior—even if only in a small way—that action will change the incentives of the people around you, causing them to change their behavior in response. If you invent a new product, competitors will copy it. If you raise prices, consumers will buy less. If you tax a good or service, people will produce less of it.

Asking *how others will respond* can help prevent bad decisions by predicting the undesirable side-effects of a change in prices or policies. The question can also be used to design changes that elicit positive responses. When Muhammad Yunus was setting up Grameen Bank, he had to think carefully about the incentives that both rural villagers and traditional banks faced and to consider how those incentives could be changed without incurring negative side-effects.

One reason that banks saw rural villagers as risky customers is that they were too poor to have anything to offer to the bank as collateral. *Collateral* is a possession pledged by a borrower to a lender, like a house or a car. If the borrower cannot repay the loan, the lender keeps the collateral. The threat of losing the collateral increases the cost of choosing to not repay the loan, giving the borrower a positive incentive to repay. When traditional banks thought about lending to poor Bangladeshis, they concluded that without the threat of losing collateral, the villagers would be less likely to repay their loans.

Yunus needed to think up a different way of creating a positive incentive for poor customers to repay their loans. His best-known solution was to require borrowers to apply for loans in five-person groups. Every person in the group would have a stake in the success of the other members. If one person didn't repay a loan, no one else in the group could borrow from the bank again.

Yunus's idea, called *group responsibility*, was simple, but hugely significant. Yunus concluded that borrowers would have a strong incentive to repay their loans: They wouldn't want to ruin relationships with other members of the group—their fellow villagers, whom they live with every day and rely on for mutual support in hard times. This, in turn, changed the trade-off faced by banks, and they responded by being more willing to lend to the poor at lower rates. By asking himself how villagers would respond to the new kind of loan and how banks in turn would respond to the villagers' response, Yunus was able to predict that his idea could be the key to spreading banking services to the poor.

Dr. Yunus's predictions proved to be correct. Seeing that poor villagers nearly always repaid their loans under Grameen's system gave other banks confidence that small borrowers could be reliable customers. Banks offering microloans, savings accounts, and other services to the very poor have spread around the world. As a result of Yunus's creativity and thoughtfulness about incentives, the poor have better access to financial services and banks earn money from providing them. Today, other ideas have proved even more effective in providing the right incentives for small borrowers, continuing in the tradition of experimentation and innovation pioneered by Yunus and Grameen Bank.

Throughout this book, you will see many examples of how the power of incentives can be harnessed to accomplish everything from increasing a company's profits to protecting the environment. But before we get carried away with brilliant economic innovations, we have to ask ourselves one more question, the final test of any solutions that come out of our problem-solving process.

Efficiency

Question 4: Why isn't everyone already doing it?

LO 1.4 Explain the economic concept of efficiency.

People tend to behave rationally. We clip coupons, compare car models before buying, and think hard about which major to choose in college. Although people are not calculating machines, we usually weigh trade-offs, respond to incentives, and are on the lookout for opportunities to get what we want in the most effective way possible.

The same goes for businesses. There are millions of businesses in the world, each trying to make a profit. When consumers want a good or service, some business will take the opportunity to earn money by providing it. That fact leads to our final assumption: *Under normal circumstances, individuals and firms will act to provide the things people want.* If a genuine profit-making opportunity exists, someone will take advantage of it, and usually sooner rather than later.

This final assumption comes from the idea of **efficiency**. Efficiency describes a situation in which resources are used in the most productive way possible to produce the goods and services that have the greatest total economic value to society. Increasing efficiency means finding a way to better use resources to produce the things that people want.

efficiency use of resources in the most productive way possible to produce the goods and services that have the greatest total economic value to society

The definition of efficiency might raise some questions. How do we determine *value,* for example? What exactly do we mean by *resources?* Over the course of the book, we'll dive deeper into these issues. For now, we'll take a broad view: Something is valuable if someone wants it, and a resource is anything that can be used to make something of value, from natural resources (such as water and trees) to human resources (such as talents and knowledge). This broad view leads to an important idea: When the economy is working efficiently, resources are *already* getting allocated to valuable ends.

So when you think you see a big, unexploited opportunity—a new product, policy, technology, or business model that could change the world or earn you millions of dollars—ask yourself: If it's such a great idea, *why isn't everyone* already *doing it?* One possible answer is simply that nobody has thought of it before. That's possible. But, if *you* have seen the opportunity, doesn't it seem likely that at least one of the billions of other smart, rational people in the world will have seen it too?

Don't get us wrong: We're not saying there is never an opportunity to do something new in the world. Great new ideas happen all the time—they drive progress. But there's a strong possibility that other people have already thought about the idea, and if they chose not to take advantage of it, that's a hint that you might be missing something. The first thing to do is backtrack to the first three economists' questions: Have you misjudged people's wants and constraints, miscalculated the trade-offs they face, or misunderstood how people will respond to incentives?

If you think back through those questions and still think you're on to something, here are some more possibilities to consider. We said that *under normal circumstances,* the economy is operating efficiently, and individuals or firms provide the things people want. What are some ways in which circumstances might not be normal?

- *Innovation:* Innovation is the explanation you're hoping is correct. Maybe your idea has not been used yet because it is too new. If you have come up with a truly new idea, whether it is new technology or a new business model, people cannot have taken advantage of it yet, because it didn't exist before.

- *Market failure:* Market failures are an important cause of inefficiency. Sometimes people and firms fail to take advantage of opportunities because something prevents them from capturing the benefits of the opportunity, or imposes additional costs on them. For instance, maybe your great new idea won't work because it would be impossible to prevent others from quickly copying it or because a few big companies have already got the market sewn up. Economists call such situations *market failure,* and we will discuss them in much greater depth later in the book.

- *Intervention:* If a powerful force—often the government—intervenes in the economy, transactions cannot take place the way they normally would. We'll see later in this book that many government economic policies intentionally or unintentionally interfere with people's ability to take advantage of profit-making opportunities.

- *Goals other than profit:* Maybe your idea won't produce a profit. Individuals and governments have goals other than profit, of course—for example, creating great art or promoting social justice. But if your idea doesn't also generate a profit, then it is less surprising that no one has taken advantage of it.

When Muhammad Yunus asked himself the question, "Why isn't everyone already lending to the poor?" he first identified a market failure involving lack of collateral and came up with the idea of group responsibility to fix it. But then he had to ask himself, "Why aren't all the banks already using the group responsibility idea?"

Maybe there was another market failure Yunus hadn't spotted. Maybe some government policy prevented it. Maybe traditional banks had considered it and decided it still wouldn't generate a profit. Yunus wasn't primarily interested in making profit, of course—he was interested in helping the poor. But if microloans weren't going to earn a profit for the banks even with group responsibility, then that would explain why no one was already doing it.

Fortunately, none of those answers were correct. This was a case in which the answer to *why isn't everyone already doing it?* was that the idea was genuinely new. Grameen Bank was able to help very poor people in Bangladesh by lending them money, while making enough profit to expand and serve more customers. Today, over 20 million people in Bangladesh can get small loans from Grameen Bank and other organizations. Around the world, over 200 million low-income customers enjoy the same opportunity. Sometimes, something that seems like a great new idea really is exactly that.

✓ CONCEPT CHECK

In every chapter of this book you will find a few Concept Checks. These questions test your understanding of the concepts presented in the preceding section. If you have trouble answering any of the questions, go back and review the section. Don't move forward until you understand these ideas.

❑ How do constraints affect decision making? **[LO 1.1]**

❑ What do opportunity costs represent? **[LO 1.2]**

❑ What is the name for something that changes the trade-offs that people face when making a decision? **[LO 1.3]**

❑ Give four reasons that might explain why a product isn't already in the market. **[LO 1.4]**

An Economist's Problem-Solving Toolbox

The four questions we've just discussed are some of the fundamental insights of economics. Using them to understand how the world *might* work is only half the battle. In the second part of this chapter we will describe some tools economists use to apply these insights to real situations.

Accurately spotting the fundamental economic concepts at work in the world is sometimes less obvious than you might think. Throughout history, people have observed the world around them and drawn conclusions that have proved hilariously—or sometimes tragically—wrong. We now know that the sun doesn't revolve around the earth. Droughts are not caused by witches giving people the evil eye. Yet, intelligent people once believed these things. It's human nature to draw meaning from the patterns we observe around us, but our conclusions are not always correct.

Economic analysis requires us to combine theory with observations and to subject both to scrutiny before drawing conclusions. In this section we will see how to put theories and facts together to determine what causes what. We will also distinguish between the way things *are* and the way we think they *should be*. You can apply these tools to various situations, from personal life choices to business decisions and policy analysis.

Correlation and causation

LO 1.5 Distinguish between correlation and causation.

Many sports fans have a lucky jersey that they wear to help their team win a game. A die-hard fan might insist that his jersey is obviously lucky, because he was wearing it when his team won the NBA finals or the Super Bowl. This superstition is an exaggeration of a common human tendency: When we see that two events occur together, we tend to assume that one causes the other. Economists, however, try to be particularly careful about what causes what.

To differentiate between events that simply occur at the same time and events that share a clear cause-and-effect relationship, we use two different terms. When we observe a consistent relationship between two events or variables, we say there is a **correlation** between them. If both tend to occur at the same time or move in the same direction, we say they are *positively correlated*. Wearing raincoats is positively correlated with rain. If one event or variable increases while a related event or variable decreases, we say they are *negatively correlated*. They move in opposite directions. High temperatures are negatively correlated with people wearing down jackets. If there is no consistent relationship between two variables, we say they are *uncorrelated*.

Correlation differs from causation. **Causation** means that one event brings about the other. As the preceding examples show, causation and correlation often go together. Weather and clothing are often correlated, because weather *causes* people to make certain choices about the clothing they wear.

Unfortunately, correlation and causation do not always go together in a straightforward way. Correlation and causation can be confused in three major ways: correlation without causation, omitted variables, and reverse causation.

correlation
a consistently observed relationship between two events or variables

causation
a relationship between two events in which one brings about the other

Economists try to be particularly careful to differentiate between correlation and causation.

Correlation without causation. Does the result of the Super Bowl predict the performance of the stock market? A few years ago, some people started to think it might. The Super Bowl pits the top team from the American Football Conference against the top team from the National Football Conference. For a long time, when a team from the AFC won, the stock market had a bad year; when a team from the NFC won, the stock market had a great year. In fact, this pattern held true 85 percent of the time between 1967 and 1997.

Would it have been a good idea to base your investment strategy on the results of the Super Bowl? We think not. There is no plausible cause-and-effect relationship here. Stock market outcomes happened to be *correlated with* Super Bowl outcomes for a number of years, but there is no logical way they could be *caused by* them. If you search long enough for odd coincidences, you will eventually find some.

Omitted variables. Consider the following statement: There is a positive correlation between the presence of firefighters and people with serious burn injuries. Does this statement mean that firefighters cause burn injuries? Of course not. We know that firefighters are not burning people; they're trying to save them. Instead, there must be some common underlying factor, or *variable,* behind both observed outcomes—fires, in this case.

Sometimes, two events that are correlated occur together because both are caused by the same underlying factor. Each has a causal relationship with a third factor, but not with each other. The underlying factor is called an *omitted variable,* because despite the fact that it is an important part of the cause-and-effect story, it has been left out of the analysis. The From Another Angle box "Does ice cream cause polio?" tells the story of an omitted variable that convinced some doctors to mistakenly campaign against a staple of summer fun: ice cream.

FROM ANOTHER ANGLE

Does ice cream cause polio?

From Another Angle boxes show you a different way of looking at an economic concept. Sometimes they will be a humorous story, sometimes a different way of thinking about a situation, and sometimes just an unusual application of a standard idea. We find that a little bit of weirdness goes a long way in helping us to remember things, and we hope it will work for you too.

A disease called polio once crippled or killed thousands of children in the United States every year. Before it was known what caused polio, doctors observed that polio infections seemed to be more common in children who had been eating lots of ice cream. Observing this *correlation* led some people to assume that there was a *causal* relationship between the two. Some doctors recommended an anti-polio diet that avoided eating ice cream. Many fearful parents understandably took their advice.

We now know that polio is caused by a virus that is transmitted from one person to another. The virus was spread through contaminated food and water—for example, dirty swimming pools or water fountains. It had nothing at all to do with how much ice cream a child ate. A polio vaccine was developed in 1952.

The ice cream confusion was caused by an *omitted variable*: warm weather. In warm weather, children are more likely to use swimming pools and water fountains. And in warm weather, children are also more likely to eat ice cream. Polio was therefore *correlated* with eating ice cream, but it certainly wasn't *caused* by it.

Source: http://www.nytimes.com/2009/08/06/technology/06stats.html?_r=1.

Reverse causation. A third common source of confusion between correlation and causation is called *reverse causation:* Did A cause B, or did B cause A? When two events always happen together, it can be hard to say which caused the other.

Let's return to the correlation between rain and raincoats. If we knew nothing about rain, we might observe that it often appears together with raincoats, and we might conclude that wearing a raincoat (A) causes rain (B). In this case, we all know that the causation goes the other way, but observation alone does not tell us that.

Looking at the timing of two correlated events can sometimes provide clues. Often, if A happens before B, it hints that A causes B rather than vice versa. But grabbing a raincoat as you leave home in the morning frequently happens *before* it rains in the afternoon. The timing notwithstanding, taking your raincoat with you in the morning clearly does not *cause* rain later in the day. In this case, your *anticipation* of B causes A to happen.

An important lesson for economists and noneconomists alike is never to take observations at face value. Always make sure you can explain *why* two events are related. To do so, you need another tool in the economist's toolbox: a model.

Models

LO 1.6 List the characteristics of a good economic model.

A **model** is a simplified representation of a complicated situation. In economics, models show how people, firms, and governments make decisions about managing resources, and how their decisions interact. An economic model can represent a situation as basic as how people decide what car to buy or as complex as what causes a global recession.

model a simplified representation of the important parts of a complicated situation

Because models simplify complex problems, they allow us to focus our attention on the most important parts. Models rarely include every detail of a given situation, but that is a good thing. If we had to describe the entire world with perfect accuracy before solving a problem, we'd be so overwhelmed with details that we'd never get the answer. By carefully simplifying the situation to its essentials, we can get useful answers that are *approximately* right.

One of the most basic models of the economy is the **circular flow model**. The economy involves billions of transactions every day, and the circular flow model helps show how all of those transactions work together. The model slashes through complexity to show important patterns. Figure 1-1 shows the circular flow of economic transactions in a graphic format called the *circular flow diagram*.

circular flow model a simplified representation of how the economy's transactions work together

The first simplification of the circular flow model is to narrow our focus to the two most important types of actors in the economy, households and firms:

- *Households* are vital in two ways. First, they supply land and labor to firms and invest capital in firms. (Land, labor, and capital are called the *factors of production*.) Second they buy the goods and services that firms produce.

FIGURE 1-1
Circular flow diagram

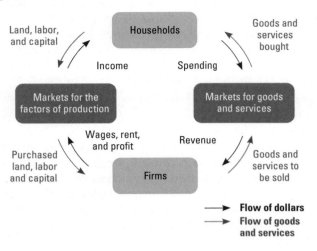

- *Firms* too are vital, but do the opposite of households: They buy or rent the land, labor, and capital supplied by households, and they produce and sell goods and services. The model shows that firms and households are tightly connected through both production and consumption.

In another helpful simplification, the circular flow model narrows the focus to two markets that connect households and firms:

- The *market for goods and services* is exactly what it sounds like: It reflects all of the activity involved in the buying and selling of goods and services. In this market, households spend their wages from labor and their income from land and capital, and firms earn revenue from selling their goods and services.
- The second market is the *market for the factors of production*. Here, households supply land, labor, and capital, and firms hire and purchase or rent these inputs.

The model puts all of this together. The transactions we have described are part of two loops. One is a loop of inputs and outputs as they travel throughout the economy. The *inputs* are the land, labor, and capital firms use to produce goods. The *outputs* are the goods and services that firms produce using the factors of production.

Another loop represents the flow of dollars. Households buy goods and services using the money they get from firms for using their factors of production. Firms get revenues from selling these goods and services—and, in turn, firms can then use the money to buy or rent factors of production.

You might be a little dizzy at this point, with everything spinning in loops. To help straighten things out, let's follow $5 from your wallet as it flows through the economy. You could spend this $5 in any number of ways. As you're walking down the street, you see a box of donuts sitting in the window of your local bakery. You head in and give the baker your $5, a transaction in the market for goods. The money represents revenue for the baker and spending by you. The donuts are an output of the bakery.

The story of your $5 is not over, though. In order to make more donuts, the baker puts that $5 toward buying inputs in the market for the factors of production. This might include paying rent for the bakery or paying wages for an assistant. The baker's spending represents income for the households that provide the labor in the bakery or rent out the space. Once the baker pays wages or rent with that $5, it has made it through a cycle in the circular flow.

As the circular flow model shows, an economic model approximates what happens in the real economy. Later in the book, we'll discuss other models that focus on specific questions—like how much gasoline prices will go up when the government raises taxes or how fast the economy is likely to grow in the next decade. The best models lead us to clearer answers about complicated questions. What makes a good economic model? We have already said that good models can leave out details that are not crucial, and focus on the important aspects of a situation. To be useful, a model *should* also do three things:

1. *A good model predicts cause and effect.* The circular flow model gives a useful description of the basics of the economy. Often, though, we want to go further. Many times we want a model not only to describe economic connections but also to predict how things will happen in the future. To do that, we have to get cause and effect right. If your model says that A causes B, you should be able to explain why. In Chapter 3 we'll learn about a central model in economics that shows that for most goods and services, the quantity people want to buy goes down as the price goes up. Why? As the cost of an item rises but the benefit of owning it remains the same, more people will decide that the trade-off is not worth it.

2. *A good model makes clear assumptions.* Although models are usually too simple to fit the real world perfectly, it's important that they be clear about the simplifying assumptions. Doing so helps us to know when the model will predict real events accurately and when it will not. For example, we said earlier that economists often assume that people behave rationally. We know that isn't always true, but we accept it as an assumption because it is *approximately* accurate in many situations. As long as we are clear that we are making this assumption, we will know that the model will not be accurate when people fail to behave rationally.

3. *A good model describes the real world accurately.* If a model does not describe what actually happens in the real world, something about the model is wrong. We've admitted that models are not perfectly accurate, because they are intentionally simpler than the real world. But if a model predicts things that are not usually or approximately true, it is not useful. How do we tell if a model is realistic? Economists test their models by observing what happens in the real world and collecting data, which they use to verify or reject the model. In the Real Life box "Testing models against history," take a look at a model that has been tested over and over again in the last few hundred years.

REAL LIFE

Testing models against history

Real Life boxes show how the concept you're reading about relates to the real world. They are your chance to test models against the data. Often these boxes will describe a situation in which people used an economic idea to solve a business or policy question, or they present interesting research ideas or experiences. Watch for links to online content, such as videos or news stories.

Thomas Malthus, an early nineteenth-century economist, created a model that described the relationship between population growth and food production. The model predicted that mass starvation would occur as populations outgrew food supplies. In his famous work, *An Essay on the Principle of Population,* Malthus wrote:

> The power of population is so superior to the power of the earth to produce subsistence for man, that premature death must in some shape or other visit the human race. . . . [G]igantic inevitable famine stalks . . .

Since Malthus wrote these words, famines have in fact killed millions of people. However, they have not been related to population growth in the way that Malthus predicted. Instead, the population of the world has increased from under a billion in 1800 to almost seven billion today. At the same time, nutrition standards have risen in almost every country.

Malthus's model left out a crucial part of the story: human ingenuity and technological progress. As the world's population has grown, people have found new ways to grow better food more efficiently, on more land. They have also found better ways to limit population growth.

Malthus's idea has not died out, though. Today, neo-Malthusian theory predicts that population will still outstrip the world's productive capacity. This theory updates Malthus's model to address more modern concerns, such as increasing environmental degradation which makes land unfit for farming. Others argue that nonrenewable resources, such as oil, will be depleted. Still others warn that even if the world's farmers can produce enough food, unequal access to resources like fresh water will cause local famines and wars.

Critics of these arguments point out that human ingenuity has somehow averted catastrophe at every point in recent history when a Malthusian disaster seemed imminent. The population boom that followed World War II was supposed to lead to starvation, but it was counteracted by the Green Revolution, which increased food production manyfold.

Is the neo-Malthusian model accurate, then, or is it too missing some critical factor? Time will provide the data to answer this question.

Source: T. R. Malthus, *An Essay on the Principle of Population*, 1798.

Positive and normative analysis

LO 1.7 Distinguish between positive and normative analysis.

Economics is a field of study in which people frequently confuse facts with judgments that are based on beliefs. Think about the following example:

Statement #1: Income taxes reduce the number of hours that people want to work.

Statement #2: Income taxes should be reduced or abolished.

Many people have trouble separating these two statements. Some feel that the second statement flows logically from the first. Others disagree with the second statement, so they assume the first can't possibly be true.

If you read carefully, however, you'll see that the first sentence is a statement about cause and effect. Thus, it can be proved true or false by data and evidence. A statement that makes a factual claim about how the world *actually* works is called a **positive statement**.

The second sentence, on the other hand, cannot be proved true or false. Instead, it indicates what *should be* done—but only if we share certain goals, understandings, and moral beliefs. A statement that makes a claim about how the world *should be* is called a **normative statement**.

To see how important the distinction between positive and normative statements can be, consider two claims that a physicist might make:

Positive statement: A nuclear weapon with the explosive power of 10 kilotons of TNT will have a fallout radius of up to 6 miles.

Normative statement: The United States was right to use nuclear weapons in World War II.

positive statement a factual claim about how the world actually works

normative statement a claim about how the world should be

Although people could disagree about both of these statements, the first is a question of scientific fact, while the second depends heavily on a person's ethical and political beliefs. The first statement may inform your opinion of the second, but you can still agree with one and not the other.

Earlier in this chapter, we introduced a feature called What Do You Think? that asks for your opinion about an important policy or life decision. From this point forward, you can use your understanding of the differences between normative and positive analysis to untangle the questions asked in these boxes and combine the two kinds of analysis to arrive at a conclusion. Begin trying your hand at this with the What Do You Think? box "The cost of college cash."

WHAT DO YOU THINK?

The cost of college cash

In 2009–2010, the average yearly cost of a college education ranged from $12,804 at public universities to $32,184 at private universities. Students have a number of options for paying the bill. They can take out federal loans, private loans, or a combination of the two to defer payments until later, or they can use savings or earnings to foot the bill.

Students who qualify for federal loans enjoy benefits such as limits on the interest rate they can be charged or the total payments they can be expected to make, and the possibility of loan forgiveness if they enter certain fields after graduation.

Lending to students is a controversial topic. Some people argue for more controls on private lending institutions, such as interest-rate caps and greater protection for students who default. They reason that lending programs should support students who would not otherwise be able to afford college. Furthermore, they argue, graduating with a lot of debt discourages students from going into lower-paid public service jobs.

Other people maintain that the existing lending system is fine. Getting a college degree, they argue, increases a person's future earning power so much that graduates should be able to handle the debt, even at high interest rates. They worry that overregulation will discourage private lenders from offering student loans, defeating the purpose of giving students better access to financial assistance.

What do you think?

Use the four basic questions economists ask to break down the problem. Remember that your answer can draw on both positive analysis (what *will* happen if a certain policy is followed) and normative analysis (what *should* be done, given your values and goals). You should be able to say which parts of your answers fall into each category.

1. What motivations and constraints apply to students who are considering different schools and loan options? What motivations and constraints apply to private lenders?
2. What opportunity costs do students face when deciding how to pay for college? Should they avoid loans by skipping college altogether or by working their way through college?
3. How would prospective students respond to government limits on the interest rate on student loans? How would private banks that offer student loans respond?
4. Why do you think the federal government has not yet implemented interest-rate caps on private student loans? Do you anticipate any unintended side effects of that policy?
5. Consider your arguments in response to questions 1 through 4. Which parts were based on normative statements and which on positive statements?

Sources: "Trends in college pricing," http://nces.ed.gov/fastfacts/display.asp?id=76; "How much student debt is too much?" http://roomfordebate.blogs.nytimes.com/2009/06/14/how-much-student-debt-is-too-much/?scp=1&sq=student%20loans&st=cse.

Throughout this book, remember that *you don't have to buy into a particular moral or political outlook in order for economics to be useful to you.* Our goal is to provide you with a toolbox of economic concepts that you can use to engage in positive analysis. We will also highlight important decisions you may face that will require you to engage in normative thinking, informed by economic analysis. Economics can help you to make better decisions and design more effective policies regardless of your goals and beliefs.

✓ CONCEPT CHECK

- ❑ What does it mean when two variables are positively correlated? **[LO 1.5]**
- ❑ What are the characteristics of a good economic model? **[LO 1.6]**
- ❑ What is the difference between a positive statement and a normative statement? **[LO 1.7]**

Conclusion

Economists approach problems differently from many other people. Underlying economics is the basic principle of rational behavior—that people make choices to achieve their goals in the most effective way possible.

In this chapter we have introduced the basic concepts economists use, as well as four questions they ask to break down problems. Throughout this book, you will see these concepts and questions over and over again:

1. Scarcity: *What are the wants and constraints of those involved?*
2. Opportunity cost: *What are the trade-offs?*
3. Incentives: *How will others respond?*
4. Efficiency: *Why isn't everyone already doing it?*

In later chapters, as we progress to more complicated problems, try using these four questions to break down problems into manageable pieces, ones you can understand using the fundamental concepts presented in this chapter.

 ◄ Mobile Window on the World—Scan this code with your smartphone to find more applications of the chapter content. (Need a barcode reader? Try ScanLife, available in your app store.)

Visit your mobile app store and download ► the Karlan and Morduch Study Econ app.

Key Terms

economics, p. 4

microeconomics, p. 4

macroeconomics, p. 4

rational behavior, p. 5

scarcity, p. 5

opportunity cost, p. 7

marginal decision making, p. 8

sunk costs, p. 9

incentive, p. 10

efficiency, p. 11

correlation, p. 13

causation, p. 13

model, p. 15

circular flow model, p. 15

positive statement, p. 18

normative statement, p. 18

Summary

LO 1.1 Explain the economic concept of scarcity.

Economists usually assume that people behave rationally and live within a condition of scarcity. Answering the question, *What are the wants and constraints of those involved?* tells you what to expect from each player in the situation you are analyzing. Given rational behavior and scarcity, you can expect people to work to get what they want (their motivations) using the limited resources at their disposal (their constraints).

LO 1.2 Explain the economic concepts of opportunity cost and marginal decision making.

Trade-offs arise when you must give up something to get something else. Answering *What are the trade-offs?* will tell you about the costs and benefits associated with a decision. The full cost of doing something is the *opportunity cost*. Economists assume that rational people make decisions "at the margin," by comparing any additional benefits from a choice to the extra costs it brings. If people are behaving rationally when they face trade-offs, they will always choose to do something if the marginal benefit is greater than the opportunity cost. They will never do it if the opportunity cost is greater than the marginal benefit.

LO 1.3 Explain the economic concept of incentives.

The collective reaction to changing trade-offs is a central idea in economics. Asking *How will others respond?* will give you a complete picture of how a particular decision affects the world. You can assume that any action will bring a response, because people react to changes in their incentives.

LO 1.4 Explain the economic concept of efficiency.

Efficiency occurs when resources are used in the most productive way possible to produce the goods and services that have the greatest total economic value to society. In other words, efficiency means using resources to produce the things that people want. Under normal circumstances, markets are efficient.

So when you see what seems to be unexploited opportunity, you should ask: If it's such a great idea, *Why isn't everyone already doing it?* Markets usually allocate resources efficiently. When they don't, a market failure may have occurred, government may have intervened in the economy, there may be goals other than profit involved, or there may be a genuine opportunity for innovation.

LO 1.5 Distinguish between correlation and causation.

When there is a consistently observed relationship between two events, we say they are *correlated.* This is different from a *causal* relationship, in which one event brings about the other. Three common ways in which correlation and causation are confused are correlation without causation, omitted variables, and reverse causation.

LO 1.6 List the characteristics of a good economic model.

A model is a simplified representation of the important parts of a complicated situation. In economics, models usually show how people, firms, and governments make decisions about managing resources and how their decisions interact. The circular flow model is a representation of how the transactions of households and firms flow through the economy. A good economic model should predict cause and effect, describe the world accurately, and state its assumptions clearly. Economists test their models by observing what happens in the world and collecting data that can be used to support or reject their models.

LO 1.7 Distinguish between positive and normative analysis.

A statement that makes a factual claim about how the world actually works is called a *positive* statement. A statement that makes a claim about how the world should be is called a *normative* statement. Economics is a field in which people frequently confuse positive statements with normative statements. However, you do not have to adopt a particular moral or political point of view to use economic concepts and models.

Review Questions

1. Suppose you are shopping for new clothes to wear to job interviews, but you're on a tight budget. In this situation, what are your wants and constraints? What does it mean to behave rationally in the face of scarcity? **[LO 1.1]**

2. You are a student with a demanding schedule of classes. You also work part-time and your supervisor allows you to determine your schedule. In this situation, what is your scarce resource? How do you decide how many hours to work? **[LO 1.1]**

3. Think about the definition of scarcity that you learned in this chapter. Name three ways that you confront scarcity in your own life. **[LO 1.1]**

4. When shopping for your interview clothes, what are some trade-offs you face? What is the opportunity cost of buying new clothes? What are the benefits? How do you balance the two? **[LO 1.2]**

5. You have an 8:30 class this morning but you are feeling extremely tired. How do you decide whether to get some extra sleep or go to class? **[LO 1.2]**

6. It's Friday night. You already have a ticket to a concert, which cost you $30. A friend invites you to go out for a game of paintball instead. Admission would cost you $25, and you think you'd get $25 worth of enjoyment out of it. Your concert ticket is nonrefundable. What is your opportunity cost (in dollars) of playing paintball? **[LO 1.2]**

7. Suppose you have two job offers and are considering the trade-offs between them. Job A pays $45,000 per year and includes health insurance and two weeks of paid vacation. Job B pays $30,000 per year and includes four weeks of paid vacation but no health insurance. **[LO 1.2]**
   a. List the benefits of Job A and the benefits of Job B.
   b. List the opportunity cost of Job A and the opportunity cost of Job B.

8. Your former neighbor gave you his lawnmower when he moved. You are thinking of using this gift to mow lawns in your neighborhood this summer for extra cash. As you think about what to charge your neighbors and whether this idea is worth your effort, what opportunity costs do you need to consider? **[LO 1.2]**

9. Think of a few examples of incentives in your daily life. How do you respond to those incentives? **[LO 1.3]**

10. You supervise a team of salespeople. Your employees already receive a company discount. Suggest a positive incentive and a negative incentive you could use to improve their productivity. **[LO 1.3]**

11. Your boss decides to pair workers in teams and offer bonuses to the most productive team. Why might your boss offer team bonuses instead of individual bonuses? **[LO 1.3]**

12. Think of a public policy—a local or national law, tax, or public service—that offers an incentive for a particular behavior. Explain what the incentive is, who is offering it, and what they are trying encourage or discourage. Does the incentive work? **[LO 1.3]**

13. Why do individuals or firms usually provide the goods and services people want? **[LO 1.4]**

14. You may have seen TV advertisements for products or programs that claim to teach a surefire way to make millions on the stock market. Apply the *Why isn't everyone already doing it?* test to this situation. Do you believe the ads? Why or why not? **[LO 1.4]**

15. Describe an innovation in technology, business, or culture that had a major economic impact in your lifetime. **[LO 1.4]**

16. Why do people confuse correlation with causation? **[LO 1.5]**

17. Name two things that are positively correlated and two things that are negatively correlated. **[LO 1.5]**

18. Why is it important for a good economic model to predict cause and effect? **[LO 1.6]**

19. Why is it important for a good economic model to make clear assumptions? **[LO 1.6]**

20. Describe an economic model you know. What does the model predict about cause and effect? **[LO 1.6]**

21. Describe an economic model you know. What assumptions does the model make? Are the assumptions reasonable? **[LO 1.6]**

22. What is the difference between disagreeing about a positive statement and disagreeing about a normative statement? **[LO 1.7]**

23. Would a good economic model be more likely to address a positive statement or a normative statement? Why? **[LO 1.7]**

24. Write a positive statement and a normative statement about your favorite hobby. **[LO 1.7]**

Problems and Applications

1. Think about how and why goods and resources are scarce. Goods and resources can be scarce for reasons that are inherent to their nature at all times, temporary or seasonal, or that are artificially created. Separate the goods listed below into

two groups; indicate which (if any) are artificially scarce (AS), and which (if any) are inherently scarce (IS). **[LO 1.1]**

a. air of any quality ____
b. land ____
c. patented goods ____
d. original Picasso paintings ____

2. You are looking for a new apartment in Manhattan. Your income is $4,000 per month, and you know that you should not spend more than 25 percent of your income on rent. You have come across the following listing for one-bedroom apartments on craigslist. You are indifferent about location, and transportation costs are the same to each neighborhood. **[LO 1.1]**

Chelsea	$1,200
Battery Park	2,200
Delancey	950
Midtown	1,500

a. Which apartments fall within your budget? (Check all that apply.)
b. Suppose that you adhere to the 25 percent guideline but also receive a $1,000 cost-of-living supplement since you are living and working in Manhattan. Which apartments fall within your budget now?

3. Suppose the price of a sweater is $15. Julia's benefit from purchasing each additional sweater is given in the table below. Julia gets the most benefit from the first sweater and less benefit from each additional sweater. If Julia is behaving rationally, how many sweaters will she purchase? **[LO 1.2]**

	Marginal benefit ($)
1st sweater	50
2nd sweater	35
3rd sweater	30
4th sweater	23
5th sweater	12
6th sweater	8

4. Sweaters sell for $15 at the crafts fair. Allie knits sweaters and her marginal costs are given in the table below. Allie's costs increase with each additional sweater. If Allie is behaving rationally, how many sweaters will she sell? **[LO 1.2]**

	Marginal cost ($)
1st sweater	5
2nd sweater	8
3rd sweater	12
4th sweater	18
5th sweater	25
6th sweater	32

5. Last year, you estimated you would earn $5 million in sales revenues from developing a new product. So far, you have spent $3 million developing the product, but it is not yet complete. Meanwhile, this year you have new sales projections that show expected revenues from the new product will actually be only $4 million. How much should you be willing to spend to complete the product development? **[LO 1.2]**

a. $0.
b. Up to $1 million.
c. Up to $4 million.
d. Whatever it takes.

6. Consider the following examples. For each one, say whether the incentive is positive or negative. **[LO 1.3]**

a. Bosses who offer time-and-a-half for working on national holidays.
b. Mandatory minimum sentencing for drug offenses.
c. Fines for littering.
d. Parents who offer their children extra allowance money for good grades.

7. Consider the following events that change prices. For each one, say whether the opportunity cost of consuming the affected good increases or decreases. **[LO 1.3]**

		Affected good
a.	A local movie theater offers a student discount.	Movie tickets
b.	A tax on soft drinks passes in your state.	Soft drinks
c.	Subsidies on corn are cut in half.	Corn subsidies
d.	Your student health center begins offering flu shots for free.	Flu shots

8. Your best friend has an idea for a drive-thru bar. Indicate the best explanation for why others have not taken advantage of her idea: true innovation, market failure, government intervention, unprofitable. **[LO 1.4]**

9. Your best friend has an idea for a long-distance car service to drive people across the country. Indicate the best explanation for why others have not taken advantage of her idea: true innovation, market failure, intervention, unprofitable. **[LO 1.4]**

10. Determine whether each of the following questionable statements is best explained by correlation without causation, an omitted variable, or reverse causation. **[LO 1.5]**
    a. In cities that have more police, crime rates are higher.
    b. Many retired people live in states where everyone uses air conditioning during the summer.
    c. More people come down with the flu during the Winter Olympics than during the Summer Olympics.
    d. For the last five years, Punxsutawney Phil has seen his shadow on Groundhog Day, and spring has come late.

11. For each of the pairs below, determine whether they are positively correlated, negatively correlated, or uncorrelated. **[LO 1.5]**
    a. Time spent studying and test scores
    b. Vaccination and illness
    c. Soft drink preference and music preference
    d. Income and education

12. Each statement below is part of an economic model. Indicate whether the statement is a prediction of cause and effect or an assumption. **[LO 1.6]**
    a. People behave rationally.
    b. If the price of a good falls, people will consume more of that good.

    c. Mass starvation will occur as population outgrows the food supply.
    d. Firms want to maximize profits.

13. From the list below, select the characteristics that describe a good economic model. **[LO 1.6]**
    a. Includes every detail of a given situation.
    b. Predicts that A causes B.
    c. Makes approximately accurate assumptions.
    d. Fits the real world perfectly.
    e. Predicts things that are usually true.

14. Determine whether each of the following statements is positive or normative. (Remember that a positive statement isn't necessarily *correct*; it just makes a factual claim rather than a moral judgment.) **[LO 1.7]**
    a. People who pay their bills on time are less likely than others to get into debt.
    b. Hard work is a virtue.
    c. Everyone should pay his or her bills on time.
    d. China has a bigger population than any other country in the world.
    e. China's One-Child Policy (which limits families to one child each) helped to spur the country's rapid economic growth.
    f. Lower taxes are good for the country.

15. You just received your midterm exam results and your professor wrote the following note: "You received a 70 on this exam, the average score. If you want to improve your grade, you should study more." Evaluate your professor's note. **[LO 1.7]**
    a. Is the first sentence positive or normative?
    b. Is the second sentence positive or normative?

Chapter Endnote

1. "Grameen Bank at a glance," Grameen Bank, October 2011, http://www.grameen-info.org/index.php?option=com_content&task=view&id=453&Itemid=527.

Specialization and Exchange

Chapter

2

LEARNING OBJECTIVES

LO 2.1   Construct a production possibilities graph and describe what causes shifts in production possibilities curves.

LO 2.2   Define absolute and comparative advantage.

LO 2.3   Define specialization and explain why people specialize.

LO 2.4   Explain how the gains from trade follow from comparative advantage.

THE ORIGINS OF A T-SHIRT

How can we get the most out of available resources? It's one of the most basic economic questions. Factory managers ask it when looking for ways to increase production. National leaders ask it as they design economic policy. Activists ask it when they look for ways to reduce poverty or conserve the environment. And, in a different way, it's a question we all ask ourselves when thinking about what to do in life and how to make sure that we're taking full advantage of our talents.

To get a handle on this question, we start by thinking about resources at the highest level: the logic of international trade and the specialization of production between countries. By the end of the chapter, we hope that you'll see how the same ideas apply to decisions at any scale, right down to whether it makes more sense to fix your own computer or pay a specialist to do it for you.

We'll start with what seems to be a simple question: Where did your T-shirt come from? Look at the tag. We're betting it was made in a place you've never been to, and maybe never thought of visiting. China? Malaysia? Honduras? Sri Lanka?

That "made in" label tells only part of the story. Chances are that your shirt's history spans other parts of the globe. Consider a standard T-shirt: The cotton might have been grown in Mali and then shipped to Pakistan, where it was spun into yarn. The yarn might have been sent to China, where it was woven into cloth, cut into pieces, and assembled into a shirt. That shirt might then have traveled all the way to the United States, where it was shipped to a store near you. A couple of years from now, when you are cleaning out your closet, you may donate the shirt to a charity, which may ship it to a secondhand clothing vendor in Mali—right back where your shirt's travels began.

Of course, this is not only the story of shirts. It is remarkably similar to the story of shoes, computers, and cars, among many other manufactured goods. Today, the products and services most of us take for granted come to us through an incredibly complex global network of farms, mines, factories, traders, and stores. Why is the production of even a simple T-shirt spread across the world? Why is the cotton grown in Mali and the sewing done in China, rather than vice versa? Why isn't the whole shirt made in the United States, so that it doesn't have to travel so far to reach you?

25

This chapter addresses fundamental economic questions about who produces which goods and why. The fact that millions of people and firms around the globe coordinate their activities to provide consumers with the right combination of goods and services seems like magic. This feat of coordination doesn't happen by chance, nor does a superplanner tell everyone where to go and what to do. Instead, the global production line is a natural outcome of people everywhere acting in their own self-interest to improve their own lives. Economists call this coordination mechanism the *invisible hand,* an idea that was first suggested by the eighteenth-century economic thinker Adam Smith.

To get some insight into the *who* and *why* of production, consider how the story of shirts has changed over the last few centuries. For most of the 1800s, Americans wore shirts made in the United States. Today, however, most shirts are made in China, Bangladesh, and other countries where factory wages are low. Have American workers become worse at making shirts over the last two centuries? Definitely not. In fact, as we'll see in this chapter, it doesn't even mean that Chinese workers are better than American workers at making shirts. Instead, each good tends to be produced by the country, company, or person with the lowest opportunity cost for producing that good.

Countries and firms *specialize* in making goods for which they have the lowest opportunity cost, and they trade with one another to get the combination of goods they want to consume. The resulting *gains from trade* can be split up so that everyone ends up better off. It's no surprise, then, that as transportation and communication between countries have improved, trade has taken off.

The concepts in this chapter apply not just to the wealth of nations and international trade. They also illuminate the daily choices most people face. Who should cook which dishes at Thanksgiving dinner? Should you hire a plumber or fix the pipes yourself? Should you become a rock star or an economist? The concepts these questions raise can be subtle and are sometimes misunderstood. We hope this chapter will provide insights that will help you become a better resource manager in all areas of your life.

Production Possibilities

In Chapter 1, we talked about models. Good models help us understand complex situations through simplifying assumptions that allow us to zero in on the important aspects. The story of why China now produces shirts for Americans that Americans themselves were producing 200 years ago is a complex one, as you'd expect. But by simplifying it into a model, we can reach useful insights.

Let's assume the United States and China produce only two things—shirts and, say, bushels of wheat. (In reality, of course, they produce many things, but we're trying not to get bogged down in details right now.) The model uses wheat to stand in for "stuff other than shirts," allowing us to focus on what we're really interested in—shirts.

Using this model we'll perform a thought experiment about production using a tool called the *production possibilities frontier*. This tool is used in other contexts as well, many of which have no connection to international trade. Here we use it to show what has changed over the last couple of centuries to explain why Americans now buy shirts from China.

Drawing the production possibilities frontier

LO 2.1 Construct a production possibilities graph and describe what causes shifts in production possibilities curves.

Let's step back in time to the United States in 1800. In our simple model, there are 2 million American workers, and they have two choices of where to work: shirt factories or wheat farms. In shirt factories, each worker produces one shirt per day. On wheat farms, each worker produces two bushels of wheat per day.

What would happen if everyone worked on a wheat farm? The United States would produce 4 million bushels of wheat per day (2 bushels of wheat per worker × 2 million workers). This is one "production possibility." We represent it by point A in panel A of Figure 2-1. Alternatively, what would happen if everyone went to work in a shirt factory? The United States would produce 2 million shirts per day (1 shirt per worker × 2 million workers). This production possibility is represented by point E in Figure 2-1.

Of course, the United States wouldn't want just shirts or just wheat—and there is no reason that all workers have to produce the same thing. There are many different combinations of shirts and wheat that American workers could produce, as panel B of Figure 2-1 shows. For example, if one-quarter of the workers go to the shirt factory, they can make 500,000 shirts (1 shirt per worker × 500,000 workers) and the remaining workers can produce 3 million bushels of wheat (2 bushels per worker × 1.5 million workers). This production possibility is represented by point B in panel B. Or maybe 1 million workers make shirts (1 million shirts) and 1 million grow wheat (2 million bushels). That's point C.

We can continue splitting the workforce between shirts and wheat in different ways, each of which can be plotted as a point on the graph in Figure 2-1. If we fill in enough points, we create the solid green line shown in Figure 2-2. This is the **production possibilities frontier (PPF)**. It is a line or curve that shows all the possible combinations of outputs that can be produced using all available resources. In this case, the frontier plots all combinations of shirts and wheat that can be produced using all available workers in the United States. Points inside the frontier (such as point T) are achievable, but don't make full use of all available resources.

The production possibilities frontier helps us answer the first of the economists' questions that we discussed in Chapter 1: *What are the wants and constraints of those involved?* People in the United States *want* to consume shirts and wheat (and other things, of course; remember, we're simplifying). The production possibilities frontier gives us a way to represent the *constraints* on production. The United States cannot produce combinations of shirts and wheat that lie outside the frontier—such as point U in Figure 2-2. There just aren't enough workers or hours in the day to produce at point U, no matter how they are allocated between shirts and wheat.

The production possibilities frontier also addresses the second economists' question: *What are the trade-offs?* Each worker can make *either* one shirt *or* two bushels of wheat per day. In other words, there is a trade-off between the quantity of wheat produced and the quantity of shirts produced. If we want an extra shirt, one worker has to stop growing wheat for a day. Therefore, the opportunity cost of one shirt is two bushels of wheat. Growing another bushel of wheat takes one worker half a day, so the opportunity cost of a bushel of wheat is half a shirt. This opportunity cost is represented graphically by

production possibilities frontier (PPF) a line or curve that shows all the possible combinations of two outputs that can be produced using all available resources

FIGURE 2-1

Possible production combinations

(A) Producing one good

Production possibilities	Bushels of wheat (millions)	Shirts (millions)
A	4	0
E	0	2

(B) Producing both goods

Production possibilities	Bushels of wheat (millions)	Shirts (millions)
B	3	0.5
C	2	1.0
D	1	1.5

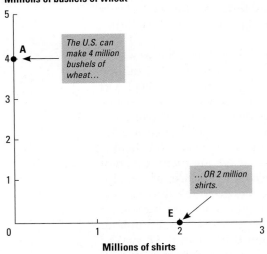

Millions of bushels of wheat

The U.S. can make 4 million bushels of wheat...

...OR 2 million shirts.

Millions of shirts

The United States can produce the maximum number of shirts or the maximum amount of wheat by devoting all its resources to one good or the other.

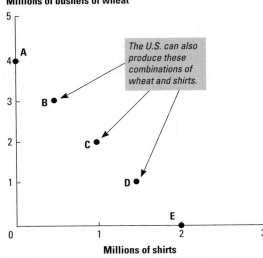

Millions of bushels of wheat

The U.S. can also produce these combinations of wheat and shirts.

Millions of shirts

By allocating some resources to the production of each good, the United States can also produce many different combinations of wheat and shirts.

the slope of the production possibilities frontier. Moving up the frontier means getting more wheat at the cost of fewer shirts. Moving down the frontier means less wheat and more shirts. Looking at Figure 2-2, you'll notice that the slope of the line is −2. This is the same as saying that the opportunity cost of one shirt is always two bushels of wheat.

We can also express the production possibilities frontier as an equation. Let's call the quantity of shirts produced each day X and the quantity of wheat Y. There are 2 million total workers, so the number making shirts plus the number growing wheat will always add up to 2 million. Since each worker takes one day to make a shirt or half a day to grow a bushel of wheat, the number making shirts equals X, and the number growing wheat equals $\frac{1}{2}$ of Y. We can write this in equation form as $X + \frac{1}{2}Y = 2$ million. Any combination of X and Y that make this equation hold true represents a point on the frontier.

More generally, where X and Y are two goods, and a is a number that represents how many workers are needed to produce one unit of good X (in our example, shirts), and b represents the amount of workers that are needed to produce one unit of good Y (in our example, wheat), then we can say in an equation that:

For a refresher on calculating and interpreting slopes, see Appendix A, "Math Essentials: Understanding Graphs and Slope," which follows this chapter.

Equation 2-1

$$aX + bY = \text{Total resources}$$

FIGURE 2-2

Production possibilities frontier

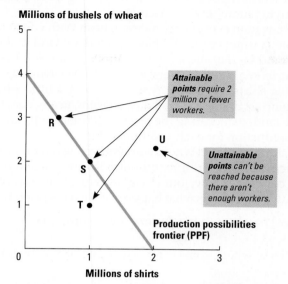

Millions of bushels of wheat

Attainable points require 2 million or fewer workers.

Unattainable points can't be reached because there aren't enough workers.

Production possibilities frontier (PPF)

Millions of shirts

Points on or below the production possibilities frontier, such as R, S, and T, represent combinations of goods that the United States can produce with available resources. Points outside the frontier, such as U, are unattainable because there aren't enough resources.

This equation can also be solved for Y in order to show the slope of the production possibilities curve. Subtracting the aX term from both sides and dividing through by b gives the equation in what is called *point-slope* form. The name refers to the fact that in this form the equation is written in terms of the slope and one point on the line. The $-\left(\frac{a}{b}\right)$ constant in front of the X term is the slope of the production possibilities frontier, which is the same as the opportunity cost of good X.

Equation 2-2

$$Y = -\left(\frac{a}{b}\right)X + \left(\frac{\text{Total resources}}{b}\right)$$

So far, we've made the assumption that all workers are able to make the same amount of each good. In reality, some workers will probably be nimble-fingered and great at making shirts, while others will be more naturally gifted at farming. What happens if we adjust our simple model to reflect this reality?

Let's start off with all workers growing wheat and nobody making shirts. If we reallocate the workers who are best at making shirts, we can get a lot of shirts without giving up too much wheat. In other words, the opportunity cost of making the first few shirts is very low. Now imagine almost all the workers are making shirts, so that only the very best farmers are left growing wheat. If we reallocate most of the remaining workers to shirt making, we give up a lot of wheat to get only a few extra shirts. The opportunity cost of getting those last few shirts is very high.

We can add a little more nuance to the model, to include land and machinery as resources also needed for production. We would find that the same pattern holds: The opportunity cost of producing an additional unit of a good typically increases as more of each resource is allocated to it. For instance, growing more wheat probably requires

For a refresher on linear equations, see Appendix B, "Math Essentials: Working with Linear Equations," which follows Chapter 3.

reallocating not only workers but also farm land. Making more shirts means setting up new factories and buying more sewing machines.

Once again, let's start with everyone growing wheat. With wheat production pushed to the maximum, some farmers probably have to work on land that isn't well-suited to growing wheat. It could be that the land is swampy, or the soil has been overfarmed and depleted of nutrients. When farmers who had been working on this poor land switch over to making shirts, the economy will lose only a little wheat and gain many shirts in return. In contrast, if only a small amount of wheat is being grown using only the best, most fertile land, reallocating the last few farmers will cause a relatively large decrease in wheat production for each additional shirt.

Returning to the simplest model where workers are the only input to production, we can translate this increasing opportunity cost into the production possibilities frontier. Doing so, we get a curve that bows out (a convex curve) instead of a straight line, as shown in Figure 2-3. Panel A shows what happens if we have just three types of workers:

- For every bushel of wheat, some can make one shirt; they're the ones between points C_1 and C_2.
- For every bushel of wheat, some can make only $\frac{1}{2}$ of a shirt (between points C_2 and C_3).
- For every bushel of wheat, some can make only $\frac{1}{4}$ of a shirt (between points C_3 and C_4).

FIGURE 2-3
Bowed-out (convex) production possibilities frontier

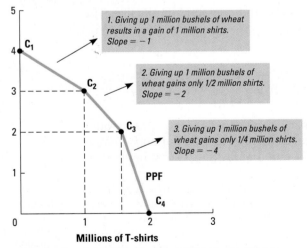

(A) Constructing the PPF

At point C_1, all workers produce wheat, and switching the best sewers to making shirts will result in a big gain in the quantity of shirts. As more and better farmers switch to making shirts, however, the gain in shirts produced decreases relative to the loss in the quantity of wheat. As a result the slope of the PPF is steeper from C_2 to C_3, and again from C_3 to C_4.

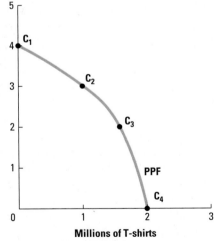

(B) The PPF

In reality, each worker has slightly different skills and therefore a slightly different opportunity cost of making shirts in terms of wheat. As a result, we get a smoothly curved production possibilities frontier.

In other words, as we go down the curve, we move from those who are better at making shirts to those who are better at growing wheat. As we do so, the opportunity cost of making shirts in terms of growing wheat increases, and the slope of the curve gets steeper (-1 between C_1 and C_2, -2 between C_2 and C_3, and -4 between C_3 and C_4).

In reality there aren't just three types of workers—each worker will have slightly different skills. The many possibilities will result in a curve that looks smooth, as in panel B of Figure 2-3. At each point of the curved production possibilities frontier, the slope represents the opportunity cost of getting more wheat or more shirts, based on the skills of the next worker who could switch.

Choosing among production possibilities

What can the production possibilities frontier tell us about what combination of goods an economy will choose to produce? Earlier, we noted that economies can produce at points inside the frontier, as well as points on it. However, choosing a production point inside the frontier means a country could get more wheat, more shirts, or both, just by using all available workers. For instance, in Figure 2-4, the United States can get more wheat without giving up any shirts, by moving from point B_1 to point B_2. It can do the same by moving from point B_2 to point B_3. But once at the frontier, it will have to give up some of one good to get more of the other. Points like B_3 that lie *on* the frontier are called **efficient**, because they squeeze the most output possible from all available resources. Points *within* (inside) the frontier are *inefficient* because they do not use all available resources.

efficient points combinations of production possibilities that squeeze the most output possible from all available resources

FIGURE 2-4
Choosing an efficient production combination

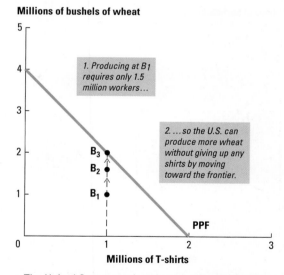

The United States needs only 1.5 million workers to reach point B_1. If the country employs more workers, it can reach point B_2 and get more wheat without giving up any shirts. The country can keep employing more workers until it reaches point B_3 (or any other point on the frontier) and there are no more workers left. Once the frontier is reached, getting more of one good requires giving up some of the other.

In the real world, economies aren't always efficient. A variety of problems can cause some workers to be unemployed or other resources to be left idle. We'll return to these issues in detail in future chapters. For now, we'll assume that production is always efficient. People and firms usually try to squeeze as much value as they can out of the resources available to them, so efficiency is a reasonable starting assumption.

Based on the assumption of efficiency, we can predict that an economy will choose to produce at a point on the frontier rather than inside it. What the production possibilities frontier cannot tell us is *which* point on the frontier that will be. Will it be F_1 in Figure 2-5, for example? Or will the U.S. choose to move down the curve to F_2, producing more shirts at the expense of less wheat? We can't say whether point F_1 or F_2 is better without knowing more about the situation. If the U.S. economy is completely self-sufficient, the decision depends on what combination of shirts and wheat people in the United States want to consume. If trade with other countries is possible, it also depends on consumers and production possibilities in those countries, as we'll see later in the chapter.

Shifting the production possibilities frontier

Thus far, we've built a simple model that tells us what combinations of T-shirts and wheat the United States could produce in 1800. However, a lot of things have changed since 1800, including an incredible explosion in productive capacity. The production possibilities frontier is a useful tool for illustrating this change and understanding how it affects the constraints and trade-offs the country faces. Two main factors drive the change in U.S. production possibilities.

FIGURE 2-5

Choosing between efficient combinations

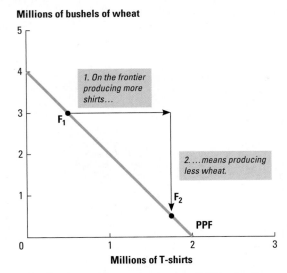

At all points on the production possibilities frontier, the United States employs the entire workforce. Because the country uses all its resources fully at each point, choosing between points on the frontier is a matter of preference when there is no trade with other countries. The U.S. may choose to produce more wheat and fewer shirts (point F) or more shirts and less wheat (point F_2), depending on what its consumers want.

First, there are more workers. The U.S. population now is much larger than it was in 1800. Having more workers means more people available to produce shirts and wheat. Graphically, we can represent this change by shifting the entire frontier outward. Panel A of Figure 2-6 shows what happens to the frontier when the U.S. population doubles, with each worker still able to produce one shirt or two bushels of wheat per day.

However, the real magic of expanded productive capacity lies in the incredible technological advances that have taken place over the last few centuries. In 1810, a businessman from Boston named Francis Cabot Lowell traveled to England to learn about British textile factories and to copy their superior technology. He brought back the power loom, which enabled workers to weave much more cotton fabric every day than they could before.

We can model this change in technology through the production possibilities frontier by changing the rate of shirt production from one to three shirts per day, as shown in panel B of Figure 2-6. As the rate of shirt production increases, while the rate of wheat production remains the same, the shape of the curve changes. In this case, it pivots outward along the x-axis, because for any given number of workers assigned to shirt-making, more shirts are produced than before. At every point except one (where all workers are growing wheat), the country can produce more with the same number of workers, thanks to improved technology.

> For a refresher about shifts and pivots in graphs, see Appendix B, "Math Essentials: Working with Linear Equations," which follows Chapter 3.

FIGURE 2-6

Shifting the production possibilities frontier

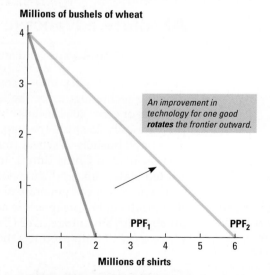

(A) Change in resources: Population growth

(B) Change in technology: Invention of the power loom

Production possibilities expand when resources increase. If the working population grows, the country can make more of everything by producing at the same rate as before. This *causes the frontier to shift outward*. If the population doubled, so would the maximum possible quantities of shifts and wheat.

Production possibilities expand when technology improves. If the textile industry adopts the power loom, workers can make more shirts in the same amount of time. This causes the frontier to rotate outward. The rate of wheat production remains constant while the rated of shirt production increases, so the slope of the frontier changes.

✓ CONCEPT CHECK

- ❐ Could a person or country ever produce a combination of goods that lies outside the production possibilities frontier? Why or why not? **[LO 2.1]**
- ❐ Would an increase in productivity as a result of a new technology shift a production possibilities frontier inward or outward? **[LO 2.1]**

Absolute and Comparative Advantage

In 1810, armed with power looms and a growing population, the United States was a highly effective producer of cotton shirts. For more than a century, it was the world's biggest clothing manufacturer. Since then, the U.S. population has grown larger, and manufacturing technology has improved even more. So, why are 30 percent of the world's clothing exports made in China today?

Up to now, we have worked with a very simple model of production to highlight the key trade-offs faced by individual producers. If there is no trade between countries, then the United States can consume only those goods that it produces on its own. In the real world, however, goods are made all over the world. If Americans want to buy more shirts than the United States produces, they can get them from somewhere else. Under these conditions, how can we predict which countries will produce which goods?

Understanding how resources are allocated among multiple producers is a step toward understanding why big firms work with specialized suppliers, or why a wealthy, productive country like the United States trades with much poorer, less-productive countries. In this section we will see that trade actually increases total production, which can benefit everyone involved. To see why, let's turn to the question of why most T-shirts sold in the United States today are made in China.

Absolute advantage

LO 2.2 Define absolute and comparative advantage.

Suppose that taking into account all the improvements in shirt-making and wheat-growing technology over the last two centuries, an American worker can now make 50 shirts or grow 200 bushels of wheat per day. A Chinese worker, on the other hand, can produce only 25 shirts (perhaps because U.S. workers use faster cloth-cutting technology) or 50 bushels of wheat (maybe because U.S. farmers use fertilizers and pesticides that farmers in China don't). In other words, given the same number of workers, the United States can produce twice as many shirts or four times as much wheat as China.

absolute advantage the ability to produce more of a good or service than others can with a given amount of resources

If a producer can generate more output than others with a given amount of resources, that producer has an **absolute advantage**. In our simplified model, the United States has an absolute advantage over China at producing both shirts and wheat, because it can make more of both products than China can per worker.

Comparative advantage

Absolute advantage is not the end of the story, though. If it were, the United States would still be producing the world's shirts. The problem is that for every T-shirt the United States produces, it uses resources that could otherwise be spent growing wheat. Of course, the same could be said of China. But in our model of T-shirt and wheat production, the opportunity cost of making one shirt in the U.S. is four bushels of wheat (200 bushels ÷ 50 shirts = 4 bushels per shirt); the opportunity cost of making one shirt in China is only two bushels of wheat (50 bushels ÷ 25 shirts = 2 bushels per shirt). The U.S. has to give up more to make a shirt than China does.

When a producer can make a good at a lower opportunity cost than other producers, we say it has a **comparative advantage** at producing that good. In our model, China has a comparative advantage over the United States at shirt-making, because its opportunity cost of producing a shirt is only two bushels of wheat, compared to four bushels of wheat for the United States.

The United States, on the other hand, has a comparative advantage over China at growing wheat. Each time the U.S. produces a bushel of wheat, it gives up the opportunity to produce one-quarter of a shirt (50 shirts ÷ 200 bushels = $\frac{1}{4}$ shirt per bushel). For China, however, the opportunity cost of growing a bushel of wheat is larger: it's one-half of a shirt (25 shirts ÷ 50 bushels = $\frac{1}{2}$ shirt per bushel). The United States has a lower opportunity cost for producing wheat than China ($\frac{1}{4}$ shirt is less than $\frac{1}{2}$ shirt), and therefore we say it has a comparative advantage at wheat production.

A country can have a comparative advantage without having an absolute advantage. In our scenario, the United States has an absolute advantage over China at producing both shirts and wheat. But it has a bigger advantage at producing wheat than at making shirts: It can make four times as much wheat per worker as China (200 versus 50 bushels) but only twice as many shirts per worker (50 versus 25). It's better at both—but it's "more better," so to speak, at producing wheat. (We know that "more better" is not good grammar, but it nicely expresses the idea.) China has a comparative advantage at the good it is "less worse" at producing shirts, even without an absolute advantage.

You may have noticed that for each country, the opportunity cost of growing wheat is the *inverse* of the opportunity cost of producing shirts. (For the United States, $\frac{1}{4}$ is the inverse of 4; for China, $\frac{1}{2}$ is the inverse of 2.) Mathematically, this means that it is impossible for one country to have a comparative advantage at producing both goods. Each producer's opportunity cost depends on its *relative* ability at producing different goods. Logic tells us that you can't be better at A than at B and also better at B than at A. (And mathematically, if X is bigger than Y, then $\frac{1}{X}$ will be smaller than $\frac{1}{Y}$.) The United States can't be better at producing wheat than shirts relative to China and at the same time be better at producing shirts than wheat relative to China. As a result, no producer has a comparative advantage at everything, and each producer has a comparative advantage at something.

We can check this international trade scenario against an example closer to home. When your family makes Thanksgiving dinner, does the best cook make everything? If you have a small family, maybe one person can make the whole dinner. But if your family is anything like our families, you will need several cooks. Grandma is by far the most experienced cook, yet the potato peeling always gets outsourced to the kids. Is that because the grandchildren are better potato peelers than Grandma? We think that's probably not the case. Grandma has an absolute advantage at everything having to do with Thanksgiving dinner. Still, the kids may have a *comparative* advantage at potato peeling, which frees up Grandma to make those tricky pie crusts.

We can find applications of comparative advantage everywhere in life. Sports is no exception; look at the From Another Angle box "Babe Ruth, star pitcher" for another example.

comparative advantage the ability to produce a good or service at a lower opportunity cost than others

FROM ANOTHER ANGLE

Babe Ruth, star pitcher

How should baseball managers decide who should play at different positions? One approach is to assign the best player to each position. But the skills required for many positions are similar. What to do when one player has an absolute advantage at multiple positions? One answer is to turn to comparative advantage.

Consider the choice that New York Yankees manager Miller Huggins faced when he acquired a player named Babe Ruth in 1920. Ruth was an excellent pitcher. In 1918 he had set a record for the most consecutively scoreless innings pitched in the World Series—a record that was not broken until 1961. He could easily have become one of the best pitchers of his generation. But Ruth didn't end up as a pitcher. Babe Ruth was both the best pitcher *and* the best hitter on the team. From a practical point of view, he couldn't do both (pitching takes too much energy), so Miller Huggins had to make a choice.

Although Ruth had an *absolute* advantage at both positions, he had a *comparative* advantage as a hitter. The opportunity cost of having Ruth pitch was the number of games the Yankees would win by having him bat. Huggins decided the opportunity cost of Ruth's pitching was higher than the opportunity cost of his batting. Ruth went on to become one of the greatest hitters of all time. In 1920 he hit 54 home runs. That year, only one other *team* collectively hit as many home runs as Ruth *alone* did.

A good manager should, as Miller Huggins did, assign players to positions according to their comparative advantage. The question is not which player is best at a particular position, but which player the team can most afford to lose at any other position. For a player seeking a particular spot on the field, the right argument may be not that he is the best at that position, but that he is worth less at any other!

Source: "Biography," BabeRuth.com, http://www.baberuth.com/biography/.

✓ CONCEPT CHECK

- ❒ What does it mean to have an absolute advantage at producing a good? **[LO 2.2]**
- ❒ What does it mean to have a comparative advantage at producing a good? **[LO 2.2]**
- ❒ Can more than one producer have an absolute advantage at producing the same good? Why or why not? **[LO 2.2]**

Why Trade?

The United States is perfectly capable of producing its own shirts and its own wheat. In fact, in our simple model, it has an absolute advantage at producing both goods. So, why buy shirts from China? We are about to see that both countries are actually able to consume more when they specialize in producing the good for which they have a comparative advantage and then trade with one another.

Specialization

LO 2.3 Define specialization and explain why people specialize.

If you lived 200 years ago, your everyday life would have been full of tasks that probably never even cross your mind today. You might have milked a cow, hauled water from a well, split wood, cured meat, mended a hole in a sock, and repaired a roof. Contrast that with life today. Almost everything we use comes from someone who specializes in providing a particular good or service. We bet you don't churn the butter you put on your toast and that you wouldn't even begin to know how to construct the parts in your computer. We are guessing you don't usually sew your own clothes or grow your own wheat. In today's world, all of us are dependent on one another for the things we need on a daily basis.

In our model, when the United States and China work in isolation, each produces some shirts and some wheat, each in the combinations that its consumers prefer. Suppose the United States has 150 million workers and China has 800 million. As before, each U.S. worker can make 50 shirts or 200 bushels of wheat, and each Chinese worker can make 25 shirts or 50 bushels of wheat. Suppose that based on U.S. consumers' preferences, U.S. workers are split so that they produce 5 billion shirts and 10 billion bushels of wheat. In China, workers are allocated to produce 10 billion shirts and 20 billion bushels of wheat. Even though China's productivity per worker is lower, it has more workers and so is able to produce a larger total quantity of goods. (The quantities of shirts and wheat are unrealistically large, because we are assuming they are the only goods being produced. In reality, of course, countries produce many different goods, but this simplifying assumption helps us to zero in on a real-world truth.)

If each country focuses on producing the good for which it has a comparative advantage, total production increases. Focusing in this way is called **specialization**, the practice of spending all of your resources producing a particular good. When each country specializes in making a particular good according to its comparative advantage, total production possibilities are greater than if each produced the exact combination of goods its own consumers want.

specialization
spending all of your time producing a particular good

We have seen that if the United States and China are self-sufficient (each producing what its people want to consume), then together the two countries can make 15 billion T-shirts and 30 billion bushels of wheat, as shown at the top of Table 2-1 ("without specialization"). What would happen if, instead, China put all its resources into making shirts, and the United States put all its resources into growing wheat? The bottom section of Table 2-1 ("with specialization") shows us:

United States

200 bushels per worker × 150 million workers = 30 billion bushels

China

25 shirts per worker × 800 million workers = 20 billion shirts

	Country	Wheat (billions of bushels)	T-shirts (billions)
Without specialization	United States	10	5
	China	20	10
	Total	**30**	**15**
With specialization	United States	30	0
	China	0	20
	Total	**30**	**20**

TABLE 2-1

Production with and without specialization

When China and the United States each specialize in the production of one good, the two countries can produce an extra 5 billion T-shirts using the same number of workers and the same technology.

By specializing, the two countries together can produce just as much wheat as before, *plus* 5 billion more shirts. Specialization increases total production, using the same number of workers and the same technology.

This rule applies to all sorts of goods and services. It explains why dentists hire roofers to fix a roof leak and why roofers hire dentists to fill a cavity. See the Real Life box "Specialization sauce" for an example of the power of specialization in a setting you probably know well—McDonald's.

REAL LIFE
Specialization sauce

Henry Ford pioneered the assembly-line method of automobile manufacturing, in which each worker does just one small task on each car before it moves down the line to the next worker, who does a different small task. Ford proved that he could build more cars in less time when each employee specialized in this way. Restaurants use the same principle: They can serve more customers faster if they split the work among managers, waitstaff, and chefs. Fast-food restaurants take specialization even further.

Fast food as we know it was born in 1948, when McDonald's founders Dick and Mac McDonald decided to implement a radically new method of preparing food. Inspired by factory assembly lines, they applied Ford's concept of specialization to the restaurant business. Instead of assigning several employees to general food preparation, they split each order into parts, parceling out the steps required to prepare a meal. One employee became the grilling specialist; another added mustard and ketchup. A different employee operated the potato fryer, and yet another mixed the milkshakes.

Any single employee would almost certainly have been able to learn how to grill a hamburger, add condiments, make fries, *and* mix a milkshake. In each restaurant, one particularly skilled employee was probably faster than everyone else at all the steps in making a meal. Even so, specialization was more efficient. By assigning only one specific task to each employee, McDonald's founders revolutionized the speed and quantity of food preparation. Harnessing the power of specialization allowed them to grill more burgers, fry more potatoes, and feed more hungry customers.

Source: Eric Schlosser, *Fast Food Nation* (Boston: Houghton Mifflin, 2002), pp. 19–20.

Gains from trade

LO 2.4 Explain how the gains from trade follow from comparative advantage.

When countries specialize in producing the goods for which they have a comparative advantage, total production increases. The problem with specialization is that each producer ends up with only one good—in our model, wheat in the United States, shirts in China. If Americans don't want to go naked and the Chinese don't want to starve, they must trade.

Suppose that China and the United States agree to trade 20 billion bushels of wheat for 7.5 billion T-shirts. As a result, each country ends up with just as much wheat as before, plus 2.5 billion more shirts. This improvement in outcomes that occurs when specialized producers exchange goods and services is called the **gains from trade**.

gains from trade
the improvement in outcomes that occurs when producers specialize and exchange goods and services

Figure 2-7 shows how the gains from trade affect a country's consumption. Before the trade, it was impossible for the United States and China to consume any combination of goods outside their production possibilities frontiers. After the trade between the two specialized producers, each country's consumption increases to a point that was previously unachievable. If the United States and China both consume the same amount of wheat as before, they are able to consume 2.5 million more T-shirts after opening up to trade.

FIGURE 2-7

Specialization and gains from trade

(A) United States' gains from trade

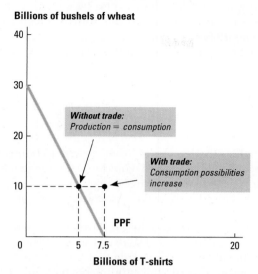

Billions of bushels of wheat

If a country does not specialize and trade, its production and consumption are both limited to points along its production possibilities frontier. By specializing and achieving gains from trading, the United States gains 2.5 million T-shirts.

(B) China's gains from trade

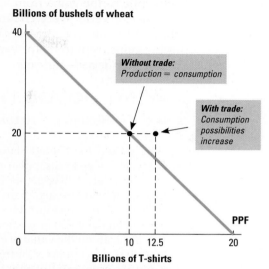

Billions of bushels of wheat

By opening up to trade, China also gains 2.5 million T-shirts compared to what it could produce on its production possibilities frontier.

In Figure 2-7, the gains from the U.S.–China trade are distributed equally—2.5 billion more shirts for the U.S. and 2.5 billion more for China. In reality, the distribution can vary; the gains do not have to be equal for the trading arrangement to benefit everyone. If China takes an extra 4 billion shirts and the United States an extra 1 billion (or vice versa), both countries will still be better off than if they worked alone.

Overall, there is room for trade as long as the two countries differ in their opportunity costs to produce a good and they set a trading price that falls between those opportunity costs. In our example, the price at which China and the U.S. are willing to trade T-shirts must fall between China's opportunity cost for producing T-shirts and the U.S.'s opportunity cost for producing T-shirts. If China is the country that has specialized in T-shirts, it cannot charge a price greater than the U.S.'s opportunity cost. If it does, the U.S. will simply make the T-shirts itself. Conversely, China must receive a price that covers its opportunity costs for making T-shirts, or it will not be willing to trade.

Consider the *wants* that drive people to engage in exchanges. When people specialize and trade, everyone gets more of the things they want than they would if they were self-sufficient. Thus, trade can be driven entirely by self-interest. Just as the United States benefits from trading with China (even though the U.S. may have an absolute advantage at producing both wheat and shirts), an experienced worker or large firm benefits from trading with a less experienced employee or a small, specialized company.

For example, when Bill Gates was the CEO of Microsoft, he probably got IT assistants to fix bugs on his computer, even though he could have done it faster himself. Let's say Bill can fix the bug in an hour, but for every hour he's distracted from running Microsoft, the company's profits go down by $1,000. The IT assistant earns only $50 an hour, so even if he takes two to three times as long to do the work, it's still worth it for Bill to hire him and spend his own time keeping Microsoft's productivity up. Bill has an absolute advantage at fixing computer bugs, but the opportunity cost in lost profits means the IT assistant has a comparative advantage. (Bill's comparative advantage is at running Microsoft.) Everyone ends up better off if they specialize.

In spite of the gains from specializing and trading, not everyone considers this an obvious choice in every circumstance—which brings us to our fourth question from Chapter 1: *Why isn't everyone already doing it?* Some people argue that it's worth giving up the gains from trade for various reasons. For some examples, see the What Do You Think? box "Is self-sufficiency a virtue?"

WHAT DO YOU THINK?

Is self-sufficiency a virtue?

Why should the United States trade with other countries? If every other country in the world were to disappear tomorrow, the United States would probably manage to fend for itself. It has plenty of fertile land, natural resources, people, and manufacturing capacity. In fact, many observers consider the value Americans place on self-sufficiency to be a cultural trait.

Based on what you now know about specialization and the gains from trade, what do you think about the value of exchange versus the value of self-sufficiency? Economists tend to line up in favor of free international trade; they argue that trade makes both countries economically better off. Serious and worthwhile arguments have also been made on the other side. The following are some reasons that have been proposed for developing national self-sufficiency.

- **National heritage.** Many people feel that a line has been crossed when a country loses its family farms or outsources a historically important industry—for example, automaking in the United States. Does a country lose its culture when it loses these industries?
- **Security.** Some people worry that trade weakens a country if it goes to war with a country that it depends on for critical goods. Is it safe to rely on other countries for your food supply, or does that kind of dependency pose a security risk? What about relying on another country for steel or uranium or oil?
- **Quality control and ethics.** When goods are imported from other countries, production standards are harder to control than if the goods are made at home. Some people argue that international trade undermines consumer safety and environmental regulations, or that it fosters labor conditions that would be considered unethical or illegal in the United States.

What do you think?

1. Do you agree with any of these objections to free trade? Why? When is self-sufficiency more valuable than the gains from trade?
2. Is the choice between trade and self-sufficiency an either/or question? Is there a middle-of-the-road approach that would address concerns on both sides of this issue?

Comparative advantage over time

Our simplified model of production possibilities and trade helps us to understand why Americans now buy shirts from China. But we noted at the beginning of the chapter that this wasn't always the case—200 years ago, the United States was selling shirts to the rest of the world. To understand why this changed, we can apply our model to shifts in comparative advantage over time. These shifts have caused significant changes in different countries' economies and trade patterns.

c. Is the opportunity cost of producing hammers higher between points A and B or between points B and C?

d. Is the opportunity cost of producing screwdrivers higher between points A and B or between points B and C?

6. For each point on the PPF in Figure 2P-3, note whether the point is: **[LO 2.1]**
   - attainable and efficient
   - attainable and inefficient
   - unattainable

7. For each point on the PPF in Figure 2P-4, note whether the point is: **[LO 2.1]**
   - attainable and efficient
   - attainable and inefficient
   - unattainable

8. The Red Cross and WIC (Women, Infants, and Children) program both provide emergency food

FIGURE 2P-3

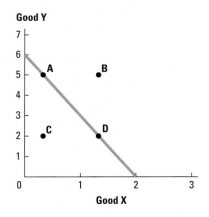

FIGURE 2P-4

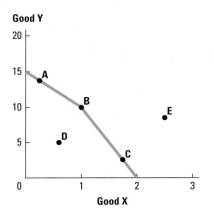

TABLE 2P-1

	Red Cross	WIC
Food packages	300	200
First-aid kits	50	20

packages and first-aid kits to New York City homeless shelters. Table 2P-1 shows their weekly production possibilities in providing emergency goods to NYC homeless shelters. **[LO 2.1]**

NYC homeless shelters need a total of 20 first-aid kits per week. Currently, they get 10 kits from the Red Cross and 10 kits from WIC. With their remaining resources, how many food packages can each organization provide to NYC homeless shelters?

9. Suppose that three volunteers are preparing cookies and cupcakes for a bake sale. Diana can make 27 cookies or 18 cupcakes per hour; Andy can make 25 cookies or 17 cupcakes; and Sam can make 10 cookies or 12 cupcakes. **[LO 2.2]**

   a. Who has the absolute advantage at making cookies?

   b. At making cupcakes?

10. Paula and Carlo are coworkers. Their production possibilities frontiers for counseling clients and writing memos are given in Figure 2P-5. **[LO 2.2]**

    a. Which worker has an absolute advantage in counseling clients?

    b. Which worker has an absolute advantage in writing memos?

    c. Which worker has a comparative advantage in counseling clients?

    d. Which worker has a comparative advantage in writing memos?

11. Two students are assigned to work together on a project that requires both writing and an oral presentation. Steve can write 1 page or prepare 3 minutes of a presentation each day. Anna can write 2 pages or prepare 1 minute of a presentation each day. **[LO 2.2]**

    a. Who has a comparative advantage at writing?

    b. Suppose that Steve goes to a writing tutor and learns some tricks that enable him to write 3 pages each day. Now who has a comparative advantage at writing?

12. Suppose that the manager of a restaurant has two new employees, Rahul and Henriette, and is trying to decide which one to assign to which task. Rahul can chop 20 pounds of vegetables or wash

FIGURE 2P-5

Paula

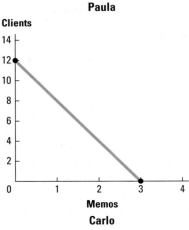

Carlo

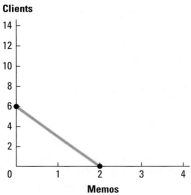

100 dishes per hour. Henriette can chop 30 pounds of vegetables or wash 120 dishes. **[LO 2.3]**

a. Who should be assigned to chop vegetables?

b. Who should be assigned to wash dishes?

13. The Dominican Republic and Nicaragua both produce coffee and rum. The Dominican Republic can produce 20 thousand tons of coffee per year or 10 thousand barrels of rum. Nicaragua can produce 30 thousand tons of coffee per year or 5 thousand barrels of rum. **[LO 2.3]**

a. Suppose the Dominican Republic and Nicaragua sign a trade agreement in which each country would specialize in the production of either coffee or rum. Which country should specialize in coffee? Which country should specialize in producing rum?

b. What are the minimum and maximum prices at which these countries will trade coffee?

14. Eleanor and her little sister Joanna are responsible for two chores on their family's farm, gathering eggs and collecting milk. Eleanor can gather 9 dozen eggs or collect 3 gallons of milk per week. Joanna can gather 2 dozen eggs or collect 2 gallons of milk per week. **[LO 2.3]**

a. The family wants 2 gallons of milk per week and as many eggs as the sisters can gather. Currently, Eleanor and Joanna collect one gallon of milk each and as many eggs as they can. How many dozens of eggs does the family have per week?

b. If the sisters specialized, which sister should gather the milk?

c. If the sisters specialized, how many dozens of eggs would the family have per week?

15. Suppose Russia and Sweden each produce only paper and cars. Russia can produce 8 tons of paper or 4 million cars each year. Sweden can produce 25 tons of paper or 5 million cars each year. **[LO 2.4]**

a. Draw the production possibilities frontier for each country.

b. Both countries want 2 million cars each year and as much paper as they can produce along with 2 million cars. Find this point on each production possibilities frontier and label it "A."

c. Suppose the countries specialize. Which country will produce cars?

d. Once they specialize, suppose they work out a trade of 2 million cars for 6 tons of paper. Find the new *consumption* point for each country and label it "B."

16. Maya and Max are neighbors. Each grows lettuce and tomatoes in their gardens. Maya can grow 45 heads of lettuce or 9 pounds of tomatoes this summer. Max can grow 42 heads of lettuce or 6 pounds of tomatoes this summer. If Maya and Max specialize and trade, the price of tomatoes (in terms of lettuce) would be as follows: 1 pound of tomatoes would cost between _____ and _____ pounds of lettuce. **[LO 2.4]**

Chapter Sources

http://www.agclassroom.org/gan/timeline/farm_tech.htm

http://www.nber.org/chapters/c8007.pdf?new_window=1

https://www.cia.gov/library/publications/the-world-factbook/geos/us.html

Math Essentials: Understanding Graphs and Slope

LEARNING OBJECTIVES

LO A.1   Create four quadrants using *x*- and *y*-axes, and plot points on a graph.

LO A.2   Use data to calculate slope.

LO A.3   Interpret the steepness and direction of slope, and explain what that says about a line.

Creating a Graph

LO A.1 Create four quadrants using *x*- and *y*-axes, and plot points on a graph.

A graph is one way to visually represent data. In this book, we use graphs to describe and interpret economic relationships. For example, we use a graph called a production possibilities frontier to explore opportunity costs and trade-offs in production. We use graphs of average, variable, and marginal costs to explore production decisions facing a firm. And—the favorite of economists everywhere—we use graphs to show supply and demand and the resulting relationship between price and quantity.

Graphs of one variable

Graphs of a single variable come in three main forms: the bar chart, the pie chart, and the line graph. In school, you've probably made all three, and plastered them on science-fair posters and presentations or used them in reports. These graphs are versatile; they can be used to present all sorts of information. Throughout economics, and in this book, you'll come across these graphs frequently.

Probably the most common single-variable graph is the *bar graph*, an example of which is shown in Figure A-1. The bar graph shows the size or frequency of a variable using bars—hence the name. The size of the bar on the *y*-axis shows the value of the variable, while the *x*-axis contains the categories of the variables. In Figure A-1, for example, the bar graph shows the number of visits received by five major news sites each month. Since the bars stack up next to each other, a bar graph makes it clear exactly where each news site stands in comparison to the others. As you can see, the larger bars for Yahoo! News and CNN mean that these sites get more visits than NYTimes.com.

FIGURE A-1

Top five news sites in 2010 As you can see, Yahoo! News gets the most visits as recorded by Nielsen. The top five news sites include both traditional new sources and sources that only exist online.

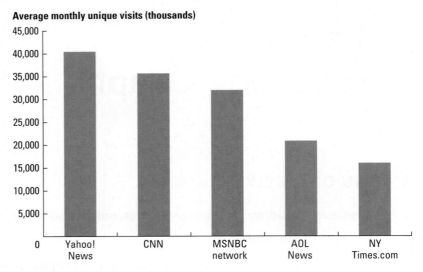

Average monthly unique visits (thousands)

Source: http://www.journalism.org/analysis_report/top_25.

In general, bar graphs are versatile. You can show the distribution of letter grades in a class or the average monthly high and low temperatures in your city. Any time the size of a variable is important, you are generally going to want to use a bar graph.

Pie charts are generally used to show how much certain components make up a whole. Pie charts are usually a circle, cut into wedges which represent how much each makes up of the whole. Figure A-2 shows the sales of the 10 largest car manufacturers (Toyota, GM, Ford, etc.) as a percentage of overall new-car sales. The large wedges of General Motors and Toyota show that these are large automakers compared to the small wedge representing Mercedes-Benz.

FIGURE A-2

Automaker market share This pie chart shows the relative market share of each automaker. The size of the wedge gives the share of each automaker. General Motors has a large wedge, while Mercedes-Benz has a much smaller share of the market.

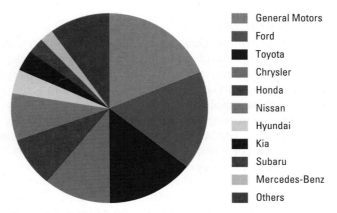

- General Motors
- Ford
- Toyota
- Chrysler
- Honda
- Nissan
- Hyundai
- Kia
- Subaru
- Mercedes-Benz
- Others

Source: WSJ Markets Data Center, http://online.wsj.com/mdc/public/page/2_3022-autosales.html

The slope of a line

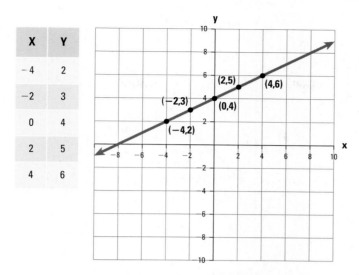

X	Y
-4	2
-2	3
0	4
2	5
4	6

Slope refers to the shape of the line and is determined by the change in *y* and *x*.

When the relationship between *x* and *y* is linear (which means that it forms a straight line), the slope is constant. That is, for each one-unit change in the *x*-variable, the corresponding *y*-variable always changes by the same amount. Therefore, we can use any two points to calculate the slope of the line—it doesn't matter which ones we pick, because the slope is the same everywhere on the line.

Slope gives us important information about the relationship between our two variables. As we are about to discuss, slope tells us something about both the direction of the relationship between two variables (whether they move in the same direction) and the magnitude of the relationship (how much *y* changes in response to a change in *x*).

Calculating slope

LO A.2 Use data to calculate slope.

In Figure A-8, the run or horizontal distance between point (2,3) and point (4,5) is 4 minus 2, which equals 2. The rise or vertical distance is 5 minus 3, which equals 2. Therefore, the slope of the line in Figure A-8 is calculated as:

$$\text{Slope} = \frac{(y_2 - y_1)}{(x_2 - x_1)} = \frac{(5 - 3)}{(4 - 2)} = \frac{2}{2} = 1$$

Let's return to Figure A-7 and apply this same calculation. Because the relationship between *x* and *y* is linear, we can use any two points to calculate the slope. Let's pick the point (2,5) to be point 1, which we call (x_1, y_1). Then, pick the point (4,6) to be point 2, which we call (x_2, y_2).

$$\frac{(y_2 - y_1)}{(x_2 - x_1)} = \frac{(6 - 5)}{(4 - 2)} = \frac{1}{2} = 0.5$$

Calculating slope

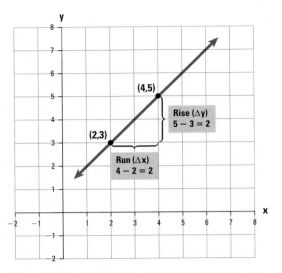

You can calculate the slope by dividing the change in the *y* value over the change in *x*—the rise over the run.

Note that it doesn't matter which point we pick as point 1 and which as point 2. We could have chosen 5 as y_2 and 6 as y_1 rather than vice versa. All that matters is that y_1 is from the same ordered pair as x_1 and y_2 from the same pair as x_2. To prove that this is true, let's calculate slope again using (2,5) as point 2. The slope still comes out to 0.5:

$$\frac{(y_2 - y_1)}{(x_2 - x_1)} = \frac{(5 - 6)}{(2 - 4)} = \frac{(-1)}{(-2)} = \frac{1}{2} = 0.5$$

Use two different points from the table in Figure A-7 to calculate slope again. Try using the points $(-4,2)$ and $(0,4)$. Do you get 0.5 as your answer?

The direction of a slope

LO A.3 Interpret the steepness and direction of slope, and explain what that says about a line.

The direction of a slope tells us something meaningful about the relationship between the two variables we are representing. For instance, when children get older, they grow taller. If we represented this relationship in a graph, we would see an upward-sloping line, telling us that height increases as age increases, rather than decreasing. Of course, it is common knowledge that children get taller, not shorter, as they get older. But if we were looking at a graph of a relationship we did not already understand, the slope of the line would show us at a glance how the two variables relate to one another.

To see how we can learn from the direction of a slope and how to calculate it, look at the graphs in panels A and B of Figure A-9.

In panel A, we can see that when *x* increases from 1 to 2, *y* also increases, from 2 to 4. If we move the other direction down the line, we see that when *x* decreases from 2 to 1,

The direction of a slope

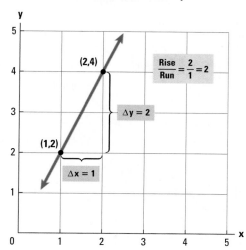

(A) Positive relationship

If a line slopes upward, its slope is positive; *y* increases as *x* increases, or *y* decreases as *x* decreases.

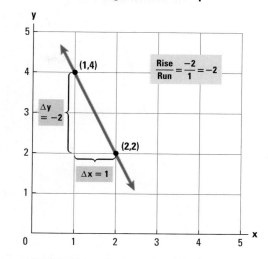

(B) Negative relationship

If a line slopes downward, its slope is negative: *y* decreases as *x* increases, or *y* increases as *x* decreases.

y also decreases, from 4 to 2. In other words, *x* and *y* move in the same direction. Therefore, *x* and *y* are said to have a *positive relationship*. Not surprisingly, this means that the slope of the line is a positive number:

$$\text{Slope} = \frac{\Delta y}{\Delta x} = \frac{2}{1} = 2$$

When the slope of a line is positive, we know that *y* increases as *x* increases, and *y* decreases as *x* decreases. If a line leans upward, then its slope is positive.

Now, turn to the graph in panel B. In this case, when *x* increases from 1 to 2, *y* decreases from 4 to 2. Reading from the other direction, when *x* decreases from 2 to 1, *y* increases from 2 to 4. Therefore, *x* and *y* move in opposite directions and are said to have a *negative relationship*. The slope of the line is a negative number:

$$\text{Slope} = \frac{\Delta y}{\Delta x} = \frac{-2}{1} = -2$$

When the slope of a line is negative, we know that *y* decreases as *x* increases, and *y* increases as *x* decreases. If a line leans downward, then its slope is negative.

In Chapter 3, you will see applications of these positive and negative relationships between the variables price and quantity. Here's a preview:

- You will see a positive relationship between price and quantity when you encounter a *supply curve*. You will learn the meaning of that positive relationship: As the price of a good increases, suppliers are willing to supply a larger quantity to markets. Supply curves, therefore, are upward-sloping.
- You will see a negative relationship between price and quantity when you encounter a *demand curve*. You will learn the meaning of that negative relationship: As the price of a good increases, consumers are willing to purchase a smaller quantity. Demand curves are downward-sloping.

The steepness of a slope

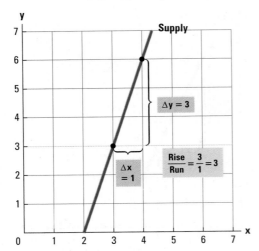

(A) Steeper slope

The larger the number representing slope is, the steeper the curve will be. The slope in panel A is steeper than the slope in panel B.

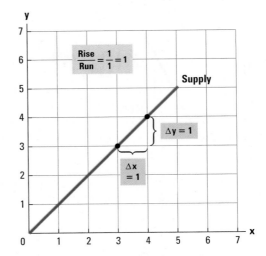

(B) Flatter slope

The closer the slope is to zero, the flatter the curve will be. The slope in panel B is flatter than the slope in panel A.

From these examples, you can see that two variables (such as price and quantity) may have more than one relationship with each other, depending on whose choices they represent and under what circumstances.

The steepness of a slope

In addition to the *direction* of the relationship between variables, the *steepness* of the slope also gives us important information. It tells us how much y changes for a given change in x.

In both panels of Figure A-10, the relationship between x and y is positive (upward-sloping), and the distance between the x values, Δx, is the same. However, the change in y that results from a one-unit change in x is greater in panel A than it is in panel B. In other words, the slope is *steeper* in panel A and *flatter* in panel B.

Numerically, the closer the number representing the slope is to zero, the flatter the curve will be. Remember that both positive and negative numbers can be close to zero. So, a slope of -1 is equally steep as a slope of 1, although one slopes downward and the other upward. Correspondingly, a line with a slope of -5 is steeper than a line with a slope of -1 or one with a slope of 1.

In general, slope is used to describe how much y changes in response to a one-unit change in x. In economics, we are sometimes interested in how much x changes in response to a one-unit change in y. In Chapter 4, for example, you will see how quantity (on the x-axis) responds to a change in price (on the y-axis).

Key Terms

slope, p. 46F

rise, p. 46F

run, p. 46F

Problems and Applications

1. Create four quadrants using *x*- and *y*-axes. Use your graph to plot the following points. **[LO A.1]**
   a. (1,4)
   b. (−2,1)
   c. (−3,−3)
   d. (3,−2)

2. Create four quadrants using *x*- and *y*-axes. Use your graph to plot the following points. **[LO A.1]**
   a. (0,4)
   b. (0,−2)
   c. (1,0)
   d. (−3,0)

3. Use the curve labeled "Demand" in Figure AP-1 to create a table (schedule) that shows Price in one column and Quantity in another. What is the slope of the curve labeled "Demand"? **[LO A.2]**

4. Use the curve labeled "Demand" in Figure AP-2 to create a table (schedule) that shows Price in one column and Quantity in another. What is the slope of the curve labeled "Demand"? **[LO A.2]**

5. Use the information about price and quantity in Table AP-1 to create a graph, with Price on the *y*-axis and Quantity on the *x*-axis. Label the resulting curve "Demand." What is the slope of that curve? **[LO A.2]**

6. Use the information about price and quantity in Table AP-2 to create a graph, with Price on the *y*-axis and Quantity on the *x*-axis. Label the resulting curve "Demand." What is the slope of that curve? **[LO A.2]**

7. Use the curve labeled "Supply" in Figure AP-3 to create a table (schedule) that shows Price in one column and Quantity in another. What is the slope of the curve labeled "Supply"? **[LO A.2]**

FIGURE AP-2

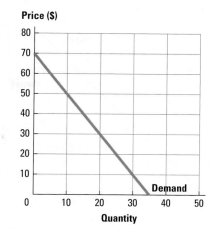

Price ($)

FIGURE AP-1

Price ($)

TABLE AP-1

Price ($)	Quantity
0	120
2	100
4	80
6	60
8	40
10	20
12	0

TABLE AP-2

Price ($)	Quantity
0	5
5	4
10	3
15	2
20	1
25	0

FIGURE AP-3

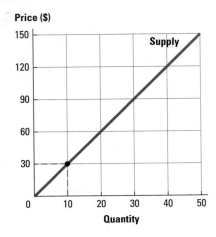

Price ($)

TABLE AP-3

Price ($)	Quantity
0	0
25	5
50	10
75	15
100	20
125	25

TABLE AP-4

Price ($)	Quantity
0	0
2	8
4	16
6	24
8	32
10	40
12	48

8. Use the curve labeled "Supply" in Figure AP-4 to create a table (schedule) that shows Price in one column and Quantity in another. What is the slope of the curve labeled "Supply"? **[LO A.2]**

9. Use the information about price and quantity in Table AP-3 to create a graph, with Price on the y-axis and Quantity on the x-axis. Label the resulting curve "Supply." What is the slope of that curve? **[LO A.2]**

10. Use the information about price and quantity in Table AP-4 to create a graph, with Price on the y-axis and Quantity on the x-axis. Label the resulting curve "Supply." What is the slope of that curve? **[LO A.2]**

11. What is the direction of slope indicated by the following examples? **[LO A.3]**
    a. As the price of rice increases, consumers want less of it.
    b. As the temperature increases, the amount of people who use the town pool also increases.
    c. As farmers use more fertilizer, their output of tomatoes increases.

12. Rank the following equations by the steepness of their slope from lowest to highest **[LO A.3]**
    a. $y = -3x + 9$
    b. $y = 4x + 2$
    c. $y = -0.5x + 4$

FIGURE AP-4

Price ($)

Part Two

Supply and Demand

The four chapters in Part 2 will introduce you to ...

the basics of markets, which form the baseline for most economic analysis. Chapter 3 introduces supply and demand. Any time we go into the store and decide to buy something, we act on our demand for that good. On the other side, the store figured out that it made sense for them to supply that good to us. The interaction between the forces of supply and demand determines the price we pay and how much gets bought and sold.

   The rest of the chapters in Part 2 will use supply and demand to answer a variety of questions: Why do people rush to the store when Apple slashes the price of an iPhone? Why would the government ever want to set limits on prices in the market?

   Together with Part 1, the chapters in this part introduce the basic concepts of economic problem solving. To start, we've stripped these ideas down to their simplest form. These same concepts will return throughout the text, and we will build on them as we turn to different problems.

Markers

LEARNING OBJECTIVES

LO 3.1   Identify the defining characteristics of a competitive market.

LO 3.2   Draw a demand curve and describe the external factors that determine demand.

LO 3.3   Distinguish between a shift in and a movement along the demand curve.

LO 3.4   Draw a supply curve and describe the external factors that determine supply.

LO 3.5   Distinguish between a shift in and a movement along the supply curve.

LO 3.6   Explain how supply and demand interact to drive markets to equilibrium.

LO 3.7   Evaluate the effect of changes in supply and demand on the equilibrium price and quantity.

MOBILES GO GLOBAL

For many people, a cell phone is on the list of things never to leave the house without, right up there with a wallet and keys. For better or worse, cell phones have become a fixture of everyday life.

It's hard to believe that as recently as the late 1990s, cell phones were a luxury that only a third of Americans enjoyed. Before that, in the 1980s, they were big, heavy devices, seldom bought for personal use at all. In less than a quarter of a century, this expensive sci-fi technology became a relatively cheap, universal convenience. Today there are approximately 90 cell phones for every 100 people in the United States. In fact, more than half of the world's 7 billion people now have a cell phone subscription.[1] In Africa, for instance, cell phone use has been growing by 20 percent a year and in 2011 topped 400 million users.[2] This phenomenal growth makes it easier to keep up with friends and family. It also connects small-town merchants to businesses in distant cities, opening up new economic possibilities.

How does a product move from expensive to cheap, from rare to commonplace, so quickly? The answer partly lies in the relationship between supply and demand. This chapter shows how the forces of supply and demand interact to determine the quantities and prices of goods that are bought and sold in competitive markets.

The basic story of how a new product takes hold is a familiar one. In the beginning, cell phones were expensive and rare. Over time, the technology improved, the price

dropped, the product caught on, and sales took off. Throughout this process of change, markets allow for ongoing communication between buyers and producers, using prices as a signal. The up and down movement of prices ensures that the quantity of a product that is available stays in balance with the quantity consumers want to buy.

To explain the leap in usage that cell phones have made over time, however, we need to go further than just price signals. Outside forces that influence supply and demand, such as changes in technology, fashion trends, and economic ups and downs, have driven that transformation. Markets have the remarkable ability to adjust to these changes without falling out of balance.

In this chapter, we'll step into the shoes of consumers and producers to examine the trade-offs they face. We'll see that the issues that drive supply and demand in the cell phone industry are not unique. In fact, the functioning of markets, as summarized in the theory of supply and demand, is the bedrock of almost everything in this book. Mastering this theory will help you to solve all kinds of problems, from what price to sell your product for as a businessperson, to how to find the cheapest gasoline, to the causes of a shortage of hybrid cars.

Markets

In Chapter 2, we discussed the power of the "invisible hand" to coordinate complex economic interactions. The key feature of an economy organized by the invisible hand is that private individuals, rather than a centralized planning authority, make the decisions. Such an economy is often referred to as a **market economy**.

market economy an economy in which private individuals, rather than a centralized planning authority, make the decisions

What is a market?

What do we mean by a *market?* The word might make you think of a physical location where buyers and sellers come together face-to-face—like a farmers' market or a mall. But people do not have to be physically near each other to make an exchange. For example, think of online retailers like Amazon.com or of fruit that is grown in South America but sold all over the world. The term **market** actually refers to the buyers and sellers who trade a particular good or service, not to a physical location.

market buyers and sellers who trade a particular good or service

Which buyers and sellers are included in the market depends on the context. The manager of a clothing store at your local mall might think about the market for T-shirts in terms of people who live locally and the other places they could buy T-shirts, like competing stores, garage sales, or online retailers. The CEO of a major clothing brand, on the other hand, might include garment factories in China and the fashion preferences of customers living all over the world in her idea of a market. Which boundaries are relevant depends on the scope of trades that are being made.

What is a competitive market?

LO 3.1 Identify the defining characteristics of a competitive market.

competitive market a market in which fully informed, price-taking buyers and sellers easily trade a standardized good or service

Making simplifying assumptions can help us zero in on important ideas. In this chapter, we will make a big simplifying assumption—that markets are *competitive*. A **competitive market** is one in which fully informed, price-taking buyers and sellers easily trade a standardized good or service. Let's unpack this multipart definition: Imagine you're driving up to an intersection where there is a gas station on each corner. This scenario demonstrates the four important characteristics of a perfectly competitive market.

First, the gas sold by each station is the same—your car will run equally well regardless of *where* you fill your tank. This means that the gas being sold is a **standardized good**—a good or service for which any two units of it have the same features and are interchangeable. In a competitive market, the good being bought and sold is standardized.

Second, the price at each gas station is prominently displayed on a big sign. As you drive by, you can immediately see how much a gallon of each type of gas costs at each station. In a competitive market, you have *full information* about the price and features of the good being bought and sold.

Third, it's easy for you to choose any of the four gas stations at the intersection. The stations are very near each other, and you don't have to have special equipment to fill up your tank or pay an entrance fee to get into the station. In competitive markets, there are no **transaction costs**—the costs incurred by buyer and seller in agreeing to and executing a sale of goods or services. Thus, in competitive markets, you don't have to pay anything for the privilege of buying or selling in the market. You can easily do business in this four-station market for gasoline.

Finally, we bet you'd find that a gallon of gas costs the same in each station at the intersection. Why? Recall the third economists' question from Chapter 1: If one station tries to raise its price, *how will others respond?* Assuming the stations are offering standardized gallons of gas, customers should be indifferent between buying from one station or another at a given price. If one raises its price, all the drivers will simply go to a cheaper station instead. The gas station that raised prices will end up losing customers. For this reason, no individual seller has the power to change the market price. In economic terminology, a buyer or seller who cannot affect the market price is called a **price taker**.

The drivers going by are also price takers. If you try to negotiate a discount at one of the gas stations before filling your tank, you won't get far—the owner would rather wait and sell to other customers who will pay more. The price is the price; your choice is to take it or leave it. In competitive markets, both buyers and sellers are price takers.

By thinking about the gas stations at a single intersection, you have learned the four characteristics of perfectly competitive markets. Table 3-1 summarizes the four characteristics of a perfectly competitive market: a standardized good, full information, no transaction costs, and price-taking participants.

In reality, very few markets are truly *perfectly* competitive. Even gas stations at the same intersection might not be: Maybe one can charge a few cents more per gallon because it uses gas with less ethanol or offers regular customers an attractive loyalty scheme or has a Dunkin' Donuts to entice hungry drivers. In future chapters, we'll spend a lot of time thinking about the different ways that markets in the real world are structured and why it matters when they fall short of perfect competition.

The market for cell phones is not perfectly competitive either. Cell phones are not standardized goods—some models look cooler, or have better cameras, or have access to different apps or calling plans. You're unlikely to be completely indifferent between two different cell phones at the same price, as you are between two gallons

standardized good a good for which any two units have the same features and are interchangeable

transaction costs the costs incurred by buyer and seller in agreeing to and executing a sale of goods or services

price taker a buyer or seller who cannot affect the market price

Standardized good	Any two units of the good have the same features and are interchangeable.
Full information	Market participants know everything about the price and features of the good.
No transaction costs	There is no cost to participating in exchanges in the market.
Participants are price takers	Neither buyers nor sellers have the power to affect the market price.

TABLE 3-1
Four characteristics of perfectly competitive markets

of gas. Furthermore, the fact that there are a limited number of service providers means that sellers aren't always price takers. If only one network has good coverage in your area or has an exclusive deal with a popular type of phone, it can get away with charging a premium.

So, why *assume* perfect competition if markets in the real world are rarely perfectly competitive? The answer is that the simple model of competitive markets we will develop in this chapter leads us to useful insights, even in markets that aren't perfectly competitive. Taking the time now to make sure you understand perfect competition inside and out will better prepare you to understand why it matters when markets aren't perfectly competitive. As we go through this chapter we'll note some ways in which the real cell phone market departs from perfect competition. By the end of the chapter, we hope you'll agree that the simple model of perfect competition tells us a lot, if not everything, about how the real cell phone market works.

✓ CONCEPT CHECK

❏ What is a market? What are the characteristics of a competitive market? **[LO 3.1]**
❏ Why are participants in competitive markets called *price takers?* **[LO 3.1]**

Demand

Demand describes how much of something people are willing and able to buy under certain circumstances. Suppose someone approached you and asked if you would like a new cell phone. What would you answer? You might think, "Sure," but as a savvy person, you would probably first ask, "For how much?" Whether you want something (or how much of it you want) depends on how much you have to pay for it.

These days most people in the United States have cell phones, but that hasn't been the case for very long. Let's assume for the sake of our model that cell phones are standardized—one model, with given features and calling plans. Now, put yourself in the position of a consumer in the mid-1990s. Maybe you've seen cell phones advertised at $499 and think it's not worth it to you. As the price goes down over time to $399, and $299, you're still not tempted to buy it. At $199, you start to consider it. Then, the first time you see a cell phone advertised for less than $125, you decide to buy.

Different people bought their first cell phone at different prices: At any given time, with any given price, some people in the population are willing to buy a phone and others aren't. If we add up all of these individual choices, we get overall *market demand*. The amount of a particular good that buyers in a market will purchase at a given price during a specified period is called the **quantity demanded**. For almost all goods, the lower the price goes, the higher the quantity demanded.

quantity demanded the amount of a particular good that buyers will purchase at a given price during a specified period

This inverse relationship between price and quantity demanded is so important that economists refer to it as the **law of demand**. The first requirement for the law of demand is the idea sometimes known as *ceteris paribus,* the Latin term for "all other things being the same." In other words, the law of demand says that, when all else is held equal, quantity demanded rises as price falls. Economists frequently rely on the idea of *ceteris paribus* to isolate the effect of a single change in the economy. If all else is not held equal, it is very difficult to see the true effect of something like a price change, because it may be accompanied by other changes that also affect quantity demanded. For instance, studies show that the demand for cell phones increases with people's incomes. So when we see both incomes *and* prices rising at the same time, we cannot immediately predict what will happen to cell phone sales. When we talk about the law of demand, therefore, it is important to remember that we are implying that nothing *other than* price changes.

law of demand a fundamental characteristic of demand which states that, all else equal, quantity demanded rises as price falls

The law of demand isn't a made-up law that economists have imposed on markets. Rather, it holds true because it describes the underlying reality of individual people's decisions. The key is to think about the *trade-offs* that people face when making the decision to buy.

What happens when the price of something falls? First, the benefit that you get from purchasing it remains the same, because the item itself is unchanged. But the opportunity cost has fallen, because when the price goes down you don't have to give up as many other purchases in order to get the item. When benefits stay the same and opportunity cost goes down, this trade-off suddenly starts to look a lot better. When the trade-off between costs and benefits tips toward benefits, more people will want to buy the good.

Of course, falling prices will not have been the only consideration in people's decisions to buy their first cell phone. Some might have decided to buy one when they got a pay raise at work. Others might have bought one at the point when most of their friends owned one. Incomes, expectations, and tastes all play a role; economists call these factors *nonprice determinants* of demand. We'll discuss their potential effects later in this chapter. First, let's focus on the relationship between price and quantity demanded.

The demand curve

LO 3.2 Draw a demand curve and describe the external factors that determine demand.

The law of demand says that the quantity of cell phones demanded will be different at every price level. For this reason, it is often useful to represent demand as a table, called a **demand schedule**, which shows the quantities of a particular good or service that consumers are willing to purchase (demand) at various prices. Figure 3-1 shows, in panel A, a hypothetical annual demand schedule for cell phones in the United States. (Remember, we're assuming that cell phones are a standardized good. This isn't quite right, but the basic principle holds true: When cell phone prices are lower, you're more likely to buy a new one.) The demand schedule assumes that factors other than price remain the same.

Panel B of Figure 3-1 shows another way to represent demand, by drawing each price-quantity combination from the demand schedule as a point on a graph. That graph, called a **demand curve**, visually displays the demand schedule. That is, it is a graph that shows the quantities of a particular good or service that consumers will demand at various prices. The demand curve also represents consumers' *willingness to buy:* It shows the highest amount consumers will pay for any given quantity.

On the demand curve, quantity goes on the *x*-axis (the horizontal axis) and price on the *y*-axis (the vertical axis). The result is a downward-sloping line that reflects the inverse relationship between price and quantity. The demand curve in Figure 3-1 represents exactly the same information as the demand schedule.

Determinants of demand

The demand curve represents the relationship between price and quantity demanded *with everything else held constant*. If everything else is *not* held constant—that is, if one of the nonprice factors that determines demand changes—the curve will shift.

The downward-sloping demand curve reflects the trade-offs that people face between (1) the benefit they expect to receive from a good and (2) the opportunity cost they face for buying it. Therefore, any factor that changes this balance at a given price will change people's willingness to buy, and thus their purchasing decisions.

demand schedule
a table that shows the quantities of a particular good or service that consumers will purchase (demand) at various prices

demand curve
a graph that shows the quantities of a particular good or service that consumers will demand at various prices

Since demand curves and other material in this chapter make extensive use of lines and linear equations, you may want to review those concepts in Appendix B, "Math Essentials: Working with Linear Equations" which follows this chapter.

FIGURE 3-1
Demand schedule and the demand curve

(A) Demand schedule

Cell phones (millions)	Price ($)
30	180
60	160
90	140
120	120
150	100
180	80
210	60
240	40
270	20

This demand schedule shows the quantity of cell phones demanded each year at various prices. As prices decrease, consumers want to purchase more cell phones.

(B) Demand curve

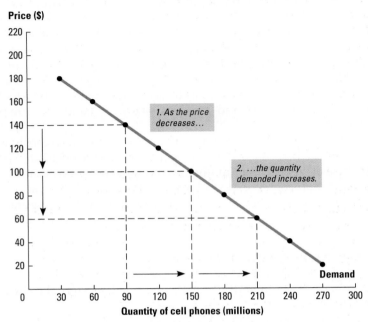

This demand curve is a graphic representation of the demand schedule for cell phones in the United States. Each entry in the demand schedule is plotted on this curve.

The nonprice determinants of demand can be divided into five major categories: consumer preferences, the prices of related goods, incomes, expectations of future prices, and the number of buyers in the market. Table 3-2 summarizes the impact of each factor on demand. Each of these nonprice determinants affects either the benefits or the opportunity cost of buying a good, even if the price of the good itself remains the same.

POTENTIALLY CONFUSING

Although these five factors include price-related issues such as the price of related goods and expectations about future prices, we refer to them as *nonprice determinants* to differentiate them from the effect of the current price of the good on demand for that good.

Consumer preferences. Consumer preferences are the personal likes and dislikes that make buyers more or less inclined to purchase a good. We don't need to know *why* people like what they like or to agree with their preferences; we just need to know that these likes and dislikes influence their purchases. At any given price, some consumers will get more enjoyment (i.e., benefits) out of a cell phone than others, simply based on how much they like talking to friends, or whether they use their phones for work, or any number of other personal preferences.

Some consumer preferences are fairly constant across time, such as those that arise from personality traits or cultural attitudes and beliefs. For example, a recluse may have little desire for a cell phone, while an on-the-go executive may find a cell phone (or two)

TABLE 3-2 **Determinants of demand**

Determinant	Examples of an increase in demand	Examples of a decrease in demand
Consumer preferences	A "Buy American" ad campaign appeals to national pride, increasing the demand for U.S.-made sneakers.	An outbreak of *E. coli* decreases the demand for spinach.
Prices of related goods	A decrease in the price of hot dogs increases the demand for relish, a complementary good.	A decrease in taxi fares decreases the demand for subway rides, a substitute good.
Incomes	An economic downturn lowers incomes, increasing the demand for ground beef, an inferior good.	An economic downturn lowers incomes, decreasing the demand for steak, a normal good.
Expectations	A hurricane destroys part of the world papaya crop, causing expectations that prices will rise and increasing the current demand for papayas.	An announcement that a new smartphone soon will be released decreases the demand for the current model.
Number of buyers	An increase in life expectancy increases the demand for nursing homes and medical care.	A falling birthrate decreases the demand for diapers.

to be essential. Other preferences will change over time, in response to external events or fads. For instance, it's more useful to own a cell phone when all your friends already have one. The demand for cell phones also jumped after the World Trade Center attacks on September 11, 2001, because people wanted to make sure they could reach their families in emergencies.[3]

Prices of related goods. Another factor that affects the demand for a particular good is the prices of related goods. There are two kinds of related goods—substitutes and complements.

We say that goods are **substitutes** when they serve similar-enough purposes that a consumer might purchase one in place of the other—for example, rice and pasta. If the price of rice doubles while the price of pasta stays the same, demand for pasta will increase. That's because the *opportunity cost* of pasta has decreased: You can buy less rice for the same amount of money, so you give up less potential rice when you buy pasta. If the two goods are quite similar, we call them *close substitutes*. Similar fishes, such as salmon and trout, might be considered close substitutes.

substitutes goods that serve a similar-enough purpose that a consumer might purchase one in place of the other

For many Americans deciding whether to buy their first cell phone, the nearest substitute would have been a landline phone. Cell phones and landlines are not very close substitutes: You can use them for the same purposes at home or the office, but only one of them can go for a walk with you. Still, if the price of U.S. landline phone service had suddenly skyrocketed, we can be sure that change would have increased the demand for cell phones.

In fact, the very high cost of landline phone services in many developing countries is one reason why cell phones spread very quickly. In the United States, almost every household had a landline phone before it had a cell phone. In many poor countries landlines are so expensive that very few people can afford one. That's why cell phones are often called a *leapfrog technology:* People go straight from no phone to cell phone, hopping over an entire stage of older technology.

Related goods that are consumed together, so that purchasing one will make a consumer more likely to purchase the other, are called **complements**. Peanut butter and jelly, cereal and milk, cars and gasoline are all complements. If the price of one of the two goods increases, demand for the other will likely decrease. Why? As consumers purchase less of the first good, they will want less of the other to go with it.

complements goods that are consumed together, so that purchasing one will make consumers more likely to purchase the other

Conversely, if the price of one of the two goods declines, demand for the other will likely increase. For example, when the prices of new cell phones fall, consumers will be more likely to buy new accessories to go with them.

Incomes.   Not surprisingly, the amount of income people earn affects their demand for goods and services: The bigger your paycheck, the more money you can afford to spend on the things you want. The smaller your paycheck, the more you have to cut back. Most goods are **normal goods**, meaning that an increase in income causes an increase in demand. Likewise, for normal goods a decrease in income causes a decrease in demand. For most people, cell phones are a normal good. If someone cannot afford a cell phone, she's more likely to buy one when her income rises. If someone already has a cell phone, she's more likely to upgrade to a newer, fancier cell phone when her income rises.

For some goods, called **inferior goods**, the opposite relationship holds: As income increases, demand decreases. Typically, people replace inferior goods with more expensive and appealing substitutes when their incomes rise. For many people, inexpensive grocery items like instant noodles, some canned foods, and generic store brands might be inferior goods. When their incomes rise, people replace these goods with fresher, more expensive ingredients. Decreases in income occur for many people during economic downturns; thus, the demand for inferior goods reflects the overall health of the economy. For an example, see the Real Life box "Can instant-noodle sales predict a recession?"

normal goods
goods for which demand increases as income increases

inferior goods
goods for which demand decreases as income increases

REAL LIFE

Can instant-noodle sales predict a recession?

If you were to open a typical college student's kitchen cupboard, what would you find? Many students rely on a decidedly unglamorous food item: ramen instant noodles. Packed with cheap calories, this tasty snack is famously inexpensive.

Ramen noodles are an example of an inferior good. When people's budgets are tight (as are those of most students), these noodles sell well. When incomes rise, ramen sales drop and more expensive foods replace them.

In Thailand, ramen noodles have even been used as an indicator of overall economic health. The Mama Noodles Index tracks sales of a popular brand of instant ramen noodles. Because the demand for inferior goods increases when incomes go down, an increase in ramen sales could signal a downturn in incomes and an oncoming recession. In fact, observers of the Thai economy say that the Mama Noodles Index does a pretty good job of reflecting changing economic conditions.

Even the demand for inferior goods may decrease during severe economic downturns, however. Although the Mama Noodles Index has risen as expected when the Thai economy falters, the index unexpectedly dropped 15 percent during the deep recession of early 2009.

So are instant noodles an inferior good or a normal good? In Thailand, the answer may depend on who you are or how severely your income has dropped. For the middle class, who choose between ramen and more expensive foods, ramen may indeed be an inferior good. For the poor, whose choice more likely is whether or not they will get enough to eat, ramen may be a normal good. When their incomes rise they may buy more ramen; when their incomes fall, even noodles may be a luxury.

Sources: "Using their noodles," Associated Press, September 5, 2005, http://www.theage.com.au/news/world/using-their-noodles/2005/09/04/1125772407287.html; "Downturn bites into instant-noodle market as customers tighten belts," *The Nation,* March 20, 2009, http://www.nationmultimedia.com/business/Downturn-bites-into-instant-noodle-market-as-custo-30098402.html.

Expectations. Changes in consumers' expectations about the future—especially future prices—can also affect demand. If consumers expect prices to fall in the future, they may postpone a purchase until a later date, causing current demand to decrease. Think about waiting to buy a new cell phone until it goes on sale, or holding off on purchasing a smartphone in the hope that the next model will be cheaper and faster than the prior one. When prices are expected to drop in the future, demand decreases.

Conversely, if consumers expect prices to rise in the future, they may wish to purchase a good immediately, to avoid a higher price. This reasoning often occurs in speculative markets, like the stock market or sometimes the housing market. Buyers purchase stock or a house expecting prices to rise, so they can sell at a profit. In these markets, then, demand increases when prices are low and are expected to rise.

Number of buyers. The demand curve represents the demand of a particular number of potential buyers. In general, an increase in the number of potential buyers in a market will increase demand; a decrease in the number of buyers will decrease it. Major population shifts, like an increase in immigration or a drop in the birthrate, can create nationwide changes in demand. As the number of teenagers and college students increases, the demand for cell phones increases too.

Shifts in the demand curve

LO 3.3 Distinguish between a shift in and a movement along the demand curve.

What happens to the demand curve when one of the five nonprice determinants of demand changes? The entire demand curve shifts, either to the right or to the left. The shift is horizontal rather than vertical, because nonprice determinants affect the quantity demanded at *each* price. The quantity demanded at a given price is now higher (or lower), so the point on the curve corresponding to that price is now further right (or left).

Consider what happens, for example, when the economy is growing and people's incomes are rising. The price of cell phones does not necessarily change, but more people will choose to buy a new one at any given price, causing quantity demanded to be higher at every possible price. Panel A of Figure 3-2 shows the resulting shift of the demand curve to the right, from D_A to D_B. In contrast, if the economy falls into a recession and people begin pinching pennies, quantity demanded will decrease at every price, and the curve will shift to the left, from D_A to D_C.

It is important to distinguish between these *shifts* in demand, which move the entire curve, and *movements along* a given demand curve. Remember this key point: *Shifts in the demand curve are caused by changes in the nonprice determinants of demand.* A recession, for example, would lower incomes and move the whole demand curve left. When we say "demand decreases," this is what we are talking about.

In contrast, suppose that the price of phones increases but everything else stays the same—that is, there is no change in the nonprice determinants of demand. Because the demand curve describes the quantity consumers will demand at any possible price, not just the current market price, we don't have to shift the curve to figure out what happens when the price goes up. Instead, we simply look at a different point on the curve to describe what is actually happening in the market right now.

To find the quantity that consumers will want to purchase at this new price, we move along the existing demand curve from the old price to the new one. If, for instance, the price of cell phones increases, we find the new quantity demanded by moving up along the demand curve to the new price point, as shown in panel B of Figure 3-2. The price change does not shift the curve itself, because the curve already describes what consumers will do at any price.

FIGURE 3-2

Movement along the demand curve versus shifts in the demand curve

(A) Shifts in the demand curve

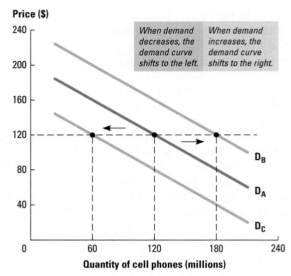

(B) Movement along the demand curve

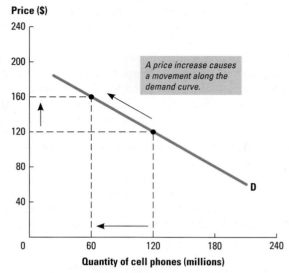

Changes in external factors cause the entire demand curve to shift. The shift from D_A to D_B represents an increase in demand, meaning that consumers want to buy more cell phones at each price. The shift from D_A to D_C represents a decrease in demand, meaning that consumers want to buy fewer cell phones at each price.

A price change causes a movement along the demand curve, but the curve itself remains constant.

To summarize, panel A of Figure 3-2 shows a *shift in demand* as the result of a change in the nonprice determinants; panel B shows a *movement along the demand curve* as the result of a change in price.

Economists use very specific terminology to distinguish between a shift in the demand curve and movement along the demand curve. We say that a change in one of the nonprice determinants of demand causes an *"increase in demand"* or *"decrease in demand"*—that is, a shift of the entire demand curve. To distinguish this from movement along the demand curve, we say that a change in price causes an *"increase in quantity demanded"* or *"decrease in the quantity demanded."* Just keep in mind that a "change in demand" is different from a "change in the quantity demanded." Observing this seemingly small difference in terminology prevents a great deal of confusion.

Understanding the effects of changes in both price and the nonprice determinants of demand is a key tool for businesspeople and policymakers. Suppose you are in charge of the Cell Phone Manufacturers' Association, an industry lobby group, and your members want to spur demand for phones. One idea might be to start an advertising campaign. If you understand the determinants of demand, you know that an advertising campaign aims to change consumer preferences, increasing the real or perceived benefits of owning a cell phone. In other words, a successful advertising campaign would shift the demand curve for cell phones to the right. Similarly, if you are a congressional representative who is considering a tax cut to stimulate the economy, you know that a tax cut increases consumers' disposable incomes, increasing the demand for all normal goods. In other words, you are hoping that the resulting increase in incomes will shift the demand curve for cell phones to the right.

✓ CONCEPT CHECK

❏ What are the five determinants of demand? **[LO 3.2]**

❏ What is the difference between a change in quantity and a change in quantity demanded? **[LO 3.3]**

Supply

We've discussed the factors that determine how many phones consumers want to buy at a given price. But are cell phone producers necessarily willing to sell that many? The concept of *supply* describes how much of a good or service producers will offer for sale under given circumstances. The **quantity supplied** is the amount of a particular good or service that producers will offer for sale at a given price during a specified period.

As with demand, we can find overall market supply by adding up the individual decisions of each producer. Imagine you own a factory that can produce cell phones or other consumer electronics. If the price of cell phones is $110, you might decide there's good money to be made and use your entire factory space to produce cell phones. If the price is only $80, you might produce some cell phones but decide it will be more profitable to devote part of your factory to producing laptop computers. If the cell phone price drops to $55, you might decide you'd make more money by producing only laptops. Each producer will have a different price point at which it decides it's worthwhile to supply cell phones. This rule—all else held equal, quantity supplied increases as price increases, and vice versa—is called the **law of supply**.

(In reality, it's costly to switch a factory from making cell phones to laptops or other goods. However, the simple version illustrates a basic truth: The higher the price of a good, the more of that good producers will want to sell.)

As with demand, supply varies with price because the decision to produce a good is about the *trade-off* between the benefit the producer will receive from selling the good and the opportunity cost of the time and resources that go into producing it. When the market price goes up and all other factors remain constant, the benefit of production increases relative to the opportunity cost, and the trade-off involved in production makes it more favorable to produce more. For instance, if the price of phones goes up and the prices of raw materials stay the same, existing phone producers may open new factories, and new companies may start looking to enter the cell phone market. The same holds true across other industries. If air travelers seem willing to pay higher prices, airlines will increase the frequency of flights, add new routes, and buy new planes so they can carry more passengers. When prices drop, they cut back their flight schedules and cancel their orders for new planes.

The supply curve

LO 3.4 Draw a supply curve and describe the external factors that determine supply.

Like demand, supply can be represented as a table or a graph. A **supply schedule** is a table that shows the quantities of a particular good or service that producers will supply at various prices. A **supply curve** is a graph of the information in the supply schedule. Just as the demand curve showed consumers' willingness to buy, so the supply curve shows producers' *willingness to sell:* It shows the minimum price producers must receive to supply any given quantity. Figure 3-3 shows U.S. cell phone providers' supply schedule and their supply curve for cell phones.

quantity supplied the amount of a particular good or service that producers will offer for sale at a given price during a specified period

law of supply a fundamental characteristic of supply which states that, all else equal, quantity supplied rises as price rises

supply schedule a table that shows the quantities of a particular good or service that producers will supply at various prices

supply curve a graph that shows the quantities of a particular good or service that producers will supply at various prices

FIGURE 3-3
Supply schedule and the supply curve

(A) Supply schedule

Cell phones (millions)	Price ($)
270	180
240	160
210	140
180	120
150	100
120	80
90	60
60	40
30	20

This supply schedule shows the quantity of cell phones supplied each year at various prices. As prices decrease, suppliers want to produce fewer cell phones.

(B) Supply curve

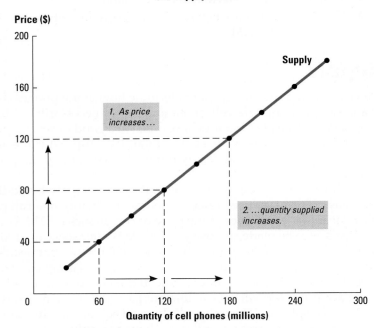

This supply curve is a graphic representation of the supply schedule for cell phones in the United States. It shows the quantity of cell phones that suppliers will produce at various prices.

Determinants of supply

The law of supply describes how the quantity that producers are willing to supply changes as price changes. But what determines the quantity supplied at any given price? As with demand, a number of nonprice factors determine the opportunity cost of production and therefore producers' willingness to supply a good or service. *When a nonprice determinant of supply changes, the entire supply curve will shift.* Such shifts reflect a change in the quantity of goods supplied at *every* price.

The nonprice determinants of supply can be divided into five major categories: prices of related goods, technology, prices of inputs, expectations, and the number of sellers. Each of these factors determines the opportunity cost of production relative to a given benefit (i.e., the price) and therefore the trade-off that producers face. Table 3-3 shows how the supply of various products responds to changes in each determinant.

Prices of related goods. Return to your factory, where you can produce either cell phones or laptops. Just as you chose to produce more laptops and fewer cell phones when the price of cell phones dropped, you would do the same if the price of laptops increased while the price of cell phones stayed constant.

The price of related goods determines supply because it affects the opportunity cost of production. When you choose to produce cell phones, you forgo the profits you would have earned from producing something else. If the price of that something else increases, the amount you forgo in profits also increases. For instance, imagine a farmer who can grow wheat or corn (or other crops, for that matter) on his land. If the price of corn increases, the quantity of wheat (the substitute crop) he is willing to grow falls, because each acre he devotes to wheat is one fewer acre he can use to grow corn.

TABLE 3-3 Determinants of supply

Determinant	Examples of an increase in supply	Examples of a decrease in supply
Price of related goods	The price of gas rises, so an automaker increases its production of smaller, more fuel-efficient cars.	The price of clean energy production falls, so the power company reduces the amount of power it supplies using coal power plants.
Technology	The installation of robots increases productivity and lowers costs; the supply of goods increases.	New technology allows corn to be made into ethanol, so farmers plant more corn and fewer soybeans; the supply of soybeans decreases.
Prices of inputs	A drop in the price of tomatoes decreases the production cost of salsa; the supply of salsa increases.	An increase in the minimum wage increases labor costs at food factories; the supply of processed food decreases.
Expectations	Housing prices are expected to rise, so builders increase production; the supply of houses increases.	New research points to the health benefits of eating papayas, leading to expectations that the demand for papayas will rise. More farmers plant papayas, increasing the supply.
Number of sellers	Subsidies make the production of corn more profitable, so more farmers plant corn; the supply of corn increases.	New licensing fees make operating a restaurant more expensive; some small restaurants close, decreasing the supply of restaurants.

Technology. Improved technology enables firms to produce more efficiently, using fewer resources to make a given product. Doing so lowers production costs, increasing the quantity producers are willing to supply at each price.

Improved technology has played a huge role in the changing popularity of cell phones. As technological innovation in the construction of screens, batteries, and mobile networks and in the processing of electronic data has leapt forward, the cost of producing a useful, consumer-friendly cell phone has plummeted. As a result, producers are now willing to supply more cell phones at lower prices.

Prices of inputs. The prices of the inputs used to produce a good are an important part of its cost. When the prices of inputs increase, production costs rise, and the quantity of the product that producers are willing to supply at any given price decreases.

Small amounts of silver and gold are used inside cell phones, for example. When the prices of these precious metals rise, the cost of manufacturing each cell phone increases, and the total number of units that producers collectively are willing to make at any given price goes down. Conversely, when input prices fall, supply increases.

Expectations. Suppliers' expectations about prices in the future also affect quantity supplied. For example, when the price of real estate is expected to rise in the future, more real estate developers will wait to embark on construction projects, decreasing the supply of houses in the near future. When expectations change and real estate prices are projected to fall in the future, many of those projects will be rushed to completion, causing the supply of houses to rise.

Number of sellers. The market supply curve represents the quantities of a product that a

In 1980, this cutting-edge technology cost $4,000.

61

particular number of producers will supply at various prices in a given market. This means that the number of sellers in the market is considered to be one of the fixed parts of the supply curve. We've already seen that the sellers in the market will decide to supply more if the price of a good is higher. This does not mean that the number of sellers will change based on price in the short run.

There are, however, nonprice factors that cause the number of sellers to change in a market and move the supply curve. For example, suppose cell phone producers must meet strict licensing requirements. If those licensing requirements are dropped, more companies may enter the market, willing to supply a certain number of cell phones at each price. These additional phones must be added to the number of cell phones existing producers are already willing to supply at each price point.

Shifts in the supply curve

LO 3.5 Distinguish between a shift in and a movement along the supply curve.

Just as with demand, changes in price cause suppliers to move to a different point on the same supply curve, while changes in the nonprice determinants of supply shift the supply curve itself. A change in a nonprice determinant increases or decreases *supply*, while a change in price increases or decreases the *quantity supplied*.

A change in one of the nonprice determinants increases or decreases the supply at any given price. These shifts are shown in panel A of Figure 3-4. An increase in supply shifts the curve to the right. A decrease in supply shifts the curve to the left. For instance,

FIGURE 3-4

Movement along the supply curve versus shifts in the supply curve

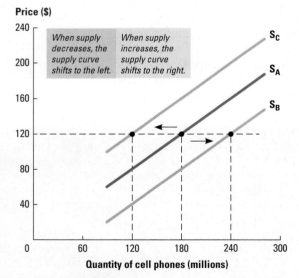

(A) Shifts in the supply curve

Changes in external factors cause the entire supply curve to shift. The shift from S_A to S_B represents an increase in supply, meaning that producers are willing to supply more cell phones at each price. The shift from S_A to S_C represents a decrease in supply, meaning that producers are willing to supply fewer cell phones at each price.

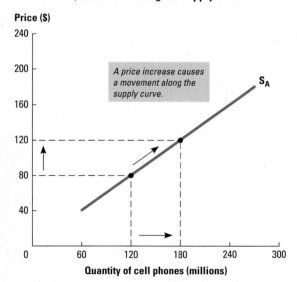

B) Movement along the supply curve

A price change causes a movement along the supply curve, but the curve itself remains constant.

an improvement in battery technology that decreases the cost of producing cell phones will shift the entire supply curve to the right, from S_A to S_B, so that the quantity of phones supplied at every price is higher than before. Conversely, an increase in the price of the gold needed for cell phones raises production costs, shifting the supply curve to the left, from S_A to S_C.

As with demand, we differentiate these shifts in the supply curve from a movement along the supply curve, which is shown in panel B of Figure 3-4. If the price of cell phones changes, but the nonprice determinants of supply stay the same, we find the new quantity supplied by moving along the supply curve to the new price point.

✓ CONCEPT CHECK

- ❒ What does the law of supply say about the relationship between price and quantity supplied? **[LO 3.4]**
- ❒ In which direction does the supply curve shift when the price of inputs increases? **[LO 3.5]**

Market Equilibrium

We've discussed the factors that influence the quantities supplied and demanded by producers and consumers. To find out what actually happens in the market, however, we need to combine these concepts. The prices and quantities of the goods that are exchanged in the real world depend on the *interaction* of supply with demand.

Bear with us for a moment as we point out the obvious: There is no sale without a purchase. You can't sell something unless someone buys it. Although this point may be obvious, the implication for markets is profound. When markets work well, the quantity supplied exactly equals the quantity demanded.

Graphically, this convergence of supply with demand happens at the point where the demand curve intersects the supply curve, a point called the market **equilibrium**. The price at this point is called the **equilibrium price**, and the quantity at this point is called the **equilibrium quantity**. We can think of this intersection, where quantity supplied equals quantity demanded, as the point at which buyers and sellers "agree" on the quantity of a good they are willing to exchange at a given price. At higher prices, sellers want to sell more than buyers want to buy. At lower prices, buyers want to buy more than sellers are willing to sell. Because every seller finds a buyer at the equilibrium price and quantity, and no one is left standing around with extra goods or an empty shopping cart, the equilibrium price is sometimes called the *market-clearing price*.

In reality, things don't always work so smoothly: Short-run "friction" sometimes slows the process of reaching equilibrium, even in well-functioning markets. As a result, smart businesspeople may hold some inventory for future sale, and consumers may need to shop around for specific items. On the whole, though, the concept of equilibrium is incredibly accurate (and important) in describing how markets function.

Figure 3-5 shows the market equilibrium for cell phones in the United States. It was constructed by combining the market supply and demand curves shown in Figures 3-1 and 3-3. In this market, the equilibrium price is $100, and the equilibrium quantity supplied and demanded is 150 million phones.

Reaching equilibrium

LO 3.6 Explain how supply and demand interact to drive markets to equilibrium.

How does a market reach equilibrium? Do sellers know intuitively what price to charge? No. Instead, they tend to set prices by trial and error, or by past experience

equilibrium the situation in a market when the quantity supplied equals the quantity demanded; graphically, this convergence happens where the demand curve intersects the supply curve

equilibrium price the price at which the quantity supplied equals the quantity demanded

equilibrium quantity the quantity that is supplied and demanded at the equilibrium price

FIGURE 3-5

Market equilibrium in the U.S. market for cell phones

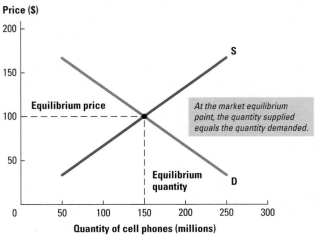

The point where the supply curve intersects the demand curve is called the equilibrium point. In this example, the equilibrium price is $100, and the equilibrium quantity is 150 million cell phones. At this point, consumers are willing to buy exactly as many cell phones as producers are willing to sell.

with customers. The incentives buyers and sellers face will naturally drive the market toward equilibrium, as sellers raise or lower their prices in response to customers' behavior.

Figure 3-6 shows two graphs, one in which the starting price is above the equilibrium price and the other in which it is below the equilibrium price. In panel A, we imagine that cell phone suppliers think they'll be able to charge $160 for a cell phone, so they produce 240 million phones, but they find that consumers will buy only 60 million. (We can read the quantities demanded and supplied at a price of $160 from the demand and supply curves.) When the quantity supplied is higher than the quantity demanded, we say that there is a **surplus** of phones, or an **excess supply**. Manufacturers are stuck holding extra phones in their warehouses; they want to sell that stock and must reduce the price to attract more customers. They have an incentive to keep lowering the price until quantity demanded increases to reach quantity supplied.

In panel B of Figure 3-6, we imagine that cell phone producers make the opposite mistake—they think they'll be able to charge only $40 per phone. They make only 60 million cell phones, but discover that consumers actually are willing to buy 240 million cell phones at that price. When the quantity demanded is higher than the quantity supplied, we say there is a **shortage**, or **excess demand**. Producers will see long lines of people waiting to buy the few available cell phones, and will quickly realize that they could make more money by charging a higher price. They have an incentive to increase the price until quantity demanded decreases to equal quantity supplied, and no one is left standing in line.

Thus, at any price above or below the equilibrium price, sellers face an incentive to raise or lower prices. No one needs to engineer the market equilibrium or share secret information about what price to charge. Instead, money-making incentives drive the market toward the equilibrium price, at which there is neither a surplus nor a shortage. The Real Life box "The Prius shortage of 2003" describes a case in which a producer started out charging the wrong price, but the market solved the problem.

surplus (excess supply) a situation in which the quantity of a good that is supplied is higher than the quantity demanded

shortage (excess demand) a situation in which the quantity of a good that is demanded is higher than the quantity supplied

FIGURE 3-6
Reaching equilibrium in the market for cell phones

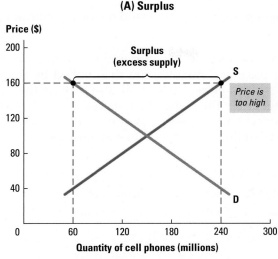

(A) Surplus

When the initial price for cell phones is above the equilibrium point, producers want to supply more cell phones than consumers want to buy. The gap between the quantity supplied and the quantity demanded is called a surplus, or excess supply.

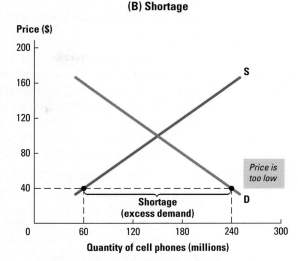

(B) Shortage

When the initial price for cell phones is below the equilibrium point, consumers want to buy more cell phones than sellers want to produce. The distance between the quantity demanded and the quantity supplied is called a shortage, or excess demand.

REAL LIFE

The Prius shortage of 2003

In 2003, Toyota introduced the first mainstream "hybrid" car, the Prius, to the U.S. auto market. A hybrid car runs on a combination of gasoline and electric power, using the engine to charge an electric battery in stop-and-go traffic. The Prius got much better gas mileage than its competitors—usually between 40 and 50 miles to the gallon. But for most families the gas savings were more than offset by the car's higher price. The car's main appeal was its environmentally friendly design.

When the Prius hit the U.S. market in October 2003, dealerships sold out immediately. Toyota had significantly underestimated the demand. Prospective buyers had to put their names on a waiting list, often for more than six months. A few years later, when gasoline prices spiked, demand was driven even higher as consumers grew more interested in good gas mileage. In the short run, Toyota could not do much to address the shortage; increasing plant capacity would take time.

Instead, the market found a way to solve the problem. As we know, price acts as a signal between buyers and sellers trying to match demand with supply. When demand is higher than supply, the price will rise. As we might expect, Prius buyers began to bid up the price of the car. Dealerships were soon charging thousands of dollars more than the manufacturer's suggested price. For a while, even the price of a *used* Prius was higher than the suggested price for a new car.

Eventually, Toyota responded to the shortage by increasing production capacity of the Prius. The company moved production of the car to progressively larger plants; in 2008, total production topped 1 million. Shortages persisted, however, as increases in demand outstripped the increases in supply. As Toyota scrambled to catch up with demand, sellers happily charged a premium to clear the market.

Source: "Wait time for Prius buyers diminishing," *CNNMoney*, November 6, 2006, http://money.cnn.com/2006/11/06/autos/prius/index.htm.

Changes in equilibrium

LO 3.7 Evaluate the effect of changes in supply and demand on the equilibrium price and quantity.

We've seen what happens to the supply and demand curves when a nonprice factor changes. Because the equilibrium price and quantity are determined by the interaction of supply and demand, a shift in either curve will also change the market equilibrium. Some changes will cause only the demand curve to shift; some, only the supply curve. Some changes will affect both the supply and demand curves.

To determine the effect on market equilibrium of a change in a nonprice factor, ask yourself a few questions:

1. Does the change affect demand? If so, does demand increase or decrease?
2. Does the change affect supply? If so, does supply increase or decrease?
3. How does the combination of changes in supply and demand affect the equilibrium price and quantity?

HINT

Remember, when we say that supply or demand increases or decreases, we're referring to a *shift in the entire curve*, not a movement along it, which is a change in quantity demanded.

Shifts in demand. We suggested earlier that landline service is a *substitute* for cell phones and that if the price of landline service suddenly skyrockets, then demand for cell phones increases. In other words, the demand curve shifts to the right. The price of landline service probably doesn't affect the supply of cell phones, because it doesn't change the costs or expectations that cell phone manufacturers face. So the supply curve stays put. Figure 3-7 shows the effect of the increase in landline price on the market equilibrium for cell phones. Because the new demand curve intersects the supply curve at a different point, the equilibrium price and quantity change. The new equilibrium price is $120, and the new equilibrium quantity is 180 million.

We can summarize this effect in terms of the three questions to ask following a change in a nonprice factor:

1. *Does demand increase/decrease?* Yes, the change in the price of landlines phone service increases demand for cell phones at every price.
2. *Does supply increase/decrease?* No, the change in the price of landline phone service does not affect any of the nonprice determinants of supply. The supply curve stays where it is.
3. *How does the combination of changes in supply and demand affect equilibrium price and quantity?* The increase in demand shifts the demand curve to the right, pushing the equilibrium to a higher point on the stationary supply curve. The new point at which supply and demand "agree" represents a price of $120 and a quantity of 180 million phones.

To improve your understanding of shifts in demand, try the online interactive graphing tutorial.

Shifts in supply. What would happen if a breakthrough in battery technology enabled cell phone manufacturers to construct phones with the same battery life for less money? Once again, asking *How will others respond?* helps us predict the market response. We can see that the new technology does not have much impact on demand: Customers probably have no idea how much the batteries in their phones cost to make, nor will they care as long as battery life stays the same. However, cheaper batteries definitely

FIGURE 3-7
Shift in the demand for cell phones

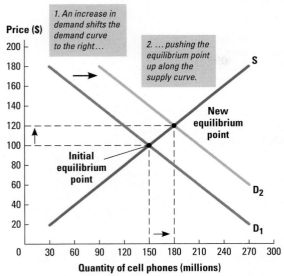

When an external factor increases the demand for cell phones at all prices, the demand curve shifts to the right. This increase in demand results in a new equilibrium point. Consumers purchase more cell phones at a higher price.

FIGURE 3-8
Shift in the supply of cell phones

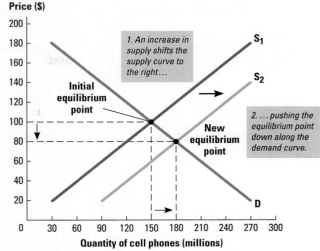

When an external factor affects the supply of cell phones at all prices, the supply curve shifts. In this example, supply increases and the market reaches a new equilibrium point. Consumers purchase more phones at a lower price.

decrease production costs, increasing the number of phones manufacturers are willing to supply at any given price. So the demand curve stays where it is, and the supply curve shifts to the right. Figure 3-8 shows the shift in supply and the new equilibrium point. The new supply curve intersects the demand curve at a new equilibrium point, representing a price of $80 and a quantity of 180 million phones.

Once again, we can analyze the effect of the change in battery technology on the market for cell phones in three steps:

1. *Does demand increase/decrease?* No, the nonprice determinants of demand are not affected by battery technology.

2. *Does supply increase/decrease?* Yes, supply increases, because the new battery technology lowers production costs.

3. *How does the combination of changes in supply and demand affect equilibrium price and quantity?* The increase in supply shifts the supply curve to the right, pushing the equilibrium to a lower point on the stationary demand curve. The new equilibrium price and quantity are $80 and 180 million phones.

Table 3-4 summarizes the effect of some other changes in demand or supply on the equilibrium price and quantity.

Shifts in both demand and supply. In our discussion so far, we've covered examples in which only demand or supply shifted. However, it's possible that factors that shift demand (such as a hike in landline cost) and supply (such as an improvement in battery technology) in the market for cell phones could coincidentally happen at the same time. It's also possible that a single change could affect both supply and demand.

For instance, suppose that in addition to reducing the cost of production, the new battery technology makes cell phone batteries last longer. We already know that cheaper batteries will increase supply. As we saw before with increases in supply, price decreases

To improve your understanding of shifts in supply, try the online interactive graphing tutorial.

TABLE 3-4 Effect of changes in demand or supply on the equilibrium price and quantity

Example of change in demand or supply	Effect on equilibrium price and quantity	Shift in curve
A successful "Buy American" advertising campaign increases the demand for Fords.	The demand curve shifts to the right. The equilibrium price and quantity increase.	
An outbreak of *E. coli* reduces the demand for spinach.	The demand curve shifts to the left. The equilibrium price and quantity decrease.	
The use of robots decreases production costs.	The supply curve shifts to the right. The equilibrium price decreases, and the equilibrium quantity increases.	
An increase in the minimum wage increases labor costs.	The supply curve shifts to the left. The equilibrium price increases, and the equilibrium quantity decreases.	

while the quantity increases. Asking *how consumers will respond* allows us to see that the improvement in battery life will also increase demand, because longer-lasting batteries will make a cell phone more valuable to consumers at any given price. As a result, both the demand curve and the supply curve shift to the right. Panel A and B of Figure 3-9 both show that the effect of a double change is a new equilibrium point at a higher price and a higher quantity.

Even without looking at a graph, we could have predicted that in this case the equilibrium *quantity* would rise. Increases in demand and increases in supply both independently lead to a higher equilibrium quantity—and the combination will certainly do so as well. Without more information, however, we cannot predict the change in equilibrium *price*. Holding all else equal, an increase in demand leads to an increase in price, but an increase in supply leads to a decrease in price. To find the net effect on equilibrium price, we would have to know whether the shift in demand outweighs the shift in supply shown in panel A of Figure 3-9, or vice versa, which is shown in panel B.

We can state this idea more generally: When supply and demand shift together, it is possible to predict *either* the direction of the change in quantity *or* the direction of the change in price without knowing how much the curves shift. Table 3-5 shows some rules you can use to predict the outcome of these shifts in supply and demand. When supply and demand move in the *same* direction, we can predict the direction of the change in

FIGURE 3-9

Shifts in both demand and supply

> An increase in supply and demand shifts both curves to the right, resulting in a higher quantity traded.
> However, the direction of the price shift depends on whether supply or demand increases more.

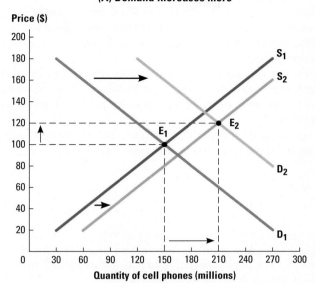

(A) Demand increases more

Sometimes, supply and demand shift together. In this example, both curves shift to the right, but demand increases more. At the new equilibrium point, E_2, consumers purchase more cell phones at a higher price.

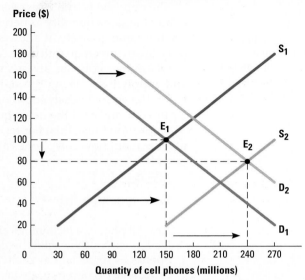

(B) Supply increases more

Sometimes, supply and demand shift together. In this example, both curves shift to the right, but supply increases more. At the new equilibrium point, E_2, consumers purchase more cell phones at a lower price.

Supply change	Demand change	Price change	Quantity change
Decrease	Decrease	?	↓
Decrease	Increase	↑	?
Increase	Increase	?	↑
Increase	Decrease	↓	?

TABLE 3-5

Predicting changes in price and quantity when supply and demand change simultaneously

quantity but not the direction of the change in price. When supply and demand move in *opposite* directions, the change in price is predictable, but not the change in quantity.

Thinking about the intuition behind these rules may help you to remember them. Any time you are considering a situation in which supply and demand shift at the same time, ask yourself, "What do buyers and sellers agree on?" For instance, when both supply and demand increase, buyers and sellers "agree" that at any given price, the quantity they are willing to exchange is higher. The reverse is true when both supply and demand decrease: Buyers and sellers agree that at a given price, the quantity they are willing to exchange is lower.

Applying this reasoning to opposite shifts in supply and demand—when one increases but the other decreases—is trickier. To find out what buyers and sellers "agree" on, try rephrasing what it means for demand to increase. One way to say it is that consumers are willing to buy a *higher* quantity at the *same* price. Another way to say it is that consumers are willing to pay a *higher* price to buy the *same* quantity. So, when demand increases and supply decreases, buyers are willing to pay more for the same quantity; also, sellers are willing to sell the same quantity only if they receive a higher price. In other words, they can "agree" on a higher price at any given quantity. We can therefore predict that the equilibrium price will increase.

The opposite is true when demand decreases and supply increases. Buyers are willing to buy the same quantity as before only if the price is lower, and sellers are willing to supply the same quantity at a lower price. Because the two groups can "agree" on a lower price at any given quantity, we can predict that the price will decrease.

Of course, you can always work out the effect of simultaneous shifts in demand and supply by working through the three questions described in the previous section. Draw the shifts in each curve on a graph, as is done in two cases in panels A and B in Figure 3-9, and find the new equilibrium.

Before you finish this chapter, read the Real Life box "Give a man a fish" for some information about how cell phones affected supply and demand in one developing country.

> To improve your understanding of simultaneous shifts in demand and supply, try the online interactive graphing tutorial.

REAL LIFE

Give a man a fish

Are cell phones a technological luxury or a practical necessity? Maybe you can't imagine life without the ability to call or text your friends anywhere, any time. But are cell phones as important as shelter, food, or water? A recent study in India showed that being able to communicate may help people to meet their basic needs.

In a competitive market, the price of a particular good is found at the point where the quantity supplied equals the quantity demanded. This model assumes that everywhere in the market, buyers and sellers are fully informed about prices and can adjust their behavior accordingly. If buyers and sellers do not have good information about prices, shortages can develop in some locations and surpluses in others.

When the economist Robert Jensen studied the market for fish in Kerala, a state in southwestern India, he found that it did not reach one equilibrium price. Instead, each local fish market has its own equilibrium. In this area, many people rely on fishing for their daily income. Fishermen tend to sell their fish at a single local market; they take the price that prevails at that market on a particular day. If that market has only a few buyers that day, the fishermen end up with too much fish. At the same time, if the fishermen in a neighboring village have a poor catch that day, some buyers at that market will go home empty-handed—even if they are willing to pay a high price. Without a way to know if there is a shortage or surplus in a nearby market, the fishermen can't adjust their prices to reach equilibrium with customers.

Jensen found that the fishermen could solve this problem using cell phones. By communicating with one another and with people on land while out fishing, they were able to find out where their catches would be most profitable that day. They used that information to travel to the right village to sell their fish. Supply began to better match the demand in each village, and prices became more uniform across villages. Access to the right information allowed the market for fish to reach an efficient equilibrium. Sellers earned an average of 8 percent more in profits, and buyers paid an average of 4 percent less for their fish. Fishermen increased their incomes, and consumers stretched their incomes further.

As the saying goes, "Give a man a fish and he will eat for a day. Teach a man to fish and he will eat for a lifetime." To this wisdom, we might add, "Give a man a cell phone. . . ."

Source: R. Jensen, "The digital provide: Information (technology), market performance, and welfare in the South Indian fisheries sector," *The Quarterly Journal of Economics,* vol. CXXII (2007), issue 3.

❐ What is the market equilibrium? **[LO 3.6]**

❐ What happens to the equilibrium price and quantity if the supply curve shifts right but the demand curve stays put? **[LO 3.7]**

Conclusion

By the time you reach the end of this course, you'll be quite familiar with the words *supply* and *demand*. We take our time on this subject for good reason: An understanding of supply and demand is the foundation of economic problem solving. You'll be hard-pressed to make wise economic choices without it.

Although markets are not always perfectly competitive, you may be surprised at how accurately many real-world phenomena can be described using the simple rules of supply and demand. In the next chapters we'll use these rules to explain how consumers and producers respond to price changes and government policies.

 ◄ Mobile Window on the World—Scan this code with your smartphone to find more applications of the chapter content. (Need a barcode reader? Try ScanLife, available in your app store.)

Visit your mobile app store and download ► the Karlan and Morduch Study Econ app.

Key Terms

market, p. 50

market economy, p. 50

competitive market, p. 50

standardized good, p. 51

transaction costs, p. 51

price taker, p. 51

quantity demanded, p. 52

law of demand, p. 52

demand schedule, p. 53

demand curve, p. 53

substitutes, p. 55

complements, p. 55

normal goods, p. 56

inferior goods, p. 56

quantity supplied, p. 59

law of supply, p. 59

supply schedule, p. 59

supply curve, p. 59

equilibrium, p. 63

equilibrium price, p. 63

equilibrium quantity, p. 63

surplus (excess supply), p. 64

shortage (excess demand), p. 64

Summary

LO 3.1 Identify the defining characteristics of a competitive market.

A market is the group of buyers and sellers who trade a particular good or service. In competitive markets, a large number of buyers and sellers trade standardized goods and services. They have full information about the goods, and there is no cost to participating in exchanges in the market. Participants in competitive markets are called price takers because they can't affect the prevailing price for a good.

LO 3.2 Draw a demand curve and describe the external factors that determine demand.

A demand curve is a graph that shows the quantities of a particular good or service that consumers will demand at various prices. It also shows consumers' highest willingness to pay for a given quantity. The law of demand states that for almost all goods, the quantity demanded increases as the price decreases. This relationship results in a downward-sloping demand curve.

Several nonprice factors contribute to consumers' demand for a good at a given price: Consumer preferences, the prices of related goods, incomes, and expectations about the future all affect demand. On a marketwide level, the number of buyers can also increase or decrease total demand. When one of these underlying factors changes, the demand curve will shift to the left or the right.

LO 3.3 Distinguish between a shift in and a movement along the demand curve.

When one of the nonprice factors that drives demand changes, the entire curve *shifts* to the left or the right. With this shift, the quantity demanded at any given price changes. When demand increases, the curve shifts to the right; when demand decreases, it shifts to the left.

When the underlying demand relationship *stays the same*, a change in the price of a good leads to a *movement along* the curve, rather than a shift in the curve.

LO 3.4 Draw a supply curve and describe the external factors that determine supply.

A supply curve is a graph that shows the quantities of a particular good or service that producers will supply at various prices. It shows the minimum price producers must receive to supply any given quantity. The law of supply states that the quantity supplied increases as the price increases, resulting in an upward-sloping supply curve.

Several nonprice factors determine the supply of a good at any given price: They include the prices of related goods, technology, prices of inputs, expectations about the future, and the number of sellers in the market. If one of these underlying factors changes, the supply curve will shift to the left or the right.

LO 3.5 Distinguish between a shift in and a movement along the supply curve.

Just as with demand, a change in the nonprice determinants of supply will cause the entire supply curve to shift to the left or the right. As a result, the quantity supplied is higher or lower at any given price than it was before. When supply increases, the curve shifts to the right; when supply decreases, it shifts to the left.

A shift in the supply curve differs from movement along the supply curve. A movement along the curve happens when the price of a good increases but the nonprice determinants of supply stay the same.

LO 3.6 Explain how supply and demand interact to drive markets to equilibrium.

When a market is in equilibrium, the quantity supplied equals the quantity demanded. The incentives that individual buyers and sellers face drive a competitive market toward equilibrium. If the prevailing price is too high, a surplus will result, and sellers will lower their prices to get rid of the excess supply. If the prevailing price is too low, a shortage will result, and buyers will bid up the price until the excess demand disappears.

LO 3.7 Evaluate the effect of changes in supply and demand on the equilibrium price and quantity.

When one or more of the underlying factors that determine supply or demand changes, one or both curves will shift, leading to a new market equilibrium price and quantity.

To calculate the change in the equilibrium price and quantity, you must first determine whether a change affects demand, and if so, in which direction the curve will shift. Then you must determine whether the change also affects supply, and if so, in which direction that curve will shift. Finally, you must determine the new equilibrium point where the two curves intersect.

Review Questions

1. Think about a competitive market in which you participate regularly. For each of the characteristics of a competitive market, explain how your market meets these requirements. **[LO 3.1]**

2. Think about a noncompetitive market in which you participate regularly. Explain which characteristic(s) of competitive markets your market does not meet. **[LO 3.1]**

3. Explain why a demand curve slopes downward. **[LO 3.2]**

4. In each of the following examples, name the factor that affects demand and describe its impact on your demand for a new cell phone. **[LO 3.2]**
   a. You hear a rumor that a new and improved model of the phone you want is coming out next year.
   b. Your grandparents give you $500.
   c. A cellular network announces a holiday sale on a text-messaging package that includes the purchase of a new phone.
   d. A friend tells you how great his new cell phone is and suggests that you get one, too.

5. Consider the following events:
   a. The price of cell phones goes down by 25 percent during a sale.
   b. You get a 25 percent raise at your job.

   Which event represents a shift in the demand curve? Which represents a movement along the curve? What is the difference? **[LO 3.3]**

6. What is the difference between a change in demand and a change in quantity demanded? **[LO 3.3]**

7. Explain why a supply curve slopes upward. **[LO 3.4]**

8. In each of the following examples, name the factor that affects supply and describe its impact on the supply of cell phones. **[LO 3.4]**
   a. Economic forecasts suggest that the demand for cell phones will increase in the future.
   b. The price of plastic goes up.
   c. A new screen technology reduces the cost of making cell phones.

9. Consider the following events:
   a. A maggot infestation ruins a large number of apple orchards in Washington state.
   b. Demand for apples goes down, causing the price to fall.

   Which event represents a shift in the supply curve? Which represents a movement along the curve? What is the difference? **[LO 3.5]**

10. What is the difference between a change in supply and a change in quantity supplied? **[LO 3.5]**

11. What is the relationship between supply and demand when a market is in equilibrium? Explain how the incentives facing cell phone companies and consumers cause the market for cell phones to reach equilibrium. **[LO 3.6]**

12. Explain why the equilibrium price is often called the market-clearing price. **[LO 3.6]**

13. Suppose an economic boom causes incomes to increase. Explain what will happen to the demand and supply of phones, and predict the direction of the change in the equilibrium price and quantity. **[LO 3.7]**

14. Suppose an economic boom drives up wages for the sales representatives who work for cell phone companies. Explain what will happen to the demand and supply of phones, and predict the direction of the change in the equilibrium price and quantity. **[LO 3.7]**

15. Suppose an economic boom causes incomes to increase and at the same time drives up wages for the sales representatives who work for cell phone companies. Explain what will happen to the demand for and supply of phones and predict the direction of the change in the equilibrium price and quantity. **[LO 3.7]**

Problems and Applications

1. Consider shopping for cucumbers in a farmers' market. For each statement below, note which characteristic of competitive markets the statement describes. *Choose from:* standardized good, full information, no transaction costs, and participants are price takers. **[LO 3.1]**
   a. All of the farmers have their prices posted prominently in front of their stalls.
   b. Cucumbers are the same price at each stall.
   c. There is no difficulty moving around between stalls as you shop and choosing between farmers.
   d. You and the other customers all seem indifferent about which cucumbers to buy.

2. Suppose two artists are selling paintings for the same price in adjacent booths at an art fair. By the end of the day, one artist has nearly sold out of her paintings while the other artist has sold nothing. Which characteristic of competitive markets has not been met and best explains this outcome? **[LO 3.1]**
   a. Standardized good.
   b. Full information.
   c. No transaction costs.
   d. Participants are price takers.

3. Using the demand schedule in Table 3P-1, draw the daily demand curve for slices of pizza in a college town. **[LO 3.2]**

4. Consider the market for cars. Which determinant of demand is affected by each of the following events? *Choose from:* consumer preferences, prices of related goods, incomes, expectations, and the number of buyers. **[LO 3.2]**
   a. Environmentalists launch a successful One Family, One Car campaign.
   b. A baby boom occurred 16 years ago.
   c. Layoffs increase as the economy sheds millions of jobs.
   d. An oil shortage causes the price of gasoline to soar.
   e. The government offers tax rebates in return for the purchase of commuter rail tickets.

TABLE 3P-1

Price ($)	Quantity demanded (slices)
0.00	350
0.50	300
1.00	250
1.50	200
2.00	150
2.50	100
3.00	50
3.50	0

FIGURE 3P-1

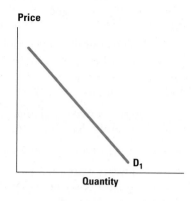

TABLE 3P-2

Price ($)	Quantity supplied (slices)
0.00	0
0.50	50
1.00	100
1.50	150
2.00	200
2.50	250
3.00	300
3.50	350

f. The government announces a massive plan to bail out the auto industry and subsidize production costs.

5. If a decrease in the price of laptops causes the demand for cell phones to increase, are laptops and cell phones substitutes or complements? **[LO 3.2]**

6. If rising incomes cause the demand for beer to decrease, is beer a normal or inferior good? **[LO 3.2]**

7. Consider the market for corn. Say whether each of the following events will cause a shift in the demand curve or a movement along the curve. If it will cause a shift, specify the direction. **[LO 3.3]**

   a. A drought hits corn-growing regions, cutting the supply of corn.

   b. The government announces a new subsidy for biofuels made from corn.

   c. A global recession reduces the incomes of consumers in poor countries, who rely on corn as a staple food.

   d. A new hybrid variety of corn seed causes a 15 percent increase in the yield of corn per acre.

   e. An advertising campaign by the beef producers' association highlights the health benefits of corn-fed beef.

8. The demand curve in Figure 3P-1 shows the monthly market for sweaters at a local clothing store. For each of the following events, draw the new outcome. **[LO 3.3]**

   a. Sweaters fall out of fashion.

   b. There is a shortage of wool.

   c. The winter is particularly long and cold this year.

   d. Sweater vendors offer a sale.

9. Using the supply schedule found in Table 3P-2, draw the daily supply curve for slices of pizza in a college town. **[LO 3.4]**

10. Consider the market for cars. Which determinant of supply is affected by each of the following events? *Choose from:* prices of related goods, technology, prices of inputs, expectations, and the number of sellers in the market. **[LO 3.4]**

    a. A steel tariff increases the price of steel.

    b. Improvements in robotics increase efficiency and reduce costs.

    c. Factories close because of an economic downturn.

    d. The government announces a plan to offer tax rebates for the purchase of commuter rail tickets.

    e. The price of trucks falls, so factories produce more cars.

f. The government announces that it will dramatically rewrite efficiency standards, making it much harder for automakers to produce their cars.

11. Consider the market for corn. Say whether each of the following events will cause a shift in the supply curve or a movement along the curve. If it will cause a shift, specify the direction. **[LO 3.5]**

    a. A drought hits corn-growing regions.

    b. The government announces a new subsidy for biofuels made from corn.

    c. A global recession reduces the incomes of consumers in poor countries, who rely on corn as a staple food.

    d. A new hybrid variety of corn seed causes a 15 percent increase in the yield of corn per acre.

    e. An advertising campaign by the beef producers' association highlights the health benefits of corn-fed beef.

12. The supply curve in Figure 3P-2 shows the monthly market for sweaters at a local craft market. For each of the following events, draw the new outcome. **[LO 3.5]**

    a. The price of wool increases.

    b. Demand for sweaters decreases.

    c. A particularly cold winter is expected to begin next month.

    d. Demand for sweaters increases.

13. Refer to the demand and supply schedule shown in Table 3P-3. **[LO 3.6]**

    a. If pizza parlors charge $3.50 per slice, will there be excess supply or excess demand? What is the amount of excess supply or excess demand at that price?

    b. If pizza parlors charge $1.00 per slice, will there be excess supply or excess demand? What is the amount of excess supply or excess demand at that price?

    c. What are the equilibrium price and quantity in this market?

The graph in Figure 3P-3 shows the weekly market for compact discs in a small town. Use this graph to answer Problems 14–16.

14. Which of the following events will occur at a price of $20? **[LO 3.6]**

    a. Equilibrium.

    b. Excess demand.

    c. Excess supply.

TABLE 3P-3

Price ($)	Quantity demanded (slices)	Quantity supplied (slices)
0.00	350	0
0.50	300	50
1.00	250	100
1.50	200	150
2.00	150	200
2.50	100	250
3.00	50	300
3.50	0	350

FIGURE 3P-2

Price

S_1

Quantity

FIGURE 3P-3

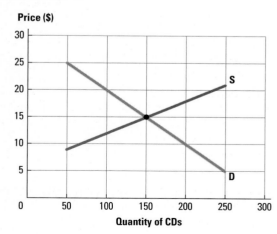

Price ($)

Quantity of CDs

d. No CDs supplied.

e. No CDs demanded.

15. Which of the following events will occur at a price of $10? **[LO 3.6]**

a. Equilibrium.

b. Excess demand.

c. Excess supply.

d. No CDs supplied.

e. No CDs demanded.

16. What are the equilibrium price and quantity of CDs? **[LO 3.6]**

17. The graph in Figure 3P-4 shows supply and demand in the market for automobiles. For each of the following events, draw the new market outcome, and say whether the equilibrium price and quantity will increase or decrease. **[LO 3.7]**

FIGURE 3P-4

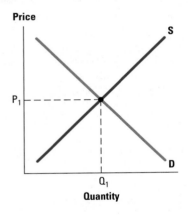

a. Environmentalists launch a successful One Family, One Car campaign.

b. A steel tariff increases the price of steel.

c. A baby boom occurred 16 years ago.

d. An oil shortage causes the price of gasoline to soar.

e. Improvements in robotics increase efficiency and reduce costs.

f. The government offers a tax rebate for the purchase of commuter rail tickets.

18. Say whether each of the following changes will increase or decrease the equilibrium price and quantity, or whether the effect cannot be predicted. **[LO 3.7]**

a. Demand increases; supply remains constant.

b. Supply increases; demand remains constant.

c. Demand decreases; supply remains constant.

d. Supply decreases; demand remains constant.

e. Demand increases; supply increases.

f. Demand decreases; supply decreases.

g. Demand increases; supply decreases.

h. Demand decreases; supply increases.

Chapter Endnotes

1. http://www.itu.int/ITU-D/ict/statistics/at_glance/KeyTelecom.html.

2. Ibid.

3. G. Wright and M. Groppe, "Some businesses benefiting from 9–11," *The Baxter Bulletin*, August 29, 2002, http://www.biometricgroup.com/in_the_news/baxter_bulletin.html, retrieved June 14, 2009.

Math Essentials: Working with Linear Equations

LEARNING OBJECTIVES

LO B.1   Use linear equations to interpret the equation of a line.

LO B.2   Use linear equations to explain shifts and pivots.

LO B.3   Use linear equations to solve for equilibrium.

· ·

Relationships between variables can be represented with algebraic equations, as well as graphs and tables. You should be comfortable moving among all three representations. We addressed graphs in Appendix A (following Chapter 2); if you didn't read it then, you might want to do so now.

Interpreting the Equation of a Line

LO B.1 Use linear equations to interpret the equation of a line.

If the relationship between two variables is linear, it can be represented by the equation for a line, which is commonly written as:

Equation B-1

$$y = mx + b$$

In this form, called the *slope intercept form*, m is the slope of the line, and b is the y-intercept.

All linear equations provide information about the slope and y-intercept of the line. From our discussion in Appendix A, we already know that slope is the ratio of vertical distance (change in y) to horizontal distance (change in x). So what does the y-intercept tell us? It is the point at which the line crosses the y-axis. Put another way, it is the value of y when x is 0. Knowing these values is useful in turning an equation into a graph. Also, as we'll see, they can allow us to get information about the real economic relationship being represented without even having to graph it.

Although you might see the equation for a line rearranged in several different forms, just remember that if y is on the left-hand side of the equation, whatever number is multiplying x (known as the *coefficient of x*) is your slope. If you don't see a number in front of x, the slope is 1. The number being added to or subtracted from a multiple of x is a constant that represents the y-intercept. If you don't see this number, you know that the y-intercept is zero. Take a look at a few examples in Table B-1.

TABLE B-1

Examples of linear equations

The steepness and position of a line in the Cartesian coordinate system is determined by two things: its slope and its intercept. Slope refers to steepness; the intercept determines where the line is positioned.

Equation	Slope	y-intercept
$y = 6x + 4$	6	4
$y = -x - 2$	-1	-2
$y = 10 - 2x$	-2	10
$y = -4x$	-4	0

Turning a graph into an equation

To see how to translate a graph into an algebraic equation, look at Figure B-1. What is the equation that represents this relationship?

To derive this equation, we need to find the values of the slope and the y-intercept. We can calculate the slope at any point along the line:

$$\text{Slope} = \frac{\Delta y}{\Delta x} = \frac{(y_2 - y_1)}{(x_2 - x_1)}$$

$$= \frac{(6 - 5)}{(4 - 2)} = \frac{1}{2} = 0.5$$

By looking at the graph to see where the line intersects the y-axis, we can tell that the y-intercept is 4. Therefore, if we write the equation in the form $y = mx + b$, we get $y = 0.5x + 4$. Our table, graph, and equation all give us the same information about the relationship between x and y.

Turning an equation into a graph

Let's work in the opposite direction now, starting with an equation and seeing what information it gives us.

The following equation takes the form $y = mx + b$, with P and Q substituted for y and x, respectively.

$$P = -5Q + 25$$

We know from looking at this equation that it represents a line with a slope of -5 and a y-intercept of 25. Suppose that we know this equation represents supply or demand, but we're not sure which. How can we tell whether this is a demand equation or a supply equation? Easy. The slope is negative. We don't need a graph to tell us that the relationship between P and Q is negative and the line will be downward-sloping. Therefore, the equation must represent demand rather than supply.

Because the y-intercept in our equation is 25, we know that the demand curve will cross the y-axis at 25. This tells us that when price is 25, quantity demanded is 0. In order for consumers to demand a positive quantity, price must be lower than 25.

If we need to know more about the relationship represented by the equation, we can graph the demand curve. Since we know that 25 is the y-intercept, we can use the point (0,25) to begin plotting our graph as shown in Figure B-2.

It takes only two points to define a line, and we already have one from the y-intercept. To find a second point, we can plug in any value of Q and solve for the corresponding P (or vice versa). For example, if we let Q = 2 and solve for P we get:

$$P = -5(2) + 25$$

$$P = -10 + 25$$

$$P = 15$$

FIGURE B-1

Translating a graph into an algebraic equation

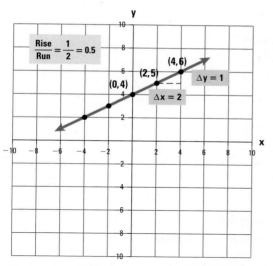

By using information provided on a graph, you can easily construct an equation of the line in the form $y = mx + b$. The slope, m, is calculated by taking the rise of a line over its run. The value of the y-intercept provides the b part of the equation.

FIGURE B-2

Translating an algebraic equation into a graph

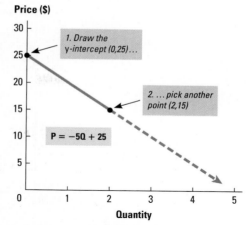

The first step in graphing the equation of a line in the form $y = mx + b$ is to plot the y intercept, given by b. Then pick another point by choosing any value of x or y, and solving the equation for the other variable to get an ordered pair that represents another point on the line. Connecting these two points gives the line.

We can now plot the point (2,15) and connect it to the y-intercept at (0,25).

Rather than plugging in random points, though, it is often useful to know the x-intercept as well as the y-intercept. On a demand curve, this will tell us what quantity is demanded when price is 0. To find this intercept, we can let P = 0 and solve for Q:

$$0 = -5Q + 25$$

$$-25 = -5Q$$

$$5 = Q$$

We can now plot the point (5,0) and connect it to (0,25) to graph the demand curve.

Finding intercepts is useful for interpreting other types of graphs as well. In a production possibilities frontier, the intercepts tell you how much of one good will be produced if all resources are used to produce that good and none are used to produce the other good. In the production possibilities frontier shown in Figure B-3, for example, we can find the y-intercept to see that by devoting all workers to making shirts and none to producing wheat, 2 million T-shirts can be produced. Alternatively, we can find the x-intercept to see that if all workers grow wheat and none make shirts, 4 million bushels of wheat can be produced.

We saw in Chapter 2 that the slope of the frontier represents the trade-off between producing two goods. We can use our intercepts as the two points we need to calculate the slope.

$$\text{Slope} = \frac{\Delta y}{\Delta x} = \frac{(4 \text{ million} - 0)}{(0 - 2 \text{ million})} = \frac{4}{-2} = -2$$

You know from Chapter 2 that the slope of the frontier will be negative because it represents a trade-off: You can't make more wheat without giving up some shirts. Because an increase in wheat means a decrease in shirts, the two variables move in opposite directions and have a negative relationship. This frontier has a constant slope, which

FIGURE B-3

Using intercepts to interpret a production possibilities frontier

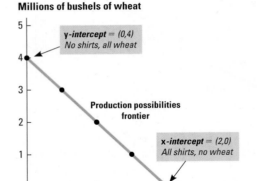

Millions of bushels of wheat

y-intercept = (0,4)
No shirts, all wheat

Production possibilities
frontier

x-intercept = (2,0)
All shirts, no wheat

Millions of shirts

The intercepts of a production possibilities frontier give the maximum amount of a good a country can produce by dedicating all resources in the economy to the production of that good. In this case, with all workers dedicated to the production of one good or the other, the economy can make either 4 million bushels of wheat or 2 million shirts.

means that the trade-off between the two goods—which we can also think of as the opportunity cost of producing shirts in terms of wheat—is also constant.

Equations with x and y reversed

Thus far, we have represented demand and supply equations with P (or y) isolated on the left side of the equation. For example, our demand equation was given as P = −5Q + 25. You may find, however, that in some places, demand and supply equations are given with Q (or x) isolated on the left side of the equation instead.

When you see this, you cannot read the equation as giving you the slope and the y-intercept. Instead, when an equation is in this form, you have the inverse of slope and the x-intercept.

Look at our demand equation again. If we rearrange the equation to solve for Q, we have an equation of the form $x = ny + a$:

$$P = -5Q + 25$$
$$P - 25 = -5Q$$
$$-\frac{1}{5}P + 5 = Q \quad \text{or} \quad Q = -\frac{1}{5}P + 5$$

We know that the starting equation represents the same underlying relationship as the final equation. For instance, we know that our slope is −5, but in the rearranged form where we have solved for Q, the coefficient multiplying P is the inverse of slope, or $-\frac{1}{5}$. We can generalize this observation to say that when we have an equation of the form $x = ny + a$, $n = \frac{1}{m}$ where m is the slope of the line from the same equation expressed in the form $y = mx + b$. We also know that 25 is the y-intercept.

FIGURE B-4

Same line, different equation forms

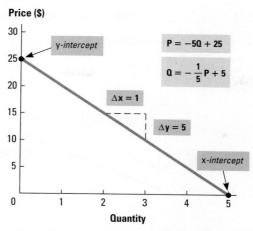

Price ($)

y-intercept

$P = -5Q + 25$

$Q = -\dfrac{1}{5}P + 5$

$\Delta x = 1$

$\Delta y = 5$

x-intercept

Quantity

Regardless of whether you solve an equation for P or Q, the resulting line is the same.

But in our rearranged form, a represents the x-intercept, which is 5. The graph in Figure B-4 shows that these two equations represent different aspects of the same line.

Keep in mind that $P = -5Q + 25$ is the same equation as $Q = -\frac{1}{5}P + 5$; we have simply rearranged it to solve for Q instead of P.

Shifts and Pivots

LO B.2 Use linear equations to explain shifts and pivots.

Imagine that your campus cafeteria has a deli with a salad bar and that the price of a salad depends on the number of ingredients you add to it. This relationship is represented by the following equation:

$$y = 0.5x + 4$$

where

y = total price of the salad

x = number of added ingredients

Because our variables are the price of a salad and the number of ingredients, negative quantities do not make sense: You can't have negative carrots in your salad, and we doubt that the cafeteria is paying you to buy salads. Therefore, we can isolate the graph of this equation to the first quadrant, as shown in panel A of Figure B-5.

Our y-intercept of 4 represents the price of a salad if you add zero ingredients. In other words, a plain bowl of lettuce costs $4. The slope of 0.5 represents the cost of adding ingredients to the salad. Each additional ingredient costs 50 cents. The fact that (2,5) is a point along the line shows that the price of a salad with two added ingredients is $5.

Shifting a line to change the intercept

(A) Restrict the graph to Quadrant I

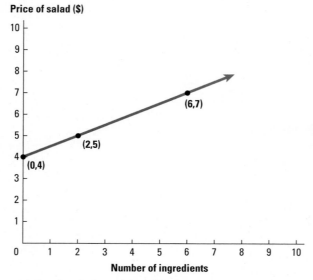

Price of salad ($)

Number of ingredients

In order to easily change the intercept, first restrict the line to values in the first quadrant. This will clearly show the *y*-intercept of the line.

(B) Shift the line upward by moving the intercept

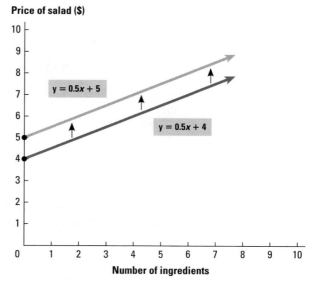

Price of salad ($)

Number of ingredients

Once the *y*-intercept is clear, you can shift the line to the new intercept indicated by the equation of the line.

How much is a salad with six added ingredients?

$$y = 0.5(6) + 4$$
$$y = 3 + 4$$
$$y = 7$$

A salad with six added ingredients is $7, and (6,7) is another point on the graph.

Now, let's see what happens to our graph when the baseline price of a bowl of lettuce without additional ingredients increases to $5. This baseline price is represented by the *y*-intercept, which changes from 4 to 5. The slope of the graph does not change, because each additional ingredient still costs 50 cents.

Thus, our equation changes to $y = 0.5x + 5$. Rather than re-graphing this new question from scratch, we can simply *shift* the original line to account for the change in the *y*-intercept, as shown in panel B of Figure B-5.

Suppose, instead, that the price of lettuce remains at $4, but the price of additional ingredients increases to $1 each. How will this change the graph and equation?

If the price of lettuce with zero additional ingredients remains at $4, the *y*-intercept will also stay the same. However, the slope will change, increasing from 50 cents to $1. Figure B-6 shows that this change of slope will *pivot* the line in our graph.

Our equation changes as well. This time, we substitute 1 in place of 0.5 for the slope. Thus, $y = x + 4$. (Remember that no coefficient on *x* indicates that the slope is 1.)

What happens if the baseline price of lettuce goes up to $5 *and* the price of toppings goes up to $1? We have to both *shift and pivot* the line to represent the change in the intercept and the slope. (Sounds like a fitness routine, doesn't it?) Figure B-7 shows both changes.

FIGURE B-6

Pivoting a line to change the slope

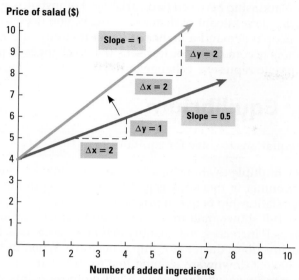

Changes in slope will pivot the equation of a line. Increases in slope will rotate the line upward; decreases in slope will rotate the line downward.

FIGURE B-7

Shift and pivot

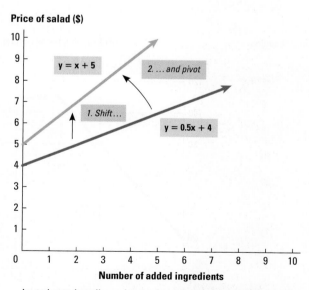

In order to handle a change in slope and intercept, you first shift the line to the new intercept and then pivot the line to reflect the new slope.

You will need to shift and pivot lines in many places throughout this book to represent changes in the relationship between two variables. For instance, we saw in Chapter 3 that when a nonprice determinant of demand changes, you need to *shift* the demand curve to show that people demand a higher or lower quantity of a good at any given price. When consumers become more or less sensitive to changes in price, you need to *pivot* the demand curve to represent a change in slope.

Solving for Equilibrium

LO B.3 Use linear equations to solve for equilibrium.

One graph can show multiple relationships between the same two variables. The most frequent case we encounter in this book is graphs showing both the demand relationship and the supply relationship between price and quantity.

Panel A of Figure B-8 shows data from supply and demand schedules. Remember from Chapter 3 that as P increases, the quantity *demanded* decreases. Since P and Q are moving in opposite directions, the relationship is negative. When these values are plotted in panel B, we have a downward-sloping line for the demand curve. Conversely, as P increases, the quantity *supplied* increases. Plotting these points yields an upward-sloping supply curve.

When we use one graph to show multiple equations of the same variables, we do so in order to show something meaningful about the relationship between them. For instance, when we show supply and demand on the same graph, we usually want to find the equilibrium point—the point at which the quantity supplied and the quantity demanded are equal to one another at the same price.

FIGURE B-8
Supply and demand

(A) Supply and demand schedules

Price ($)	Q_{demand}	Q_{supply}
20	180	0
30	160	10
40	140	20
50	120	30
80	60	60
90	40	70
100	20	80
110	0	90

(B) Graphing the schedules

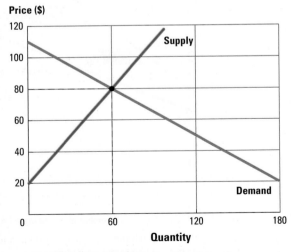

The supply and demand schedules show the quantities demanded and supplied for a given price.

Graphing the values from the schedules gives a downward-sloping demand curve and an upward-sloping supply curve.

We can find the equilibrium point in several ways. If we have schedules showing both demand and supply data, the easiest way to find equilibrium is to locate the price that corresponds to *equal supply and demand quantities*. What is that price in panel A of Figure B-8? At a price of 80, Q is 60 in the demand schedule as well as in the supply schedule.

We can also find the equilibrium point easily by looking at a graph showing both supply and demand. The one-and-only point where the two lines intersect is the equilibrium.

Sometimes, however, it is useful to find equilibrium from equations alone, without having to graph them or to calculate a whole schedule of points by plugging in different prices. Usually you'll want to use this method when you are given equations but no graph or schedule. However, just for practice, let's first derive the supply and demand equations from Figure B-8 and then figure out the equilibrium point.

We want to start by representing supply and demand as equations of the form $y = mx + b$. Let y = price and x = quantity. We need to determine the slope (m) and the y-intercept (b) for each equation.

First, the demand equation: What is the y-intercept? It is the value of y when x is 0. Looking at panel A in Figure B-8, we can see that when Q is zero, P is 110. The y-intercept of the demand equation is 110. Now we need the slope. Because this is a linear relationship and the slope is constant, we can determine the slope using any two points. Let's use the points (180,20) and (160,30).

$$\frac{\Delta y}{\Delta x} = \frac{(P_2 - P_1)}{(Q_2 - Q_1)} = \frac{(20 - 30)}{(180 - 160)} = \frac{-10}{20} = -0.5$$

Thus, our demand equation is: P = −0.5Q + 110.

We'll use the same procedure to derive the supply equation. Looking at the supply schedule, we can see that when Q is zero, P is 20. The y-intercept is 20. To determine slope, let's use the points (0,20) and (10,30).

$$\frac{\Delta y}{\Delta x} = \frac{(P_2 - P_1)}{(Q_2 - Q_1)} = \frac{(20 - 30)}{(0 - 10)} = \frac{-10}{-10} = 1$$

Thus, our supply equation is: P = Q + 20.

Now that we have our equations, we can use them to solve for equilibrium. Equilibrium represents a point that is on both the demand and supply curves; graphically, it is where the two curves intersect. This means that P on the demand curve must equal P on the supply curve, and the same for Q. Therefore, it makes sense that we find this point by setting the two equations equal to each other.

$$P_D = -0.5Q + 110$$

$$P_S = Q + 20$$

$$P_D = P_S,$$

therefore,

$$-0.5Q + 110 = Q + 20$$

This allows us to solve for a numeric value for Q.

$$1.5Q + 20 = 110$$

$$1.5Q = 90$$

$$Q = 60$$

Now that we have a value for Q, we can plug it in either the supply or demand equation to get the value for P. Let's use our supply equation.

$$P = 20 + Q$$

$$P = 20 + 60$$

$$P = 80$$

Solving for equilibrium using the equations gives us the same point we found using the demand and supply schedules: P = 80 and Q = 60 ($80,60).

Problems and Applications

1. Use the demand curve in Figure BP-1 to derive a demand equation. **[LO B.1]**

2. Use the demand schedule in Table BP-1 to derive a demand equation. **[LO B.1]**

3. Use the supply curve in Figure BP-2 to derive a supply equation. **[LO B.1]**

4. Use the supply schedule in Table BP-2 to derive a supply equation. **[LO B.1]**

5. Graph the equation P = 2Q + 3. Is this a supply curve or a demand curve? **[LO B.1]**

6. Graph the equation P = −8Q + 10. Is this a supply curve or a demand curve? **[LO B.1]**

7. Rearrange the equation Q = 5 − 0.25P and sketch the graph. Is this a supply curve or a demand curve? **[LO B.1]**

8. Rearrange the equation Q = 0.2P and sketch the graph. Is this a supply curve or a demand curve? **[LO B.1]**

TABLE BP-1

Price ($)	Quantity
0	320
10	280
20	240
30	200
40	160
50	120
60	80
70	40
80	0

FIGURE BP-2

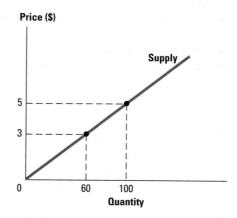

Price ($)

Supply

5

3

0   60   100
            Quantity

9. The entrance fee at your local amusement park is $20 for the day. The entrance fee includes all rides except roller coasters. Roller coasters cost an extra $2 per ride. **[LO B.2]**

FIGURE BP-1

Price ($)

90

45

Demand

0   10   25
            Quantity

TABLE BP-2

Price ($)	Quantity
100	0
200	25
300	50
400	75
500	100
600	125

a. Write an equation that represents how much money you will spend on rides as a function of the number of rides you go on: S = total spending on rides; Q = the quantity of roller coaster rides.

b. What is your total spending on rides if you ride 4 roller coasters?

c. Draw a graph of the relationship between total spending on rides and the number of roller coaster rides.

d. Redraw the graph from part (c) to show what changes if the entrance fee increases to $25.

e. Rewrite the equation from part (a) to incorporate the increased entrance fee of $25.

f. After the entrance fee increases to $25, what is your total spending on rides if you ride 4 roller coasters?

10. Use the following two equations: **[LO B.3]**
   (1) $P = 12 - 2Q$
   (2) $P = 3 + Q$

   a. Find the equilibrium price and quantity.
   b. Graph the demand and supply equations. Illustrate the equilibrium point.

11. With reference to Table BP-3: **[LO B.3]**

   a. Use the information from the table to create the demand and supply equations.
   b. Use your demand and supply equations to solve for equilibrium.
   c. Graph supply and demand curves. Illustrate the equilibrium point.

TABLE BP-3

Price ($)	Quantity demanded	Quantity supplied
0	12	0
20	10	4
40	8	8
60	6	12
80	4	16
100	2	20
120	0	24

Elasticity

LEARNING OBJECTIVES

LO 4.1	Calculate price elasticity of demand using the mid-point method.
LO 4.2	Explain how the determinants of price elasticity of demand affect the degree of elasticity.
LO 4.3	Calculate price elasticity of supply using the mid-point method.
LO 4.4	Explain how the determinants of price elasticity of supply affect the degree of elasticity.
LO 4.5	Calculate cross-price elasticity of demand, and interpret the sign of the elasticity.
LO 4.6	Calculate income elasticity of demand, and interpret the sign of the elasticity.

COFFEE BECOMES CHIC

In the 1990s, a coffeehouse craze rippled through middle-class communities in the United States, as a strong economy bolstered sales of high-priced espresso drinks. Soon, Americans were making daily pilgrimages to a place called Starbucks, where a cup of coffee had been transformed into the "Starbucks experience," complete with soundtrack, mints, and charity-themed water bottles. For 15 years the Starbucks business model was highly successful. From 1992 through 2007, the company expanded by over 15,000 stores.

When the U.S. economy stumbled in 2008, however, Starbucks's growth rate dropped to an all-time low. Competitors and customers began to ask, "How much is too much for a cup of coffee?" Presumably, Starbucks executives had asked themselves that very question over the course of more than a decade. Given the company's phenomenal rate of expansion, they must have had the right answer—at least until the economy started having problems.

How do businesses like Starbucks make pricing decisions? How do they anticipate and react to changing circumstances? We learned in the last chapter that if Starbucks raised the price of its lattes—perhaps due to a coffee supply shortage caused by poor weather in Ethiopia—this would reduce the quantity demanded by consumers. This chapter introduces the idea of elasticity, which describes how much this change in prices will affect consumers.

Like the market for cell phones, the market for gourmet coffee is not perfectly competitive. Managers of a big company like Starbucks have some ability to set prices, and they try to choose prices that will earn the largest profits. They also try to respond to changing market conditions: How much will sales fall if the price of coffee beans drives up the cost of a latte? How much will people decrease their coffee consumption during a recession? How many customers will be lost if competitors like Dunkin' Donuts and McDonald's offer less-expensive coffee? Even in perfectly competitive markets, producers want to predict how their earnings will change in response to economic conditions and changes in the market price.

Nonprofit service providers also often need to think about price elasticity. For instance, a nonprofit hospital wants to set the price of care so as to cover costs without driving away too many patients. Similarly, nonprofit colleges and universities want to cover costs and keep education affordable for students. The ability to address issues like these is critical for any public or private organization. Understanding how to price a Starbucks latte requires the same kind of thinking as figuring out whether to raise entrance fees to national parks to cover the costs of maintaining the wilderness. Solving these challenges relies on a tool called *elasticity,* a measure of how much supply and demand will respond to changes in price and income.

In this chapter, you will learn how to calculate the effect of a price change on the quantity supplied or demanded. You will become familiar with some rules that businesses and policy-makers follow when they cannot measure elasticity exactly. Using what you know about supply and demand, you will be able to categorize different types of goods by noting whether their elasticities are positive or negative. You will also learn how to use a rough approximation of price elasticity to tell whether raising prices will raise or lower an organization's total revenue.

What Is Elasticity?

If Starbucks raises the price of a latte, we can expect the quantity of lattes demanded to fall. But by how much? Although we saw in Chapter 3 that price increases cause the quantity demanded to fall in a competitive market, we have not yet been able to say *how big* that movement will be. That question is the subject of this chapter.

elasticity a measure of how much consumers and producers will respond to a change in market conditions

Elasticity is a measure of how much consumers and producers will respond to a change in market conditions. The concept can be applied to supply or demand, and it can be used to measure responses to a change in the price of a good, a change in the price of a related good, or a change in income.

The concept of elasticity allows economic decision makers to anticipate *how others will respond* to changes in market conditions. Whether you are a business owner trying to sell cars or a public official trying to set sales taxes, you need to know how much a change in prices will affect consumers' willingness to buy.

The most commonly used measures of elasticity are *price elasticity of demand* and *price elasticity of supply.* These two concepts describe how much the quantity demanded and the quantity supplied change when the price of a good changes. The *cross-price elasticity of demand* describes what happens to the quantity demanded of one good when the price of another good changes. Another helpful measure, *income elasticity of demand,* measures how much the quantity demanded reacts to changes in consumers' incomes. Let's begin with price elasticity of demand.

Price Elasticity of Demand

price elasticity of demand the size of the change in the quantity demanded of a good or service when its price changes

Price elasticity of demand describes the size of the change in the quantity demanded of a good or service when its price changes. We showed in Chapter 3 that quantity demanded generally decreases when the price increases, but so far we have not been able to say *how much* it decreases. Price elasticity of demand fills this gap in our understanding of supply and demand.

Another way to think about price elasticity of demand is as a measure of consumers' sensitivity to price changes. When consumers' buying decisions are highly influenced by price, we say that their demand curve is *more elastic,* meaning that a small change in price causes a large change in the quantity demanded. When consumers are not very sensitive to price changes—that is, when they will buy approximately the same quantity, regardless of the price—we say that their demand curve is *less elastic.*

Calculating price elasticity of demand

LO 4.1 Calculate price elasticity of demand using the mid-point method.

Consider the challenge Starbucks faced in shoring up falling sales during the recession. In this situation, a business might lower its prices by offering a sale. But would a sale work? How much could Starbucks's managers expect purchases to increase as a result of the sale? In other words, *How will customers respond* to a sale? The ability to answer this question is a critical tool for businesses. To do so, we need to know the price elasticity of demand for Starbucks coffee.

Let's say that Starbucks usually charges $2 for a cup of coffee. What might happen if it offers a special sale price of $1.50? Suppose that before the sale, Starbucks sold 10 million cups of coffee each day. Now, say that consumers react to the sale by increasing the quantity demanded to 15 million cups per day. Figure 4-1 shows the quantity demanded before and after the sale as two points on the demand curve for coffee. Based on the results of this sale, what can we say about consumers' sensitivity to the price of coffee at Starbucks?

FIGURE 4-1

Elasticity of the demand for coffee

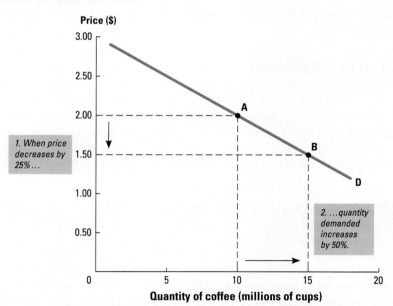

When the price of coffee is $2 a cup, consumers demand 10 million cups. If the price falls to $1.50 per cup, the quantity demanded increases to 15 million cups.

Mathematically, price elasticity is the percentage change in the quantity of a good that is demanded in response to a given percentage change in price. The formula looks like this:

Equation 4-1

$$\text{Price elasticity of demand} = \frac{\%\text{ change in Q demanded}}{\%\text{ change in P}}$$

HINT

A *percentage change* is the difference between the starting and ending levels divided by the starting level, expressed as a percentage. So a percentage change in quantity would be expressed as:

$$\text{Percentage change in quantity} = \left[\frac{(Q_2 - Q_1)}{Q_1}\right] \times 100$$

Similarly, a percentage change in price would be expressed as:

$$\text{Percentage change in price} = \left[\frac{(P_2 - P_1)}{P_1}\right] \times 100$$

If we plug the original and sale quantities and prices into Equation 4-1, what do we find? The price was cut by 25 percent, and the quantity demanded rose by 50 percent. That tells us that the price elasticity of demand is −2.0.

$$\text{Price elasticity of demand} = \frac{(15 \text{ million} - 10 \text{ million})/10 \text{ million}}{(1.50 - 2.00)/2.00} = \frac{50\%}{-25\%} = -2.0$$

Note that the *price elasticity of demand will always be a negative number.* Why? Because price and quantity demanded move in opposite directions. That is, a positive change in price will cause a negative change in the quantity demanded, and vice versa. However, be aware that economists often drop the negative sign and express the price elasticity of demand as a positive number, just for the sake of convenience. Don't be fooled! Under normal circumstances, price elasticity of demand is always negative, whether or not the negative sign is printed.

POTENTIALLY CONFUSING

Some books print the negative sign of elasticity estimates; others do not. Another way to think of an elasticity measure is as an absolute value. The *absolute value* of a number is its distance from zero, or its numerical value without regard to its sign. For example, the absolute values of 4 and −4 are both 4. The absolute value of elasticity measures the "size" of the response, while the sign measures its direction. Sometimes only the absolute value will be printed, when it is assumed that you know the direction of the change.

You might be wondering why we work with percentages in calculating elasticity. Why not just compare the change in the quantity demanded to the change in price? The answer is that percentages allow us to avoid some practical problems. Think about what would happen if one person measured coffee in 12-ounce cups, while another measured it by the pot or the gallon. Without percentages, we would have several different measures of price elasticity, depending on which unit of measurement we used. To avoid this problem, economists use the *percentage change* in quantity rather than the *absolute change* in quantity. That way, the elasticity of demand for coffee is the same whether we measure the quantity in cups, pots, or gallons.

Using the mid-point method

Unfortunately, even when using percentages, we still have a measurement problem: The answer changes depending on which direction we move along the demand curve. We saw that when the price dropped from $2 to $1.50, the elasticity of demand was −2.0:

$$\text{Price elasticity of demand} = \frac{(15 \text{ million} - 10 \text{ million})/10 \text{ million}}{(1.50 - 2.00)/2.00} = \frac{50\%}{-25\%} = -2.0$$

What happens if we calculate the price elasticity from the other direction? Suppose that Starbucks ends the sale and puts the price of coffee back up from $1.50 to $2. This action causes the quantity demanded to fall from 15 million cups back down to 10 million. Note that while dropping from $2 to $1.50 was a 25 percent reduction in price ($0.50/$2.00 = 25 percent), increasing from $1.50 to $2 is a 33 percent increase ($0.50/$1.50 = 33 percent). Similarly, going from a quantity of 15 million to 10 million is a 33 percent decrease, whereas going from 10 million to 15 million is a 50 percent increase. Plugging these figures into our equation, we find that the elasticity of demand now seems to be −1.0:

$$\text{Price elasticity of demand} = \frac{(10 \text{ million} - 15 \text{ million})/15 \text{ million}}{(2.00 - 1.50)/1.50} = -\frac{33\%}{33\%} = -1.0$$

This is a headache. We're moving between the same two points on the demand curve, with the same change in price and quantity ($0.50 and 5 million cups), but in one direction we find an elasticity of demand of −2.0 and in the other direction it's −1.0. We'd like to have a consistent way to estimate the elasticity of demand between two points on the demand curve, regardless of the direction of the movement.

The **mid-point method** solves our problem: It measures the percentage change relative to a point *midway between the two points*. Using the mid-point method, we find the percentage change in quantity by dividing the change in quantity by the average of (that is, the mid-point between) the old and new quantities:

mid-point method method that measures percentage change in demand (or supply) relative to a point midway between two points on a curve; used to estimate elasticity

Equation 4-2

$$\% \text{ change in Q} = \frac{\text{Change in Q}}{\text{Average of Q}}$$

In the denominator of this expression, the mid-point (average) quantity is equal to the sum of the two quantities divided by 2. We can find the mid-point price in the same way:

$$\text{Mid-point of Q} = \frac{(Q_1 + Q_2)}{2}$$

$$\text{Mid-point of P} = \frac{(P_1 + P_2)}{2}$$

In our example, the demand for coffee went from 10 million cups at $2 to 15 million cups at $1.50. So the average (mid-point) quantity was 12.5 million, and the average (mid-point) price was $1.75.

The formula for the price elasticity of demand using the mid-point method is shown in Equation 4-3.

Equation 4-3 Mid-point method

$$\text{Price elasticity of demand} = \frac{(Q_2 - Q_1)/[(Q_1 + Q_2)/2]}{(P_2 - P_1)/([P_1 + P_2)/2]}$$

Using Equation 4-3, we find that the price elasticity of demand is the same whether we move from a lower price to a higher one or vice versa. For a price decrease, the elasticity is:

$$\text{Price elasticity of demand} = \frac{(15 \text{ million} - 10 \text{ million})/12.5 \text{ million}}{(1.50 - 2.00)/1.75} = \frac{40\%}{-29\%} = -1.38$$

For a price increase, the elasticity is:

$$\text{Price elasticity of demand} = \frac{(10 \text{ million} - 15 \text{ million})/12.5 \text{ million}}{(2.00 - 1.50)/1.75} = \frac{-40\%}{29\%} = -1.38$$

Our measure for the price elasticity of demand is now consistent.

Determinants of price elasticity of demand

LO 4.2 Explain how the determinants of price elasticity of demand affect the degree of elasticity.

How would the quantity demanded of lattes (or your drink of choice) change if the price fell from $3 to $1.50? Now, how much would the quantity demanded of cotton socks change if the price fell from $10 per pack to $5? Although both represent a 50 percent price reduction, we suspect that the former might change your buying habits more than the latter. Socks are socks, and $5 savings probably won't make you rush out and buy twice as many.

Would you expect this price change to reduce the quantity demanded of lobsters?

"Great idea, Pete!"

www.CartoonStock.com. Used with permission.

The underlying idea here is that consumers are more sensitive to price changes for some goods and services than for others. Why isn't price elasticity of demand the same for all goods and services? Many factors determine consumers' responsiveness to price changes. The availability of substitutes, relative need and relative cost, and the time needed to adjust to price changes all affect price elasticity of demand.

Availability of substitutes. Recall from Chapter 3 that substitutes are goods that are distinguishable from one another, but have similar uses. When the price of a good with a close substitute increases, consumers will buy the substitute instead. If close substitutes are available for a particular good, then the demand for that good will be *more elastic* than if only distant substitutes are available. For example, the price elasticity of demand for cranberry juice is likely to be relatively elastic; if the price gets too high, many consumers may switch to grape juice.

Degree of necessity. When a good is a basic necessity, people will buy it even if prices rise. The demand for socks probably is not very elastic, nor is the demand for home heating during the winter. Although people may not like it when the prices of these goods rise, they will buy them to maintain a basic level of comfort. And when prices fall, they probably won't buy vastly more socks or make their homes a lot hotter.

In comparison, the demand for luxuries like vacations, expensive cars, and jewelry is likely to be much more elastic. Most people can easily do without these goods when their prices rise. Note, however, that the definition of a necessity depends on your standards and circumstances. In Florida, air conditioning may be a necessity and heating a luxury; the opposite is likely to be true in Alaska.

Cost relative to income. All else held equal, if consumers spend a very small share of their incomes on a good, their demand for the good will be less elastic than otherwise. For instance, most people can get a year's supply of salt for just a few dollars. Even if the price doubled, a year's supply would still cost less than $10, so consumers probably would not bother to adjust their salt consumption.

The opposite is also true: If a good costs a very large proportion of a person's income, like going on a luxury three-week vacation to the beach, the demand for the good will be more elastic. If the price of rooms at high-end beach-front hotels doubles, then a lot of people will decide to do something else with their vacations.

Adjustment time. Goods often have much more elastic demand over the long run than over the short run. Often, adjusting to price changes takes some time. Consider how you might react to an increase in the price of gasoline. In the short run, you might cancel a weekend road trip, but you would still have to do the same amount of driving as usual to school, work, or the grocery store. Over a year, however, you could consider other choices that would further reduce your consumption of gas, such as buying a bus pass or a bicycle, getting a more fuel-efficient car, or moving closer to work or school.

Scope of the market. A major caveat to the determinants just described is that each depends on how you define the market for a good or service. The price elasticity of demand for bananas might be high, but the price elasticity of demand for *fruit* could still be low, because there are more substitutes for bananas than for the broader category of fruit. Similarly, although water might have a very low price elasticity of demand as a basic necessity, the demand for *bottled* water could be extremely elastic.

Using price elasticity of demand

When we make decisions in the real world, we often don't know the exact price elasticity of demand. But we don't always need to estimate elasticity precisely to know that consumers will react differently to price changes for lattes than for socks. Instead, businesses and other decision makers often know something general about the shape of the demand curve they are facing. Being able to place goods into several broad categories of elasticity can facilitate real pricing decisions in situations without full information.

At the extremes, demand can be perfectly elastic or perfectly inelastic. When demand is **perfectly elastic**, the demand curve is horizontal, as shown in panel A of Figure 4-2. This graph indicates that consumers are very sensitive to price, because demand drops to zero when the price increases even a minuscule amount. When demand is **perfectly inelastic**, the demand curve is vertical, as shown in panel B of Figure 4-2. In this case, the quantity demanded is the same no matter what the price. These two extremes rarely occur in real life.

Between these two extremes, elasticity is commonly divided into three quantifiable categories: elastic, inelastic, and unit-elastic. When the absolute value of the price elasticity of demand is greater than 1, we call the associated demand **elastic**. With elastic demand, a given percentage change in the price of a good will cause an even larger percentage change in the quantity demanded. For example, a 40 percent change in price might lead to a 60 percent change in the quantity demanded. Panel A of Figure 4-3 illustrates elastic demand.

When the absolute value of the price elasticity of demand is less than 1, we say that demand is **inelastic**. With inelastic demand, a given percentage change in price will cause a smaller percentage change in the quantity demanded. For example, a 40 percent change in price might lead to a 20 percent change in the quantity demanded. Panel B of Figure 4-3 illustrates inelastic demand.

perfectly elastic demand demand for which the demand curve is horizontal, in a way such that demand could be any quantity at the given price, but drops to zero if the price increases

perfectly inelastic demand demand for which the demand curve is vertical, in a way such that that the quantity demanded is always the same no matter what the price

elastic demand that has an absolute value of elasticity greater than 1

inelastic demand that has an absolute value of elasticity less than 1

FIGURE 4-2

Perfectly elastic and perfectly inelastic demand

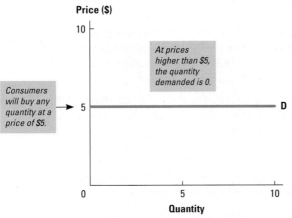

(A) Perfectly elastic demand (Elasticity = infinite)

Price ($)

Consumers will buy any quantity at a price of $5.

At prices higher than $5, the quantity demanded is 0.

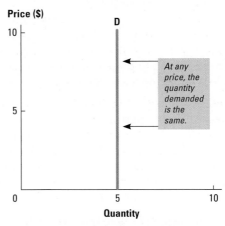

(B) Perfectly inelastic demand (Elasticity = 0)

Price ($)

At any price, the quantity demanded is the same.

When demand is perfectly elastic, the demand curve is horizontal. At prices above $5, consumers will not buy any quantity of the good.

When demand is perfectly inelastic, the demand curve is vertical. Consumers will always demand the same quantity of a good, regardless of the price.

FIGURE 4-3

Elastic, inelastic, and unit-elastic demand

1. After price decreases by 40% under...

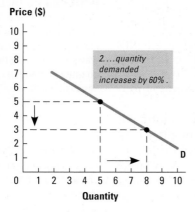

(A) Elastic demand

Price ($)

2. ...quantity demanded increases by 60% .

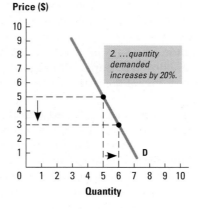

(B) Inelastic demand

Price ($)

2. ...quantity demanded increases by 20%.

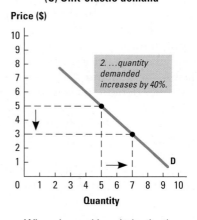

(C) Unit-elastic demand

Price ($)

2. ...quantity demanded increases by 40%.

With an elastic demand curve, a small change in price leads to a big change in the quantity demanded. As a result, the price elasticity of demand is greater than 1.

With an inelastic demand curve, even a large price change has a small effect on the quantity demanded. As a result, the price elasticity of demand is less than 1.

When demand is unitelastic, the percentage change in price equals the percentage change in quantity, so that the price elasticity of demand is exactly 1.

If the absolute value of elasticity is exactly 1—that is, if a percentage change in price causes the same percentage change in the quantity demanded—then we say that demand is **unit-elastic**. In this case, a 40 percent change in price leads to a 40 percent change in the quantity demanded. Panel C of Figure 4-3 illustrates unit-elastic demand.

unit-elastic demand that has an absolute value of elasticity exactly equal to 1

As we'll see later in this chapter, these terms—elastic, inelastic, and unit-elastic—can be used to describe any sort of elasticity, not just the price elasticity of demand. Although these categories may sound academic, they can have serious implications for real-world business and policy decisions. The Real Life box "Does charging for bednets decrease malaria?" describes a case in which knowing whether the price elasticity of demand is elastic or inelastic is a matter of life and death.

To improve your understanding of elastic, inelastic, and unit-elastic demand, try the online interactive graphing tutorial.

REAL LIFE

Does charging for bednets decrease malaria?

Around the world, malaria kills millions of young people every year. There is no vaccine to protect children from malaria. There is a way to escape the disease, though: sleep under a bednet that has been treated with insecticide. Bednets prevent malaria by shielding people from disease-carrying mosquitoes.

Organizations that want to promote the use of bednets to fight malaria face a practical question: Would charging a fee for bednets be more effective in reducing the illness than handing out the nets for free?

Those who advocate charging a fee argue that people who pay for the nets will value them more, and will probably use them more, than those who receive the nets for free. These advocates expect that fewer nets will be wasted on people who don't really want them and that people who do buy them will be more likely to use them. Moreover, if people pay for their bednets, provider organizations will be able to afford to distribute more of them. On the other hand, the law of demand states that the higher the price, the lower the quantity demanded is likely to be. Even if charging a fee would make some people more likely to use the nets, it might dissuade others from getting them, thus undermining the aim of the anti-malaria campaign.

To settle this question, health organizations needed to know the price elasticity of the demand for bednets. Working in Kenya, economists Jessica Cohen of the Harvard School of Public Health and Pascaline Dupas of Stanford set up an experiment to try both methods and to measure the price elasticity of demand for bednets. As it turned out, charging a fee greatly reduced the quantity of the nets demanded. In the experiment, the number of people who took bednets dropped by 75 percent when the price increased from zero to $0.75. Nor did people who bought bednets at that price use them more effectively than those who received them for free.

If profit were the goal in this campaign, a few bednets sold at $0.75 would generate more revenue than a lot of bednets given away for free. But the goal was to protect people from malaria, not to make a profit. For organizations with a social mission, free distribution of bednets seems more effective than charging a fee.

Source: J. Cohen and P. Dupas, "Free distribution or cost sharing? Evidence from a randomized malaria prevention experiment," *Quarterly Journal of Economics* 125, no. 1 (February 2010): 1–45.

Knowing whether the demand for a good is elastic or inelastic is extremely useful in business, because it allows a manager to determine whether a price increase will cause total revenue to rise or fall. **Total revenue** is the amount that a firm receives from the sale of goods and services, calculated as the quantity sold multiplied by the price paid for each unit. This number is important for an obvious reason: It tells us how much money sellers receive when they sell something.

total revenue the amount that a firm receives from the sale of goods and services, calculated as the quantity sold multiplied by the price paid for each unit

An increase in price affects total revenue in two ways:

To improve your understanding of the quantity and price effects of a price change, try the online interactive graphing tutorial.

- It causes a *quantity effect*, or a decrease in revenue that results from selling fewer units of the good.
- It causes a *price effect*, or an increase in revenue that results from receiving a higher price for each unit sold.

Figure 4-4 shows both the quantity effect and the price effect. When the quantity effect outweighs the price effect, a price increase will cause a drop in revenue, as it does in Figure 4-4. When the price effect outweighs the quantity effect, a price increase will raise total revenue.

When demand is elastic, a price increase causes total revenue to fall. We already know that when demand is elastic, a change in price will cause a larger percentage change in quantity demanded. Another way of saying this is that the quantity effect outweighs the price effect. So when demand is elastic, a price increase causes a proportionally larger decrease in the quantity demanded, and total revenue falls.

Conversely, when demand is inelastic, the percentage change in price is larger than the percentage change in quantity demanded. The price effect outweighs the quantity effect, and total revenue increases. With inelastic demand, then, consumers will purchase less of a good when prices rise, but the change in the quantity demanded will be proportionally less than the change in price. Figure 4-5 shows this trade-off between the price and quantity effects. As you can see, panel A shows an elastic demand in which a $1 change in price causes the quantity demanded to increase by 4,000. With the inelastic demand curve in panel B, a $2 decrease in price increases quantity demanded by only 1,000.

FIGURE 4-4

Effect of a price increase on total revenue

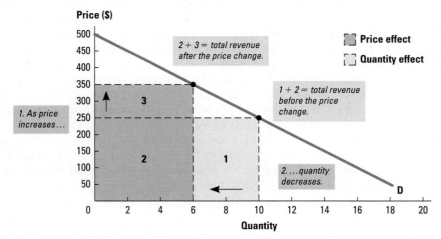

The colored rectangles represent total revenue at two different prices. As the price increases from $250 to $350, total revenue is affected in two ways. The blue rectangle represents the increase in revenue received for each unit sold (the price effect). The yellow rectangle represents the decrease in total revenue as the number of units sold drops (the quantity effect). The elasticity of demand determines which effect is larger. In this case, the yellow area is larger than the blue area, meaning that the quantity effect outweighs the price effect, and total revenue decreases.

FIGURE 4-5

Elasticity and changes in total revenue

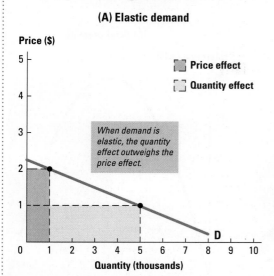

(A) Elastic demand

In this market, demand is elastic. At a price of $1, 5,000 units are sold for a total revenue of $5,000. If the price increases to $2, only 1,000 units are sold for a total revenue of only $2,000. The quantity effect outweighs the price effect.

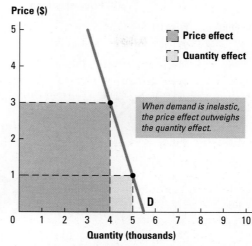

(B) Inelastic demand

In this market, demand is inelastic. At a price of $1, 5,000 units are sold for a total revenue of $5,000. If the price increases to $3, the number of units sold drops by only 1,000, to 4,000 units. Because the price effect outweighs the quantity effect, total revenue climbs to $12,000, an increase of $7,000.

There is one final point to make. So far, everything we've said has described elasticity *at a particular spot on the demand curve.* For most goods, however, elasticity varies along the curve. So when we said that the price elasticity of demand for coffee was 1.38, we meant that it was 1.38 for a price change from $1.50 to $2 a cup. If the price changes from $2 to $2.50, the elasticity will be different.

The reasoning behind this fact is common sense. Imagine that the price of lattes plummets to 10 cents, and you get into the habit of buying one every morning. What would you do if you showed up one morning and found that the price had doubled overnight, to 20 cents? We bet you'd shrug and buy one anyway.

Now, imagine the price of lattes is $10, and you buy them only as occasional treats. If you arrive at the coffee shop and find the price has doubled to $20, what will you do? You'd probably consider very carefully whether you really need that latte. In both cases, you would be responding to a 100 percent increase in price for the same product, but you would react very differently. This makes perfect sense: In one case, the latte costs you only 10 more cents, but in the other, it costs an additional $10.

Your reactions to the latte illustrate a general rule: Demand tends to be more elastic when price is high and more inelastic when price is low. This brings us to an important caveat about the three graphs shown in Figure 4-3. Although the example of an elastic demand curve in panel A has a steeper *slope* than the inelastic demand curve in panel B, we now know that slope is not the same as elasticity.

In fact, the elasticity of demand is different at different points along a linear demand curve. The reasoning is nonintuitive, but straightforward when you think about it graphically. Look at Figure 4-6. The line in panel B has a constant slope, but the percentage changes in price and quantity are very different at either end of the curve. For instance, going from $45 to $40 is a much smaller difference (in percentage terms) than from $10 to $5, but the slope of the curve is the same between both sets of points.

87

FIGURE 4-6

Changes in elasticity along the demand curve

(A) Demand and revenue schedule

Price ($)	Quantity	Total revenue ($)
50	0	0
45	1	45
40	2	80
35	3	105
30	4	120
25	5	125
20	6	120
15	7	105
10	8	80
5	9	45
0	10	0

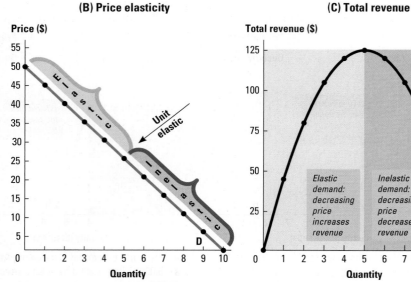

(B) Price elasticity

(C) Total revenue

This table lists the data shown in the graphs in panels A and B. Quantity demanded always increases as price falls. Total revenue rises until the price falls to $25, then falls at lower prices.

Price elasticity of demand varies along the demand curve. Above a certain price, demand is elastic; below it, demand is inelastic.

This graph shows total revenue along the demand curve shown above. Total revenue first rises, but then begins to fall as demand moves from elastic to inelastic.

For a refresher on slope versus elasticity, see Appendix C, "Math Essentials: Calculating Percentage Change, Slope, and Elasticity," which follows this chapter.

The result is that as we move along a linear demand curve, revenue first increases and then decreases with higher prices. Panel C graphs out the total revenue curve associated with the demand curve in panel B, using calculations from the schedule in Panel A. Note that when the price is high, lowering the price will increase revenue. For example, when the price decreases from $45 to $40 (see the schedule), total revenue almost doubles, from $45 to $80. When the price is low, however, lowering it further decreases total revenue. Moving from $10 to $5, for example, decreases total revenue from $80 to $45.

Price elasticity of demand has all sorts of real-world applications. See, for example, the issue discussed in the What Do You Think? box "Should entrance fees at national parks be raised?"

WHAT DO YOU THINK?

Should entrance fees at national parks be raised?

The National Park Service is the steward of 84 million acres of America's most famous natural spaces, including Yellowstone, the Grand Canyon, and the Everglades. In 2008, the Park Service proposed higher fees at some parks. Writer John Krist argued in favor of the price increases:

> A day at Disneyland costs a family of four at least $232, not counting Mickey Mouse ears. At Six Flags Magic Mountain, the admission price would be at least $180. A seven-day pass to enter Yellowstone National Park costs $25 per car, which means that the same family spending a week among bison, elk, geysers and grizzlies would pay the equivalent of 89 cents per person, per day.

88

Which is why it's perplexing to see such an outcry over news that the Park Service wants to raise entrance fees at 135 sites over the next two years. . . . Their principal arguments are economic: Tourism-dependent communities fret that higher fees will reduce visitation and cut into profits, while others argue that the increases will keep out those of limited financial means. It's true, in theory at least, that raising the price of something should decrease demand for it.* . . .

On the other hand, it's absurd to expect a finite amount of parkland to accommodate a continually increasing number of people. Anyone who has driven into Yosemite Valley on a holiday weekend is unlikely to regard a drop in park visitation as entirely a bad thing.

Slightly higher user fees are unlikely to have much effect on park use, but they could have a significant effect on the quality of the park experience. Most of that money will stay at individual parks, where it can be spent on upkeep and repairs—the sort of unglamorous expenditures that typically get short-changed in the politically driven federal budget process. Smaller crowds and plumbing that works—what's not to like?

* You can tell that the author of this piece hadn't read Chapter 3 of this book. If he had, he would have been careful to say that raising the price decreases the quantity demanded, rather than that it decreases demand.

What do you think?

1. Do you agree with Krist's argument that the demand for national park visits is inelastic at current price levels, so that higher fees are "unlikely to have much effect on park use"? Think about the factors that affect price elasticity, such as the availability and price of substitutes.
2. How would you weigh the following trade-offs?
   a. Should the Park Service intentionally try to shrink the demand for visits in order to reduce crowding? In order to protect parks from environmental damage?
   b. Does the Park Service have a responsibility to keep national parks accessible to families who cannot afford to pay higher fees?
   c. Should the Park Service be concerned about the economic impact of a reduced demand for visits on surrounding communities?

Source: "So what if park fees go up?" John Krist, *High Country News*, July 16, 2008. Used with permission.

✔ CONCEPT CHECK

- ❏ What is the formula for calculating the price elasticity of demand? **[LO 4.1]**
- ❏ Why should you use the mid-point method to calculate the price elasticity of demand? **[LO 4.1]**
- ❏ If demand is inelastic, will an increase in price increase or decrease revenue? **[LO 4.2]**

Price Elasticity of Supply

What happens when an increase in coffee consumption drives up the price of coffee beans? *How will the coffee market respond* to the price change? We can predict based on the law of supply that coffee growers will respond to an increase in price by increasing their production—but by how much?

Price elasticity of supply is the size of the change in the quantity supplied of a good or service when its price changes. Price elasticity of supply measures producers' responsiveness to a change in price, just as price elasticity of demand measures consumers' responsiveness to a change in price.

price elasticity of supply the size of the change in the quantity supplied of a good or service when its price changes

89

Chapter 3 showed that when prices rise, producers supply larger quantities of a good; when prices fall, they supply smaller quantities. Just as the price elasticity of demand for a good tells us how much the quantity demanded changes as we move along the demand curve, the price elasticity of supply tells us how much the quantity supplied changes as we move along the supply curve.

Calculating price elasticity of supply

LO 4.3 Calculate price elasticity of supply, using the mid-point method.

Price elasticity of supply is measured in the same way as price elasticity of demand: as the percentage change in quantity divided by the percentage change in price (see Equation 4-4).

Equation 4-4

$$\text{Price elasticity of supply} = \frac{\% \text{ change in quantity supplied}}{\% \text{ change in price}}$$

To ensure that elasticity will be the same whether you move up or down the supply curve, you should use the mid-point method, as in Equation 4-5.

Equation 4-5 Mid-point method

$$\text{Price elasticity of supply} = \frac{(Q_2 - Q_1)/[(Q_1 + Q_2)/2]}{(P_2 - P_1)/[(P_1 + P_2)/2]}$$

Suppose that when the price of coffee beans goes from $1 to $1.20 per pound, production increases from 90 million pounds of coffee beans per year to 100 million pounds. Using the mid-point method, the percentage change in quantity supplied would be:

$$\% \text{ change in quantity supplied} = \frac{(100 \text{ million} - 90 \text{ million})}{95 \text{ million}} = 11\%$$

The percentage change in price would be:

$$\% \text{ change in price} = \frac{(1.2 - 1)}{1.1} = 18\%$$

So the price elasticity of supply at this point on the supply curve is:

$$\text{Price elasticity of supply} = \frac{11\%}{18\%} = 0.6$$

An elasticity of 0.6 tells us that the supply of coffee beans is relatively inelastic, at least in the short run. Does this result make sense? As it turns out, coffee takes a long time to grow. Coffee plants don't produce a full yield for four to six years after they are planted. Because coffee growers can't increase production quickly, it makes sense that the supply of coffee would be inelastic. (Remember that if prices had fallen from $1.20 to $1, instead of rising from $1 to $1.20, the elasticity would be the same using the mid-point method.)

HINT

- The elasticity of demand is calculated by dividing a positive number by a negative number, or by dividing a negative number by a positive number, so the answer is always negative.
- The elasticity of supply, on the other hand, is calculated by dividing either a positive number by another positive number, or a negative number by another negative number. In either case, the answer is always positive.

Remembering this rule can help you to check your arithmetic.

There is one important difference between the elasticities of supply and demand: The price elasticity of demand is always negative, and the price elasticity of supply is always positive. The reason is simple: The quantity demanded always moves in the *opposite direction* from the price, but the quantity supplied moves in the *same direction* as the price.

As with the price elasticity of demand, we can describe the price elasticity of supply using three categories:

- *Elastic*, if it has an absolute value greater than 1.
- *Inelastic*, if it has an absolute value less than 1.
- *Unit-elastic*, if it has an absolute value of exactly 1.

In extreme cases, we can also describe supply as being *perfectly elastic* (if the quantity supplied could be anything at a given price, and is zero at any other price), or *perfectly inelastic* (if the quantity supplied is the same, regardless of the price).

To improve your understanding of price elasticity, try the online interactive graphing tutorial.

Determinants of price elasticity of supply

LO 4.4 Explain how the determinants of price elasticity of supply affect the degree of elasticity.

Whether supply is elastic or inelastic depends on the supplier's ability to change the quantity produced in response to price changes. Three factors affect a supplier's ability to expand production: the availability of inputs, the flexibility of the production process, and the time needed to adjust to changes in price. Recall that this last factor—time—is also a determinant of the elasticity of demand. Just as consumers take time to change their habits, suppliers need time to ramp up production.

Availability of inputs. The production of some goods can be expanded easily, just by adding extra inputs. For example, a bakery can easily buy extra flour and yeast to produce more bread, probably at the same cost per loaf. Increasing the supply of other goods is more difficult, however, and sometimes is impossible. If the price of Picasso paintings goes up, there isn't much anyone can do to produce more of them, since we cannot bring the artist back to life.

In other words, the elasticity of supply depends on the elasticity of the supply of inputs. If producing more of a good will cost a lot more than the initial quantity did, because the extra inputs will be harder to find, then the producer will be reluctant to increase the quantity supplied. Higher and higher prices will be needed to convince the producer to go to the extra trouble.

Flexibility of the production process. The easiest way for producers to adjust the quantity supplied of a particular good is to draw production capacity away from other goods when prices rise, or to reassign capacity to other goods when prices fall. Farmers may find this sort of substitution relatively simple: When corn prices are high they will plant more acres with corn; when corn prices are low they will reassign acres to more profitable crops. Other producers have much less flexibility. If you own a company that manufactures specialized parts for Toyota, you might need to buy new machinery to begin making parts for Ford, let alone switch to another type of product entirely.

Adjustment time. As with demand, supply is more elastic over long periods than over short periods. That is, producers can make more adjustments in the long run than in the short run. In the short run, the number of hotel rooms at Disneyland is fixed; in the medium and long run, old rooms can be renovated and new hotels can be built. Production capacity can also increase or decrease over time as new firms start up or old ones shut down.

❏ How would you calculate the price elasticity of supply? **[LO 4.3]**
❏ What are the three determinants of the price elasticity of supply? **[LO 4.4]**

Other Elasticities

The quantity of a good that is demanded is sensitive to more than just the price of the good. Because people are clever, flexible, and always on the lookout for ways to make the most of opportunities, the quantity demanded also responds to changing circumstances, such as the prices of other goods and the incomes consumers earn. Let's consider two other demand elasticities, the *cross-price elasticity of demand* and the *income elasticity of demand*.

Cross-price elasticity of demand

LO 4.5 Calculate cross-price elasticity of demand, and interpret the sign of the elasticity.

We have noted that the substitutability of goods affects price elasticity. That is, consumers' willingness to start or stop buying a good depends on the availability of other goods that serve the same purpose. For example, we might expect a Starbucks latte to have relatively price-elastic demand, because some people will buy regular coffee from Dunkin' Donuts when the price of a Starbucks latte rises. Once again, recalling the four economists' questions we presented in Chapter 1, asking *"How will others respond?"* is the key to understanding the situation.

cross-price elasticity of demand a measure of how the quantity demanded of one good changes when the price of a different good changes

What happens if the price of Dunkin' Donuts coffee falls but the price of a Starbucks latte stays the same? **Cross-price elasticity of demand** describes how the quantity demanded of one good changes when the price of a *different* good changes. Because lattes and regular coffee are substitutes, we expect the quantity of lattes demanded to go down when the price of regular coffee falls, as some people switch from lattes to coffee. The reverse also holds: If the price of a cup of Dunkin' Donuts coffee rises, while the price of a Starbucks latte doesn't, we expect the quantity of lattes demanded to rise as some people switch from coffee to the relatively cheaper latte. Equation 4-6 gives the formula for the cross-price elasticity of demand.

Equation 4-6

$$\text{Cross-price elasticity of demand between A and B} = \frac{\%\text{ change in quantity of A demanded}}{\%\text{ change in price of B}}$$

When two goods are substitutes, we expect their cross-price elasticity of demand to be positive. That is, an increase in the price of one will cause an increase in the quantity demanded of the other. On the other hand, a decrease in the price of one good will cause a decrease in the quantity demanded of the other. Just how elastic it is depends on how close the two substitutes are. If they are very close substitutes, a change in the price of one will cause a large change in the quantity demanded of the other, so that cross-price elasticity will be high. If they are not close substitutes, cross-price elasticity will be low.

Cross-price elasticity can also be negative. Unlike the price elasticity of demand, which can be expressed as an absolute value because it is always negative, the sign of a cross-price elasticity tells us about the relationship between two goods. We have seen that when two goods are substitutes, their cross-price elasticity will be positive.

However, when two goods are complements (that is, when they are consumed together), cross-price elasticity will be negative.

For example, when people drink more coffee, they want more cream to go with it. Coffee and cream are complements, not substitutes. So when the demand for coffee increases, the demand for cream will increase, all else held equal. When two goods are linked in this way, their cross-price elasticity will be negative, because an increase in the price of one good will decrease the quantity demanded of both goods. Again, the relative size of the elasticity tells us how strongly the two goods are linked. If the two goods are strong complements, their cross-price elasticity will be a large negative number. If the two goods are loosely linked, their cross-price elasticity will be negative but not far below zero.

Income elasticity of demand

LO 4.6 Calculate income elasticity of demand, and interpret the sign of the elasticity.

There are some goods that people buy in roughly the same amounts, no matter how wealthy they are. Salt, toothpaste, and toilet paper are three examples. These are not the sort of products people rush out to buy when they get a raise at work. Other goods, though, are very sensitive to changes in income. If you got a raise, you might splurge on new clothes or a meal at a fancy restaurant.

The **income elasticity of demand** for a good describes how much the quantity demanded changes in response to a change in consumers' incomes. As Equation 4-7 shows, it is expressed as the ratio of the percentage change in the quantity demanded to the percentage change in income:

income elasticity of demand a measure of how much the quantity demanded changes in response to a change in consumers' incomes

Equation 4-7

$$\text{Income elasticity of demand} = \frac{\%\ \text{change in quantity demanded}}{\%\ \text{change in income}}$$

Recall from Chapter 3 that increases in income raise the demand for normal goods and lower the demand for inferior goods. Income elasticity tells us how much the demand for these goods changes.

For example, a Starbucks Frappuccino® is a normal good that might be fairly responsive to changes in income. When people become wealthier, they will buy more of a small luxury item like this. Therefore, we would guess that the income elasticity of demand for fancy iced coffee drinks is positive (because the drink is a normal good) and relatively large (because the drink is a nonnecessity that has many cheaper substitutes).

Regular coffee is also generally a normal good, so its income elasticity should be positive. However, we might guess that it will be less elastic than a Frappuccino's. Many people consider their standard cup of coffee every day before work to be more of a necessity than a luxury and will buy it regardless of their incomes. Another way to put it is that the demand for Frappuccinos is income-elastic, while the demand for plain coffee is relatively income-inelastic. For normal goods like these, income elasticity is positive, because the quantity that is demanded increases as incomes rise. Both necessities and luxuries are normal goods. If the good is a necessity, income elasticity of demand will be positive but less than 1. If the good is a luxury, income elasticity will be positive but more than 1.

As with the cross-price elasticity of demand, the income elasticity of demand can be negative as well as positive. The income elasticity of demand is negative for inferior goods because quantity demanded decreases as incomes increase.

In 2009 Starbucks introduced a new retail product, VIA® instant coffee. Although some coffee enthusiasts sneered, others thought it was a shrewd move at a time of

TABLE 4-1 Four measures of elasticity

Measure	Equation	Negative	Positive	More elastic	Less elastic
Price Elasticity of Demand	$\dfrac{\text{\% change in quantity demanded}}{\text{\% change in price}}$	Always	Never	Over time, for substitutable goods and luxury items	In the short run, for unique and necessary items
Price Elasticity of Supply	$\dfrac{\text{\% change in quantity supplied}}{\text{\% change in price}}$	Never	Always	Over time, with flexible production	In the short run, with production constraints
Cross-Price Elasticity	$\dfrac{\text{\% change in quantity demanded of A}}{\text{\% change in price of B}}$	For complements	For substitutes	For near-perfect substitutes and strong complements	For loosely related goods
Income Elasticity	$\dfrac{\text{\% change in quantity demanded}}{\text{\% change in income}}$	For inferior goods	For normal goods	For luxury items with close substitutes	For unique and necessary items

economic hardship. Instant coffee mix may be an inferior good in some places: As incomes increase, people will drink more expensive beverages and *decrease* their consumption of instant coffee. During a recession, however, budgets tighten, and people may increase their consumption of instant coffee as they cut back on more expensive drinks. At least, that is what Starbucks was hoping. In this scenario, the income elasticity of instant coffee would be small and negative. A less-appealing inferior good that people quickly abandon as they grow richer would have a large, negative income elasticity.

Once again, the sign and size of a good's elasticity tell us a lot about the good. Table 4-1 summarizes what we have learned about the four types of elasticity.

If you find this discussion particularly interesting, you might want to consider work as a pricing analyst. You can read more about this in the Where Can It Take You? box "Pricing analyst."

WHERE CAN IT TAKE YOU?
Pricing analyst

In most industries, keeping an eye on competitors' prices and responding accordingly is a major task. Large businesses hire *pricing analysts* to perform this critical function. Pricing analysts use their knowledge of elasticity and markets to help businesses determine the right price to charge for their products.

To learn more, continue reading by scanning the QR code near the end of the chapter or by going online.

✔CONCEPT CHECK

❏ Why is the cross-price elasticity of demand positive for substitutes? **[LO 4.5]**

❏ Why does the income-elasticity of demand depend on whether a good is normal or inferior? **[LO 4.6]**

Conclusion

Supply and *demand* may be the most common words in economics, but applying these concepts to the real world requires a bit of elaboration. Elasticity is the first of several concepts we will study that will help you to apply the concepts of supply and demand to business and policy questions. In this chapter we saw how elasticity can be used to set prices so as to maximize revenue. In the coming chapters we will use elasticity to predict the effects of government intervention in the market, and we will dig deeper into the consumer and producer choices that drive elasticity.

 ◄ Mobile Window on the World—Scan this code with your smartphone to find more applications of the chapter content. (Need a barcode reader? Try ScanLife, available in your app store.)

Visit your mobile app store and download ► the Karlan and Morduch Study Econ app.

Key Terms

elasticity, p. 78

price elasticity of demand, p. 78

mid-point method, p. 81

perfectly elastic demand, p. 83

perfectly inelastic demand, p. 83

elastic, p. 83

inelastic, p. 83

unit-elastic, p. 85

total revenue, p. 85

price elasticity of supply, p. 89

cross-price elasticity of demand, p. 92

income elasticity of demand, p. 93

Summary

LO 4.1 Calculate price elasticity of demand using the mid-point method.

Elasticity is a measure of consumers' and producers' responsiveness to a change in market conditions. Understanding the elasticity for a good or service allows economic decision makers to anticipate the outcome of changes in market conditions and to calibrate prices so as to maximize revenues.

Price elasticity of demand is the size of the change in the quantity demanded of a good or service when its price changes. Elasticity should be calculated as a percentage using the mid-point method to avoid problems with conflicting units of measurement and with the direction of a change. Price elasticity of demand is almost always negative, because the quantity demanded falls as the price rises. It is usually represented as an absolute value, without the negative sign.

LO 4.2 Explain how the determinants of price elasticity of demand affect the degree of elasticity.

In general, demand is inelastic for goods that have no close substitutes, are basic necessities, or cost a relatively small proportion of consumers' income.

Demand is also inelastic over short periods and for broadly defined markets. When demand is elastic, a percentage change in the price of a good will cause a larger percentage change in the quantity demanded; the absolute value of the elasticity will be greater than 1. When demand is inelastic, a percentage change in price will cause a smaller percentage change in the quantity demanded; the absolute value of the elasticity will be less than 1. When demand is unit-elastic, the percentage changes in price and quantity will be equal, and the elasticity will be exactly 1.

LO 4.3 Calculate price elasticity of supply using the mid-point method.

Price elasticity of supply is the size of the change in the quantity supplied of a good or service when its price changes. Price elasticity of supply is almost always positive, because the quantity supplied increases as the price increases.

LO 4.4 Explain how the determinants of price elasticity of supply affect the degree of elasticity.

Supply is generally inelastic when additional inputs to the production process are difficult to get and the production process is inflexible. Supply is also inelastic over short periods. Supply is considered elastic when the absolute value of its price elasticity is greater than 1; inelastic when the absolute value is less than 1; and unit-elastic when it is exactly 1.

LO 4.5 Calculate cross-price elasticity of demand, and interpret the sign of the elasticity.

Cross-price elasticity of demand is the percentage change in the quantity demanded in response to a given percentage change in the price of a *different* good. The cross-price elasticity of demand between two goods will be positive if they are substitutes and negative if they are complements.

LO 4.6 Calculate income elasticity of demand, and interpret the sign of the elasticity.

Income elasticity of demand is the percentage change in the quantity of a good demanded in response to a given percentage change in income. Income elasticity of demand will be positive for normal goods and negative for inferior goods.

Review Questions

1. You are advising a coffee shop manager who wants to estimate how much sales will change if the price of a latte rises. Explain why he should measure elasticity in percentage terms rather than in terms of dollars and cups. **[LO 4.1]**

2. Explain why the coffee shop manager should measure elasticity using the mid-point method in his calculations. **[LO 4.1]**

3. You are working as a private math tutor to raise money for a trip during spring break. First explain why the price elasticity of demand for math tutoring might be elastic. Then explain why the price elasticity of demand for math tutoring might be inelastic. **[LO 4.2]**

4. You are working as a private math tutor to raise money for a trip during spring break. You want to raise as much money as possible. Should you should increase or decrease the price you charge? Explain. **[LO 4.2]**

5. You have been hired by the government of Kenya, which produces a lot of coffee, to examine the supply of gourmet coffee beans. Suppose you discover that the price elasticity of supply is 0.85. Explain this figure to the Kenyan government. **[LO 4.3]**

6. You have noticed that the price of tickets to your university's basketball games keeps increasing but the supply of tickets remains the same. Why might supply be unresponsive to changes in price? **[LO 4.3]**

7. Which will have a more price-elastic supply over six months: real estate in downtown Manhattan or real estate in rural Oklahoma? Explain your reasoning. **[LO 4.4]**

8. Certain skilled labor, such as hair cutting, requires licensing or certification, which is costly and takes a long time to acquire. Explain what would happen to the price elasticity of supply for haircuts if this licensing requirement were removed. **[LO 4.4]**

9. Although we could describe both the cross-price elasticity of demand between paper coffee cups and plastic coffee lids and the cross-price elasticity of demand between sugar and artificial sweeteners as highly elastic, the first cross-price elasticity is negative and the second is positive. What is the reason for this? **[LO 4.5]**

10. Name two related goods you consume which would have a positive cross-price elasticity. What happens to your consumption of the second good if the price of the first good increases? **[LO 4.5]**

11. Name two related goods you consume which would have a negative cross-price elasticity. What happens to your consumption of the second good if the price of the first good increases? **[LO 4.5]**

12. In France, where cheese is an important and traditional part of people's meals, people eat about six times as much cheese per person as in the United States. In which country do you think the demand for cheese will be more income-elastic? Why? **[LO 4.6]**

13. Name a good you consume for which your income elasticity of demand is positive. What happens when your income increases? **[LO 4.6]**

14. Name a good you consume for which your income elasticity of demand is negative. What happens when your income increases? **[LO 4.6]**

Problems and Applications

1. When the price of a bar of chocolate is $1, demand is 100,000 bars. When the price rises to $1.50, demand falls to 60,000 bars. Calculate the price elasticity of demand according to the instructions below and express your answer in absolute value. **[LO 4.1]**

   a. Suppose price increases from $1 to $1.50. Calculate the price elasticity of demand in terms of percent change, as described on pages 79–80.

b. Suppose price decreases from $1.50 to $1. Calculate the price elasticity of demand in terms of percent change, as described on pages 79–80.

c. Suppose the price increases from $1 to $1.50. Calculate the price elasticity of demand using the mid-point method.

d. Suppose the price decreases from $1.50 to $1. Calculate the price elasticity of demand using the mid-point formula.

2. If the price elasticity of demand for used cars priced between $3,000 and $5,000 is −1.2 (using the mid-point method), what will be the percent change in quantity demanded when the price of a used car falls from $5,000 to $3,000? **[LO 4.1]**

3. Three points are identified on the graph in Figure 4P-1. **[LO 4.2]**

   a. At point A, demand is _____.

   b. At point B, demand is _____.

   c. At point C, demand is _____.

4. Which of the following has a more elastic demand in the short run? **[LO 4.2]**

   a. Pomegranate juice or drinking water?

   b. Cereal or Rice Krispies®?

   c. Speedboats or gourmet chocolate?

5. In each of the following instances, determine whether demand is elastic, inelastic, or unit-elastic. **[LO 4.2]**

   a. If price increases by 10 percent and quantity demand decreases by 15 percent, demand is _____.

   b. If price decreases by 10 percent and quantity demanded increases by 5 percent, demand is _____.

6. In each of the following instances, determine whether quantity demanded will increase or decrease, and by how much. **[LO 4.2]**

a. If price elasticity of demand is −1.3 and price increases by 2 percent, quantity demanded will _____ by _____ percent.

b. If price elasticity of demand is −0.3 and price decreases by 2 percent, quantity demanded will _____ by _____ percent.

Problems 7 and 8 refer to the demand schedule shown in Table 4P-1. For each price change, say whether demand is elastic, unit-elastic, or inelastic, and say whether total revenue increases, decreases, or stays the same.

7. Price increases from $10 to $20. Demand is _____ and total revenue _____. **[LO 4.2]**

8. Price decreases from $70 to $60. Demand is _____ and total revenue _____. **[LO 4.2]**

Problems 9–12 refer to Figure 4P-2.

9. Draw the price effect and the quantity effect for a price change from $60 to $50. Which effect is larger? Does total revenue increase or decrease? No calculation is necessary. **[LO 4.2]**

10. Draw the price effect and the quantity effect for a price change from $30 to $20. Which effect is larger? Does total revenue increase or decrease? No calculation is necessary. **[LO 4.2]**

11. Draw the price effect and the quantity effect for a price change from $60 to $70. Which effect is larger? Does total revenue increase or decrease? No calculation is necessary. **[LO 4.2]**

12. Draw the price effect and the quantity effect for a price change from $10 to $20. Which effect is larger? Does total revenue increase or decrease? No calculation is necessary. **[LO 4.2]**

FIGURE 4P-1

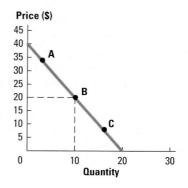

TABLE 4P-1

Price ($)	Quantity demanded
80	0
70	50
60	100
50	150
40	200
30	250
20	300
10	350
0	400

FIGURE 4P-2

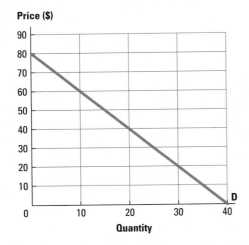

13. Use the graph in Figure 4P-3 to calculate the price elasticity of supply between points A and B using the mid-point method. **[LO 4.3]**

14. If the price of a haircut is $15, the number of haircuts provided is 100. If the price rises to $30 per haircut, barbers will work much longer hours, and the supply of haircuts will increase to 300. What is the price elasticity of supply for haircuts between $15 and $30? **[LO 4.3]**

15. Which of the following has a more elastic supply in the short run? **[LO 4.4]**

    a. Hospitals or mobile clinics?

    b. Purebred dogs or pet rabbits?

    c. On-campus courses or online courses?

16. In each of the following instances, determine whether supply is elastic, inelastic, or unit-elastic. **[LO 4.4]**

    a. If price increases by 10 percent and quantity supplied increases by 15 percent, supply is _____.

FIGURE 4P-3

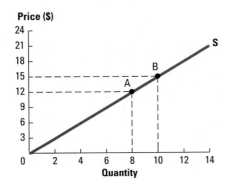

b. If price decreases by 10 percent and quantity supplied decreases by 5 percent, supply is _____.

17. In each of the following instances, determine whether quantity supplied will increase or decrease, and by how much. **[LO 4.4]**

    a. If price elasticity of supply is 1.3 and price increases by 2 percent, quantity supplied will _____ by _____ percent.

    b. If price elasticity of supply is 0.3 and price decreases by 2 percent, quantity supplied will _____ by _____ percent.

18. Suppose that the price of peanut butter rises from $2 to $3 per jar. **[LO 4.5]**

    a. The quantity of jelly purchased falls from 20 million jars to 15 million jars. What is the cross-price elasticity of demand between peanut butter and jelly? Are they complements or substitutes?

    b. The quantity of jelly purchased rises from 15 million jars to 20 million jars. What is the cross-price elasticity of demand between peanut butter and jelly? Are they complements or substitutes?

19. For each of the following pairs, predict whether the cross-price elasticity of demand will be positive or negative: **[LO 4.5]**

    a. Soap and hand sanitizer.

    b. CDs and MP3s.

    c. Sheets and pillowcases.

20. Suppose that when the average family income rises from $30,000 per year to $40,000 per year, the average family's purchases of toilet paper rise from 100 rolls to 105 rolls per year. **[LO 4.6]**

    a. Calculate the income-elasticity of demand for toilet paper.

    b. Is toilet paper a normal or an inferior good?

    c. Is the demand for toilet paper income-elastic or income-inelastic?

21. In each of the following instances, determine whether the good is normal or inferior, and whether it is income-elastic or income-inelastic. **[LO 4.6]**

    a. If income increases by 10 percent and the quantity demanded of a good increases by 5 percent, the good is _____ and _____.

    b. If income increases by 10 percent and the quantity demanded of a good decreases by 20 percent, the good is _____ and _____.

Math Essentials: Calculating Percentage Change, Slope, and Elasticity

LEARNING OBJECTIVES

LO C.1   Understand how to calculate percentage changes.

LO C.2   Use slope to calculate elasticity.

The math associated with the concept of elasticity covers a wide variety of topics. In order to be able to calculate elasticity, you need to be able to calculate percentage changes. In order to talk about shape of a line, and its elasticity, you need to be able to understand slope and the relationship between variables, particularly price and quantity.

Percentage Change

LO C.1 Understand how to calculate percentage changes.

In Chapter 4, we calculated elasticity in all its forms. If you're not entirely comfortable calculating percentage change, though, elasticity can be a daunting idea. Percentage changes represent the relative change in a variable from an old value to a new one. In general, the formula can be reduced in plain English to saying, "New minus old, divided by old, times 100."

The mathematical equivalent is shown as Equation C-1. There, X_1 represents the original value of any variable X, and X_2 is the new value of this variable.

Equation C-1

$$\text{Percentage change} = \left[\frac{(X_2 - X_1)}{X_1}\right] \times 100$$

Overall, you can use this method to calculate the percentage change in variables of various kinds. A percentage change in quantity, for example, would be expressed as:

$$\text{Percentage change in quantity} = \left[\frac{(Q_2 - Q_1)}{Q_1}\right] \times 100$$

where Q_2 represents the new value of quantity demanded and Q_1 the original quantity demanded.

Similarly, a percentage change in price would be expressed as:

$$\text{Percentage change in price} = \left[\frac{(P_2 - P_1)}{P_1}\right] \times 100$$

Let's try an example for practice: For weeks, you have been watching the price of a new pair of shoes. They normally cost $80, but you see that the store has a sale and now offers them for $60. You find the percentage change in the price of the shoes by first subtracting the old price ($80) from the new one ($60) to find the change in price, which is −$20. To find how much of a change this is, you take this −$20 price change and divide it by the original cost of the shoes ($80). This gives you the decimal that you multiply by 100 to get the percentage change:

$$\frac{\$60 - \$80}{\$80} = -0.25$$

$$-0.25 \times 100 = -25\%$$

In this case, the $20 price reduction was a 25 percent decrease in price. Not a bad sale!

Notice that in this case, the percentage change is negative, which indicates that the new value is less than the original. If the prices of shoes had increased instead, the associated percentage change would be a positive value.

The best way to do get comfortable with calculating percentage changes is through lots of practice. You can find a few extra problems to try on your own at the end of this appendix, and you also could challenge yourself to calculate price changes you see in your everyday life.

Slope and Elasticity

LO C.2 Use slope to calculate elasticity.

In Appendix A, "Math Essentials: Understanding Graphs and Slope," we showed that the direction of a slope tells us something meaningful about the relationship between the two variables we are representing: When x and y move in the same direction, they are said to have a *positive* relationship. Not surprisingly, this means that the slope of the line is a positive number. When the slope of a line is positive, we know that y increases as x increases, and y decreases as x decreases. Similarly, when x and y move in opposite directions, they are said to have a *negative* relationship. The slope of the line is a negative number. When the slope of a line is negative, we know that y decreases as x increases, and y increases as x decreases.

In Chapter 3, we saw a positive relationship between price and quantity in the supply curve. We saw a negative relationship between price and quantity in the demand curve. Two variables (such as price and quantity) may have more than one relationship to each other, depending on whose choices they represent and under what circumstances.

The steepness of a slope is also important. Numerically, the closer the number representing the slope is to zero, the flatter the curve will be. Remember that both positive and negative numbers can be close to zero. So, a slope of −1 is equally steep as a slope of 1, although one slopes downward and the other upward. Correspondingly, a line with a slope of −5 is steeper than a line with a slope of −1 or one with a slope of 1. You can tell just from looking at an equation how steep the line will be. If this idea is still a little hazy, you might want to page back to Appendix A to refresh your memory, as the steepness of slope is important to understanding the concept of elasticity.

FIGURE C-1

Measuring a change in Q in response to a change in P

(A) Steeper slope

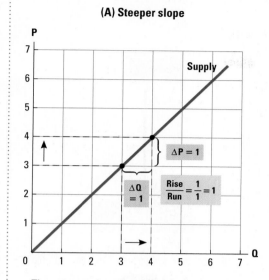

The steeper slope in panel A indicates that price changes less in panel A than in panel B in response to a change in quantity demanded.

(B) Flatter slope

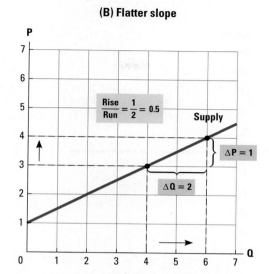

The flatter slope in panel B indicates that price changes more in panel B than in panel A in response to a change in quantity demanded.

Although the ideas of slope and elasticity are related, there are two basic mathematical distinctions between them:

1. Slope describes the change in y per the change in x, whereas elasticity measures are based on the change in x per the change in y.

2. We usually measure elasticity in terms of *percentage changes,* rather than absolute (unit-based) changes.

Why would we be interested in how much x changes in response to a one-unit change in y? To get at this difference, let's look at Figure C-1. It is similar to Figure A-10 (in Appendix A, p. 46J), but replaces the variables x and y with the quantity of a good (Q) and its price (P).

In Chapter 4 you learned that *price elasticity* is a measure of the responsiveness of supply (or demand) to changes in price. In other words, it is a measure of how quantity (on the x-axis) responds to a change in price (on the y-axis). So this time, let's make the change in price (vertical distance) the same and look at how much quantity changes (horizontal distance).

Looking at Figure C-1, we can see that when price moves from P_1 to P_2, quantity supplied changes by less in panel A than it does in panel B. When price increases from P_1 to P_2 in panel A, quantity increases by one unit, from Q_1 to Q_2. In contrast, panel B shows an increase of two units from Q_1 to Q_2 for the same change in P. This means supply is less responsive to a price change in panel A compared to panel B.

X over Y, or Y over X?

We have noted that slope is indicated by $\frac{\Delta y}{\Delta x}$. In contrast, elasticity is commonly indicated by $\frac{\%\Delta Q}{\%\Delta P}$, which corresponds to $\frac{\Delta x}{\Delta y}$. In some sense, then, elasticity is computed as the mirror image of slope. The easiest way to picture this is to see the difference between slope and elasticity for vertical and horizontal lines.

FIGURE C-2

Slope versus elasticity of horizontal and vertical lines

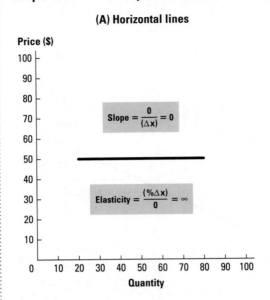

(A) Horizontal lines

When a line is horizontal, the slope is zero and the associated elasticity is infinite. In other words, demand or supply only occurs at a single price.

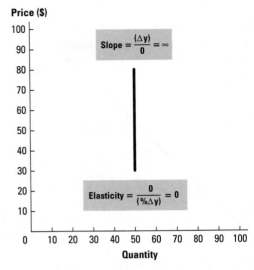

(B) Vertical lines

When a line is vertical, the slope is infinite and the elasticity is zero. Regardless of the price, quantity supplied or demanded is going to be the same.

In Figure C-2, the horizontal line pictured in panel A has a slope of zero. This is because a one-unit change in x results in zero change in y. Therefore, slope is calculated as $\frac{0}{\Delta x}$. Zero divided by any number is zero. If we think of the horizontal line as a demand curve mapping price to quantity demanded, however, the price elasticity is infinity.

How can slope be zero and elasticity infinity? Remember that slope measures how much y changes in response to a change in x. Elasticity, however, measures the sensitivity of P (on the y-axis) to a change in Q (on the x-axis). Whereas x is in the denominator when calculating slope, it is in the numerator when calculating elasticity. For a horizontal line, then, elasticity will be %ΔQ/0, since there is no change in P. Division by 0 is mathematically undefined, or known as infinity.

The reverse is true when we look at a vertical line. When a graph is vertical, there is zero change in x for any change in y. Therefore, slope is calculated as $\frac{\Delta y}{0}$. In this case, slope is undefined (infinity). But elasticity will be 0/%ΔP. Again, zero divided by any number is zero.

Elasticity changes along lines with constant slope

The second important mathematical difference between slope and elasticity is that we usually measure slope in terms of absolute changes, but we measure elasticity in terms of percent changes. This means that at different points along a straight line, slope is constant, but elasticity varies.

As an example, take a look at the demand schedule in Table C-1. First, let's calculate the slope between two different sets of points. Using the first two prices and quantities at the top of the demand schedule, we see that the slope between these points is −1.

Price ($)	Quantity
80	0
70	10
60	20
50	30
40	40
30	50
20	60
10	70
0	80

TABLE C-1
Demand schedule

$$\text{Slope \#1} = \frac{\Delta P_1}{\Delta Q_1} = \frac{(0 - 10)}{(80 - 70)} = \frac{-10}{10} = -1$$

Then, pick another two points. Using the quantities 30 and 20 and their respective prices, we can calculate that the slope is still −1.

$$\text{Slope \#2} = \frac{\Delta P_2}{\Delta Q_2} = \frac{(30 - 20)}{(50 - 60)} = \frac{10}{-10} = -1$$

No matter what two points along the demand curve we choose, the slope is the same. *Slope is constant because the demand curve is linear.*

Now let's calculate elasticity between these same two sets of points. We will use the mid-point method described in Chapter 3 to calculate elasticity:

$$\text{Elasticity} = \frac{\%\Delta Q}{\%\Delta P} = \frac{\Delta Q/Q_{\text{midpoint}}}{\Delta P/P_{\text{midpoint}}}$$

Let's start with the top of the demand curve and calculate the price elasticity of demand for a price change from 80 to 70. Using the midpoint method, we have:

$$\frac{\Delta Q/Q_{\text{midpoint}}}{\Delta P/P_{\text{midpoint}}} = \frac{(0 - 10)/5}{(80 - 70)/60} = \frac{-10/5}{10/60} = \frac{-2}{0.17} = -11.8$$

Now let's calculate the price elasticity of demand at the bottom of the demand curve for a price change of 30 to 20.

$$\frac{\Delta Q/Q_{\text{midpoint}}}{\Delta P/P_{\text{midpoint}}} = \frac{(50 - 60)/55}{(30 - 20)/25} = \frac{-10/55}{10/25} = \frac{-0.18}{0.4} = -0.45$$

Even though both of these calculations represented a 10-unit change in quantity in response to a $10 change in price, along a linear demand curve, elasticity changes. Moving down along the demand curve means less elasticity. This is because the same change in Q or P is a different *percentage* of the midpoint at different points on the line.

Problems and Applications

1. Calculate the percentage change in each of the following examples. **[LO C.1]**
   a. 8 to 12.
   b. 16 to 14.
   c. 125 to 120.
   d. 80 to 90.

2. Find the percentage change in price in these examples **[LO C.1]**
   a. The price of a $4 sandwich increases to $5.
   b. A sale discounts the price of a sofa from $750 to $500.

3. Use the demand curve in Figure CP-1 to answer the following questions. Use the mid-point method in your calculations. **[LO C.2]**
   a. What is the price elasticity of demand for a price change from $0 to $20?
   b. What is the price elasticity of demand for a price change from $20 to $40?
   c. What is the price elasticity of demand for a price change from $40 to $60?

4. Use the demand schedule in Table CP-1 to answer the following questions. Use the mid-point method in your calculations. **[LO C.2]**
   a. What is the price elasticity of demand for a price change from $4 to $8?
   b. What is the price elasticity of demand for a price change from $8 to $16?
   c. What is the price elasticity of demand for a price change from $20 to $24?

TABLE CP-1

Price ($)	Quantity
0	60
4	50
8	40
12	30
16	20
20	10
24	0

TABLE CP-2

Price ($)	Quantity
0	56
1	48
2	42
3	35
4	28
5	21
6	14
7	7
8	0

5. Use the demand schedule in Table CP-2 to answer the following questions. Use the mid-point method when calculating elasticity. **[LO C.2]**
   a. What is the price elasticity of demand for a price change from $2 to $3? What is the slope of the demand curve for a price change from $2 to $3?
   b. What is the price elasticity of demand for a price change from $3 to $5? What is the slope of the demand curve for a price change from $3 to $5?
   c. What is the price elasticity of demand for a price change from $6 to $7? What is the slope of the demand curve for a price change from $6 to $7?

FIGURE CP-1

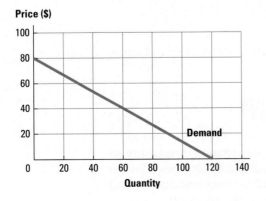

Efficiency

LEARNING OBJECTIVES

LO 5.1	Use willingness to pay and willingness to sell to determine supply and demand at a given price.
LO 5.2	Calculate consumer surplus based on a graph or table.
LO 5.3	Calculate producer surplus based on a graph or table.
LO 5.4	Calculate total surplus based on a graph or table.
LO 5.5	Define efficiency in terms of surplus, and identify efficient and inefficient situations.
LO 5.6	Describe the distribution of benefits that results from a policy decision.
LO 5.7	Define and calculate deadweight loss.
LO 5.8	Explain why correcting a missing market can make everyone better off.

A BROKEN LASER POINTER STARTS AN INTERNET REVOLUTION

In 1995, a young software developer named Pierre Omidyar spent his Labor Day weekend building a website he called AuctionWeb. His idea was to create a site where people could post their old stuff for sale online and auction it off to the highest bidder. Soon after, he sold the first item on AuctionWeb for $14.83. It was a broken laser pointer, which he had posted on the site as a test, never expecting anyone to bid on it. When Pierre pointed out that the pointer was broken, the bidder explained that he was "a collector of broken laser pointers."

As you might have guessed, AuctionWeb became the wildly successful company we now know as eBay. In 2011, the total value of items sold on eBay was nearly $68.6 billion; 100 million people around the world were active users.

Like many creation stories, the tale of eBay's first sale gives us insight into what makes it tick. People are interested in some pretty odd things (like broken laser pointers), but given a big enough audience, someone who wants to sell can usually find someone who wants to buy. When buyers and sellers are matched up and they trade, each is made better off. The buyer gets an item he wants, and the seller gets money. Because both parties benefit from engaging in such transactions, they are willing to pay eBay to provide the marketplace where they can find one another.

eBay's success is based on one of the most fundamental ideas in economics, and its importance stretches far beyond the company itself: *Voluntary exchanges create value and can make everyone involved better off.* This principle drives a range of businesses that do not manufacture or grow anything themselves, but instead facilitate transactions between producers and consumers—from grocery stores, to investment banks, to online retailers.

But this principle raises a question: How do we know that people are better off when they buy and sell things? Can we say anything about *how much* better off they are?

To answer these questions, we need a tool to describe the size of the benefits that result from transactions and who receives them. In this chapter we will introduce the concept of *surplus*, which measures the benefit that people receive when they buy something for less than they would have been willing to pay or sell something for more than they would have been willing to accept. *Surplus* is the best way to look at the benefits people receive from successful transactions.

Surplus also shows us why the equilibrium price and quantity in a competitive market are so special: They maximize the total well-being of those involved. Even when we care about outcomes other than total well-being (like inequality in the distribution of benefits), surplus gives us a yardstick for comparing different ideas and policies. For instance, calculations of surplus can clearly show who benefits and who loses from policies such as taxes and minimum wages. As we'll see, *efficiency*, in the sense of maximizing total surplus, is one of the most powerful features of a market system. Even more remarkable is that it is achieved without centralized coordination.

Surplus also shows us how simply enabling people to trade with one another can make them better off. Often, creating a new market for goods and services (as the Grameen Bank did in Bangladesh, in the example in Chapter 1) or improving an existing market (as eBay did on the Internet) can be a good way to help people. Knowing how and when to harness the power of economic exchanges to improve well-being is an important tool for businesspeople and public-minded problem solvers alike.

Willingness to Pay and Sell

LO 5.1 Use willingness to pay and willingness to sell to determine supply and demand at a given price.

eBay is an online auction platform that allows people to create a web page advertising an item for sale. People who want to buy the item make bids offering to pay a particular price. This decentralized marketplace supports all sorts of transactions: from real estate, to used cars, to rare books, to (in one extraordinary case) a half-eaten cheese sandwich said to look like the Virgin Mary (which sold for $28,000).

Who uses eBay? What do they want? At the most basic level, they are people who want to buy or sell a particular good. We're not sure what's going on with people who want broken laser pointers or decade-old cheese sandwiches, so let's stick with something a little more typical. How about digital cameras? (Just as we did in Chapter 3, we'll make the simplifying assumption that there is just one kind of digital camera rather than thousands of slightly different models.)

Imagine you see a digital camera posted for sale on eBay. Who might bid on it? What are their *wants and constraints?* Most obviously, people who bid will be those who *want* a camera. But they will also care about the price they pay: Why spend $200 for a camera if you can get it for $100 and spend the other $100 on something else? Potential buyers *want* to pay as little as possible, but on top of this general preference, each buyer has a maximum price she is willing to pay.

Economists call this maximum price the buyer's **willingness to pay** or **reservation price**. Economists use these two terms interchangeably; in this book, we'll stick with "willingness to pay." This price is the point above which the buyer throws up her hands and says, "Never mind, I'd rather spend my money on something else." Each potential buyer wants to purchase a camera for a price that is as low as possible and no higher than her maximum *willingness to pay*. On eBay, we can see willingness to pay in action. When the price of a product remains below a bidder's willingness to pay, he'll continue to bid on it. When the going price passes his willingness to pay, he'll drop out.

Of course, buyers are only half the story. Who posted the camera for sale on eBay in the first place? To create a functioning market for digital cameras, someone has to want to sell them. Whereas buyers want to buy a camera for as low a price as possible, sellers want to sell for as high a price as possible. Why take less money if you could get more? Just as each potential buyer has a willingness to pay, each potential seller has a *willingness to sell*. **Willingness to sell** is the minimum price that a seller is willing to accept in exchange for a good or service. A seller always wants to sell for a price that is as high as possible, but never lower than his minimum. We can see willingness to sell in action on eBay through the "reserve price" that sellers can set when they post an item. This reserve price sets a bar below which the seller will not accept any bids. If she doesn't get any higher bids, she simply keeps the item.

So far, so good: Buyers want to buy low, sellers want to sell high. What does this have to do with markets? We're about to see that willingness to pay and willingness to sell are actually the forces that drive the shape of demand and supply curves.

Willingness to pay and the demand curve

Let's return to potential camera buyers and take a closer look at how they choose to bid on the camera posted on eBay. To keep things simple, let's imagine that there are five buyers who are considering bidding on this particular camera.

- The first potential buyer is a bird watcher, who cares passionately about having a good camera to document the rare birds she finds. She is willing to pay up to $500 for the camera.
- The next bidder is an amateur photographer; he has an outdated camera and is willing to pay $250 for this newer model.
- The third bidder is a real estate agent, who will be willing to pay $200 or less to be able to take better pictures of her properties.
- Next is a journalist, who wouldn't mind having a newer camera than the one her newspaper provided, but would pay no more than $150 for it.
- Finally there is a teacher, who will spend no more than $100—the amount of the eBay gift certificate given to him by appreciative parents for his birthday.

We can plot each potential buyer's willingness to pay on a graph. In panel A of Figure 5-1, we've graphed possible prices for the camera against the number of buyers who would be willing to bid that price for it. Remember that each person's willingness to pay is a *maximum*—he or she would also be willing to buy the camera at any lower price. Therefore, at a price of $100, all five buyers are willing to bid; at $350, only one will bid.

willingness to pay (reservation price) the maximum price that a buyer would be willing to pay for a good or service

willingness to sell the minimum price that a seller is willing to accept in exchange for a good or service

FIGURE 5-1

Willingness to pay and the demand curve

(A) Willingness to pay with few buyers

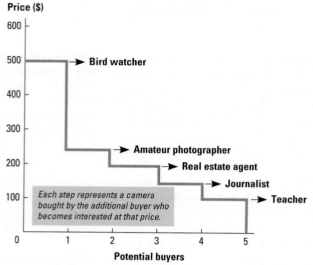

At any given price, buyers with a higher willingness to pay will buy and those with a lower willingness to pay will not. If the price were $350, only one buyer would buy. If it were $50, all five people would buy. This demand curve has a step-like shape rather than a smooth line because there are a limited number of buyers whose prices are expressed in round dollar amounts.

(B) Willingness to pay with many buyers

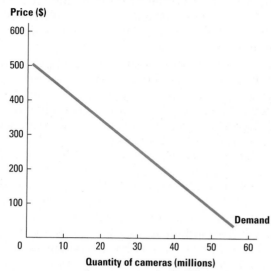

In the real market for a particular model of a digital camera, there are millions of cameras demanded at a particular price. The steps that we see in panel A get smaller and smaller until they disappear into a smooth curve.

If you squint a bit, you might notice that the graph in panel A looks a lot like a demand curve—price on the *y*-axis, quantity on the *x*-axis, and a line showing that quantity demanded increases as price decreases. In fact this *is* a demand curve, albeit one representing only five potential buyers. If we conducted the same exercise in a bigger market and plotted out the willingness to pay of millions of people rather than just five, we'd get a smooth demand curve, as shown in panel B of Figure 5-1.

Notice that although each buyer's willingness to pay is driven by different factors, we can explain the motivations behind all of their decisions by asking, *What are the trade-offs?* Money that is spent to buy a camera on eBay cannot be spent on other things. Willingness to pay is the point at which the benefit that a person will get from the camera is equal to the benefit of spending the money on another alternative—in other words, the opportunity cost.

At prices above the maximum willingness to pay, the opportunity cost is greater than the benefits; at lower prices, the benefits outweigh the opportunity cost. For instance, $250 is the point at which the enjoyment that the amateur photographer gets from a camera is the same as the enjoyment he would get from, say, buying $250 worth of stamps for his stamp collection instead. Since everyone has things they want other than cameras, this same logic applies to each of the potential buyers represented in the demand curve.

To figure out which of our five individual buyers will actually purchase a camera, we have to know the market price. To find the market price, we have to know something about the supply of digital cameras. Therefore, we turn next to investigating the supply curve.

Willingness to sell and the supply curve

As you may have guessed, just as the shape of the demand curve was driven by potential buyers' willingness to pay, the shape of the supply curve for digital cameras is driven by potential sellers' willingness to sell. To simplify things, let's imagine five particular sellers who have posted their cameras for sale on eBay.

- The first prospective seller is a comic book collector. He was given a camera as a birthday present, but all he really cares about is having money to spend on comic books. He's willing to part with his camera for as little as $50.
- Then there's a sales representative from a big company that makes digital cameras. She's authorized to sell for anything $100 or higher.
- Next is a professional nature photographer, who owns several cameras but won't sell for anything less than $200; at a lower price he'd rather give it as a gift to his nephew.
- Another seller is a sales representative at a smaller company which is just setting up in the camera business and has much higher costs of production than the larger company; it can make money only by selling its cameras for $300 or more.
- The fifth seller is an art teacher who is sentimentally attached to her camera, given to her by a friend. She won't give it up unless she can get at least $400.

We can represent these five individuals by plotting their willingness to sell on a graph. Panel A of Figure 5-2 shows a graph of potential prices and the number of cameras that

FIGURE 5-2

Willingness to sell and the supply curve

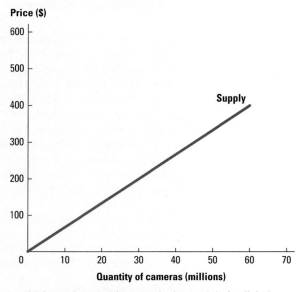

At any given price, sellers with a lower willingness to sell will sell, while those with a higher willingness to sell will not. At a price of $400, all five people will sell their cameras, while at a price of $200, only three sell. This rough supply curve would look smooth if there were many sellers, each with a different willingness to sell.

In the real market for a particular model of a digital camera, there are millions of cameras supplied at a particular price. The steps that we see in panel A get smaller and smaller until they disappear into a smooth curve.

will be up for bid at each price. This graph is a supply curve representing only five potential sellers. As with the demand curve, if we added all of the millions of digital cameras that are actually for sale in the real world, we see the smooth supply curve we're accustomed to, as in panel B.

Sellers' willingness to sell is determined by the *trade-offs* they face, and in particular, the opportunity cost of the sale. The opportunity cost of selling a camera is the use or enjoyment that the seller could get from keeping the camera—or, in the case of the two camera manufacturers, from doing something else with the money that would be required to manufacture it. Each seller's opportunity cost will be determined by different factors—not all of them strictly monetary, as in the case of the teacher who is sentimentally attached to her camera.

For items that the seller just wants to get rid of, the starting price might be one cent. If opportunity cost is zero, anything is better than nothing! On the other hand, in a market where manufacturers are producing and selling new products, the minimum price will have to be high enough to make it worth their while to continue making new products. If the sale price didn't cover their costs of production, the manufacturers would simply stop making the item—otherwise, they would actually lose money every time they made a sale. (Occasionally, we do see manufacturers selling below the cost of production, but only when they've made a mistake and have to get rid of already-produced goods.)

Having met five potential buyers and five potential sellers, we're now in a position to understand what happens when the two groups come together in the market to make trades. But first, take a look at the Real Life box "Haggling and bluffing" to consider how buyers' willingness to pay interacts with sellers' willingness to sell in the real world.

REAL LIFE

Haggling and bluffing

If you've ever visited a flea market or bought a used car, you have probably haggled over price. In much of the world haggling for goods is an integral part of daily life. Even in wealthy countries, bargaining over salaries and promotions is commonplace—employees offer to sell their time and skills, and employers offer to buy them. In any bargaining situation, the seller wants to sell for as high a price as possible, and the buyer wants to buy for as low a price as possible. How do they reach an agreement?

The idea of willingness to pay explains a lot of bargaining strategies. Usually, the seller will start with a price much higher than the minimum she is actually willing to accept. Likewise, the buyer starts with an offer much lower than what he is actually willing to pay. Neither will reveal the price he or she thinks is reasonable. Isn't this a waste of time? They both know that they'll end up somewhere in the middle. Why not just start there?

Put yourself in the shoes of a flea-market vendor. If you knew for certain how much a potential customer was willing to pay, would you accept anything short of that amount? Probably not. As the would-be buyer, then, you have a strong incentive to make sure that the vendor doesn't know your true willingness to pay. The same is true for the vendor, who wants to hide from the potential buyer the minimum price he'll accept. Both parties start bidding far from their actual reservation price, hoping to end up with the most favorable price possible.

The same principle also explains a trick that is sometimes used by hagglers: bluffing about your willingness to pay. What would you do if the cost of an item were above your maximum willingness to pay? On eBay, you'd stop bidding; in the flea market, you'd walk away. Walking away from the bargaining table signals that the current price is higher than your willingness to pay—whether or not that is truly the case. If the seller realizes he won't get a higher price, he will sometimes settle rather than lose the sale entirely. On the other hand, if you're a bad bluffer or if your offered price is below the seller's willingness to sell, you lose the deal.

The next time you hear that "labor has walked out on talks" in a union wage negotiation or that a party to a civil lawsuit has "withdrawn from mediation," you will know that they're signaling their minimum or maximum price. The question is, are they bluffing?

✓ CONCEPT CHECK

❑ How is willingness to pay determined by opportunity cost? **[LO 5.1]**
❑ What is the relationship between willingness to pay and the demand curve? **[LO 5.1]**

Measuring Surplus

Surplus is a way of measuring who benefits from transactions and by how much. Economists use this word to describe a fairly simple concept: If you get something for less than you would have been willing to pay, or sell it for more than the minimum you would have accepted, that's a good thing. Think about how nice it feels to buy something on sale that you would have been willing to pay full price for. That "bonus" value that you would have paid if necessary, but didn't have to, is *surplus*. We can talk about surplus for both buyers and sellers, individually and collectively.

surplus a way of measuring who benefits from transactions and by how much

Surplus is the difference between the price at which a buyer or seller would be *willing* to trade and the actual price. Think about willingness to pay as the price at which someone is completely indifferent between buying an item and keeping his money. At a higher price, he would prefer to keep the money; at a lower price, he would prefer to buy. By looking at the distance between this "indifference point" and the actual price, we can describe the extra value the buyer (or the seller) gets from the transaction.

Surplus is a simple idea, but a surprisingly powerful one. It turns out that this is a better measure of the value that buyers and sellers get from participating in a market than price itself. To see why this is true, read the From Another Angle box "How much would you pay to keep the Internet from disappearing?"

FROM ANOTHER ANGLE

How much would you pay to keep the Internet from disappearing?

Why is surplus a better measure of value than how much we pay for something? Consider the difference between what we pay for the Internet versus a particular model of computer.

Most people can access the Internet for very little, or even for free. You might pay a monthly fee for high-speed access at home, but almost anyone can use the Internet for free at schools, libraries, or coffee shops. Once you're online there are millions of websites that will provide information, entertainment, and services at no charge. Computer owners, on the other hand, pay a lot for particular types of computers. For instance, consumers might pay $999 for a MacBook laptop. Does this mean that we value access to the Internet less than a MacBook? Probably not.

To see why simply measuring price falls short of capturing true value, think about how much you would pay to prevent the particular type of computer you own from disappearing from the market. You might pay something: After all, there's a reason you chose it in the first place, and you might be willing to cough up a bit extra to get your preferred combination of technical specifications, appearance, and so on. But if the price got very steep, you'd probably rather switch to another, similar type of computer instead of paying more money. That difference—the maximum extra amount you would pay over the current price to maintain the ability to buy something—is your consumer surplus. It is the difference between your willingness to pay and the actual price.

Now consider the same question for the Internet. Imagine that the Internet is going to disappear tomorrow, or at least, that you will be unable to access it in any way. How much would you pay to keep that from happening? Remember, that means no e-mail, no Google search or maps, no Facebook, no Twitter, no YouTube, no video streaming, and no online shopping. We suspect that you might be willing to pay a lot. The amount that you're willing to pay represents the true value that you place on the Internet, even though the amount that you currently spend on it might be very little. That's the magic of surplus.

Consumer surplus

LO 5.2 Calculate consumer surplus based on a graph or table.

Let's go back to our five eBay buyers and calculate the surplus they would receive from buying a camera at a given price. Suppose it turns out that the going rate for cameras on eBay is $160. The bird watcher was willing to bid up to $500. Therefore, her **consumer surplus** from buying the camera is $340—the difference between her willingness to pay and the $160 she actually pays. Two other potential buyers will also buy a camera if the price is $160: the real estate agent (willing to pay up to $200) and the amateur photographer (willing to pay $250). The consumer surplus they receive is $40 and $90, respectively. The other two potential buyers will have dropped out of bidding when the price rose above $100 and then above $150, so they buy nothing and pay nothing. Their consumer surplus is zero.

consumer surplus the net benefit that a consumer receives from purchasing a good or service, measured by the difference between willingness to pay and the actual price

We can add up each individual's consumer surplus to describe the overall benefits that buyers received in a market. (Confusingly, economists use the same term for individual and collective surplus, but you should be able to tell from the context whether we mean one person's consumer surplus or total consumer surplus for all buyers in the market.) If the market for digital cameras consisted only of our five individuals, then the total consumer surplus would be:

$$\$340 + \$90 + \$40 + \$0 + \$0 = \$470$$

Panel A in Figure 5-3 shows consumer surplus for these five individuals when the price is $160. Consumer surplus is represented graphically by the area underneath the demand curve and above the horizontal line of the equilibrium price.

For a refresher on the area under a linear curve, see Appendix D, "Math Essentials: The Area under a Linear Curve," which follows this chapter.

How does a change in the market price affect buyers? Since buyers would always prefer prices to be lower, a decrease in price makes them better off, and an increase in price makes them worse off. Some people will choose not to buy at all when prices rise—which means that their surplus becomes zero. Those who do buy will have a smaller individual surplus than they had at the lower price. The opposite is true when prices fall. Measuring consumer surplus tells us *how much* better or worse off buyers are when the price changes.

Panel B of Figure 5-3 shows what happens to total consumer surplus if the going price of cameras on eBay falls to $100. You can see by comparing panel A and panel B that when the price level falls, the area representing consumer surplus gets bigger. The consumer surplus of each of the three buyers who were already willing to buy increases by $60 each, and an additional two buyers join the market. The journalist gains consumer

Government Intervention

Chapter

6

LEARNING OBJECTIVES

LO 6.1 Calculate the effect of a price ceiling on the equilibrium price and quantity.

LO 6.2 Calculate the effect of a price floor on the equilibrium price and quantity.

LO 6.3 Calculate the effect of a tax on the equilibrium price and quantity.

LO 6.4 Calculate the effect of a subsidy on the equilibrium price and quantity.

LO 6.5 Explain how elasticity and time period influence the impact of a market intervention.

FEEDING THE WORLD, ONE PRICE CONTROL AT A TIME

In the spring of 2008, a worldwide food shortage caused food prices to skyrocket. In just a few months, the prices of wheat, rice, and corn shot up as much as 140 percent. In the United States, the number of people living on food stamps rose to the highest level since the 1960s. By June, low-income Americans were facing tough choices, as the prices of basics like eggs and dairy products rose. Many reported giving up meat and fresh fruit; others said they began to buy cheap food past the expiration date.[1]

Rising food prices caused trouble all over the world. The *Economist* magazine reported on the political fallout:

> [In Côte d'Ivoire,] two days of violence persuaded the government to postpone planned elections. . . . In Haiti, protesters chanting "We're hungry" forced the prime minister to resign; 24 people were killed in riots in Cameroon; Egypt's president ordered the army to start baking bread; [and] the Philippines made hoarding rice punishable by life imprisonment. [2]

Faced with hunger, hardship, and angry outbursts, many governments felt obliged to respond to the crisis. But what to do? Responses varied widely across countries. Many countries made it illegal to charge high prices for food. Others subsidized the price of basic necessities. In the United States and Europe, policy-makers tried to alleviate the shortage by paying farmers to grow more food. Were these responses appropriate? What, if anything, should governments do in such a situation?

Food is a tricky issue for policy-makers because it's a basic necessity. If prices rise too high, people go hungry. If prices fall too low, farmers go out of business, which raises the risk of food shortages in the future. So, while policy-makers aren't too concerned if the prices of many goods—like digital cameras or lattes—jump up and down, they often do care about food prices. But attempts to lower, raise, or simply stabilize prices can backfire or create unintended side effects. Sometimes the cure ends up being worse than the problem itself.

In this chapter, we'll look at the logic behind policies that governments commonly use to intervene in markets and their consequences—both intended and unintended. We will start with *price controls,* which make it illegal to sell a good for more or less than a certain price. Then we will look at *taxes* and *subsidies,* which discourage or encourage the production of particular goods. These tools are regularly applied to a broad range of issues, from unemployment to home ownership, air pollution to education. For better or worse, they have a huge effect on our lives as workers, consumers, businesspeople, and voters.

Why Intervene?

In Chapter 3, we saw that markets gravitate toward equilibrium. When markets work well, prices adjust until the quantity of a good that consumers demand equals the quantity that suppliers want to produce. At equilibrium, everyone gets what they are willing to pay for. In Chapter 5, we saw that equilibrium price and quantity also maximize total surplus. Thus, at equilibrium, there is no way to make some people better off without harming others.

So, why intervene? Why not let the invisible hand of the market determine prices and allocate resources? Some would argue that's exactly what should be done. Others believe the government has to intervene sometimes—and the fact is that every single government in the world intervenes in markets in some fashion.

Three reasons to intervene

The arguments for intervention fall into three categories: correcting market failures, changing the distribution of surplus, and encouraging or discouraging consumption of certain goods. As we discuss different policy tools throughout the chapter, ask yourself which of these motivations is driving the intervention.

Correcting market failures. Our model of demand and supply has so far assumed that markets work efficiently—but in the real world, that's not always true. For example, sometimes there is only one producer of a good, who faces no competition and can charge an inefficiently high price. In other cases, one person's use of a product or service imposes costs on other people that are not captured in prices paid by the first person, such as the pollution caused by burning the gas in your car. Situations in which the assumption of efficient, competitive markets fails to hold are called **market failures.** When there is a market failure, intervening can actually increase total surplus. We'll have much more to say about market failures in future chapters. In this chapter, we will stick to analyzing the effect of government interventions in efficient, competitive markets.

market failures
situations in which the assumption of efficient, competitive markets fails to hold

Changing the distribution of surplus. Efficient markets maximize total surplus, but an efficient outcome may still be seen as unfair. (Of course, the definition of fairness is up for debate.) Another reason to intervene in the market, therefore, is to change the distribution of surplus.

For example, even if the job market is efficient, wages can still drop so low that some workers fall below the poverty line while their employers make healthy profits. The government might respond by intervening in the labor market to impose a minimum wage. This policy will change the distribution of surplus, reducing employers' profits and lifting workers' incomes. Reasonable people can—and often do—argue about whether a policy that benefits a certain group (such as minimum-wage workers) is justified or not. Our focus will be on accurately describing the benefits and costs of such policies. Economics can help us predict whose well-being will increase, whose well-being will decrease, and who may be affected in unpredictable ways.

Encouraging or discouraging consumption. Around the world, many people judge certain products to be "good" or "bad" based on culture, health, religion, or other values. At the extreme, certain "bad" products are banned altogether, such as hard drugs. More often, governments use taxes to discourage people from consuming bad products, without banning them altogether. Common examples are cigarettes and alcohol; many governments tax them heavily, with the aim of reducing smoking and drinking. In some cases, minimizing costs imposed on others (such as from pollution or second-hand smoke) is also part of the motivation for discouraging consumption.

On the other hand, governments use *subsidies* to encourage people to consume "good" products or services. For instance, many governments provide public funding for schools to encourage education and for vaccinations to encourage parents to protect their children against disease.

Four real-world interventions

In this chapter we'll look at four real-world examples of how governments have intervened or could intervene in the market for food. For each, we'll consider the motives for the intervention and what its direct and indirect consequences were or could be. These four interventions are:

1. For many Mexican families, tortillas are an important food. What happened when the Mexican government set a *maximum price* for tortillas, in an effort to keep them affordable?

2. To ensure supplies of fresh milk, the U.S. government wanted to protect dairy farmers. What happened when the government set a *minimum price* for milk?

3. Many Americans struggle with health problems caused by overeating and poor nutrition. Several states have responded by banning the use of certain fats in food products; others require that restaurants post nutritional information

about the foods they serve. What would happen if governments *taxed* high-fat or high-calorie foods?

4. What would happen if, instead of setting a maximum price for tortillas, the Mexican government *subsidized* tortillas?

As we walk through these examples of real policies, we want you to apply both positive and normative analysis. Remember the difference:

- *Positive* analysis is about facts: Does the policy actually accomplish the original goal?
- *Normative* analysis is a matter of values and opinions: Do you think the policy is a good idea?

Few policies are all good or all bad. The key question is, *What are the trade-offs* involved in the intervention? Do the benefits outweigh the costs?

✓**CONCEPT CHECK**

❏ What are three reasons that a government might want to intervene in markets?

Price Controls

Suppose you are an economic policy advisor and food prices are rising. What should you do? If you were living in a region with many low-income consumers, you might want to take action to ensure that everyone gets enough to eat. One policy tool you might consider using is a **price control**—a regulation that sets a maximum or minimum legal price for a particular good. The direct effect of a price control is to hold the price of a good up or down when the market shifts, thus preventing the market from reaching a new equilibrium.

price control
a regulation that sets a maximum or minimum legal price for a particular good

Price controls can be divided into two opposing categories: *price ceilings* and *price floors.* We encountered this idea already in the chapter on surplus, when we imagined an interfering eBay manager setting prices for digital cameras. In reality, eBay would never do such a thing, but governments often do, particularly when it comes to markets for food items. What are the effects of using price controls to intervene in a well-functioning, competitive market?

Price ceilings

LO 6.1 Calculate the effect of a price ceiling on the equilibrium price and quantity.

price ceiling
a maximum legal price at which a good can be sold

A **price ceiling** is a maximum legal price at which a good can be sold. Many countries have price ceilings on staple foods, gasoline, and electricity, as policy-makers try to ensure everyone can afford the basic necessities.

Historically, the government of Mexico has set a price ceiling for tortillas, with the intent of guaranteeing that this staple food will remain affordable. Panel A of Figure 6-1 illustrates a hypothetical market for tortillas without a price ceiling. The equilibrium price is $0.50 per pound, and the equilibrium quantity is 50 million pounds.

Let's say that the government of Mexico responded to rising tortilla prices by setting a price ceiling of approximately $0.25 per pound, as shown in panel B of Figure 6-1. How should we expect producers and consumers to respond to this intervention? When price falls, consumers will want to buy more tortillas. In this example, the price fell from $0.50 to $0.25, and as a result, quantity demanded increased from 50 million to 75 million pounds.

FIGURE 6-1

A market with and without a price ceiling

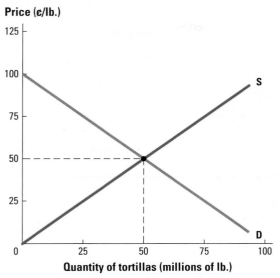

(A) Market without price ceiling

Without government intervention, the market for tortillas in Mexico would reach equilibrium at a price of 50 cents per pound and a quantity of 50 million pounds.

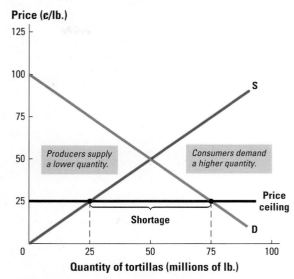

(B) Market with price ceiling

After government intervention, a price ceiling of 25 cents keeps the price of tortillas below the equilibrium point. At this new price, consumers want to buy more tortillas (75 million pounds) than producers want to supply (25 million pounds), resulting in a shortage of tortillas.

Predictably, however, a lower price means fewer producers will be willing to sell tortillas. When the price fell to $0.25, the quantity supplied dropped from 50 million to 25 million pounds. A lower price means higher quantity demanded but lower quantity supplied. Supply and demand were no longer in equilibrium. The price ceiling created a *shortage* of tortillas, equal to the 50 million pound difference between the quantities supplied and demanded.

Did the price ceiling meet the goal of providing low-priced tortillas to consumers? Yes and no. Consumers were able to buy *some* tortillas at the low price of $0.25 a pound—but they wanted to buy three times as many tortillas as producers were willing to supply. We can assess the full effect of the price ceiling by looking at what happened to consumer and producer surplus. Without looking at the graph, we already know that a price ceiling will cause producer surplus to fall: Sellers are selling fewer tortillas at a lower price. We also know that total surplus—that is, producer and consumer surplus combined—will fall, because the market has moved away from equilibrium. Some trades that would have happened at the equilibrium price do not happen, and the surplus that would have been generated by those mutually beneficial trades is lost entirely. This area is known as *deadweight loss* and is represented by area 1 in Figure 6-2. As we discussed in Chapter 5, **deadweight loss** represents the loss of total surplus that occurs because the quantity of a good that is bought and sold is below the market equilibrium quantity.

What we can't tell without looking at the graph is whether consumer surplus will increase or decrease—that response depends on the shape of the supply and demand curves. Consumers lose surplus from trades that no longer take place. But for the trades that still do take place, consumers gain surplus from paying $0.25 instead of $0.50 (while producers lose the same amount of surplus from receiving the lower price).

deadweight loss a loss of total surplus that occurs because the quantity of a good that is bought and sold is below the market equilibrium quantity

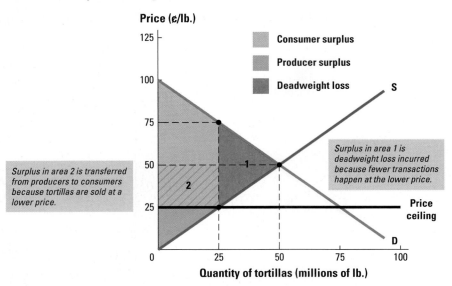

FIGURE 6-2
Welfare effects of a price ceiling

Price (¢/lb.)

- Consumer surplus
- Producer surplus
- Deadweight loss

Surplus in area 2 is transferred from producers to consumers because tortillas are sold at a lower price.

Surplus in area 1 is deadweight loss incurred because fewer transactions happen at the lower price.

Price ceiling

S

D

Quantity of tortillas (millions of lb.)

The price ceiling causes the total quantity of tortillas traded to fall by 25 million relative to equilibrium. This results in deadweight loss. The price ceiling also causes surplus to be transferred from producers to consumers: Consumers win because they pay a lower price, and producers lose because they sell at a lower price.

This direct transfer of surplus from producers to consumers is represented by area 2 in Figure 6-2. The fact that area 2 is larger than half of area 1 (the portion of deadweight loss that would have gone to consumers at equilibrium) represents the goal the price ceiling was intended to achieve: a net increase in the well-being of consumers. Was the policy worthwhile? On the one hand, consumers gained surplus. On the other hand, the surplus lost by producers was greater than that gained by consumers, meaning that total surplus decreased. Is it a price worth paying? That is a normative question about which reasonable people can disagree.

Another factor we may want to consider in our overall analysis of the price ceiling is how the scarce tortillas are allocated. Because a price ceiling causes a shortage, goods must be rationed. This could be done in a number of ways. One possibility is for goods to be rationed equally, with each family entitled to buy the same amount of tortillas per week. This is what happened when food was rationed in the United States during World War II.

Another possibility is to allocate goods on a first-come, first-served basis. This forces people to waste time standing in lines. In still other cases, rationed goods might go to those who are given preference by the government, or to the friends and family of sellers. Finally, shortages open the door for people to bribe whoever is in charge of allocating scarce supplies, which would mean even more deadweight loss than in the example shown in Figure 6-2. Economists call this *rent-seeking behavior,* and it is often cited as an argument against imposing price ceilings.

Price ceilings are sometimes used with noble intentions. The What Do You Think? box "Put a cap on payday lending?" asks you to weigh the costs and benefits of a controversial price ceiling on the interest rates of payday loans.

WHAT DO YOU THINK?

Put a cap on payday lending?

After the global financial crisis that began in 2008, policy-makers considered many proposals to reform financial practices. Small loans to consumers got a lot of attention, as some people felt that irresponsible borrowing—through credit cards, mortgages, and consumer loans—was in part to blame for the crisis.

One of the most controversial types of borrowing is the *payday loan,* a short-term cash loan—usually for less than $1,000—that is intended to be repaid with the borrower's next paycheck. Many borrowers like these loans because they can walk out of the loan center with cash in their pockets in 30 minutes or less. Because payday loans are often used by people with poor credit, lenders often charge high fees or interest rates (reflecting the higher risk of loan default). Payday loan centers tend to be located in low-income neighborhoods, where people have few other options for borrowing.

In 2008, the U.S. Congress considered putting a price ceiling of 36 percent per year on the interest rates lenders could charge for payday loans. Since the interest rate is effectively the "price" of taking out a loan, this measure amounted to a price ceiling on a certain sort of loan service. Supporters of the proposed price ceiling argued that limiting interest rates would protect vulnerable consumers from "predatory" lenders who offer loans people can't afford, thus trapping borrowers in a cycle of taking out loans simply to repay prior loans.

Critics of the price ceiling countered that capping interest rates would force many payday lenders out of business. People who make informed decisions to take out payday loans would be hurt by the resulting loss of credit. Those borrowers who have no other options could be driven to stop paying their bills or to overdraw their checking accounts. Building up debt and penalties in these ways, critics argued, could be even more expensive than a payday loan.

As we write this book, 15 states have banned payday loans or set a ceiling on the interest rates that are charged for them. In 2008, for example, Ohio capped payday loan rates at 28 percent per year. Other states still allow less restricted payday loans. In Missouri, lenders can charge up to 75 percent over a short loan period. You can learn about short-term loan regulations in your state by visiting http://www.payday loaninfo.org/state-information.

What do you think?

1. An Internet search for *payday loan* turns up dozens of websites that promise "instant," "easy," or "no hassle" loans. What's the cheapest rate you can find in your state? Would you consider borrowing at this price?
2. Price ceilings hold down prices, but also cause shortages and transfer surplus from payday-loan store owners to borrowers. Knowing that, would you support a cap on payday loan interest rates?
3. What would you expect the outcome of such a policy to be for buyers (borrowers) and sellers (lenders)?
4. Can you think of a way to protect potential victims of high interest rates without hurting borrowers who make informed borrowing decisions?

Source: "Payday loan consumer information," Consumer Federation of America's PayDay Loan website, http://www.paydayloaninfo.org.

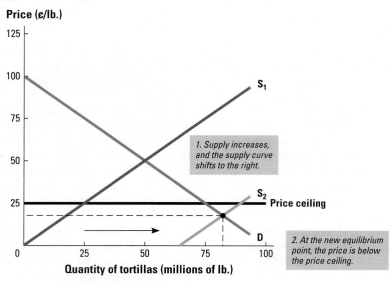

FIGURE 6-3

Nonbinding price ceiling

Price (¢/lb.)

1. Supply increases, and the supply curve shifts to the right.

S₁

S₂

Price ceiling

2. At the new equilibrium point, the price is below the price ceiling.

D

Quantity of tortillas (millions of lb.)

A price ceiling is intended to keep prices below the equilibrium level. However, changes in the market can reduce the equilibrium price to a level below the price ceiling. When that happens, the price ceiling no longer creates a shortage, because the quantity supplied equals the quantity demanded.

A price ceiling does not always affect the market outcome. If the ceiling is set above the equilibrium price in a market, it is said to be *nonbinding*. That is, the ceiling doesn't "bind" or restrict buyers' and sellers' behavior because the current equilibrium is within the range allowed by the ceiling. In such cases, the equilibrium price and quantity will prevail.

Although price ceilings are usually binding when they are first implemented (otherwise, why bother to create one?), shifts in the market over time can render the ceilings nonbinding. Suppose the price of corn decreases, reducing the cost of making tortillas. Figure 6-3 shows how the supply curve for tortillas would shift to the right in response to this change in the market, causing the equilibrium price to fall below the price ceiling. The new equilibrium is 80 million pounds of tortillas at $0.20 a pound, and the price ceiling becomes nonbinding.

Price floors

LO 6.2 Calculate the effect of a price floor on the equilibrium price and quantity.

price floor a minimum legal price at which a good can be sold

A **price floor** is a minimum legal price at which a good can be sold. The United States has a long history of establishing price floors for certain agricultural goods. The rationale is that farming is a risky business—subject to bad weather, crop failure, and unreliable prices—but also an essential one, if people are to have enough to eat. A price floor is seen as a way to guarantee farmers a minimum income in the face of these difficulties, keeping them in business and ensuring a reliable supply of food.

The United States has maintained price floors for dairy products for over 60 years; the Milk Price Support Program began with the Agricultural Act of 1949. What effect has this program had on the market for milk? In panel A of Figure 6-4, we show a hypothetical unregulated market for milk in the United States, with an annual equilibrium quantity of 15 billion gallons and an equilibrium price of $2.50 per gallon.

Now suppose the U.S. government implements a price floor, so that the price of milk cannot fall below $3 per gallon, as shown in panel B of Figure 6-4. *How will producers and consumers respond?* At $3 per gallon, dairy farmers will want to increase milk production from 15 to 20 billion gallons, moving up along the supply curve. At that price, however, consumers will want to *decrease* their milk consumption from 15 to 10 billion gallons, moving up along the demand curve. As a result, the price floor creates an excess supply of milk that is equal to the difference between the quantity supplied and the quantity demanded—in this case, 10 billion gallons.

Has the government accomplished its aim of supporting dairy farmers and providing them with a reliable income? As with price ceilings, the answer is yes and no. Producers who can sell all their milk will be happy, because they are selling more milk at a higher price. However, producers who cannot sell all their milk because demand no longer meets supply will be unhappy. Consumers will be unhappy because they are getting less milk at a higher price.

Again, we can apply the concept of surplus to formally analyze how this change in total surplus is distributed between consumers and producers. Before the price floor, 15 billion gallons of milk were sold and bought; afterward, only 10 billion. Five billion gallons of milk that could have been traded were not, reducing total surplus. This dead-weight loss is represented by area 1 in Figure 6-5.

FIGURE 6-4

A market with and without a price floor

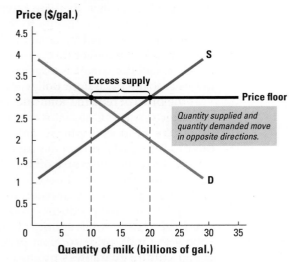

(A) Market without price floor

Price ($/gal.)

Without government intervention, the equilibrium point in the market for milk would be 15 billion gallons at a price of $2.50 per gallon.

(B) Market with price floor

Price ($/gal.)

Excess supply

Price floor

Quantity supplied and quantity demanded move in opposite directions.

A price floor raises the price of milk above the equilibrium point. At the new price of $3 per gallon, consumers want to buy less than suppliers want to produce, resulting in a 10 billion-gallon surplus.

Quantity of milk (billions of gal.)

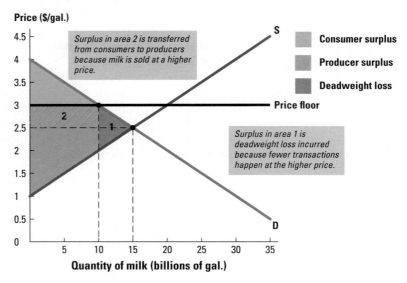

FIGURE 6-5

Welfare effects of a price floor

Price ($/gal.)

Surplus in area 2 is transferred from consumers to producers because milk is sold at a higher price.

Surplus in area 1 is deadweight loss incurred because fewer transactions happen at the higher price.

Price floor

Consumer surplus

Producer surplus

Deadweight loss

Quantity of milk (billions of gal.)

The price floor causes the total quantity of milk traded to fall by 5 billion gallons relative to equilibrium. This results in deadweight loss. The price floor also causes surplus to be transferred from consumers to producers: In this example, producers win because they sell at a higher price, and consumers lose because they pay a higher price.

Like price ceilings, price floors change the distribution of surplus, but in this case producers win at the expense of consumers. When the price floor is in effect, the only consumers who buy are those whose willingness to pay is above $3. Their consumer surplus falls, because they are buying the same milk at a higher price, and their lost surplus is transferred directly to the producers who sell milk to them. This transfer of surplus is represented by area 2 in Figure 6-5. Whether producers gain or lose overall will depend on whether this area is bigger or smaller than their share of the deadweight loss. The fact that area 2 is larger than the section of area 1 lost to producers shows that in this case the price floor policy increased well-being for producers.

Is the price of reduced total and consumer surplus worth paying to achieve increased producer surplus? One factor to consider is how the extra surplus is distributed among producers. Producers who are able to sell all their milk at the higher price will be happy. But producers who do not manage to sell all of their goods will be left holding an excess supply. They may be worse off than before the imposition of the price floor. With excess supply, customers may choose to buy from firms they like based on familiarity, political preference, or any other decision-making process they choose.

To prevent some producers from being left in the lurch, the government may decide to buy up all the excess supply of milk, ensuring that *all* producers benefit. In fact, that is how the milk price support program works in the United States. The Department of Agriculture guarantees producers that it will buy milk at a certain price, regardless of the market price. Of course, paying for the milk imposes a cost on taxpayers and is often cited as an argument against price floors. How much milk will the government have to buy? The answer is the entire amount of the excess supply created by the price floor. In the case of the hypothetical milk price floor, the government will have to buy

FIGURE 6-6

Nonbinding price floor

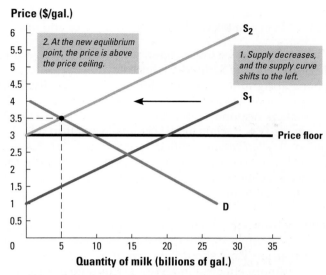

Price ($/gal.)

2. At the new equilibrium point, the price is above the price ceiling.

1. Supply decreases, and the supply curve shifts to the left.

S_2

S_1

Price floor

D

Quantity of milk (billions of gal.)

Although a price floor is usually set so as to raise prices above the equilibrium level, changes in the supply can raise the equilibrium price above the price floor. When that happens, the surplus that was created by the price floor disappears, and the quantity supplied equals the quantity demanded.

10 billion gallons at a price of $3. The cost to taxpayers of maintaining the price floor in this example would be $30 billion each year.

Price floors are not always binding. In fact, in recent years, the market prices for dairy products in the United States have usually been above the price floor. The price floor may become binding, however, in response to changes in the market. Consider the effect of the increased demand for ethanol in 2007 on the market for milk. Ethanol is a fuel additive made from corn. The sudden rise in demand for ethanol pushed up the price of corn, which in turn pushed up the cost of livestock feed for dairy farmers. As a result, the supply curve for milk shifted to the left, pushing the equilibrium price for milk above the $3 price floor to $3.50. Figure 6-6 shows how such a decrease in supply could render a price floor nonbinding.

✓CONCEPT CHECK

❑ Why does a price ceiling cause a shortage? **[LO 6.1]**

❑ What can cause a price ceiling to become nonbinding? **[LO 6.1]**

❑ Explain how a government can support a price floor through purchases. **[LO 6.2]**

Taxes and Subsidies

Taxes are the main way that governments raise revenue to pay for public programs. Taxes and subsidies can also be used to correct market failures and encourage or discourage production and consumption of particular goods. As we will see, like price floors and price ceilings, they can have unintended consequences.

Taxes

LO 6.3 Calculate the effect of a tax on the equilibrium price and quantity.

We began this chapter by discussing hunger, which is usually a minor problem in wealthy countries. Indeed, the United States has the opposite problem: diseases associated with overeating and poor nutrition, such as obesity, heart disease, and diabetes.

How can policy-makers respond to this new type of food crisis? In 2008, the state of California banned the use of trans fats in restaurants in an effort to reduce heart disease and related problems. Trans fats are artificially produced ("partially hydrogenated") unsaturated fats. Used in many fried and packaged foods because they extend products' shelf lives, they are believed to be unhealthy if consumed in excess. For decades, trans fats have been the key to making commercially produced french fries crispy and pastries flaky.

Rather than banning trans fats, what would happen if California taxed them? When a good is taxed, either the buyer or seller must pay some extra amount to the government on top of the sale price. How should we expect people to *respond* to a tax on trans fats? Taxes have two primary effects. First, they discourage production and consumption of the good that is taxed. Second, they raise government revenue through the fees paid by those who continue buying and selling the good. Therefore, we would expect a tax both to reduce consumption of trans fats and to provide a new source of public revenue.

Figure 6-7 illustrates this scenario by showing the impact of a trans-fat tax on the market for Chocolate Whizbangs. A delicious imaginary candy, Chocolate Whizbangs are unfortunately rather high in trans fats. Suppose that, currently, 30 million Whizbangs are sold every year, at $0.50 each.

A tax on sellers. Let's say that the government of California enacts a trans-fat tax of $0.20, which the seller must pay for every Whizbang sold. *How will buyers and sellers respond?* The impact of a tax is more complicated than the impact of a price control, so let's take it one step at a time.

1. **Does a tax on sellers affect supply?** *Yes, supply decreases.*

    When a tax is imposed on sellers, they must pay the government $0.20 for each Whizbang sold. At any market price, sellers will behave as if the price they are receiving is actually $0.20 lower. Put another way, for sellers to be willing to supply any given quantity, the market price must be $0.20 higher than it was before the tax.

    Figure 6-7 shows this change in supply graphically, by adding a new supply curve (S_2). (Technically, this "shift" isn't really a shift of the curve, but a way of showing the new equilibrium price; see the nearby Potentially Confusing box.) Note that the new supply curve is $0.20 higher, the exact amount of the tax. At any given market price, sellers will now produce the same quantity as they would have at a price $0.20 lower before the tax. At $0.60 on curve S_2, the quantity supplied will be the same as at a price of $0.40 on curve S_1. At a price of $0.50 on curve S_2, the quantity supplied will be the same as at a price of $0.30 on curve S_1, and so on.

2. **Does a tax on sellers affect demand?** *No, demand stays the same.*

    Demand remains the same because the tax does not change any of the non-price determinants of demand. At any given price, buyers' desire to purchase Whizbangs is unchanged. Remember, however, that the *quantity demanded* may still change—does change, in fact—although the curve itself doesn't change.

FIGURE 6-7

Effect of a tax paid by the seller

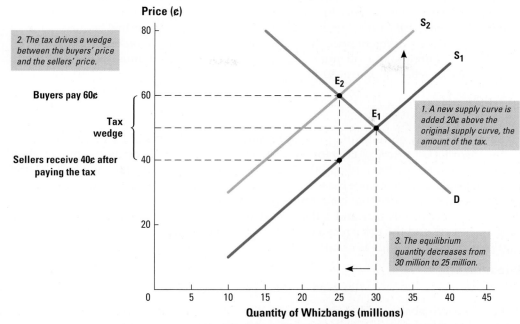

2. The tax drives a wedge between the buyers' price and the sellers' price.

Buyers pay 60¢

Tax wedge

Sellers receive 40¢ after paying the tax

1. A new supply curve is added 20¢ above the original supply curve, the amount of the tax.

3. The equilibrium quantity decreases from 30 million to 25 million.

A tax levied on the seller adds a new supply curve that is 20 cents higher than the original, which is the amount of the tax. As a result, the equilibrium quantity decreases and the equilibrium price increases. At the equilibrium quantity, the price paid by buyers is now different from the amount received by sellers after the tax is paid. This "tax wedge" is equal to the amount of the tax, or 20 cents.

3. **How does a tax on sellers affect the market equilibrium?** *The equilibrium price rises, and quantity demanded falls.*

   The new supply curve causes the equilibrium point to move up along the demand curve. At the new equilibrium point, the price paid by the buyer is $0.60. Because buyers now face a higher price, they demand fewer Whizbangs, so the quantity demanded falls from 30 million to 25 million. Notice that at the new equilibrium point, the quantity demanded is lower and the price is higher. Taxes usually reduce the quantity of a good or service that is sold, shrinking the market.

POTENTIALLY CONFUSING

In Chapter 3, "Markets," we distinguished between a curve *shifting* to the left or right and *movement along* the same curve. A shift represents a fundamental change in the quantity demanded or supplied at any given price; a movement along the same curve simply shows a switch to a different quantity and price point. Does a tax cause a *shift* of the demand or supply curve or a *movement along* the curve?

The answer is neither, really. Here's why: When we add a tax, we're not really shifting the curve; rather, we are adding a second curve. The original curve is still needed to understand what is happening. This is because the price that sellers receive is actually $0.20 lower than the price at which they sell Whizbangs, due to the tax. So we need one curve to represent what sellers receive and another curve to represent what buyers pay. Notice in Figure 6-7 that the price suppliers receive is on the original supply curve, S_1, but the price buyers pay is on the new supply curve, S_2. The original curve *does not actually move,* but we add the second curve to indicate that because of the tax, buyers face a different price than what the sellers will get. In order for the market to be in equilibrium, the quantity that buyers demand at $0.60 must now equal the quantity that sellers supply at $0.40.

Look at the new equilibrium price in Figure 6-7. The price paid by buyers to sellers is the new market price, $0.60. However, sellers do not get to keep all the money they receive. Instead, they have to pay the tax to the government. Since the tax is $0.20, the price that sellers receive once they have paid the tax is only $0.40. Ultimately, sellers do not receive the full price that consumers pay, because the tax creates what is known as a *tax wedge* between buyers and sellers. A **tax wedge** is the difference between the price paid by buyers and the price received by sellers, which equals the amount of the tax. In Figure 6-7, the tax wedge is calculated as shown in Equation 6-1.

tax wedge the difference between the price paid by buyers and the price received by sellers in the presence of a tax

Equation 6-1

$$\text{Tax wedge} = P_{buyers} - P_{sellers} = \text{Tax}$$

For each Whizbang sold at the new equilibrium point, the government collects tax revenue, as calculated in Equation 6-2. Specifically, the government receives $0.20 for each of the 25 million Whizbangs sold, or $5 million total. Graphically, the government revenue equals the green-shaded area in Figure 6-8.

Equation 6-2

$$\text{Government tax revenue} = \text{Tax} \times Q_{post\text{-}tax}$$

Just like a price control, a tax causes deadweight loss and redistributes surplus. We can see the deadweight loss caused by the reduced number of trades in Figure 6-8. It is surplus lost to buyers and sellers who would have been willing to make trades at the pre-tax equilibrium price.

The redistribution of surplus, however, is a little trickier to follow. Under a tax, *both* producers and consumers lose surplus. Consumers who still buy pay more for the same candy than they would have under equilibrium, and producers who still sell receive less for the same candy. The difference between this lost surplus and deadweight loss, however, is that it doesn't "disappear." Instead, it becomes government revenue. In fact, the area representing government revenue in Figure 6-8 is exactly the same as the surplus lost to buyers and sellers still trading in the market after the tax has been imposed. This revenue can pay for services that might transfer surplus back to producers or consumers, or both, or to people outside of the market.

A tax on buyers. What happens if the tax is imposed on buyers instead of sellers? Surprisingly, the outcome is exactly the same. Suppose California enacts a sales tax of $0.20, which the buyer must pay for every Whizbang bought. In this case the demand curve, rather than the supply curve, moves by the amount of the tax, but the resulting equilibrium price and quantity are the same (see Figure 6-9).

To double-check this result, let's walk step by step through the effect of a tax levied on buyers.

1. **Does a tax on buyers affect the supply curve?** *No, supply stays the same.*

    The supply curve stays the same because the tax does not change the incentives producers face. None of the nonprice determinants of supply are affected.

FIGURE 6-8

Government revenue and deadweight loss from a tax

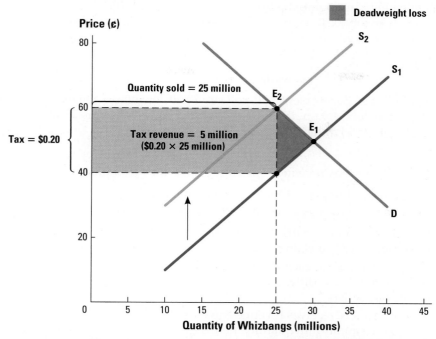

The revenue from a per-unit tax is the amount of the tax multiplied by the number of units sold at the post-tax equilibrium point. The amount of tax revenue directly corresponds to the surplus lost to consumers and producers. The trades that no longer happen under the tax represent deadweight loss.

2. **Does a tax on buyers affect the demand curve?** *Yes, demand decreases.*

   Demand decreases because the price buyers must pay per unit, including the tax, is now $0.20 higher than the original price. As Figure 6-9 shows, we take the original demand curve D_1 and factor in the amount of the tax to get a second demand curve D_2, which represents the price buyers pay under the tax. At any given price, buyers will now behave as if the price were actually $0.20 higher. For example, at $0.40 on curve D_2, the quantity demanded is as if the price were $0.60 on curve D_1. At $0.30 on curve D_2, the quantity demanded is as if the price were $0.50.

3. **How does a tax on buyers affect the market equilibrium?** *The equilibrium price and quantity both fall.*

   As a result, the equilibrium point with the new demand curve is further down the supply curve. The equilibrium price falls from $0.50 to $0.40, and the quantity demanded and supplied falls from 30 million to 25 million. Although the market equilibrium price goes down instead of up, as it does with a tax on sellers, the actual amount that buyers and sellers pay is the same no matter who pays the tax. When buyers pay the tax, they pay $0.40 to the seller and $0.20 to the government, or a total of $0.60. When sellers pay the tax, buyers pay $0.60 to the seller, who then pays $0.20 to the government. Either way, buyers pay $0.60 and sellers receive $0.40.

As Figure 6-9 shows, a tax on buyers creates a tax wedge just as a tax on sellers does. At the new equilibrium point, the price sellers receive is $0.40. The buyer pays $0.40 to the seller and then the $0.20 tax to the government, so that the total effective price is $0.60. Once again, the tax wedge is $0.20, exactly equal to the amount of the tax.

Equation 6-3

$$\text{Tax wedge} = \$0.60 - \$0.40 = \$0.20$$

Furthermore, the government still collects $0.20 for every Whizbang sold, just as under a tax on sellers. Again, the post-tax equilibrium quantity is 25 million, and the government collects $5 million in tax revenue.

Equation 6-4

$$\text{Tax revenue} = \$0.20 \times 25 \text{ million} = \$5 \text{ million}$$

What is the overall impact of the tax on Whizbangs? Regardless of whether a tax is imposed on buyers or sellers, there are four effects that result from all taxes:

1. Equilibrium quantity falls. The goal of the tax has thus been achieved— consumption of Whizbangs has been discouraged.
2. Buyers pay more for each Whizbang and sellers receive less. This creates a tax wedge, equal to the difference between the price paid by buyers and the price received by sellers.
3. The government receives revenue equal to the amount of the tax multiplied by the new equilibrium quantity. In this case, the California state government

FIGURE 6-9

Effect of a tax paid by the buyer

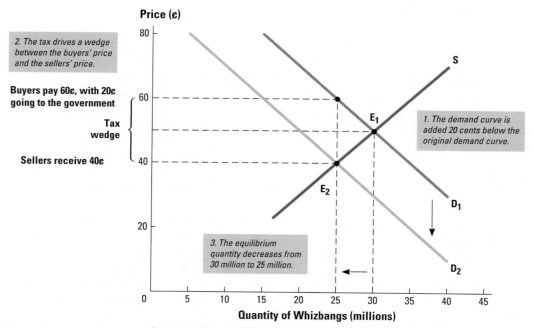

A tax levied on the buyer adds a new demand curve 20 cents below the original curve. As a result, the equilibrium quantity decreases and the equilibrium price paid by the buyer increases. These results are the same as those of a tax levied on the seller.

receives an additional $5 million in revenue from the tax on Whizbangs—which could be used to offset the public health expenses caused by obesity-related diseases.

4. The tax causes deadweight loss. This means that the value of the revenue the government collects is always less than the reduction in total surplus caused by the tax.

In evaluating a tax, then, we must weigh its goal—in this case, reducing the consumption of trans fats—against the loss of surplus in the market.

Who bears the burden of a tax? We've seen that the outcome of a tax does not depend on who pays it. Whether a tax is levied on buyers or on sellers, the cost is shared. But which group bears more of the burden?

In our example, the burden was shared equally. Buyers paid $0.50 for a Whizbang before the tax; after the tax, they pay $0.60. Therefore, buyers bear $0.10 of the $0.20 tax burden. Sellers received $0.50 for each Whizbang before the tax; after the tax, they receive $0.40. Therefore, sellers also bear $0.10 of the $0.20 tax burden. The shaded rectangles in panel A of Figure 6-10 represent graphically this 50 – 50 split.

Often, however, the tax burden is not split equally. Sometimes one group carries much more of it than the other. Compare the example just given to another possible market for Whizbangs, represented in panel B of Figure 6-10. In this case, buyers paid $0.50 before the tax. After the tax, they pay $0.54, so their tax burden is $0.04 per Whizbang. Sellers, on the other hand, receive only $0.34 after the tax, so their tax burden, at $0.16 per Whizbang, is four times as large as that of buyers. Panel C shows the opposite

FIGURE 6-10

Tax incidence and relative elasticity

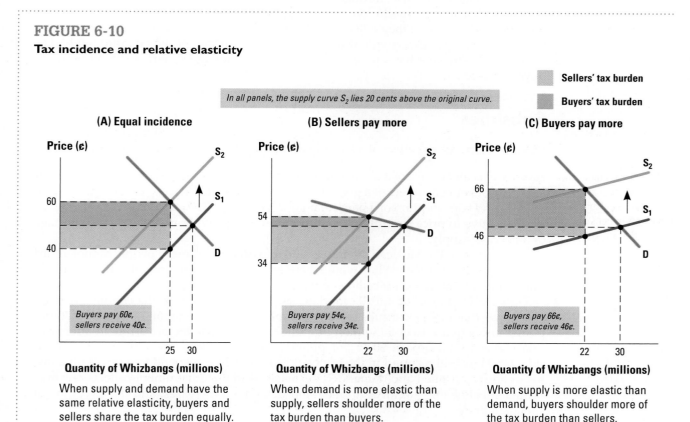

In all panels, the supply curve S₂ lies 20 cents above the original curve.

Sellers' tax burden
Buyers' tax burden

(A) Equal incidence

When supply and demand have the same relative elasticity, buyers and sellers share the tax burden equally.

(B) Sellers pay more

When demand is more elastic than supply, sellers shoulder more of the tax burden than buyers.

(C) Buyers pay more

When supply is more elastic than demand, buyers shoulder more of the tax burden than sellers.

tax incidence the
relative tax burden
borne by buyers and
sellers

case, in which buyers bear more of the burden than sellers. Thus, buyers pay $0.66 and sellers receive $0.48. The relative tax burden borne by buyers and sellers is called the **tax incidence**.

What determines the incidence of a tax? The answer has to do with the relative elasticity of the supply and demand curves. Recall from Chapter 4 that price elasticity describes how much the quantity supplied or demanded changes in response to a change in price. Since a tax effectively changes the price of a good to both buyers and sellers, the relative responsiveness of supply and demand will determine the tax burden. Essentially, the side of the market that is more price elastic will be more able to adjust to price changes and will shoulder less of the tax burden.

Panel B of Figure 6-10 imagines a market in which demand is more elastic: Many consumers easily give up their Whizbang habit and buy healthier snacks instead. In that case, Whizbang producers pay a higher share of the tax. Panel C imagines a market in which demand is less elastic: Consumers are so obsessed with Whizbangs that they will buy even at the higher price. In that case, buyers pay a higher share of the tax.

Recall that the market outcome of a tax—the new equilibrium quantity and price—is the same regardless of whether a tax is imposed on buyers or on sellers. Thus, the tax burden will be the same no matter which side of the market is taxed. Note in panel C of Figure 6-10 that buyers bear the greater part of that burden, even though the tax is imposed on sellers. The actual economic incidence of a tax is unrelated to the "statutory incidence"—that is, the person who is legally responsible for paying the tax.

This is an important point to remember during public debates about taxes. A politician may say that companies that pollute should be held accountable for the environmental damage they cause, through a tax on pollution. Regardless of how you may feel about the idea of taxing pollution, remember that levying the tax on companies that pollute does not mean that they will end up bearing the whole tax burden. Consumers who buy from those producers will also bear part of the burden of the tax, through higher prices. Policy-makers have little control over how the tax burden is shared between buyers and sellers.

Subsidies

LO 6.4 Calculate the effect of a subsidy on the equilibrium price and quantity.

subsidy a requirement
that the government
pay an extra amount to
producers or consumers
of a good

A **subsidy** is the reverse of a tax: a requirement that the government pay an extra amount to producers or consumers of a good. Governments use subsidies to encourage the production and consumption of a particular good or service. They can also use subsidies as an alternative to price controls to benefit certain groups without generating a shortage or an excess supply.

Let's return to the Mexican dilemma—what to do when hungry people cannot afford to buy enough tortillas. What would happen if the government subsidized tortillas rather than imposed a price ceiling on them?

Figure 6-11 shows the tortilla market we discussed earlier in the chapter. The figure shows that before the subsidy, the market is in equilibrium at a price of $0.70 per pound and a quantity of 50 million pounds. Now suppose the government offers tortilla makers a subsidy of $0.35 per pound. *How will buyers and sellers respond to the subsidy?* They will respond in the opposite way that they respond to a tax: With a tax, the quantity supplied and demanded decreases, and the government collects revenue. With a subsidy, the quantity supplied and demanded increases, and the government spends money.

FIGURE 6-11

Effect of a subsidy to the seller

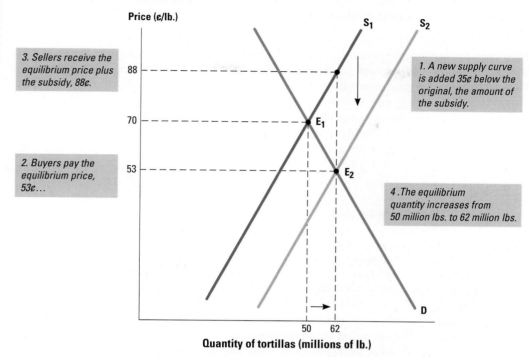

A subsidy has the opposite effect of a tax. A new supply curve
is added 35 cents below the original supply curve. This decreases
the equilibrium price and increases the equilibrium quantity
supplied and demanded.

We can calculate the effect of a $0.35 tortilla subsidy by walking through the same three steps we used to examine the effect of a tax.

1. **Does a subsidy to sellers affect the supply curve?** *Yes, supply increases.*

   When producers receive a subsidy, the real price they receive for each unit sold is higher than the market price. At any market price, therefore, they will behave as if the price were $0.35 higher. Put another way, for sellers to supply a given quantity, the market price can be $0.35 lower than it would have to be without the subsidy. As a result, the new supply curve is drawn $0.35 below the original. In Figure 6-11, S_2 shows the new supply curve that is the result of the subsidy.

2. **Does a subsidy to sellers affect the demand curve?** *No, demand stays the same.*

   The demand curve stays where it is, because consumers are not directly affected by the subsidy.

3. **How does a subsidy to sellers affect the market equilibrium?** *The equilibrium price decreases and the equilibrium quantity increases.*

   The equilibrium quantity with the new supply curve increases as consumers move down along the demand curve to the new equilibrium point. At the new, post-subsidy equilibrium, the quantity supplied increases from 50 million pounds of tortillas to 62 million pounds. As with a tax, the price buyers pay for tortillas differs from the price sellers receive after the subsidy, because the subsidy creates a wedge between the two prices. This time, however, sellers receive a *higher* price than the pre-subsidy equilibrium of $0.70, and buyers pay

141

a *lower* one. Buyers pay $0.53 per pound and sellers receive $0.88 per pound. The government pays the $0.35 difference.

A subsidy benefits both buyers and sellers, increasing total surplus *within* the market. However, the subsidy imposes a cost on the government, and ultimately on taxpayers. In this example, the government must pay $0.35 for each of the 62 million pounds of tortillas produced, for a total expenditure of $21.7 million. Is the subsidy worth the cost? That depends on how much we value the increased production of tortillas and the reduced cost to consumers versus the opportunity cost of the subsidy—that is, whatever other use the government or taxpayers might have made of that $21.7 million. And as the Real Life box "The unintended consequences of biofuel subsidies" shows, the obvious benefits of a subsidy can sometimes be swamped by unexpected costs.

REAL LIFE

The unintended consequences of biofuel subsidies

The United States subsidizes the production of "biofuels" such as ethanol, a cleaner fuel than gasoline. The professed goal of the subsidy is to reduce pollution—and as hoped, the subsidy has caused a huge increase in the production of ethanol. Unfortunately, it has also had some unintended effects. In *Time* magazine, Michael Grunwald argues that, indirectly, biofuels can actually increase pollution:

> [T]he basic problem with most biofuels is amazingly simple, given that researchers have ignored it until now: using land to grow fuel leads to the destruction of forests, wetlands and grasslands that store enormous amounts of carbon. . . . More deforestation results from a chain reaction so vast it's subtle: U.S. farmers are selling one-fifth of their corn to ethanol production, so U.S. soybean farmers are switching to corn, so Brazilian soybean farmers are expanding into cattle pastures, so Brazilian cattlemen are displaced to the Amazon.

Through a complex chain of market reactions that policy-makers probably didn't anticipate, Grunwald argues, ethanol subsidies are having the opposite of the hoped-for reduction in air pollution. Unfortunately, unintended consequences aren't always just a postscript to market interventions. Sometimes, they can change the whole story.

Source: M. Grunwald, "The clean energy scam," *Time,* March 27, 2008, http://www.time.com/time/magazine/article/0,9171,1725975,00.html. The *New York Times* had a follow-up in its environmental blog: http://green.blogs.nytimes.com/2008/11/03/the-biofuel-debate-good-bad-or-too-soon-to-tell/.

As with a tax, the effect of a subsidy is the same regardless of whether it is paid to producers or consumers. If consumers received a $0.35 subsidy for every pound of tortillas they bought, their demand curve would be $0.35 above the original, the supply curve would remain unchanged, and the equilibrium outcome would be the same as if producers received the subsidy: Quantity increases from 50 million pounds to 62 million pounds, buyers pay $0.53 per pound, and sellers receive $0.88.

Also as with a tax, the way in which the benefits of a subsidy are split between buyers and sellers depends on the relative elasticity of the demand and supply curves. The side of the market that is more price elastic receives more of the benefit. In our example, both have almost the same benefit: Buyers are better off by $0.17 per pound of tortillas, and producers by $0.18. As with taxes, it is important to note that who gets what share of benefit from the subsidy does not depend on who receives the subsidy. Sometimes in debates about subsidies you will hear someone argue that a subsidy should be given either to buyers or sellers because they deserve it more. This argument doesn't make much sense in a competitive market (although it might in a noncompetitive market).

In sum, a subsidy has the following effects, regardless of whether it is paid to buyers or sellers:

1.   Equilibrium quantity increases, accomplishing the goal of encouraging production and consumption of the subsidized good.
2.   Buyers pay less and sellers receive more for each unit sold. The amount of the subsidy forms a wedge between buyers' and sellers' prices.
3.   The government has to pay for the subsidy, the cost of which equals the amount of the subsidy multiplied by the new equilibrium quantity.

✓ CONCEPT CHECK

❑ What is a tax wedge? **[LO 6.3]**

❑ How does a subsidy affect the equilibrium quantity? How does it affect the price that sellers receive and the price that buyers pay? **[LO 6.4]**

❑ Does it matter whether a subsidy is paid to buyers or sellers? Why or why not? **[LO 6.4]**

Evaluating Government Interventions

LO 6.5 Explain how elasticity and time period influence the impact of a market intervention.

We began this chapter with a discussion of three reasons why policy-makers might decide to intervene in a market. To decide whether policy-makers have achieved their goals by implementing a price control, tax, or subsidy, we need to assess the effects of each intervention, including its unintended consequences.

We've established a few rules about the expected outcomes of market interventions. Table 6-1 summarizes the key effects of price controls, taxes, and subsidies. In general, we can say the following:

•   Price controls have opposing impacts on the quantities supplied and demanded, causing a shortage or excess supply. In contrast, taxes and subsidies move the quantities supplied and demanded in the same direction, allowing the market to reach equilibrium at the point where the quantity supplied equals the quantity demanded.
•   Taxes discourage people from buying and selling a particular good, raise government revenue, and impose a cost on both buyers and sellers.
•   Subsidies encourage people to buy and sell a particular good, cost the government money, and provide a benefit to both buyers and sellers.

In the following sections we will consider some of the more complicated details of market interventions. These details matter. Often the details of an intervention make the difference between a successful policy and a failed one.

How big is the effect of a tax or subsidy?

Regardless of the reason for a market intervention, it's important to know exactly *how much* it will change the equilibrium quantity and price. Can the effect of a tax or subsidy on the equilibrium quantity be predicted ahead of time? The answer is yes, if we know the price elasticity of supply and demand. The more elastic supply or demand is, the greater the change in quantity. This rule follows directly from the definition of price elasticity, which measures buyers' and sellers' responsiveness to a change in price—and a tax or subsidy is effectively a change in price.

TABLE 6-1 Government interventions: a summary

Intervention	Reason for using	Effect on price	Effect on quantity	Who gains and who loses?
Price floor	To protect producers' income	Price cannot go below the set minimum.	Quantity demanded decreases and quantity supplied increases, creating excess supply.	Producers who can sell all their goods earn more revenue per item; other producers are stuck with an unwanted excess supply.
Price ceiling	To keep consumer costs low	Price cannot go above the set maximum.	Quantity demanded increases and quantity supplied decreases, creating a shortage.	Consumers who can buy all the goods they want benefit; other consumers suffer from shortages.
Tax	To discourage an activity or collect money to pay for its consequences; to increase government revenue	Price increases.	Equilibrium quantity decreases.	Government receives increased revenue; society may gain if the tax decreases socially harmful behavior. Buyers and sellers of the good that is taxed share the cost. Which group bears more of the burden depends on the price elasticity of supply and demand.
Subsidy	To encourage an activity; to provide benefits to a certain group	Price decreases.	Equilibrium quantity increases.	Buyers purchase more goods at a lower price. Society may benefit if the subsidy encourages socially beneficial behavior. The government and ultimately the taxpayers bear the cost.

Figure 6-12 shows the effect of a $0.20 tax on the quantity demanded under four different combinations of price elasticity of supply and demand—again, for Whizbangs.

- In panel A, both supply and demand are relatively inelastic. In this case the tax causes the equilibrium quantity to decrease, but not by much. Both buyers and sellers are willing to continue trading, even though they now must pay the tax.
- In panel B, demand is more elastic than supply, so when the supply curve is $0.20 higher, the change in quantity is much larger than in panel A.
- In panel C, supply is elastic but demand is relatively inelastic. Again, because suppliers are highly responsive to the cost of the tax, the quantity changes more than in panel A.
- Finally, panel D shows what happens if supply and demand are both elastic. In this case, the quantity goes down even more than in the second and third examples.

To predict the size of the effect of a tax or subsidy, then, policy-makers need to know the price elasticity of both supply and demand. As we have seen, they can also use that information to determine who will bear more of the burden or receive more of the benefit.

If you are interested in the role of government in the economy, read the Where Can It Take You? box "Public economics" to learn more about the field.

FIGURE 6-12
Price elasticity and the effect of a $0.20 tax

(A) Inelastic supply and demand	(B) Inelastic supply and elastic demand	(C) Elastic supply and inelastic demand	(D) Elastic supply and demand
The equilibrium quantity decreases by 3 million.	*The equilibrium quantity decreases by 7 million.*	*The equilibrium quantity decreases by 4 million.*	*The equilibrium quantity decreases by 20 million.*

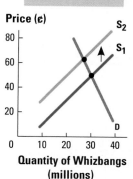
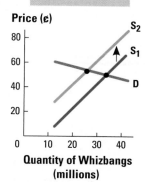
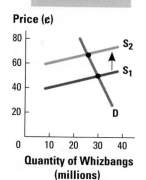
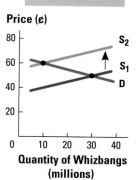

When both supply and demand are relatively price-inelastic, the equilibrium quantity does not decrease significantly because of a tax.	When supply is inelastic but demand is relatively elastic, the equilibrium quantity decreases more than it does in panel A in response to a tax.	When supply is relatively elastic compared to inelastic demand, the equilibrium quantity decreases more than it does in panel A in response to a tax.	The greatest decrease in the equilibrium quantity occurs when both demand and supply are relatively elastic; both buyers and sellers react strongly to the change in price that is caused by a tax.

WHERE CAN IT TAKE YOU?
Public economics

Are you more interested in elections and legislation than in how to run a business? If so, we hope you are beginning to realize that understanding the economics behind public policy is incredibly important. Although well-designed policies can accomplish great things, well-intentioned but poorly designed policies can backfire badly.

To learn more about the economics of public policy, consider taking a *public economics* course. We will discuss policy issues throughout this book, but there is a lot more to learn, whether you want to be a politician, an analyst at a think tank, or just an informed voter.

Long-run versus short-run impact

We have seen that in addition to changing the price of a good or service, price controls cause shortages or excess supply. Because buyers and sellers take time to respond to a change in price, sometimes the full effect of price controls becomes clear only in the long run.

Suppose the U.S. government imposed a price floor on gasoline in an attempt to reduce air pollution by discouraging people from driving. Panel A of Figure 6-13 shows the short-run impact of a price floor in the market for gasoline. Note that in the short run, the quantity of gas demanded might not change very much. Although people would cut down on unnecessary driving, the greater part of demand would still be

FIGURE 6-13

Government intervention in the long and short run

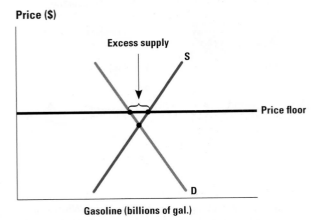

(A) Short run

In the short run, neither the supply nor the demand for gasoline is very elastic, so the effect of a price floor on the quantity supplied is relatively small.

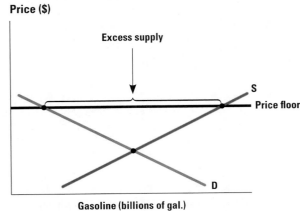

(B) Long run

In the long run, both the supply and the demand for gasoline will change in response to price controls. As a result, the long-run effect on the quantity supplied is much greater than the short-run effect.

based on driving habits that are difficult to change, such as commuting to work or going to the grocery store. And unless gasoline producers have a lot of unused oil wells sitting around, sellers might have trouble ramping up production quickly. In the short run, demand and supply are not very elastic, and the price floor results in only a small excess supply.

Recall that for both supply and demand, one of the determinants of price elasticity is the period over which it is measured. On both sides of the market, elasticity is often greater over a long period than over a short one. On the demand side, consumers might make small lifestyle changes over the medium term, such as buying a bus pass or shopping closer to home. Over the long run, they might make even bigger changes. When they need to buy a new car, for example, they will be inclined to buy a model that offers high gas mileage. If they move to a new job or home, they may place more weight than in the past on commuting distance.

Supply will also be more elastic over the long run. Because a higher price gives suppliers an incentive to produce more, they may invest in oil exploration, dig new wells, or take steps to increase the pumping capacity of existing wells. Panel B of Figure 6-13 shows the long run impact of a price floor in the market for gasoline. Because both supply and demand are more elastic in the long run than in the short run, the excess supply of gasoline is much larger in the long run than in the short run.

If the goal of the price floor was to reduce air pollution by giving consumers an incentive to cut down on driving, the impact might look disappointing in the short run: The quantity of gas burned will decrease very little. Over the long run, however, the quantity of gas burned will decrease further, and the policy will look more successful. If, on the other hand, the reason for the price floor was to support gasoline suppliers, the short-run response would look deceptively rosy, because suppliers will sell almost the same quantity of gas at a higher price. As the quantity falls over the long run, however, more producers will be stuck with an excess supply and the policy will start to look less successful.

In the European Union and the United States, farmers are given very generous subsidies. Without these subsidies, many farmers would be forced to quit farming. Critics argue that subsides distort the market by keeping prices of certain foods much higher than they would be without subsidies. Read the full debate in the What Do You Think? box "Farm subsidies."

WHAT DO YOU THINK?

Farm subsidies

Many wealthy countries spend a lot of money on price floors and subsidies that encourage domestic agricultural production. For instance, the costs associated with Europe's Common Agricultural Policy (CAP) currently account for almost half the European Union's budget, or approximately $50 billion per year.

CAP was established in 1957 with the following objectives:

1. To increase agricultural productivity by developing technical progress and by ensuring the rational development of agricultural production and the optimum utilization of the factors of production, particularly labor.
2. To ensure thereby a fair standard of living for the agricultural population, particularly by the increasing of the individual earnings of persons engaged in agriculture.
3. To stabilize markets.
4. To guarantee regular supplies.
5. To ensure reasonable prices in supplies to consumers.

Supporters believe that these are important and worthwhile policy goals. However, CAP has come under heavy criticism for many reasons. Critics say that CAP imposes a huge cost on taxpayers; creates excess supplies of crops by distorting farmers' incentives; hurts farmers in poor countries, whose produce must compete with Europe's subsidized crops; and channels public funds to big agribusinesses.

The European Union is not alone in its policies. Every year the United States Farm Bill allocates many billions of dollars to crop price supports. Japan also intervenes heavily in agricultural markets.

What do you think?

1. Do you approve of the stated objectives of Europe's Common Agricultural Policy? Which, if any, do you think merit the market distortions they may create?
2. Do wealthy nations have a responsibility to consider the impact of their agricultural policies on poorer countries, or are domestic farming interests more important?

Source: "Cap explained," European Commission website, 2009, http://ec.europa.eu/agriculture/publi/capexplained/cap_en.pdf.

✔ CONCEPT CHECK

❏ If the demand for a good is inelastic, will a tax have a large or small effect on the quantity sold? Will buyers or sellers bear more of the burden of the tax? **[LO 6.5]**
❏ Would you expect a tax on cigarettes to be more effective over the long run or the short run? Explain your reasoning. **[LO 6.5]**

Conclusion

If you listen to the news, it might seem as if economics is all about business and the stock market. Business matters, but many of the most important, challenging, and useful applications of economic principles involve public policy.

This chapter gives you the basic tools you need to understand government interventions and some of the ways they can affect your everyday life. Of course, the real world is complicated, so this isn't our last word on the topic. Later, we discuss how to evaluate the benefits of both markets and government policies. We'll also discuss market failures and whether and when governments can fix them.

 ◄ Mobile Window on the World—Scan this code with your smartphone to find more applications of the chapter content. (Need a barcode reader? Try ScanLife, available in your app store.)

Visit your mobile app store and download ► the Karlan and Morduch Study Econ app.

 Study Econ
McGraw Hill

Key Terms

market failures, p. 125

price control, p. 126

price ceiling, p. 126

deadweight loss, p. 127

price floor, p. 130

tax wedge, p. 136

tax incidence, p. 140

subsidy, p. 140

Summary

LO 6.1 Calculate the effect of a price ceiling on the equilibrium price and quantity.

Government usually intervenes in a market for one or more of the following reasons: to correct a market failure, to change the distribution of a market's benefits, or to encourage or discourage the consumption of particular goods and services. Governments may also tax goods and services in order to raise public revenues.

A price ceiling is a maximum legal price at which a good can be sold. A binding price ceiling causes a shortage, because at the legally mandated price, consumers will demand more than producers supply. This policy benefits some consumers, because they are able to buy what they want at a lower price, but other consumers are unable to find the goods they want. Producers lose out because they sell less at a lower price than they would without the price ceiling.

LO 6.2 Calculate the effect of a price floor on the equilibrium price and quantity.

A price floor is a minimum legal price at which a good can be sold. A price floor causes an excess supply, because at the minimum price, sellers will supply more than consumers demand. This policy benefits some producers, who are able to sell their goods at a

higher price, but leaves other producers with goods they can't sell. Consumers lose because they buy less at a higher price. Maintaining a price floor often requires the government to buy up the excess supply, costing taxpayers money.

LO 6.3 Calculate the effect of a tax on the equilibrium price and quantity.

A tax requires either buyers or sellers to pay some extra price to the government when a good is bought and sold. A tax shrinks the size of a market, discouraging the consumption and production of the good being taxed. The effect is the same regardless of whether the tax is levied on buyers or sellers. The tax burden is split between consumers and producers, and the government collects revenues equal to the amount of the tax times the quantity sold.

LO 6.4 Calculate the effect of a subsidy on the equilibrium price and quantity.

A subsidy is a payment that the government makes to buyers or sellers of a good for each unit that is sold. Subsidies increase the size of a market, encouraging the consumption and production of the good being subsidized. The effect is the same regardless of whether the subsidy is paid to buyers or sellers. Both consumers and producers benefit from a subsidy, but taxpayers must cover the cost.

LO 6.5 Explain how elasticity and time period influence the impact of a market intervention.

In evaluating the effects of a government intervention in the market, it is important to consider both the intended and unintended consequences of the policy. The size of the impact of a tax or subsidy and the distribution of the burden or benefit will depend on the price elasticities of supply and demand. Furthermore, the impact of a government intervention is likely to change over time, as consumers and producers adjust their behavior in response to the new incentives.

Review Questions

1. You are an advisor to the Egyptian government, which has placed a price ceiling on bread. Unfortunately, many families still cannot buy the bread they need. Explain to government officials why the price ceiling has not increased consumption of bread. **[LO 6.1]**

2. Suppose there has been a long-standing price ceiling on housing in your city. Recently, population has declined, and demand for housing has decreased. What will the decrease in demand do to the efficiency of the price ceiling? **[LO 6.1]**

3. Suppose the United States maintains a price floor for spinach. Why might this policy decrease revenues for spinach farmers? **[LO 6.2]**

4. Suppose Colombia maintains a price floor for coffee beans. What will happen to the size of the deadweight loss if the price floor encourages new growers to enter the market and produce coffee? **[LO 6.2]**

5. Many states tax cigarette purchases. Suppose that smokers are unhappy about paying the extra charge for their cigarettes. Will it help smokers if the state imposes the tax on the stores that sell the cigarettes rather than on smokers? Why or why not? **[LO 6.3]**

6. Consider a tax on cigarettes. Do you expect the tax incidence to fall more heavily on buyers or sellers of cigarettes? Why? **[LO 6.3]**

7. In the Philippines, rice production is lower than rice consumption, resulting in a need to import rice from other countries. In this situation, the Philippine government might consider subsidizing rice farmers. What are the potential benefits of such a policy? What are the costs? **[LO 6.4]**

8. A subsidy will increase consumer and producer surplus in a market and will increase the quantity of trades. Why, then, might a subsidy (such as a subsidy for producing corn in the United States) be considered inefficient? **[LO 6.4]**

9. Suppose the government imposes a price ceiling on gasoline. One month after the price ceiling, there is a shortage of gasoline, but it is much smaller than critics of the policy had warned. Explain why the critics' estimates might still be correct. **[LO 6.5]**

10. A state facing a budget shortfall decides to tax soft drinks. You are a budget analyst for the state. Do you expect to collect more revenue in the first year of the tax or in the second year? Why? **[LO 6.5]**

Problems and Applications

1. Many people are concerned about the rising price of gasoline. Suppose that government officials are thinking of capping the price of gasoline below its current price. Which of the following outcomes do you predict will result from this policy? Check all that apply. **[LO 6.1]**
   a. Drivers will purchase more gasoline.
   b. Quantity demanded for gasoline will increase.
   c. Long lines will develop at gas stations.
   d. Oil companies will work to increase their pumping capacity.

2. Figure 6P-1 shows a market in equilibrium.
   a. Draw a price ceiling at $12. What is the amount of shortage at this price? Draw and calculate the deadweight loss. **[LO 6.1]**
   b. Draw a price ceiling at $4. What is the amount of shortage at this price? Draw and calculate the deadweight loss. **[LO 6.1]**

3. Decades of overfishing have dramatically reduced the world supply of cod (a type of whitefish).

FIGURE 6P-1

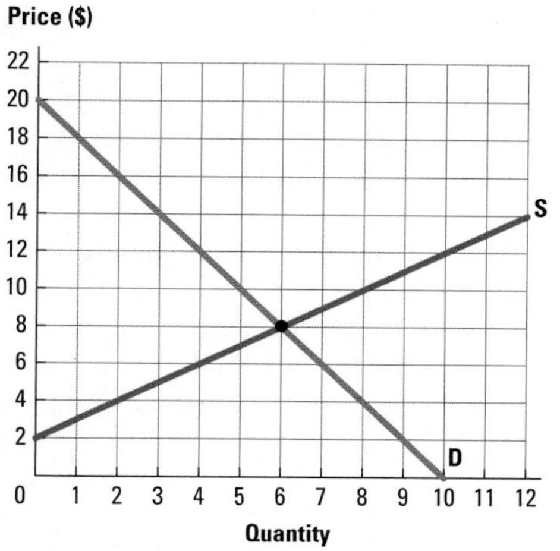

Price ($)

[Graph showing a downward-sloping demand curve (D) from (0, 20) to (10, 2) and an upward-sloping supply curve (S) from (0, 2) rising to (12, 14), intersecting at equilibrium around (6, 8). X-axis labeled Quantity from 0 to 12; Y-axis labeled Price ($) with values 2, 4, 6, 8, 10, 12, 14, 16, 18, 20, 22.]

FIGURE 6P-2

Market for farmed halibut

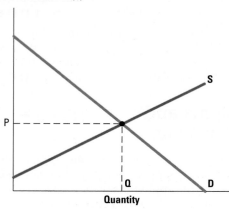

Farm-raised halibut is considered a close substitute for ocean-fished cod. **[LO 6.1]**

a. On the graph in Figure 6P-2, show the effect of overfishing cod on the market for farmed halibut.

A fast-food chain purchases whitefish for use in its Fish 'n' Chips meals. Already hurt by the reduced supply of cod, the fast-food chain has lobbied aggressively for price controls on farmed halibut. As a result, Congress has considered imposing a price ceiling on halibut at the former equilibrium price—the price that prevailed before overfishing reduced the supply of cod.

b. On your graph, show what will happen in the market for farmed halibut if Congress adopts the price control policy. Draw and label the price ceiling, quantity demanded, quantity supplied, and deadweight loss.

4. The Organization for the Promotion of Brussels Sprouts has convinced the government of Ironia to institute a price floor on the sale of brussels sprouts, at $8 per bushel. Demand is given by $P = 9 - Q$ and supply by $P = 2Q$, where Q is measured in thousands of bushels. **[LO 6.2]**

a. What will be the price and quantity of brussels sprouts sold at market equilibrium?

b. What will be the price and quantity sold with the price floor?

c. How big will be the excess supply of brussels sprouts produced with the price floor?

5. The traditional diet of the citizens of the nation of Ironia includes a lot of red meat, and ranchers make up a vital part of Ironia's economy. The government of Ironia decides to support its ranchers through a price floor, which it will maintain by buying up

TABLE 6P-1

Price ($)	Quantity demanded (thousands of lbs.)	Quantity supplied (thousands of lbs.)
6	5	80
5	20	70
4	35	60
3	50	50
2	65	40
1	80	30

excess meat supplies. Table 6P-1 shows the supply and demand schedule for red meat; quantities are given in thousands of pounds. **[LO 6.2]**

a. How many thousands of pounds of meat would you recommend that the government purchase to keep the price at $4/pound?

b. How much money should the government budget for this program?

6. Suppose you have the information shown in Table 6P-2 about the quantity of a good that is supplied and demanded at various prices. **[LO 6.3]**

a. Plot the demand and supply curves on a graph, with price on the y-axis and quantity on the x-axis.

b. What are the equilibrium price and quantity?

c. Suppose the government imposes a $15 per unit tax on sellers of this good. Draw the new supply curve on your graph.

TABLE 6P-2

Price ($)	Quantity demanded	Quantity supplied
45	10	160
40	20	140
35	30	120
30	40	100
25	50	80
20	60	60
15	70	40
10	80	20
5	90	0

d. What is the new equilibrium quantity? How much will consumers pay? How much will sellers receive after the tax?

e. Calculate the price elasticity of demand over this price change.

f. If demand were less elastic (holding supply constant), would the deadweight loss be smaller or larger? **[LO 6.5]**

7. The weekly supply and demand for fast-food cheeseburgers in your city is shown in Figure 6P-3. In an effort to curb a looming budget deficit, the mayor recently proposed a tax that would be levied on sales at fast-food restaurants. **[LO 6.3]**

   a. The mayor's proposal includes a sales tax of 60 cents on cheeseburgers, to be paid by consumers. What is the new outcome in this market (how many cheeseburgers are sold and at what price)? Illustrate this outcome on your graph.

   b. How much of the tax burden is borne by consumers? How much by suppliers?

   c. What is the deadweight loss associated with the proposed tax?

   d. How much revenue will the government collect?

   e. What is the loss of consumer surplus from this tax?

8. Demand and supply of laptop computers are given in Figure 6P-4. The quantity of laptops is given in thousands. Suppose the government provides a

FIGURE 6P-4

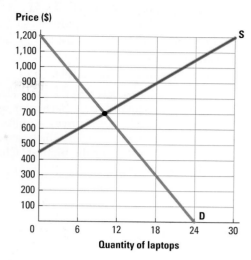

$300 subsidy for every laptop computer that consumers purchase. **[LO 6.4]**

   a. What will be the quantity of laptops bought and sold at the new equilibrium?

   b. What will be the price consumers pay for laptops under the subsidy?

   c. What will be the price that sellers receive for laptops under the subsidy?

   d. How much money should the government budget for the subsidy?

9. Suppose government offers a subsidy to laptop sellers. Say whether each group of people gains or loses from this policy. **[LO 6.4]**

   a. Laptop buyers.

   b. Laptop sellers.

   c. Desktop computer sellers (assuming that they are different from laptop manufacturers).

   d. Desktop computer buyers.

10. Suppose that for health reasons, the government of the nation of Ironia wants to increase the amount of broccoli citizens consume. Which of the following policies could be used to achieve the goal? **[LO 6.1, 6.4]**

   a. A price floor to support broccoli growers.

   b. A price ceiling to ensure that broccoli remains affordable to consumers.

   c. A subsidy paid to shoppers who buy broccoli.

   d. A subsidy paid to farmers who grow broccoli.

11. The following scenarios describe the price elasticity of supply and demand for a particular good. In

FIGURE 6P-3

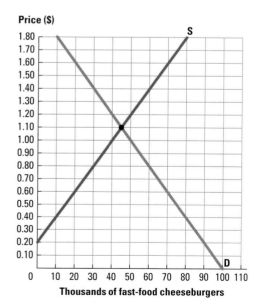

which scenario will a subsidy increase consumption the most? Choose only one. **[LO 6.5]**

    a. Elastic demand, inelastic supply.

    b. Inelastic demand, inelastic supply.

    c. Elastic demand, elastic supply.

    d. Inelastic demand, elastic supply.

12. The following scenarios describe the price elasticity of supply and demand for a particular good. All else equal (equilibrium price, equilibrium quantity, and size of the tax), in which scenario will government revenues be the highest? Choose only one. **[LO 6.5]**

    a. Elastic demand, inelastic supply.

    b. Inelastic demand, inelastic supply.

    c. Elastic demand, elastic supply.

    d. Inelastic demand, elastic supply.

Chapter Endnotes

1. http://www.time.com/time/magazine/article/0,9171,1727720,00.html; and http://www.nytimes.com/2008/06/22/nyregion/22food.html.

2. "The new face of hunger," *The Economist*, April 17, 2008.

Part Three

Individual Decisions

The five chapters in Part 3 will introduce you to ...

how consumers make decisions. Every day we make lots of choices. Some are relatively small, like deciding whether to splurge on a dinner out or to donate a few dollars to a particular cause. Some are large and important. At some point, you'll meet with your advisor to discuss possible careers. One day, you may consider buying a house, and—although it might not seem like economics— you might choose someone with whom you want to spend the rest of your life.

How can we be sure of the right choices? What about the decisions of others? The five chapters in this part show how economics can help in getting a handle on these questions

Chapter 7 introduces a fundamental concept that economists use to understand how people make decisions. Regardless of size or cost, decisions are made based on what is called *utility*. For the most part, the desire to maximize utility is what guides people when they make decisions.

Still, it is not always easy to translate good intentions into effective outcomes. Almost all of us make some decisions that we don't follow through on. Sometimes we make choices that may not seem completely rational. Chapter 8 will explain why we sit through movies that aren't so good, or order a plate of fajitas instead of the healthy salad we had planned to eat. This is part of the field of behavioral economics. Behavioral economics enriches the understanding of decision making by bringing in social and psychological factors that influence decision making. It can help us turn good ideas into good outcomes—and it's as relevant to public policy and business as it is to choices you make every day.

When making decisions, in daily life or in politics and business, it is important to consider what others are doing. This is called thinking *strategically*. Chapter 9 introduces the tools of game theory and the advantages of thinking strategically. A winning strategy is key when running a tight political campaign, or picking a location for a new store, or handling a tricky negotiation with a boss. Making the right decisions wins elections, earns profit, and gets you the raise you deserve.

Overall, one of the most important parts of making a decision is having the relevant information—the topic of Chapter 10. If you are new in a city, how can you decide where to eat? If you are a manager, how can you make sure everyone's working hard—even when you're not around? What should you think about when you buy a used car or select an insurance plan? We'll see how information affects decisions and contracts, and how markets require good information. When information isn't available, markets can fail to deliver an efficient outcome, opening up possible ways that public policy might help.

Chapter 11 considers two other elements of decision making: time and risk. Some decisions have benefits and costs that will come in the future (like saving, or going to college). And some decisions also involve risk: The car you drive off the lot could strand you on the side of the road tomorrow, or it could be a champ and run perfectly for years. The successes of businesses and governments often hinge on how well they are prepared for unknowns that emerge over time. Chapter 11 gives you conceptual tools to organize your thinking about life's uncertainties.

The problems we deal with in Part 3 are at the heart of economics. They show the power of economics to help you make better choices in everyday life, and, as a society, to help us better reach shared goals.

Consumer Behavior

LEARNING OBJECTIVES

LO 7.1   Explain how revealed preferences indicate which goods or activities give a person the most utility.

LO 7.2   Show how the budget constraint affects utility maximization.

LO 7.3   Show how a change in income affects consumption choices.

LO 7.4   Show how a change in price affects consumption choices, and distinguish between the income and substitution effects.

LO 7.5   Outline the ways in which utility is influenced by outside perceptions, and describe how people get utility from altruism and reciprocity.

THE SEASON FOR GIVING

Every holiday season, millions of Americans engage in a frenzy of gift-giving. Shopping malls fill with excited consumers, searching for gifts that friends and family will treasure.

There is another way of telling this happy holiday story though: Every holiday season millions of Americans engage in a frenzy of inefficient spending. Gift-giving, according to this second story, is wasteful. The giver spends money to buy something that the receiver may or may not want. In the best-case scenario, the gift is something the receiver would have purchased for himself had he been given money instead. In most cases, though, the gift-giver is an imperfect judge of what the receiver really wants. And if the giver is especially clueless, the gift ends up stuffed in the back of a closet, never to be seen again (or regifted to somebody else).

Although people don't usually like to admit it, the second story might be closer to reality than the first. Economist Joel Waldfogel surveyed students in his class and found that on average the personal value they placed on the gifts they received was between 65 and 90 percent of the original price. In other words, someone who bought a $20 gift would often have done better to hand that person $18 in cash (and keep the difference). Waldfogel wrote about the inefficiency of gift-giving in *Scroogenomics*—a book that was, no doubt, wrapped and ironically gifted to thousands of people during the holidays.

Which holiday story is more accurate? The answer requires us to talk more carefully about a concept—utility—that is at the heart of all microeconomic thinking. *Utility* is a way of describing the value that a person places on something, like receiving a gift, eating a meal, or experiencing something fun. The tough thing about gift-giving is that it's hard to know exactly how much value another person will place on something. Some people would like an iPod, others a pair of running shoes. (There are probably even a few people who actually want those sweaters from Aunt Mildred.) If you're

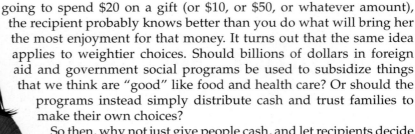

going to spend $20 on a gift (or $10, or $50, or whatever amount), the recipient probably knows better than you do what will bring her the most enjoyment for that money. It turns out that the same idea applies to weightier choices. Should billions of dollars in foreign aid and government social programs be used to subsidize things that we think are "good" like food and health care? Or should the programs instead simply distribute cash and trust families to make their own choices?

So then, why not just give people cash, and let recipients decide what to do with it? If we take a broader view, cash might *not* turn out to be better than a gift. In the case of government social programs, there's a worry that when handing out cash, the money might get diverted to the wrong people or be spent on purchases that taxpayers think are not essential.

But what of your own gift-giving? The receiver might derive sentimental value from your gift, precisely because you cared enough to choose it. Or, a gift might be important as a signal about your relationship with the recipient and how well you know his or her likes and dislikes. In the best case of all, you might buy a gift that is better than cash, giving something the receiver didn't know about or wouldn't have thought to buy for himself. When you surprise a friend with a movie she's never heard of but that quickly becomes her favorite, it's clear that gift-giving can be utility-enhancing.

In this chapter, we will explore the full meaning of *utility* and how it drives decision making—from simple pleasures like eating and sleeping to complex social values like behaving morally or meeting others' expectations. We'll see how economists define *utility* and how they use an abstract idea about the subjective value individuals place on things to do practical economic analysis. Utility is part of what defines economics as unique from other areas of study. Although we didn't call it by name, it's at the root of most of the questions we explored in Chapters 1 through 6. If you look back after reading this chapter, you'll see that underpinning the choices about satisfying *wants* and making *trade-offs* is the most important idea in economics: the quest to maximize utility.

The Basic Idea of Utility

The challenges of gift-giving bring up a point that is crucial to economic analysis: $20 isn't valuable in and of itself. Instead, it represents the things you could choose to buy for $20—food, music, a haircut, part of a rent payment, or savings that will let you get these things somewhere down the road. If someone gave you $20, you could probably, without too much trouble, figure out how to spend it in a way that benefits you. Most of us are pretty good at knowing our own likes and dislikes, at least when it comes to everyday things.

But it is much harder to figure out what *someone else* would want with that $20. If you could simply buy them whatever you would have wanted for yourself, that would be easy. But what makes you happiest is probably not the same as what will make them the happiest. Everyone has different likes and dislikes, situations in life, incomes, and so on. Those differences make us appreciate and prioritize different purchases and activities.

Utility and decision making

For now, let's stick with the easier scenario: Forget about what other people might like, and just think about what makes *you* happy. Imagine that it's the weekend. You have a completely free day, with no obligations. What will you do with it? Remember the first question economists ask: What are your *wants and constraints?* Here, your *constraints* are pretty clear. You have the hours available in one day and access to however much money is available in your bank account. But what can we say about your *wants?* In this chapter, we'll look more closely at the question of what it means to "want" something.

Your possibilities for what to do on a free day are almost endless. You could spend all day watching TV. You could read a thick Russian novel. You could go to the mall and buy some new running shoes. You could study. You could work the phones for your favored candidate in the upcoming election. You could buy 300 cans of tomato soup and take a bath in them. Out of these and a million other possibilities, how do you decide what you *want* to do the most with the time and money available?

This is a surprisingly complex question. Each possible way of spending your day probably involves very different mixtures of good and bad feelings. If you spend all day watching TV, you might feel very relaxed. On the other hand, if you spend the day reading a Russian novel, you might feel proud of yourself for improving your mind and experience a little thrill every time you anticipate casually discussing *The Brothers Karamazov* with that attractive literature major.

Somehow, you need to decide what combination of activities—and what blend of emotions and sensations you get from those activities—is preferable to you, on the whole. Russian novels, TV, and tomato-soup baths are pretty different things. But since we all compare options about what to do with our time and what to buy with our money every day, we must have some sort of internal yardstick that allows us to compare the value we derive from different choices. Sometimes this evaluation is subconscious: You probably don't agonize daily over whether to bathe in soup, even though you *could* do it. Sometimes it's quite conscious and requires deep thinking or extensive research, like choosing whether to buy a car and if so, what model.

What we need is a universal measure that allows us to compare choices like reading to TV-watching, and TV-watching to working a second job to earn a little extra money. Clearly, something like this must exist inside your mind. Otherwise you wouldn't be able to make these types of decisions, consciously or subconsciously. Economists call this measure **utility**. Utility is a measure of the amount of satisfaction a person derives from something.

utility a measure of the amount of satisfaction a person derives from something

People get utility from the goods and services they consume and experiences they have. You can get utility from consuming a tasty snack. You can also get utility from figuratively "consuming" a pleasant sensation or experience, such as scoring a goal in a soccer game or chatting with a friend. You can get utility from things you can purchase—food, clothes, cell phones, massages—and also from things that don't usually have a dollar value, like listening to music, learning new things, or doing a good deed. In short, things you like increase your utility. If something is unpleasant and you would choose not to consume it even if it were free, we say that thing reduces your utility.

The idea of utility is fundamental to economics. Think about some of the examples discussed in earlier chapters, such as buying cell phones or Starbucks lattes. People make decisions like this by choosing to do the things they think will give them the most utility, given all of the available options. That is, if you buy a Starbucks latte, it's because you think it will give you more utility than a double espresso or a soda or anything else you could have bought with that amount of money.

Economists call this method of decision making *utility maximization.* The idea that people are *rational utility maximizers* is the baseline assumption in the way economists think about the world. Later in the book, we'll see that economists sometimes relax this assumption to account for the fact that people can be short on information or self-control when making choices. But utility maximization is always the starting point in economics for thinking about how individuals behave.

Over the course of this chapter, we hope you'll see that utility is a deep idea. It encompasses even the toughest choices we make in life and can include the ways that other people influence those choices. For instance, people do unpleasant things all the time. Is that because they are failing to maximize their utility? Not at all. If we take a broad enough view, we usually see that people are doing what they *believe* will bring them the most well-being. Often, that takes into account trade-offs between things that seem nice or feel good in the short term and things that are productive or moral or pleasant in the long term. People weigh the trade-offs between ice cream and health, personal safety and joining the army to defend their country, spending now or saving for later, and so on. The idea of utility allows us to think about this internal calculus in all its richness and complexity.

Revealed preference

LO 7.1 Explain how revealed preferences indicate which goods or activities give a person the most utility.

Unfortunately, utility is hard to measure. If you want to know how much money you've got, you can look at your bank account and put a precise figure on it. But utility is subjective and mysterious. We can't always explain to *ourselves* why we get more utility from one thing than another; we definitely can't put a scale inside *other people's* heads to see how much utility they get from something—although scientists are hard at work to develop something that will do this. For more about methods that scientists use to paint a picture of happiness around the world and at the neural level, read the Real Life box "The science of happiness."

REAL LIFE
The science of happiness

How to measure utility is a question that interests more than just economists. Psychologists and neuroscientists also want to find meaningful ways to compare people's mental states when they're doing different activities or living in different kinds of cultures. Increasingly, economists are teaming up with researchers in these fields to study what has become known as the "science of happiness."

For example, researchers have compiled survey data in a "World Database of Happiness." You can view their Average Happiness map, at http://www1.eur.nl/fsw/happiness/hap_nat/maps/Map_AverageHappiness.php. Costa Rica ranks highest in average happiness, while Tanzania, Togo, and Zimbabwe tie for the lowest average happiness. Potentially, such studies can help us understand what features of life in different countries make people more happy or unhappy. That knowledge could help us design public policies that make citizens happier.

Survey questions such as the ones used to compile the world map of average happiness often ask people to report how happy they are, or how satisfied they feel with their lives. Researchers also ask how happy people are during different activities: Study participants carry a diary with them and receive reminder messages at random points during each day. They write down what they are doing and how happy they feel on a numerical scale. This allows researchers to compare whether, on average, people are happier while commuting to work or looking after their children or playing sports or cooking dinner.

Neuroscientists gather information on happiness using brain-imaging technology that allows researchers to directly observe which regions of the brain are activated in different contexts, including economic decision-making contexts. These data are increasing our understanding of how a subjective feeling of well-being emerges from observable neural activities.

Economists who study happiness hope that by borrowing techniques from neuroscience, they can change the study of utility. In the future it will use more objective data about the actual brain processes involved in decision making. Although it's a tall order, some researchers even hope to create measures of utility that are comparable across people. If this sounds interesting to you, investigate interdisciplinary work in fields like behavioral economics, neuroeconomics, or economic psychology.

Sources: The World Database of Happiness, http://worlddatabaseofhappiness.eur.nl; D. Kahneman et al., "The Day Reconstruction Method: Instrument documentation," 2004, http://www.krueger.princeton.edu/drm_documentation_july_2004.pdf.

How can we say anything meaningful about the utility other people experience? The answer is surprisingly simple: We observe what people actually do, and we assume that, as rational individuals, they're doing what gives them the most utility. If you observe someone pausing at the ice-cream counter and then ordering a scoop of chocolate ice cream, you can conclude she thought she would get more utility from the chocolate than the strawberry or chocolate-chip cookie dough. If you observe someone buying tickets for an action movie, you can conclude that this gives him more utility than the romantic comedy he could have seen instead.

Economists call this idea **revealed preference**. We can tell what maximizes other people's utility by observing their behavior. The fact that someone chose to do something "reveals" that she preferred it to the other available options. Of course, this inference is specific to a particular person and situation. Different people prefer different ice-cream flavors. The same person might be in the mood for an action movie today and a romantic comedy tomorrow.

Revealed preference might sound obvious. But it's actually an idea that is unique to economics, and somewhat controversial. If you're interested in understanding how economics overlaps with other disciplines such as psychology, anthropology, or political science, it's important that you understand the idea and its limitations.

Continuing our earlier example, let's say that you spent your free day watching TV instead of reading that Russian novel. Later, you tell a friend, "I really wanted to finish *The Brothers Karamazov,* but somehow I ended up spending all day watching TV." As economists, we suspect you're not being entirely honest with yourself. Observing that you spent all day in front of the TV, with *The Brothers Karamazov* lying unopened on the table next to you, revealed preference suggests that what you *really* wanted to do was watch TV. If not, why did you do it?

This is a trivial example, but it's easy to think of a more serious one. Suppose someone tells you, "I really want to stop smoking, but somehow I keep buying cigarettes." Revealed preference suggests he is getting more utility from continuing to smoke than he would get from actually quitting. If you were a policy-maker deciding how heavily to tax cigarettes, or whether to ban cigarette advertising, you'd have to think seriously about whether to give more weight to what people *say* they want or to what they actually *do*. In the case of cigarettes, there's a reasonable argument that physical addiction makes it hard for people to actually do in the moment what they know they want in the long term. There might be a role for friends or policy-makers to help by taking some options out of reach. We'll come back to this issue in a later chapter.

revealed preference the idea that people's preferences can be determined by observing their choices and behavior

Despite interesting debates on tough cases like cigarettes, the idea of revealed preference can take us a long way toward understanding what people want. Notice that we're not making comparisons between people; we're looking only at what one individual prefers. In other words, we can say that two people both preferred chocolate ice cream over strawberry, but not whether one of them liked chocolate more than the other.

Utility functions

utility function
a formula for calculating the total utility that a particular person derives from consuming a combination of goods and services

bundle a unique combination of goods that a person could choose to consume

The idea of revealed preference gives us a nice framework for evaluating people's utility. But we can't just follow people around and observe all of their behavior. (That would be impractical, as well as creepy.) Instead, we need a more formal method to make revealed preferences useful in economic analysis. In order to think systematically about how people make choices, economists construct a **utility function**. A utility function is a formula for calculating the total utility that a particular person derives from consuming a combination of goods and services. Each unique combination of goods and services that a person could choose to consume is called a **bundle**. The utility function is a map that connects each possible bundle to the corresponding level of utility that a person gets from consuming it.

Earlier, we said that utility is a subjective measure that can't be readily quantified. Yet, a utility function is a way of quantitatively describing preferences. The key to understanding this contradiction is that the utility measurements that go into a utility function are *relative*, not absolute. If we say that a certain activity gives a person utility of 3, the only thing that means is that the person values the activity more highly than an activity associated with a utility measure of 2 and less than one with utility of 4. The numbers don't mean anything except an ordering for activities the person likes more or less.

Let's apply this idea to a simple utility-generating experience: eating dinner. Say that Sarah is eating a dinner of macaroni and cheese, broccoli, and ice cream. We ask her to rate the utility she gets from each part of her dinner. She gets utility of 3 from each serving of macaroni and cheese, utility of 2 from each serving of broccoli, and utility of 8 from each scoop of ice cream. (Remember that the specific numbers we use are arbitrary. What matters are the *relative numbers* attached to each good in the function, which help us understand how much more utility Sarah gets from choosing one thing over another.) For dinner, she eats one serving of mac and cheese, two servings of broccoli, and two scoops of ice cream. Her dinner utility function is therefore:

$$\text{Total utility} = (3 \times 1 \text{ mac and cheese}) + (2 \times 2 \text{ broccoli}) + (8 \times 2 \text{ ice cream})$$

$$= 3 + 4 + 16 = 23$$

This analysis raises some questions: Does it suggest that Sarah should keep eating and eating, with the idea that the more food, the more utility? Why stop, when every serving of broccoli, mac and cheese, and ice cream would add positive utility? Also, since ice cream gives her far and away the most utility, shouldn't she ditch the broccoli and mac and cheese, to have an ice-cream dinner chock full of utility? In reality, we're sure you'll agree that infinite eating of ice cream is not a good idea and is unlikely to maximize anyone's utility. What is missing from this analysis?

✓ CONCEPT CHECK

❏ What can observing people's actual choices tell us about their preferences? What is this approach called? **[LO 7.1]**

❏ What is the word for a particular combination of goods and services that a person could choose to consume? **[LO 7.1]**

Marginal Utility

To understand when and why Sarah should stop eating ice cream, we need the concept of marginal utility. In Chapter 1, we introduced the idea of making decisions *at the margin*. The change in total utility that comes from consuming one additional unit of a good or service is called **marginal utility**.

Let's go back to ice cream. Imagine how much pleasure you'd get from a scoop of your favorite flavor. Now imagine eating a second scoop. Is it just as enjoyable? Maybe it's a bit less yummy than the very first taste. In other words, the marginal utility you get from a second scoop is a little lower than the marginal utility of the first scoop. Now eat a third scoop. We bet you'll enjoy this one less than the first two. A fourth scoop? You're not getting much additional enjoyment at all. A fifth scoop, and a sixth? Less and less enjoyable; in fact, after six scoops of ice cream, it's likely that you're feeling the effects of a little too much sugar.

This principle—that the additional utility gained from consuming successive units of a good or service tends to be smaller than the utility gained from the previous unit—is called **diminishing marginal utility**. The diminishing marginal utility of food items is particularly noticeable, because our bodies have a physical reaction to additional consumption. Our stomachs start to tell us that we're full, and our sense of taste fades as the novelty of a new flavor passes. Economists believe that the principle of diminishing marginal utility applies to most goods and services. Imagine you have recently moved to a cold climate and have no sweaters. Buying one sweater makes a huge difference in your comfort. Buying a tenth sweater isn't such a big deal.

Sometimes, marginal utility diminishes so much that it actually becomes negative. When we offer you a seventh scoop of ice cream, you might feel indifferent between eating it or not. It adds nothing to your total utility, so it has zero marginal utility. And you'd rather not eat an eighth scoop, as it will make you feel slightly sick. The eighth scoop would *reduce* your total utility. In other words, it would have *negative marginal utility*.

Figure 7-1 illustrates this idea. Panel A shows the total utility you get from eating more and more scoops of ice cream. The curve slopes upward to begin with, flattening out as additional scoops add less and less to your total utility. At the point marked A, the seventh scoop, your total utility peaks—and the slope of the curve is completely flat. Beyond that point, each scoop has negative marginal utility; the curve of total utility slopes downward.

Panel B shows the same idea, plotting the marginal utility of each scoop rather than total utility. The line in this graph slopes downward, showing that your marginal utility is diminishing with each additional scoop. At point A, the marginal utility is zero: You get no extra enjoyment from the seventh scoop. At scoop 8, marginal utility is negative. Point A is a significant link between panel A and panel B: When the marginal utility of an additional unit of a good is zero, you've maxed out the total utility you can get from consuming that good.

Although many things you can do or buy have diminishing marginal utility, not all of them will end up in *negative* marginal utility. For example, most people will never get negative utility from having more savings. If you have no savings, the marginal utility of your first $1,000 is pretty high. If you already have a million dollars, the marginal utility of having another $1,000 might be pretty small. There's probably not that much difference between life with $1,000,000 and life with $1,001,000. But it's hard to imagine you'd ever get *reduced* total utility from having more money magically appear in your savings account. If you really can't think of anything else to buy, after all, you can always give it away to someone else and enjoy being a philanthropist.

For most purchasing decisions, you wouldn't get anywhere near the point of negative marginal utility. After all, it's not every day that someone offers you free unlimited

marginal utility
the change in total utility that comes from consuming one additional unit of a good or service

diminishing marginal utility
the principle that the additional utility gained from consuming successive units of a good or service tends to be smaller than the utility gained from the previous unit

FIGURE 7-1
Diminishing marginal utility

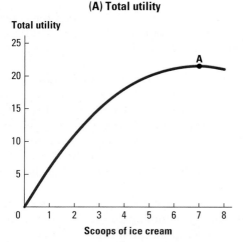

(A) Total utility

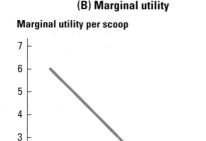

The first couple of scoops of ice cream cause big increases in utility. But as you eat more ice cream, the effect of each additional scoop on your total utility decreases until more ice cream will actually make you *un*happier, starting at point A.

(B) Marginal utility

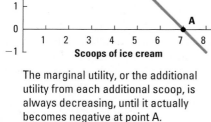

The marginal utility, or the additional utility from each additional scoop, is always decreasing, until it actually becomes negative at point A.

ice cream or sweaters or cash: Usually you have to pay or work for them. Long before you buy a seventh scoop of ice cream, you are likely to have decided you'd get higher marginal utility from spending that money on something else. This brings us to the most important point in this chapter: What happens when we combine the concept of *diminishing marginal utility* with the concept of *wants and constraints?*

Maximizing utility within constraints

LO 7.2 Show how the budget constraint affects utility maximization.

Let's go back to the example of your free day. In reality, you're very unlikely to spend the entire day doing just one thing. Instead, you might do a number of different things: drive to the mall, shop for running shoes, and eat some lunch; go for a run in your new shoes; relax for a while by watching TV; make a little progress through *The Brothers Karamazov;* and go out with friends in the evening. If that particular schedule isn't your cup of tea, there are millions of other possible combinations you could choose. How do you pick which bundle of activities to do within the time and money available?

Marginal utility helps make sense of this sort of decision by calling attention to the *trade-offs* involved. Why didn't you spend another hour at the mall? Because once you'd been there for four hours, the marginal utility of another hour was less than the marginal utility of going for an energizing run instead. Why didn't you run for a second hour? Because you were getting tired. The marginal utility of another hour of running was less than the marginal utility of watching some TV. And so on, with the rest of the day.

Of course, you don't have to make these choices consecutively, waiting until you get tired of one activity before deciding to move on. People can think ahead about the bundle of goods or activities that will give them the most combined utility, anticipating

FIGURE 7-2

The budget constraint

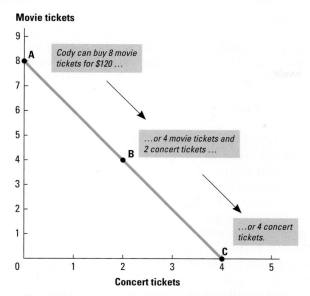

The budget constraint represents the combinations of goods that are available to Cody given his budget. Each bundle on the line costs exactly the amount of money Cody has in his budget.

that too much of one thing isn't as good as some other option. Your choice about how to spend the day is really about selecting a *combination* of goods and activities that will maximize your utility, within the limits of time and money available to you. If you have spent your day wisely, there is no other combination of activities that could have added up to greater total utility.

There are many things that might give you positive utility that you choose not to do. They may be good and enjoyable, but the opportunity cost (passing up something even more enjoyable) is higher than the benefit you'd get. People have many wants, and they are constrained by the time and money available to them. If they are rational utility maximizers, they try to optimize within those constraints by spending their resources on the bundle of goods and activities that will give them the highest possible total utility.

We can use a quantitative model to illustrate the idea of maximizing utility within constraints. Like all models, we'll have to simplify a bit. Imagine that Cody has $120 to spend each month after paying all his bills. Assume there are only two things he considers spending the money on: a night at the movies, which costs $15, and concert tickets, which are $30 each. There are several possible combinations of movie and concert tickets that Cody could buy within his budget. He could not see any concerts at all and spend $120 going to the movies, or only see four movies ($60) and two concerts ($60), and so on. We can represent these possibilities on a line called a *budget constraint* or budget line, as shown in Figure 7-2. A **budget constraint** is a line composed of all of the possible combinations of goods and services a consumer can buy with his or her income. (If this graph looks familiar to the production possibilities frontier graph of Chapter 2, that's no coincidence. They express very similar ideas—the concept of choosing between different combinations of things within the constraint of limited resources.)

If Cody is a rational consumer, making choices to achieve goals in the most effective way possible, he will spend his budget on the combination of movie and concert

budget constraint a line that is composed of all of the possible combinations of goods and services that a consumer can buy with her or his income

tickets that maximizes his utility. Cody feels that going to the movies three times in a month is very important. He'll give each of the first three movies a utility score of 95. After that, seeing a fourth movie gives him a utility of 80, and a fifth movie scores an additional 65 points of utility. (Remember that utility is an imaginary measure. These numbers don't refer to anything that's measurable outside of Cody's mind; they're just a way of getting an insight into his relative preferences.) Eventually, he'd become so sick of the cinema that he'd rather not go an eighth time: the marginal utility of movie number eight would be negative, at −10. These numbers are included on panel A of Table 7-1.

How about the concerts? Cody says he would not be happy if he went the entire month without going to a concert, so a first concert gives him utility of 100. Getting to that second concert would also be good; he'll give that second ticket an 85. After a while concerts begin to lose some of their interest, so the marginal utility Cody gets from each ticket decreases. By the time he's bought three tickets, he feels like that's enough, and additional tickets won't increase his total utility. Panel B of Table 7-1 shows the marginal total utility Cody gets from each concert ticket.

By adding up the marginal utility of each extra ticket, done in panel A of Figure 7-3, you can see that the optimal combination for Cody is to see two concerts and four movies. That's the combination out of the available options that gives him the most total utility. If Cody is a rational, utility-maximizing consumer, then we can expect to observe him do just that.

Usually, economists don't ask people to give a utility rating to the things they could buy. Instead, they try out different utility functions, and make predictions about how they expect people to behave. They might look at data about how groups of people in the real world actually did behave and compare the two. They then can assess how well they understood the wants and constraints that motivated people's choices.

As always, real life is a lot more complicated than any model. In reality people choose between thousands of different spending possibilities rather than just two, yielding millions of possible combinations. The principle, however, is the same. Rational consumers

TABLE 7-1 Maximizing total utility

(A) Utility from movie tickets			(B) Utility from concert tickets		
Number of tickets	Marginal utility	Total utility	Number of tickets	Marginal utility	Total utility
1	95	95	1	100	100
2	95	190	2	85	185
3	95	285	3	25	210
4	80	365	4	0	210
5	65	430			
6	35	465			
7	10	475			
8	−10	465			

Cody gets lots of utility from the first few concert tickets. After the third ticket, he gets no further utility.

Utility greatly increases as Cody buys the first few movie tickets, and peaks when he buys 7 movie tickets. After that, utility decreases.

FIGURE 7-3
Maximizing utility

(A) Maximizing total utility

Bundle	Concert tickets	Utility from concert tickets	Movie tickets	Utility from movie tickets	Total utility
A	0	0	8	465	465
B	1	100	6	465	565
C	2	185	4	385	570
D	3	210	2	190	400
E	4	210	0	0	210

This table shows all the bundles that Cody can potentially consume. The total utility he gets from each bundle depends on the number of concert tickets and the number of movie tickets in it.

(B) Utility along the budget constraint

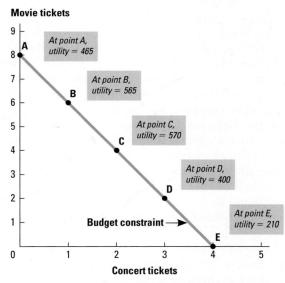

Each bundle on the budget corresponds to one of the rows in the table in panel A. While each costs the same, the utility they provide varies according to Cody's preferences.

choose to spend their budgets on the combination of goods and services that will give them the highest possible total utility.

There's another real-life complication we haven't considered in this chapter: Budgets don't fall out of the sky; they're usually determined by earlier choices about what job to apply for and how much to work. In the real world, our decisions about how to maximize utility also involve this trade-off between work and available budget: Would you get more utility from working hard and having more money to spend, or having more leisure time but less money to enjoy it with? This is an idea we'll come back to later in the book.

☐ If something has negative marginal utility, what happens to your total utility when you consume it? **[LO 7.2]**

☐ What is the budget constraint? **[LO 7.2]**

Responding to Changes in Income and Prices

Income changes all the time. You might get a raise for diligent work, or your boss, pressed by a lack of business, may be forced to cut your hours so you earn less money. Both of these changes in income are likely to change how much you decide to spend on the things you buy. The same is true for changes in prices. If lattes drop in price by $0.50 one day, you'll probably decide to buy more of them. As these examples show, rational utility maximizers will change their behavior as circumstances like income and prices change.

Changes in income

LO 7.3 Show how a change in income affects consumption choices.

When a person's income increases, more bundles of goods and services become affordable. When income decreases, fewer bundles are affordable, and consumers will probably have to cut consumption of some things. We represent these changes by shifting the entire budget line to show each new range of options available to the consumer.

Why does this happen? Let's look at what happens when Cody gets $60 for his birthday from his grandparents. Let's say he decides to use all of his money this month—including the birthday cash, for a grand total of $180—to buy concert tickets. With the extra cash, he can buy six tickets instead of only four. If he decided to buy only movie tickets instead, he could afford four more than before. With more money, he can buy more of both goods at every point; the entire budget line shifts out by the equivalent of $60, maintaining the same slope as it did before. As a result, Cody can buy more movie tickets or more concert tickets (or more of both) than he did before he received the birthday money.

Why does the slope stay the same? Even though Cody has more money, the ratio of the prices of the two goods has not changed. Movie tickets are still $15 and concert tickets $30. The only thing that has changed is that Cody is now able to buy more tickets in whatever combination he chooses. Figure 7-4 shows the effect of this increase in income.

Changes in prices

LO 7.4 Show how a change in price affects consumption choices, and distinguish between the income and substitution effects.

What about when income stays the same but the prices of goods change? In general, changes in the price of a good have two important effects, called the *income effect* and the *substitution effect*.

Before thinking about the difference between the two, this is a good time for a quick refresher on normal goods and inferior goods. Remember that *normal goods* are those for which demand increases as income increases. If Cody chose to increase his consumption of both movie and concert tickets when his income increased, this

FIGURE 7-4

The effect of an increase in income

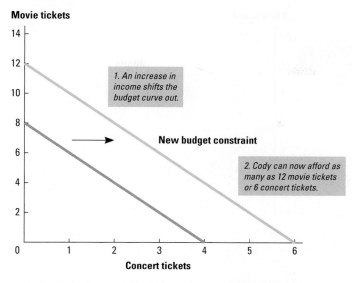

When Cody's income increases as a result of a gift, he is able to afford more goods. This shifts the budget constraint outward, and he can now buy 12 movie tickets or 6 concert tickets.

would imply they are both normal goods. In contrast, *inferior goods* are those for which demand decreases as income increases. (Instant ramen noodles, that staple of college diets everywhere, are a classic inferior good.)

Income effect. The **income effect** describes the change in consumption that results from increased effective wealth due to lower prices. In other words, if Cody normally pays $15 for each movie ticket, but they now cost only $10, he is $5 "richer" for each ticket he buys. If he continues to buy his usual four movie tickets a month, he now has an extra $20 in comparison to last month.

Any price decrease causes the budget line to rotate outward, as shown in Figure 7-5. Why does the curve rotate outward instead of shifting right in a parallel fashion? Let's return to Cody's pre-birthday budget constraint of $120. If he puts all of his money into movie tickets, he is able to afford 12 tickets at the new lower price, four more than he was originally able to buy. But if he puts all of his money into concert tickets, he is still able to afford only six of them, since their price has stayed the same.

In general, consumers can buy more things when the price of a good they usually purchase decreases. When goods get cheaper, the consumer's money goes farther. This is the income effect.

Substitution effect. The **substitution effect** describes the change in consumption that results from a change in the relative price of goods. In our example, movies became cheaper *relative to* concerts, as represented by the change in the slope of the budget line. This relative change causes Cody to choose more movies and fewer concerts. He substitutes the good that has become cheaper in relative terms for the one that has become more expensive, which is why it's called the "substitution" effect.

Another way to say this is that the *opportunity cost* of concerts and movies has changed. When movies cost $15 and concerts $30, the opportunity cost of a concert was two movies. When the price of a movie ticket decreases to $10, the opportunity cost of a

income effect the change in consumption that results from increased effective wealth due to lower prices

substitution effect the change in consumption that results from a change in the relative price of goods

FIGURE 7-5

The effect of a price change

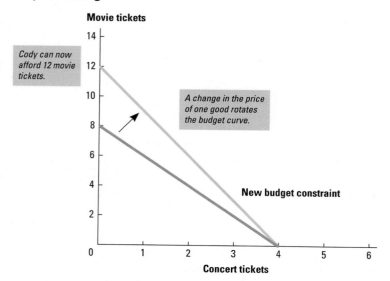

When the price of one good changes, the budget constraint rotates out to demonstrate the new consumption bundles that are available. The change in slope reflects the change in the relative prices of the two goods.

concert increases to three movies. The flip-side is that the opportunity cost of movies in terms of forgone concerts has decreased (from $\frac{1}{2}$ to $\frac{1}{3}$).

Why? Think about the situation as a change in the marginal utility per dollar that Cody gets for each good. When the price of movies decreases, the marginal utility per dollar for movie tickets goes up; the marginal utility per dollar for concert tickets stays the same. Cody now gets more utility bang for his buck from movies, so he wants to spend more of his budget on them.

Occasionally, though, people may actually choose to consume *more* of a good when its price increases. This occurs for goods known as *Veblen goods.* Veblen goods are items for which the quantity demanded is higher when prices are higher. They are something that people buy *because* they are flashy and expensive. Buyers choose them to show others that they can afford flashy and expensive goods.

The idea of Veblen goods conflicts with the idea of utility we presented earlier in this chapter; there we assumed that you would make the same choices whether you were alone or not. Would you buy a luxury watch when a basic one tells time just fine if you were the only person who could see it? Why buy a $200 handbag when a $50 one will hold all of your stuff, if no one else will see you with it? Although you may also enjoy the high quality, durability, or design of luxury items, these goods sell at least in part because people get utility from the reaction others have to items known to be expensive or exclusive. The Veblen good suggests that utility may be far from the individual measure we have talked about so far.

This example illustrates one of the many instances in which your utility is affected by other people. The perceptions of others help explain why people buy luxury items. They also influence how we donate to charity and what gifts we give to others, and even how we interact with others in everyday situations. Such examples show the remarkable breadth of the concept of utility, and we explore this idea further in the next section.

✔**CONCEPT CHECK**

- ❐ What happens to the budget constraint when income increases? **[LO 7.3]**
- ❐ What happens to consumption of a normal good when its price increases? **[LO 7.4]**
- ❐ What is the difference between the income effect and the substitution effect of a price increase for a normal good? **[LO 7.4]**

Utility and Society

A common misconception about economics is that utility maximization assumes people are inward-looking consumption machines. In fact, the idea of utility is much broader and more flexible than that. Utility can help us think about envy, status, kindness, and a range of other very human emotions.

Here's an example: To avoid Scroogenomics-style waste during the holidays, why not give your aunt and uncle what anyone would want—a goat? We don't mean giving the actual goat to your relatives as an affordable and earth-friendly lawn care solution. Instead, charities like Oxfam will send a goat to a poor family in Africa or South America in your aunt's and uncle's names. A single goat can be a great help. Goats can provide milk for the family and fertilizer for crops. They can even act as a source of savings that can be sold when times are tough. Oxfam sends a friendly card to the "recipients" letting them know that you have given something on their behalf.

Many organizations offer the opportunity to give these "charity-gifts"—sending a goat or other useful items to a stranger in need, while giving the credit for the donation as a gift to someone else. What can the idea of utility tell us about this three-party exchange? Your aunt and uncle get a warm glow knowing that they were at least partially responsible for your donation. You get the same good feeling that accompanies a good deed. It's also possible that you get a little kick from knowing that your aunt and uncle find you both socially conscious and generous. And, of course, the family that receives the goat receives something that they will undoubtedly use.

As the Oxfam example shows, people can get utility from a variety of sources, in a way that weaves together both psychology and economics. Some people do good deeds only when others are looking because they're interested only in their reputation. Of course, many others do good deeds because they're good—every year, people give to perfect strangers, who may live in the same town or thousands of miles away. In the next few sections, we'll look at all of these motivations.

Utility and status

LO 7.5 Outline the ways in which utility is influenced by outside perceptions, and describe how people get utility from altruism and reciprocity.

The utility we get from consuming something is not always about our direct benefit alone. If it were, those designer handbags would be a far tougher sell. Chocolate ice cream is a rare example of something we'd probably enjoy just as much whether or not anybody else knew we were consuming it. More often, utility comes from two sources: One is the *direct effect* the product has on us, and the other is the effect that *other people's reactions* to it have on us. In the end, overall utility is a mix of outside perceptions and inner preferences, both of which contribute to decision making. Your choice of which cell phone you use, which brands of clothes you wear, or which car you drive is likely to be partly influenced by your efforts to signal personality traits, aesthetics, or social status.

Take the decision to buy a new car. There are many obvious differences between an off-road sport utility vehicle (SUV) and a Prius. The SUV grinds over rough terrain with ease; the Prius would struggle as off-road conditions get hairy. While the Prius might not be the ideal car for your next dirt-road adventure, it sips gas—generally getting 50 miles per gallon—compared to the sub-20 miles per gallon for the rugged SUV. If your internal preference was the only thing that mattered, you would likely make your final decision based on characteristics such as these.

However, utility calculations include much more than that. Sure, gas mileage is an important consideration, but there are other reasons that people buy cars. As you silently whir through town in a Prius, for instance, the people who see you probably associate other traits with you (that you may or may not have): It's not out of line to assume that the average Prius driver lives a healthy and earth-friendly life, although any particular individual may not. We'd guess that every person who owns a Prius has at least once gotten a little kick out of knowing that they are perceived to have these traits.

Even more important than the opinion of random strangers, though, will be the perceptions of those who are close to you. If you're a long-time member of an environmental group, you may get more utility from showing up to a meeting in a brand-new Prius than you would if you rumbled up in a large SUV. The SUV, though, may score more points at the local outdoors club.

The idea that utility is influenced by others' opinions is not new. Since utility can be related to status and some people get lots of utility from showing off how wealthy they are, they buy goods that best show off this wealth. For more about this phenomenon and how it relates to charity, read the From Another Angle box "Conspicuous consumption and conspicuous charity."

FROM ANOTHER ANGLE
Conspicuous consumption and conspicuous charity

Do people really buy Ferraris for their top-of-the-line engineering, or Cristal champagne because it tastes better, or Louis Vuitton handbags because they're more efficient for transporting lipstick and keys? In general, when the price of a good rises, people want to buy less of it. Sometimes, though, people get a buzz from buying more expensive things because it shows off how wealthy they are.

Thorstein Veblen called this phenomenon "conspicuous consumption." As an economist writing during America's Gilded Age at the end of the nineteenth century, Veblen saw wealthy people around him living in unbelievable luxury, to show off their power and status. More recently, evolutionary psychologist Geoffrey Miller has argued that conspicuous consumption has its roots in biology. *To learn more, continue reading by scanning the QR code near the end of the chapter or by going online.*

Frames of reference. Utility is sometimes influenced not just by what others think, but by how much others have. Would you rather make $36,000 at a firm where the average salary is $40,000, or $34,000 at a firm where the average salary is $30,000, assuming the jobs are exactly the same? It seems like an easy question. You might think it's your own salary that affects your utility, not anyone else's, so you'd get more utility from the extra money. Yet when researchers presented people with this scenario, 80 percent said that someone in the second position would be happier with her job situation.

What can account for this? If the only utility we get comes from pleasures like eating ice cream, then a higher salary would give us more utility: We can buy more ice cream with \$36,000 than with \$34,000. But if we also get utility from how others see us, that starts to explain why we might prefer to earn \$4,000 more than the people we spend most of our time with. Perhaps we'd get utility from driving to the office every day in a slightly newer car than our coworkers', taking calls on a slightly fancier cell phone, and being able to talk about planning slightly more impressive vacations.

Utility may also depend on whom you compare yourself with. If your frame of reference is coworkers earning \$30,000, you'll get more utility from earning \$34,000 than if your frame of reference is former schoolmates who are earning \$40,000 at other firms. If you compare yourself with CEOs of Fortune 500 companies, then earning \$34,000 will make you positively miserable. This line of thought has an unsettling implication: Simply by changing our frame of reference, we might gain or lose utility. See the What Do You Think? box "Choosing a League" to read more about this debate.

WHAT DO YOU THINK?

Choosing a league

Would you rather be the worst player in the major leagues or the best player in the minor leagues? Would you rather be the star soloist in your local choir or a below-average voice in a prestigious, big-city choir?

Before the age of modern communications, these questions didn't matter so much. Everyone's frame of reference was fairly local and limited. Technology has changed all that: Thanks to downloadable MP3s and streaming radio through Pandora and Spotify, our frame of reference for good music is much broader. The local diva in the church choir was probably much more exciting in a time when you couldn't compare her to Madonna—and the local diva might have been much happier when she didn't have Madonna to compare herself to.

The same is true of good local athletes, actors, chefs, comedians, politicians, and many other professions. To the extent that utility in these pursuits comes from relative status, there are fewer and fewer winners as our frame of reference becomes wider and wider. The same goes for material wealth in general: Some people argue that introducing television to remote communities can make them less happy by allowing comparisons with much more wealthy societies.

Then again, we all have some power to choose our own frames of reference. It's up to the local diva whether she chooses to enjoy performing to a small but appreciative audience at church, or stay at home feeling sad that she was turned down when she auditioned for *American Idol*.

What do you think?

1. Would you rather be the best player on a bad team or the worst player on a good team? Why?
2. Are there benefits to comparing ourselves to superstars? How do those benefits weigh against the negatives?

Of course, utility maximization is only as selfish or unselfish as we ourselves are. As you plink a few coins in the tin in front of the grocery store during the holidays and see the warm smile from the bell-ringer, it is likely that you are getting utility from that as well. It's a mutually beneficial exchange. You get a fuzzy glow while shopping, and charities receive needed donations. Utility can come from following through on our best inclinations as well as our pettiest ones, and can help explain some very noble actions.

Utility and altruism

In 2010, a 7.0 magnitude earthquake shook Haiti, killing over 300,000 people; it left millions more homeless, without access to food or clean water. In the following two weeks, people in North America donated over $500 million to relief efforts. And, of course, charity is not limited to sympathetic reactions to calamitous disaster. Even in the midst of the deep economic recession in 2008, Americans gave more than $300 billion to charities of every kind. They gave to religious groups and schools, arts organizations, and disaster relief. That's not counting the donations of time and expertise that people made as volunteers. Nor does it include the countless acts of everyday kindness and selflessness that people perform for family and friends and strangers.

How does economics account for this evidence of mass caring for others? How does it account for doctors who travel overseas to treat sick people in refugee camps? For people who care for their elderly relatives? For volunteers in after-school programs who help kids do their homework? When people behave "selflessly" by doing something for others, with no obvious benefit for themselves, we say they are behaving *altruistically*. Economists use the term **altruism** to describe a motive for action in which a person's utility increases simply because someone else's utility increases.

altruism a motive for action in which a person's utility increases simply because someone else's utility increases

When we do good things, we often get utility from multiple sources. A doctor who travels overseas to treat sick people in refugee camps will get utility from helping others. If she is like most people, she also will probably get utility when she tells people at parties about her charitable work. Desires like this are also an undeniable part of giving behavior. Altruistic and selfish or image-conscious motivations can coexist perfectly well; a single action might produce utility for many different reasons. For instance, imagine buying an extra concert ticket for a friend: It's entirely reasonable for you to get utility both from your altruistic enjoyment of your friend's happiness and from your own increased enjoyment of the experience due to sharing it with good company.

The Product RED campaign, started in 2006, gives a couple dollars to fight global AIDS for every Product-RED-branded good you buy. If people cared only about altruism, this campaign wouldn't exist. Instead of spending $20 dollars on a T-shirt, with $5 dollars given to charity, a truly altruistic person would forgo the more-expensive T-shirt, spend $10 on cheaper threads, and give $10 to charity. Even further, someone probably wouldn't buy a T-shirt at all but would instead write a check for $20 directly to the RED Global Fund. In buying that T-shirt, unless you think that the only way you can inspire others to donate is by wearing the T-shirt, then you are showing that you get some sort of utility beyond the simple altruism in fighting AIDS. Maybe you get a warm glow from wearing that shirt. Or maybe you just liked the design.

Economists have done experiments to get at the underlying reasons for giving. The results of these efforts are presented in the Real Life box "Why we give."

REAL LIFE

Why we give

Economists have recently used experiments to gain insight into the psychology of charity. In one experiment, researchers varied the person who went door to door soliciting donations for charity. Young, attractive people visited some houses; dowdier solicitors visited others. The result? The attractive solicitors got significantly more donations. The impact of attractiveness was more pronounced than any other single factor that the experimenters examined. The appearance of the person collecting donations might seem like something that shouldn't matter in our conscious decisions about charity, but it's possible that people respond to beauty on a subconscious level, something that psychologists call the "halo effect."

In another experiment, researchers randomly assigned each potential donor to a certain level of matching donations. Some were told that every $1 they donated would be matched by a $3 donation from a third party. Others were offered a match of $2; others got a simple $1 to $1 match. Another group was not offered any matching donation at all. Those who were offered matching donations gave more than those who weren't, but the level of matching was irrelevant. Those offered 2:1 or 3:1 matches did not give significantly more than those offered the 1:1 match. This result suggests people saw the match as a reason to give to the charity, even if the size of the match didn't matter.

The question of the *impact* of charitable giving is one that economists are also researching, and with startling results. Experimenting with different ways of using international aid money show that some projects do much more good per dollar given than others. (You can read more about these experiments in the chapter titled "Development Economics.")

Yet this raises a troubling possibility: The charities that raise the most money won't necessarily be the ones that are having the greatest impact on those in need, but rather those with the flashiest fundraising techniques. As economic research increases our understanding of why people give, and about which charities do the most good, we may also find ways to bring the two together and encourage people to give more money to the most effective charities. For example, the website GuideStar rates the efficiency of charities (www.guidestar.org). Similarly, GiveWell (www.givewell.org) aims to help individuals find charities that will do the most good for their money.

Sources: Dean Karlan and John List, "Does price matter in charitable giving? Evidence from a large-scale natural field experiment," *American Economic Review* 97, no. 5 (December 2007), pp. 1774–1793; Craig Landry et al., "Toward an understanding of the economics of charity: Evidence from a field experiment," *The Quarterly Journal of Economics* 121, no. 2 (May 2006), pp. 747–782.

In the end, when economists say things like, "We assume people are rational and act in their self-interest," they aren't saying they assume people are selfish. They mean only that people maximize their utility. Revealed preferences show us that many people get utility from doing things that really aren't selfish at all.

Utility and reciprocity

Revealed preference also suggests that many people get utility from punishing bad behavior and rewarding good. Imagine that a researcher asks you to take part in an experiment. You will do the experiment with a partner; you know nothing about him or her, and you will never meet. The researcher then gives you $10 and tells you that you can give any amount of the money to your partner, or decide to keep it all for yourself. The researcher lets you know that he will triple the amount that you decide to transfer—so, for example, a $3 transfer becomes a $9 transfer. Your partner will get the opportunity to transfer money back to you. If you could talk to the other person, you might agree that you'll transfer the full $10; she'll receive $30 and transfer $15 back to you. But you can't talk to each other. What would you do?

When researchers ask people to play this game in real experiments, they find that, on average, the more the first person shares with a partner, the more the partner will send back in response. This suggests that people get utility from rewarding kindness with kindness in return, even when there's nothing in it for them.

We call this tendency **reciprocity**. Reciprocity means responding to another's action with a similar action. Reciprocity involves doing good things for people who did good things for us. (Note the difference from altruism, which involves simply wanting others to be better off.)

reciprocity
responding to another's action with a similar action

Reciprocity also occurs when we respond in kind to bad treatment. When people make an effort to decrease someone else's utility in response to being harmed themselves, they are engaging in *negative reciprocity*. When you steal toothpaste from that guy down the hall whose music has kept you up at night for a week, you're engaging in negative reciprocity.

People frequently engage in reciprocal actions even when they stand to lose out on some benefit. To see how this works, let's return to the game from the research experiment. Like before, you choose how much money to transfer to your partner, but now the researcher allows the partner to accept or reject the offer. If she rejects, then neither of you gets to keep *any* of the money.

In theory, you might expect the partner to accept any offer: Even if you transfer only one cent, the partner is better off accepting it than rejecting it. But that's not what happens when this experiment is played in practice. The partner regularly rejects the money if she deems the amount offered to be "too low." The partner willingly forfeits free money as a way to punish the other who has acted "unfairly." This outcome occurs despite the fact that the punishment has no future implications—the two participants don't know who the other person is, and there will be no further rounds of the experiment. As the experiment shows, fairness is an ideal that people often are willing to sacrifice for, even when it's not rational to do so.

Reciprocity guides everyday interactions. When you bring over a pizza in exchange for help studying for an exam, or buy the food that you were offered as a free sample in the store, you are engaging in reciprocity. Along with ideas such as altruism and status, reciprocity adds depth to our concept of utility into something quirky and altogether human.

✔CONCEPT CHECK

❏ Name two ways that an action may provide utility, other than the direct effect of consuming a good or service? **[LO 7.5]**

Conclusion

The ideas in this chapter are at the very heart of economic analysis. Everything in the following chapters (and for that matter, the preceding chapters) is in some way based on the assumption that people attempt to maximize their utility within the limitations of the resources available to them.

We'll enrich this picture in the coming chapters, seeing that individuals have to answer a lot of tough questions when making even commonplace decisions. When will the costs arrive relative to the benefits? What are the risks? Am I fully informed about the situation? Are others competing with me for the same goal?

The idea of utility maximization is remarkably flexible. We'll see that people often have preferences that extend far beyond a narrow definition of their own benefit. Sometimes they pursue their goals in unexpected or not entirely rational ways. Nonetheless, the essential idea of individuals pursuing the things they want in the face of scarcity drives economic analysis from A to Z.

 ◄ Mobile Window on the World—Scan this code with your smartphone to find more applications of the chapter content. (Need a barcode reader? Try ScanLife, available in your app store.)

Visit your mobile app store and download ► the Karlan and Morduch Study Econ app.

Key Terms

Summary

LO 7.1 Explain how revealed preferences indicate which goods or activities give a person the most utility.

Utility is an imaginary measure of the amount of satisfaction a person derives from something. People get utility from things they can purchase but also from things that don't usually have a dollar value. People make decisions by choosing to do the things they think will give them the most utility, given all of the available options. Economists use the term utility maximization to describe this method of decision making. Economists generally assume that individuals' preferences are demonstrated through the choices that they make, a concept known as revealed preference. We observe what people actually do, and assume that, as rational individuals, they're doing what gives them most utility.

LO 7.2 Show how the budget constraint affects utility maximization.

The budget constraint is a line that shows all the possible consumption bundles available to an individual given a fixed budget. The slope of the budget line is equivalent to the ratio of prices of the two goods. A rational individual will maximize utility given the amount of goods he or she can afford.

LO 7.3 Show how a change in income affects consumption choices.

An increase in an individual's income will cause the budget line to shift outward, allowing a consumer to buy more goods on average. A decrease in income on the other hand will cause a person to consume fewer goods on average.

LO 7.4 Show how a change in price affects consumption choices, and distinguish between the income and substitution effects.

A change in the price of goods can have two effects on optimal consumption. The change in consumption that results from increased effective wealth due to lower prices is called the income effect. When prices decrease, a consumer is able to afford larger quantities, just as if her income had increased. The substitution effect describes the change in consumption that results from a change in the relative price of goods. When one good becomes relatively less expensive compared to the other good than it was before the price change, consumers will be inclined to buy more of it

LO 7.5 Outline the ways in which utility is influenced by outside perceptions, and describe how people get utility from altruism and reciprocity.

How much utility consumers get from a good can be influenced by how others perceive their choice. Some people choose to consume expensive goods to signal to others that they can afford these goods. Utility can also be influenced by your frame of reference—you're far more likely to be happy with a salary if it's in line with what everyone around you earns.

Altruism is a motive for action in which a person's utility increases simply because someone else's utility increases. Reciprocity is the idea that some people get utility from punishing bad behavior and rewarding good, even when it comes at some cost to them.

Review Questions

1. Which of the following activities give you positive utility? **[LO 7.1]**
   a. Playing sports
   b. Receiving a prestigious scholarship
   c. Buying a new TV
   d. Eating brussels sprouts
   e. All of the above

2. Your gym offers two classes at the same time: weightlifting and yoga. Both classes are included in your membership and have space available. Your friend tells you he wants to work on his strength and take the weightlifting class, but you always see him in yoga class. Which class gives him more utility? How do you know this? **[LO 7.1]**

3. Evie has a gift pass for unlimited rollercoaster rides on her birthday. Given the information about Evie's utility in Table 7P-1, explain why she chooses to ride only three times. [LO 7.1]

TABLE 7P-1

Number of roller-coaster rides	Total utility
1	20
2	35
3	45
4	40

4. Dan likes to spend his allowance on two things: candy and toys. What are the three constraints that determine the possible consumption bundles of toys and candy available to Dan? [LO 7.2]

5. Evan has $40 to spend at an amusement park. The roller coaster costs $10 per ride. Given the information about Evan's utility in Table 7P-2, explain why he chooses to ride only three times. [LO 7.2]

TABLE 7P-2

Number of roller-coaster rides	Total utility
1	20
2	35
3	45
4	40

6. Suppose a wedge of cheese is $10, and a loaf of bread is $5. What is the opportunity cost of purchasing a wedge of cheese (in terms of bread)? Explain what happens to the opportunity cost of purchasing a wedge of cheese (in terms of bread) if your income decreases by 20 percent. [LO 7.3]

7. Simone spends $200 a month on voice lessons and dance lessons. She just learned that starting next month her favorite dance instructor is moving out of town and the monthly rent for her apartment is increasing. How will each of these events affect

Simone's budget constraint for voice and dance lessons? [LO 7.3]

8. Julian buys plants and flowers every month. Both are normal goods. When the price of flowers fell, Julian purchased fewer plants. Which effect was stronger for Julian, the income effect or the substitution effect? [LO 7.4]

9. Sarah spends her monthly entertainment budget on books and movies. Sarah's initial utility-maximizing combination of books and movies is five movies and two books a month. Assume the price of books falls. Sarah's new utility-maximizing combination of books and movies is five movies and four books. Given this information, can we say whether movies are a normal good? [LO 7.4]

10. An organization that raises money to provide meals for seniors gives tote bags to its donors. Sami thinks it is wasteful to spend donated money on tote bags for donors because the money could be used to provide more meals. Explain to Sami why giving tote bags could make financial sense for the organization. [LO 7.5]

11. Your friend says, "I'd rather be a big fish in a small pond than a small fish in a big pond." What concept does this comment illustrate? [LO 7.5]

Problems and Applications

1. Total utility is maximized when marginal utility becomes (positive, zero, negative) _____. [LO 7.1]

2. Table 7P-3 shows the total utility that John gets from ice cream, for each quantity he consumes. Fill in the third column showing the marginal utility he gets from each additional scoop. [LO 7.1]

TABLE 7P-3

Quantity of ice cream (scoops)	Total utility	Marginal utility of the last scoop eaten
1	10	
2	17	
3	21	
4	23	
5	23	

3. You love going to the movies. For your birthday, your friend offers to take you to a triple feature without popcorn or a double feature with two bags of popcorn. Table 7P-4 shows your utility for movies and popcorn. Which option should you choose? **[LO 7.1]**

TABLE 7P-4

# Movies	Total utility	# Popcorn bags	Total utility
1	10	1	5
2	15	2	5
3	18	3	4

4. Refer to the budget constraint for jeans and T-shirts in Figure 7P-1. Which of the following consumption bundles is attainable? **[LO 7.2]**
   a. 3 pairs of jeans, 1 T-shirt.
   b. 2 pairs of jeans, 4 T-shirts.
   c. 2 pairs of jeans, 3 T-shirts.
   d. 1 pair of jeans, 4 T-shirts.

5. Petra has $480 to spend on DVDs and books. A book costs $24 and a DVD costs $15. **[LO 7.2]**
   a. Write an equation for the budget constraint. Let x = books. Let y = DVDs.
   b. Use your equation to determine how many books Petra can buy if she buys 8 DVDs.

FIGURE 7P-1

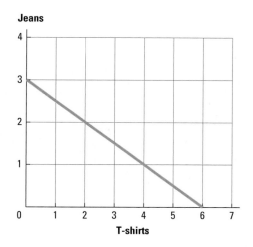

6. Jordan visits her sister several times a year. Jordan's travel budget is $600, which she uses to buy bus tickets and train tickets. The train costs $120 per trip, and the bus costs $40. **[LO 7.2, 7.3]**
   a. Graph Jordan's budget constraint.
   b. How many total trips can Jordan take if she takes the train three times?
   c. Suppose Jordan's travel budget is cut to $360. Draw her new budget constraint.
   d. How many train trips can she take if she doesn't want to reduce the total number of trips she takes each year?

7. Maria has a $300 gift certificate at a spa that she can use on massages or manicures. A massage costs $100, and a manicure costs $30. **[LO 7.3, 7.4]**
   a. Write the equation for Maria's budget constraint. Let x = massages. Let y = manicures.
   b. Suppose Maria decides to split her gift certificate with a friend and transfers half of the value of her gift certificate to her friend. Write the equation for her new budget constraint.
   c. After giving away half of her gift certificate, suppose the price of massages increases by 50 percent before Maria can use her gift certificate. Write the equation for her new budget constraint.

8. Every year, Heather hosts a holiday party for her friends. Her party budget is $200. Heather spends her budget on food platters that cost $25 each and on entertainment, which costs $50 per hour. **[LO 7.4]**
   a. Graph Heather's budget constraint for food and entertainment.
   b. To reward her loyal business, the entertainment company Heather hires has offered her a 50 percent discount on entertainment purchases for this year's party. On your graph, illustrate Heather's new budget constraint for food and entertainment.
   c. Assuming that food platters and entertainment are normal goods, what can you say about the quantity of each good that Heather will purchase after the discount? Will the quantity of entertainment increase or decrease, or is the change uncertain? Will the quantity of food increase or decrease, or is the change uncertain?

9. Hideki attends baseball games and goes to movie theaters. Baseball tickets cost $15, and movie tickets cost $10. His entertainment budget is $180. **[LO 7.4]**
   a. Graph Hideki's budget constraint for baseball and movie tickets.

177

b. Suppose the home team is having a good season, and the price of baseball tickets goes up to $20 per game. Graph the new budget constraint.

c. Assuming that baseball and movie tickets are normal goods, what can you say about the quantity of each good that Hideki will consume after the price of baseball tickets goes up? Will the quantity of baseball games he attends increase or decrease, or is the change uncertain? Will the quantity of movies he watches increase or decrease, or is the change uncertain?

10. For which of the following goods is the utility you get from consuming them likely to be affected by the opinions of others? [LO 7.5]

a. MP3s.

b. A new car.

c. Running shoes.

d. A new laptop for class.

11. Say whether each of the following situations is an example of altruism or reciprocity. [LO 7.5]

a. Giving a few canned goods to the local food bank for its annual food drive.

b. Helping someone move her couch after she helped you study for an upcoming exam.

c. The biological relationship between cleaner fish and large predators in the ocean, in which cleaner fish keep the predator free from parasites and the predator keeps the cleaner fish safe.

Chapter Sources

http://www.slate.com/articles/business/money-box/2011/12/scarves_no_surfing_lessons_yes_the_economist_s_guide_to_efficient_gift_giving_.html

https://www.amherst.edu/media/view/104699/original/christmas.pdf

Using Indifference Curves

LEARNING OBJECTIVES

LO E.1   Explain how the marginal rate of substitution relates to the shape of the indifference curve.

LO E.2   Outline the four properties that apply to all indifference curves.

LO E.3   Describe the point at which a consumer maximizes utility.

LO E.4   Show how changes in income and prices affect utility maximization.

- -

Representing Preferences Graphically

The chapter titled "Consumer Behavior" presented utility in all of its complexity. We learned how people decide how much to give, how the consumption of goods is affected by the opinion of others, and how people maximize their utility given how much they are able to spend. In this appendix, we describe an important tool that economists use when looking at how people make decisions—indifference curves.

Indifference curves are a way to represent utility graphically. We'll describe how they work and show that indifference curves come in many shapes and sizes. As you'll see, indifference curves can be applied to many different problems of consumer choice, including how people maximize their utility, how they respond to changes in both income and prices, and how they relate to some fundamental concepts in economics.

Consumption bundles and indifference curves

LO E.1 Explain how the marginal rate of substitution relates to the shape of the indifference curve.

To start, we'll bring back Cody and again look at the decision he has to make about how to best spend his money for the month. Like before, he has $120 dollars to spend on movie and concert tickets. Movies now cost $10, and concert tickets cost $40 each. This presents a lot of choices. He could spend most of his money on movie tickets, leaving comparatively little for concert tickets, or he could splurge on three concert tickets and not see any movies. He could also choose combinations of tickets in between.

Each of these possible combinations he could choose is called a *consumption bundle.* In the chapter "Consumer Behavior," we put these consumption bundles into a utility function, which produced a number that represented the amount of utility a person receives from a certain combination of goods. This was a laborious process, going through each consumption bundle and doing the arithmetic needed to find the utility that would be gained from each possible choice.

FIGURE E-1
Indifference curves

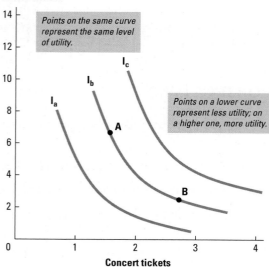

Indifference curves represent the utility provided by different combinations of goods and services. Points on the same indifference curve give the same utility. Higher indifference curves represent greater utility.

Fortunately, there's another way, in which graphs come into play. By representing the utility from various bundles on curves, we can easily compare the bundles visually. An **indifference curve** fulfills this need, linking all the different bundles that provide a consumer with equal levels of utility. It is called an indifference curve because it shows all of the options between which a consumer is truly indifferent. By "indifferent," economists don't mean that the consumer doesn't care about the options. Instead, "indifferent" means that the consumer experiences no real difference between one bundle of goods or services over another. In other words, any of the bundles would be equally acceptable.

Figure E-1 shows a set of indifference curves for our model consumer, Cody. Each point on one of the curves represents a consumption bundle that gives Cody the same amount of satisfaction as the other bundles on that curve. If his consumption moves from point A on curve I_b to point B, he loses some movie tickets, but gets enough extra concert tickets to compensate him so that he feels indifferent between the two options. If he moved to a point on a different curve, though, he would not be indifferent. Specifically, moving to a point on a higher indifference curve, such as I_c, gives him higher utility. Moving to a point on a lower indifference curve, such as I_a, gives him lower utility.

Indifference curves gain their shape from the principle of diminishing marginal utility. At each end of the curve, Cody is indifferent between bundles that trade lots of one good for very little of the other. This is due to diminishing marginal utilities. When he has a lot of movie tickets, he doesn't get very much utility from the last few tickets he buys. Buying one more concert ticket, on the other hand, gives him a lot of utility. As a result, the slope of the curve is very steep. At the other end of the curve, the opposite is true. In order to maintain the same amount of utility, he would have to give away lots of concert tickets in order to compensate for the utility he gets from an extra movie ticket.

At any point, the slope of the indifference curve tells you how much more of one good Cody requires to compensate him for the loss of the other. In other words, it

indifference curve a curve showing all the different consumption bundles that provide a consumer with equal levels of utility

tells you the rate at which he would be willing to trade or substitute between the two goods. This is called the **marginal rate of substitution (MRS)**. Because the marginal rate of substitution is the relative satisfaction the consumer gets from two goods—in general, we'll call them X and Y—at any point, it can also be represented as the ratio of the marginal utilities of the two goods. The marginal rate of substitution is also equal to the absolute value of the slope of the indifference curve at any given point. After all, the slope is just the ratio of how much the y variable changes for one unit of movement along the x-axis.

marginal rate of substitution the rate at which a consumer is willing to trade or substitute between two goods

Equation E-1

$$\text{Absolute value of slope} = \text{MRS} = \frac{MU_X}{MU_Y}$$

Properties of indifference curves

LO E.2 Outline the four properties that apply to all indifference curves.

There are a few properties about indifference curves that are essential to the way they work. Later economics classes (if you take them, which we hope you will do) will prove these rules using math, but for now, we will show why they make sense intuitively.

- *A consumer prefers a higher indifference curve to a lower one.* Since higher indifference curves contain more goods, and the average consumer gets more utility from consuming more, a higher indifference curve represents bundles of goods that provide the consumer with more utility than the bundles on lower indifference curves. Without constraints, it simply doesn't make any sense to pick a bundle on a lower indifference curve when you could pick a bundle with more goods, and more utility.

- *Indifference curves do not cross one another.* Each indifference curve represents all the bundles that provide the consumer with a certain level of utility. Suppose that one curve represents bundles with utility of 10 and a second curve is bundles with utility of 20. If these curves crossed, the bundle at the point of intersection would simultaneously have utility of 10 and 20. That's not possible!

- *Indifference curves usually slope downward.* Assuming that both goods are desirable, then the consumer would always prefer more of each good to less of it. A downward-sloping indifference curve—one with a negative slope—shows that when a consumer gets less of one good, her utility decreases and she requires more of the other good in order to compensate.

- *Indifference curves usually curve inward.* This inward curve, like the side of a bowl, follows from the property of diminishing marginal utility. At the top of the curve, the slope is steep, because the consumer has a lot of the good on the y-axis and is willing to trade more of it for even a little of the good on the x-axis. As the curve goes downward, the consumer has less of the good represented on the y-axis and requires more and more of the good on the x-axis to compensate for the loss of that good, and the slope flattens out.

Just as utility functions are unique to a consumer and represent his personal preferences, so too there is no such thing as a universal set of indifference curves for particular goods. There are only indifference curves for a particular person. Even if Cody and his friend Tasha are both trying to decide how many movie tickets to buy with the same amount of money, if Tasha gets more utility from movies, she will be willing to trade many more concert tickets for movie tickets at every point along the curve.

Perfect substitutes and perfect complements

In two special cases, indifference curves become straight lines. In Chapter 3 we mentioned that many goods have substitutes and complements. Remember, *substitutes* are two goods that have similar qualities and fulfill similar desires. These include tangerines and oranges, tea and coffee, or coal and natural gas, for example. While many goods are general substitutes for each other like these, some are so similar that they can be called *perfect substitutes*. Different brands of milk are a good example. We'd wager that you can't tell the difference between any two brands in the store that are roughly the same price. Different brands of tomatoes, potatoes, and many other types of produce are also often perfect substitutes.

Since both goods are essentially the same, the rules of diminishing marginal utility simply don't apply to perfect substitutes. For example, let's say you have five cartons of Farmer John milk; a friend offers to trade you two cartons of his Happy Cow milk for two cartons of your Farmer John milk. If you can't tell the difference between the two brands, you'd have very little reason to make the trade. There'd be no benefit to giving up some of your Farmer John milk for the same amount of Happy Cow milk.

If the price is the same, you'd always be indifferent to having one brand versus the other, no matter how many cartons you already have of each brand. You are perfectly indifferent between the two. You could spend all of your milk money on each, or split it 50–50 between the two, or trade one Farmer John for one Happy Cow at any point along the curve and still get the same utility. This represents a marginal rate of substitution of 1 at every point. As a result, the indifference curve for perfect substitutes, shown in panel A of Figure E-2, is always linear. In the case of the two milks, since you are willing to trade one carton for the other, the slope of the indifference curve is 1.

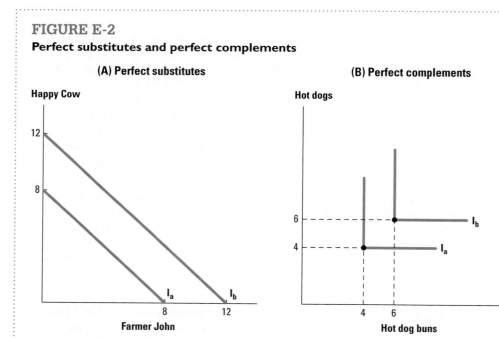

FIGURE E-2
Perfect substitutes and perfect complements

(A) Perfect substitutes

(B) Perfect complements

Since the two goods are perfect substitutes, a consumer is willing trade one for the other in order to maintain the same amount of utility.

Once a consumer has one of each good, adding extras on either side doesn't actually add any further utility. This is because perfect complements are useless without the other good.

The marginal rate of substitution is not always going to be 1, though. In general, the slope of the indifference curve is going to depend on the relative value of the two goods. Take the example of money. In the vast majority of cases, you'd be indifferent toward having a $5 bill or five $1 bills; in the end you buy $5 worth of stuff with either combination. If you don't mind making the trade between the two, the marginal rate of substitution between $1 bills and $5 bills is 5 (or $\frac{1}{5}$ depending on which is on the y-axis), making for a much steeper indifference curve than what was the case for similarly priced milk.

Perfect complements, unlike substitutes, are goods that have to be consumed together. Pairs of shoes, socks, and gloves are all perfect complements. In each of these cases, having just one of a good without its complement isn't useful at all (unless, like Michael Jackson, you favor the single-glove look). If you are having a cookout, you're generally going to want to have enough buns for your hot dogs. Having more buns than hot dogs doesn't increase your utility, as they aren't really good for much besides holding hot dogs, and they just sit around until you get more hot dogs. (Of course, this wouldn't be true if you have trouble with gluten and have to eat hot dogs without the buns.)

The relationship between complements creates an L-shaped indifference curve, part horizontal and part vertical. Let's say that you buy six hot dogs and six buns. Now imagine that you get another bun. Since you can't do anything with the extra bun, you still have the same amount of utility as when you had six hot dogs and six buns. The same is true whether you have eight buns or 12. You still only get the same amount of utility as when you had six of each. The same is also true for when you get more hot dogs. In most cases, it doesn't do you any good to have more hot dogs without buns. This relationship between perfect complements gives the L-shaped indifference curve shown in panel B of Figure E-2.

Understanding Consumer Choice

Even though indifference curves come in many different shapes, their relation to utility maximization is always the same. In the "Consumer Behavior" chapter, we worked through an example—movie and concert tickets—to find what bundle maximizes utility. We looked at each bundle on the budget line, and added up the utility that a consumer (in that case, Cody) got from each good in the bundle. Whichever bundle resulted in the higher amount of utility was the correct choice.

This is a long and tedious process, though. The concepts of marginal rates of substitution and indifference curves presented in this appendix allow for a much clearer picture of how to find where a consumer maximizes his utility. Not to spoil the surprise, but you'll find that these two methods, along with the method of finding the optimal consumption bundle presented in the chapter, end up providing the same answer.

Equalizing the marginal utility of the last purchase

LO E.3 Describe the point at which a consumer maximizes utility.

Another way to think about optimal consumption is to imagine that you are buying utility and trying to get the best value for your money. That is, you want to maximize your marginal utility per dollar spent. How would you choose a consumption bundle that fits this criterion?

Let's approach this challenge from a *marginal decision-making* viewpoint. As a rational consumer, before Cody buys anything, he has to ask himself, "Could I do better by spending my dollar on something else?" Suppose he starts his purchases from scratch, and chooses which good to buy next based on which will bring him the greatest marginal utility per dollar. Marginal utility per dollar spent is calculated by taking the extra utility gained from consuming one more unit of a good and dividing it by the cost of that unit. Panel A of Table E-1 shows the marginal utility of attending concerts, and panel B shows the marginal utility of going to the movies.

If you look at panel C in Table E-1, you'll see that starting with nothing, Cody's best move is to buy a concert ticket. After that, the good that brings him the highest marginal utility per dollar for his next purchase is a movie ticket, and so on. Cody continues to choose each purchase based on what gets him the most bang for his buck—the highest marginal utility for the next dollar he spends. When does this stop? When Cody reaches his budget limit. It's not a coincidence that at this point, the marginal utility of the next dollar spent on each good is the same.

Suppose that instead of starting his purchases from scratch, Cody picks a random consumption bundle, and then analyzes whether he could switch one of his purchases to achieve more utility. If he started with 12 movie tickets and no concert tickets, he could get more utility by switching some of his money over to buy a concert ticket. We can see that the marginal utility per dollar he would get from buying his first concert ticket is greater than the marginal utility per dollar he receives from his last $40 worth of movie tickets. He can continue to make these trades until he reaches a point where he can no longer get more marginal utility by switching his last dollar spent. At this point, the marginal utilities are the same for each of his choices.

Optimal consumption occurs at the point where the marginal utility gained from the dollar spent on good X equals the marginal utility gained from the last dollar spent on good Y.

The marginal utility per dollar spent on good X can be written as the marginal utility divided by the price: $\frac{MU_X}{P_X}$. So, optimal consumption occurs where:

Equation E-2
$$\text{Optimal consumption} = \frac{MU_X}{P_X} = \frac{MU_Y}{P_Y}$$

In our example, Cody reaches the point where the marginal utilities per dollar for concerts and for movies are equal when he watches four movies and two concerts. Notice that this is the same consumption bundle we found to be optimal using the "maximize utility" approach in the "Consumer Behavior" chapter.

Finding the highest indifference curve

You know that consumers prefer bundles on higher indifference curves to lower ones, because those bundles give them greater utility. A final way to think about optimal consumption, therefore, is to find the highest possible indifference curve that still contains bundles within the budget constraint.

Figure E-3 shows Cody's budget constraint and several indifference curves. There are many bundles on curve I_1 that lie within his budget constraint, and even a few that fall on the budget line. But you can see that the highest possible indifference curve he can reach with the given budget constraint is I_2, which just grazes up against the budget line, intersecting it at only one point. He has no reason to choose a bundle on a lower curve, and bundles on higher curves like I_3 are unreachable given his budget.

At the optimal consumption bundle at point C, the slope of the budget line is the same as the slope of the indifference curve—they are tangent to one another. In order to find where the two meet, we need some math.

TABLE E-1
Equalizing marginal utility

(A) Calculating marginal utility of concert tickets

# tickets	Utility	$ spent	Marginal utility/$
0	0	0	—
1	70	40	1.75
2	130	80	1.5
3	185	120	1.375

(B) Calculating marginal utility of movie tickets

# tickets	Utility	$ spent	Marginal utility/$
0	0	0	—
1	17	10	1.7
2	34	20	1.7
3	50	30	1.6
4	65	40	1.5
5	79	50	1.4

The tables show the calculation of the marginal utility Cody would get from the purchase of each ticket. These numbers are used in the next panel to determine the optimal amount of tickets to purchase.

(C) Purchase decisions

Choice	Potential marginal utility/$ from next movie ticket	Potential marginal utility/$ from next concert ticket	Buy?	Total $ spent
1	1.7	1.75	Concert	40
2	1.7	1.5	Movie	50
3	1.7	1.5	Movie	60
4	1.6	1.5	Movie	70
5	1.5	1.5	Buy both!	120

Each purchase gives Cody a certain marginal utility per dollar spent. As he makes each consumption choice, he chooses the good that will bring him the highest marginal utility per dollar. At the point where the marginal utility of the next purchase of each good is equal, Cody buys one of each, and has maximized total utility.

FIGURE E-3

The optimal consumption bundle

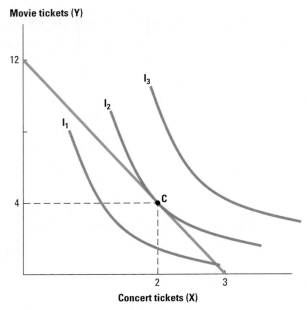

This graph shows several of Cody's indifference curves. Curves I_1 and I_2 are both within his budget. I_3 provides the most utility but will cost more than his budget allows. I_2, which just grazes the budget constraint, provides the most utility that Cody can afford.

In general, the formula for the slope of the budget line for goods X and Y is:

Equation E-3

$$\text{Slope of the budget line} = \frac{P_X}{P_Y}$$

The formula for the slope of the indifference curve between those same goods is:

Equation E-4

$$\text{Slope of the indifference curve} = \text{MRS} = \frac{MU_X}{MU_Y}$$

Since the slope of the budget line is equal to the slope of the indifference curve at the optimal consumption point and they are equal at the point where they are tangent, we can put these two formulas together:

Equation E-5

$$\text{Optimal consumption} = \frac{P_X}{P_Y} = \frac{MU_X}{MU_Y}$$

We can reduce this equation by rearranging terms to put X on one side of the equation and Y on the other. Doing so, we can confirm that this is exactly the same formula that we just found in Equation E-2:

$$\text{Optimal consumption} = \frac{MU_X}{P_X} = \frac{MU_Y}{P_Y}$$

Finding the highest possible indifference curve turns out to be the same thing as equalizing the marginal utility per dollar for each good. Cody can rest easy: No matter which approach he uses to make his consumption choice, he will arrive at the same answer.

In the next few sections, maximizing utility by using indifference curves will be instrumental to figuring out how consumers respond to change. In the "Consumer Behavior" chapter, we were able to make only very general statements about how changes in prices and income affect overall consumption. Now we'll be able to form a more complete picture of how consumers make decisions in response to change.

How Consumers Respond to Change

Budgets change. Prices also go up and down. Consumers respond to changes in income and prices by adjusting their consumption decisions. In this section, we'll describe how to apply the optimal-choice approaches to changes in income and prices. Although in the end we will find the same results as we did in the chapter, we now do so with a more complete conception of consumer decisions using indifference curves.

Responding to a change in income

LO E.4 Show how changes in income and prices affect utility maximization.

From the chapter on "Consumer Behavior," you'll remember that an increase in income shifts the budget constraint out, and a decrease in income has the opposite effect. It was determined that an increase in income leads to more consumption—as long as both goods are normal, meaning that the consumer demands more of them as income increases. This result was taken on faith that since more is better, it is only logical that a consumer would buy more when she receives more income.

Adding indifference curves to this analysis allows us to see why this is true. Although this will be similar to what happened in the "Consumer Behavior" chapter, we'll run through another example of a change in income—this time using indifference curves. Like before, we're back to movie and concert tickets.

When Cody gets $80 dollars for his birthday, the increase in his income means that Cody has access to higher indifference curves that contain more tickets than before. As is the case with any optimization, the goal is to find the indifference curve that is tangent to the new budget constraint. This process is shown in Figure E-4. When his income increases by $80, he ends up buying eight movie tickets and three concert tickets.

Responding to a change in prices

As you'll remember from the chapter, a change in price rotates the budget constraint. In a sense, the change in price is similar to a change in income: When the price of a good increases, for example, you can't afford the same amount of goods as before. The effect is the same as if you'd lost some income.

Although we'll go through and break the effect of a price change into its two parts, we'll first show the overall effect of a change in prices. Starting from our movie/concert ticket setup, let's say that the local movie theater has a special discount that decreases the price of tickets to $5, and the budget constraint rotates outward. The collection of goods that was optimal before the price change is no longer available. The consumer has to move down to a lower indifference curve. Figure E-5 shows this effect: Cody moves from indifference curve I_1 to I_2. Thankfully, the process of optimization is still the same, even as the budget constraint changes. All you need to do is find the indifference curve that is tangent to new budget constraint.

The income and substitution effects. If you'll remember from the body of the chapter, the change in consumption that occurs with a change in prices can be broken into two

Increases in income with normal goods

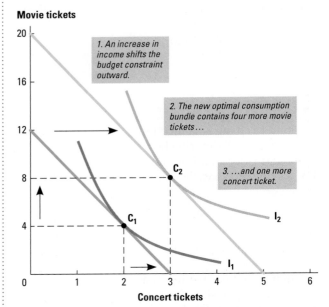

When Cody's income increases, his budget constraint shifts outward, keeping the same slope. Cody will choose to consume at the highest indifference curve possible that intersects the budget line, at point C_2. The new consumption bundle contains both more concert tickets and more movie tickets, meaning that they are both normal goods.

Overall effect of a price decrease

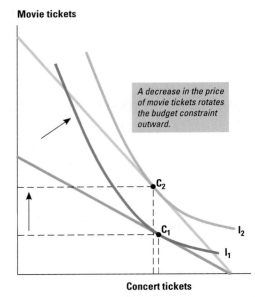

When the price of one good decreases, the budget constraint rotates outward to demonstrate the new consumption bundles that are available. The change in slope reflects the change in the relative prices of the two goods.

parts, the *income effect* and the *substitution effect*. Depending on the type of good, the income and substitution effects will have different impacts on the optimal consumption bundle of the consumer when prices change. For normal goods, a price increase will lead to a larger change in the income effect versus the substitution effect, and so a consumer will consume less.

Let's see what happens when we add indifference curves: Figure E-6 shows the overall response to the price change with indifference curves, in two steps. One corresponds to the substitution effect, and the other to the income effect.

Panel A shows the first step, in which consumption responds to the changes in relative prices (substitution effect) by moving along the original indifference curve to the point where the marginal rate of substitution is equal to the new slope of the budget line, which is shown by the dashed green line (parallel to the original budget line). Panel B shows the second step, when consumption shifts up to the highest indifference curve that is now accessible due to the increase in purchasing power (income effect). This new consumption bundle is at point C_2, which includes more of both goods.

Indifference curves help make sense of the income and substitution effects. Before, we could only make general statements about the impact of a change in prices, but indifference curves allow us to see exactly how much the consumption changes under the income and substitution effects.

Deriving the demand curve using indifference curves

Indifference curves can also fill in our understanding of one of the more fundamental concepts in economics: the individual demand curve. When the demand curve was

FIGURE E-6

The income and substitution effects of a price decrease

(A) Substitution effect

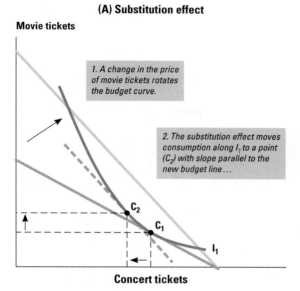

Movie tickets

1. A change in the price of movie tickets rotates the budget curve.

2. The substitution effect moves consumption along I_1 to a point (C_2) with slope parallel to the new budget line...

C_2

C_1

I_1

Concert tickets

The substitution effect moves the optimal consumption point along the *same* indifference curve, increasing consumption of the good whose price has been reduced (movie tickets), and decreasing consumption of the other good (concert tickets). If the substitution effect alone were at work, consumption would move to C_2. The dashed green line reflects the new slope of the budget line.

(B) Income effect

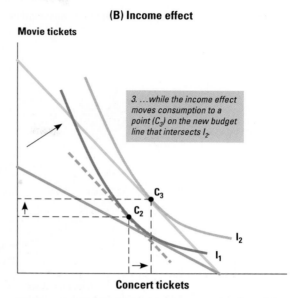

Movie tickets

3. ...while the income effect moves consumption to a point (C_3) on the new budget line that intersects I_2.

C_3

C_2

I_2

I_1

Concert tickets

The income effect will also increase consumption of the good with the newly reduced price (movie tickets), but it has the opposite effect on the item whose price has not changed (concert tickets.) In this particular example, the income and substitution effects happen to have opposite effects on the number of concert tickets purchased. The combined impact of the income and substitution effect in this example is to increase the number of movie tickets purchased.

originally presented in the "Markets" chapter, we simply said the consumer would demand a certain quantity based on price. Did you wonder, Where did those numbers come from? They are actually derived from indifference curves.

Since the indifference curves show where a consumer gets the most utility, it makes sense that any consumer would demand the quantity of a good that gives her the most utility. Remember that indifference curves are intrinsic to a person, and that the demand curves we are making are demand curves *for the individual.* They do not represent full-market demand. With that caveat, we'll bring back, one more time, Cody and his decision to buy concert and movie tickets.

Starting from the original $120 and $10 price for movie tickets, we know that Cody's optimal consumption bundle includes four movie tickets. That is the same as saying that at a price of $10, he demands four movie tickets. What happens if we decrease the price to $5? After the budget constraint rotates inward, his optimal consumption bundle includes five movie tickets. At the lower price, he now demands (is willing to buy) nine tickets. This information is all that we need to build the demand curve. Demanding four tickets when the price is $10 represents one point on the demand schedule, and demanding nine when the price is $5 represents another. Finding the slope between these two points fleshes out the rest of Cody's demand curve. Figure E-7 shows how his demand curve for movie tickets is built in this way.

FIGURE E-7
Deriving the demand curve using indifference curves

(A) Optimal consumption

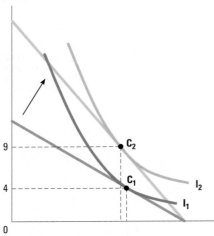

(B) The demand curve for movie tickets

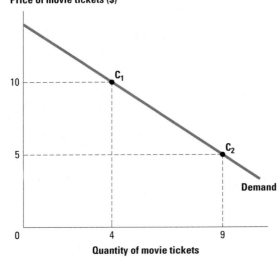

When the price of movie tickets falls from $10 to $5, rotating the budget constraint, the optimal number of movie tickets Cody wants to consume increases from 4 to 9 tickets.

These two optimal consumption bundles provide enough information to build a demand curve for movie tickets.

Conclusion

The idea that individuals maximize utility is one of the most powerful concepts in economics. Indifference curves, though they may seem complex at first, can make understanding this concept far easier. From demand curves to price changes, indifference curves can help explain how consumers decide how much to buy and how satisfied they are with their choices.

Key Terms

indifference curve, p. 178B
marginal rate of substitution (MRS), p. 178C

Summary

LO E.1 Explain how the marginal rate of substitution relates to the shape of the indifference curve.

An indifference curve links all the different bundles that provide a consumer with equal levels of utility. It is called an indifference curve because it shows all of the options among which a consumer is truly indifferent.

At any point, the slope of the indifference curve tells you how much more of one good a consumer requires

to compensate for the loss of the other. In other words, it tells you the rate at which a consumer would be willing to trade or substitute between the two goods. This is the marginal rate of substitution (MRS). Because the marginal rate of substitution is the relative satisfaction the consumer gets from the two goods at any point, it can also be represented as the ratio of the marginal utilities of the two goods. The marginal rate of substitution is also equal to the absolute value of the slope of the indifference curve at any given point. The slope is just the ratio of how much the y variable changes for one unit of movement along the x-axis.

LO E.2 Outline the four rules that apply to all indifference curves.

Indifference curves generally follow four rules: Consumers prefer higher indifference curves to lower ones; indifference curves do not cross; indifference curves usually slope downward; and they bow inward.

LO E.3 Describe the point at which a consumer maximizes utility.

A consumer maximizes utility at the point where the highest indifference curve is tangent to the budget constraint. That is, the utility-maximization point is where the slope of the indifference curve equals the slope of the budget constraint.

This point can also be found through two other methods: (1) Count the utility gained from each bundle on the budget constraint, to see which is the greatest; (2) find the point where the marginal utilities for the goods in the bundle are equal.

LO E.4 Show how changes in income and prices affect utility maximization.

Changes in income shift the budget constraint. Increases in income will, on average, increase the optimal consumption of goods in a bundle. The opposite is true for decreases in income: Changes in prices rotate the budget constraint. On average, when prices decrease, the optimal consumption bundle includes more goods than before; when prices increase, the optimal consumption bundle includes fewer goods than before.

Review Questions

1. If an indifference curve is a vertical line, does the amount of the good on the *y*-axis influence the consumer's utility? **[LO E.1]**

2. Two friends are discussing their plans for the month. One works at a movie theater and gets 10 free movie tickets; the other works at a concert venue and gets 10 free concert tickets. What can we predict about the first person's marginal rate of substitution between movies and concerts? What can we predict about the second person's marginal rate of substitution between the two? How does this relate to the slope of each of their indifference curves? **[LO E.1]**

3. Your friend tells you that although she has a large amount of M&Ms and just a few Skittles, she would still be willing to give up the rest of her Skittles, just to get one last M&M. What characteristic of indifference curves is your friend going against? **[LO E.2]**

4. Suppose that a budget constraint intersects an indifference curve at two separate points. Can either of these consumption bundles be optimal? Explain why or why not. **[LO E.3]**

5. Dan consumes two goods: peanut butter and jelly sandwiches, which are an inferior good, and chicken salad sandwiches, which are a normal good. He gets a raise at work. Will the ratio of peanut butter and jelly sandwiches to chicken salad sandwiches that he consumes increase or decrease? **[LO E.4]**

Problems and Applications

1. Your baby cousin Hubert loves lollipops and bouncy balls. Look at the indifference curves in Figure EP-1 that represent his preferences among various bundles of the two goods. Assuming the indifference curves follow the four properties outlined in this appendix, rank bundles A through D from the highest utility to the lowest, including ties. **[LO E.1]**

2. Table EP-1, shows some possible consumption bundles for a person who consumes MP3s and lattes. **[LO E.2]**
   a. Which bundles fall on the lowest indifference curve?
   b. Which bundles fall on the highest indifference curve?

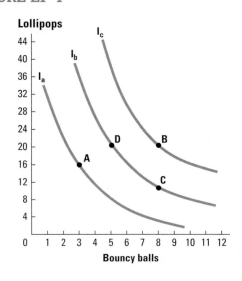

FIGURE EP-1

TABLE EP-1

Bundle	Number of MP3s	Number of lattes	Total utility
A	13	8	20
B	3	2	12
C	13	10	23
D	6	3	15
E	9	4	17
F	6	1	12
G	17	9	23
H	4	0	11

TABLE EP-2

Quantity of a good	Marginal utility of a soda	Marginal utility of a sports drink
1	10	8
2	8	7
3	6	6
4	5	5
5	4	4
6	3	3
7	2	2

3. Determine whether the preferences described below would be represented by an indifference curve that is L-shaped, bows inward, or is a straight line. **[LO E.2]**

   a. Edgar will eat carrots only if he has hummus to go with them.

   b. Andrew likes to start his day right with oatmeal, but he's just as happy starting it with steel-cut oats as he is with rolled oats.

   c. Ezekiel really enjoys coffee and donuts together, but he's also happy eating just one or the other.

4. A consumer is stocking up on sodas and sports drinks at the dollar store. As you might expect at a dollar store, each bottle of each drink costs $1. He has a $10 bill to spend. Based on Table EP-2 of marginal utilities, find the optimal consumption bundle. **[LO E.3]**

5. A consumer is buying steaks for $4 each and potatoes for $1 per pound. She has $40. Plot her budget constraint on Figure EP-2, and find her optimal consumption bundle. **[LO E.3]**

6. Under utility maximization, is it possible that after an increase in income, a consumer would remain

FIGURE EP-2

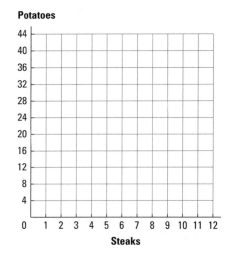

on the same indifference curve? What about after a decrease in the price of one of the goods? **[LO E.4]**

7. *True or false?* The income effect is represented by the shift in consumption of a good as the bundle moves along the old indifference curve before moving to another indifference curve tangent to the new budget line. **[LO E.4]**

Behavioral Economics: A Closer Look at Decision Making

LEARNING OBJECTIVES

LO 8.1 Define time inconsistency, and explain how it accounts for procrastination and other problems with self-control.

LO 8.2 Explain why sunk costs should not be taken into account in deciding what to do next.

LO 8.3 Identify the types of opportunity cost that people often undervalue, and explain why undervaluing them distorts decision making.

LO 8.4 Define fungibility, and explain why it matters in financial decision making.

. . . .

WHEN IS $20 NOT QUITE $20?

Imagine yourself in the following situation: Earlier today, you bought a ticket for a concert this evening. The ticket cost $20. You arrive at the concert venue, reach into your pocket for the ticket, and . . . it's not there. You must have dropped it somewhere on the way. How annoying! Tickets are still available at the door for $20. Which of the following is your reaction?

#1: "Oh well, never mind. These things happen. I'll just buy another ticket."
#2: "No way I'm going to spend $40 on this concert! I'd rather go do something else instead."

   If you said #2, many are like you: 46 percent of people presented by researchers with a similar situation said they'd do something else with their evening. The others, 54 percent, said they'd swallow their annoyance enough to buy a replacement ticket.

   Now imagine an alternative scenario. This time you arrive at the concert venue intending to buy your ticket at the door. You reach into your pocket for the money to pay, and . . . hold on, what's this? You definitely had five $20 bills in your pocket this morning, but now you have only four. You must have lost one of them somewhere today. How annoying! Which of the following do you then say?

#1: "Oh well, never mind. These things happen. I'll get my ticket for the concert."
#2: "You know what? Forget the concert."

This time only 12 percent chose #2 and said they'd abandon their evening plans. Fully 88 percent of people said they'd buy the ticket anyway.

You may have noticed that these two situations are *exactly the same*. In both scenarios, you arrive at the venue intending to see a concert you had previously decided was worth $20 to you, only to make the unwelcome discovery that you are $20 less well off than you'd thought you were.

If you are very short of cash, it would make sense to skip the concert in *either* case. If you're not short of cash, it wouldn't make sense to do so in *either* case. What difference does it make if you lost the $20 bill *before* or *after* you'd converted it into a concert ticket? Objectively, it doesn't matter at all. Emotionally, however, it does seem to matter. (Even if you'd have bought a ticket in both scenarios, wouldn't you have felt just a little bit more annoyed about losing the ticket?) To a significant minority of people, that emotional difference is so great it would make them abandon their plans if they'd lost the ticket, but *not* if they'd lost the $20 bill.

This is not rational behavior. Other examples of apparently irrational behavior are common:

- Saying you want to lose weight, but ordering dessert.
- Being willing to pay more for something if you use a credit card than if you use cash.
- Stubbornly watching to the end of a movie you've decided you're not enjoying at all.

Rational (as defined in economics) people wouldn't behave in these ways, but many people do. Yet, haven't we said throughout this book that economists assume people behave rationally to maximize their utility? Yes, we have. So what's going on?

The assumption that people are rational utility maximizers gets us a long way. It's true enough often enough to be useful. But it's not true all the time, and how much the exceptions matter is a hotly debated question in economics right now. In the past few decades economists have been learning a lot from psychologists and biologists about how real people make everyday decisions that translate economic ideas into action. The resulting theories have developed into a branch of economics that expands our models of decision making. This field is called *behavioral economics*, the topic of this chapter.

Behavioral economists are not just advancing our academic knowledge of how people make decisions. They also have developed some practical, easy-to-use tools that can help people enact the choices they *say* they would like to make: save more money, get healthier, give more to charity. You may even be using some of these tools without realizing it.

behavioral economics a field of economics that draws on insights from psychology to expand models of individual decision making

Formally, **behavioral economics** is a field of economics that draws on insights from psychology to expand models of individual decision making. Behavioral economics is wide-ranging, and in this chapter we'll cover just three of its more interesting applications: time inconsistency, thinking irrationally about costs, and forgetting the fungibility of money.

d. Enrolling in an automatic-transfer program that will move a specified amount of money from your checking account to your savings account each month.

3. You're seated at a banquet that is beginning to become boring. Which of the following pieces of information are relevant to your decision to stay or go somewhere else? [LO 8.2]

   a. Another party is happening at the same time, and you've heard that it's fun.

   b. The dinner you were served was only so-so.

   c. You haven't eaten dessert yet, and it looks delicious.

   d. You paid $30 to attend the banquet.

   e. The other party has a cover charge of $10.

4. You just spent $40 on a new movie for your collection. You would have preferred the director's cut but discovered when you got home that you bought the theatrical version. The store you bought the movie from has an "all sales final" policy, but you could resell the movie online for $30. The director's cut sells for $50. By how much would you need to value the director's cut over the theatrical version for it to make sense for you to sell the version you bought and buy the director's cut? [LO 8.2]

5. Suppose you're bowling with friends. You've already played one game and are trying to decide whether to play another. Each game costs $6 per person, plus a one-time rental fee of $5 for the bowling shoes. It would take another hour to play the next game, which would make you late to work. Missing an hour of work would mean that you would lose pay at a rate of $12 per hour. Based on this information, how much would you have to enjoy the next bowling game, expressed in terms of dollars, to play another game? [LO 8.3]

6. During a holiday party at work, you pay $2 to buy a raffle ticket for a 160-gigabyte iPod. You win the drawing. Based on a little research online, you discover that the going rate for a hardly used 160-gigabyte iPod is $200. [LO 8.3]

   a. What was the opportunity cost of acquiring the iPod?

   b. What is the opportunity cost of choosing to keep the iPod?

7. Jamie is saving for a trip to Europe. She has an existing savings account that earns 2 percent interest and has a current balance of $4,500. Jamie doesn't want to use her current savings for vacation, so she decides to borrow the $1,500 she needs for travel expenses. She will repay the loan in exactly one year. The annual interest rate is 5 percent. [LO 8.4]

   a. If Jamie were to withdraw the $1,500 from her savings account to finance the trip, how much interest would she forgo?

   b. If Jamie borrows the $1,500, how much will she pay in interest?

   c. How much does the trip cost her if she borrows rather than dips into her savings?

8. Suppose you have accumulated a credit card balance of $500, at an annual interest rate of 10 percent. You are also planning to open a new savings account that accumulates interest at an annual rate of 3 percent. You just got your paycheck and have $200 that you can use either to pay down your debt or open your savings account. [LO 8.4]

   a. If you use the full $200 to pay down your debt, what will your credit card balance be in one year? Assume no additional credit card payments during this time.

   b. If, instead, you put the full $200 into your savings account, what will be the balance in your savings account in one year, assuming you make no additional deposits during this time? What will your credit card balance be, assuming you make no additional payments during this time because your payment requirements have been deferred for one year?

   c. In one year, how much money will you have lost if you deposit the $200 in your savings account compared to paying down your credit card?

Chapter Endnote

1. http://duke.edu/~dandan/Papers/PI/deadlines.pdf.

Game Theory and Strategic Thinking

LEARNING OBJECTIVES

LO 9.1 Define strategic behavior and describe the components of a strategic game.

LO 9.2 Explain why noncooperation is a dominant strategy in the prisoners' dilemma.

LO 9.3 Explain how repeated play can enable cooperation.

LO 9.4 Explain how backward induction can be used to make decisions.

LO 9.5 Use a decision tree to solve a sequential game.

LO 9.6 Define first-mover advantage and identify it in practice.

LO 9.7 Explain why patient players have more bargaining power in repeated games.

LO 9.8 Explain how a commitment strategy can allow players to achieve their goals by limiting their options.

LITTERBUGS BEWARE

Litter is an eyesore, whether it's a candy bar wrapper on the sidewalk or a plastic bag caught on a fence along the highway. Most people would prefer clean streets, parks, and oceans over messy ones, so why is there litter?

Imagine that it's a sunny day and that you've had lunch at a table outside. You're just finishing up when the wind blows your sandwich wrapper to the ground. You could go chase it, but the wind is blowing the paper even farther away. You're in a hurry, and it's unlikely that you will get caught and punished for not putting the wrapper in a trash can. Besides, there's other trash around; your wrapper is not going to make much difference to the overall environment. So, with a bit of guilt, you walk away.

The trouble is that once others see your garbage blowing about, they're more likely to decide to litter as well. That then can lead to even more litter. The result is an increasingly dirty, trash-strewn community.

That's the paradox. Everyone would like to have a clean environment, but incentives push us to sometimes make things just a little bit worse. Over time, with everyone making things just a little bit worse, the outcome adds up to being a lot worse. Once

everyone's littering, you'll litter more too. It's not the best outcome, but somehow that's how things unwind. The problem escalates because it's impossible to get everyone to agree, voluntarily, to not litter.

How can the problem be fixed? One idea is to create strong norms against littering. One way to do that is to encourage families, schools, churches, and other civic organizations to reinforce the shared sense that it's good to keep communities clean. The now-iconic "Don't Mess with Texas" slogan was originally created at the request of the Texas Department of Transportation to try to create social norms against roadside litter.

The government of Singapore in Southeast Asia took a different route; it used a strong dose of economic incentives. It made a choice to stop the problem before it started. If you're caught in Singapore tossing trash anywhere but in the trash can, it will cost you $1,400. In addition to the fine, the Singaporean authorities usually impose what is called a "corrective work order." This order forces you to collect trash outside in bright green vests under the full scrutiny of public humiliation. If you try to dump something a little bigger, say, by tossing a full garbage bag from your car—you face up to $35,000 in fines or a year in jail, plus the loss of your vehicle.

With these harsh punishments, it's not surprising that Singapore is generally cleaner than large cities in the United States. In New York City, for example, you sometimes have to walk for blocks to find a trash can, and the fine for littering in New York (from $50 to $250) doesn't have the same sting as in Singapore. By making littering very costly, Singapore left its citizens with little choice but to put their trash in the can, solving the littering problem. Singapore's policy is tough, but authorities argue that the high fines help citizens obtain the clean outcome that they want. That outcome had been impossible to achieve because of a collective failure to voluntarily quit littering. What's more, in the end the authorities rarely have to enforce the fines. With effective incentives in place, few people end up littering.

While Singapore has found a way to reduce litter, many other places have problems with trash that simply cannot be solved through heavy fines and rules. When trash moves across borders or floats open in the sea, it is hard to create workable international solutions. Deep within state or national parks and wilderness areas, it's hard to catch litterers. But as the Singapore example shows, taking people's motivations and incentives seriously is a helpful way to start piecing together responses.

In this chapter, we'll see that the littering problem is an example of the *prisoners' dilemma*—a game of strategy in which people make rational choices that lead to a less-than-ideal result for all. It might seem to trivialize choices to think of them as a "game," but economists use the term *game* in a broader sense than its everyday use: To economists, *games* are not just recreational pursuits like chess, Monopoly, or poker, but any situation in which players pursue strategies designed to achieve their goals. As we'll see in this chapter, these kind of games pop up in all kinds of real-world situations, ranging from environmental protection to business to war.

Information

LEARNING OBJECTIVES

LO 10.1 Define information asymmetry and explain why it matters for economic decision making.

LO 10.2 Define adverse selection and explain how it is caused by asymmetric information.

LO 10.3 Define moral hazard and explain how it is caused by asymmetric information.

LO 10.4 Differentiate between screening and signaling and describe some applications of each.

LO 10.5 Explain how reputations can help to solve information problems.

LO 10.6 Explain how statistical discrimination might be used to solve information problems.

LO 10.7 Discuss the uses and limitations of education and regulation in overcoming information asymmetry problems.

A SOLUTION FOR STUDENT LOANS?

In the 1970s, administrators at Yale University thought they had come up with a student loan program that solved many of the problems faced by students trying to pay for an education. Here's how it worked: Students could choose to join a plan whereby, instead of paying back individual loans, they would owe a small percentage of their income every year after graduation. They would stop owing payments when the debt for their *entire graduating class* was paid off.

The idea was to remove the disincentive for students to go into worthwhile public-service careers, which tend not to pay well. The university realized that these students had a harder time paying off individual loans. Under their new plan, graduates with low incomes would pay only a small amount; those with higher incomes would make up the difference. University administrators figured that every class would have some captains of industry and some social workers and missionaries. By pooling everyone's debt, things would even out. The investment bankers and corporate lawyers would hardly miss the extra money they had to pay, but teachers and artists would benefit tremendously from their lower monthly payments.

Chapter 10

Good idea? If you said yes, you wouldn't be the only one to think so. The plan was supported by Yale economist James Tobin who subsequently won a Nobel Prize—and it drew on an idea put forward earlier by Milton Friedman, a University of Chicago economist (and another Nobel winner). Unfortunately, almost 30 years later, not a single graduating class had succeeded in paying off its collective debt. The program was deemed a total flop, and the university was pressured into canceling much of the debt.

What went wrong? There were two problems. The first was that the program was optional: Students could choose to opt out and pay off their debt individually in the usual way. Administrators had assumed that a representative cross-section of students would want to participate in the program. They overlooked the fact that many students have plans for life after college and have a fairly good sense of whether their incomes are likely to be high or low. Those who are drawn to banking or medicine can expect to earn a lot of money; those called to teaching or preaching can expect to earn less. To a student expecting to earn a low income, the program looked like a great deal—pay only what you can afford. For a student expecting a higher income, it wasn't such an attractive prospect: She'd probably end up paying off not only her own loan, but also those of her less-wealthy peers. Not surprisingly, then, many students who anticipated a higher income chose not to join the program. The planned pooling of big and small contributions did not take place.

As if this wasn't bad enough, a second problem soon became apparent: Unlike the Internal Revenue Service (IRS), the university could not automatically collect payments from alumni's paychecks. The university had to rely on program participants to feel so good about their alma mater that they would willingly report their income and pay what they owed. You may not be surprised to hear that this did not work out so well. Not all participants held up their end of the deal. The university had to try to hunt down its alumni, find out how much money they had made, and force them to pay. It was not well-equipped to do this.

These two problems have a common theme—an imbalance of information. When students were deciding whether to join the program, they knew how likely it was that they would become investment bankers, but the university didn't. (Even if the university had known about students' career intentions, that wouldn't have forced the future investment bankers to participate—but alarm bells might have rung when they noticed that the program was disproportionately packed with education and art majors, without any finance majors.) And then, as the program participants graduated and started work, the university couldn't know how much they were earning and if they were underpaying on what they owed. The problems caused by the missing information weren't just flukes or the result of lax enforcement; they were inherent in the program's design.

Up to this point, we have mostly assumed that economic decision makers are fully informed when they make decisions. We will see in this chapter that imbalances in information can cause problems in all kinds of transactions—between lenders and borrowers, buyers and sellers, and employers

b. You are purchasing your car from a local dealership.

11. In college admissions, which of the following are examples of statistical discrimination? Choose all that apply. **[LO 10.6]**

   a. A college has minimum required scores on standardized tests.

   b. A college is an all-women's school.

   c. A college uses high-school GPA to rank students for scholarship offers.

   d. A college requires three letters of recommendation.

12. In a market for car insurance, which of the following are examples of statistical discrimination? Choose all that apply. **[LO 10.6]**

   a. Premiums are adjusted based on the zip code of the insured.

   b. Premiums are adjusted based on the color of the car.

   c. Premiums are adjusted based on the driving record of the insured.

   d. Premiums are adjusted based on the model of the car.

13. Say which public regulation approach is likely to be more effective in providing information to consumers of pharmaceuticals. **[LO 10.7]**

   a. Requiring pharmaceutical companies to list major side effects of their medications in television advertisements.

   b. Requiring pharmaceutical companies to post online the full text of research results from medical testing done during the development of new drugs.

14. Say which public regulation approach is likely to be more effective in providing information to consumers of restaurant meals. **[LO 10.7]**

   a. Filing a notice at city hall when a restaurant fails a health and sanitation inspection.

   b. Posting a public notice on the door of a restaurant that fails a health and sanitation inspection.

Chapter Endnote

1. For the record: The alternative scenario is totally hypothetical—the IRS is not legally allowed to engage in the activity described in the scenario.

Time and Uncertainty

LEARNING OBJECTIVES

LO 11.1	Explain why money is worth more now than in the future, and how the interest rate represents this relationship.
LO 11.2	Calculate compounding over time with a given interest rate.
LO 11.3	Calculate the present value of a future sum.
LO 11.4	Evaluate the costs and benefits of a choice using expected value.
LO 11.5	Explain how risk aversion makes a market for insurance possible.
LO 11.6	Explain the importance of pooling and diversification for managing risk.
LO 11.7	Describe the challenges that adverse selection and moral hazard pose for insurance.

IS COLLEGE WORTH IT?

As the 2012 presidential campaign swung into gear, there was at least one thing that Republican Mitt Romney and Democrat Barack Obama could agree on: Both believed the interest rate on federal student loans should be frozen at 3.4 percent per year.[1] Both candidates seemed to feel that the government should limit the financial burden associated with the choice to attend college.

For most students, college loans are not just political talking points. The total amount of student loan debt has now climbed to about $1 trillion dollars, and about two-thirds of U.S. college students leave college with some debt.[2] The interest on loans means eventually paying back a lot more than the amount you borrowed. Is it worth it? In 2011 just over half of people under age 25 with bachelor's degrees were not able to find a job in line with their qualifications.[3]

How should you think about borrowing for college? The decision to attend college means weighing the trade-offs involved and deciding that the costs and benefits of a college degree make it more worthwhile than other things you could be doing with your time and money. If you borrow to go to college, you have to decide that it's worth paying a future fee (called *interest* payments) to get your hands on a chunk of money right now. Whether or not you borrow, you have to believe that your time and tuition money are better spent on college than other options, like investing an equal amount of money in real estate or a business start-up, or spending more time working rather than studying.

For most people, at least part of the decision to go to college depends on anticipated future earnings. You expect a college education to pay off down the road by enriching your mind and teaching you skills that will increase your chances of getting a high-paying job. You're betting that your extra earnings will more than cover the interest

costs of your loan. You also are betting that those earnings will be greater than what you could have accrued by investing borrowed money somewhere else and starting to work right away instead. For most people these are good bets. But there's always uncertainty, especially when the economy is shaky. Economics provides a way to think about choices like this, which have uncertain future costs and benefits.

When you make decisions that require you to weigh uncertain future costs and benefits, you face two complications. The first is that you can't directly compare costs and benefits that show up now (such as college tuition) with those that show up in the future (such as higher salaries), because the value of money changes over time. In this chapter, we'll show how to use interest rates to make these comparisons accurately.

The second complication is that the future is uncertain. For instance, there is always the possibility that you might *not* end up earning more, despite your college degree. In the following section we look at how to account for risk when making decisions about the future. In the final part of the chapter, we'll see how some risks can be managed through diversifying and pooling.

You can put the ideas in this chapter to work to understand many important life decisions: whether to take out a loan to buy a house or a car or to start a business; whether to purchase insurance against car accidents or theft, or to provide for your children if you get too sick to work; and whether you should invest in some opportunity or other—the stock market, real estate, retirement funds—in the hope of getting income in the future.

Value Over Time

In previous chapters we've talked about making decisions by weighing the benefits and opportunity cost of each option. Conveniently, many decisions involve immediate trade-offs—that is, costs and benefits that occur at the same time. You give the barista your money, and in return you get handed a coffee, right away.

In this chapter, we'll apply the question *What are the trade-offs?* to a trickier set of decisions—those that involve costs that occur at one time and benefits that occur at another.

Timing matters

LO 11.1 Explain why money is worth more now than in the future, and how the interest rate represents this relationship.

Why does it matter if the costs and benefits of a choice occur at different times? Consider the following scenario: You have won first prize in a competition. Congratulations! For your prize, you can choose one of the following options.

Option A: You can have $100,000 now.

Option B: You can have $100,000 ten years from now.

Which would you choose? We're guessing you'd take option A. If you take the $100,000 now, you can do fun or useful things with it right away—like pay for your college education, or treat yourself to a brand new Porsche, or donate tens of thousands of insecticide-treated bednets to help people living in malarial areas of Africa stay healthy. Why would you wait 10 years to do any of these things?

Even if you don't intend to do anything with the money right away, you're still better off taking option A—you can always just save it while you think about what to do with it. Pretty much everyone would rather have money now than the same amount of money later. Conversely, most people prefer *costs* that are delayed to those they have to bear immediately. That's why so many people buy things on credit.

These preferences—for immediate benefits and delayed costs—are another way of saying that money is worth more to us *now* than in the future. This means we cannot simply equate costs and benefits that occur at different times. To be able to weigh trade-offs that happen over time, we need a way of reflecting the changing value of money over time.

Interest rates

How *much* more is money worth now than in the future? Suppose that you now get the following prize options for winning the competition:

Option A: You can have $100,000 now.

Option B: You can have $1,000,000 ten years from now.

Which would you choose? Tempting as it would be to take $100,000 now, we bet most people would probably be willing to wait 10 years to get their hands on a million. Now ask yourself this: How much would we have to offer to convince you to take option B over option A? $105,000? $200,000? $350,000? $500,000? Not everyone will have the same answer. It depends on how much more it is worth to you to have money now, rather than 10 years from now. If you strongly prefer to have cash in hand, then we'll have to offer you a lot more money in the future in order to convince you to wait. If you're more patient, we won't have to offer you so much.

But where do these individual preferences come from? Think about this question in terms of opportunity cost. *What is the opportunity cost* of waiting until the future to get your money? It's the value of whatever you could otherwise have done with the money in the meantime.

When a bank lends you money to attend college, for example, it passes up the opportunity to do something else productive with that money instead. Thus, if you want the bank to give you money now, you have to agree to pay something extra when you repay the loan in future. The opportunity cost to the bank of lending you money is represented by the **interest rate** it charges you on the loan—the price of borrowing money for a specified period of time, expressed as a percentage per dollar borrowed and per unit of time. The interest rate tells us how much more the money is worth to the bank today than in the future. Different banks may offer loans at different interest rates, depending on how strongly they prefer to have cash in hand.

interest rate the price of borrowing money for a specified period of time, expressed as a percentage per dollar borrowed and per unit of time

POTENTIALLY CONFUSING

In the real world, interest rates also reflect the risk that a borrower will default on a loan, and the risk of inflation. For the sake of simplicity, we are ignoring inflation and assuming that all loans are certain to be paid back. This enables us to zero in on what interest rates fundamentally represent: the *opportunity cost* of having to wait to get your money.

On the flip-side, when you save money at a bank, the bank usually pays you interest on your deposit. In essence, the bank is borrowing money from you, the depositor. You, too, have an opportunity cost—the value of whatever else you could have done with that money instead of depositing it with the bank. Again, for each individual this will be different. Some will be happy to deposit money at 1 percent interest, while others would prefer to do something else with their money unless they are offered 5 percent. Interest rates are an important concept in macroeconomics as well as microeconomics, and we'll return to them in greater detail later in the book. For now, we'll focus on why they matter for individual decision making.

Typically, the interest rate is expressed as a percentage of the sum of money in question, over a specified time period—usually one year. For instance, if the interest rate on a loan of $1,000 is 5 percent per year, it means that after one year the borrower will owe the original $1,000 plus 5 percent of $1,000 in interest:

$$\$1,000 + (\$1,000 \times 5\%) = \$1,000 \times 1.05 = \$1,050$$

The general formula for the value of a loan of amount X at the end of one period of time with an interest rate r is:

Equation 11-1

$$\text{Value of a loan with interest} = (X \times 1) + (X \times r) = X \times (1 + r)$$

You can also think of interest as a cost per unit, just like other prices. An annual interest rate of 5 percent is the same thing as saying that the price of borrowing money is $0.05 per year for every dollar you owe. Interest is a price per dollar, *per unit of time*.

Equation 11-2

$$\text{Interest rate: } r = \frac{\text{Price per \$}}{\text{Time}}$$

Compounding

LO 11.2 Calculate compounding over time with a given interest rate.

An annual interest rate of 5 percent tells us that the cost of borrowing $1,000 for one year is $50. So what's the cost of borrowing $1,000 for two years, or five years, or 10 years?

Unfortunately, it's not as simple as just $50 a year. That's because interest also accumulates on interest, not just on the original sum. Let's say you deposit $1,000 in a bank account that offers 5 percent interest (remember, effectively the bank is borrowing the money from you). After one year, you have $1,050. In the second year, you earn 5 percent interest on $1,050 (not the original $1,000), which is $52.50. After two years you have $1,102.50, not $1,100.

$$
\begin{aligned}
\text{1st year:} \quad & (\$1,000 \times 1.05) = \$1,050 \\
\text{2nd year:} \quad & (\$1,000 \times 1.05) \times 1.05 \\
& = \$1,000 \times (1.05)^2 = \$1,102.50
\end{aligned}
$$

compounding the process of accumulation that results from the additional interest paid on previously earned interest

This process of accumulation, as interest is paid on interest that has already been earned, is called **compounding**. Over time, compounding can have a big effect. If you were expecting your initial $1,000 deposit to grow by a steady $50 per year, then after 20 years you would expect to have $2,000 in the bank. But thanks to compounding, your

5 percent interest earnings help you accumulate $1,000 \times (1.05)^{20} = \$2,653.29$. With compounding, the general formula for finding the future value of an initial deposit (*PV*) over a time period of *n* years at interest rate *r* is:

Equation 11-3

$$\text{Future value of a sum} = FV = PV \times (1 + r)^n$$

Compounding is welcome news for investors, because it means your money grows at a greater rate than you might have expected. Instead of taking 20 years to double your money, as it would if your $1,000 grew by just $50 a year, it takes just a little over 14 years for your deposit to double in value at an interest rate of 5 percent. See "The rule of 70" in the Real Life box for a quick way to estimate compounding over time.

REAL LIFE
The rule of 70

The "rule of 70" is a quick and easy tool for estimating the effects of compounding over time. It states that the amount of time it will take an investment to double in value is roughly 70 time periods divided by the interest rate per period. Therefore, if you are earning 5 percent interest per year on your savings account, it will take about $70 \div 5 = 14$ years for the value of your account to double. *To learn more about the rule of 70, continue reading by scanning the QR code near the end of the chapter or by going online.*

As nice as compounding is for savers, it can be dangerous territory for borrowers—especially when interest rates are much higher than 5 percent, as they often are for credit cards and personal loans. While federally guaranteed student loans currently top out at 6.8 percent per year, private student loans can cost as much as 18 percent. If you don't keep up with payments on your loans, unpaid interest incurs more interest due to compounding, and debts can rapidly spiral out of control.

Present value

LO 11.3 Calculate the present value of a future sum.

The decision to go to college means accepting immediate costs—such as tuition, room and board, and time spent studying rather than earning a salary—in return for the anticipated benefit of earning higher salaries down the road. Knowing that interest rates represent the opportunity cost of delaying benefits, we can come closer to answering the question with which we started this chapter: How can you know whether the delayed benefits of college will outweigh the immediate costs?

Economists use interest rates to compare the present value and future value of a sum. Earlier, we asked how much you'd have to be offered before you'd prefer to wait 10 years than to have $100,000 right now. Let's say you think you could invest the money for an 8 percent annual return. We can calculate that the future value of $100,000 in 10 years with an 8 percent interest rate is $100,000 \times (1.08)^{10} = \$215,892.50$.

If we know the future value, we can also rearrange this equation to calculate **present value**. Present value is how much a certain amount of money that will be obtained in the future is worth today. So if you knew that an investment was going to pay you $215,892.50 in 10 years, and you knew that the interest rate over that time would be 8 percent, then you

present value how much a certain amount of money that will be obtained in the future is worth today

could calculate the present value of that investment as \$215,892.50 ÷ $(1.08)^{10}$ = \$100,000. More generally, if r is the annual interest rate, then the formula for calculating the present value of a sum FV received in n years at interest rate r is as follows:

Equation 11-4

$$\text{Present value of a sum} = PV = \frac{FV}{(1 + r)^n}$$

Notice that this formula is simply another way of writing Equation 11-3. The relationship between present value and future value is always given by the interest rate and the time period. If you know the present value, you can multiply by the compound interest rate to find the future value. If you know the future value, you can divide by the compound interest rate to find the present value. Present value translates future costs or benefits into the equivalent amount of cash in hand today. That information enables us to compare the future amounts directly with the immediate amounts.

Let's go back to your college-loan decision. Say you expect that if you *don't* have a college degree, you'll earn a total career income of \$1.2 million (that equates to an average of \$40,000 a year over 30 years). If you *do* have a degree, you expect to earn an extra \$20,000 a year, raising your total career income to \$1.8 million. So if you go to college, you expect to have earned an extra \$600,000 after working for 30 years (\$20,000 × 30). What is that future \$600,000 worth in today's money? Let's say that your first job starts five years from now, and that you expect to be able to invest your money at a 5 percent interest rate. You can calculate that the present value of the extra \$600,000 you earn by going to college is equivalent to having \$252,939 in hand right now, by the following calculation:[4]

$$\$20,000/(1.05)^5 + \$20,000/(1.05)^6 + \$20,000/(1.05)^7 + \ldots + \$20,000/(1.05)^{34}$$

According to the calculation, as long as you are paying less than \$252,939 to attend college, then the future benefit will exceed the present cost. In fact, a more realistic version of this calculation would show college in an even more favorable light, since you don't have to pay all the tuition money at once. This is just an example, of course. With your own predictions about your likely earnings (based on your expected career, where you're going to live, and other relevant variables), you can calculate a comparison that's tailor-made for your own situation.

Knowing how to translate between present and future value can be useful in many other decisions when the benefits and opportunity cost occur at different times. If you want a certain level of income when you retire, how much should you save into your retirement fund now? If you run a business, what value of future sales would be needed to make it worthwhile to invest in a new piece of machinery? You can compare these kinds of costs and benefits as long as you know three of the four variables in Equations 11-3 and 11-4: time period, interest rate, and either the present or future value of the costs and benefits.

It's surprising to learn that many people earn a million dollars over a lifetime of work. (However, at \$8 an hour, you'd have to work about 16 hours a day for over 30 years.)

© Dan Piraro, May 20, 2009, bizarrocomics.com. Used with permission.

✓ CONCEPT CHECK

❏ What does the interest rate on a loan represent to the lender? **[LO 11.1]**

❏ What is the "rule of 70"? **[LO 11.2]**

❏ What two factors determine the relationship between a future sum of money and its present value? **[LO 11.3]**

Risk and Uncertainty

If you are the worrying sort, you may have noticed a limitation of, or problem with, our analysis of the costs and benefits of college. What happens if your income doesn't increase as much as you expect it to as a result of attending college?

Just as in this example, some of the most important life decisions you will face involve weighing uncertain future costs and benefits against today's costs and benefits. We can make educated guesses about what will happen in the future, but there is always the chance that these guesses will turn out to be off. The changing value of money over time is only one challenge when making decisions about the future; risk is another.

What is risk?

Risk exists when the costs or benefits of an event or choice are uncertain. Everything in life involves some uncertainty. When you fly, there might be a delay that means missing an important connection. When you buy a used car, it might turn out to need expensive repairs. When you invest in a company, its stock price could tumble. When you invest in a college education, you might graduate just as the economy is tanking and well-paying jobs are hard to find. Evaluating risk requires that we think about different possible outcomes and accept that our best guess about future costs and benefits could be wrong.

risk exists when the costs or benefits of an event or choice are uncertain

```
POTENTIALLY CONFUSING
```

Although they may seem like similar ideas, some economists often distinguish between "risk" and "uncertainty." They use *risk* to refer to situations in which the probabilities that different outcomes will happen *are known*. We know, for example, that a coin has a 50 percent chance of coming up heads when it's flipped. Making a bet on a coin flip thus entails risk. Or, consider airline safety: Although you may not want to look at the numbers (they are actually quite reassuring), the Federal Aviation Administration collects extensive statistics on the safety of airplanes; anyone can make a reasonable guess of the chance of the next flight crashing.

Those examples contrast with situations of *uncertainty*, in which the probabilities are *not known*, and may not even be measurable. The decision to go to college, for example, involves uncertainties about your future earnings and happiness in different kinds of careers. Even the best economists can't accurately predict what the health of the economy will be 10 or 20 years down the road.

The distinction may matter when you take courses focused on risk and uncertainty. But in the rest of the chapter, we'll use the terms *risk* and *uncertainty* interchangeably to refer to choices for which the probabilities of the event occurring are known.

Expected value

LO 11.4 Evaluate the costs and benefits of a choice using expected value.

Even when we can't know for *certain* how something will turn out, we can often say something about the *likelihood* that it will turn out one way versus another. If we can estimate how likely different outcomes are, and the financial implications of each outcome, then we can come up with a single cost or benefit figure that takes risk into account. That figure is called **expected value**. Expected value is the average of each possible outcome of a future event, weighted by its probability of occurring.

expected value the average of each possible outcome of a future event, weighted by its probability of occurring

We can use expected value to make the analysis of the benefits of a college education a bit more realistic. In reality, of course, you could follow countless possible career paths. But for the sake of simplicity, let's say there are just two possibilities open to you *without* a college degree. Without a college degree, you have:

- A 50 percent chance of a career in which you make $1.5 million over 30 years ($50,000 a year).
- A 50 percent chance of making $900,000 over 30 years ($30,000 a year).

Then suppose that getting a college degree opens up a new range of job options. *With* a college degree, you have:

- A 50 percent chance of making $2.4 million.
- A 25 percent chance of making $1.5 million.
- A 25 percent chance of making $900,000.

Table 11-1 shows these possibilities. We can't know for sure which of these possible career paths will come true. But since we know the probability of each, we can measure the expected value of your future income with and without college. The general formula for the expected value of a decision is found by multiplying each possible outcome of an event (which we will call *S*) by the probability *P* of it occurring, and then adding together each of these terms for *n* different outcomes:

Equation 11-5

$$\text{Expected value} = EV = (P_1 \times S_1) + (P_2 \times S_2) + \ldots + (P_n \times S_n)$$

Using this formula, we find that the expected value of your income without a college degree is:

$$EV = (50\% \times \$1,500,000) + (50\% \times \$900,000) = \$1,200,000$$

Applying the same method to find the expected value of your income with a college degree, you get:

$$EV = (25\% \times \$1,500,000) + (25\% \times \$900,000) + (50\% \times \$2,400,000)$$
$$= \$1,800,000$$

Unlike our earlier estimates, these figures incorporate the risk that your income might actually be lower with a college degree than it would have been without. It's always a possibility—you might get unlucky. But since you cannot know ahead of time whether you will be lucky or not, you can still make a choice based on your *expected* income, which is $600,000 higher with a degree.

Expected value can be a useful tool for making decisions whenever future outcomes are uncertain. For example, when investing in a retirement fund, you won't know for certain how quickly that fund will grow, but calculating an expected value can help you to decide how much you need to be saving. When choosing between different options, though, you won't necessarily always want to choose the option with the highest expected value. As we will see, you will also want to consider the worst-case outcome for each option, and decide whether the risk of the worst-case outcome is unacceptably high.

TABLE 11-1
Probability of outcomes

Lifetime earnings by education level	$0.9 million	$1.5 million	$2.4 million
No college degree	50%	50%	0%
College degree	25%	25%	50%

Propensity for risk

LO 11.5 Explain how risk aversion makes a market for insurance possible.

Some things are riskier than others. There's a very low risk of injury when playing golf, for example, and a more significant risk when skiing. Similarly, some things that you can do with your money involve a higher risk of loss than others. Putting your money in a savings account or government bonds carries a very low risk of loss; investing in a start-up company or playing the stock market usually carries a much higher risk.

People have different levels of willingness to engage in risky activities. Those who generally have low willingness to take on risk are said to be **risk-averse**. Those who enjoy a higher level of risk are **risk-seeking**. These attitudes toward risk are an aspect of an individual's preferences—as is a preference for a certain ice-cream flavor, or a preference to spend your spare income on clothes or concerts.

> **risk-averse** having a low willingness to take on situations with risk
>
> **risk-seeking** having a high willingness to take on situations with risk

Some people have different preferences for risk.

Although individuals have varying tastes for taking on financial risks, economists believe that people are generally risk-averse in the following sense: When faced with two options with equal expected value, they will prefer the one with lower risk. Let's say we run a competition, and you're the winner. As a prize, we offer you these options:

Option A: We flip a coin. Heads, and your prize is $100,001. Tails, and your prize is $99,999.

Option B: We flip a coin. Heads, and your prize is $200,000. Tails, and you get nothing at all.

Both options have an expected value of $100,000. (Try writing out this calculation to make sure.) When economists say that people are generally risk-averse, it implies that most people prefer option A, even though both options have the same expected value. (Clearly, though, not *everyone* would choose option A. If that was the case, nobody would ever go to a casino and take big chances by piling their bets on red or black on the roulette wheel.)

To put it another way, the *expected value* of option B would have to be greater before most people would accept the risk of winning nothing. If you chose option A, ask yourself *how much* would the value in option B have to rise to tempt you to switch to B? Perhaps to $250,000? (The expected value of option B would then rise to $125,000.) How about $1,000,000 (for an expected value of $500,000 for option B)? The answer depends on your personal taste for risk, and it will differ for each individual. Although it may seem unlikely (alas) that you will ever win such a prize in a competition, this trade-off between risk and expected value is exactly the kind of choice you have to make whenever you think about investing money in stocks, retirement funds, bonds, or real estate.

✓ CONCEPT CHECK

❏ How is the expected value of a future event calculated? **[LO 11.4]**

❏ Why do economists say that people tend to be risk-averse? **[LO 11.5]**

Insurance and Managing Risk

People cope with uncertainty about the future in many ways. One approach is to simply avoid taking greater risks than are strictly necessary. If you don't want to risk hurting yourself while skiing, then don't go skiing! But some risks in life are unavoidable, and some risky activities—like skiing—are avoidable but fun. So people have also developed ways to *manage* the risks they face in their lives.

One common way to manage risk is to buy insurance. An insurance policy is a product that lets people pay to reduce uncertainty in some aspect of their lives. For instance, if you enjoy skiing, you can buy insurance to cover the cost of being airlifted to a hospital if you break your leg in a fall on the slopes. Insurance products usually involve paying a regular fee in return for an agreement that the insurance company will cover any unpredictable costs that arise.

The market for insurance

You've probably encountered many types of insurance associated with common risks that people face in life. There is auto insurance to manage the risk of having your car damaged or causing damage to someone else. Medical insurance manages the risk of becoming ill or injured. Homeowner's or renter's insurance manages the risk of having your belongings destroyed or stolen. Companies that provide these insurance products collect a fee—called a *premium*—in return for covering the costs that clients would otherwise have to pay if they experienced any of these unfortunate events.

In general, the amount people pay for insurance is higher than its *expected value*. For instance, suppose that you pay $1,000 per year for auto insurance. Suppose also that in any given year there is a 1 percent likelihood that you will get into an accident that costs $10,000, and a 0.1 percent likelihood of an accident that costs $200,000. If we assume that your insurance policy would cover the full cost of these accidents, then the expected value of coverage in any given year is $300:

$$EV = (1\% \times \$10{,}000) + (0.1\% \times \$200{,}000)$$

$$= \$100 + \$200 = \$300$$

Does paying $1,000 for something with a $300 expected value make people suckers? Not really. Most people are risk-averse enough to find insurance worth the extra expense. The $700 doesn't go down the drain. It buys the utility that comes from peace of mind, knowing that if you do get into an expensive auto accident, you will not be ruined by the costs. The reason people are generally willing to pay for insurance is that they would have trouble finding enough money to replace their homes and all of their possessions following, say, a fire, or to cover the cost of long-term hospital care if they fell ill. Insurance allows people to feel confident that if they are suddenly faced with these huge expenses, they won't face bankruptcy or be unable to pay for the services they need.

In fact, if the expected value of insurance policies were equal to the premiums paid, insurance companies would not stay in business very long: The insurers would be paying out approximately the same amount they received in premiums, with nothing left over. The industry exists only because it can make a profit from the extra amount that people are willing to pay for the service of managing risk.

Some people are willing to pay for coverage of very unusual risks. To read about some unusual insurance policies, read the From Another Angle box "Hole-in-one insurance?"

FROM ANOTHER ANGLE

Hole-in-one insurance?

Auto, home, and medical insurance are some of the most common insurance products because they relate to risks that most people face. However, insurance can be appropriate for anything that involves large and unexpected expenses, and markets have developed to cover some much more unusual risks, from insurance on body parts to insurance against the risk of hitting a hole in one in golf. *To learn more, continue reading by scanning the QR code near the end of the chapter or by going online.*

Pooling and diversifying risk

LO 11.6 Explain the importance of pooling and diversification for managing risk.

Insurance does not reduce the risks inherent in life. Having car insurance will not make you less likely to be in an accident. (As we will see in the next section, it may actually make accidents *more* likely.) Instead, insurance works because it reallocates the costs of such an event, sparing any individual from taking the full hit. This reallocation occurs through two mechanisms.

The first mechanism for reallocating risk is called pooling. **Risk pooling** occurs when people organize themselves in a group to collectively absorb the cost of the risk faced by each individual. This is the foundational principle that makes insurance companies work. The company is able to easily absorb the cost of one person's emergency, because at any given time, it will have many other clients who are paying their premiums and not making claims.

risk pooling
organizing people into a group to collectively absorb the risk faced by each individual

Suppose, for example, a company has 1,000,000 clients. Putting aside the question of the company's profits, this is equivalent to every client agreeing that he or she will pay $\frac{1}{1,000,000}$ of the cost of catastrophes that happen to other clients. In return, all clients have the assurance that they won't have to pay $\frac{999,999}{1,000,000}$ of the cost if a catastrophe happens to them. Pooling doesn't reduce the risk of catastrophes happening; it just reallocates the costs when they do.

An example of risk pooling comes from the method used by the United Kingdom and other countries to pay for student loans. Rather than making individual students responsible for the costs of their education, all students get their loans from a government-backed company. That company must be repaid only if students earn enough money out of college to do so. You can read about the merits and problems of this system in the What Do You Think? box "Who should bear the risk that a college degree doesn't pay off?"

WHAT DO YOU THINK?

Who should bear the risk that a college degree doesn't pay off?

Suppose you could buy insurance against the possibility that despite your college degree, you will never get a high-paying job: If your salary never rises above a certain level, the insurance company will pay off the loan you took out to go to college. Would you be interested in buying such an insurance product?

Actually, this is exactly the kind of student loan system in place in some countries, such as the United Kingdom. Students borrow from a government-backed company and repay their loans only once they start earning above a certain amount. If their earnings never reach that level, the loan is eventually written off.

Supporters of this system say it encourages more young people to go to college: Nobody needs to fear that by getting an education, they will incur debts that they will struggle to pay off. Critics point out that taxpayers—including people who never went to college—end up subsidizing graduates who fail to get high-paying jobs.

Some people have proposed replacing this system with a "graduate tax." Under this proposal, college education would be free, and paid for by levying an additional income tax on all college graduates earning above a certain sum. Instead of asking all taxpayers to foot the bill for college, only people who attend college would be on the hook.

Effectively, this is a debate about who should bear the risk that a college education doesn't pay off. In the UK, it's currently the taxpayers. Under the graduate-tax proposal, the risk would be pooled among everyone who attends college. In the U.S., the responsibility usually falls on the individual student or student's family. Should others be required to pay for the education of people who decide to be social workers or poets? On the other hand, does society as a whole lose something by discouraging students from pursuing their passions for social services or the arts?

What do you think?

1. Who should bear the costs of a college education for those people who do not earn enough money to pay back their loans?
2. Should the tuition for those who go into certain majors or professions be forgiven? If you think so, how should we choose which majors or professions should be chosen for this type of program?

diversification the process by which risks are shared across many different assets or people, reducing the impact of any particular risk on any one individual

The second mechanism for managing risk is diversification. Risk **diversification** refers to the process by which risks are shared across many different assets or people, reducing the impact of any particular risk on any one individual. Diversification is about not putting all your eggs in one basket, and it can be practiced by individuals or firms. For instance, if you invest all of your money in one company, you are completely dependent on that company's fortunes. If it goes bankrupt, so will you. Instead, many people choose to diversify by investing smaller amounts in many companies. If one company fails, they will lose some money, but not all of it. Like pooling your risks, diversifying your risks does not change the likelihood that bad things will happen. It just means that you're not going to be completely ruined by a single unfortunate event.

The key to diversification is that the risks should be as unrelated as possible. For instance, suppose an insurance company sells only one type of insurance—home insurance against earthquakes in San Francisco. This would not be a sensible way for homeowners in San Francisco to pool their risks because if one client's home is destroyed by an earthquake, that same earthquake is likely to destroy many other clients' homes as well. The insurance company could face all of its clients making claims at once, and would go bankrupt. In other words, the risk of earthquake damage to one home in San Francisco is *highly correlated* with the risk of earthquake damage to other homes in San Francisco. (Remember that *positive correlation* means things tend to occur together.)

To avoid this problem, the insurance company might choose also to sell, say, car insurance in New Jersey and hurricane insurance in Florida. Earthquakes, car crashes, and hurricanes in different parts of the country are *uncorrelated:* None of them are more or less likely to occur if one of the others occurs. The insurance company has diversified its risk by selling different products in different places. If it has to pay out after an earthquake in San Francisco, those costs will be covered by the premiums it continues to collect in other places.

These days, you're offered insurance quite often, whether on a new tennis racquet or a cell phone. At the time, you have no idea whether it's a good idea to buy it or not. If the cell phone breaks, the insurance is totally worth it; if the phone lasts for years, you didn't need insurance at all. As "Hindsight is 20/20" in the From Another Angle box describes, though, it's not best to look at a decision to buy insurance many years after the fact.

FROM ANOTHER ANGLE

Hindsight is 20/20

Say you bought an extended warranty that guarantees the replacement of your washing machine if it breaks, and then the washing machine actually does break. You might feel quite pleased with yourself. Now imagine that after living in the Mississippi delta and paying flood insurance for 20 years, you move away without having experienced a single flood. You might feel like you threw away your money. Was the washing machine warranty the right decision, and the flood insurance the wrong decision? Don't be too hasty to draw that conclusion. In both cases, the way things actually turned out has nothing to do with whether the initial decision was a good one.

Decisions that seem right when you make them can seem horribly wrong in retrospect. It's tempting to think that you need the benefit of hindsight to judge whether a decision about the future was right. But that's the wrong way to think about such decisions. You have to judge whether they were right or wrong by considering the best information available *at the time.*

In decisions about insurance, two pieces of information are crucial: How likely is the event you're insuring against, and how catastrophic would it be if it happened? The Mississippi delta is quite likely to flood, and recovering from flood damage can be ruinously expensive. So, buying flood insurance in this instance was probably the right decision, even if you didn't end up using it. On the other hand, flood insurance is probably not such a smart purchase if you live on the top of a hill in Denver—flood damage would be just as ruinously costly, but the likelihood is minuscule.

How about the washing machine? Suppose it costs $450, and the salesperson offers you insurance at $12.50 a month. This comes to $150 a year, so if the washing machine works well for at least three years—which is quite likely—you've already saved enough to buy a new one. If you're unlucky and it does break down before then, it wouldn't be a disaster: It would be annoying to have to fork out $450 for another washing machine, but it probably wouldn't bankrupt you. Unless you're extremely risk-averse, refusing the insurance at that price is the right decision—even if it turns out that the washing machine then breaks down in its second year.

After the fact, the uncertainty about the future that drove you to buy insurance has been resolved. But that doesn't mean that you should second-guess your decisions. If your hilltop Denver home suffers damage in a flash-flood, you're an unlucky person—but you didn't necessarily make the wrong decision about whether or not to buy flood insurance.

Problems with insurance

LO 11.7 Describe the challenges that adverse selection and moral hazard pose for insurance.

Managing risks by pooling and diversifying them sounds great. There are two big problems, however: adverse selection and moral hazard. Although we discussed these ideas at length in the "Information" chapter, they are particularly crucial for thinking about insurance and risk management.

The first problem insurance companies face is **adverse selection**. This concept describes a state that occurs when buyers and sellers have different information about the quality of a good or the riskiness of a situation, and this asymmetric information results in failure to complete transactions that would have been possible if both sides had the same information. In the context of insurance, adverse selection refers to the tendency for people with higher risk to be drawn toward insurance. For example, in car insurance, the hidden information is that insurers don't know who the bad drivers are, and the unattractive good is an insurance policy on a reckless driver. If you know you're a terrible driver, you're going to try to buy as much car insurance as you can; if you smoke, live on fast food, and do not exercise, you might be an enthusiastic customer for health insurance, and so on.

If insurance companies knew everything about their clients, adverse selection would not be a problem. The insurers would simply charge higher premiums to higher-risk clients. Insurance companies can and do ask potential clients seemingly endless questions about their driving records, smoking habits, and so on. But the clients still often know

adverse selection a state that occurs when buyers and sellers have different information about the quality of a good or the riskiness of a situation; results in failure to complete transactions that would have been possible if both sides had the same information

much more about their relevant risk factors than the insurance company. The result is that insurers have a hard time accurately assessing how risky a particular customer will be and charging the right price. To cover their costs, insurance companies usually end up charging higher prices to *all* customers. That decision can make insurance a much less good deal for low-risk individuals. If not kept in check, adverse selection can make it hard for less-risky individuals to find an insurance contract that's worth buying.

moral hazard the tendency for people to behave in a riskier way or to renege on contracts when they do not face the full consequences of their actions

The second problem is **moral hazard**—the tendency for people to behave in a riskier way or to renege on contracts when they do not face the full consequences of their actions. If your car is insured against theft, for example, you may be more relaxed about parking it in an unsafe-looking neighborhood. This problem is especially acute with medical insurance: People who know that their medical costs are covered may demand treatments and tests that they would never purchase if they had to pay for them on their own. In these cases, insurance can actually *increase* the expected cost of risks, as discussed in the What Do You Think? box "Should health insurance include preventive care?"

WHAT DO YOU THINK?

Should health insurance include preventive care?

One of the highest-profile political debates in America is about how to rein in the steadily increasing costs of medical care. Skyrocketing medical expenditures have been attributed to many factors, including the increased prevalence of obesity, an aging population, and steadily rising malpractice liabilities for doctors.

One strategy that many have suggested to rein in costs is to increase the incentives for people to seek preventive care. With many diseases—including cancer and diabetes, two of the costliest to treat—spending money on early detection and preventive care can prevent much higher costs from being incurred down the road. Preventive care can also reduce the suffering that comes with chronic illness.

On the other hand, moral hazard comes into play. If people with medical insurance are entitled to preventive care, they may demand all kinds of expensive tests and preventive treatments that they really don't need. Some people worry that this increase in spending might negate the benefit of future savings.

What do you think?
1. Should government policy encourage insurance companies to cover preventive care?
2. Should insurance companies be able to choose which procedures they cover?

✓CONCEPT CHECK

❒ Why are people often willing to pay more for insurance than the expected value of the coverage? **[LO 11.5]**
❒ What's the difference between risk pooling and risk diversification? **[LO 11.6]**
❒ Why can moral hazard increase the costs of insurance coverage? **[LO 11.7]**

Conclusion

Some of life's most important decisions involve weighing uncertain *future* costs and benefits against costs and benefits *today.* In this chapter, we looked at tools that can help with these decisions. Interest rates enable you to compare apples to apples when you think about costs and benefits that occur at different times. Expected value can help you think about what is the best option given uncertainty. Managing risk through pooling or diversification can allow you to avoid bearing the full cost of a worst-case scenario if it happens.

◄ Mobile Window on the World—Scan this code with your smartphone to find more applications of the chapter content. (Need a barcode reader? Try ScanLife, available in your app store.)

Visit your mobile app store and download ► the Karlan and Morduch Study Econ app.

 Study Econ McGraw Hill

Key Terms

interest rate, p. 239

compounding, p. 240

present value, p. 241

risk, p. 243

expected value, p. 243

risk-averse, p. 245

risk-seeking, p. 245

risk pooling, p. 247

diversification, p. 248

adverse selection, p. 249

moral hazard, p. 250

Summary

LO 11.1 Explain why money is worth more now than in the future, and how the interest rate represents this relationship.

Money is worth more in the present than in the future because it can be immediately spent or invested in productive opportunities. The interest rate is the cost of borrowing money for a certain unit of time. It is usually expressed as a percentage per time period. The interest rate is the amount needed to compensate the lender for the opportunity cost of loaning out money—in other words, the amount of money the lender could have earned from investing in something else if he or she weren't lending it.

LO 11.2 Calculate compounding over time with a given interest rate.

Compounding is the process of accumulation that results from the additional interest paid on previously earned interest. With compound interest, the amount of interest earned increases each period, since interest payments earned in the past themselves accumulate interest in future periods. We calculate the future value of a sum of money, including compound interest, as $FV = PV \times (1 + r)^n$.

LO 11.3 Calculate the present value of a future sum.

Present value refers to how much a certain amount of money in the future is worth today. It can be calculated by rearranging the formula for the future value of a sum, to $PV = \frac{FV}{(1 + r)^n}$. Translating cost or benefits that occur at different times into their present value gives you a common unit of value, allowing you to compare apples to apples.

LO 11.4 Evaluate the costs and benefits of a choice using expected value.

Risk exists with uncertainty about the future—the possibility that things won't turn out as you expect. In order to understand the likely value of a choice with multiple possible outcomes, we calculate its expected value. Expected value is the average of all possible future values, weighted by their probability of occurring. Expected value allows us to account for risk when comparing options.

LO 11.5 Explain how risk aversion makes a market for insurance possible.

People have varying degrees of willingness to take on risk. Those who have a high willingness to take on risk are known as risk-seeking; those with a low willingness to take on risk are risk-averse. People are generally risk-averse in the limited sense that when two choices have the same expected value, they will prefer the less risky one. This tendency is explained by the concept of diminishing marginal utility: The loss of utility caused by losing a large sum is greater than the benefit of gaining the same amount.

Insurance is a common strategy for managing risk. An insurance policy lets people pay to reduce uncertainty in some aspect of their lives. Such products usually involve paying a regular fee (premium) in return for an agreement that someone else will cover any unpredictable costs that arise. Insurance does not reduce the risk of something bad happening; it simply guarantees that the cost of the event to the insured person will be low. Risk aversion makes a market for insurance profitable: People are willing to pay to shield themselves from the cost of bad things happening, above and beyond the actual expected cost of those things.

LO 11.6 Explain the importance of pooling and diversification for managing risk.

Risk pooling is a strategy for managing risk that involves many people organizing themselves in a group in order to collectively absorb the cost of the risk faced by each individual. Risk pooling doesn't decrease the risk that a bad event will occur; it only reduces the cost to a particular individual in the event that it does occur.

Diversification is another strategy for managing risk that involves replacing large risks with smaller unrelated ones. That way, the cost of failure for any one investment is not so great, and the chance of many different investments all failing together is small, so the risk of losing a large amount is reduced. Like pooling, diversification does not change the likelihood that bad things will happen; it just reduces the costs associated with any single event.

LO 11.7 Describe the challenges that adverse selection and moral hazard pose for insurance.

One challenge faced by insurance schemes is adverse selection—the tendency for people with higher risk to be drawn toward insurance. If insurance companies were able to accurately identify risky clients, adverse selection would not be a problem; insurers would simply charge more for higher-risk clients. But clients often know much more about their relevant risk factors than the insurance company does.

Moral hazard is another challenge for insurance companies. Moral hazard means that people will behave in a riskier way when they know that their risks are covered by insurance.

Review Questions

1. Anna is indifferent between receiving $200 today or $230 in a month. What does this imply about her opportunity cost in the coming month? How much interest would Anna need to charge to lend $200 for the month in order to break even? **[LO 11.1]**

2. Colton has a choice between $100 today and $150 in three months. Farah has a choice between $100 today and $125 in three months. Colton chooses $100 today. Farah chooses $125 in three months. Explain why Farah is the one who delays payment even though Colton stands to earn more by waiting. **[LO 11.1]**

3. Suppose your aunt invests $2,000 for you. You are not allowed to have the money until the original amount doubles. Your aunt's investment earns 10 percent, compounded annually. Give a rough estimate of how long it will take before you can access the money your aunt invested for you. **[LO 11.2]**

4. You are considering taking out a two-year loan of $1,000 from a bank, on which you can pay either compound yearly interest of 1 percent or a flat rate of 2 percent for the whole two-year period. Which option is a better deal, and why? **[LO 11.2]**

5. Suppose you know that an investment will earn a positive return in the future. Why is it important to know the present value of the investment? **[LO 11.3]**

6. Suppose you are selling a piece of furniture to a friend who can't afford to pay you upfront but offers to pay you in monthly installments for the next year. What information do you need to calculate the present value of this offer? (*Hint:* Think about the formula for present value.) **[LO 11.3]**

7. A pharmaceutical company is considering investing in the development of a new drug. The company stands to make a lot of profit if the drug is successful. However, there is some risk that the drug will not be approved by government regulators. If this happens, the company will lose its entire investment. Advise the company how to take this risk into account as managers evaluate whether to invest. **[LO 11.4]**

8. You have a big exam tomorrow. You were planning to study tonight, but your friend has tickets to a concert and has invited you to join her. You would be willing to accept a B on the exam in order to go to the concert. You estimate that if you don't study you have a 35 percent chance of scoring a 90, a 35 percent chance of scoring an 80 (the score required to earn a B), a 25 percent chance of earning a 75, and a 5 percent chance of earning a 60. Will you go to the concert? Explain why or why not. **[LO 11.4]**

9. Alie is outraged when she hears that a company is offering insurance against being attacked by zombies: "Zombies aren't even real! This company is just taking advantage of people." Without acknowledging the possible existence of zombies, provide an alternative perspective on the insurance company's ethics. **[LO 11.5]**

10. Julia pays $500 for an insurance policy with an expected value of $120. Explain why this is a rational choice for Julia. **[LO 11.5]**

11. Suppose that the crop yield of corn farmers in Iowa depends solely on rainfall levels. Also suppose that every part of the state gets approximately the

same amount of rain as every other part in any given year. Will the corn farmers of Iowa be able to effectively use pooling to reduce their exposure to risk? Why or why not? **[LO 11.6]**

12. An insurance company that faces fierce competition from other providers is considering a strategy to sell more policies by simplifying its portfolio and becoming the expert in flood insurance for the state. The company managers reason, "Everyone buys flood insurance in this state, so let's focus our efforts on becoming the preferred provider." Evaluate this strategy. **[LO 11.6]**

13. Suppose the economy is suffering and many people are afraid they will be laid off from their jobs. Workers would like to protect against this risk with insurance. Identify and explain two problems that prevent insurance companies from offering layoff insurance. **[LO 11.7]**

14. BackPedal is a bike-rental shop that rents bicycles, helmets, and other gear by the day. **[LO 11.7]**

    a. BackPedal offers an optional helmet rental for $10/day with the rental of a bicycle. To his surprise, the store manager has noticed that cycling accidents are higher among customers who rent helmets than those who do not. Explain this phenomenon using economic concepts. Assume that customers who do not rent helmets also do not own helmets.

    b. BackPedal is considering offering helmets for free with a bike rental. Explain how this new policy will affect the issues you identified in part *a*.

Problems and Applications

1. Your bank offers 3 percent annual interest on savings deposits. If you deposit $560 today, how much interest will you have earned at the end of one year? **[LO 11.1]**

2. You have $350, which a friend would like to borrow. If you don't lend it to your friend, you could invest it in an opportunity that would pay out $392 at the end of the year. What annual interest rate should your friend offer you to make you indifferent between these two options? **[LO 11.1]**

3. If you deposit $500 in a savings account that offers 3 percent interest, compounded annually, and you don't withdraw any money, how much money should you expect to have in the account at the end of three years? **[LO 11.2]**

4. Suppose you run up a debt of $300 on a credit card that charges an annual rate of 12 percent, compounded annually. How much will you owe at the end of two years? Assume no additional charges or payments are made. **[LO 11.2]**

5. Your savings account currently has a balance of $32,300. You opened the savings account two years ago and have not added to the initial amount you deposited. If your savings have been earning an annual interest rate of 2 percent, compounded annually, what was the amount of your original deposit? **[LO 11.3]**

6. You run a business and are considering offering a new service. If you offer the new service, you expect it to generate $60,000 in profits each year for your business over the next two years. In order to offer the new service, you will need to take out a loan for new equipment. Assume a 5 percent annual interest rate. **[LO 11.3]**

7. You are driving home from work, and get stuck in a traffic jam. You are considering turning off from your usual route home and taking a longer route that might have less traffic. However, you know that there is some chance that the traffic on your usual, shorter route will clear up. Based on Table 11P-1, calculate the expected value (in minutes until you arrive home) of each option. **[LO 11.4]**

8. Books for Kids is a not-for-profit organization that runs after-school reading programs in four school districts. Books for Kids is planning a fundraiser to buy new books. Last time it held a fundraiser, donors were allowed to specify which district program they wanted to receive their donation. Table 11P-2 shows the average donations and the

TABLE 11P-1

	Light traffic	Moderate traffic	Heavy traffic
Probability of encountering on Route 1	30%	20%	50%
Duration of drive on Route 1	10 minutes	30 minutes	60 minutes
Probability of encountering on Route 2	50%	50%	0%
Duration of drive on Route 2	20 minutes	40 minutes	80 minutes

TABLE 11P-2

	Average donation ($)	Percent of donations (%)
Northwest district	25	15
Southeast district	50	30
West district	15	20
South district	12	35

percent of all donations that went to each district. Using the last fundraiser as a projection, what is the expected value of the average donation across all four programs? **[LO 11.4]**

9. Cora had two options when buying car insurance. Option A had a higher expected value, but Cora chose option B. From the list below, what can we assume about these policies and Cora's willingness to take on risk? Check all that apply. **[LO 11.5]**
   a. Option B was riskier.
   b. Option A was risker.
   c. Cora is risk-seeking.
   d. Cora is risk-averse.

10. You are considering buying one of two types of health insurance. You guess that in the next year there is a 1 percent chance of serious illness that will cost you $67,500 in health care; a 9 percent chance of a moderate illness that will cost you $2,500; and a 90 percent chance of regular health care needs that will cost you $500. One type of health insurance is emergency-only coverage; it will cover your expenses for serious illness but not moderate illness or regular care. The other type covers moderate illness and regular expenses, but its payout is capped, so it will not cover the cost of a serious illness. **[LO 11.5]**
    a. What is the expected value of payouts from the emergency-only insurance?
    b. What is the expected value of payouts from the capped-coverage insurance?
    c. Which is the more risk-averse option?

11. For each of the following scenarios, say whether *pooling* or *diversification* is a more promising risk-mitigation strategy. **[LO 11.6]**
    a. Employees of a company who receive their salaries and health insurance from their employer and also invest their savings in that company's stocks.
    b. Families who are worried about losing their possessions if their houses burn down.

    c. Neighboring farmers who grow the same crop, which is prone to failure in dry years.

12. You have two possessions you would like to insure against theft or damage: your new bicycle, which cost you $800, and a painting you inherited, which has been appraised at $55,000. The painting is more valuable, but your bicycle must be kept outdoors and is in much greater danger of being stolen or damaged. You can afford to insure only one item. Which should you choose? Why? **[LO 11.6]**

13. Say whether each of the following scenarios describes an insurance problem caused by *adverse selection* or by *moral hazard*. **[LO 11.7]**
    a. People who have homeowners insurance are less likely than others to replace the batteries in their smoke detectors.
    b. People who enjoy dangerous hobbies are more likely than others to buy life insurance.
    c. People whose parents died young are more likely than others to enroll in health insurance.
    d. People who have liability coverage on their car insurance take less care than others to avoid accidents.

14. Requiring every American to get mandatory health care insurance has been a controversial part of health care reform debates in the United States. Putting aside other arguments for or against mandatory coverage, would this policy reduce adverse selection, moral hazard, both, or neither? **[LO 11.7]**

Chapter Endnotes

1. B. Greene, "Obama, Romney Agree on Extending Student Loan Interest Rate Cut," *U.S. News and World Report*, April 23, 2012, http://www.usnews.com/news/articles/2012/04/23/obama-romney-agree-on-extending-stafford-interest-rate-cut.
2. Ibid.
3. H. Yen, Associated Press, cited in *U.S. News and World Report*, April 23, 2012, http://www.usnews.com/news/articles/2012/04/23/obama-romney-agree-on-extending-stafford-interest-rate-cut.
4. The reason the superscripts in the denominators in the computation begin with 5 is that in the example, you don't start earning your salary until year 5—that is, after college is over.

Chapter Sources

http://professionals.collegeboard.com/profdownload/cb-policy-brief-college-stu-borrowing-aug-2009.pdf
http://www.census.gov/prod/2002pubs/p23-210.pdf

Math Essentials: Compounding

LEARNING OBJECTIVES

LO F.1   Use compounding to calculate time value of money.

· ·

Compounding

LO F.1 Use compounding to calculate time value of money.

In Chapter 11, you learned how to compute the future value of money using compound interest. Compounding occurs because the interest your money earns in one time period itself earns interest in the next time period. Multiplying a single investment by an interest rate is simple enough, but calculating the growth of an investment over time is more complicated, because the base keeps changing. In every period, we have to multiply the interest rate by the initial investment *plus* any interest earned in earlier time periods.

Future Value

Let's say that you invest $100 right now at an interest rate of 10 percent. You plan to withdraw your money in four years, and the interest compounds annually. What will be the value of your investment in four years?

Let's first calculate the value year by year, accounting for the compounding interest. This calculation is essentially calculating percentage change. The 10 percent in interest represents how much the original amount you invest will change in one time period (in this case, one year).

Year 1:	$100.00 + ($100.00 × 0.10) = $110.00
Year 2:	$110.00 + ($110.00 × 0.10) = $121.00
Year 3:	$121.00 + ($121.00 × 0.10) = $133.10
Year 4:	$133.10 + ($133.10 × 0.10) = $146.41

Notice that each year we incorporate the interest earned in the previous year into the base investment for the next year. In other words, we multiply the interest rate not by the initial investment, but by the initial investment *plus* any previously earned interest.

Instead of these year-by-year calculations, we can use a formula. The general formula for computing the future value of money using compounding is:

Equation F-1

$$\text{Future value} = FV = PV \times (1 + r)^n$$

PV is the amount (present value) of the initial investment, *FV* is the future value of the investment, *r* is the interest rate, and *n* is the number of time periods between now and the future.

Let's try the problem again using the formula for compound interest. First, remember the order of operations:

PEMDAS

P: Parentheses, from the innermost outward

E: Exponents

MD: Multiplication and Division from left to right

AS: Addition and Subtraction from left to right

Therefore, we plug in your initial investment of $100 for PV_1 and the time period of 4 years for *n*, and solve for *FV* in the following order. (*Hint:* You might want a calculator for this.)

$$FV = PV \times (1 + r)^n$$

$$FV = 100 \times (1 + 0.1)^4$$

$$FV = 100 \times (1.1)^4 \qquad \text{(Remember to \textit{start with the operations inside the parentheses}.)}$$

$$FV = 100 \times 1.4641 \qquad \text{(Now you \textit{apply the exponent}.)}$$

$$FV = \$146.41$$

After four years, your investment of $100 will be worth $146.41.

Let's see how the problem changes when we change the interest rate. This time, let's calculate the future value of your $100 investment if the interest rate is 5 percent. We will still invest for four years with interest compounded annually.

Year 1: $100.00 + ($100.00 × 0.05) = $105.00

Year 2: $105.00 + ($105.00 × 0.05) = $110.25

Year 3: $110.25 + ($110.25 × 0.05) = $115.76

Year 4: $115.76 + ($115.76 × 0.05) = $121.55

Now, let's do the problem again using the formula.

$$FV = 100 \times (1 + 0.05)^4$$

$$FV = 100 \times (1.05)^4$$

$$FV = 100 \times 1.2155$$

$$FV = \$121.55$$

After four years, your investment of $100 is worth $121.55.

This same method can be used to calculate the value of a borrowed sum of money, as well as an invested one. Instead of an initial investment, we can plug in the initial amount borrowed. The interest rate is the rate at which the debt increases, rather than the rate at which your investment grows; otherwise the calculations are exactly the same.

Suppose you borrow $1,000 at a monthly interest rate of 10 percent, and wait for five months to pay it off. Let's assume that interest is compounded monthly. How will your debt accumulate each month?

Month 1: $1,000.00 + ($1,000.00 × 0.10) = $1,100.00

Month 2: $1,100.00 + ($1,100.00 × 0.10) = $1,210.00

Month 3: $1,210.00 + ($1,210.00 \times 0.10) = $1,331.00$

Month 4: $1,331.00 + ($1,331.00 \times 0.10) = $1,464.10$

Month 5: $1,464.10 + ($1,464.10 \times 0.10) = $1,610.51$

Let's do the problem again using the formula.

$$FV = 1,000 \times (1 + 0.1)^5$$
$$FV = 1,000 \times (1.1)^5$$
$$FV = 1,000 \times 1.61051$$
$$FV = 1,610.51$$

After five months, you will owe $1,610.51, or more than one and a half times your initial debt.

Problems and Applications

1. If you invest $250 at an annually compounded interest rate of 10 percent, how much will you have in 3 years? **[LO F.1]**

2. Suppose you invest $500 at an annually compounded interest rate of 3 percent. **[LO F.1]**
   a. How much will you have in 10 years?
   b. How much will you have in 20 years?
   c. How much will you have in 50 years?

3. Suppose you borrow $50 from a payday lender, who charges a monthly interest rate of 5 percent, compounded monthly. **[LO F.1]**
   a. If you pay back the loan in one month, how much will you owe?
   b. If you pay back the loan in one year, how much will you owe?
   c. If the interest rate is raised to 6 percent rather than 5 percent, how much *more* will you owe if you wait for a year to pay off the debt?

Part Four

Firm Decisions

The six chapters in Part 4 will introduce you to ...

the choices and decisions that companies make. Every day, about 120 million Americans get up and go to work in over 6 million different offices, stores, factories, and other businesses. These 6 million firms are diverse in what they do and how they do it, but there are important common threads.[1] Most firms focus on meeting customers' needs while managing employees and physical resources. While doing that, they're usually working hard to keep up with the competition. A lot of tough choices have to be made along the way. Imagine being a CEO at a large firm and having to decide which product to invest in, where to locate a new factory, which employees to hire, or whether to cut prices after the competition drops theirs. The next chapters explain how firms—big and small—make these kinds of choices.

We begin in Chapter 12 with a simple look at revenues and costs. Understanding the form that costs take can give insight into the choices the firm faces. The types of costs a business has to pay drive its decisions about how much to produce to maximize profits and when to stay in business or shut down.

Firms also have to know about the competition they face in the market. Some markets are a fierce battleground, with many companies trying to sell the exact same thing. Other markets have only a few companies. Other markets are dominated by one firm that faces no competition at all. Chapters 13, 14, and 15 describe the features of these different kinds of markets, and how firms behave in each.

Regardless of what they are selling, businesses need to pay for inputs like raw materials, equipment, and workers to produce goods or services. These are called the factors of production and are the focus of Chapter 16. Thinking about the markets for factors of production can explain why some professions earn more than others, as well as how businesses make decisions about how much to produce and what inputs to use.

Chapter 17 describes what happens when businesses go global. International trade connects American consumers and businesses to people and producers all over the world. In this chapter, we take a look at why certain goods are made in one country and shipped to another, as well as how globalization, trade, and government policies affect the well-being of workers and consumers in different countries.

Endnote

1. Data on firms and employment are from U.S. Bureau of the Census, Statistics of U.S. Business for 2009, http://www.census.gov/econ/susb/.

Perfect Competition

LEARNING OBJECTIVES

LO 13.1   Describe the characteristics of a perfectly competitive market.

LO 13.2   Calculate average, marginal, and total revenue.

LO 13.3   Find a firm's optimal quantity of output.

LO 13.4   Describe a firm's decision to shut down and when to exit the market, and explain the difference between these choices.

LO 13.5   Draw a short-run supply curve for a competitive market with identical firms.

LO 13.6   Draw a long-run supply curve for a competitive market with identical firms, and describe its implications for profit-seeking firms.

LO 13.7   Explain why a long-run supply curve might slope upward.

LO 13.8   Calculate the effect of a shift in demand on a market in long-run equilibrium.

TRAINSIDE VARIETY

When we think about markets in action, one image that comes to mind is the bustling trading floor of the New York Stock Exchange. But let's travel for a moment to an interesting market scene that's much farther away. Imagine sitting on a long-distance train in West Africa, on a journey from Yaoundé in the south of Cameroon to Maroua in the north. Every now and then, the train grinds to a halt near a town. Not many passengers get on or off—most are simply going from one of these big cities to the other. This journey takes many, many hours, and there is no restaurant car on board the train. The travelers need food and drink, and at each stop local merchants rush toward the train, offering refreshments for sale.

There is a limited range of goods being offered. Some vendors are selling bunches of small, ripe bananas. Some sell bags of oranges, partially skinned so you can crush them in your hand and sip the juice. Others offer bags of peanuts, which have been soaked in salty water and dried in the sun. You will be able to find corn on the cob or plantain (a less-sweet kind of banana), roasted over an open fire. Vendors jostle for position along the train as passengers take turns to hang out of the window, peruse the choice of snacks, and hand down money to the vendors.

You won't see much bargaining going on. Everyone seems to know and accept the prices as given. After all, if a vendor tries to charge more than the going rate for a roasted plantain, a passenger has many other vendors to choose from. And if a passenger tries to

pay less for a roasted plantain, vendors can easily sell to someone else. Eventually, all the passengers have bought the snacks they want, the train rolls off again, and the local merchants head back home and wait for the next train to come by with a new batch of customers.

For reasons we will explain in this chapter, this scene is probably about as close as you will come in the real world to observing a situation that economists call *perfect competition.* Like many of the concepts we've explored in this book, a *perfectly* competitive market is a simplified model that is rarely an exact fit with messy reality. It nonetheless tells us a lot about how the real world works. It also represents one of the miracles of economics: how well-functioning markets can deliver goods and services at wide scale and at low prices—with price signals determining the appropriate supply and demand, and without the government ever stepping in.

In this chapter, we'll describe the behavior of firms in a perfectly competitive market. We'll investigate how firms in such markets make decisions about what quantity of output to produce, and when to stop producing altogether. We'll see that although firms are driven to seek profits, in the long run we can expect that firms in a perfectly competitive market *won't* earn *economic* profits. Understanding the decisions made by firms takes us behind the market supply curve we've used in previous chapters, to analyze the forces that shape it in the short run and in the long run.

In showing how competition works, we'll also see why it can bring benefits to consumers. The forces of competition help make millions of products and services available and affordable to billions of people, just as competition makes cheap, refreshing snacks available to passengers on a long train journey.

A Competitive Market

In this chapter, we'll discuss how firms make production decisions. Before we can begin this analysis, we have to break down one of the most important and powerful assumptions frequently made by economists: that firms are operating in competitive markets. We can analyze the importance of competitive markets through the lens of the first economists' question, *What are firms' wants and constraints?* In the previous chapter we identified what firms *want:* to maximize their profits. Participation in a competitive market, however, places some very specific *constraints* on their ability to achieve this goal, as we're about to see.

Characteristics of a competitive market

LO 13.1 Describe the characteristics of a perfectly competitive market.

We touched on the idea of a **competitive market** in Chapter 3, where we discussed its two essential features. First, buyers and sellers are fully informed **price takers**. They can't affect prices—the going price is the going price. Second, goods are standardized. Many markets have some degree of competitiveness but don't meet the full standards. Economists use the idea of *perfectly competitive markets* to refer to an idealized model of markets in which the two essential features hold true.

Let's briefly review the two essential characteristics of a perfectly competitive market. We'll then add a third feature that is nonessential but important.

Individuals can't affect the going price. If you were the only seller of roasted plantains to a train full of hungry passengers, you'd be in a pretty good position. You could charge a very high price, knowing that some people would be hungry enough to pay it. Similarly, if you were the only passenger on a train and were facing dozens of roasted plantain sellers, you'd be in a great position. You could offer a very low price, confident that some seller would be desperate enough to sell you a plantain.

Most sellers and buyers in most markets are not in the happy position of being able to set their own price. Instead, most face some degree of competition. Nonetheless, they may still have some ability to decide what price to set. Say you're the only plantain seller at this train stop, but passengers know there will be many more at the next stop in half an hour's time. You may be able to charge a little bit of a premium to very hungry passengers who can't wait that long; but the presence of competition constrains your ability to charge what you like.

The first essential characteristic of a *perfectly* competitive market is that buyers and sellers have *so much* competition, they have *no ability at all* to set their own price. Usually this implies that the market contains a very large number of buyers and sellers. In such markets, the decisions of individual participants are so small relative to the total size of the market that they can't affect market prices. Instead, buyers and sellers have to accept the going rate. Buyers and sellers are price takers, who must "take" (accept) the prevailing price as they find it. The opposite of being a price taker is having **market power**, or the ability to noticeably affect market prices.

Goods and services are standardized. The second essential characteristic of a *perfectly* competitive market is that the goods and services being traded are standardized. When goods are standardized, they are interchangeable. Buyers have no reason to prefer those sold by one producer over those sold by another, provided that they are the same price. This means that producers have to sell at the market price. They'd lose all of their business if they charged more, and they have no incentive to charge less.

This is usually not the case in real life, where goods are differentiated by quality, brand name, or characteristics that appeal to different tastes. Imagine an American equivalent of the Cameroonian train stop: turning off the interstate for a burger. Do you go to McDonald's or Burger King? Your choice is probably not determined solely by the price of the burgers, but also by your knowledge of whether you happen to prefer one over the other: A McDonald's burger is similar to a Burger King burger, but they are not the same. When goods are not standardized, producers will be able to charge different prices. Sellers of roasted plantains to Cameroonian train passengers, though, are not in this position. There are no brand names here—one roasted plantain is the same as any other.

competitive market a market in which fully informed price-taking buyers and sellers easily trade a standardized good or service

price taker a buyer or seller who cannot affect the market price

market power the ability to noticeably affect market prices

There is so much competition in perfectly competitive markets that buyers and sellers cannot affect the market price, assuming that the goods offered for sale are relatively the same. Buyers can turn to the next seller if the price is too high, and as long as there are plenty of buyers, sellers have no incentive to lower prices.

Many natural resources, such as metals and lumber, can be considered standardized goods. At the same price, buyers don't care whether their gold comes from a mine in the United States or Uzbekistan, or whether their crude oil comes from a well in the Saudi Arabian desert or tar sands in Canada: As long as it meets certain defined characteristics, then gold is gold, and crude oil is crude oil. Standardized goods like this are often referred to as *commodities*.

Note that one implication of goods being standardized is that there are *no information asymmetries* in a perfectly competitive market; everyone knows exactly what they are trading. For one illustration of the importance of knowledge in keeping markets competitive, see the Real Life box "Bazaar competition."

REAL LIFE

Bazaar competition

Bazaars are often the most vibrant and colorful places in towns and cities around the world. International travelers are sometimes surprised to see massive bazaars that specialize in one very specific type of product, such as fruit, flowers, furniture, or fabric. In many cities, there are huge markets where hundreds and even thousands of vendors all sell exactly the same goods for exactly the same prices.

This tendency may seem perplexing. We sometimes see something similar in the United States: All the auto dealers in town may locate on the same road, for example. This increases their chances of attracting potential customers who want to test-drive different brands of cars. But having a Honda dealership next to a Ford dealership next to a Chevrolet dealership is not the same as having a hundred small shops all selling the *exact same thing*, for the *exact same price*. To find a different product, you will have to go to a different bazaar. Wouldn't it be easier for consumers to have a single location where they could go to buy all the different things they need, like the typical American mall or shopping center? And wouldn't sellers find it easier to operate in a location where they were the *only* ones selling their particular type of goods, rather than facing so much competition?

The answer to these questions may be that the bazaar is an ancient way of ensuring healthy market competition. In the days before you could search Google to see how much different sellers are charging for a particular good, the vast majority of people had no way to know the price of something without going to the shop to ask. Moreover, just getting to a market can require a significant time investment. Therefore, if there is only one shop selling a good in a particular location, customers will be stuck buying whatever they can find there. Knowing this, the shopkeeper has a strong incentive to increase prices.

As a consumer, would you shop at the store located all by itself, or the one next to a hundred other identical stores? If they all sell standardized goods, you should feel confident that competition between the hundred stores will bring down the price as far as possible. Shop owners, in turn, know that customers will prefer to shop in a location where competition flourishes. Thus it makes sense for stores to locate next to the hundred other stores selling the exact same things.

In short, bazaars aren't so bizarre—they're an old fashioned way of ensuring that competition works.

Source: John McMillan, *Reinventing the Bazaar: A Natural History of Markets* (New York: W.W. Norton, 2002).

Firms can freely enter and exit. Having price-taking buyers and sellers trading standardized goods is sufficient to define a perfectly competitive market. But another characteristic of perfectly competitive markets is important to understanding the way they function in the long run: Firms are able to freely enter and exit the market. This means that new firms can be created and begin producing goods and services, and existing firms can decide to shut down.

The extent to which firms can freely enter and exit explains some differences among markets. It helps us see why the market for roasted plantains at train stations comes close to a perfectly competitive market, but the market for, say, crude oil does not. It's pretty easy to set up as a plantain roaster. All you need is charcoal, a grill, and some plantains. It's a lot more difficult to set up as an oil producer. You need all kinds of expensive machinery and expertise. These entry requirements make it relatively easy for existing producers of oil to collude with each other to keep prices artificially high— causing the oil market to fail the "price-taking" requirement of perfect competition. It would be difficult for sellers of roasted plantains to do the same. New firms would enter the plantain market and undercut the colluders' prices.

In general, free entry into a market keeps existing firms on their toes. It can help drive innovation, cost-cutting, and quality improvements, as firms respond to the entry of new competitors. In theory free entry and exit is not an *essential* condition for a competitive market, but in practice the threat of collusion means that markets tend not to stay competitive when this condition is not present.

Remember that in real life, few markets meet all the assumptions of perfect competition. Nonetheless, perfect competition is a useful beginning assumption; it provides a base for describing interactions between buyers and sellers and plays a significant role in most markets. We'll work with this simplification for now, but keep in mind that the picture will become more complicated as we continue.

Revenues in a perfectly competitive market

LO 13.2 Calculate average, marginal, and total revenue.

The characteristics of perfect competition lead to a less-than-obvious conclusion: *In a perfectly competitive market, producers are able to sell as much as they want without affecting the market price.* This follows from the definition of being a price taker and the fact that consumers are indifferent between the standardized goods sold by different producers. These two very important assumptions mean that when firms make decisions about the quantity they will produce, they don't have to worry about whether their actions will cause the market price to rise or fall, or whether they will find buyers. As we analyze the revenue that firms can expect to bring in, we can assume that firms in a competitive market will be able to sell any quantity of output at the market price.

POTENTIALLY CONFUSING

How can every firm in a competitive market sell as much as it wants? If every firm produced more and more, wouldn't the quantity for sale outstrip the quantity demanded, pushing the price down?

In theory, yes. But there are two reasons why this doesn't interfere with our conclusion. First, firms will not want to produce an infinite quantity. Remember the principle of diminishing marginal product (from "The Costs of Production" chapter): As firms produce more, their costs tend to go up. As we'll see later in this chapter, that means there will come a point for every firm at which it doesn't want to produce any more.

Second, remember that we are thinking about decisions made by individual firms. By definition, in a perfectly competitive market, each individual firm is so small relative to the size of the whole market that an increase in its output causes a negligibly small increase in the total quantity supplied. Any individual firm's choice about the quantity to produce has such a tiny effect on the total quantity supplied to the market that the change in price is essentially zero.

Let's imagine that you live in a Cameroonian town and you are setting up a plantain-roasting enterprise to cater to passing train travelers. What can we say about your firm's revenue? In "The Costs of Production" chapter, we talked about *total revenue:* the price that a firm receives for each good, multiplied by the quantity of that good it sells. In this case, the firm sells only one good: roasted plantains. Its total revenue is therefore equal to the price of roasted plantains times the quantity it sells, or $P \times Q$. For instance, if the price is 1,000 CFA francs (the Cameroonian currency) per bunch of plantains, and the firm produces 5 bunches of roasted plantains, its total revenue will be 5,000 CFA francs.

Table 13-1 shows revenue for a firm in a competitive market—in this case, the plantain firm. The third column in the table shows total revenue at various quantities. Price remains the same regardless of the quantity that the firm produces, because the firm is a price taker in a competitive market. So, if the quantity produced triples, from 1 bunch of plantains to 3 bunches of plantains, revenue also triples from 1,000 CFA francs to 3,000 CFA francs.

We also need to consider two other measures of revenue: average revenue and marginal revenue. **Average revenue** is total revenue divided by the quantity sold. Total revenue is $P \times Q$. So average revenue is $(P \times Q)$ divided by Q, or simply P. In other words, *for any firm selling one product, average revenue is equal to the price of the good.*

Marginal revenue is the revenue generated by selling an additional unit of a good. In our example, this is simply the market price, because one unit of the good always generates revenue of $1 \times P = P$. *For a firm in a competitive market, marginal revenue is equal to the price of the good.* (If the market were not competitive, however, producing an additional unit of a good might affect the market price.)

We can check these rules in Table 13-1 by calculating average and marginal revenue directly from quantity and price. Average revenue, shown in column 4, is equal to the

average revenue
total revenue divided by the quantity sold

marginal revenue
the revenue generated by selling an additional unit of a good

FIGURE 13-2

The short-run supply curve and the shutdown rule

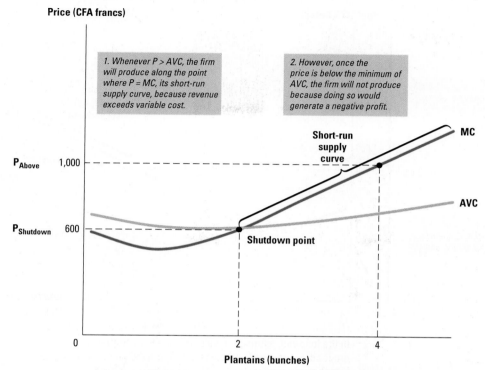

Price (CFA francs)

1. Whenever P > AVC, the firm will produce along the point where P = MC, its short-run supply curve, because revenue exceeds variable cost.

2. However, once the price is below the minimum of AVC, the firm will not produce because doing so would generate a negative profit.

Short-run supply curve

MC

P_{Above} 1,000

AVC

$P_{Shutdown}$ 600

Shutdown point

0   2   4

Plantains (bunches)

The section of the marginal cost curve that is above AVC describes the firm's short-run supply curve. At any price above that point, the firm will produce the quantity where price intersects the MC curve. At prices below the minimum of AVC, the firm produces nothing, because it would generate a negative profit.

We can state the short-run shutdown rule as follows:

Equation 13-1 Shutdown rule

$$\text{Shut down if } P < AVC$$

Above the shutdown price, a firm's short-run supply curve is the same as its MC curve, as shown in Figure 13-2. At each price, the firm will supply the profit-maximizing quantity. The profit-maximizing quantity is the one at which marginal cost equals marginal revenue. Since marginal revenue is the same as price in a perfectly competitive market, we can take a shortcut by simply reading the quantity corresponding to each price along the MC curve. Below the shutdown price, however, the firm will not produce at all.

When the firm makes long-run decisions, the reasoning is different. In the long run, all costs become variable. Leases can expire and not be renewed; machinery can be sold. Therefore, when deciding whether to exit in the long run, the firm should consider whether average revenue is greater than average *total* cost. If the market price is less than the lowest point on the ATC curve, the firm should make a long-run decision to exit the market for good. We can state the exit rule as:

Equation 13-2 Exit rule

$$\text{Exit if } P < ATC$$

FIGURE 13-3

The long-run supply curve and the exit rule

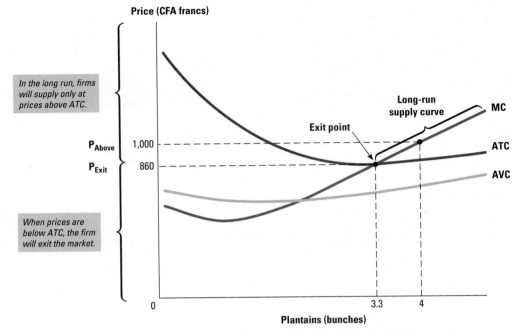

In the long run, a firm can avoid not only the variable costs of production, but also fixed costs, by exiting the market. If price is less than average total cost, the firm should exit the market. Conversely, if price is more than average total cost, a firm should enter the market.

Figure 13-3, which shows the firm's long-run supply curve, illustrates the exit rule. At prices above average total cost, the firm will produce at the point where price intersects marginal cost. At lower prices, the firm will choose to produce nothing and will exit the market.

In making the long-run decision, the firm will consider whether the market price is likely to remain low *in the long run*. If it believes that the market price has fallen only in the short run, and will increase again in the long run, then it would not make sense to exit the market permanently. This reasoning explains why a firm might decide to halt production temporarily in the short run when price dips below AVC, but might not make the long-run decision to exit the market permanently. The firm could stop its variable costs (lay off workers, buy no more raw materials), but keep open the possibility of restarting production by retaining its machinery and premises, in the hope that the price goes back up again.

✓CONCEPT CHECK

❑ What is the relationship between cost and revenue at the profit-maximizing quantity of output? **[LO 13.3]**

❑ How do sunk costs affect a firm's decision to shut down? **[LO 13.4]**

❑ When should a firm exit the market in the long run? **[LO 13.4]**

Behind the Supply Curve

So far in this book, we've used the supply curve to describe the relationship between price and the quantity supplied on a market level. So far in this chapter, we've seen how an individual firm's costs determine its decisions about how much it is willing to supply at a given price. It's time to connect the two. By doing so, we will see how the supply curve for the market reflects the sum of the choices of many individual suppliers, each willing to produce a certain quantity of a good at each price. We've seen that firms think differently about their production decisions in the short run and the long run. The individual choices also generate differences between market supply curves in the short run and the long run.

Short-run supply

LO 13.5 Draw a short-run supply curve for a competitive market with identical firms.

In the short run, we assume that the number of firms in the market is fixed. The total quantity of a good that is supplied at a given price is therefore the sum of the quantities that each individual producer is willing to supply. To simplify things a bit, let's assume that each plantain-roasting firm currently in the market is the same. Each has the same resources, same technology, and so on, such that each is willing to supply the same quantity at a given price as all of the others.

Panel A of Figure 13-4 shows the supply curve for one of these roasted-plantain firms. (Note that it's the same short-run supply curve we established in Figure 13-2: It is the firm's MC curve at points after it intersects the AVC curve.) Suppose that there are 100 producers currently operating in the roasted-plantain market, each with the same supply curve. The total quantity supplied is simply the sum of the quantities that each firm supplies. Panel B of Figure 13-4 shows the market supply curve. At every price level, the total quantity supplied in the market is 100 times the quantity supplied by each firm.

Long-run supply

LO 13.6 Draw a long-run supply curve for a competitive market with identical firms, and describe its implications for profit-seeking firms.

The key difference between supply in the short run and supply in the long run is that we assume that firms are able to enter and exit the market in the long run. The number of firms is not fixed, but changes in response to changing circumstances. We've already seen what makes a firm decide to exit the market—price falling below the lowest point on the ATC curve. At that point, the firm would be operating at a loss. Conversely, a firm would want to enter the market if it sees it could produce at a level of ATC that is below the market price. In other words, more firms will enter a market if the existing firms are making a profit.

At this point we need to remember the difference between *accounting profit* and *economic profit*. If firms are making an economic profit, their revenues are higher than their total costs. Those total costs *include opportunity costs* such as the money they could have made if they had invested their resources in other business opportunities. Understanding that the ATC curve also includes opportunity costs helps us to understand what makes firms want to enter and exit a market.

The existence of economic profits in a market signals that there is money to be made. *How will others respond* to this signal? They will enter the market to take advantage of the profit-making opportunity. If firms supplying roasted plantains to Cameroonian

FIGURE 13-4
Firm and market supply curves

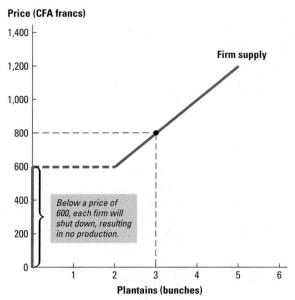

(A) Firm supply: One firm

Price (CFA francs)

Firm supply

Below a price of 600, each firm will shut down, resulting in no production.

Plantains (bunches)

Each firm is willing to supply a higher quantity as price increases. Price equals MR, and the optimal quantity at any price is where MR equals MC. Each optimal quantity-price pair adds a point on the supply curve.

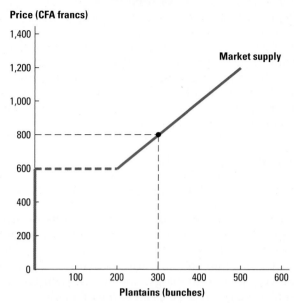

(B) Market supply: 100 firms

Price (CFA francs)

Market supply

Plantains (bunches)

The total quantity supplied is the sum of the quantity that each firm supplies. If there are 100 identical firms in the market, the market supply at any price is 100 times the quantity supplied by each firm.

train travelers are making more money than firms supplying salted peanuts or skinned oranges, we can expect orange-skinning firms and peanut-salting firms to switch their resources toward roasting plantains instead, if the costs of doing so are not very large.

But as more firms enter the roasted-plantain market, what happens? The total quantity offered for sale at any given price increases. Remember from Chapter 3 that the number of firms in the market is one of the nonprice determinants of supply: More firms means an increase in supply, and the whole supply curve shifts to the right. As supply increases, and demand stays constant, the market equilibrium moves to a lower price and higher quantity.

What does the new equilibrium imply for the profits made by firms in the market? Remember that profits are revenues minus costs. As the equilibrium market price falls, revenues fall—and so do profits. As long as *economic* profits are positive, however, more firms still have an incentive to enter the market to take advantage of them. Thus, the process continues, with firms entering the market and driving quantity up and price down. Eventually, the price will be so low that economic profits are reduced to zero—in other words, $P = ATC$. At this point, firms are indifferent between the roasted-plantain market and other business opportunities; they no longer have an incentive to enter the market.

When we understand that ATC also includes *opportunity costs*, we can understand better why firms decide to make the opposite decision—to exit a market. If price falls below ATC, a firm may still be making accounting profits. But at that point the firm is making negative economic profits. It could be making more money by pursuing other opportunities. It thus has an incentive to exit the market to invest its resources elsewhere.

What happens when some firms exit the market? The quantity supplied at any given price decreases, the supply curve shifts to the left, and the new market equilibrium is at a lower quantity and higher price. As price increases, profits also increase. The process continues until economic profits are zero, at which point no more firms exit the market; they are indifferent between the roasted-plantain market and other business opportunities.

Understanding the process of market entry and exit leads us to several conclusions. In the long run in a perfectly competitive market: (1) Firms earn zero economic profits. (2) Firms operate at an efficient scale. (3) Supply is perfectly elastic. Let's consider each.

Firms earn zero economic profits. This first conclusion might sound surprising: *In the long run, firms in a perfectly competitive market earn zero economic profit.* This doesn't mean that a business is not earning *accounting* profit. It simply means that the firm could not earn greater accounting profit by choosing to operate in a different market instead.

Remember, though, that *perfectly* competitive markets do not often exist in the real world. In the next section, we'll see why this first conclusion rarely holds in reality.

Firms operate at an efficient scale. The second conclusion about firms in competitive markets is less counterintuitive than the first, but powerful nonetheless: *In the long run, firms in a competitive market operate at an efficient scale.* Remember from "The Costs of Production" chapter that a firm's *efficient scale* is the quantity that minimizes average total cost.

To reach this conclusion, we need to bring together three pieces of information discussed earlier. First, remember that a firm's optimal production is the point at which price (i.e., marginal revenue) equals marginal cost. Second, remember that the marginal cost curve intersects the average total cost curve at its lowest point. Finally, we just established that in the long run, economic profits are zero, meaning that price is equal to average total cost. What happens when we put these three rules together?

$$P = MR = MC$$
$$MC = ATC \text{ at the minimum of ATC (at its lowest point)}$$
$$P = ATC$$

This tells us that P = MC = ATC. The intersection of all three lines takes place at only one point, as shown in Figure 13-5. As we know, MC = ATC at the minimum of ATC. When a firm produces at a point that satisfies this condition, it is therefore necessarily producing the quantity that minimizes average total cost in the long run. In other words, it is operating at its efficient scale.

Supply is perfectly elastic. Our third conclusion about competitive markets in the long run follows directly from the first two. We have established that economic profits are zero. In order for this to be true, price must be equal to the minimum of ATC. If anything causes the market equilibrium to move away from this price, the resulting positive or negative profits will cause firms to enter or exit the market. Such entry and exit will increase or decrease the quantity supplied, until price returns to the level that yields zero economic profits. Thus, in the long run, price is the same at any quantity. This causes the supply curve to be horizontal, as shown in Figure 13-6. Remember from Chapter 4 that a horizontal supply curve is *perfectly elastic*—producers will supply any quantity at the market price. In theory, therefore, in a competitive market, the price of a good should never change in the long run.

Why the long-run market supply curve shouldn't slope upward, but does

LO 13.7 Explain why a long-run supply curve might slope upward.

We've just put together a tidy theory about how suppliers will behave in the long run. But our theory makes a few predictions that don't quite match what we actually observe

FIGURE 13-5

Firms operate at efficient scale in the long run

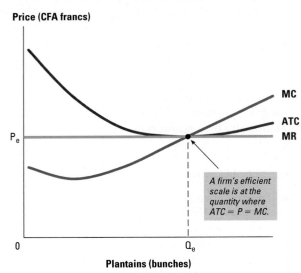

In the long run, firms in a competitive market operate at an efficient scale. A firm's efficient scale is the quantity that minimizes average total cost, which occurs where $P = MC = ATC$.

FIGURE 13-6

Perfectly elastic long-run supply curve

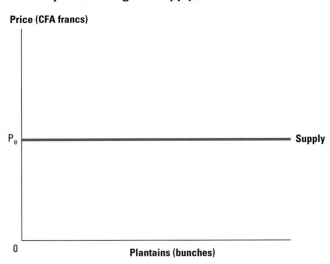

If anything causes the market to move away from the minimum-of-ATC price, the resulting positive or negative profits will cause firms to enter or exit the market, increasing or decreasing the quantity supplied until it returns to the equilibrium price. Thus, in the long run, price is the same at any quantity, and the supply curve is horizontal.

to be true. Assuming that the price of a good or service never changes doesn't seem very realistic. Here, we'll add a few nuances to the model just discussed, to explain why price doesn't stay perfectly constant in the long run.

The main tweak to the model from the previous section removes the assumption that all firms have the same cost structure. In the real world, this is hardly ever true: Some firms are simply more efficient than others at converting inputs into outputs. It would not be realistic to expect new entrants to an industry to achieve the same low costs as firms that have built up expertise over the years. The newer firms with higher costs will enter only markets with higher prices. In practice, therefore, the long-run supply curve will slope upward, because price has to rise to entice new firms to enter and increase the total quantity supplied.

In reality, price is equal to the minimum of ATC for the least-efficient firm in the market, not for every firm currently in the market. Dropping the simplifying assumption that every firm's costs are the same also overturns the surprising conclusion we came to in the last section—that firms in a perfectly competitive market earn zero economic profit. The last firm to enter the market earns zero economic profit, because its ATC is equal to price. But more efficient firms, with lower ATC, are able to earn positive economic profit.

Even if every firm in a market has the same ATC, there is a second reason why prices will still change in the long run. Over time, average total cost itself may change. Innovative firms are always searching for better production processes and new technologies that enable them to produce goods at lower cost. Imagine that a new form of efficient barbecue enables plantains to be roasted using half the amount of charcoal. This will reduce the variable costs of plantain-roasting firms, lowering both the MC and the ATC curves as shown in Figure 13-7. This in turn will increase profits, which will incentivize new firms to enter the market, which will increase the quantity supplied, which will drive down price.

For a real-world example of technological innovation driving down costs in the long run, see the Real Life box "How Ford changed the world."

FIGURE 13-7

Market entry due to changing production costs

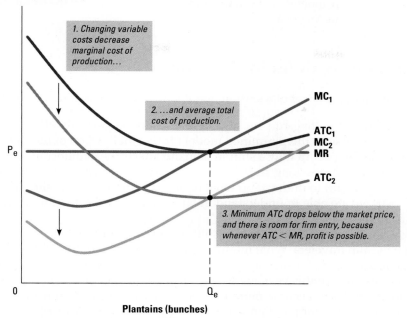

Price (CFA francs)

1. Changing variable costs decrease marginal cost of production...

2. ...and average total cost of production.

MC₁
ATC₁
MC₂
MR
ATC₂

Pₑ

3. Minimum ATC drops below the market price, and there is room for firm entry, because whenever ATC < MR, profit is possible.

0

Qₑ

Plantains (bunches)

As technology and production processes improve, ATC can decrease. Since price must be equal to the minimum of ATC in the long run, price will fall as production costs fall.

REAL LIFE

How Ford changed the world

Although the market for cars is not *perfectly* competitive (brands and styles of cars differ, so the goods are not standardized), it still comes close to meeting our definition in other ways. There are many buyers and sellers: In the early years of the automobile industry, when cars were less complex, and simpler to manufacture, it was relatively easy for new firms to enter the market. As a result, early on there were many more American car companies than there are today.

About 100 years ago, the Ford Company's pioneering use of the factory assembly line revolutionized the automobile industry and drove down costs. On an assembly line, each worker specializes in one small step of production, such as tightening a single bolt or welding a particular piece. The goods under production move along the line, with a worker at each station completing a single step, until the product is finished. An assembly line allows each worker to learn one task very well—to specialize.

In the early 1900s, Ford pioneered the use of assembly lines to produce its flagship automobile, the Model T. Ford spent seven years tweaking its production process to be as efficient as possible. The result was that Ford was able to produce the Model T at a dramatically lower cost than competitors' cars, and to sell it at a lower price, thereby reaching a much larger market. Ford's technological innovation in the production process enabled the company to quickly become the dominant auto producer in the world.

Ford's competitors had no choice but to adopt the assembly line to stay competitive. By 1930, over 250 auto manufacturers that did not adopt the assembly line had gone bankrupt. Ford's surviving competitors, who adopted the assembly line themselves, became able to compete with Ford on price, creating incentives for further innovation. The net result of this competition and innovation was that cars became cheap enough for middle-class consumers—a development that radically changed the social and geographic landscape of America.

Responding to shifts in demand

LO 13.8 Calculate the effect of a shift in demand on a market in long-run equilibrium.

We have seen why the long-run supply curve will not be perfectly elastic in practice. However, we'll stay with this simplified model for the final section of the chapter. It can still tell us something about how a shift in demand affects the equilibrium of a perfectly competitive market in the long run. Although we rarely see *perfect* competition in the real world, it is helpful to understand what happens in theory in this simplified model. Knowing that, we are able to understand in later chapters why it matters when reality diverges from the model.

Suppose, for instance, that there is a shift in demand for roasted plantains among Cameroonian train travelers. What might cause such a shift in demand? One possibility is a change in the price of a substitute good—for instance, roasted corn. Suppose there is a poor harvest of corn this year, increasing its price. Faced with more expensive corn, travelers in general will become more interested in buying plantain instead. This will shift the demand curve for plantain to the right. *How will the market respond to this shift?*

Panel A of Figure 13-8 shows the market for roasted plantains before the demand curve shifts. Notice that it shows both the short-run supply curve, which slopes upward, and the long-run supply curve, which—in theory at least—is horizontal in a perfectly

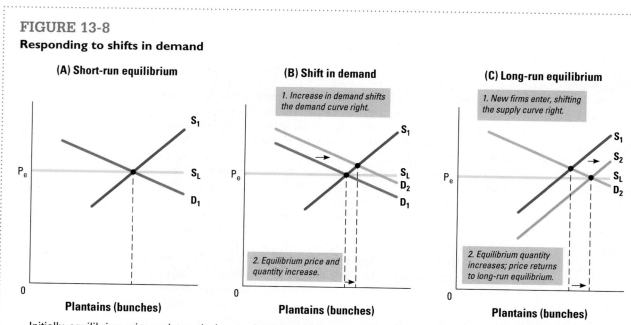

FIGURE 13-8

Responding to shifts in demand

(A) Short-run equilibrium

S_1
P_e
S_L
D_1
0
Plantains (bunches)

(B) Shift in demand

1. Increase in demand shifts the demand curve right.
S_1
P_e
S_L
D_2
D_1
2. Equilibrium price and quantity increase.
0
Plantains (bunches)

(C) Long-run equilibrium

1. New firms enter, shifting the supply curve right.
S_1
S_2
P_e
S_L
D_2
2. Equilibrium quantity increases; price returns to long-run equilibrium.
0
Plantains (bunches)

Initially, equilibrium price and quantity in a market fall at the intersection of the demand curve and the long-run supply curve (panel A). When an external change in market conditions increases demand, the price and quantity move away from the long-run equilibrium in the short term (panel B). In the long run, however, market entry increases supply, pushing price back down to the long-run equilibrium level (panel C).

competitive market. With the increased price of corn, the short-run demand curve for plantains shifts to the right, from D_1 to D_2, as shown in panel B. The equilibrium point slides up the short-run supply curve—a higher quantity of roasted plantains is traded, at a higher price.

This higher price means that plantain-roasting firms are making economic profit, creating an incentive for more firms to enter the market. As shown in panel C, the short-run supply curve shifts to the right, from S_1 to S_2 as more firms enter the market. The market equilibrium price slides down the new demand curve until it reaches the long-run supply curve. At that point, plantain-roasting firms are no longer making economic profit, so no new firms enter the market.

In the long run, then, the end result of the demand curve shifting to the right is to increase the quantity traded, but without any change in the price, which remains at the minimum level of average total cost.

✓ CONCEPT CHECK

- ❑ What induces new firms to enter a market? **[LO 13.6]**
- ❑ Why do firms operate at their efficient scale in the long run in a perfectly competitive market? **[LO 13.6]**
- ❑ Why might the long-run supply curve slope upward if firms don't have identical cost structures? **[LO 13.7]**
- ❑ What happens to the equilibrium price and quantity supplied in a perfectly competitive market if the market demand curve shifts to the right? **[LO 13.8]**

Conclusion

In this chapter, we dug into the wants and constraints that drive firm behavior in competitive markets. Firms will choose to produce a quantity that maximizes their profits. In the short run, they will shut down if their revenues don't cover their *variable* costs of production. In the long run, they will exit the market if their revenues don't cover their *total* costs of production.

This analysis leads to some surprising conclusions about long-run supply in competitive markets: Firms earn zero economic profit; they operate at their efficient scale; and long-run supply is, in theory, perfectly elastic. Firms are able to enter and exit the market freely to adjust the quantity supplied at a given price.

These choices by firms benefit consumers by keeping prices low and ensuring that supply is responsive to needs. As we have noted, however, real-world markets are not guaranteed to be perfectly competitive. Firms may wield market power, or offer products that are not perfectly standardized. There may be barriers that prevent firms from freely entering or exiting the market. Understanding what perfect competition looks like, we can now spend the next few chapters looking at how firms behave when we relax the assumptions of perfect competition.

 ◄ Mobile Window on the World—Scan this code with your smartphone to find more applications of the chapter content. (Need a barcode reader? Try ScanLife, available in your app store.)

Visit your mobile app store and download ► the Karlan and Morduch Study Econ app.

Key Terms

competitive market, p. 285

price taker, p. 285

market power, p. 285

average revenue, p. 288

marginal revenue, p. 288

Summary

LO 13.1 Describe the characteristics of a perfectly competitive market.

A perfectly competitive market has two essential characteristics and one that is nonessential but important. The first essential characteristic of a perfectly competitive market is that it contains a large number of buyers and sellers. The second is that sellers offer standardized goods, so that buyers have no reason to prefer one producer over another at a given price. Finally, firms in competitive markets are usually able to enter and exit the market freely.

LO 13.2 Calculate average, marginal, and total revenue.

Total revenue is equal to the quantity of each good that is sold, multiplied by its price. *Average revenue* is total revenue divided by quantity, or in other words, average revenue is equal to the price of the good. *Marginal revenue* is the revenue generated by selling an additional unit of a good. For a firm in a competitive market, marginal revenue is also equal to the price of the good.

LO 13.3 Find a firm's optimal quantity of output.

The profit-maximizing quantity is the one at which the marginal revenue of the last unit was exactly equal to the marginal cost. Another way of putting this is that it's the quantity at which the marginal cost curve intersects the marginal revenue curve. Producing any more or less would decrease profits.

LO 13.4 Describe a firm's decision to shut down and when to exit the market, and explain the difference between these choices.

There are two ways that a firm can choose to produce nothing. First, it can shut down its operations temporarily, producing a quantity of zero, but leaving open the possibility of restarting production in the future. Second, it can shut down permanently by exiting the market, choosing to produce nothing not only in the present but also in the future. If average revenue is less than the average variable cost of production, then the firm should shut down. In the long run, if price is less than average total cost, the firm should exit the market.

LO 13.5 Draw a short-run supply curve for a competitive market with identical firms.

In the short run, we assume that the number of firms in the market is fixed. The total quantity of goods that are supplied at a given price is therefore simply the sum of the quantity that each existing individual producer is willing to supply.

LO 13.6 Draw a long-run supply curve for a competitive market with identical firms, and describe its implications for profit-seeking firms.

The key difference between supply in the short run and supply in the long run is that we assume that firms are able to enter and exit the market in the long run. Thus, if economic profits are nonzero, firms will be induced to enter or exit the market, driving supply up or down until profits are zero. This leads us to three conclusions about competitive markets in the long run: Firms earn zero economic profits, firms operate at their efficient scale, and supply is perfectly elastic.

LO 13.7 Explain why a long-run supply curve might slope upward.

The assumption of perfectly elastic supply is based on the idea that in the long run, price must equal the minimum of average total cost. Over time, however, average total cost itself may change. New production processes and technologies enable firms to produce goods at lower cost. Also, if firms face different costs of production due to scarce resources or skills, prices will have to be higher at higher quantities to induce higher-cost firms to enter the market.

LO 13.8 Calculate the effect of a shift in demand on a market in long-run equilibrium.

In the short run, firms in a competitive market respond to a shift in demand (in the way described in Chapter 3). If demand increases, price increases and quantity supplied goes up. However, this pushes firms that are already in the market to earn a positive economic profit and operate at a size larger than their efficient scale. In the long run, other firms respond to this by entering the market, which pushes price back down to its long-run equilibrium level.

Review Questions

1. You stop by a crafts fair and you notice consumers haggling with vendors over prices. What does this tell you about the competitiveness of this market? Suppose you plan to go to a farmers' market next. Do you expect to find more or less haggling at this market than you did at the crafts fair? Why? **[LO 13.1]**

2. In the market for gold jewelry (unlike the market for gold ore), products come in a range of designs, styles, and levels of quality. Which of the characteristics of a competitive market is violated in the jewelry market? What does this imply for consumers' willingness to buy from different producers? **[LO 13.1]**

3. Suppose that the manager of a donut shop tells you that he sold 220 donuts today, for a total revenue of $220 and average revenue of $0.90. What's wrong with this story? **[LO 13.2]**

4. Suppose a firm's output is small relative to the size of its market. Explain why this means the firm's marginal revenue will be equal to the market price. **[LO 13.2]**

5. The manager of the donut shop tells you that he sells donuts for $1 each, and that if he were to make additional donuts, based on his current level of output, it would cost him $0.80 per donut. Do you recommend that the manager increase or decrease the number of donuts he makes? **[LO 13.3]**

6. Suppose a firm is operating in a competitive market and is maximizing profit by producing at the point where marginal revenue = marginal cost. Now suppose that consumer wealth decreases in this market (and the good is a normal good). What might you expect to happen to the profit-maximizing output quantity for the firm? **[LO 13.3]**

7. A restaurant owner is trying to decide whether to stay open at lunchtime. She has far fewer customers at lunch than at dinner, and the revenue she brings in barely covers her expenses to buy food and pay the staff. What do you recommend that she do? Explain your reasoning to her. **[LO 13.4]**

8. In what ways are profit-maximizing and loss-minimizing the same? In what ways are they different? **[LO 13.4]**

9. Suppose that the profit-maximizing quantity of output for a firm in the competitive textile industry is 1 million yards of cloth. If this firm is representative of others in the industry, how can you describe total supply in the market, with respect to the number of firms? **[LO 13.5]**

10. What would you expect to happen to market supply if variable costs decreased for individual firms in the market? **[LO 13.5]**

11. Suppose that the airline industry is in long-run equilibrium when the price of gasoline increases, raising the cost of operating airplanes. In the long run, what do you expect to happen to the number of airlines in business? Why? **[LO 13.6]**

FIGURE 13Q-1

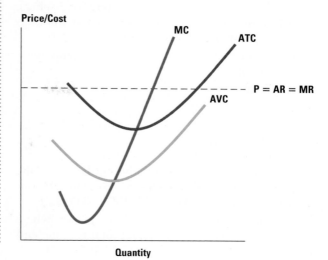

12. The firm in Figure 13Q-1 represents the cost structure for all firms in the industry. Describe the steps that will lead to long-run equilibrium in this market. **[LO 13.6]**

13. Corn farmers in Iowa are producers in a highly competitive global market for corn. They also have some of the most fertile, productive land in the entire world. Could Iowa's farmers be earning a positive economic profit in the long run? Why or why not? **[LO 13.7]**

14. Suppose that firms in an industry have identical cost structures and the industry is in long-run equilibrium. Explain how the profit motive could lead to *lower* market prices. **[LO 13.7]**

15. A market is in long-run equilibrium and firms in this market have identical cost structures. Suppose demand in this market decreases. Describe what happens to the profit-maximizing output quantity for individual firms as the market leaves and then returns to long-run equilibrium. **[LO 13.8]**

16. A market is in long-run equilibrium and firms in this market have identical cost structures. Suppose demand in this market decreases. Describe what happens to the market quantity as the market leaves and then returns to long-run equilibrium. **[LO 13.8]**

Problems and Applications

1. Suppose the market for bottled water and the market for soft drinks both have large numbers of buyers and sellers. Which of these markets is likely to be more competitive? **[LO 13.1]**

2. Suppose the market for steel and the market for cars both have large numbers of buys and sellers. Which market is likely to be affected by information asymmetries? **[LO 13.1]**

3. Check all that apply. In a perfectly competitive market, MR = **[LO 13.2]**
   a. Price
   b. Average revenue
   c. Total revenue
   d. $\dfrac{\Delta \text{ in total revenue}}{\Delta \text{ in quantity}}$

4. Darla sells roses in a competitive market where the price of a rose is $5. Use this information to fill out the revenue columns in Table 13P-1. **[LO 13.2]**

5. Paulina sells beef in a competitive market where the price is $5 per pound. Her total revenue and total costs are given in Table 13P-2. **[LO 13.3]**
   a. Fill out the table.
   b. At what quantity does marginal revenue equal marginal cost?

6. On Figure 13P-1, show the profit-maximizing quantity when price is P_1. Label this point Q_{max1}. Show the profit-maximizing quantity when price is P_2. Label this point Q_{max2} **[LO 13.3]**

FIGURE 13P-1

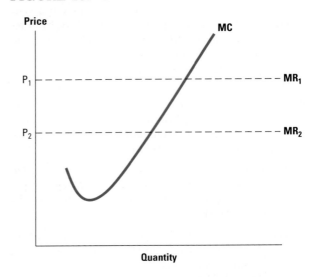

7. The data in Table 13P-3 are the monthly average variable costs (AVC), average total costs (ATC), and marginal costs (MC) for Alpacky, a typical alpaca wool-manufacturing firm in Peru. The alpaca wool industry is competitive. **[LO 13.4]**

TABLE 13P-3

Output (units of wool)	AVC ($)	ATC ($)	MC ($)
0	—	—	—
1	20.00	30.00	20.00
2	17.00	22.00	14.00
3	16.70	20.00	16.00
4	17.00	19.50	18.00
5	18.00	20.00	22.00
6	22.33	24.00	44.00

TABLE 13P-1

Quantity of roses	Total revenue ($)	Average revenue ($)	Marginal revenue ($)
1			
2			
3			
4			
5			

TABLE 13P-2

Quantity of beef (lb.)	Total revenue ($)	Total cost ($)	Profit ($)	Marginal revenue ($)	Marginal cost ($)	Marginal profit ($)
0	0	4		—	—	—
1	5	6				
2	10	9				
3	15	14				
4	20	22				

For each market price given below, give the profit-maximizing output quantity and state whether Alpacky's profits are positive, negative, or zero. Also state whether Alpacky should produce or shut down in the short run.

Q_{max}	Profit (+,−, 0)	Produce in SR? (Y/N)
a. $16.00: ____	_____	_____
b. $18.00: ____	_____	_____
c. $22.00: ____	_____	_____

8. The marginal costs, average variable costs (AVC), and average total costs (ATC) for a firm are shown in Figure 13P-2. In the figure, mark the quantity the firm will choose to produce in the short run given this cost structure and the market price. Does the firm earn positive or negative profits? Graph the area that defines the firm's profit (or loss). **[LO 13.4]**

9. The cost curves for an individual firm are given in Figure 13P-3. **[LO 13.4]**
   a. In Figure 13P-3 (A), highlight the firm's short-run supply curve.
   b. In Figure 13P-3 (B), highlight the firm's long-run supply curve.

10. Suppose the quantity of apples supplied in your market is 2,400. If there are 60 apple producers, each with identical cost structures, how many apples does each producer supply to the market? **[LO 13.5]**

11. Suppose an industry consists of many firms with identical cost structures, represented by the

FIGURE 13P-3

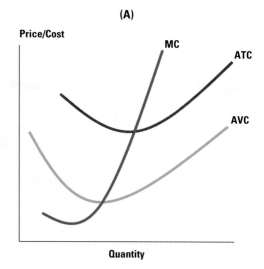

12. The monthly average variable costs, average total costs, and marginal costs for Alpacky, a Ztypical alpaca wool manufacturing firm in Peru, are shown in Table 13P-3 (above). All firms in the industry share the same costs as Alpacky, and the industry is in long-run equilibrium. What is the market price? **[LO 13.6]**

13. The industry in Figure 13P-5 consists of many firms with identical cost structures, and the

"typical individual firm" in panel A of Figure 13P-4. Price is P_1. With the aid of panel A, draw the short-run market supply curve in panel B, and show the firm and market output quantities at the equilibrium price in each panel. Label the firm output q_1 and the market output Q_1. **[LO 13.5]**

FIGURE 13P-2

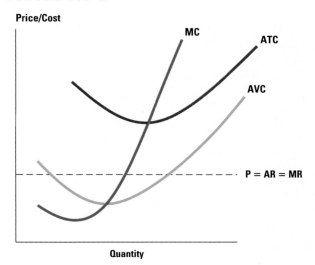

FIGURE 13P-4

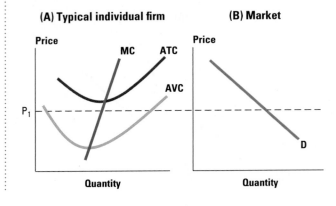

(A) Typical individual firm   **(B) Market**

FIGURE 13P-5

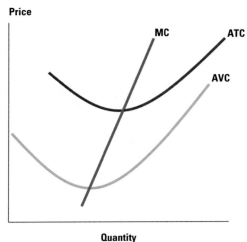

(A) Typical individual firm

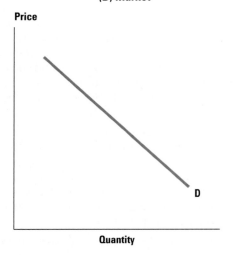

(B) Market

industry experiences constant returns to scale. **[LO 13.6]**

   a. Draw the short-run market supply curve.

   b. Draw the long-run market supply curve.

14. A firm's costs are represented in Table 13P-4. Suppose the price in the market is $110. Is the market in long-run equilibrium—yes, no, or can't determine? **[LO 13.7]**

15. Curling is a sport that involves sliding a granite stone over a patch of ice. The Winter Olympics has generated a lot of excitement about the fascinating sport of curling. As a result, demand for curling stones has increased. Curling stones are made from blue Trefor granite. There are limited deposits of blue Trefor, and other types of granite are poor substitutes. If the increase in demand for curling stones persists, do you expect the long-run equilibrium price to increase, decrease, or stay the same? **[LO 13.7]**

16. The industry in Figure 13P-6 consists of many firms with identical cost structures, and the industry experiences constant returns to scale. Consider a change in demand from D_1 to D_2 which increases price from P_1 to P_2 in the short run. **[LO 13.8]**

   a. Draw the new short-run supply curve after the market adjusts and returns to long-run equilibrium.

   b. Draw the long-run supply curve.

17. Suppose the market for gourmet chocolate is in long-run equilibrium, and an economic downturn has reduced consumer discretionary incomes. Assume chocolate is a normal good, and the chocolate producers have identical cost structures. **[LO 13.8]**

   a. What will happen to demand—shift right, shift left, no shift?

   b. What will happen to profits for chocolate producers in the short run—increase, decrease, or no change?

   c. What will happen to the short-run supply curve—increase, decrease, or no change?

   d. What will happen to the long-run supply curve—increase, decrease, or no change?

TABLE 13P-4

Quantity	VC ($)	MC ($)	AVC ($)	TC ($)	ATC ($)
0	0	—	—	1,000	—
10	500	50	50	1,500	150
20	900	40	45	1,900	95
30	1,700	80	57	2,700	90
40	4,400	270	110	5,400	135
50	8,000	360	160	9,000	180
60	14,000	600	233	15,000	250

FIGURE 13P-6

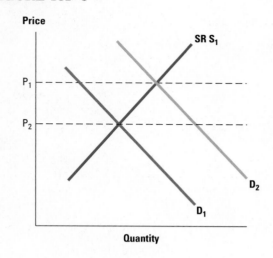

Monopoly

14

LEARNING OBJECTIVES

LO 14.1	List several reasons that monopolies exist, and explain how each causes barriers to entry.
LO 14.2	Explain why a monopolist is constrained by demand.
LO 14.3	Calculate the profit-maximizing production price and quantity for a monopolist.
LO 14.4	Calculate the loss in total social welfare associated with a monopoly.
LO 14.5	Describe the pros and cons of common public policy responses to monopoly.
LO 14.6	Explain why a firm has an incentive to use price discrimination when possible.

DIAMONDS WEREN'T ALWAYS FOREVER

Diamonds are, perhaps, the ultimate symbol of luxury. For reasons we will discover in this chapter, they have become nearly synonymous with romantic commitment. More than 80 percent of brides-to-be in the United States receive a diamond engagement ring, at an average cost of more than $3,000. Across society, they are also synonymous with conspicuous consumption. From swanky New York society to Los Angeles hip-hop stars, people use diamond jewelry to display wealth and status.

Why do diamonds carry such social cachet? They're expensive. People wearing diamonds show that they can afford the best. And why are diamonds expensive? You might assume it's because they are scarce and therefore precious. As it turns out, diamonds are not so rare. Tens of thousands of pounds of diamonds are produced every year.

Why, then, do we pay so much for diamonds? The answer lies in the story of one of the most successful companies of all time: De Beers. For more than a century, De Beers used aggressive business tactics to control almost all of the international market for diamonds. It also used ingenious marketing methods to boost demand for its product. By controlling the production and sale of most of the world's diamonds, De Beers became the opposite of a price-taking firm in a competitive market. It had so much market power that it was effectively able to set the market price of diamonds; it did this by choosing the quantity it released into the market at any given time.

The story of De Beers starts in the 1870s, when diamonds were truly rare. Just a few diamonds were found every year, scooped out of riverbeds and jungles in India and Brazil. They were expensive and only the truly elite could afford diamond jewelry. Then, British miners discovered enormous deposits of high-quality diamonds in South

Africa. This must have seemed like a fabulous opportunity to make huge amounts of money. But there was also a danger: If companies flooded the market with diamonds, the quantity supplied would shoot up and the price would be forced down. Soon it would no longer be so exclusive and prestigious to own a diamond, reducing people's willingness to pay for them. This change in preferences would shift demand, which would result in even lower prices. People would buy a lot of diamonds—but the sellers wouldn't make as much money.

A businessman named Cecil Rhodes joined with other mine owners to form a single corporation, De Beers. By controlling all of the newly discovered diamond mines—and almost all of the world's diamond production—De Beers ensured that smaller amounts of diamonds came onto the market, keeping prices high. In this way, DeBeers made much more money than they would have if they'd produced lots of diamonds but sold them at vastly lower prices.

In this chapter we'll see how monopolists such as De Beers calculate the optimal quantity and price to maximize their profits. We'll also see that a monopolist profits from its control of the market, but consumers lose—and, in general, total surplus decreases. For these reasons, governments usually try to limit monopoly power, using a range of policies that we'll discuss. Even the mighty De Beers has been unable to resist these pressures. It now controls only about 40 percent of the world diamond market—still a huge share, but a far cry from its heyday.

This look at monopolies takes us away from the model of perfect competition. In looking beyond markets with lots of firms competing against each other, we start to see the range and diversity of markets that make up the economy.

Why Do Monopolies Exist?

Most firms face some degree of competition. In the "Perfect Competition" chapter, we considered what would happen if a firm faced so much competition that it had no choice but to accept the going market price for its products. In this chapter, we'll ask what happens if a firm faces *no competition at all,* and is therefore able to have total control over how much it charges for its products.

monopoly a firm that is the only producer of a good or service with no close substitutes

Economists call such a firm a **monopoly**. The word *monopoly* comes from a root meaning *single seller,* and it describes a firm that is the only producer of a good or service that has no close substitutes. A firm is a *perfect monopoly* if it controls 100 percent of the market in a product. Firms can still have a large degree of *monopoly power* if they control slightly less than 100 percent of the market. For example, throughout the twentieth century, De Beers controlled 80 to 90 percent of the diamond market. It wasn't a perfect monopoly, but it wielded so much monopoly power that it was almost totally able to exert control over diamond prices.

The lack of a close substitute for a product is an essential part of the definition of monopoly. For example, if you are a monopoly seller of water, you can pretty much set your own price and people have no choice but to pay it. Water has no close substitutes.

If you are a monopoly seller of orange juice, you don't have the same power. Set your price too high, and people will buy apple juice instead.

One of the keys to De Beers's success is that it persuaded many people that diamonds are a good with no close substitutes. This is quite an impressive feat. After all, when it comes down to it, a diamond is simply a sparkly stone that looks nice in jewelry. It ought to have some close substitutes, such as rubies, sapphires, and emeralds (and also synthetic diamonds, which are practically indistinguishable from ones dug out of the ground). If De Beers ensures that the price of diamonds is high, why don't people buy these other stones instead? The answer is that De Beers has marketed diamonds very cleverly. The famous phrase "A diamond is forever" was the invention of a De Beers advertising campaign that ran in the U.S. from 1938 to the late 1950s. Within one generation, De Beers created the idea that the diamond is the recognized symbol of betrothal. Pursuing the same strategy in Japan, it advertised diamonds as representing modern, Western style. Between 1967 and 1981, the number of Japanese brides wearing diamond engagement rings went from 5 percent to 60 percent.

Many women nowadays would feel disappointed if they received an engagement ring containing another kind of stone or an artificial diamond. Diamonds are truly beautiful, but the strength of our preference for them reflects decades of clever marketing by the people at De Beers.

Barriers to entry

LO 14.1 List several reasons that monopolies exist, and explain how each causes barriers to entry.

It's easy to see why any firm would love to be a monopoly. But we can also see how the forces of competition are usually stacked against any one firm gaining that much market power. After all, when a firm charges high prices in a competitive market, some other enterprising firm will generally come along charging a lower price. In a monopoly situation such as the diamond market, other firms could make profits by entering the market and undercutting the monopolist's high prices. So we have to ask, *why isn't everyone doing it?*

The key characteristic of a monopoly market is that there are barriers that prevent firms other than the monopolist from entering the market. The barriers allow the monopolist to set prices and quantities without fear of being undercut by competitors. *Barriers to entry* contradict the *free entry and exit* feature that characterizes perfectly competitive markets.

Barriers to entry take four main forms: scarce resources, economies of scale, government intervention, and aggressive business tactics on the part of market-leading firms.

Scarce resources. The most straightforward cause of barriers to entry is scarcity in some key resource or input into the production process. Though not an especially common source of monopoly power, it was the case, at first, in the diamond market. Diamonds come out of the ground in only a limited number of places, after all. If a firm owns all the diamond mines (as De Beers effectively did in the 1870s), it has control of the production process. A new firm cannot simply enter the market without somehow gaining control of a mine.

Sometimes a single country, rather than a single firm, controls scarce resources with no close substitutes. When this happens, economic policy issues can become entangled in diplomatic relations, as described in the Real Life box "China's rare earth."

REAL LIFE

China's rare earth

Touchscreen devices such as iPads and smartphones are an everyday part of life. They currently rely on a metallic compound called indium tin oxide. Nor is it just touchscreens that need "rare earth" elements; so does a great deal of cutting-edge green-energy and defense technology. China controls 95 percent of all of all rare earth elements; it is effectively a monopoly supplier to the rest of the world. *To learn more, continue reading by scanning the QR code near the end of the chapter or by going online.*

Economies of scale. In the "Perfect Competition" chapter, we discussed the idea of *economies of scale*—instances when, as a firm produces more output, its average costs go down. In some industries, economies of scale are so powerful that competition between two or more firms simply doesn't make much sense; in these cases, the required infrastructure is too costly to replicate.

Imagine what would be needed to create competition in the electricity-supply industry, for example: Multiple firms would have to build power plants and huge systems of distribution poles and wires to serve the same area. Building such a system is prohibitively expensive for a firm. The electric industry has high fixed costs relative to the variable cost of supplying another unit of electricity. Because of this, the firm that can sell the most electricity can spread its fixed costs more widely. By doing so, the firm can achieve a lower cost per unit than a firm with the same fixed costs but lower output. The result is that one big firm can have a large cost advantage in providing all of the electricity for a given region.

natural monopoly
a market in which a single firm can produce, at a lower cost than multiple firms, the entire quantity of output demanded

Electricity supply is an example of a **natural monopoly**. This is a market in which a single firm can produce, at a lower cost than multiple firms, the entire quantity of output demanded. Drinking-water supply and natural gas are other examples of natural monopolies; these depend on a network of pipes that would be immensely expensive for new market entrants to duplicate. Yet another example is public transport: Imagine trying to enter the railways business by constructing new sets of tracks between major cities.

The term *natural monopoly* comes from the fact that, paradoxically, monopoly can be the "natural" outcome of competitive forces. An electricity supplier or a railway company doesn't have to worry about new firms entering the market to compete. Other firms have no incentive to enter, because they would face higher costs of production than the monopoly. Thus, high fixed costs create an effective barrier to entry.

Governments often get involved in natural monopolies to try to protect the public from abuse of monopolistic power. We'll see how later in the chapter.

Government intervention. Governments may create or sustain monopolies where they would not otherwise exist. In many U.S. states, for example, the government has created a monopoly on the sale of alcoholic beverages. In Iran, an elite branch of the army called the Revolutionary Guard Corps controls the construction industry as well as the oil and gas industries. Governments usually say they are creating monopolies in the public interest. In some cases, though, critics wonder if the real reason is to use monopoly power to benefit insiders.

Sometimes governments create monopoly power for state-owned firms. They can do this through a legal prohibition on other firms entering the market, or by subsidizing a state-owned enterprise so heavily that private companies effectively cannot compete. Not all state-owned enterprises are monopolies, though. For instance, some governments own airlines that compete against privately owned airlines.

Governments can also create or support private monopolies through regulation of intellectual property rights. Patents and copyrights give people who invent or create something the exclusive right to produce and sell it for a given period of time. For instance, by forbidding the use of a chemical formula by other manufacturers, patents allow pharmaceutical companies to act temporarily as monopolists in the market for a particular drug. This allows the patent-holder to raise prices and earn higher profits. When the patent expires, government protection of the monopoly ends; competitors can then drive down prices by producing a generic version of the same drug.

Creative works like art, movies, and music are also frequently protected by intellectual property laws. By making it illegal to distribute unauthorized copies of movies, for example, governments grant movie-making companies a legal monopoly over selling downloads of the movies they make. The result is that downloads of movies are more expensive than they would be if anyone could legally copy the movie and sell it.

Creating monopolies through intellectual property protection has costs and benefits for society. On the plus side, it gives firms an incentive to invest in research and creative activities that lead to products that enrich people's lives. Movie companies wouldn't spend millions of dollars on special effects if anyone could legally copy the download of the finished movie and sell it at any price. On the negative side, as we will see later in this chapter, monopolies drive down consumer surplus by setting higher prices than would be charged in a competitive market. In most cases, they reduce total surplus. Whether the social costs outweigh the social benefits is hotly debated and likely depends on the scenario at hand.

Aggressive tactics. The limited number of diamond mines in the world is not the only explanation for how De Beers managed to exert monopoly power over the diamond industry for so long. As new deposits of diamonds were found by other companies in other countries, De Beers had to constantly protect its monopoly power from the forces of competition. How could it prevent those new companies from undercutting its prices?

De Beers employed a number of tactics. It offered to buy up the companies that discovered new sources of diamonds. It entered into exclusive agreements with diamond-producing countries. And it was not afraid to employ aggressive methods of persuasion. De Beers punished anyone who did business with independent diamond producers. The punishment it meted out could be deadly for a smaller player in the diamond market.

For example, in the 1970s, Israeli diamond merchants began amassing stockpiles of diamonds as a safe way to store their wealth. De Beers didn't like this. It feared that the price of diamonds might collapse if the Israeli merchants chose to sell their stockpiles all at once. De Beers sent a representative to tell the Israeli merchants to stop stockpiling their gems. If they did not do so, De Beers threatened to bar them from its "sightings," its exclusive invitation-only diamond sales. Many of the diamond merchants resisted, before eventually giving in. Those who resisted paid a high price for their rebellion: The Israeli diamond industry suffered so badly, a quarter of its employees lost their jobs.

A more recent example of a company accused of employing aggressive tactics to gain or maintain monopoly power in local markets is Walmart. The company has been sued on several occasions for *predatory pricing*—that is, temporarily slashing prices until rival local stores are forced out of business. The results of the suits have been mixed: Courts in Arkansas and Mexico found no evidence of wrongdoing, but courts in Germany ultimately found that Walmart was undermining competition with its low prices. Other suits were settled out of court. Predatory pricing is a way for a large company, which can sustain short-term losses, to force smaller rivals out of the market. By doing so it can create monopoly power, which then enables the company to dictate its own prices.

Not all tactics to maintain monopoly power are so unwelcome to smaller competitors, however. For example, although Google controls around four-fifths of the world's Internet searches, it knows that a new company with a better search algorithm could overtake it. It tries to preserve its dominant position by buying promising-looking inventions in search technology. Many web entrepreneurs set up in business actively hoping that one of the giants of the industry—Google, Facebook, Microsoft, or Apple—will come along with a lucrative offer to buy them out.

✓ CONCEPT CHECK

- ❏ How do scarce resources create barriers to entry? **[LO 14.1]**
- ❏ How do economies of scale create barriers to entry? **[LO 14.1]**
- ❏ Give examples of government policies that create barriers to entry. **[LO 14.1]**

How Monopolies Work

We have to begin our analysis of a monopoly's behavior by understanding its *wants and constraints*. Just like any other firm, a monopoly *wants* to maximize its profits. As we saw in the "Perfect Competition" chapter, a firm in a perfectly competitive market is constrained by the fact that its production decisions cannot affect the prevailing market price. A monopoly does not face this constraint—but it is *constrained* by the market demand curve. In this section, we'll first see why this constraint exists and then how the monopolist makes production choices to maximize profits.

Monopolists and the demand curve

LO 14.2 Explain why a monopolist is constrained by demand.

In a perfectly competitive market, each individual firm faces a horizontal demand curve, even though the demand curve for the market as a whole slopes downward. This is because each firm is assumed to be too small for its production decisions to affect the market price. It can sell as much as it wants at the market price. But, if it tries to charge more, it will be undercut by competitors and won't be able to sell anything. We can depict this graphically with a horizontal line, as in panel A of Figure 14-1, which shows a horizontal demand curve for violet diamonds. Violet diamonds are the rarest of colored diamonds. Each year, only a select few are mined from the Argyle diamond mine in Australia. Panel A shows the demand faced by a firm selling violet diamonds in a perfectly competitive market where the market price is $2,500 per carat.

In contrast, as the only producer in the market, a monopolist faces the downward-sloping market demand curve, shown in panel B. The monopolist can choose to sell at any price it wants without fear of being undercut, because there are no other firms to do the undercutting. However, it is still constrained by market demand. Naturally, it would love to sell a huge quantity of goods at a high price. But *how would consumers respond to a high price?* The law of demand says that, all else equal, quantity demanded falls as price rises. The monopoly can choose any price-quantity combination on the demand curve, but is unable to choose points that are not on the curve. (It can't force customers to buy more or less than the quantity they demand at any given price.) The monopolist can choose to sell at a high price of $5,000 per diamond, but only by selling a small quantity—three diamonds. Or, it can choose to sell five more diamonds, reaching a total of eight, but only by lowering its price to $2,500 per diamond.

De Beers recognized the fact that its sales were limited by demand. That's why it went beyond controlling the supply side of the market, and invested heavily in shifting

FIGURE 14-1

Competitive versus monopolistic demand curves

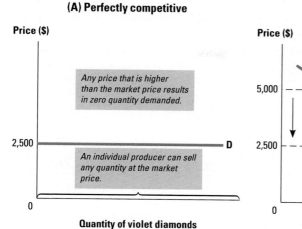

(A) Perfectly competitive

Price ($)

Any price that is higher than the market price results in zero quantity demanded.

2,500 ————————————— D

An individual producer can sell any quantity at the market price.

0

Quantity of violet diamonds

In a perfectly competitive market, an individual producer cannot deviate from the market price. The quantity the firm chooses to sell at that price does not affect the quantity demanded.

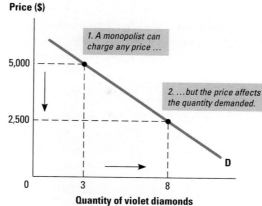

(B) Monopolistic

Price ($)

1. A monopolist can charge any price ...

5,000

2. ...but the price affects the quantity demanded.

2,500

D

0   3   8

Quantity of violet diamonds

In a monopolistic market, the monopolist can choose to charge a higher or lower price and still sell some quantity of goods. However, the pricing decision affects the quantity demanded.

the demand curve outward through the marketing methods we discussed earlier. Only by increasing demand would it be able to sell a higher quantity of diamonds at a higher price.

POTENTIALLY CONFUSING

Sometimes in this chapter we'll refer to a monopoly "picking a price." At other times, we'll say that it controls the quantity of goods available for sale. It's important to understand that these two decisions are equivalent. Each possible price corresponds to one specific quantity on the demand curve, and vice versa. The monopoly can control the market by setting a price and allowing customers to buy the quantity they demand at that price. Or it can control the market by restricting the quantity supplied, and allowing prices to adjust so that the quantity demanded meets the quantity supplied. Thus, the resulting price-quantity combination is the same, regardless of whether the monopoly picks a price or a quantity to supply.

Monopoly revenue

LO 14.3 Calculate the profit-maximizing production price and quantity for a monopolist.

The first step in understanding a monopolist's quest for profits is to map out the revenues it can bring in. Suppose that De Beers can choose the price of the diamonds it offers for sale in the United States. To simplify our model, let's assume for now that De Beers sells diamonds of uniform size (one-carat violet diamonds) and quality. What revenue can it expect to bring in at each possible price?

Column 1 of Table 14-1 shows the range of prices De Beers is considering. Because it is constrained by demand, DeBeers has to accept the quantity that American consumers

TABLE 14-1 Monopolist's revenue

The price a monopolist chooses to charge affects the quantity demanded, and therefore total revenue.

(1) Price ($/diamond)	(2) Quantity sold (Violet diamonds)	(3) Total revenue ($)	(4) Average revenue ($/diamond)	(5) Marginal revenue ($)
6,500	0	0	—	—
6,000	1	6,000	6,000	6,000
5,500	2	11,000	5,500	5,000
5,000	3	15,000	5,000	4,000
4,500	4	18,000	4,500	3,000
4,000	5	20,000	4,000	2,000
3,500	6	21,000	3,500	1,000
3,000	7	21,000	3,000	0
2,500	8	20,000	2,500	−1,000
2,000	9	18,000	2,000	−2,000
1,500	10	15,000	1,500	−3,000

are willing to buy at a given price. Column 2 shows the quantity of diamonds demanded at various prices. When price is high, consumers demand a small quantity of diamonds. For example, if De Beers chose to charge $6,000 per diamond, only one person would purchase a diamond. As price decreases, consumers demand higher and higher quantities. At a price of $1,500, consumers will purchase 10 violet diamonds. If we graphed the price and corresponding quantity sold from the first two columns of the table, we would have the market demand curve.

The *total revenue* that De Beers could earn at each price is simply price times quantity sold, which is the amount shown in column 3. As price increases and quantity sold decreases, total revenue first rises, and then falls. Remember from Chapter 4 that total revenue increases on sections of the demand curve where demand is price-elastic; it decreases on sections of the curve where demand is price-inelastic.

Average revenue, shown in column 4, is the revenue De Beers receives per diamond sold. It is calculated by dividing total revenue by quantity sold. This is simply a rearrangement of the equation that total revenue is quantity times price. Thus, just as in a competitive market, average revenue is equal to price.

Unlike a firm in a competitive market, however, a monopolist's *marginal revenue* is not equal to price. Marginal revenue is the revenue generated by selling each additional unit. We calculate marginal revenue by taking total revenue at a certain quantity and subtracting the total revenue when quantity is one unit lower. For instance, based on Table 14-1, total revenue from five diamonds is $20,000, and total revenue from four diamonds is $18,000. So, the marginal revenue from selling a fifth diamond is $20,000 − $18,000 = $2,000.

In a competitive market, a firm can sell as much as it wants without changing the market price. The additional revenue brought in by one unit is always simply the price of that unit. Thus, in a competitive market, marginal revenue is equal to price. In a market dominated by a monopoly, however, the monopoly's choice to produce an additional unit drives down the market price. Because of this effect, producing an additional unit of output has two separate effects on total revenue:

1. *Quantity effect:* First, total revenue increases due to the money brought in by the sale of an additional unit.
2. *Price effect:* Second, total revenue decreases, because all units sold now bring in a lower price than they did before.

Depending on which of these effects is larger, total revenue might increase or decrease when De Beers increases the quantity of diamonds it sells. If there were no price effect (as in a perfectly competitive market), then marginal revenue would be determined solely by the quantity effect; it would be equal to price. But the price effect always works in the opposite direction of the quantity effect—it decreases revenue. Thus, *marginal revenue in a monopoly market is always less than the price,* except for the very first unit sold. For that first unit, average revenue and marginal revenue are both equal to the price.

Figure 14-2 shows De Beers's total, average, and marginal revenue at various prices in the U.S. market for violet diamonds. Average revenue is equal to price at any quantity sold. In other words, the average revenue curve is the same as the market demand curve. The marginal revenue curve lies below the average revenue curve, because marginal revenue is always less than price after the very first unit sold.

Table 14-1 and Figure 14-2 show that marginal revenue can sometimes be negative. This occurs in our example at quantities above seven diamonds (the point at which the

FIGURE 14-2

Monopolist's total, average, and marginal revenue

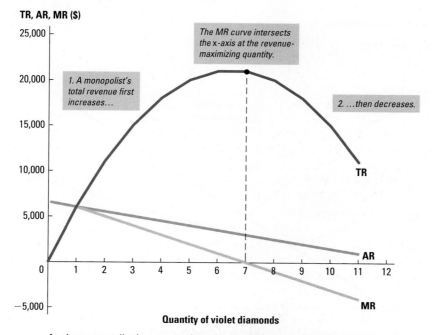

As the monopolist increases the price, total revenue (TR) first increases and then decreases. Total revenue is maximized when marginal revenue (MR—the lightest green line) equals zero. Average revenue (AR, or price) is always greater than marginal revenue, because each additional unit sold brings less revenue than the last unit.

marginal revenue curve crosses the *x*-axis in Figure 14-2). What does it mean when marginal revenue drops below zero in Figure 14-2? Think back to the price effect. Negative marginal revenue means that the price effect has become bigger than the quantity effect, and so each additional unit of output decreases total revenue. Thus, the point at which the MR curve crosses the *x*-axis represents the revenue-maximizing quantity. In our example, total revenue is maximized at a quantity of seven. (Table 14-1 shows that, in this example, the same total revenue can also be obtained by producing a quantity of six.)

Revenue is important, but as we know, what firms really care about is maximizing profit. So how do monopolists go about maximizing their profit?

Maximizing profits by picking price and quantity sold. De Beers exerted control over the diamond market through the quantity of diamonds it released for sale at any given time. The company held back stockpiles of diamonds worth billions of dollars for years at a time to maintain this control.

The purpose of this stockpiling was to ensure that the quantity of diamonds for sale was always the quantity that maximized De Beers's profits. Sometimes, the profit-maximizing quantity was lower than the total quantity of diamonds available, and so it was in De Beers's interest to hold some back from the market. How can a monopolist choose the price-quantity combination that maximizes its profits? Perhaps surprisingly, it can approach this problem in exactly the same way that a firm in a competitive market would.

Figure 14-3 shows hypothetical cost and revenue curves for De Beers. The general appearance of these curves should be familiar from the "Perfect Competition" chapter. The only relevant difference between the curves for a monopoly and the equivalent

FIGURE 14-3

Monopolist's cost curves

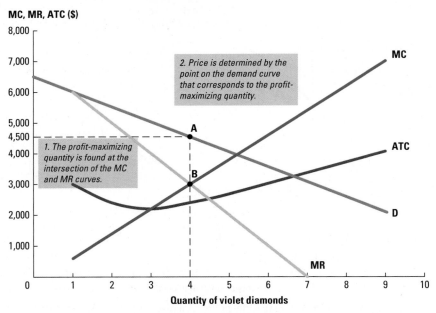

A monopolist can choose both the quantity and the price at which to produce. To maximize profit, the monopolist will always produce that quantity at which marginal cost equals marginal revenue. It then sets the price based on the demand for that quantity.

ones for a firm in a competitive market is that marginal and average revenue slope downward for the monopolist. (In a competitive market, those curves are horizontal at the market-price level.) Just as in a competitive market, the profit-maximizing quantity of output for a monopoly is the point at which the marginal revenue curve intersects the marginal cost curve. Why is this so?

Remember that the contribution of each additional unit of output to a firm's profit is the difference between marginal revenue and marginal cost. If the marginal revenue of a unit of output is higher than its marginal cost, then the unit brings in more money in sales than it costs the firm to produce it. Thus, it contributes to the firm's profit. What if, on the other hand, marginal revenue is lower than marginal cost? In that case, the unit costs more to produce than it brings in, and the firm loses money by producing it.

The same marginal decision-making analysis we used in the "Perfect Competition" chapter applies here:

- At any quantity of output *below* the intersection of the marginal revenue and marginal cost curves, MR is higher than MC. At that point, De Beers could earn more profits by offering an additional diamond for sale.

- At any quantity of output *above* the intersection, the company loses profits on each additional diamond offered for sale. At that point, De Beers could earn more profits by offering fewer diamonds for sale.

Therefore, De Beers should increase the quantity of output up to the point where it can no longer earn more profits by increasing output. (That is where MR = MC, shown at point B in Figure 14-3.) It should then stop producing output, before it starts losing money.

There is an important difference between a firm in a competitive market that produces at the point where MR = MC and a monopoly that does the same thing. In a competitive market, marginal revenue is equal to price. For a monopolist, price is greater than marginal revenue; therefore price is also greater than marginal cost at the optimal production point. The profit-maximizing price is the price on the demand curve that corresponds to the profit-maximizing quantity of output. This is shown as point A in Figure 14-3.

This fact—that a monopoly's profit-maximizing price is higher than its marginal costs—is key to understanding how monopolies are able to earn positive economic profits in the long run. Remember that a firm in a competitive market produces at the point where P = MC = ATC in the long run. If price is higher than MC, other firms will enter the market, increasing supply and driving down the price, until profits are zero and there is no longer an incentive for more firms to enter. In a monopoly market, however, other firms can't enter the market, due to the barriers to entry that allowed the firm to become a monopolist in the first place. The result is that a monopolist is able to maintain a price higher than average total cost.

Remember that the formula for calculating profit is:

$$\text{Profit} = (P - ATC) \times Q$$

So, if price is greater than ATC, profits will be positive, even in the long run.

We can also observe this same fact graphically, as shown in Figure 14-4. De Beers's profit is equal to the area of the shaded box. The box's length is equal to the profit-maximizing quantity of output. The box's height is the distance between the profit-maximizing price and average total cost. We can also think of that amount ($2,250, the difference between A and B in the figure) as the profit earned on the average diamond sold.

This analysis shows us why De Beers had such a strong incentive to maintain its monopoly power. The fact that there were no other diamond producers to enter the market and drive down the price of diamonds gave De Beers the ability to maintain a

To improve your understanding of how to calculate profit-maximizing price and quantity, try the online interactive graphing tutorial.

FIGURE 14-4
Monopoly profit

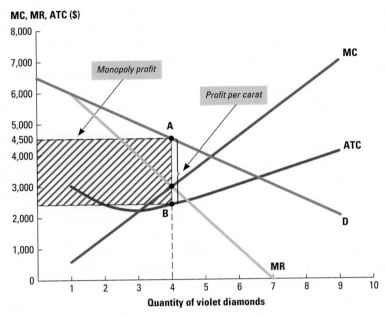

The monopolist sets the price at point A on the demand curve, which corresponds to the profit-maximizing quantity. The monopolist's profit equals the difference between the price and the average total cost (point B), multiplied by the quantity sold. Put another way, Profit = (P − ATC) × Q, or the area of the shaded box.

price higher than its costs. This market power in turn allowed it to earn economic profits in the long run.

✓ CONCEPT CHECK

- ❑ Why can't a monopoly choose to sell at any price-quantity combination it wants? **[LO 14.2]**
- ❑ Why is marginal revenue lower than price for a monopoly? **[LO 14.3]**
- ❑ Why are monopolies able to earn positive economic profits in the long run? **[LO 14.3]**

Problems with Monopoly and Public Policy Solutions

Since 2000, De Beers's grip on the diamond industry has lessened: Its market share has dropped from more than 80 percent of the world diamond trade to near 40 percent. This is partly due to large-scale mining of diamonds in Canada and Russia, outside of De Beers's range of control. It is also due in part to increased pressure from governments and diamond consumers to stop De Beers from exercising its monopoly power. Following a series of lawsuits in the United States and Europe, De Beers was banned from operating in certain countries, and forced to pay large fees or change its practices in others. Until 2004, De Beers executives weren't even allowed to travel to the United States on business.

Monopolies are great for the monopolist, and not so great for everyone else. Consumers get fewer diamonds, at a higher price. This market inefficiency reduces total surplus. In this section, we'll see how the existence of monopolies has welfare costs. We'll also look at the range of public policies governments use to try to discourage monopolies and mitigate their effect on consumers. As we'll see, these policy responses are imperfect, and often highly controversial. Before we weigh the costs and benefits of different policy responses, let's consider the welfare costs of monopoly power.

The welfare costs of monopoly

LO 14.4 Calculate the loss in total social welfare associated with a monopoly.

Why do policy-makers get riled up about monopolies? A monopoly's ability to keep quantity low and prices high hurts society in general and consumers in particular. Let's dig back into the monopolist's production decision to show why this is so.

The equilibrium price and quantity in a competitive market maximize total surplus. In other words, the market is efficient. Figure 14-5 shows the market demand curve for diamonds, as well as hypothetical marginal revenue and marginal cost curves. What is the efficient production level in this market? Remember from the "Perfect Competition" chapter that a competitive firm's supply curve is equivalent to the section of the marginal cost curve that lies above average total cost. The efficient quantity lies at the

FIGURE 14-5

Deadweight loss in a monopoly market

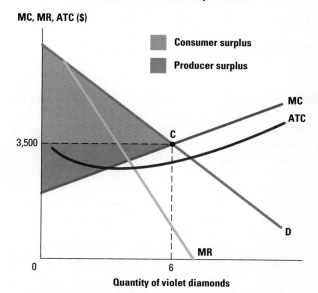

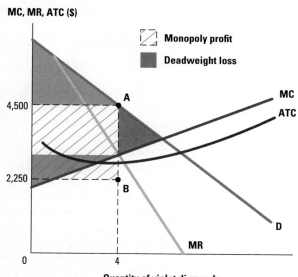

A competitive market produces the equilibrium price and quantity (point C). When the market is in equilibrium, total surplus is maximized, and there is no deadweight loss.

A monopoly market produces the quantity at which marginal revenue equals marginal cost (point B). Because that quantity is lower than the market equilibrium quantity, the monopoly's profit cuts into consumer surplus. Fewer trades take place, and society suffers a deadweight loss.

intersection of supply (marginal cost) and demand, at point C in panel A. At any higher quantity, total surplus is reduced, because the increase in consumer surplus is less than the decrease in producer surplus. At any lower quantity, total surplus is also reduced—the decrease in consumer surplus is greater than the increase in producer surplus.

A monopoly, however, will produce the quantity found at point B in panel B of Figure 14-5, where marginal revenue intersects marginal cost. This quantity is lower than the efficient quantity that would prevail in a competitive market, which tells us that total surplus is not maximized. It also tells us that producer surplus is higher than the level in a competitive market, while consumer surplus is lower. Monopolies earn profit, while consumers lose surplus. Panel B represents the loss of total surplus as a deadweight loss (exactly as we did in the "Efficiency" chapter when discussing the welfare cost of taxes).

It's important to remember that this description of the costs of monopoly is a positive statement—a statement about how things *are.* That is different from a normative judgment—a statement about how things *should* be. There can be cases in which people believe that the advantages to maintaining a particular monopoly outweigh the total welfare costs due to lost surplus. This is similar to the feeling many people have that it is worth accepting some deadweight loss from taxes in order to achieve goals such as providing benefits to the poor or supporting military or police forces. There is no principle that tells us that maximizing efficiency trumps other goals.

However, voters and policy-makers in many countries have made the normative judgment that monopolies are usually a bad thing. This isn't so surprising: Maximizing total surplus means that society's resources are being used efficiently, and few people are excited to provide extra profits to monopolies. After all, voters are more likely to be consumers than owners of monopolies.

This does not mean that monopolists are always wealthy, large-scale enterprises. For an example of a monopolist toward whom we might feel more than usually sympathetic, check out the From Another Angle box "Poor monopolists."

FROM ANOTHER ANGLE
Poor monopolists

When Muhammad Yunus won the Nobel Peace Prize in 2006, the Grameen Bank became a household name around the world. The bank is credited with bringing access to financial services to millions of rural Bangladeshis. It is less widely known that Grameen was also the first to bring access to phones within reach of the same population.

Grameen used an ingenious business model to accomplish this, in a country known for its strained rural infrastructure and limited resources. The bank recruited long-standing clients to act as local phone operators. It loaned them the $420 necessary to start a small phone kiosk and trained them to operate it as a business. Grameen also sold the operators discounted telephone airtime on credit, which the operators in turn sold to villagers.

The demand for phone services in Bangladeshi villages was tremendous, and the phone kiosks flourished. Farmers and traders used the phones to manage business orders and keep track of prices in local markets. Families used the phones to stay in touch with relatives who had left home to find work in the city.

Because Grameen's operators were the first to bring phone services to rural villages, they had no competitors. Grameen initially established a single phone-kiosk operator in each village. By doing so, it inadvertently created a local monopoly in this previously missing market. This turned out to be a huge windfall for the operators; they were able to earn profits often amounting to double or triple the average Bangladeshi income. Needless to say, this new stream of income enabled the operators to pay off their loans in record time. Recognizing the demand for phone services, and perhaps that the new rural telecom market would benefit from healthy competition, Grameen began establishing multiple operators in each village.

When you hear the word "monopolist," you might think of a massive corporation getting rich by quashing the competition. The reality of Grameen phone operators couldn't be further from this stereotype. The phone operators were indeed monopolists, but they were also impoverished villagers, just trying to improve their families' lives. Remember—there's nothing inherently evil about monopoly. The important thing is to weigh the social welfare benefits that accrue to monopolists against the efficiency losses to the rest of society.

Source: http://www.grameentelecom.net.bd/about.html.

Public policy responses

LO 14.5 Describe the pros and cons of common public policy responses to monopoly.

Policy-makers have developed a range of policy responses to monopolies. These tools aim to break up existing monopolies, prevent new ones from forming, and ease the effect of monopoly power on consumers. Each comes with costs as well as benefits; some economists argue that the best response is often to do nothing at all. As we discuss each type of policy, keep a critical eye on its pros and its cons.

Antitrust laws. The regulation of monopolies has been a high-profile political issue in America for quite a while. In the late nineteenth century, massive corporations called "trusts" were beginning to dominate entire industries. To check their growing power, Congress passed the Sherman Antitrust Act in 1890. The act requires the federal government to investigate and prosecute corporations that engage in anti-competitive practices. This includes practices such as price fixing and bid rigging. The early twentieth century was also a period of major antitrust activity in the United States. President Theodore Roosevelt, in particular, became known as a "trustbuster." Using the Sherman Act, he vigorously prosecuted corporations that used monopolistic practices to stifle competition. Over the years, the government has used the Sherman Act to break up monopolies in various industries, including railroads, oil, aluminum, tobacco, and telecommunications.

The Sherman Act still has an impact. As recently as the late 1990s, it was uncommon to use an Internet browser other than Microsoft's Internet Explorer. In 1999, the U.S. government sued Microsoft for anti-competitive behavior. The suit alleged that by bundling Internet Explorer with Microsoft Windows, the company was unfairly pushing competing web browsers out of the market. (Microsoft eventually reached a settlement with the government, and agreed to stop certain business practices perceived to be anti-competitive.) Today, there are lots of Internet browsers, including Chrome, Firefox, Safari, and improved versions of Internet Explorer.

For another case concerning an area in which the antitrust law has not yet had much impact, read the Real Life box "Rockers vs. Ticketmaster."

REAL LIFE
Rockers vs. Ticketmaster

Anyone who has been to a major concert or show in the U.S. has probably experienced the hefty pile of fees and charges that come with buying a ticket through Ticketmaster. These fees can add up to between 20 and 40 percent of the face value of the tickets themselves.

Ticketmaster is the single dominant player in the lucrative U.S. ticket business. For example, 27 of 30 NHL teams and 28 of 30 NBA teams sell tickets only through Ticketmaster. Many of the nation's leading concert and theater venues have similar agreements. These exclusive agreements are a crucial element of Ticketmaster's business strategy. Because of them, competitors have difficulty gaining a foothold in the market. Many feel that Ticketmaster has thus become a de facto monopoly in the market for tickets.

This has infuriated many musicians who want to keep prices of tickets low for their fans' sake. Two groups have even pursued lawsuits against Ticketmaster. In 1994, Pearl Jam complained to the U.S. Justice Department about Ticketmaster's allegedly monopolistic practices and high markups. The group's lawsuit was unsuccessful. In 2003, jam band String Cheese Incident sued Ticketmaster. The suit alleged that the exclusive agreements with venues were monopolistic and violated the Sherman Antitrust Act. This case settled out of court, and the results were not publicly disclosed.

The power of Ticketmaster may not last long, though. A slew of new sites that sell concert tickets online, including Etix and Ticketfly, are trying to compete against Ticketmaster. Since they can offer cheaper booking fees for bands and ticket prices for fans, these competitors may prove to be a win for everyone—except, of course, Ticketmaster.

Sources: http://www.rollingstone.com/music/news/string-cheese-incident-eliminate-service-charges-for-summer-tour-20120302; http://latimesblogs.latimes.com/music_blog/2010/08/ticketmaster-a-new-era-of-transperancy-or-smoke-mirrors-.html.

The U.S. government has also used the Sherman Antitrust Act and its partner the Clayton Antitrust Act of 1914 to prevent monopolies from forming in the first place. The Justice Department can block two firms from merging if the merger would result in a company with too much market power. Two examples include a proposed merger between office-supply giants Office Depot and Staples, which the Justice Department blocked in 1997, and a failed AT&T merger with T-Mobile in 2011.

In recent years, however, the government has only infrequently used the power to block mergers. More often, the government investigates a potential merger and allows it to go forward. For instance, in 2008, Delta Airlines merged with Northwest Airlines to become the largest airline in the world. Then, in 2012, the merger of United and Continental created a new global number one. These mergers occurred with the full blessing of the Justice Department, which determined that there was sufficient pressure from other airlines to maintain competition. Further, the mergers were seen as actually generating benefits for customers due to cost savings in airport operations and the organization of plane fleets.

People sometimes criticize antitrust actions as being politically motivated or causing more inefficiency than they create. How could antitrust action cause inefficiency in the market? It could accidentally break up a natural monopoly. Or, it could break a large company into several firms that operate at a smaller-than-efficient scale. Different regulators handle these decisions differently. For instance, Microsoft still faced antitrust lawsuits in Europe long after it settled its case in the United States.

Public ownership. Natural monopolies pose a particular problem for policy-makers. On the one hand, the monopolist is able to achieve lower costs of production than multiple competing producers would. On the other hand, even a natural monopoly chooses to produce at a price that is higher than marginal cost, causing deadweight loss.

One possible solution for governments is to run natural monopolies as public agencies. Examples of public ownership of natural monopolies include the U.S. Postal Service to deliver mail and Amtrak to provide train services. The rationale behind public ownership of natural monopolies is that governments are supposed to serve the public interest rather than maximize profit. They could choose to provide broader service than

FIGURE 14-6

Price regulation of a natural monopoly

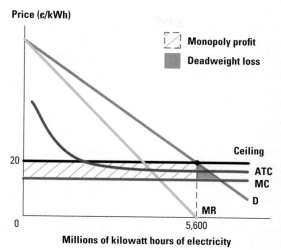

(A) Price ceiling above MC but below full monopoly pricing

Price (¢/kWh)

Monopoly profit
Deadweight loss

Ceiling
20
ATC
MC
D
MR
0   5,600

Millions of kilowatt hours of electricity

When the price ceiling (20 cents) is set above the natural monopoly's average total cost, the firm will produce at the point where the price intersects the average revenue to maximize its profits. Some deadweight loss remains.

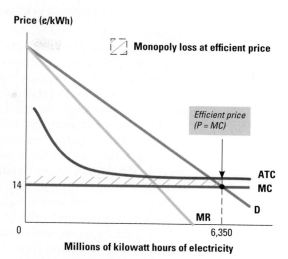

(B) Price ceiling at efficient price

Price (¢/kWh)

Monopoly loss at efficient price

Efficient price
(P = MC)

ATC
14
MC
MR   D
0   6,350

Millions of kilowatt hours of electricity

In a competitive market, there is no deadweight loss, and the efficient price occurs at the point where P = MC. A publicly owned natural monopoly producing at this point loses money.

a private monopolist might. For example, a government-supported monopoly might deliver mail to any postal address in the country; a private monopolist might prefer not to deliver to remote addresses that are more expensive to reach.

A publicly owned monopoly could also set prices lower than an unregulated monopolist would. Panel A of Figure 14-6 shows an example. In this case, the regulated price is higher than average total cost, but is lower than the price that an unregulated monopoly would set. Even though price is lower than it would be if the monopoly were unregulated, there is still some deadweight loss. Panel B shows how governments often regulate prices for a natural monopoly in order to diminish deadweight loss. Recall that in a competitive market, where deadweight loss is zero, firms produce at the point where P = MC. However, a natural monopoly is defined by the fact that ATC falls as quantity increases, which means that MC must be below ATC at all possible quantities. As a result, a natural monopolist that sets price equal to marginal cost will incur losses, as shown in panel B.

However, public ownership of a natural monopoly has its problems. Politicians may feel pressure to lower prices even further, below the level they would be in a competitive market. As we saw in the "Efficiency" chapter, doing so will create shortages and people will demand more than it makes sense for the producer to supply at that price. Publicly owned companies may also make business decisions—such as where to locate or what types of products to offer—on the basis of political concerns. Perhaps most importantly, the loss of the profit motive could reduce the publicly owned monopolist's motivation to improve efficiency and to provide better service or lower costs. After all, there is no rule stating that all monopolies must make a profit. (Amtrak and the U.S. Postal Service both lost money in 2011.) If an inefficient public monopoly cannot provide a service at a price that sufficient numbers of people are willing to pay, it can remain in operation by covering its losses with revenue from taxes.

These concerns explain why public ownership of monopolies has become much less common. Since the 1980s, especially in Europe, many government-operated agencies such as state airlines, telecoms, and utilities have been privatized (that is, sold to private companies) and regulated instead.

Regulation. If policy-makers don't want to go all the way to public ownership, one common intermediate step is to regulate the behavior of natural monopolies. Such regulation takes the form of controls on the prices natural monopolies are allowed to charge. This is frequently the case in utility markets. For instance, many governments allow private monopolies to exist in the supply of electricity, tap water, or natural gas, but cap the price these companies can charge.

In theory, such controls could have the same effect as public ownership: By capping the price at ATC, regulators can force natural monopolies to earn zero economic profits, reducing deadweight loss as much as possible without causing the firm to incur losses and exit the market. Unfortunately, it is rarely so simple in practice. Firms have an incentive to avoid giving regulators useful information about their true costs of production. Lack of information makes it difficult for regulators to determine the appropriate price level. The idea behind privatizing natural monopolies relates to incentives: A private firm should be more motivated than a public one to increase its profits by innovating and reducing costs, and those savings should result in lower prices for consumers. But if the regulator sets a price so low that *all* of the cost savings go to consumers, the firm will have no incentive to reduce costs. If the regulator sets the price at a level insufficient to cover the monopolist's costs, it could even drive the firm out of business.

Vertical splits. Another common response to natural monopolies is to look for ways to split an industry "vertically" and introduce competition into parts of it. Rather than splitting a monopolist "horizontally" into multiple companies that compete to sell the same product, a "vertical" split divides the original firm into companies that operate at different points in the production process. For example, the supply of electricity is a natural monopoly, but the generation of electricity is not. Policy-makers in countries such as New Zealand have split the electricity industry vertically, separating generation from supply. Firms compete to generate electricity, but then all use the same wires to supply the electricity to people's homes and businesses.

Similarly, countries such as the UK have split the railway industry vertically. Several competing providers of train services run their trains on the same sets of tracks. This requires active regulation to make sure that different companies do not try to run trains in different directions at the same time. Critics also say that the system enables the operators of train services and the monopoly that manages the tracks to blame each other for delays.

No response. Looking at the pros and cons of various interventions in monopoly markets, some economists conclude that the best response to a monopoly is sometimes no response at all. When might the right solution be to do nothing? Doing nothing might be preferable if regulation is too difficult to create or manage effectively. If government interventions in the market are subject to corruption or political mishandling, it might be better not to act. This view doesn't deny that monopoly power causes inefficiency. Instead, it simply holds that sometimes the problems caused by intervention might be worse.

✓ CONCEPT CHECK

- ❏ Why does monopoly cause deadweight loss? **[LO 14.4]**
- ❏ What are some of the potential problems with public ownership of monopolies? **[LO 14.5]**

Market Power and Price Discrimination

In any market, some consumers typically would be willing to pay more for the good than the market price. They enjoy consumer surplus when they buy at a price lower than their willingness to pay. If you were a firm, wouldn't you like to be able to charge different individuals different prices for the same good? You could charge a higher price to customers with higher willingness to pay, transforming their consumer surplus into your producer surplus. The more monopoly power a firm has, the more able it is to do exactly this.

What is price discrimination?

LO 14.6 Explain why a firm has an incentive to use price discrimination when possible.

The practice of charging customers different prices for the same good is called **price discrimination**. It involves "discriminating" between customers on the basis of their willingness to pay. Examples of price discrimination are all around us. Have you ever used your student ID card to claim discounts on public transport or theater tickets? That's an example of price discrimination. You are getting exactly the same product as people who are being charged full price, but you receive a discount because companies assume that, on average, students have lower willingness to pay for many goods.

How can a firm charge different customers different amounts for the same good? In a perfectly competitive market, it couldn't. Remember that firms in a perfectly competitive market sell at a price equal to their average total cost, and earn zero economic profit. They couldn't afford to offer discounted prices to students; doing so would result in *negative* profit. Nor could they choose to charge nonstudents a higher price, because those customers would simply go to the competition instead.

As we move away from the model of perfect competition, price discrimination becomes possible. Whenever firms gain a degree of market power, they look for ways to exploit customers' varied willingness to pay. Consider why clothing stores hold periodic sales, for example. It enables them to charge two different prices: They charge one price to consumers who are willing to pay more to get the item when it first hits the market. They charge a lower price to those who don't mind waiting until the sales are on. Similarly, theaters tend to charge lower prices for matinee showings: They attract the cash-poor and time-rich during the day; people with busy work schedules will generally be both more willing and able to pay the higher prices charged for an evening showing.

The more monopoly power a firm has, the more it is able to price discriminate. For example, college students are often pleasantly surprised to find that they can buy computer software through their colleges for significantly lower prices than they could in a store or online. (Take a look at your school's information technology website. We bet you'll find discounts.) The Microsoft Office® suite of programs, such as Word®, Excel®, and PowerPoint®, often sells for half as much when bought through a university.

While Microsoft Office does have substitutes, such as the open source OpenOffice suite, for many people these are not close enough substitutes. These free products cannot handle the full range of Office functions; if you are sharing documents with other people who all use Microsoft Office, then you also need to own Microsoft Office.

price discrimination
the practice of charging customers different prices for the same good

Price discrimination in action: Tourists who don't read Spanish pay extra.

Microsoft can use its monopoly power to exploit differences in the willingness to pay of different groups. For simplicity, suppose Microsoft knows that there are three groups of potential Office customers: students, who are willing to pay $75; standard computer users, who are willing to pay $150; and people who use their computers to run their businesses, who are willing to pay $225. Say there are 1 million potential customers in each group, as shown in the stylized demand curve in Figure 14-7. There is a limit to the quantity Microsoft can sell at any given price.

Of course, in reality, there is variation in people's willingness to pay within these groups. For example, some students are willing to pay more than $75, and some less. But for the sake of simplicity, let's assume for now that all students, all standard users, and all business users are the same. Let's also assume that there is a fixed cost of $50 million to produce Office (for instance, to pay for research and development), and that the variable cost of production is essentially zero. (Zero isn't too far from reality—making a copy of software doesn't cost very much.) With no variable cost, the profit that Microsoft earns is simply TR − FC. (Note, too, that if variable costs are zero, marginal costs also are zero.)

What price should Microsoft set for Office? If it chooses $75, all 3 million potential customers will buy a copy of Office, and the company will earn:

$$\text{Profit} = \text{TR} - \text{FC}$$
$$= (3 \text{ million} \times \$75) - \$50 \text{ million}$$
$$= \$225 \text{ million} - \$50 \text{ million} = \$175 \text{ million}$$

FIGURE 14-7
Demand for Microsoft Office®

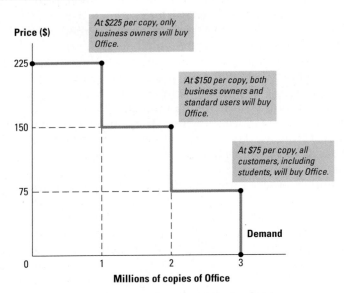

This simplified demand curve shows the demand for Office in a perfectly segmented market. In this example, all members of each group have the same willingness to pay: All business owners will pay $225 or less; all standard users will pay $150 or less; and all students will pay only $75 or less.

TABLE 14-2

Profit without price discrimination

If Microsoft can charge only one price for Office, the best option is to choose $150, which will maximize profit at $250 million. That option, however, will exclude students, who are unwilling to pay more than $75.

Price ($)	Number of copies	Total revenue ($)	Fixed cost ($)	Profit ($)
75	3,000,000	225,000,000	50,000,000	175,000,000
150	2,000,000	300,000,000	50,000,000	250,000,000
225	1,000,000	225,000,000	50,000,000	175,000,000

What if Microsoft chooses to charge $150? As the calculations in Table 14-2 show, only 2 million customers will buy at the higher price. In that case, the company will earn $250 million in profits. If it charges $225 per copy of Office, only 1 million business customers will choose to buy, and Microsoft will earn $175 million in profits.

If Microsoft can pick only one price, it should pick $150 to maximize its profits. However, by charging $150, Microsoft loses the business of students, who have a lower willingness to pay. It also misses out on the extra $75 that business customers would have been willing to pay. Microsoft does best if it can find a way to charge these three groups the exact price they are willing to pay. Then, its profits are:

Profit = TR − FC

$\quad$ = [(1 million × $225) + (1 million × $150) + (1 million × $75)] − $50 million

$\quad$ = $450 million −$50 million

$\quad$ = $400 million

Microsoft can earn an additional $150 million ($400 − $250) in profits if it can charge students less and businesses more. We can see why any firm with market power would want to price discriminate. As a student, this is good news for you too (at least if you're facing monopoly pricing).

Perfect price discrimination. Dividing its customers into just three categories—students, business owners, and others—is a blunt way of discriminating among them. In reality, there are not just three types of customer—there are millions, all with their own individual willingness to pay. What if Microsoft was able to price discriminate more accurately by charging every individual customer a price exactly equal to her willingness to pay?

Figure 14-8 shows a smooth demand curve representing the varied willingnesses to pay of many individuals (rather than just three clusters of customers). Panel A shows what happens if Microsoft does not price discriminate—if it charges just one price, $150, for Office. Its profit is represented by the green-shaded area. The gold-shaded area represents the consumer surplus enjoyed by customers who would have been willing to purchase for more than $150. The gray area shows deadweight loss. That represents the mutually beneficial trades that could have taken place, but did not. These are customers who would have been willing to purchase Office for a price between $150 and zero.

Now look at panel B, which shows what happens when Microsoft price discriminates among the three categories of customer. The size of the blue-shaded area, representing Microsoft's profits (producer surplus), has increased. At the same time, consumer surplus has decreased for the group of customers who were willing to pay over $150. Customers who were willing to pay between $75 and $150, however, now enjoy some consumer surplus. Finally, deadweight loss has been reduced to only those mutually beneficial trades that could have taken place between $75 and zero, but did not.

FIGURE 14-8
Price discrimination

(A) No price discrimination

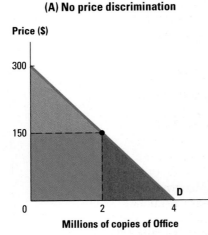

With no price discrimination, Microsoft charges one price, $150, to all customers.

(B) Imperfect price discrimination

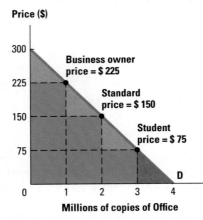

With imperfect or tiered price discrimination, Microsoft can earn a profit on sales to both students and other buyers. Because not all students have the same willingness to pay, however, some mutually beneficial trades (represented by the gray-shaded area) don't take place.

(C) Perfect price discrimination

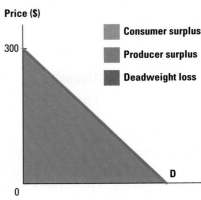

If Microsoft could charge each customer his or her exact willingness to pay, the company would profit on all exchanges, eliminating both the deadweight loss and the consumer surplus shown in panel A.

Panel C shows what would happen if Microsoft were able to price discriminate perfectly. The area representing Microsoft's profits becomes even bigger. There is no consumer surplus at all anymore; all customers are charged at the exact level of their willingness to pay. The consumer surplus that previously existed has all been transformed into producer surplus. But neither is there any deadweight loss. Instead, all possible mutually beneficial trades take place—meaning the market is *efficient.* The more perfectly a company is able to price discriminate, the more profit it makes, and the more efficiently the market works. Remember that efficiency doesn't say anything about the distribution of surplus—including whether it goes to consumers or producers—but only whether total surplus is maximized.

So why doesn't a monopoly charge every individual a different price? There are some obvious problems with this idea, as we will see.

Price discrimination in the real world. The first problem with price discrimination in the real world is defining categories of customers. Microsoft's price-discrimination strategy would not work very well if anyone could simply say "I'm a student" and be charged the lower price. The company needs some way to verify who is a student. To get around this problem, Microsoft enters into agreements with colleges, which take responsibility for identifying who is a student. In general, students have to go through their colleges' websites and enter their student ID number or other verification to purchase software at the discount price. Similarly, if you turn up at the box office of a theater asking to purchase a ticket with a student discount, the cashier will ask for your student ID card.

The second problem facing the firm that tries to price discriminate is that many products can easily be resold. If someone you know is about to pay $150 for Microsoft Office, some people might be tempted to buy student versions at a low price and illicitly resell them at a higher price. To prevent this, there needs to be some way of punishing people who cheat the system. Hence, Microsoft can use legal enforcement against anyone who uses student version of Office for their business. Similarly, theaters need some way to stop students from bulk-buying tickets and selling them to nonstudents. They may, for instance, demand to see a student ID before allowing entrance into a theater with a student ticket.

Many goods do not lend themselves to this kind of tracking as easily as software or theater tickets. Imagine if Apple sold iPhones to customers under age 18 for a 50 percent discount. This might seem like a neat way to increase its profits, if there are lots of under-18s who would love to buy an iPhone but cannot afford to pay full price. However, high school students would have a thriving business buying up the iPhones at the local Apple store and reselling them to older buyers for a profit. No one over 18 would buy their iPhones directly from Apple, which therefore has no incentive to offer different prices.

For a firm that wants to practice *perfect* price discrimination, the challenges are even more forbidding. It would need to be able to read the minds of each individual customer and form an accurate impression of how much that customer would be willing to pay. Much as Microsoft would love to be able to read the minds of potential purchasers and charge them exactly what they'd be willing to pay, the task is essentially impossible.

Still, some practitioners of price discrimination are adept at sizing up their customers before quoting a price. See the From Another Angle box "Rickshaw rides: Price discrimination and asymmetric information."

FROM ANOTHER ANGLE

Rickshaw rides: Price discrimination and asymmetric information

Tourist regions charge visitors notoriously inflated prices. Taxi and rickshaw drivers in India are especially famous for charging foreign-looking, wealthy-looking, and clueless-looking passengers significantly higher fares than they would charge to locals. This practice is the root of countless confrontations where rickshaw drivers and foreign tourists try to bargain over fares, generally in a mix of broken English and improvised sign language. What are the economic forces underlying this common scene?

One explanation is that tourists are the victims of a severe information asymmetry. Tourists often don't know how far their destination is and have no idea about the standard "local" rate for going there. Since drivers invariably know more than tourists about the "fair price" of fares, they are able to exploit this information asymmetry to boost their earnings.

Another factor contributing to the difference in the prices paid by locals and tourists is their differing willingness to pay. Tourists from wealthier countries are generally willing to pay more than most Indians would for the same goods and services. Someone from New York City might consider 100 rupees (about $2) for a rickshaw ride across Delhi to be an incredible bargain (a similar ride in a New York taxi could cost $25), even if 100 rupees is more than twice what locals pay.

But why doesn't competition between drivers push fares back down to competitive levels? Remember, price discrimination works only for producers with market power. One rickshaw driver may not have much sway in the market, but the rickshaw drivers in a particular location often operate like a cartel. Rather than competing, they have standing agreements not to undercut one another on price.

However, the days of frustrated tourists might be numbered. More and more cities across India are requiring rickshaws to start using the mortal enemy of price-discriminating drivers everywhere: the fare meter.

Conclusion

Monopolies can use their market power to hold price above the level that would prevail in a competitive market, turning consumer surplus into positive economic profits and reducing total social welfare. This poses a tricky problem for policy-makers, who want to regulate or break up monopolies to increase welfare. Practically speaking, it can be difficult to accomplish this goal without causing more inefficiency. Policies designed to address the problems associated with monopolies run the risk of setting prices at the wrong level or raising costs by breaking up a natural monopoly.

This difficult situation is complicated further by the fact that few firms are truly perfect monopolies. Instead, many markets include firms with some degree of market power, ranging on the spectrum from perfect monopoly to perfect competition. We can call markets in this range "imperfectly competitive." It turns out that small differences in the structure of imperfectly competitive markets can make big differences in how firms behave; those differences can give policy-makers headaches. In the next chapter, we'll take a close look at two specific varieties of imperfect competition.

◄ Mobile Window on the World—Scan this code with your smartphone to find more applications of the chapter content. (Need a barcode reader? Try ScanLife, available in your app store.)

Visit your mobile app store and download ► the Karlan and Morduch Study Econ app.

Study Econ
McGraw Hill

Key Terms

monopoly, p. 310

natural monopoly, p. 312

price discrimination, p. 327

Summary

LO 14.1 List several reasons that monopolies exist, and explain how each causes barriers to entry.

The key characteristic of a monopoly market is that there are barriers that prevent firms other than the monopolist from entering the market. Barriers to entry take four main forms: scarce resources, economies of scale, government intervention, and aggressive business tactics on the part of market-leading firms.

Scarcity in some key resource or input into the production process means that firms may have difficulty accessing the resources they need to enter the market. When there are large economies of scale in a market, firms have no incentive to enter; they would face higher costs of production than the monopoly. Some monopolies are created or sustained by the power of

government, through public ownership or protection of intellectual property. Finally, some monopolies use their size and various aggressive tactics to keep smaller firms from getting a toehold in the market.

LO 14.2 Explain why a monopolist is constrained by demand.

As the only firm in the market, a monopoly is constrained in the price-quantity combinations it can sell by the market demand curve. All else equal, quantity demanded falls as price rises. The monopoly can choose any price-quantity combination on the demand curve, but it is unable to choose points that are not on the curve, because it can't force customers to buy more or less than they demand at any given price.

LO 14.3 Calculate the profit-maximizing production price and quantity for a monopolist.

A monopoly chooses the profit-maximizing quantity the same way a firm in a competitive market would: by producing at the quantity for which marginal revenue is equal to marginal cost. Price is the price that corresponds to that quantity on the demand curve. Unlike a firm in a competitive market, however, the monopoly price is higher than marginal revenue, and therefore also higher than marginal cost at the profit-maximizing point. This means that a monopoly earns positive economic profits.

LO 14.4 Calculate the loss in total social welfare associated with a monopoly.

The equilibrium price and quantity in a competitive market maximize total surplus. A monopoly's profit-maximizing quantity, however, is lower than the efficient quantity that would prevail in a competitive market. This tells us that total surplus is not maximized, and that producer surplus is higher than competitive levels, while consumer surplus is lower. The deadweight loss caused by a monopoly is equal to total surplus under perfect competition minus total surplus under a monopoly.

LO 14.5 Describe the pros and cons of common public policy responses to monopoly.

Policy-makers have developed a range of policy tools aimed at breaking up existing monopolies, preventing new ones from forming, and mitigating the effect of monopoly power on consumers. Antitrust laws allow the government to sue firms that engage in anti-competitive practices and to block mergers that would result in too much market power. Public ownership of natural monopolies maintains the cost advantages of economies of scale, but removes the profit motive that might drive quality improvements and cost reductions. Price regulation may also preserve the cost advantages of natural monopoly while holding down price, but it is practically difficult to set price at the right level. In some cases, doing nothing may actually be the best policy response to monopoly.

LO 14.6 Explain why a firm has an incentive to use price discrimination when possible.

Price discrimination is the practice of charging customers different prices for the same good. Price discrimination allows a firm to charge each customer a price closer to his willingness to pay, turning consumer surplus into producer surplus and increasing the firm's profits.

Review Questions

1. If competition places discipline on costs, motivating firms to innovate and find more cost-effective ways to produce, explain why in some markets a single firm without competitors will produce at a lower cost than if the firm faced competition. **[LO 14.1]**

2. Suppose a city has a chain of fitness centers (gyms) all owned by the same company, Fit Fun. A new company is considering opening a gym in the city. Give an example of an aggressive tactic Fit Fun might take to maintain its monopoly. **[LO 14.1]**

3. Suppose that De Beers and the local water utility are both monopolists, in the markets for diamond jewelry and water, respectively. If both monopolies decided to raise prices 15 percent, which monopoly would be more likely to see its total revenue decrease? Why? **[LO 14.2]**

4. Suppose that a producer in a previously competitive market is granted the sole right to produce in the market. Given that demand in the market is unchanged but now all consumers must purchase from the same producer, why might the new monopolist produce less than the quantity that was produced when the market was competitive? **[LO 14.2]**

5. Suppose that an inventor discovers a new chemical compound that can change the color of people's eyes with no negative side effects. Since she holds a patent on this chemical, she has a monopoly over the sale of the new eye-color treatment. However, she's an inventor, not a businessperson. Explain to her how she should set the price for the eye-color treatment in order to maximize her profits. **[LO 14.3]**

6. Suppose a monopolist has to purchase new equipment and his fixed costs increase. Explain what will happen to the monopolist's profit-maximizing output quantity and the monopolist's profits. **[LO 14.3]**

7. Until the 1980s, AT&T held a monopoly over the national market for phone services. Suppose that AT&T argued that it was a natural monopoly, because the fixed cost of creating a nationwide phone network generated huge economies of scale, and that there was therefore no welfare loss associated with its monopoly. Counter this argument by explaining how even a natural monopoly causes deadweight loss. **[LO 14.4]**

8. Suppose you are advising a mayoral candidate in your town. The candidate's platform includes strong opposition to monopoly suppliers because consumer welfare is compromised by monopoly pricing. Present your candidate with an alternative view about why it may make sense to tolerate the existence of some monopoly firms. **[LO 14.4]**

9. Suppose that your state is considering a law that would force all monopolies to charge no more than their average total costs of production. Explain to your legislator the pros and cons of this approach. **[LO 14.5]**

10. Suppose that your state is considering a law that would force all monopolies to charge the efficient price that would prevail if the market were competitive. Explain to your legislator why the state will have to subsidize natural monopolies if this law goes into effect. **[LO 14.5]**

11. Suppose a small town has one theater for live performances and one Indian restaurant. Will it be easier for the theater or for the Indian restaurant to price discriminate? **[LO 14.6]**

12. Suppose a museum charges different entrance fees for children, students, adults, and seniors, but these groups all pay the same amount for souvenirs at the gift shop. Explain why the museum price discriminates on admission but not souvenirs. **[LO 14.6]**

Problems and Applications

1. The United States Postal Services maintains a monopoly on mail delivery in part through its exclusive right to access customer mailboxes. Which barrier to entry best describes this situation—scarce resources, economies of scale, government intervention, or aggressive tactics? **[LO 14.1]**

2. Which (if any) of the following scenarios is the result of a natural monopoly? **[LO 14.1]**
   a. Patent holders of genetically modified seeds are permitted to sue farmers who save seeds from one planting season to the next.
   b. Doctors in the United States are prohibited from practicing without a medical license.
   c. There is one train operator with service from Baltimore to Philadelphia.
   d. Coal is used as the primary energy in a country with abundant coal deposits.

3. Due to arduous certification requirements, Nature's Crunch is currently the only certified organic produce grower in a region that produces lots of nonorganic produce alternatives. From a profit-maximizing perspective, would it be better for Nature's Crunch to lobby the government to relax organic certification requirements or to require grocery stores to clearly label its produce as organic? **[LO 14.2]**

4. Nature's Crunch is currently the only certified organic produce grower in a region that produces lots of nonorganic produce alternatives. Which of the following scenarios would increase Nature's Crunch's profits? Check all that apply. **[LO 14.2]**
   a. A tomato blight affecting chemically treated plants.
   b. An increase in the cost of chemical pesticides.
   c. A new report about the environmental dangers of chemically treated plants.
   d. Income tax cuts for all consumers.
   e. A new report showing that there is no nutritional difference between organic and nonorganic produce.

5. Table 14P-1 presents the demand schedule and marginal costs facing a monopolist producer. **[LO 14.3]**
   a. Fill in the total revenue and marginal revenue columns.
   b. What is the profit-maximizing level of output?

TABLE 14P-1

Q	P ($)	TR ($)	MR ($)	MC ($)
0	10			—
1	9			2
2	8			2
3	7			2
4	6			2
5	5			2
6	4			2
7	3			2
8	2			2
9	1			2
10	0			2

TABLE 14P-2

Q	P ($)	TR ($)	MR ($)	MC ($)
0	8			—
1	7			1
2	6			2
3	5			3
4	4			4
5	3			5
6	2			6
7	1			7
8	0			8

FIGURE 14P-2

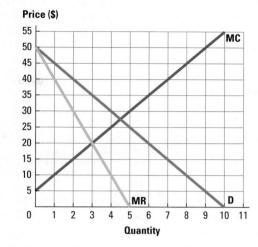

c. What price will the monopolist charge for the quantity in part *b*?

6. Table 14P-2 presents the demand schedule and marginal costs facing a monopolist producer. **[LO 14.3]**

   a. Fill in the total revenue and marginal revenue columns.

   b. What is the profit-maximizing level of output?

   c. What price will the monopolist charge for the quantity in part *b*?

7. Figure 14P-1 presents the demand curve, marginal revenue, and marginal costs facing a monopolist producer. **[LO 14.3, 14.4]**

FIGURE 14P-1

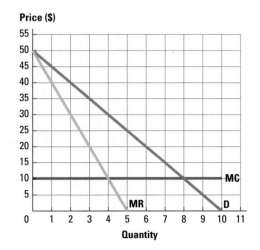

a. What is the profit-maximizing level of output?

b. What price will the monopolist charge for the quantity in part *a*?

c. What are the efficiency costs (deadweight loss) of monopoly output/pricing? Provide a numerical answer and illustrate this area on the graph.

d. What is consumer surplus under monopoly output/pricing? Illustrate this area on the graph.

e. What is the loss of consumer surplus under monopoly outcomes versus efficient outcomes? Provide a numerical answer.

8. Figure 14P-2 presents the demand curve, marginal revenue, and marginal costs facing a monopolist producer. **[LO 14.3, 14.4]**

   a. What is the profit-maximizing level of output?

   b. What price will the monopolist charge for the quantity in part *a*?

   c. What are the efficiency costs (deadweight loss) of monopoly output/pricing? Provide a numerical answer and illustrate this area on the graph.

   d. What is consumer surplus under monopoly output/pricing? Illustrate this area on the graph.

   e. What is the loss of consumer surplus under monopoly outcomes versus efficient outcomes? Provide a numerical answer.

9. Use Figure 14P-3 to answer the following questions. **[LO 14.5]**

   a. Under monopoly pricing, are profits positive, negative, or zero?

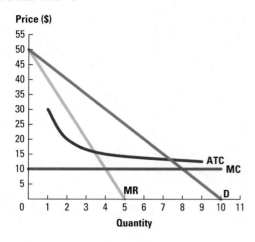

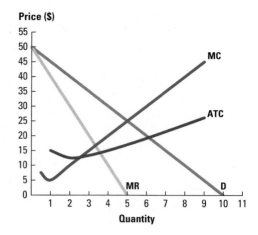

b. If government regulates average total cost pricing (P = ATC), are profits positive, negative, or zero?

c. If government regulates efficient pricing, are profits positive, negative, or zero?

d. Is this a natural monopoly?

10. Use Figure 14P-4 to answer the following questions. [LO 14.5]

a. If this monopolist were regulated, would it prefer average total cost pricing (P = ATC) or efficient pricing?

b. Is this a natural monopoly?

11. Suppose a monopolist discovers a way to perfectly price discriminate. What is consumer surplus under this scenario? What are the efficiency costs? [LO 14.6]

12. Suppose there are three types of consumers who attend concerts at your university's performing arts center: students, staff, and faculty. Each of these groups has a different willingness to pay for tickets; within each group, willingness to pay is identical. There is a fixed cost of $1,000 to put on a concert, but there are essentially no variable costs. [LO 14.6]

For each concert:

- There are 140 students willing to pay $20.
- There are 200 staff members willing to pay $35.
- There are 100 faculty members willing to pay $50.

a. If the performing arts center can charge only one price, what price should it charge?

b. What are profits at this price?

c. If the performing arts center can price discriminate and charge two prices, one for students and another for faculty/staff, what are its profits?

d. If the performing arts center can perfectly price discriminate and charge students, staff, and faculty three separate prices, what are its profits?

Chapter Sources

http://www.nytimes.com/2008/08/09/business/worldbusiness/09nocera.html?_r=1&ref=business

http://www.idexonline.com/portal FullNews.asp?id=27380

http://www.theatlantic.com/doc/198202/diamond

http://articles.latimes.com/2007/aug/26/world/fg-guards26?pg=1

http://www.washingtonpost.com/wp-dyn/content/article/2008/10/29/AR2008102903505.html

http://www.nytimes.com/1997/07/01/business/office-depot-and-staples-merger-halted.html?pagewanted=1

http://money.cnn.com/2000/08/25/europe/diamonds/

http://newsandinsight.thomsonreuters.com/Legal/News/2011/12_-_December/Court_affirms_$295_million_De_Beers_settlement/

Monopolistic Competition and Oligopoly

Chapter 15

LEARNING OBJECTIVES

LO 15.1   Name the defining features of oligopoly and monopolistic competition.

LO 15.2   Calculate the profit-maximizing price and quantity for a monopolistically competitive firm in the short run.

LO 15.3   Describe a monopolistically competitive market in the long run.

LO 15.4   Analyze the welfare costs of monopolistic competition.

LO 15.5   Explain how product differentiation motivates advertising and branding.

LO 15.6   Describe the strategic production decision of firms in an oligopoly.

LO 15.7   Explain why firms in an oligopoly have an incentive to collude, and why they might fail to do so.

LO 15.8   Compare the welfare of producers, consumers, and society as a whole in an oligopoly to monopoly and perfect competition.

WHICH ONE OF THESE IS JUST LIKE THE OTHERS?

What do the musicians Toby Keith, Björk, and Kanye West have in common? We'll give you a hint. It's the same thing that Drake has in common with Death Cab for Cutie and Tracy Chapman. It's also the same thing that Shakira shares with Bob Dylan and that the Decemberists share with the Rolling Stones.

Each of these groups of artists is on one of the four major recording labels that together account for more than 80 percent of the U.S. music market. These four labels—Universal Music Group (Universal), Sony Music Group (Sony), Warner Music Group (Warner), and EMI Group (EMI)—each control between 10 and 30 percent of the market. If you want to be a successful recording artist, you'll have a much better chance with one of them on your side.

That wasn't always the case, though. In the 1950s and 1960s, many stars were able to make their names with small record labels. An Alabama radio host named Sam Phillips started Sun Records out of a cheap storefront in Memphis. He promptly signed then-unknown artists Elvis Presley, Johnny Cash, and B.B. King. A Ford assembly-line worker, Berry Gordy, formed Motown Records in Detroit with a tiny family loan, and made stars of artists including Marvin Gaye and Stevie Wonder. In the last decade,

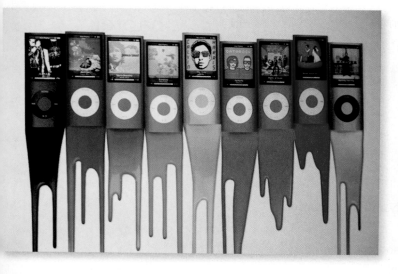

as the Internet has revolutionized music distribution, new ways have opened up again for musicians to market themselves independently of the four major labels. But it's still not as common for an artist to break through on a small label today as it was in the early days of rock and roll.

In previous chapters, we described two extreme market structures: monopoly and perfect competition. In this chapter, we'll see why the music industry—both past and present—is not a good fit for either of those two models. Instead, the music industry is a market that is somewhat competitive, but not perfectly competitive. Such a market structure is quite common in the real world.

In particular, we'll discuss two types of market structure that are *imperfectly competitive*: monopolistic competition and oligopoly. These market structures aren't mutually exclusive. As we'll see, many industries, including the music industry, display characteristics of both.

Understanding market structure is key to running a successful business. A business owner needs to know the type of market in which she is engaged in order to know how much freedom she has to set prices, or how much attention to pay to the behavior of other firms. Her business strategy may differ greatly depending on how much competition she faces and of what sort. Understanding market structure can also be valuable in making good choices as a consumer or policy-maker. It can help us to interpret a firm's choice to advertise, for example, or to decide when we should favor regulators stepping in to address "anti-competitive" business practices. The concepts that we explore in this chapter will help us understand choices faced by businesses, consumers, and policy-makers.

What Sort of Market?

What sort of market is the music industry? That's the 5-billion-dollar question for everyone from record-label executives to retailers to antitrust lawyers at the Department of Justice. In answering it, we'll focus on the two characteristics that define a range of market structures: number of firms and product variety.

Let's start by looking at the number of firms. Figure 15-1 shows that the music industry is dominated by four labels; no single one of them is big enough to dominate the industry in the way that De Beers dominated the diamond market in the twentieth century. This tells us the music industry is not a monopoly.

It's also not perfectly competitive. That's not simply because the market is dominated by a few large firms. It's also because it encompasses a wide variety of products. Even if there were thousands of small record labels competing, the market would not be perfectly competitive because music is not a standardized product. There are many similarities between, say, a Kanye West track and a music file by The Shins: They're both digitized versions of music, using data-compression technology with a common digital encoding format; both emit sounds of instruments and voices when played. They're similar enough that it makes sense for us to think of them both as products of the same

FIGURE 15-1

Market share in the music business The music industry is dominated by four big firms. Their record sales represent over 80 percent of the market. They are so big that their behavior affects the entire market for music.

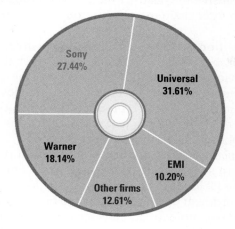

industry, the music industry. But they are certainly not a standardized product—at least, not to fans of either artist.

These two features of the music industry—a small number of large firms, and product variety—are the defining features of two market structures that lie between the extreme models of monopoly and perfect competition. Both market structures—oligopoly and monopolistic competition—are common in the real world. While many industries display features of both models, understanding each model separately allows us to make powerful predictions about how firms will behave.

Oligopoly and monopolistic competition

LO 15.1 Name the defining features of oligopoly and monopolistic competition.

Oligopoly describes a market with only a few firms. (The word itself is derived from the Greek words for "few sellers.") These companies sell a product or service that may or may not be completely standardized, but is similar enough that they're in competition. Examples of oligopolies are wireless network providers (the U.S. market is dominated by four companies—AT&T, Verizon, T-Mobile, and Sprint), and fast-food burgers (think McDonald's, Burger King, and Wendy's).

One of the defining features of an oligopoly is that strategic interactions between a firm and its rivals have a major impact on its success. In particular, we'll see that the price and quantity set by an individual firm affect the others' profits. This stands in contrast to firms in perfectly competitive markets or monopolists. In a perfectly competitive market, other firms' actions cannot affect the market. If you are a true monopolist, there *are* no other firms (unless another firm is trying to create a product that can substitute for yours).

If you are in charge of a company in an oligopoly, though, it is a vital part of your job to keep an eye on competitors. The shareholders of Wendy's would not be impressed if the CEO had no idea that McDonald's had just introduced a new kind of burger or that Burger King was offering promotional discounts on sodas.

Oligopolies are also characterized by the existence of some barriers to entry. Barriers to entry enable monopolies to exist. You couldn't set up in the diamond business to challenge De Beers without discovering a new source of diamonds. In perfect competition, by contrast, we assume there are *no* barriers to entry—it's easy for new firms to enter

oligopoly a market with only a few firms, which sell a similar good or service

the market. Oligopoly is somewhere in the middle. It would be possible to set up as a wireless carrier, but expensive to construct the infrastructure. It would be possible to break into the national burger chain market, but tough to overcome established brand loyalties.

monopolistic competition a market with many firms that sell goods and services that are similar, but slightly different

Monopolistic competition describes a market with many firms that sell goods and services that are similar, but slightly different. Remember that a feature of perfect competition is that consumers are indifferent between the products of competing firms. A feature of monopoly is that the product has no close substitutes. Between these two extremes are markets in which products have substitutes that are close but not perfect. Consumers might be willing to pay a bit extra, but if the price differential is too large, they will choose a substitute product instead.

Although the name *monopolistic competition* sounds like a contradiction in terms, it expresses the idea that firms in such a market have a kind of monopoly but in a limited sense. For example, in the 1950s Sun Records had a monopoly on selling Elvis records. If you wanted an Elvis record, you had no choice but to buy it from Sun. Devoted fans of Elvis might be willing to pay more for an Elvis record than for records by other artists. Thus, Sun had some power to set its own price, but not much. If Sun raised the price of Elvis records too high, most people would prefer to save their money or to buy records by other artists instead.

Monopolistic competition describes a great many real-world markets. For example, General Mills, the parent company of Häagen-Dazs, has a monopoly on selling Häagen-Dazs brand ice cream, but not a monopoly on ice cream in general. If you especially like Häagen-Dazs, you might be willing to pay a bit extra for it. But if the price differential becomes too great you'll switch to another brand, such as Ben & Jerry's. Similarly, you might be willing to pay a little more for a meal at your favorite restaurant, but if the price is too high, you'd be happy to settle for your second favorite.

Oligopoly and monopolistic competition are often found together, as in the music industry. Oligopoly is about the *number of firms*; monopolistic competition is about *variety of products*. Thus, you can have one without the other. Oligopolies can exist when products are standardized; monopolistic competition can exist when there are many small firms. For this reason we will now explore the two market structures separately.

✓ CONCEPT CHECK

❑ What is the difference between oligopoly and monopolistic competition? **[LO 15.1]**

Monopolistic Competition

Remember that under the model of perfect competition, firms do not make economic profits. It's not surprising, then, that firms would rather be operating under conditions of monopolistic competition, where they *can* make economic profits.

How do monopolistically competitive firms make economic profits? By making a product that consumers perceive to be different from the products of their competitors. In other words, firms must offer goods that are similar to competitors' products but more attractive in some ways. This process is called **product differentiation**. It is an essential part of the strategy of many businesses in the real world.

product differentiation the creation of products that are similar to competitors' products but more attractive in some ways

Sometimes product differentiation is accomplished through genuine innovation. The many record labels operating in the 1950s music business are an example. They competed to discover and shape new, exciting, *different* performers who could attract a following of loyal fans. The more enthusiastic Elvis fans were, the less interchangeable they considered Elvis's records to be with those of other artists. The less interchangeable the records, the more Sun could charge without fear of losing sales. The founder of Sun

Records discovered a wealth of previously overlooked talent in and around Memphis: He was happy to work with black musicians who were otherwise excluded from white-dominated parts of the music business in that era of segregation. In doing so, he helped to create rock and roll—not only recognizing talent, but shaping it into something new.

Regardless of whether or not genuine innovation is involved, firms have an interest in persuading customers that their products are unique. This is the role of advertising and branding. Even when a firm's product is not really very different from other products on the market, it may be possible to convince customers that the product *is* different, and thereby persuade them to pay more for a particular brand. We'll return to these issues later in the chapter.

Monopolistic competition in the short run

LO 15.2 Calculate the profit-maximizing price and quantity for a monopolistically competitive firm in the short run.

Product differentiation enables firms in monopolistically competitive markets to produce a good for which there are no exact substitutes. In the short run, this allows a firm to behave like a monopolist. In the long run, as we will see, the situation is different. This difference between the short and long run is the key to understanding monopolistic competition.

First, we'll look at the short run, when monopolistically competitive firms can behave like monopolists. Figure 15-2 shows these short-run production choices:

1. Firms face a downward-sloping demand curve. Just like a monopolist, a monopolistically competitive firm cannot adjust its price without causing a change in the quantity consumers demand.

FIGURE 15-2

Monopolistic competition in the short run

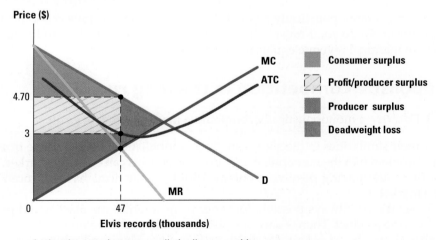

In the short run in a monopolistically competitive market, Elvis's label will produce records up to the point where marginal revenue is equal to marginal cost, and charge the corresponding price on the demand curve. The firm earns profits in this case, but also creates deadweight loss.

2. Assuming that production involves both fixed and marginal costs, firms face a U-shaped average total cost (ATC) curve.
3. The profit-maximizing production quantity is at the point where the marginal revenue (MR) curve intersects the marginal cost (MC) curve. The profit-maximizing price is determined by the point on the demand curve that corresponds to this quantity.

POTENTIALLY CONFUSING

Sun Records was a small player in a very competitive music market. So why wasn't it a price taker, facing a horizontal demand curve, as a small firm in a perfectly competitive market would be? Why did it face a downward-sloping demand curve in the short run?

The key here is how we define the scope of the market. Sun Records was small relative to the market for *records*. But it was large—in fact, a monopolist—in the market for *Elvis records*. Consumers who wanted Elvis records could buy them only from Sun. Sun was not a price taker in the market for Elvis records, and so it faced a downward-sloping demand curve.

The steepness of the demand curve is determined in part by the degree of substitutability between Elvis records and other records. What if buyers see the records as very close substitutes? In that case, people will switch to other artists if Sun raises the price even a little bit, and the demand curve will be quite flat. What if, on the other hand, fans are very loyal to Elvis? In that case, most won't stop buying Elvis records even when prices go up, and the demand curve will be steeper.

In other words, the less-differentiated the products are, the closer each firm's demand curve is to the horizontal curve faced by perfectly competitive firms. By differentiating their products more—for example, finding a very distinctive artist such as Elvis and building a loyal following of devoted fans—firms can increase the steepness of the demand curve they face in the short run.

In summary, a monopolistically competitive firm can earn positive economic profits in the short run. To do so, it must behave just like a monopolist—by producing at the point where marginal revenue equals marginal cost.

Monopolistic competition in the long run

LO 15.3 Describe a monopolistically competitive market in the long run.

For all of their similarities in the short run, the monopolistically competitive firm faces one huge problem that the monopolist does not: Other firms can enter the market. When existing firms are making positive economic profits, other firms have an incentive to enter the market.

Of course, it's not always possible for other firms to enter the market and produce *exactly* the same product. There's only one Elvis, after all, and he belongs to Sun Records. What other firms *can* do is look for artists who are *like* Elvis, and whose records will therefore be seen by music lovers as closer substitutes for Elvis records.

This explains why, in music and in many other industries, products tend to come in waves. A new musical performer with an original style comes along and makes a splash; other record labels rush to sign artists who have a similar style. A trendy high-fashion label produces a new range of clothing; other fashion labels rush to produce clothes that look similar. Apple releases the iPad, and other companies rush to produce touchscreen tablet computers. And so on.

What effect does the entry of more firms have on the demand faced by each existing firm? Remember from Chapter 3 that availability of substitute goods is one of the determinants of demand. More firms making more products that are similar to the original product means that consumers have a wider range of substitutes. With more product options from which consumers can choose, demand for the original product decreases at every price. The demand curve faced by the firm shifts to the left.

As long as firms currently in the market are earning profits, more firms will enter the market with products that are close substitutes. As a result, the demand curve will continue to shift to the left. This process will continue until the point when potential firms no longer have an incentive to enter the market. When does that happen? At the point when existing firms are no longer earning economic profits.

The opposite logic holds if firms in the market are losing money in the short run: Firms will have an incentive to exit the market when they are earning negative profits. These exits will drive up demand for the existing firms and shift the demand curves they face to the right. This process will continue until, in the long run, firms are breaking even and no longer have an incentive to exit. You may have noticed something like this happening in the music industry: Sometimes so many performers are releasing similar-sounding music, the market niche becomes oversaturated.

In the long run, firms in a monopolistically competitive market face the same situation as firms in a perfectly competitive market: Profits are driven to zero. Remember from earlier chapters that zero profit means that total revenue is exactly equal to total cost. In per-unit terms, zero profit means that price is equal to average total cost (ATC). Figure 15-3 shows this situation; the ATC curve is *tangent* to the demand curve at exactly

FIGURE 15-3

Monopolistic competition in the long run

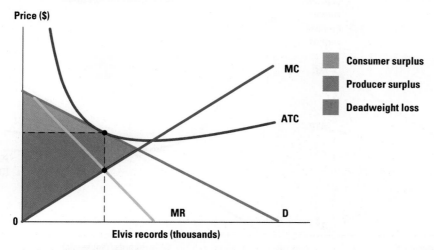

In the long run in a monopolistically competitive market, firms will enter the market, driving down demand until all market participants earn zero economic profits. Elvis's label will produce records up to the point where marginal cost equals marginal revenue. Because profits are zero, this is the same as the quantity at which average total cost curve is tangent to the demand curve.

one point, where ATC = Price. That point represents the profit-maximizing quantity and is the optimal production point.

Note that ATC touches the demand curve at the same quantity where MR intersects MC. This graphic relationship is equivalent to saying that profits are zero. If ATC is not exactly tangent to the demand curve at the optimal point, then profits are positive or negative. If the ATC is above the demand curve, for example, this would mean that costs were higher than price, and firms would lose money and exit the market. If, on the other hand, ATC hit the demand curve at multiple places, costs would be below price and firms would earn profits. This situation would induce firms to enter the market. This process of entry and exit, which moves the demand curve left or right, continues until this relationship *does* hold.

In the long run, monopolistic competition has some features in common with monopoly, and others in common with perfect competition. Just like a *monopoly*, a monopolistically competitive firm faces a downward-sloping demand curve. Such a curve means that marginal revenue is less than price; this in turn means that marginal cost is also less than price. But, like a firm in a *perfectly competitive* market, a monopolistically competitive firm earns zero economic profits in the long run.

These differences have two important implications:

1. **Monopolistically competitive firms operate at smaller-than-efficient scale.** As we've just described, the optimal production point for a monopolistically competitive firm in the long run will be where the ATC curve touches the demand curve. Because the demand curve is downward-sloping, this will always be on the decreasing section of the ATC curve, as panel A of Figure 15-4 shows.

FIGURE 15-4
Monopolistic competition versus perfect competition

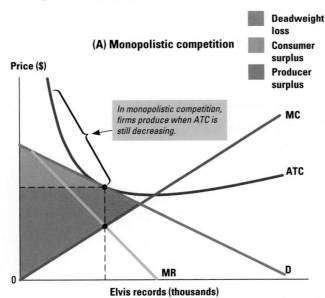
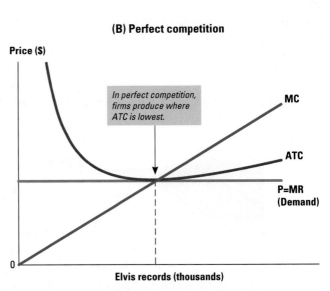

In a monopolistically competitive market, firms produce at the point where ATC is tangent to the demand curve. At this point, they could decrease ATC by producing more, but choose not to because doing so decreases profits. This results in firms producing at a smaller-than-efficient scale.

In a perfectly competitive market, firms produce at the quantity that minimizes ATC. This is the efficient choice, since they cannot produce more or less without increasing costs.

This contrasts with the situation in a perfectly competitive market, in which firms' optimal production is at the lowest point on the ATC curve, as shown in panel B.

When firms produce the quantity that minimizes average total cost (as in a perfectly competitive market), we say they are operating at their *efficient scale*. In contrast, a monopolistically competitive firm maximizes profits by operating at a smaller scale than the efficient one. Another way of saying this is that the firm has *excess capacity*.

2. **Monopolistically competitive firms want to sell more.** For a firm in a perfectly competitive market, price is equal to marginal cost. If the firm sold an additional unit at that price, marginal cost would rise above price, and profit would fall.

   In contrast, a monopolistically competitive firm sells at a price that is equal to average total cost, but higher than marginal cost. (Look again at panel A of Figure 15-4.) If the firm was able to sell an additional unit without lowering the price, that unit would generate more revenue than cost, and so increase the firm's profits. In other words, as soon as we depart from the model of perfect competition, firms have an incentive to engage in tactics for bringing in more customers, such as advertising and brand promotion.

The need for continual innovation. Our analysis of monopolistic competition in the long run has another interesting implication. Ask yourself: How will firms respond to competitors entering the market with closer and closer substitutes for existing products? Clearly, existing firms will want to step up their own attempts to differentiate their product. Only by constantly finding new ways to be different is it possible for a monopolistically competitive firm to generate profits in the long run.

The need for continual innovation explains why record labels are constantly on the lookout for new talent. It explains why firms in so many industries put so much effort into launching new products and finding new ways to advertise their products. If they don't, their competitors will catch up, and their economic profits will disappear. A truly innovative firm that manages to stay one step ahead of its competitors can continue to earn economic profits by always offering something slightly different.

For this reason, economists usually believe that competition encourages innovation. In contrast, a monopolist has far less incentive to innovate, because there is no danger of customers switching to a firm with newer and better products.

The welfare costs of monopolistic competition

LO 15.4 Analyze the welfare costs of monopolistic competition.

Like any deviation from the equilibrium price and quantity that would prevail under perfect competition, monopolistic competition is inefficient. Firms maximize profits at a price that is higher than marginal cost, and the quantity bought and sold is smaller than it would be under perfect competition. This means that there is deadweight loss—the market does not maximize total surplus.

Can anything be done about this problem? In the "Monopoly" chapter, we discussed ways that policy-makers try to address the welfare costs of monopolies, and noted that it is difficult to do so successfully. Unfortunately, regulating a monopolistically competitive market to increase efficiency is even harder. By definition, there are many firms in the market, and many slightly different products. Trying to assess firms' costs and regulate prices for every single one would be a gargantuan task.

Instead, the government could set a single price for all firms in the market and then let the natural forces of competition take over. Since monopolistically competitive firms earn zero economic profits, regulating a lower price would mean that those firms which could not figure out how to produce at a lower cost would be forced to leave the market.

Such regulation would come with a definite cost. Although consumers would get a greater quantity of similar products at a lower price, they would also lose out on some product variety. Instead of dozens or hundreds of similar products aiming to suit consumers' different tastes, everyone would have to make do with fewer options. How would you feel if instead of having five options for fast food in town, you had only three, but the burgers were a little bit cheaper?

Most governments are not too bothered about the welfare loss from monopolistic competition. Even if they could do something about it, it's not obvious whether consumers would appreciate having lower prices if it's at the expense of having many products to choose from.

Product differentiation, advertising, and branding

LO 15.5 Explain how product differentiation motivates advertising and branding.

We've seen that product differentiation enables firms to keep making economic profits in the short run. Firms therefore have an incentive to persuade customers that their products cannot easily be substituted with a rival product. They can do this either by making products truly different or by convincing consumers that they are different. Advertising is one strategy employed by firms to inform customers about—or convince them of—the differences between products. It involves creative thinking that goes beyond economics, as described in the Where Can It Take You? box "The advertising age."

WHERE CAN IT TAKE YOU?

The advertising age

What made you choose that particular brand of paper notebook? The energy drink you had on your way to class? Your favorite whitening toothpaste? That novel for summer vacation? Someone spent a lot of time and energy figuring out how to make that particular product and brand appealing to you, often in ways you might not consciously have realized. If you have a creative spirit and a love of business, then working in advertising might be a good fit. *To learn more, continue reading by scanning the QR code near the end of the chapter or by going online.*

Whether advertising is a good or bad thing is a subject for debate. On the one hand, advertising can convey useful information to consumers. You may learn about a new product or technology from an ad, or find out where something you want is sold, or when it is on sale, or what styles or flavors are available. In general, advertising provides this information in a pleasant, easy-to-understand format, free of cost and inconvenience. We don't need to trudge from store to store to find out where the sales are, or search online every day to see whether that new movie has been released yet. Instead, companies will spend money to hand us all of this information.

If we believe that the main effect of advertising is to provide useful information about products and prices, then advertising serves a valuable purpose. More information will increase competition in a marketplace. Consumers will learn when a firm is offering a cheaper product that is a close substitute for higher-priced competitors. This will drive prices down, bringing the market closer to the model of perfect competition.

On the other hand, advertising rarely consists of a bullet-pointed list of straightforward facts. Instead, advertisers go to great lengths to make viewers feel good about the thing being advertised. Ads portray beautiful people having a fabulous time, or heart-warming family moments, or adrenaline-inducing stunts and special effects. Often, this portrayal has little or nothing to do with the product being advertised. Instead, it is intended to make us associate a particular image or emotion with that product. The image of happy lovers embracing in a romantic location doesn't tell us anything about the unique qualities of a particular company's jewelry. It may, though, create a strong mental association between falling in love and receiving a new pair of earrings. For evidence that this kind of advertising can and does work, see the Real Life box "What really sells loans?"

REAL LIFE

What really sells loans?

Ads often aim to make the viewer feel good and to associate feeling good with the product. For example, an ad might try to associate a new car with shots of long sunny adventures with attractive friends. But how much of a difference does this really make? Don't potential customers just see through these ads?

Could emotions really matter as much as something economically important, such as the price of the good? Several economists (including one of the authors of this book) designed a study to answer this question in the context of advertising for consumer loans. In the experiment, a lender in South Africa sent ads by mail to tens of thousands of prior clients. The ads varied in the interest rate at which the loan was offered, as well as the appearance and content of the mailer. Different mailers included different combinations of features: an image of an attractive woman, a list of possible uses for the loan, information on interest rates, or a promotional raffle for a cell phone.

Not surprisingly, customers were more likely to take out a loan in response to mailers advertising lower interest rates. But they were also more likely to borrow if there was an attractive woman's picture on the ad. In fact, putting an attractive woman's picture on the mailer increased demand to the same degree as reducing the interest rate by 25 percent!

Of course, if you had asked loan customers directly whether they would rather have a 25 percent cheaper loan or look briefly at a picture of an attractive woman, most would likely have opted for the cheaper loan. The fact that their responses to the mailer told a different story demonstrates that economic information is only one input into people's decision making when faced with cleverly designed advertising.

Source: Marianne Bertrand, Dean Karlan, Sendhil Mullainathan, Eldar Shafir, and Jonathan Zinman, "What's Advertising Content Worth? Evidence from a Consumer Credit Marketing Field Experiment," *Quarterly Journal of Economics* 125, no. 1 (2010), pp. 263–306.

What if we believe that the main effect of advertising is not to convey useful information but to persuade customers that products are more different than they truly are? In this view, advertising decreases consumers' willingness to substitute between similar products. The result is that firms can charge a higher markup over marginal cost. This in turn drives prices up throughout the market.

So which *is* the main effect of advertising? There's no simple answer. Whether advertising serves mainly to provide useful information or to trigger gut-level reactions probably varies across markets. Sometimes, however, we can get a clue as to which effect is stronger from the reaction of producers when lawmakers consider banning advertising. (They have proposed such bans for tobacco, prescription drugs, alcohol, legal services, and even cosmetic surgery.) If producers object strongly to a ban on advertising, it is probably because they believe advertising persuades customers that products are more different than they really are. Producers' silence in the face of bans, or even support of them, may indicate that advertising in this industry serves mostly to inform consumers and promote competition—something that existing firms won't want to see happen.

Advertising as a signal. It's often hard to tell what real information about a product we're supposed to get from an ad. Why should we believe an actor who is well paid to say that a particular cellular network is faster than another? What does GEICO Insurance's green animated gecko know about car insurance? Sometimes, though, advertising may contain useful information for customers, even if it's not stated explicitly.

Think about the problem of *asymmetric information* (discussed in the "Information" chapter). Firms know more about the true quality of their products than consumers do. Consumers would like to find the best products, and the firms who make the best products would like to make themselves known to customers. But consumers can't trust a firm that simply says it has high-quality products; both high-quality and low-quality firms have an incentive to claim that their products are the best. The high-quality firms need a way to credibly signal the quality of their products. Advertising fits the bill, because advertising costs money.

Let's think, from a firm's perspective, about the choice to advertise. Suppose that a music label has signed a brilliant new artist and is sure people will love his first album if they hear it. The company calculates that if it spends a large amount of money on a high-profile TV advertising campaign, lots of people will buy the album; they will like it so much they will tell their friends and will buy concert tickets, fan merchandise, and the artist's future albums; the label will end up making $10 million in profits. If the company is wrong, and people don't like the album, the firm won't recover the cost of the money it spends on advertising—and will lose $5 million. The advertising expenditure will be a great investment for the label if the quality of the product is good, and a terrible investment if the quality is bad.

On the other hand, what does this decision look like if the label is not so confident about the quality of the new album? If the firm doesn't promote the album, there's still a chance that people who buy it will love it and tell their friends. But the sales will be much lower than if there was a huge TV campaign behind it. Let's say the label makes $2 million if people like the unadvertised album. And what if the people who buy the album don't like it? The label will lose some money it spent producing the music, but only $50,000. If the label is not so confident in the quality of the album, then it makes sense not to advertise. If people don't like it, at least the label will lose much less money than it would have done if it had advertised it. The choice to advertise or not advertise is illustrated in the decision tree in Figure 15-5.

Now let's think from a consumer's perspective about the firm's choice to advertise. Consumers can observe only the final outcome—whether the firm chooses to advertise or not—and not the true quality of the product. However, consumers can view the advertising as a credible signal. If they see that a music label is spending a lot of money on high-profile TV advertising for a new singer's album, they can reasonably conclude that the label is very confident that people will like the album. It may be perfectly reasonable, therefore, for consumers to try a product based on advertising. The important factor for consumers in assessing the usefulness of advertising as a signal is not the ad's content, but *how much it cost.* The more expensive the advertising is, the more consumers

FIGURE 15-5

Advertising as a signal of quality If the music label suspects fans will not like the album, it will actually lose money by advertising. Because rational music companies will choose to advertise an album only if they know it is good, consumers can use promotion efforts as a signal of album quality.

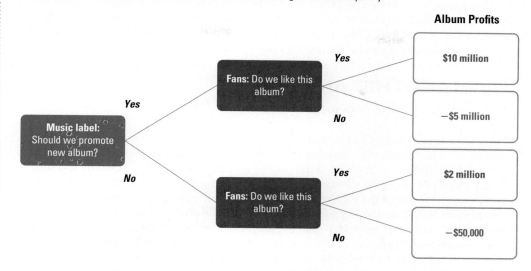

can assume the firm is confident that it has a good product that will earn repeat business from satisfied customers.

Branding. In 2009, two kitchen workers employed by Domino's Pizza uploaded videos to YouTube showing themselves contaminating food in various ways—we'll spare you the details—before allegedly giving the food to customers. (When the story was made public, the makers of the videos insisted it was a prank, and that none of the food had ever been served.) The employees responsible were immediately fired, but the damage to the Domino's brand had been done. Consumer surveys completed after the story broke showed a marked downturn in perception of the brand, moving from positive to negative in a matter of days. It needed quick action and some savvy public relations work for Domino's to help its brand recover.

This story illustrates why it may be rational for consumers to think of a strong brand as being an implicit guarantee of a product's quality. Firms with no reputation to protect may not be too concerned with the repercussions of selling a bad-quality product. But just one unfortunate incident can undo years of careful thought and hard work that a firm such as Domino's has put into building a strong brand. Because consumers know that firms stand to lose when their brand's reputation is damaged, they can conclude that firms with strong brands probably have strong quality control in all locations and levels of the company.

For this reason, a brand may also convey useful information in a confusing situation. A traveler in a strange city may have little information about the quality of food and drink available in local stores. If she sees a Starbucks, however, she can assume with confidence that she will be able to buy a familiar drink of predictable quality. The local tea shop might actually be better than Starbucks, but the traveler doesn't know that. She may rationally choose to go for the known quantity of the Starbucks brand, rather than taking a risk on the local competition.

It isn't always rational to rely on brand names to make decisions, however. Brands may also perpetuate false perceptions of quality or product differences. For instance, brand-name pharmaceuticals often command much higher prices than their generic counterparts, despite the fact that the two are made with identical active ingredients and have the same medical effect. In such cases strong brands can even form a *barrier to entry* in a market, moving it toward a structure of oligopoly in which a few leading players have a significant amount of market power. Before we look at how oligopolies work, see the From Another Angle box "Coke, Pepsi, and the not-so-secret formula" for an illustration of just how important it can be for firms to use branding to differentiate their products.

FROM ANOTHER ANGLE
Coke, Pepsi, and the not-so-secret formula

In its advertising, Coca-Cola makes a big deal about its "secret formula." When two employees tried to sell the company's confidential recipe to Pepsi in 2007, you might think Pepsi would have jumped at the chance to learn how its rival makes its product. In fact, Pepsi not only refused to buy the information, it participated in an FBI operation that led to the arrest of the would-be informants. What was going on here?

To answer that question, we have to understand the structure of the cola industry. The Coca-Cola Company and PepsiCo have been battling it out for over a century. Coke has around 80 percent of the cola market and Pepsi around 20 percent. The cola industry is therefore an oligopoly: Two firms dominate, and it would be hard for new cola manufacturers to break into the global market. This is partly because both Coke and Pepsi have successfully built such strong brands; it would be tough to persuade consumers to switch to new colas.

But the market for colas also has features of monopolistic competition: Each company tries to increase the size and loyalty of its customer base by emphasizing the differentiation of its product. Many blind taste tests have found that most people—even those who claim to be ardent fans of one brand or the other—can't distinguish between them when they don't know which they're drinking. So this seems to be a clear example of an industry in which advertising mainly serves to persuade people that products are more different than they really are.

Consider for a moment what would happen if Pepsi were to buy Coke's secret formula and publish it for the world to see. That information would make it easier for new companies to enter the cola market; they could advertise that their products are exactly identical to Coke. The entrance of new companies with undifferentiated products would bring the market closer to the model of perfect competition. The result would be to push down the price of Coke. This would be a disaster for Coke—but it would be bad news for Pepsi, too. The new colas would be close substitutes for Pepsi; some Pepsi customers would probably switch to the new wave of cheaper, undifferentiated colas. Under this scenario, Pepsi loses customers, and profits.

Why, then, didn't Pepsi buy the recipe, keep it secret, and use it to make its own cola taste exactly like Coke? After all, Coke has 80 percent of the market to Pepsi's 20 percent, so Coca-Cola must be doing something right. The problem for Pepsi was that since Coke has an established brand, Coke customers would have no reason to switch to Pepsi for the same taste at the same price. Pepsi would have to reduce its price to attract Coke customers to switch, and it would meanwhile lose the ability to charge a premium to the loyal 20 percent who actually claim to prefer the taste of Pepsi. If Pepsi made the move, it would not be able to earn as much economic profit.

Pepsi did the right thing in an ethical sense. But we also see why Pepsi's move may have been smart from an economic angle too. Pepsi's profit-maximizing decision was to ignore the chance to learn Coke's secret formula, and continue to differentiate its own product instead.

Sources: http://www.nytimes.com/ref/business/20070527_COKE_GRAPHIC.html; http://freakonomics.blogs.nytimes.com/2006/07/07/how-much-would-pepsi-pay-to-get-cokes-secret-formula/.

✓ CONCEPT CHECK

- ❑ How does product differentiation allow monopolistically competitive firms to gain market power? **[LO 15.2]**
- ❑ How does the short run differ from the long run in a monopolistically competitive market? **[LO 15.2]**
- ❑ Why are monopolistically competitive firms always willing to increase the quantity they sell? **[LO 15.3]**
- ❑ Why is it difficult to regulate a monopolistically competitive market to increase efficiency? **[LO 15.4]**
- ❑ Why might it be rational for a consumer to make purchasing decisions based on advertising? **[LO 15.5]**
- ❑ Why do firms want to develop their brands? **[LO 15.5]**

Oligopoly

Suppose you're an executive at Universal Music. Your day-to-day decisions hinge on how to make your company as profitable as possible. You have a lot to think about: Which new artists should we sign? How should we advertise upcoming releases? How much can we charge for CDs and legitimate downloads without driving customers into illegal downloading? What should we do to get more radio play for our latest singles?

One common thread runs through these decisions: You know your competition. You know you're playing to win against Sony, EMI, and Warner. You know their executives, their catalogs of artists, and at least a bit about their distribution and advertising deals. You probably also have some idea of what new releases they have coming in the pipeline. You might keep an eye on smaller, independent companies too, but your real preoccupation is with the other major players. In other words, you're playing in a game with three very identifiable competitors.

This contrasts sharply with the situation in a perfectly competitive market. As a price-taking firm in such a market, you'd be competing against dozens, hundreds, or even thousands of other firms. You probably wouldn't know the managers at those firms, and it wouldn't matter. Making business decisions with the intent of beating out any one of them would be pointless since all of the other firms would simply move in to fill the gap.

The fact that firms in an oligopoly market compete against a few identifiable rivals with market power drives our analysis. Firms in a perfectly competitive market have only one choice—what quantity to produce given the market price. Oligopolists, on the other hand, make *strategic* decisions about price and quantity that take into account the expected choices of their competitors. As we analyze oligopolies, we'll draw on our discussion of *game theory* from the "Game Theory and Strategic Thinking" chapter.

Oligopolies in competition

LO 15.6 Describe the strategic production decision of firms in an oligopoly.

Let's begin our analysis of oligopoly with a pared-down example from the music industry. For the sake of simplicity, suppose that there are only two big labels rather than four—Universal and Warner. (Technically, an oligopoly with two firms is known as a *duopoly*.) Also suppose that music is a standardized good, so that consumers are indifferent between buying music released by Universal and music released by Warner. Although we discussed earlier in the chapter why this is not entirely true, it's a reasonable simplification to clarify our analysis of oligopoly. Each label has such a large stable of artists that fans of any particular musical genre will be likely to find close substitutes for their tastes between the two rival labels.

Figure 15-6 shows the market demand schedule for albums, and the corresponding demand curve, for this two-company market. As we'd expect, the number of albums demanded increases as the price decreases. The third column of the table in panel A shows total revenue at each price-quantity combination. Remember that the quantity in the first column represents the total quantity demanded *in the whole market*, so column 3 shows the combined revenue of the two firms. Suppose that each firm pays a fixed cost of $100 million to sign artists and record albums. Let's also assume, for the sake of simplicity, that the marginal cost of producing each new album is zero.

Remember from the "Perfect Competition" chapter that in the perfect-competition model, price is driven down until it equals marginal cost. Since we're assuming the marginal cost of production is zero, the market equilibrium under perfect competition would be 140 million albums at a price of zero. (Of course, in the long run, albums couldn't remain free because music labels would not be covering their fixed costs; firms would exit the market until the price rose to a level where fixed costs were covered.) This is just another way of saying something we know already: In the model of perfect competition, no firm makes any economic profits.

In contrast, what if the market were a monopoly? We know from the "Monopoly" chapter that the monopolist would choose to sell the price and quantity combination that maximizes profits. Looking at the table, we can see this point would be 70 million albums at a price of $14. The monopolist's profit would be $880 million, which is its total revenue of $980 million minus its fixed cost of $100 million.

FIGURE 15-6
Demand for albums

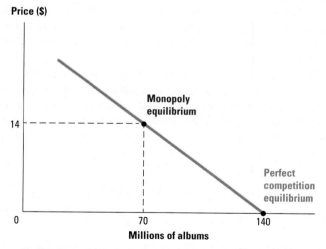

(A) Demand and revenue schedule

	Albums (millions)	Price ($)	Revenue (millions of $)
	40	20	800
	50	18	900
	60	16	960
Monopoly	70	14	980
	80	12	960
	90	10	900
	100	8	800
	110	6	660
	120	4	480
	130	2	260
Perfect competition	140	0	0

(B) Demand curve

If albums were produced by a monopoly, the firm would produce the profit-maximizing quantity. In perfect competition, price would be driven down to marginal cost, which in this case is zero.

What happens when there are *two* firms in the market—Universal and Warner? Since the monopoly production choice maximizes profits, the best the two firms could do would be to agree to act like a joint monopolist. If each produced 35 million albums, total quantity sold would equal 70 million, and the two labels could each earn profits of $390 million:

$$TR - TC$$

$$(35 \text{ million} \times \$14) - \$100 \text{ million} = \$390 \text{ million}$$

Sounds great, right? But let's say that Warner has a wily CEO, who decides to produce another 5 million albums without letting the CEO of Universal know about her plan. The total quantity of CDs sold on the market goes up to 75 million, which pushes the price down to $13. However, rather than splitting production equally, Warner is now selling 40 million albums to Universal's 35 million. As a result, Warner's profits go up to $420 million; Universal's profits are reduced by $35 million because each of the 35 million albums it sells is now going for one dollar less than it was before:

$$\text{Warner's profits} \quad = (40 \text{ million} \times \$13) - \$100 \text{ million} = \$420 \text{ million}$$

$$\text{Universal's profits} = (35 \text{ million} \times \$13) - \$100 \text{ million} = \$355 \text{ million}$$

The CEO of Universal won't be happy. What happens if he responds by sneaking an extra 5 million albums onto the market himself? The total quantity sold will be 80 million, which pushes the price down even further to $12. Now, each firm is selling 40 million albums, rather than 35 million, for a price that is $2 less per album:

$$\text{Profits for each of two firms} = (40 \text{ million} \times \$12) - \$100 \text{ million} = \$380 \text{ million}$$

Universal has gained some ground by retaliating, though each label is worse off than it was when it agreed to cooperate by producing 35 million albums each. This logic continues to drive quantity sold up and price down: Now Warner's CEO decides to produce 45 million albums, which would drive price down to $11 and increase her firm's profits to $395 million. However, the Universal CEO responds with the same decision, and each firm actually sells 45 million albums at a price of $10 each, for a lower profit of $350 million. Competition between oligopolists drives price and profits down to below the monopoly level, just as perfect competition does.

However, unlike perfect competition, oligopolistic competition does not necessarily drive profits all the way down to the efficient level. Remember from the "Monopoly" chapter that monopolists considering whether to produce an additional unit of output need to weigh two effects:

- *Quantity effect:* An additional unit of output sold at a price above marginal cost increases the firm's profit.
- *Price effect:* An additional unit of output raises the total quantity in the market and drives down the market price. The firm receives a lower price and therefore lower profit for each unit it sells.

The same thing happens in oligopoly: When the quantity effect outweighs the price effect, an increase in output will raise a firm's profit level. In this case, profit-maximizing firms will increase their output.

But when the quantity effect does not outweigh the price effect, the firm has no incentive to increase output. Consider the next quantity decision faced by Warner's CEO. If she produces another 5 million albums, she'll still make only $350 million in profits

(50 million × $9 = 45 million × $10). The quantity effect (selling an extra 5 million units) is exactly canceled out by the price effect (the price is $1 lower). She has no incentive to increase production.

Universal faces the same decision. Thus, we can predict that both companies will choose to stay at a production level of 45 million albums. The market equilibrium in this competitive duopoly is 90 million albums at a price of $10.

In reality, of course, there aren't just two big firms in the music business; there are four. But the principle remains exactly the same. Suppose we begin again with the total profit-maximizing monopoly quantity—70 million albums at a price of $14 each—with output divided equally among the four firms. Each firm produces 17.5 million albums, and brings in $245 million in revenues, minus its fixed costs of $100 million, for profits of $145 million.

$$TR - TC$$

$$(17.5 \text{ million} \times \$14) - \$100 \text{ million} = \$145 \text{ million}$$

But each firm has an incentive to raise its own profits if it can, even if it means decreasing the profits of other firms and of the market as a whole. As long as the quantity effect is greater than the price effect, each firm will keep increasing its output.

Now that there are four firms rather than two in the market, the price effect is smaller. When the market is split evenly between two firms, a 20 percent increase in one firm's output increases the total quantity in the market by 10 percent. If the two firms each produce 35 million albums, a 20 percent increase in output from one firm would increase its production by 7 million albums. Total production of albums would increase by 10 percent, from 70 million to 77 million.

In a market that is split evenly among four firms, a 20 percent increase in one firm's output increases the total quantity in the market by only 5 percent. The smaller the increase in total quantity, the smaller the downward effect on market price. The price effect is smaller when there are more firms; thus, each firm will increase its quantity by more before the quantity effect becomes equal to the price effect.

Whatever the number of firms in the market, an oligopolist will continue to increase output up to the quantity at which the positive quantity effect of an additional unit on profits is exactly equal to the negative price effect.

Analyzing an oligopolist's production decision in terms of the price and quantity effects highlights an important general idea: An oligopolist's production decision affects not only its own profits, but those of other firms as well. The profit-raising quantity effect is felt only by the individual firm that decides to produce more; the profit-lowering price effect also affects all other firms in the market. A decision that is profit-maximizing for an individual firm lowers combined profits for the market as a whole.

This is an example of a general economic truth: When an individual (person or firm) reaps all of the benefits and all of the costs of a decision, he (or it) will rationally make an optimal choice. But when a decision imposes costs or benefits on others, an individual's rational choice will not necessarily be optimal for the group. In the case of oligopoly, other firms have to bear the costs of one firm's rational decision to increase output. We'll return to this topic in much more detail in later chapters when we talk about externalities and public goods.

Compete or collude?

LO 15.7 Explain why firms in an oligopoly have an incentive to collude, and why they might fail to do so.

You don't get to be CEO of Warner or Universal if you don't understand how an oligopoly works. You can bet these are smart people who know that they are engaged in a strategic "game" like the prisoners' dilemma discussed in the "Game Theory and Strategic Thinking" chapter. In our simplified example, the firms have two options: to compete with each other, or to join forces and act like a monopolist. The act of working together to make decisions about price and quantity is called **collusion**. As we have seen, when Warner and Universal choose to compete with each other, they end up producing 45 million albums each and making profits of $350 million. If they agree to collude, they will each produce 35 million albums and make $390 million in profits. If collusion can enable firms to earn higher profits, *why isn't everyone doing it?*

collusion the act of working together to make decisions about price and quantity

When Universal's CEO decides how many albums to produce, he will think strategically and ask himself what Warner's CEO is thinking. What if Warner decides to produce 35 million albums? Look at the payoff matrix in Figure 15-7. Reading across the top row of the matrix, we see that Universal will make $390 million if it also produces 35 million albums; it will make $440 million if it produces 45 million albums. The right choice for Universal is clear—produce more albums and make more profit.

But what if Warner also decides to produce 45 million albums? Reading across the bottom row, we see that if Universal makes 35 million albums it will make $320 million; if it produces 45 million albums it will make $350 million. Again, the choice is clear. Looking at his options, the CEO of Universal will conclude that whatever Warner decides to do, Universal should produce 45 million albums.

Looking at the strategic decision illustrated in Figure 15-7, two things stand out. First, as we've already calculated, both firms do worse when they compete with each other than when they collude. This is because, by competing, they drive quantity sold above the profit-maximizing monopoly level that would be achieved by collusion.

Second, each firm has an incentive to renege on a collusion deal and compete, regardless of what the other firm does. Consider the decision from Warner's point of view. If Warner expects Universal to produce the lower, "collusion" quantity, it can earn $50 million more in profits by competing than by colluding. (How do we know? Compare Warner's profits in the top left square of Figure 15-7 to those in the bottom left square.)

FIGURE 15-7

Oligopoly production as the prisoners' dilemma Record labels' decision to collude can be modeled as a game called the prisoners' dilemma. Although both firms would be better off if they could agree to collude and produce a lower quantity, each has an incentive to defect from this agreement and earn more profits.

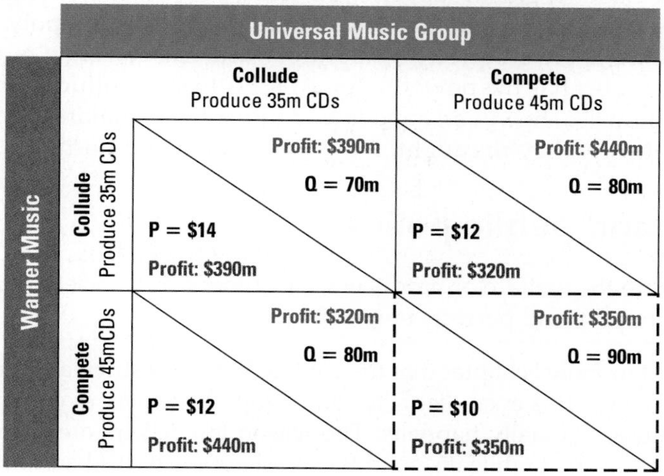

If Warner expects Universal to produce the higher, "competitive" quantity, it still earns more profits by competing than by sincerely sticking to the collusion agreement. (Compare the $350 million of the bottom right square to the $320 million of the top right square.)

dominant strategy a strategy that is the best one for a player to follow no matter what strategy other players choose

When one strategy is always the best for a player to choose, regardless of what other players do, we call it a **dominant strategy**. In an oligopoly, competition is a dominant strategy for Universal. Unfortunately, it is also a dominant strategy for Warner, whose CEO is making exactly the same calculation. As a result, both firms will choose to compete rather than collude, producing 45 million albums and making $350 million in profits.

Nash equilibrium an equilibrium reached when all players choose the best strategy they can, given the choices of all other players

When all players in a game have a dominant strategy, the result is called a **Nash equilibrium**. It is an outcome in which all players choose the best strategy they can, given the choices of all other players. (Nash equilibrium can be reached even when firms don't have a dominant strategy, but in this case they do.) Nash equilibrium is significant because when it is reached, no one has an incentive to break the equilibrium by changing his strategy.

However, as described in the "Game Theory and Strategic Thinking" chapter, there is a way out of this dilemma for the two CEOs. The key is to remember that decisions are made not once, but over and over again between the same set of firms. Once the Universal CEO considers that the interaction is a "repeated game," his incentives change. If he reneges on the deal while the CEO of Warner keeps her word, he will gain $50 million in profits for this year. But he will be sure that Warner will retaliate *next year* by going back to the competitive production levels. He therefore knows Universal will lose $40 million in profits *every year thereafter*; the firm will earn $350 million in the competitive equilibrium rather than $390 million in the collusion equilibrium. With *future* profits in mind, both companies may take an initial chance that the other will hold up its end of an initial agreement to collude. If both stand firm, they may keep cooperating, each producing 35 million CDs, year after year.

cartel a number of firms who collude to make collective production decisions about quantities or prices

This sort of strategy is often the glue that holds firms together in a **cartel**—a number of firms who collude to make collective production decisions about quantities or prices. A well-known cartel is the Organization of the Petroleum Exporting Countries (OPEC). Member countries agree to limit the amount of petroleum they produce, in order to manipulate the market price and maximize their profits. The fact that each member country knows it is in its long-term interest to collude rather than compete is enough to keep OPEC together. Interest in future profits dissuades any individual country from chasing short-term profits by producing more oil in any given year. Although OPEC does not control all of the global supply of oil, it is a powerful force in global oil prices.

If cartels are so advantageous for firms operating in an oligopoly, why don't we see more of them? There's a pretty straightforward reason: They're usually illegal. No international court has the power to force OPEC to stop colluding in the global oil market. Most countries, however, have laws against firms making agreements about prices or quantities. If they're caught, they can be fined and punished.

Oligopoly and public policy

LO 15.8 Compare the welfare of producers, consumers, and society as a whole in an oligopoly to monopoly and perfect competition.

We saw in the "Monopoly" chapter that the United States has strict laws prohibiting "anti-competitive" behavior. It is even illegal for an oligopolist to *offer* to collude, regardless of whether the collusion actually happens. The reason lawmakers are so concerned about collusion, of course, is that while it's good for the oligopolists, it's bad for the rest of us. In our hypothetical example, when Warner and Universal are colluding, the price of CDs is $14. When they are competing, the price is only $10. The music-buying public is better off if Warner and Universal compete rather than collude.

Remember that in a monopoly, there is deadweight loss—a welfare loss caused by the transactions that did not take place because the market equilibrium was at a higher price and lower quantity than would be efficient. Figure 15-8 compares the producer surplus, consumer surplus, and deadweight loss under varying amounts of competition. Note that the last two graphs—collusion and monopoly—are identical. Because the market outcomes in a competitive oligopoly are between those of a monopoly and a perfectly competitive market, deadweight loss still exists, but it is lower than when there is collusion.

It's no wonder governments are so keen to prevent firms from colluding, and no wonder firms are so keen to collude without being caught. In 1960, for example, the U.S. government reviewed its annual records for bids it had received when it invited companies to supply certain types of heavy machinery. Government agencies discovered that 47 manufacturers had submitted *identical* bids for the previous three

FIGURE 15-8

Deadweight loss under varying amounts of competition Perfect competition represents one end of the deadweight loss spectrum, and collusion/monopoly represents the other. A competitive oligopoly falls somewhere in between. There is less deadweight loss than in the case of collusion or monopoly, but it does not eliminate deadweight loss in the way that perfect competition does.

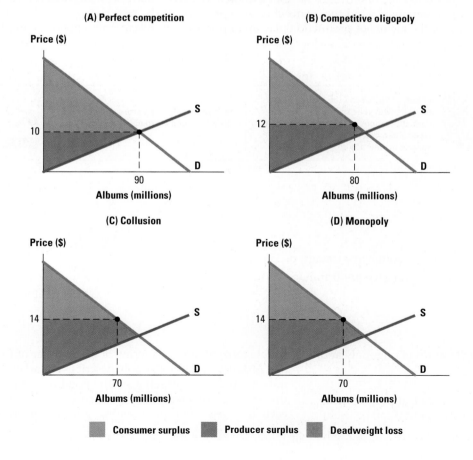

years of bidding. This showed that the manufacturers were secretly colluding on their bids. They were taking turns to submit the lowest bid, at a price that would be much higher than if they were actually competing. It is estimated that the cartel, until it was broken up, cost U.S. taxpayers $175 million each year.

✓ CONCEPT CHECK

☐ Why is the equilibrium in an oligopolistic market less efficient than a competitive market? **[LO 15.6]**

☐ Why would two companies in an oligopoly benefit from colluding? **[LO 15.7]**

☐ Why would it be difficult for companies to collude, even if doing so were legal? **[LO 15.7]**

☐ What happens to deadweight loss as the number of firms in an oligopolistic market increases? **[LO 15.8]**

Conclusion

In previous chapters, we've explored two opposite ends of the spectrum of market structures: perfect competition and monopoly. In this chapter, we've moved to the gray area in between, learning about imperfect competition and the characteristics of industries that fall into the categories of monopolistic competition and oligopoly. Knowing about these market structures helps business owners make optimal decisions about production and pricing. Such knowledge also helps consumers make sense of firms' behavior and the abundance of advertising they see in the real world.

Market structure can tell us a lot about how firms make decisions, but there are still a number of other factors that we haven't explored yet. Up until now, we've focused on the amount of any given good that firms choose to produce. In the next chapter, we'll see how markets for the factors of production play an important role in *how* firms choose to produce goods.

 ◄ Mobile Window on the World—Scan this code with your smartphone to find more applications of the chapter content. (Need a barcode reader? Try ScanLife, available in your app store.)

Visit your mobile app store and download ► the Karlan and Morduch Study Econ app.

Key Terms

Summary

LO 15.1 Name the defining features of oligopoly and monopolistic competition.

Most markets in the real world don't fit perfectly into any one model of market structure, but it can be useful to categorize markets in terms of the number of firms and product variety. Oligopoly describes a market with only a few firms that sell a similar good or service. In this setting, firms tend to know their competition and each firm has some price-setting power, but no one has total market control. Monopolistic competition, in contrast, describes a market with many firms that sell goods and services that are similar, but slightly different. These firms are not necessarily price takers, but they still face competition in the long run.

LO 15.2 Calculate the profit-maximizing price and quantity for a monopolistically competitive firm in the short run.

In the short run, monopolistically competitive firms behave just like monopolists. They face a downward-sloping demand curve and cannot change price without causing a change in the quantity consumers demand. The profit-maximizing production quantity is at the point where the marginal revenue (MR) curve intersects the marginal cost (MC) curve. The profit-maximizing price is determined by the point on the demand curve that corresponds to this quantity.

LO 15.3 Describe a monopolistically competitive market in the long run.

In the long run, monopolistic competition has some features in common with monopoly, and others in common with perfect competition. Just like a monopoly, a monopolistically competitive firm faces a downward-sloping demand curve, which means that marginal revenue is less than price. This in turn means that marginal cost is also less than price. Like a firm in a perfectly competitive market, however, a monopolistically competitive firm earns zero economic profits in the long run.

LO 15.4 Analyze the welfare costs of monopolistic competition.

Like any deviation from the equilibrium price and quantity that would prevail under perfect competition, monopolistic competition is inefficient. Because firms maximize profits at a price that is higher than marginal cost, some mutually beneficial trades never occur. This means that there is deadweight loss—the market does not maximize total surplus. However, regulating monopolistically competitive markets to increase efficiency is difficult, and usually comes at the expense of product variety.

LO 15.5 Explain how product differentiation motivates advertising and branding.

Producers invest in advertising to convince consumers that their products are different from other similar products. The less substitutable a good seems with other goods, the less likely consumers are to switch to other products if the price increases. Thus, producers have an incentive to differentiate their products—either by making them truly different or by convincing consumers that they are different. Through advertising and branding, firms either explicitly give the desired information to the consumer or signal the quality of their products.

LO 15.6 Describe the strategic production decision of firms in an oligopoly.

Oligopolists make strategic decisions about price and quantity that take into account the expected choices of their competitors. Unlike price-taking firms in a competitive market, an oligopolist produces a quantity that affects the market price. The increase in profit retained from an additional unit of output is called the quantity effect. The decrease in profit caused by an additional unit of output lowering the market price is called the price effect. Typically, an oligopolistic firm will increase output until the positive quantity effect outweighs the negative price effect.

LO 15.7 Explain why firms in an oligopoly have an incentive to collude, and why they might fail to do so.

An oligopolist has an incentive to produce more output than is profit maximizing for the market as a whole, driving down price and imposing costs on its competitors. By colluding, firms can maximize industry profits by producing the equivalent monopoly quantity and splitting revenues. However, each firm involved always has an incentive to renege on the agreement, since a firm could earn higher profits by competing.

LO 15.8 Compare the welfare of producers, consumers, and society as a whole in an oligopoly to monopoly and perfect competition.

The competitive equilibrium in an oligopoly leads to a quantity and price that are somewhere between the outcomes of a perfectly competitive market and those of a monopoly. Because the equilibrium is not the same as in a competitive market, oligopoly results in some deadweight loss and increases producer surplus at the expense of consumer surplus. When oligopolists collude, the equilibrium looks like a monopoly outcome and results in even higher deadweight loss and higher producer surplus.

Review Questions

1. Explain why an oligopolist (with few competitors) pays more attention to what its competitors are doing than a producer in a competitive market (with many competitors) does. **[LO 15.1]**

2. If a market has few barriers to entry and many firms, how might firms still have positive economic profit? Describe a strategy a firm in this type of market might use to maintain economic profits. **[LO 15.1]**

3. McDonald's, Burger King, and Wendy's all produce hamburgers, among other things. However, if you prefer burgers from McDonald's, you might consider other burgers an imperfect substitute. With this in mind, how would you expect McDonald's to set its prices in the short run? Describe the relationship between price, marginal revenue, and marginal cost. **[LO 15.2]**

4. Consider Jimmy Choo designer shoes. In what way does Jimmy Choo face many competitors? In what way does Jimmy Choo face no competitors? **[LO 15.2]**

5. Restaurants offer related but differentiated products to their consumers. In the long run, new restaurants enter the market and imitate the cuisine and atmosphere of successful competitors. How would you expect a restaurant to set its prices in the long run? Describe the relationship between price and average total cost. Does a restaurant earn economic profits? **[LO 15.3]**

6. In both perfectly competitive and monopolistically competitive markets, when firms are making positive economic profits, other firms will enter until price equals ATC and profits are zero. Despite these similarities, in a perfectly competitive market total surplus is maximized, while in a monopolistically competitive market surplus is not maximized. Explain this difference. **[LO 15.3]**

7. Suppose a perfectly competitive market for hot-dog stands in New York City becomes monopolistically competitive when gourmet, discount, and ethnic hot-dog retailers show up, making each cart slightly different. If hot dogs from different stands are now imperfect substitutes and there are numerous carts in the city, compare the producer and consumer surplus and total social welfare before and after the change. **[LO 15.4]**

8. Given that the market for smartphones is inefficient, explain why consumers of smartphones might not want the price to be regulated. **[LO 15.4]**

9. Imagine that you have a program on your cell phone that allows you to walk up to any item in the supermarket and have your phone recognize it and display all the necessary information about the product. The program tells you where and how it is made, and when it is predicted to go on sale next. Does a firm selling goods in this setting need to advertise? Why or why not? **[LO 15.5]**

10. Why might the cost of advertising be relevant to a consumer's decision about which brand of a product to purchase? **[LO 15.5]**

11. Suppose that the market for e-readers is an oligopoly controlled by Amazon.com, Barnes and Noble, Sony, and Apple. Barnes and Noble is considering increasing its output. How would this affect the market price? How would it affect the profits of each company? **[LO 15.6]**

12. Compare the efficiency of perfectly competitive markets, monopoly markets, and oligopoly markets. Explain why the same profit-maximizing behavior for the individual firm leads to different levels of efficiency in these three types of markets. **[LO 15.6]**

13. The Organization of the Petroleum Exporting Countries (OPEC) is a cartel of 12 countries that controls roughly two-thirds of the world's oil production. The cartel gives countries quotas for production. Why might a country be tempted to produce above quota for a year? How do you think other OPEC countries might respond if it did so? **[LO 15.7]**

14. Isabella runs an IT solutions business for her college peers and has only one competitor, Franco. Isabella and Franco have decided to collude and provide monopoly-level output. Given that they are both freshmen and intend to run their businesses for the next three years, is this agreement sustainable? Would your answer change if Franco knew he planned to transfer to another college next year? **[LO 15.7]**

15. The United States Postal Service (USPS) has a government monopoly on home mail delivery, but several private companies, such as FedEx, UPS, and DHL, compete with the USPS for other types of delivery service. Describe the differences in producer and consumer surplus, and in overall social welfare, that would occur in each of the following scenarios. **[LO 15.8]**

    a. The USPS has a monopoly on every type of mail or package.

    b. Consumers are allowed to choose between USPS, UPS, FedEx, and DHL for home mail delivery.

    c. There are an infinite number of local and national mail providers.

16. Explain why government is usually more concerned about regulating an oligopoly than a monopolistically competitive market. **[LO 15.8]**

Problems and Applications

1. Identify whether each of the following markets has few or many producers, and uniform or differentiated products. Which market is an oligopoly? Which market is monopolistically competitive? **[LO 15.1]**
   a. College education.
   b. Retail gas market.

2. Match the statement about goods sold in a market with the market type. **[LO 15.1]**
   a. There are imperfect substitutes for the goods.
   b. There are no substitutes for the goods.
   c. The goods may or may not be standardized.

3. Interscope sells the music of Lady Gaga, who promotes a unique public image and fashion style. Given her huge success, it is likely that by the end of the coming year, multiple performers will be imitating or borrowing heavily from her style. Suppose the current period's supply and demand for Lady Gaga MP3s is given in Figure 15P-1. **[LO 15.2, 15.3]**
   a. What are the profit-maximizing price and quantity for Lady Gaga MP3s in the short run?
   b. In the long run, what happens to the demand curve?
   c. In the long run, what happens to the profit-maximizing price?

4. Figure 15P-2 shows the monopolistically competitive market for smartphones. **[LO 15.3]**
   a. Is this producer earning positive or negative profits in the short run?

FIGURE 15P-1

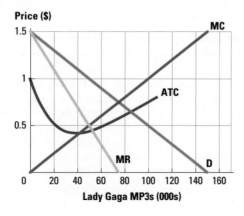

5. Figure 15P-3 shows a monopolistically competitive market for a fictional brand of shampoo called SqueakyKleen. **[LO 15.4]**

FIGURE 15P-2

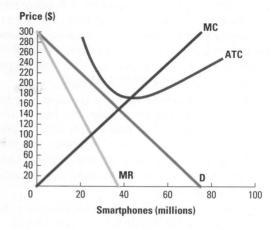

FIGURE 15P-3

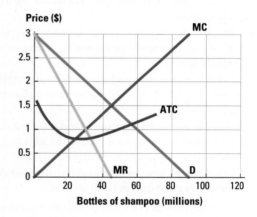

   b. In the long run, will economic profits increase or decrease for this producer?

5. Figure 15P-3 shows a monopolistically competitive market for a fictional brand of shampoo called SqueakyKleen. **[LO 15.4]**
   a. What is the price and quantity of SqueakyKleen in the short run?
   b. What is the efficient price and quantity of SqueakyKleen?
   c. Draw the deadweight loss.

6. For which good would you expect deadweight loss to be smaller relative to the total surplus in its market: Burger King hamburgers or Lady Gaga MP3s? Explain your answer. **[LO 15.4]**

7. For which product would you expect producers to have a stronger reaction to a ban on advertising: music artists or fast-food burgers? Explain your answer. **[LO 15.5]**

8. Suppose you manage a firm in a monopolistically competitive market. Which of the following strategies will do a better job of helping you maintain economic profits: obtaining a celebrity endorsement for your product or supporting the entry of firms that will compete directly with your biggest rival? Explain your answer. **[LO 15.5]**

9. Table 15P-1 shows the monthly demand schedule for a good in a duopoly market. The two producers in this market each face $5,000 of fixed costs per month. There are no marginal costs. **[LO 15.6]**

    a. What is the monthly profit for each duopolist if they evenly split the quantity a monopolist would produce?

    b. What is the monthly profit for duopolist A and duopolist B if duopolist A decides to increase production by 200 units?

10. Figure 15P-4 shows the monthly demand curve for a good in a duopoly market. There are no fixed costs. **[LO 15.6]**

    a. What is the monthly profit for each duopolist if they evenly split the quantity a monopolist would produce?

    b. What is the deadweight loss if the duopolists evenly split the quantity a monopolist would produce?

    c. What is the monthly profit for duopolist A and duopolist B if duopolist A decides to increase production by 10 units?

    d. What is the deadweight loss if duopolist A increases production by 10 units?

11. Oil Giant and Local Oil are the only two producers in a market, as shown in Figure 15P-5. They have an agreement to restrict oil output in order to keep prices high. **[LO 15.7]**

FIGURE 15P-4

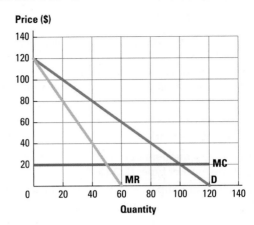

FIGURE 15P-5

		Oil Giant	
		Collude 3 million barrels	**Compete** 4 million barrels
Local Oil	**Collude** 3 million barrels	Profit: $270m Profit: $270m	Profit: $300m Profit: $225m
	Compete 4 million barrels	Profit: $225m Profit: $300m	Profit: $240m Profit: $240m

a. What is the dominant strategy for each player?

b. If this game is played once, what is the Nash equilibrium?

c. Now suppose that both players know that the game will be played multiple times. What outcome would we expect?

12. Suppose Warner Music and Universal Music are in a duopoly and currently limit themselves to 10 new artists per year. One artist sells 2 million songs at $1.25 per song. However, each label is capable of signing 20 artists per year. If one label increases the number of artists to 20 and the other stays the same, the price per song drops to $0.75, and each artist sells 3 million songs. If both labels increase the number of artists to 20, the price per song drops to $0.30, and each artist sells 4 million songs. **[LO 15.7]**

    a. Fill in the revenue payoffs for each scenario in Figure 15P-6.

TABLE 15P-1

Quantity	Price ($)
400	30
600	25
800	20
1,000	15
1,200	10
1,400	5
1,600	0

FIGURE 15P-6

b. If this game is played once, how many artists will each producer sign, and what will be the price of a song?

c. If this game is played every year, how many artists will each producer sign, and what will be the price of a song?

13. Suppose a new product is developed and is supplied by a monopolist with a patent. Compared with the monopoly outcome, indicate whether consumer surplus, producer surplus, and total surplus increase, decrease, or remain the same under the following scenarios. [LO 15.8]

a. Another producer creates a similar product and colludes with the original producer.

b. Another producer creates a similar product and competes with the original producer.

c. The patent expires.

14. For which of the following markets would there be a greater increase in total welfare if government were able to intervene and regulate prices: OPEC or the music industry? Explain your answer. [LO 15.8]

Chapter Sources

Peter J. Alexander, "Product variety and market structure: A new measure and a simple test," *Journal of Economic Behavior & Organization* 32, issue 2 (1997, pp. 207–214)

http://www.peterjalexander.com/images/Market_Structure_a nd_Product_Variety.PDF

http://query.nytimes.com/gst/fullpage.html?res =9A04E4DD173FF935A25757C0A96F9C8B63&ref =dominos-pizza-inc

Richard A. Peterson and David G. Berger, "Measuring industry concentration, diversity, and innovation in popular music," *American Sociological Review* 61, no. 1 (February 1996, pp. 175–178), http://www.jstor.org/stable/2096413

The Factors of Production

Chapter 16

LEARNING OBJECTIVES

LO 16.1 Define factors of production and describe how they contribute to output.

LO 16.2 Graph the demand curve for a factor of production, and explain its relationship to marginal productivity.

LO 16.3 Graph the supply curve for a factor of production, and explain what determines the supply of labor.

LO 16.4 Explain how to find the equilibrium price and quantity for a factor of production.

LO 16.5 Use graphs to demonstrate the effect of a shift in supply or demand and describe what causes these curves to shift.

LO 16.6 Define human capital, and justify its importance in the labor market.

LO 16.7 Describe the similarities and differences between the markets for land and capital and the market for labor.

LO 16.8 Identify two reasons why a wage might rise above the market equilibrium, and describe their effect on the labor market.

LO 16.9 Describe several causes of imperfectly competitive labor markets and their effect on workers and employers.

. . . .

THE FIELDS OF CALIFORNIA

In 2012, baseball star Albert Pujols earned $12 million a year playing for the Los Angeles Angels. The contract he signed with the Angels in 2011 guarantees him $254 million over 10 years. During the spring and summer of 2012, another group of workers were also engaged in tough, physical work—but they earned a lot less money. California's tens of thousands of farm workers earned an average salary of just over $19,000.

Of course, there are many, many differences between baseball and farm work. On a superficial level, though, baseball players have something in common with farm laborers. They are both mostly young men in their 20s and 30s, many of whom were born outside the United States. They do hard, physical, seasonal work, and they train on the job rather than in school.

So, why does Albert Pujols make over 1,000 times more money than someone who prunes orange trees or picks tomatoes? For that matter, why does Pujols make so much more than other Major League Baseball players? (Don't feel too sorry for the others; their average salary is still over $3 million a year.) Why do baseball players make more than other professional athletes, whose average salary in California is about $125,000?

We suspect that you intuitively know the answer to these questions. When he signed his huge contract with the Angels, Albert Pujols was one of the top players in baseball. Of course he gets paid a lot! Not just anyone can do what he does. The same thing goes for professional baseball players in general. If there are only a thousand people in the entire country who have a particular skill, they can demand a lot of money to do what *only* they can do.

Furthermore, Americans like to watch baseball, and they're willing to pay to see it played well. We like tomatoes and oranges too, but if farm workers earned millions of dollars a year, consumers would have to be willing to pay a lot more for dinner. Similarly, the very best professional racquetball player in California makes far less money than Albert Pujols. That happens not necessarily because he is less skilled or because there is a larger supply of great racquetball players, but because sports fans simply aren't willing to pay as much to watch racquetball.

The economic reasoning behind this intuition is that labor—whether slugging or fielding or harvesting—is an ingredient in producing a good that consumers want, such as a baseball game or a tomato. The labor that goes into producing these goods is bought and sold, in a way that is tied to the market for the goods themselves. The price that workers are paid depends on the number of people who are able to supply that type of labor and on the demand for the goods that are produced with it.

In this chapter we'll discuss the markets for *factors of production*. Economists usually lump the factors of production into three categories—labor, land, and capital. We'll see how prices in these markets are determined by markets for consumer goods, as well as by public policy. Seeing how supply and demand govern factor markets allows us to understand how firms make decisions about how much of which factors to use. This choice is important for any business owner: Is it worth buying a new machine or hiring another employee? How can you know?

Understanding factor markets—particularly labor markets—is also a key to explaining people's income. We'll describe how ownership of different factors of production affects income and why people earn different amounts. This chapter is thus a building block for understanding income inequality. Since the majority of people make their living primarily by selling their labor, we'll focus on understanding the differences between the wages people earn. What differentiates Albert Pujols from a farm worker, or a professional racquetball player, or a plumber, or you? This chapter will leave you with tools for understanding labor markets as a worker, a boss, or a voter.

The Factors of Production: Land, Labor, and Capital

LO 16.1 Define factors of production and describe how they contribute to output.

When you buy a ticket to a baseball game, what are you really paying for? A baseball game requires the time and skills of players and those of managers, umpires, coaches, ticket collectors, and janitors. It also requires a ballpark and a parking lot, training facilities, loudspeakers, jumbo screens, balls and gloves, and other equipment.

The ingredients that go into making a baseball game, or a tomato, or any other good or service, are called **factors of production**. We can think about three different types of factors: labor, land, and capital. Labor and land are exactly what they sound like: Labor is the time employees spend working, and land is the place where they work. **Capital** refers to manufactured goods that are used to produce new goods. The capital needed to produce a baseball game includes equipment like bats, lights, uniforms, and video screens. The capital needed to produce a tomato includes seeds, fertilizer, irrigation equipment, and trucks to transport harvested tomatoes.

Factors of production are bought and sold in markets, in much the same way as the goods they go into producing. The sellers in factor markets are people who own the factors of production; the buyers are firms that want to use them to produce goods and services. The price of each factor is determined by supply and demand.

In this section, we'll describe the production decisions that drive factor markets and make them slightly different from other markets. We'll see how factor markets are tied to markets for consumer goods, and how each factor's contribution to production is measured. These are tools that you will need in order to figure out how businesses make production decisions, and ultimately, to see why baseball players are paid more than farm workers.

factors of production the ingredients that go into making a good or service

capital manufactured goods that are used to produce new goods

Derived demand

How does a firm decide how much of each factor of production it wants to use? The Los Angeles Angels wanted—and were willing to pay for—Pujols's labor because it would help them win baseball games. That, in turn, would raise the value of tickets and broadcast rights to baseball games, which are then supplied to fans. The demand for baseball players is "derived" from a team's choice to supply games, and it depends on how much they contribute to the value of the end product.

Likewise, when a farmer decides how many workers to employ to pick tomatoes, or whether to invest in new irrigation equipment, or whether to buy a field which could be used to grow tomatoes, he will consider the market for tomatoes. Farmers' demand for tomato pickers, irrigation equipment, and good tomato-growing land is *derived* from the market for tomatoes. If consumers want more tomatoes, demand for the factors of production that go into tomatoes will increase. If they want fewer tomatoes, demand for those factors of production will decrease. For this reason, the demand for factors of production is referred to as *derived demand*.

Marginal productivity

In the "Costs of Production" chapter we discussed production functions, which describe the relationship between the quantity of inputs a firm uses and the resulting quantity of outputs. For example, a farm that hires more workers can produce more tomatoes. The increase in output that is generated by an additional unit of input is called **marginal product**. Graphically, we can think of the marginal product of a factor as the slope of the total production curve, when output is plotted against the quantity of the input that is used. Figure 16-1 shows the marginal product of labor in tomato production. The change in the quantity of tomatoes produced due to hiring one additional worker is that worker's marginal product. Marginal product also applies to the other factors of production, land, and capital.

Recall that inputs usually have diminishing marginal productivity. In other words, for a given amount of land, the tenth farm worker will generally contribute less to a farm's output than the first worker. This fact will become important as we describe the demand for labor.

marginal product the increase in output that is generated by an additional unit of input

FIGURE 16-1

Marginal product of labor

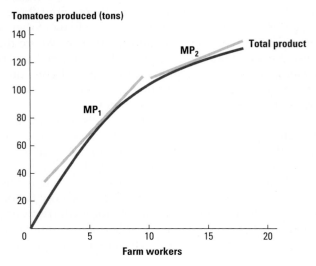

The more workers a farm employs, the more tomatoes the farm can harvest. Hiring an additional farm worker adds fewer tomatoes to the harvest than the previous worker. As the number of workers increases, total production increases, but the marginal product of labor diminishes.

Picking the right combination of inputs

In some cases, firms can choose what combination of factors to use, substituting one for another. For instance, picking tomatoes can be done either by hand or by machine. A farmer can choose to hire many workers and buy no machinery, or hire fewer workers and buy more machinery. Note that this doesn't work for all goods: You can't choose to produce a baseball game by having fewer players and more bats.

A profit-seeking firm will choose the combination of inputs that maximizes profit, based on the local price of each factor of production. The price of farm machinery is similar all over the world, but the cost of farm labor varies more widely. In poorer economies, labor is usually cheap, so farmers tend to hire lots of workers and buy fewer machines. In rich countries, labor costs more, so farmers tend to hire fewer workers and buy more machines. Another way of saying this is that farming tends to be *labor-intensive* in poor countries and *capital-intensive* in rich countries.

✓ CONCEPT CHECK

❏ Give examples of each of the factors of production that are used in an auto repair shop. **[LO 16.1]**

❏ What is labor demand "derived" from? **[LO 16.1]**

❏ What is the relationship between a worker's marginal product and a firm's total output? **[LO 16.1]**

Labor Markets and Wages

We now have some concepts to use when thinking about the markets for factors of production. We'll use them to take a closer look at the markets for labor and capital. First we'll consider the demand for labor, and then its supply.

Before we start, though, there are a few things that may take some getting used to. First, remember that individuals who work are the "suppliers" of labor. Firms that produce goods using those workers are the "buyers" of labor. This is the reverse of the usual situation, in which we think of firms as suppliers and individual people as buyers.

Second, the wage that workers earn is the "price" of labor. We rarely use the word *price* when talking about people and their skills, but wages play exactly the same role in labor markets as prices do in markets for goods and services. In the labor market, the two terms mean exactly the same thing: Wages are simply the price of labor.

Demand for labor

LO 16.2 Graph the demand curve for a factor of production, and explain its relationship to marginal productivity.

Let's consider how a tomato farmer decides how many workers to employ. For simplicity, we'll assume that the tomato farm is a profit-maximizing firm in a competitive market. That makes sense when there are many different tomato farms, each a price taker in the market for selling tomatoes and in the market for hiring farm workers. Let's also assume for now that all farm workers are equally productive.

What determines the number of workers the farm hires? Consider the owner's *wants and constraints.* The owner wants to maximize the farm's profit. Remember that a firm in a competitive market maximizes profits by producing the quantity at which the revenue it earns from the last unit is equal to the cost of producing that unit. So, a tomato farm wants to produce tomatoes up to the point where the marginal revenue from the last ton is equal to the marginal cost of producing that ton.

Since the farm is a price taker in a competitive market, the farmer cannot control the going price of tomatoes nor the going wage of tomato pickers—both of which affect how much profit is made. Therefore, maximizing profit boils down to making the right choice about the quantity to produce.

If we leave land, tractors, and other inputs fixed at a certain level, the farm's output will be determined by the number of workers hired and each worker's marginal productivity, as shown in Table 16-1 for a single hypothetical farm. For any quantity of labor (number of workers, in column 1), the table tells us the quantity of tomatoes produced (column 3) and the marginal cost of hiring the last worker (in column 6). That marginal cost of the last worker is the worker's wage; in this example, it is $20,000 for each worker, or about $10 dollars per hour for 40 hours of work per week over 50 weeks in a year.

Each worker hired adds something to total production—that worker's *marginal product* (shown in column 2). You can see that marginal product diminishes with each added worker. The first group of workers is able to harvest lots of tomatoes; as more and more workers come to the farm, they start to get in each other's way.

The question of how much labor a firm will hire comes down to whether added workers are going to generate more revenue than what it costs to hire them. Therefore, we want to find the marginal revenue associated with each worker. To find this value, we simply multiply the marginal product of labor (MPL)—that is, the quantity of additional output generated by each worker, shown in column (2)—by the market price of tomatoes (column 4). In other words, we translate the worker's marginal product into its dollar value (as shown in column 5 of the table). We call the marginal product generated by an additional unit of input times the price of the output the **value of the marginal product**. (This value is also sometimes referred to as the *marginal revenue product.*) For example, suppose that the marginal product of the eighth worker hired by the farm is 8 tons of tomatoes, and the going price for tomatoes is $2,000 per ton. Then the value of the marginal product of that worker would be $16,000.

value of the marginal product
the marginal product generated by an additional unit of input times the price of the output

TABLE 16-1 Labor productivity and cost

(1)	(2)	(3)	(4)	(5)	(6)	(7)
# of workers (L)	Marginal product of labor*	Tomatoes produced (Y)	Price ($) of tomatoes (P)	Value ($) of marginal product†	Annual wage ($) (W)	Marginal profit ($)††
0	0 tons/worker	0 tons	2,000 per ton	0	20,000	—
1	15	15	2,000	30,000	20,000	10,000
2	14	29	2,000	28,000	20,000	8,000
3	13	42	2,000	26,000	20,000	6,000
4	12	54	2,000	24,000	20,000	4,000
5	11	65	2,000	22,000	20,000	2,000
6	10	75	2,000	20,000	20,000	0
7	9	84	2,000	18,000	20,000	−2,000
8	8	92	2,000	16,000	20,000	−4,000
9	7	99	2,000	14,000	20,000	−6,000

* MPL = change of Y / change in L

† VMPL = P × MPL

†† VMPL − W

To improve your understanding of how to calculate the marginal product of labor and marginal revenue, try the online interactive graphing tutorial.

For a competitive firm, the price of the output is always going to be the same. This implies that the value of the marginal product decreases for each additional worker, because the value of the output stays constant while the marginal product of labor decreases.

As you can see in the table, hiring three workers definitely makes sense for the farm. The third worker produces $26,000 of tomatoes but costs the farmer only $20,000. Therefore, hiring the third worker yields a marginal profit (column 7) of $6,000. Hiring the next two also makes sense for the farm: Each adds more revenue than what he is paid in wages.

When should the farmer stop hiring workers? A competitive firm should keep hiring as long as the value of the marginal product is greater than or equal to the marginal cost. In our example, the tomato farmer should hire the sixth worker, whose value of marginal product is $20,000. It should not hire the seventh worker, though, who adds only $18,000—an amount less than the extra cost of the worker's $20,000 in wages.

Figure 16-2 shows in graph form the relationship between the value of the marginal product and the number of farm workers hired. The table in panel A shows the values of the marginal product for each worker, taken from Table 16-1. Panel B plots these numbers onto a graph. You can see that the curve formed by plotting the value of the marginal product for workers is downward-sloping, due to the diminishing marginal product of each additional worker. What is the profit-maximizing quantity of labor that the firm decides to hire? We find the answer by seeing where the value of the marginal product of labor intersects the market-wage level. At that point, the value of the last worker's marginal product is greater than or equal to marginal profit.

Note that at any given wage, there is only one profit-maximizing quantity of labor. As wages rise or fall, firms should adjust the quantity of labor they demand. We can plot this profit-maximizing quantity for a variety of wages, and generate a whole demand curve. This demand curve *looks* exactly the same as the VMP curve: At each point along

FIGURE 16-2

Value of the marginal product and the demand curve for labor

(A) Value of the marginal product

Labor (# workers)	VMPL ($)
1	30,000
2	28,000
3	26,000
4	24,000
5	22,000
6	20,000
7	18,000
8	16,000
9	14,000

(B) VMPL equals labor demand

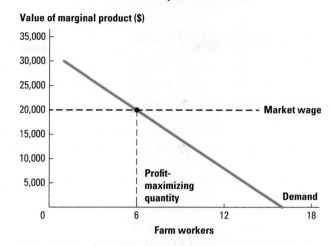

The value of the marginal product of labor decreases with the number of workers hired. The quantity of labor demanded at any given wage is the quantity at which the value of the marginal product of labor equals the wage. The result is a downward-sloping demand curve, with the quantity of labor demanded increasing as the wage decreases.

the curve the wage is equal to the VMP of the last worker hired, and therefore corresponds to a point on the VMP curve.

The curve shown in Figure 16-2 is just one demand curve—the demand curve for the tomato farmer. It's straightforward, though, to find the labor demand curve for the entire market: Add up the quantities of labor demanded by all firms in the market, just as we did with the demand for consumer goods in Chapter 3.

Supply of labor

LO 16.3 Graph the supply curve for a factor of production, and explain what determines the supply of labor.

As in all markets, the demand for labor tells only half the story. Ultimately, the equilibrium quantity and wage are determined by the interaction of demand and supply. The supply of labor is more complicated than the supply of most goods and services, but is still driven by a basic trade-off between the costs and benefits of supplying labor to firms.

Consider the choice made by an individual worker—say, a farm worker in California—who is deciding how many hours to work each week. The main benefit of working is earning a certain wage for every hour of work. Workers can choose to work a lot to earn more money, or they could choose to pass up that chance in order to have more time off.

Now, what about the cost side of the trade-off? The "cost" to an individual of supplying her labor is more difficult to calculate than the benefit. Because the worker doesn't need to buy any inputs to "produce" an hour of labor, we can't directly compare the worker's cost of supplying labor to a firm's cost of production. Instead, we need to *think about the opportunity cost* of supplying another hour of labor. If you work an extra hour, you give up the chance to spend that hour doing something else—going for a run, checking Facebook, doing your laundry. Economists usually categorize all nonwork activities under the term *leisure.* Although they may not seem relaxing or fun, doing chores around the house or errands in town are usually classified as leisure. The cost of working is therefore the forgone opportunity to enjoy leisure.

POTENTIALLY CONFUSING

For simplicity's sake, we talk about people deciding to supply their labor from hour to hour. Of course, in the real world, individuals usually can't set their own hours. A worker can't usually tell the boss that he wants to work 39 or 41 hours this week instead of 40. For an individual, real labor-supply decisions are often whether to work full-time, part-time, or not at all, and whether to work overtime or take a second job. It turns out, though, that over an extended period and a large group of workers, the *total* labor supply is quite flexible, and analyzing changes in average hours in fact captures most of the action. We'll continue to talk about workers choosing hours, but you should keep in mind that labor-supply decisions can involve a broader range of choices.

There is also another kind of opportunity cost associated with the choice to work for a particular employer. A person who decides to work an extra hour on a farm gives up the opportunity to spend that hour working at another paying job—say, as a construction worker or bartender. In deciding whether the opportunity cost of not working that other job outweighs the benefits of more farm work, the worker will have to consider not only the wages each other job offers, but also any other perks of each job. Workers value many benefits like health insurance, a pleasant work environment, and the chance to learn new skills. One job, offered by the tourism board of Queensland, Australia, offered a cost-benefit package unusually heavy on the benefits. For more on this dream job, see the From Another Angle box "The best job in the world."

FROM ANOTHER ANGLE

The best job in the world

In 2009, the tourism board of Queensland, Australia, advertised the "best job in the world"—being a "caretaker" of the beautiful Hamilton Island on the Great Barrier Reef. The caretaker would be paid 150,000 Australian dollars (around $110,000) to sunbathe, snorkel, and relax in a rent-free multimillion-dollar home. In return, he or she would be responsible for talking with reporters and blogging about adventures on the island. Many people would have done "the best job in the world" for free. *To learn more, continue reading by scanning the QR code near the end of the chapter or by going online.*

The decision to supply another hour of labor depends on the trade-off between the benefits of an hour of work (the wage plus any other perks) and the opportunity cost (lost time for leisure or other kinds of work). If the benefits outweigh the costs, we would expect a person to work an additional hour. This logic holds up to the point where the benefit of another hour of work exactly equals the opportunity cost. At that point, the worker becomes indifferent between spending the next hour on work or leisure.

What happens to the quantity of labor supplied if wages go up? In most markets, when price increases, so does quantity supplied. It makes sense then that when higher wages are being offered, the benefits of work go up, people will want to work more, and the quantity of labor supplied will increase.

The relationship is also true for *all of the workers* in the market. As wages increase, more people find that the benefits of working are greater than the costs, and so the number of people who are willing to supply labor increases. This relationship is shown in the labor-supply curve drawn in Figure 16-3. The market labor-supply curve is formed by adding up all of the individual labor-supply curves.

The price and income effects. There is one important feature of the labor-supply curve, however, that makes it different from other supply curves. While higher wages generally increase the quantity of labor supplied, this is not always true. A higher wage increases the benefit of an additional hour of work, but it also, less obviously, increases the *opportunity cost* of working.

To see why, we have to go back to the individual decision to supply labor. The key to figuring out why opportunity costs increase is the fact that leisure is usually more enjoyable when we have money to spend. If your wages go up, you have more money, so you might prefer to spend that extra hour using some of that money to enjoy your leisure time. Indeed, if you are now getting paid more per hour, you might decide that you'd rather work *fewer* hours. If this is the case, a wage increase might actually *reduce* the supply of labor.

Economists have two terms to describe the competing incentives that influence a worker's response to a change in the wage. The *price effect* describes the increase in labor supply in response to the higher wage that can be earned for each hour of work. The *income effect* describes the decrease in labor supply due the greater demand for leisure caused by a higher income.

We can see the influence of the income and price effects on labor supply decisions in Figure 16-4. This analysis is similar to that of the income and substitution effects we saw in the "Consumer Behavior" chapter when considering purchasing decisions under a budget constraint. In this case, workers are constrained by the amount of time they have available. There are 8,760 hours in a (non-leap) year; assuming that workers will spend some portion of that time sleeping and eating, let's say there are roughly 5,000 hours available for work per year. Time translates into income through work and wages. At an initial wage rate of $10 per hour, a worker faces a budget constraint represented by the dark green line in the left graph in panel A. He can choose to earn nothing and have 5,000 hours of leisure a year, choose to earn $50,000 and have no leisure time, or choose

FIGURE 16-3
Supply of labor

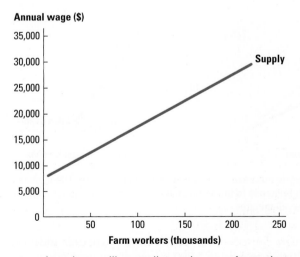

A producer will generally supply more of a good or service as its price rises. The same rule applies to workers who supply their labor, yielding the familiar upward-sloping supply curve.

FIGURE 16-4

Income and price effects of a wage increase

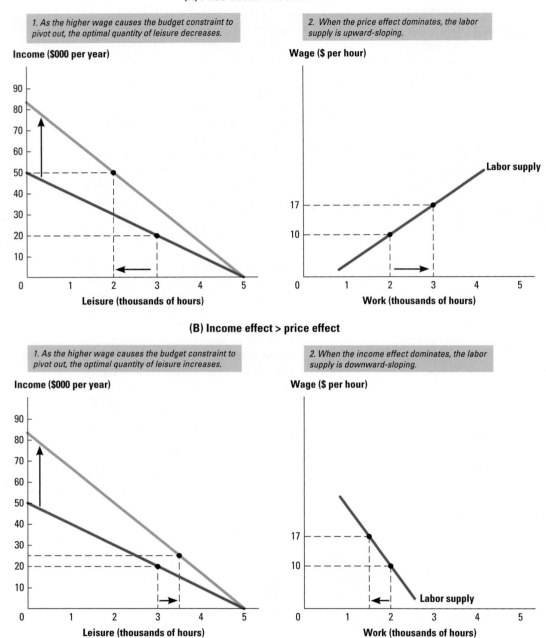

(A) Price effect > income effect

1. As the higher wage causes the budget constraint to pivot out, the optimal quantity of leisure decreases.

2. When the price effect dominates, the labor supply is upward-sloping.

Income ($000 per year)

Wage ($ per hour)

Labor supply

Leisure (thousands of hours)

Work (thousands of hours)

(B) Income effect > price effect

1. As the higher wage causes the budget constraint to pivot out, the optimal quantity of leisure increases.

2. When the income effect dominates, the labor supply is downward-sloping.

Income ($000 per year)

Wage ($ per hour)

Labor supply

Leisure (thousands of hours)

Work (thousands of hours)

The price effect causes labor supply to increase in response to a wage increase. The income effect causes labor supply to decrease in response to the same change. Whether total labor supply goes up or down depends on which effect dominates.

any point in between. Suppose that based on a particular individual's preferences, he chooses to earn $20,000 and have 3,000 hours of leisure. When the wage increases, the budget line pivots outward. Let's say the wage increases from $10 an hour to $17 an hour (quite a raise!). Now, the worker's choice is on the light green line that runs between no income with 5,000 hours of leisure and $85,000 with no leisure time per week.

Panel A shows how a worker reacts to this wage increase when the *price effect* is bigger than the income effect. This worker responds to the new budget constraint by choosing to earn $51,000 and have only 2,000 hours of leisure. In other words, by supplying 1,000 more labor hours, the worker earns $17,000 more (at the new wage). Here, an increase in the wage has caused an increase in the amount of labor supplied. The right graph translates the leisure chosen on the left into a labor supply curve, which shows the hours of labor the worker supplies at any given wage rate. The fact that the price effect outweighs the income effect is reflected in the upward-sloping labor supply curve.

Panel B shows what happens when the *income effect* is bigger than the price effect. This worker responds to the same wage increase by choosing to earn $25,500 and have 3,500 hours of leisure time. Here, an increase in the wage has caused the worker to supply 500 *fewer* hours of labor. When the income effect outweighs the price effect, the labor supply curve slopes downward.

Either of these two situations is a rational response, depending on whether the individual in question gets more utility from additional leisure or additional money. These preferences determine the relative sizes of the price and income effects.

Which of these effects dominates in the real world? While the income effect certainly plays a role in decision making, in most cases the price effect will outweigh it. In general, people respond to higher wages by wanting to work more. So, for the rest of this chapter, we will use the usual upward-sloping supply curve for labor, indicating that the labor supply increases as the wage increases.

Reaching equilibrium

LO 16.4 Explain how to find the equilibrium price and quantity for a factor of production.

A worker deciding how many hours to work can be represented with an individual labor-supply curve. A farm choosing the profit-maximizing number of employees can be represented with a firm-level demand curve. In order to see how the labor market works as a whole, however, we need to add up all the supply curves of individual workers and the demand curves of individual firms to find market level supply and demand.

The process for identifying the equilibrium wage and quantity in the labor market should look very familiar. As in all competitive markets, the equilibrium is found at the point where the supply and demand curves intersect. Figure 16-5 shows the equilibrium in a market for tomato-farm workers in California. At this point, the quantity of labor supplied equals the quantity demanded by tomato farmers in California at the market wage. Farm workers get $20,000 per year, and farmers hire 125,000 workers.

The labor market reaches equilibrium through the same process as any other market, assuming that both wages and the quantity of labor can adjust freely in response to incentives. For instance, suppose the wage for farm workers is $11.50 per hour (roughly $23,000 per year, at 40 hours of work per week for 50 weeks per year). At that price, given the value of the marginal product of labor, farmers want to hire 100,000 workers. However, 163,500 workers want to work at that wage, given their opportunity cost of labor. Because the quantity of labor supplied is greater than the quantity demanded, the market is out of balance. Some workers who want to work will be left without a job, or at least with fewer working hours than they want. In other words, at that price there is a surplus of farm labor.

If you were a farm owner, *how would you respond to this situation?* Knowing that there are plenty of underemployed and willing workers out there, you might offer a lower wage. If you can get the work done at a lower cost, you probably won't complain. When the wage falls from $11.50 to $10 per hour, the quantity of workers demanded by farm owners will increase. Some workers will be willing to work for $10 per hour, but others

FIGURE 16-5
Labor market equilibrium

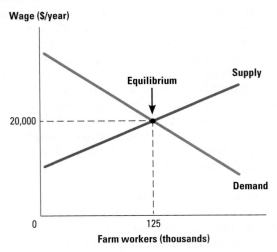

In a competitive labor market, the price of labor (that is, the wage) is determined by the intersection of the supply and demand curves for labor. Here, the labor market reaches equilibrium at a wage of $20,000 per year. At that point 125,000 workers are hired.

will find that the opportunity cost of work outweighs the benefits. The latter group will be unwilling to work for $10. Thus, the quantity of labor supplied will decrease, while the quantity demanded will increase, bringing the market into equilibrium.

If wages drop below the market equilibrium level, the opposite will happen: Farmers will demand more labor than workers are willing to supply. Farmers will have to offer higher wages to attract the workers they need, increasing the quantity of labor supplied and decreasing the quantity demanded. This process will continue until the wage brings the supply of labor into balance with demand.

> To improve your understanding of how to find the labor market equilibrium, try the online interactive graphing tutorial.

Shifts in supply and demand

LO 16.5 Use graphs to demonstrate the effect of a shift in supply or demand and describe what causes these curves to shift.

Just as in the supply and demand model in Chapter 3, the supply and demand curves for labor can shift right or left with changes in nonprice determinants. In the labor market, such factors include technology, labor market regulations, and other external forces.

For example, many of California's farm workers are in the United States illegally—most, by some accounts. Occasionally the authorities implement a crackdown on immigration, increasing the strictness of border controls with Mexico. We can think of this as an external change that decreases the supply of workers at any given wage level. To see why, we first need to ask, *How should we expect Mexican prospective farm workers to respond to stricter border controls?* The greater chance of getting caught at the border and deported, after a dangerous and expensive trip, decreases the expected value of supplying their labor to California's farmers. Faced with this choice, some workers will stay home. Others will make the trip, but will be turned back at the border.

Thus, stricter border controls will cause the total supply of labor to be lower at any given wage than it was under more lax enforcement. We can represent this decrease in

376

the supply of labor by shifting the entire supply curve to the left, as shown in Figure 16-6. The equilibrium point slides up along the demand curve, from E_1 to E_2 in the figure. At that new equilibrium point, the quantity of labor supplied is lower and wages are higher.

In the early 2000s, there was in fact a crackdown on immigration in California. But wages of California farm workers did not rise during this period—at least, no more than wages on average rose throughout the country. Why not? Does this real-world data mean our model is wrong? Not necessarily. There could have been another factor at work, shifting the demand curve to the right at the same time. For instance, consider *how farm owners might respond* to an immigration crackdown that was causing an increase in wages. As we saw earlier, firms can sometimes substitute one factor of production for another. Faced with a higher cost of labor, farmers might have decided they could maximize profits by employing fewer workers and investing in more farm machinery instead.

Adding machinery can vastly improve the productivity of a small group of farm workers. However, the marginal product of labor diminishes very quickly as the number of workers increases. Once you have the few workers you need to operate the machines, adding more workers adds little to the quantity harvested. Such a reduction in the marginal product of labor would decrease the quantity of labor demanded at any given wage, shifting the entire demand curve to the left. As Figure 16-7 shows, the equilibrium point slides down the supply curve to a new equilibrium point (E_3 in the figure) at a lower quantity and a lower wage. Note that at the new equilibrium point, there are fewer total farm workers than before the immigration crackdown (85,000 compared to 125,000). Wages, however, have returned to almost the same level as before.

This scenario has played out several times in the last half century. Immigration crackdowns threatened to raise the price of farm labor, which led farmers to increase their

To improve your understanding of shifts in labor supply and demand, try the online interactive graphing tutorial.

FIGURE 16-6

Decrease in the labor supply

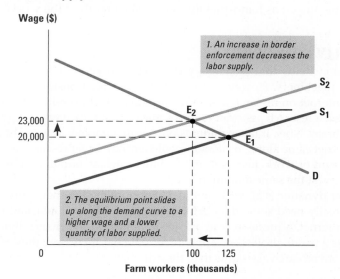

When an external change in border controls causes a change in workers' trade-offs, the labor supply curve shifts. In this case, stricter controls shift the curve to the left, decreasing the equilibrium number of farm workers supplied from 125,000 to 100,000 and increasing the equilibrium wage from $20,000 to $23,000.

FIGURE 16-7

Decrease in the demand for labor

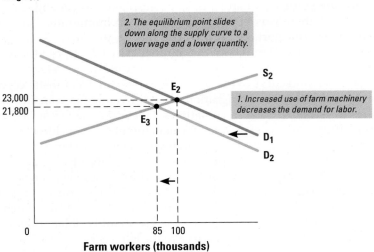

When increased use of farm machinery decreases
the marginal product of labor, the labor demand
curve shifts left. The equilibrium number of workers
falls from 100,000 to 85,000, and the equilibrium wage
falls from $23,000 to $21,800.

use of machines to reduce the labor intensity of farm work. Increased wages also provided an incentive for firms to develop new, more effective technologies for planting and harvesting crops, reducing the number of workers needed even further. Some of the cutting and sorting machines that are used today on tomato farms allow farm owners to produce the same output as hand-picking with only a tenth of the workers.

POTENTIALLY CONFUSING

Popular opinion holds that technology displaces workers. This is sometimes true, as with farm machinery. However, it is not always true. Consider, for example, the effect of the Internet on research assistants' productivity. In pre-Internet days, when a professor asked a research assistant to find some data, it took days of digging through texts at the library. Now, it takes minutes on a search engine. You might assume that when the Internet came along, professors could employ fewer research assistants to do the same amount of work, just as farm machinery means farmers can employ fewer workers to harvest the same amount of crops.

But another dynamic is at work. In the days before the Internet, a professor would have had to really need some data before she paid a research assistant to search for it. With the Internet, a professor can ask for data just on the chance that it might be interesting. As a result, professors' appetite for data has increased; they often demand more labor from research assistants than they did before.

Determinants of labor demand and supply

We've just discussed two examples of the underlying determinants of labor supply and demand—immigration policy and technological innovation. A variety of other external factors can also cause the curves to shift.

Determinants of labor demand. In thinking about the underlying determinants of the labor demand curve, the key is to remember that demand is determined by the value of the marginal product of labor. Any event that increases the value of the marginal product will increase demand. Any event that decreases the value of the marginal product will decrease demand. In general, many shifts in the labor demand curve can be traced to three determinants: supply of other factors, technology, and output prices.

Supply of other factors. The marginal product of labor itself may change, due to a *change in the supply of other factors.* For instance, suppose the supply of gasoline falls, pushing the price of gasoline up and reducing the use of gas-guzzling farm machinery. This could increase the marginal product of farm workers.

Technology. Changes in technology can also affect the marginal product of labor. Often, changes in technology are *labor-augmenting,* meaning that they increase the marginal product of labor. When the marginal product of labor increases, labor demand also increases. Other technology changes, such as tomato-picking machinery, are *labor-saving,* meaning that they reduce the marginal product of labor. When the marginal product of labor decreases, labor demand also decreases.

Output prices. Finally, labor demand can be influenced by output prices. Suppose a recession decreases the demand for fresh tomatoes, lowering the price. Even if farm workers' marginal product stays the same, the *value* of that marginal product decreases, so the labor demand curve shifts left. Likewise, if the price of tomatoes increases, the value of the marginal product of labor increases, and the labor demand curve shifts right.

Determinants of labor supply. In thinking about the determinants of *labor supply,* the key is to remember that at any given wage, the supply of labor is determined by the *number of workers* and the *opportunity cost of providing their labor.* Changes that increase the opportunity cost of work or decrease the number of workers will decrease the labor supply, shifting the supply curve left. Changes that decrease the opportunity cost of work or increase the number of workers will increase the labor supply, shifting the supply curve right. The determinants of labor supply include culture, population, and other opportunities.

Culture. One determinant of labor supply relates to *cultural attitudes* toward work. Today, for example, it is far more accepted for women to work outside the home than it was 50 years ago. Similarly, over the last century, a decline in racial discrimination has opened up new professional opportunities to people of color, allowing them to supply their labor in areas that were previously closed to them. Some commentators believe that the long hours Americans work, in comparison to many other countries, is attributable to the idea that hard work signifies social status: If you are constantly busy, you must be an important person. If these cultural influences are true, we should expect Americans to supply more hours of labor at any given wage.

Population. Another way in which the supply of labor can change is if the working-age population changes. The effect of population on labor supply is straightforward: When there are more potential workers, all else equal, the total labor supply will be higher.

Change in population can come about through changes in birth or death rates—for instance, the "baby boom" that followed World War II. The "boomer" generation entered the workforce in the 1960s and 1970s, swelling the labor supply. As the boomers reach retirement age during this decade, the labor supply may shrink, causing problems for certain industries.

Immigration into a country (or emigration out of a country) has similar effects on the labor supply. For a more nuanced discussion of the economic effects of immigration, read the What Do You Think? box "Should the United States be a country of immigrants?"

WHAT DO YOU THINK?

Should the United States be a country of immigrants?

The economy of the United States—arguably, more than any other economy in the world—has been shaped by huge waves of workers emigrating from other countries (see Figure 16-8).

German farmers settled the Midwest in the 1850s. Chinese workers built the transcontinental railroad in the 1880s. Immigrants from southern and eastern Europe powered northeastern factories during the early decades of the twentieth century.

However, millions more are turned away. To work legally in the United States, non-citizens need a permit called a visa. Unless you have rare and valuable skills—such as being a top baseball player, scientist, or doctor—you won't be guaranteed to get one. Faced with this difficulty, many people try to enter the country and work without a visa: An estimated 8 million people are working in the U.S. today without one.

Immigration stirs powerful feelings. Arguments stem from disagreements about whether immigration is economically good or bad for those already in the country. Often, immigrants are willing to work for less money than native-born workers. This is good for businesses, which can hire cheaper labor, and for consumers, who can purchase goods and services at lower cost as a result. Economists usually argue that immigration promotes efficiency and economic growth by allowing resources (in this case, people and skills) to go where they will be most productive. Therefore, most economists believe that in the long run immigration will create new jobs. However, this is not much consolation to a local worker who has lost his job and now needs to look for a new one—perhaps in another industry or another part of the country.

The problem is complicated because these disagreements are driven not just by economic concerns, but also by cultural and philosophical attitudes. Some believe that it's worth paying higher prices so that more Americans can get jobs at a slightly higher wage. Others wonder whether it is fair to withhold the ladder of opportunity that the ancestors of current citizens may have climbed up. As long as the United States continues to be a land of opportunity, attracting immigrants from around the world, this debate will surely continue.

What do you think?

1. Does the government have a responsibility to address the negative effects of immigration on native-born workers who are affected by it?
2. Should everyone who wants to work in the U.S. be legally allowed to do so? Where should the line be drawn, and why?

Sources: http://www.usafis.org/green_card/prev_years.asp; http://www.dhs.gov/files/statistics/publications/LPR09.shtm.

Other opportunities. Because the decision to work depends on the opportunity cost of labor, a *change in the next-best opportunity* available to workers can increase or decrease the labor supply in a particular industry. For instance, better wages and working conditions in retail or service jobs could lead workers to supply less labor to farms. Similarly, a slump in one industry could increase the relative attractiveness of another industry, increasing the quantity of labor supplied in the latter.

What's missing? Human capital

LO 16.6 Define human capital, and justify its importance in the labor market.

There is not a single market with a single equilibrium for all labor in an economy. Baseball players are not paid the same wage as farm workers, after all. But even within

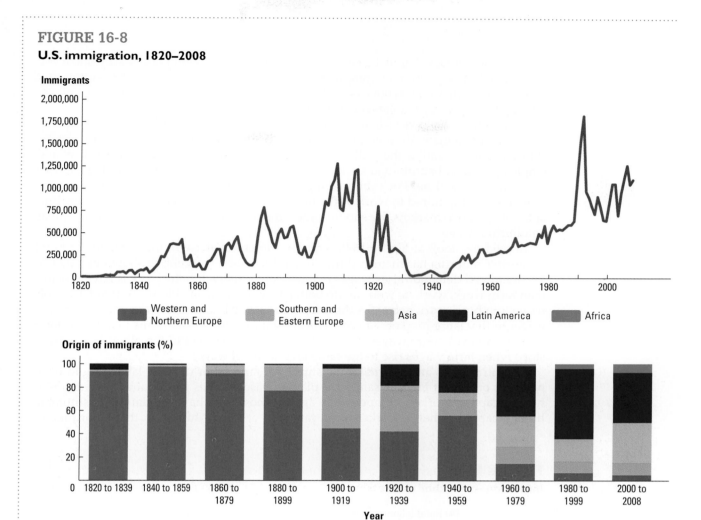

FIGURE 16-8

U.S. immigration, 1820–2008

Immigrants

Sources: http://www.migrationinformation.org/datahub/charts/historic.1.shtml; U.S. Department of Homeland Security; http://www.dhs.gov/files/statistics/publications/LPR08.shtm.

specific markets, like the market for baseball players, workers are not paid the same wage. Albert Pujols, the baseball player from the beginning of the chapter, earns 24 times the salary as center fielder Peter Bourjos, who plays a very similar position for the same team. What causes this difference?

What's missing from this picture is the idea of **human capital**, the set of skills, knowledge, experience, and talent that determine the productivity of workers. In taking courses at school, you are acquiring human capital. Human capital determines the productivity of workers. It is so crucial in determining how labor markets work that economists sometimes consider it the fourth, and possibly the most important, factor of production. Workers differ from one another, and are paid differently, because they have different amounts and types of human capital that allow them to be more or less productive than other workers at various tasks.

Is the difference between a highly paid player such as Albert Pujols and other less "productive" players due more to natural talent, or personal characteristics, or hard work, or experience? The truth is, it's hard to say. Human capital can encompass all of these considerations.

Some types of human capital make workers more productive at a wide variety of jobs—for instance, having a strong work ethic, being good with numbers, or having a knack for getting along with people. Other types of human capital are specific to a

human capital the set of skills, knowledge, experience, and talent that determine the productivity of workers

381

particular job or task. For instance, going to medical school won't necessarily make you a better plumber, painter, or computer technician. Top professional athletes often find that their human capital is not easy to transfer: They may be amazingly good as a player but hopeless as a coach, manager, or television personality.

Human capital allows us to understand that what we call the labor market is actually a collection of a many different, interconnected labor markets for workers with similar skills. The more similar the skills required to do any two jobs, the more workers and employers can substitute one skill set for the other, and the more connected the two labor markets will be. For example, many farm laborers in California may have the human capital required to work in the hotel industry instead. When labor is substitutable between two markets, we should expect the two markets to pay the same or similar equilibrium wage.

To see why, look at Figure 16-9. Suppose that an increase in the demand for hotel rooms in California has increased the demand for hotel workers, as shown in panel A. The increased demand raises wages in the hotel industry. If hotel work is paying better than farm work, workers who can do both jobs will be inclined to work at hotels. Their move into hotel work decreases the supply of farm labor, as shown in panel B, raising wages in that labor market. Workers will continue moving from farms to hotels as long as they can earn better wages by switching from one market to the other. The process stops when farm wages rise to the same level as hotel wages.

In contrast, ups and downs in the supply of farm labor or hotel labor should have no effect on Albert Pujols's salary for playing baseball. His job requires very different human capital. Workers compete only against those who have similar or substitutable human capital. When a worker has a rare skill or talent, supply in that labor market

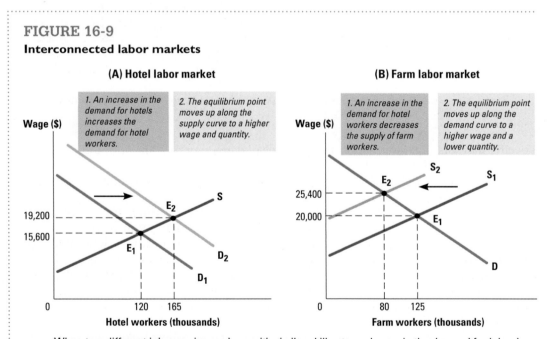

FIGURE 16-9
Interconnected labor markets

(A) Hotel labor market

1. An increase in the demand for hotels increases the demand for hotel workers.

2. The equilibrium point moves up along the supply curve to a higher wage and quantity.

Wage ($)

19,200
15,600

E_2
E_1
S
D_2
D_1

0   120   165

Hotel workers (thousands)

(B) Farm labor market

1. An increase in the demand for hotel workers decreases the supply of farm workers.

2. The equilibrium point moves up along the demand curve to a higher wage and a lower quantity.

Wage ($)

25,400
20,000

E_2
E_1
S_2
S_1
D

0   80   125

Farm workers (thousands)

When two different jobs require workers with similar skill sets, a change in the demand for labor in one industry can affect the supply of labor in another. When the demand for hotel workers increases, as shown in panel A, workers who might have been indifferent between farm work and hotel work will shift toward hotel work. Their move to a different labor market will decrease the number of farm workers, shifting the farm labor supply curve left, as shown in panel B.

is low. When the rare skill contributes to the production of something that consumers value highly, like hitting home runs, the value of the marginal product is high. Low supply and high demand leads to the equilibrium outcome we see in the Major League Baseball labor market: few workers, and high wages.

✓ CONCEPT CHECK

❏ What is the relationship between the value of the marginal product of labor, the wage, and the demand for labor? **[LO 16.2]**

❏ Under what circumstances might an increase in the wage decrease the labor supply? **[LO 16.3]**

❏ What happens to the equilibrium wage and quantity of labor when the demand for labor increases, holding all else equal? **[LO 16.4]**

❏ Which way does the labor supply curve shift after a population increase, holding all else equal? **[LO 16.5]**

❏ What are some ways that people can acquire human capital? **[LO 16.6]**

Land and Capital

We now turn from labor to the other two main factors of production: land and capital. If you were a farmer, would you be willing to pay as much for an acre of land in California's Sonoran Desert as you would for an acre of land in California's super-fertile Central Valley? If you owned a baseball team, would you pay as much for a stadium located 50 miles outside the city as you would for one in the heart of downtown? In both cases, one type of land has greater marginal productivity than the other. We can expect producers to pay more for land with higher productivity.

As these scenarios suggest, we can think about the markets for land and capital in a way that is very similar to our analysis of labor markets—with some differences. In this section we'll examine a few features of the markets for land and capital that make them unique. We'll also look at how ownership of the different factors of production determines a person's income.

Capitalists: Who are they?

Capital is a tricky concept. Sometimes the word *capital* can mean physical capital, such as machinery. At other times it can mean financial capital, as in "She needs some start-up capital for her new business." Then, of course, there's human capital, which we discussed earlier.

These uses of the term are related. The reason the word *capital* sometimes refers to financial assets is that money can be invested in a business, which then uses the money to buy physical capital. Thus a "capitalist" is someone who owns physical capital. Sometimes that ownership is direct, as in ownership of a factory. Often it is indirect, as in ownership of shares of stock, which represent partial ownership of a company and its physical capital.

In general, when people talk about investing, they mean that they have lent their money to someone who will use it to buy physical capital. Thus, anyone who puts money into the stock market, holds bonds or stocks, or opens a retirement account owns capital. This actually represents a sizable share of the population—in the United States, just over half of Americans qualify as "capitalists" by this definition.[1]

Markets for land and capital

LO 16.7 Describe the similarities and differences between the markets for land and capital and the market for labor.

Before we say anything else about the markets for land and capital, we should note one important difference from labor markets: When a firm wants to use land or capital, it has two choices—to buy or rent. When we talk about the price of land or capital, then, we need to distinguish between the rental price and the purchase price. The **rental price** is what a producer pays to use a factor of production for a certain period or task. The **purchase price** is what a producer pays to gain permanent ownership of a factor of production. The rental price and the purchase price are both important concepts for understanding markets for land and capital.

rental price the price paid to use a factor of production for a certain period or task

purchase price the price paid to gain permanent ownership of a factor of production

Rental markets. The rental prices of land and capital are determined in the same way as the wage in a labor market. When Walmart hires a full-time cashier, Walmart is actually "renting" the cashier's labor for 40 hours a week. Walmart also is renting when it leases a new building or borrows money. In the case of borrowing, the rental price of capital is the interest paid on loans.

As with labor, the demand for land or capital is determined by the value of the marginal product of each unit. No firm will rent land or machinery that contributes less to the firm's output than its rental cost. On the other side of the market, the quantity of land or capital supplied depends on the other opportunities available for using them. The market equilibrium price and quantity in the rental market is determined by the intersection of supply and demand, just as in any other market.

In the markets for factors of production, economists use the phrase **economic rent** to describe the gains that workers and owners of capital receive from supplying their labor or machinery in factor markets. In the rental markets shown in Figure 16-10, the area above the supply curve but below the equilibrium rental price is economic rent. It represents the rental price of a factor of production minus the cost of supplying it. If

economic rent the gains that workers and owners of capital receive from supplying their labor or machinery in factor markets

FIGURE 16-10

Economic rent in rental markets for land and capital

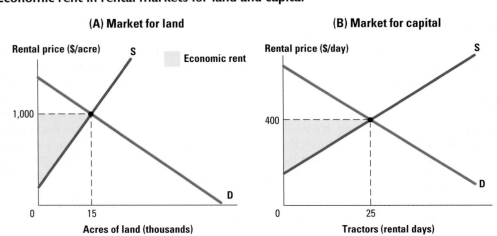

Just as in the labor market, the rental markets for land and capital reach an equilibrium price and quantity at the point where the supply curve intersects the demand curve. The area above the supply curve and below equilibrium rental price is called *economic rent.*

Albert Pujols is willing to play baseball for $9 million, the $3 million dollar difference between this willingness to play and his actual salary of $12 million is economic rent earned by Pujols.

The shaded area in the figure may seem familiar to you: In Chapter 3 (and elsewhere), we identified this as *producer surplus*. The concept is the same, but in the markets for factors of production, we use the term *economic rent*. Later, we'll discuss what role these gains (as part of something called the factor distribution of income) play in the economy.

POTENTIALLY CONFUSING

Be careful not to confuse the term *economic rent* with the everyday usage of *rent*. The everyday use has a related but more general meaning: the money paid to landlords for the privilege of using their land or capital. Sometimes, economic rent and the traditional usage of the word *rent* overlap. For example, when a contractor rents a tool (a capital good) to frame in a new house he's building for sale, the person that rents out that tool also gets some economic rent from the transaction.

Purchase markets. Renting land or capital allows a firm to use it for a certain period without worrying about its long-term value. In contrast, buying land or capital requires potential owners to think about an asset's long-run productivity. To determine the price they should pay for land or capital, potential buyers must forecast what its marginal product is likely to be over time. They can then assess the value of the expected future flows of income in order to compare them to the cost of the asset. (We explore the relevant tools in the chapter on "Time and Uncertainty.") Smart sellers will make similar calculations in order to calculate their own notion of a reasonable price.

The factor distribution of income

Most people own at least one factor of production. If you can work, you own your own labor, which can be rented to producers for a wage. Many people also own some capital or land. Ownership of these productive resources determines your income, which in turn determines your ability to consume goods and services. Who owns what, and how much income they receive from it, are therefore crucial questions.

Economists refer to the pattern of income that people derive from different factors of production as the *factor distribution of income.* In other words, the factor distribution of income shows how much income people get from labor compared to land and capital. Figure 16-11 shows the U.S. factor distribution of income. In the United States, the majority of income—about 70 percent—comes from labor (shown in the figure as "compensation of employees"). Corporate profits, interest, and rent all go to owners of physical capital. Proprietor income represents both the labor and capital factors that proprietors put into their businesses. Perhaps surprisingly, the factor distribution of income hasn't changed much in the last century, despite enormous changes in the economy and technology.

Big inequalities in earnings from the factors of production can sometimes seem unfair. Writing in the nineteenth century as new factories were transforming the economic landscape of Europe, Karl Marx unleashed his fury at the fact that workers earned so little relative to factory owners. To Marx, the owners of capital exploited those who earn their income through labor, and he urged workers to revolt against the capitalist system. Marx's ideas inspired some of the biggest political upheavals of the last two centuries,

FIGURE 16-11

The factor distribution of income In the United States, the majority of income comes from compensation for labor. Corporate profits, interest, and rent all go to owners of physical capital, while proprietor income goes to individual business owners for both the labor and capital put into their businesses.

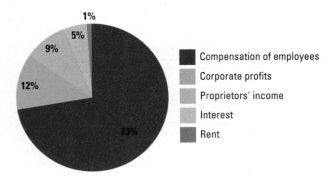

- Compensation of employees
- Corporate profits
- Proprietors' income
- Interest
- Rent

Source: Bureau of Economic Analysis, National Income and Product Accounts.

including revolutions in Europe, Russia, and China fought in the name of giving more power to workers. In each case, though, capitalism eventually returned as the dominant economic system.

The triumph of capitalism doesn't mean that all policy debates have ended. Marx's judgment was *normative*. His ideas differ from the *factual* analysis in this chapter of how income is determined in an efficient, competitive market—by the productivity of the land, labor, or capital that people own. That productivity, in turn, is defined by how much consumers will pay for the output the factors produce. Our aim is to describe how competitive factor markets allocate resources. Our analysis does not imply that the existing factor distribution of income is, or is not, *fair* in a broader sense. You have to draw on your own values to answer for yourself whether it is right or wrong that Albert Pujols and other professional athletes earn far more than a farm worker, or why owners of certain types of capital earn more than others.

For one example of a debate on the question of how productivity is rewarded, see the What Do You Think? box "Work, wages, and social value."

WHAT DO YOU THINK?

Work, wages, and social value

In most professions, people are comfortable with the idea that workers are paid according to their productivity. For example, we tend to accept that exceptionally talented professional baseball (and football, basketball, and hockey) players will earn more than their teammates, that lawyers who regularly win tough cases will charge more than other lawyers, and that salespeople who bring in lots of revenue to a firm will be rewarded accordingly. In general, we see higher pay as both a reward and an incentive for higher productivity.

In some professions, however, pay for performance may seem out of keeping with the nature of the work. For example, the idea that a pastor should be paid for each new member she brings into a congregation might strike some people as odd. That's not to say it doesn't happen, though. Looking at records from United Methodist churches in Oklahoma, researchers at the University of North Carolina found that, on average, pastors received a pay increase equal to 3 percent of the revenues generated by the new members they brought into the church. That is comparable to how much of the salary of Fortune 500 CEOs depends on their own company performance—although the typical pastor's salary is much lower.

Debates over performance pay are especially heated when it comes to teachers. Almost everywhere in the United States, teachers earn a salary that depends mainly on their years of experience. Proponents of performance pay say that teachers should be compensated largely in proportion to the results their students achieve, as measured through standardized tests. They argue that such a system rewards good teachers and encourages them to work hard. Opponents say that performance pay encourages teachers to focus too much on test scores, distracting them from teaching deeper concepts and helping struggling students.

A related debate focuses on the salaries of workers in nonprofit organizations, especially those that assist the poor. Some people argue that rewarding good performance with high salaries attracts the best workers, making nonprofits more effective at doing good for those in need of help. Opponents counter that it is inappropriate for workers in nonprofits to earn so much more than those they serve, and that the resulting income gap can make it difficult for nonprofit workers to understand their clients' situation.

What do you think?

1. Do you think that people should accept performance pay in some professions but not in others?
2. Would performance pay for teachers be less controversial if it were easier to get a more complete picture of performance, in such areas as helping students develop rounded personalities and inspiring learning?
3. Would stronger financial incentives change the fundamental nature of social professions such as teaching and preaching? Might that be a good thing? What might be lost?

Source: http://www.slate.com/id/2258794/.

✓ CONCEPT CHECK

❑ What is the difference between the rental price and the purchase price of capital? **[LO 16.7]**

❑ How is physical capital related to financial capital? **[LO 16.7]**

Real-World Labor Markets

Now that we've looked at all three factors of production, we'll return to labor for the rest of the chapter, to see how the real world looks in relation to the model of perfectly competitive labor markets we outlined above. One important dimension we consider here is the role of government policy. Another is the power of bosses or unions to influence market outcomes. Still another dimension is created by changes in population size. The simple model of perfect competition in labor markets provides an important benchmark, and here we enrich the picture to describe realities that you'll probably encounter throughout your working life.

Minimum wages and efficiency wages

LO 16.8 Identify two reasons why a wage might rise above the market equilibrium, and describe their effect on the labor market.

The model of labor supply and demand we outlined earlier in this chapter does a good job of explaining the most important determinants of wages and gives a reasonably accurate picture of many labor markets. However, two notable exceptions to the model—minimum wages and efficiency wages—can push wage rates above the market equilibrium point.

In the United States, the federal government requires that all employers pay all workers a wage that is at or above a certain minimum rate (in 2012, $7.25 per hour). Some state governments impose higher minimum wages (in 2012, up to $9.04 per hour in the state of Washington). Minimum wages are a controversial topic. Supporters usually argue that a minimum wage is needed protect low-paid workers from ruthless employers and guarantee workers an acceptable standard of living. Opponents see a minimum wage as a form of government interference in the free market, one that raises the cost of doing business, causing unemployment in the process. As economic analysts, how can we weigh these opposing claims?

First, we need to separate positive arguments from normative arguments. Let's start by asking what effect we would expect a minimum-wage law to have on the labor market. Minimum wage laws are examples of price floors, discussed in Chapter 6. Imposing a price floor means the quantity demanded decreases and the quantity supplied increases compared to equilibrium levels. In other words, more people are willing to work than there are jobs available, causing unemployment. This situation is shown in Figure 16-12. Imposing a price floor is good news for the people who keep their jobs, and bad news for the people who were employed at the equilibrium wage but are not employed any more.

However, this analysis assumes that the labor market is perfectly efficient. If the market is already inefficient and the minimum wage is below the equilibrium level, the effect of a minimum wage might not be to cause unemployment. The minimum wage might instead transfer surplus from employers to workers.

The evidence on how minimum wage laws affect the real world is mixed. In some cases, a minimum wage causes some unemployment. In others, the biggest impact is on *who* is employed. Since higher-skilled workers become cheaper relative to low-skilled workers when the minimum wage increases, employers might hire more skilled and experienced workers, and fewer young and unskilled workers. Whether or not you think that result is a good one is a normative question, which we will leave to your own judgment.

efficiency wage
a wage that is deliberately set above the market rate to increase worker productivity

Another reason that wages might rise above market equilibrium is that some employers may voluntarily choose to pay workers more, to increase their productivity. Economists call this arrangement an **efficiency wage**. There are two ways in which

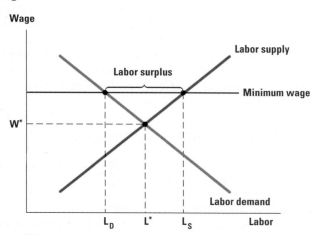

FIGURE 16-12

The minimum wage

When people are willing to supply more labor than firms are willing to hire, the labor market has a surplus of workers, which is also known as unemployment.

an efficiency wage might increase workers' productivity. First, earning more than the market wage gives workers an incentive to stay with the firm. Thus the firm gets to hold onto experienced, well-trained workers, rather than repeatedly having to spend time and resources to train new employees.

The second reason is an extension of the first. If workers have a lot to lose by leaving the firm, they will work hard to avoid getting fired. Efficiency wages make sense when a boss cannot constantly supervise workers—say, a shop owner who visits only a couple of times a week. If a salesperson at the shop receives the market wage, she may take the risk of slacking off, since if she's caught, she can hope to get another job at an equivalent wage. But if the salesperson receives a wage sufficiently larger than the going market rate, even the small probability that the boss might catch her slacking off carries a higher potential cost. She'd be fired from an especially rewarding job.

In the end, workers respond to incentives, and when it becomes more costly to leave or get fired from a job, employees are going to work harder to stay. This is good for both sides. While businesses get more productive workers, employees also get a higher wage. This is why efficiency wages have been used from the first assembly line (Henry Ford offered his workers double the going wage in 1914) to the market for high-powered lawyers today.

That said, efficiency wages are a great deal only for workers who get them. The use of efficiency wages creates unemployment by keeping wages above the equilibrium wage level, similar to the way minimum wage laws can create unemployment. If you have a well-paying job you'll be happy. But if you're unemployed and struggling to find a job, you will probably view the existence of efficiency wages with a wary eye.

Company towns, unions, and labor laws

LO 16.9 Describe several causes of imperfectly competitive labor markets and their effect on workers and employers.

Just as the markets for goods and services aren't always perfectly competitive, neither are labor markets. In some real-world labor markets, employers have market power, pushing wages down to capture more surplus. In others, workers may have market power, pushing wages up. In addition, government regulation of the workplace can impose costs or friction on a market.

Let's first consider the scenario in which employers have market power. Normally, we would call a firm with market power a monopolist or an oligopolist. But because firms are the buyers in this situation (they are buying labor in the labor market), we need a new term. A market in which there is only one buyer but many sellers is called a **monopsony**. Whereas a monopolist can maintain a price *higher* than that in a competitive market, a monopsonistic employer can push wages (that is, the price of labor) *lower* than the competitive level. In fact, the market for professional baseball players was a classic example of monopsony until league regulations changed in the 1970s; to see how this affected the market for professional baseball players, read the Real Life box "Monopsony and competition in professional baseball."

monopsony
a market in which there is only one buyer but many sellers

Sometimes, a firm that is the largest employer in a region, or one of only a few major employers, can gain market power. Historically, such situations arose when a town sprang up around the worksite for a major company. These "company towns" were common in Appalachia, where coal mines or steel plants were the main source of jobs. Often, the company literally owned everything in town, including the grocery store. More recent, less extreme examples include Detroit, with its reliance on the success of the Big Three car companies, and Redmond, Washington, home to Microsoft.

REAL LIFE

Monopsony and competition in professional baseball

Today, professional sports players seem to jump from team to team looking for the highest salary. But that has not always been true. From 1879 until 1976, professional baseball players were bound to their teams by a "reserve clause" in their contracts. That legal clause prevented them from considering offers from other teams. In other words, Major League Baseball was a monopsony.

What would we expect to happen to wages in this situation? *To find out, continue reading by scanning the QR code near the end of the chapter or by going online.*

Workers can also gain market power. When they do, they can push wages higher than the market equilibrium. Gaining market power requires that workers join together to make a collective decision about when to supply their labor, much like a cartel in the market for commodities. Labor unions are the usual mechanism for organizing workers in this way. To raise wages (or improve nonwage benefits) and capture some surplus for workers, unions must have a monopoly or near-monopoly on labor in a particular market. Otherwise, competition for jobs will push wages back down to the market equilibrium level, just as in a competitive market for goods. The importance of union monopoly was demonstrated during the 1987 NFL strike. When the football players in the league went on strike, owners simply found replacement players to take their place. Although fans weren't entirely convinced by teams made up of replacement players, the games were still aired on TV, and so teams and owners still made money. The striking NFL players realized that they did not have monopoly power and that the league could move on without them, which helped convince them to end the strike.

In general, the larger the membership of a union, the more power it has. For this reason, unions often span multiple labor markets. The AFL-CIO, the largest union organization in the United States, is a confederation of unions that represents 13 million workers, ranging from pilots and bricklayers to actors and police officers. Other large union federations include AFGE (American Federation of Government Employees), the union that represents government workers, and the NEA (National Education Association), which represents workers in many different parts of the education sector.

Finally, government intervention in the labor market can cause wages and employment to move away from the market equilibrium, much as in the markets for goods and services. We have already discussed the minimum wage; other types of regulation, summarized in Figure 16-13, can also affect the labor market. Regulations such as standards to ensure that workers won't be injured at work are relatively uncontroversial, but do impose some costs, effectively acting as a tax on employment.

Changing demographics

Earlier in this chapter, we saw how immigration can affect the labor market. Rising or falling birth rates also have a profound effect on the overall supply of labor and economic growth. Countries with a declining population may have too few workers to power production, and too few consumers to drive a healthy demand for goods and services. Excessive population growth is a concern as well. Overpopulation can strain the environment and limit the government's ability to pay for education and other services. High birth rates can also make it harder for parents to invest as much as they would like to in their children's development and education. This lack of investment ends up reducing the human capital (and therefore the productivity) of the future labor force.

FIGURE 16-13

Major labor laws of the twentieth century

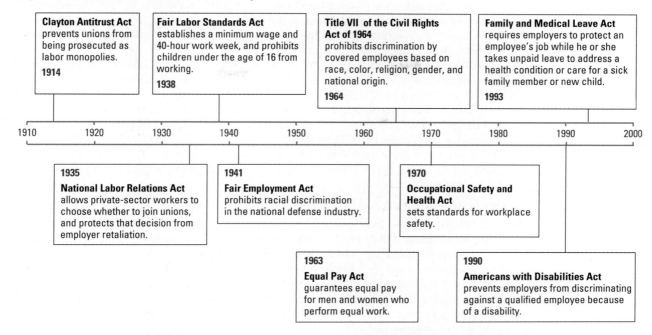

Sources: http://www.bls.gov/opub/cwc/cm20030124ar02p1.htm; http://www.library.gsu.edu/spcoll/pages/pages.asp?ldID=105&guideID=515&ID=3900.

When growing populations suddenly start to slow down, the result is often that a small number of workers ends up supporting a lot of elderly dependents. The United States has found itself in this situation, as birth rates have fallen and medical advances mean people are living longer: In 1940, 160 working people were paying into the Social Security program for every retiree who received benefits. Today, just a little more than three working people are paying into the system for every retiree. A wave of workers from the baby boom generation are reaching retirement age, while the following generations that will be entering the workforce to support them are far smaller.

Because of the serious effects of population growth on the economy, many governments have enacted policies to encourage or discourage childbearing. For a discussion of the pros and cons of such policies, see the What Do You Think? box "Population policy and the wealth of nations."

WHAT DO YOU THINK?

Population policy and the wealth of nations

When you look at a newborn baby, the child's future contribution to the economy probably is not the first thing that comes to mind. But today's birth rates determine the size of the future labor force, so many countries have adopted policies to encourage or discourage births.

Many European countries have negative population growth rates, meaning that each year more people die than babies are born. This drives European governments to encourage couples to have more children by subsidizing day care, granting generous parental leave from work, and offering tax credits for children.

China faced the opposite problem: a population explosion that threatened to outstrip the country's ability to feed and house all its citizens. Since 1979, China has enforced a one-child policy. Under that policy, those who live in urban areas face heavy fees if they choose to bear more than one child (although the government is now beginning to reverse the policy in some areas). The policy is controversial, but there's little argument about its contribution to curbing the country's population growth. In 1950, the average Chinese woman had six children; now she has just under two. Many people attribute China's incredible economic growth—the country's income has grown more than 2,000 percent in two generations—in part to its population policy.

Population policies can have some serious side effects. In China and India, local government officials have reportedly used harsh means to lower birth rates, such as intimidation and forced sterilization. In places where having sons is culturally important, some women have sex-selective abortions or even practice female infanticide to ensure that their child will be male. Opponents of China's one-child policy point to a growing gender imbalance: By 2020, men will outnumber women in China by an estimated 24 million. Defenders of the law, on the other hand, argue that it has allowed China to avoid the worst strains of overpopulation, and has encouraged families to invest fully in children's education.

What do you think?

1. Is it right for the government to discourage or encourage couples to bear children for economic reasons? How would you weigh the importance of lifting people out of poverty against the right to privacy and self-determination?
2. If the government is going to play a role in influencing population growth, what sort of policy might be appropriate? What kind of policy would cross the line?
3. What alternative to the one-child policy might China have had? What kind of policy would you propose for a country that has serious concerns about the economic effects of overpopulation?

Sources: http://data.un.org/Data.aspx?q=china&d=PopDiv&f=variableID%3A54%3BcrID%3A156%2C948; http://news.bbc.co.uk/2/hi/8451289.stm.

✓**CONCEPT CHECK**

❏ Why might an employer choose to pay an efficiency wage? **[LO 16.8]**
❏ What would you expect to happen to wages in a monopsonistic labor market? **[LO 16.9]**
❏ If birth rates go up, what happens to the size of the labor force in the future? **[LO 16.9]**

Conclusion

Why do some people earn more money than others? That is one of the most fundamental questions in economics and politics. When markets are competitive, everyone earns income in proportion to the productivity of the factors of production they control. For most people, that means their income is based on their own productivity as workers. That's usually closely tied to the skills, education, and other talents that determine our "human capital." For farmers, the productivity of land matters as well. For investors, income is determined by the productivity of their financial capital. Competitive markets have the remarkable ability to reward work according to what is contributed to the economy.

We've seen that we can use the familiar tools of supply and demand to put prices on the factors of production, and we examined how business owners decide how much of each factor to use in producing goods and services. Their choice is driven by both the marginal productivity and the price of each factor. In future chapters we'll return to the markets for land, labor, and capital, to see what happens when we add public policy and collective decision making to the picture.

Key Terms

factors of production, p. 367

capital, p. 367

marginal product, p. 367

value of the marginal product, p. 369

human capital, p. 381

rental price, p. 384

purchase price, p. 384

economic rent, p. 384

efficiency wage, p. 388

monopsony, p. 389

Summary

LO 16.1 Define factors of production and describe how they contribute to output.

The ingredients that are used to make a good or service are called factors of production. We can divide factors of production into three major categories: land, labor, and capital (a previously produced good that can be used to produce a new good). Factors of production are rented, bought, and sold in markets, at prices and in quantities that are determined by supply and demand. Firms choose to produce using the combination of factors that will maximize their profit.

LO 16.2 Graph the demand curve for a factor of production, and explain its relationship to marginal productivity.

The demand for factors of production is determined by their contribution to the value of a firm's output. We can use the marginal product of labor (or land or capital) to measure the increase in output gained by using one more unit of a factor of production. Thus, the value of the marginal product of labor is the revenue that is generated by an additional worker. Firms will hire workers up to the point where the wage equals the value of the marginal product of labor (where marginal revenue equals marginal cost). If we graph the value of the marginal product against the number of workers, we get a downward-sloping relationship that is the same as the demand curve for labor.

LO 16.3 Graph the supply curve for a factor of production, and explain what determines the supply of labor.

The supply of a factor of production is driven by the opportunity cost of using that factor in a given market. The opportunity cost of supplying labor in a particular labor market is the time you would otherwise have spent on leisure or working at another job.

An increase in wages has two effects on the labor supply, a price effect and an income effect. The price effect causes the quantity of labor supplied to increase, all else held equal. The income effect decreases the labor supply, as workers demand more leisure time. In general, the price effect outweighs the income effect, which means that the labor supply curve slopes upward.

LO 16.4 Explain how to find the equilibrium price and quantity for a factor of production.

Factor markets reach equilibrium at the point where the demand curve intersects the supply curve, and the quantity demanded equals the quantity supplied at a given price or wage.

LO 16.5 Use graphs to demonstrate the effect of a shift in supply or demand, and describe what causes these curves to shift.

If the underlying determinants of supply or demand change, the equilibrium point can shift. The determinants of labor demand include anything that affects the value of the marginal product, including the supply of other factors, changes in technology, and output prices. The determinants of labor supply include culture, population, and the availability of other opportunities.

LO 16.6 Define human capital, and justify its importance in the labor market.

In addition to the three primary factors of production, economists note a fourth critically important factor, human capital. Human capital is the set of skills, knowledge, experience, and talent that goes into the work people do. Workers differ from one another because they have different amounts and types of human capital to offer, which allow them to be more or less productive than others at different tasks. Some types of human capital make workers more productive at a wide range of jobs; others relate to very specific tasks. Differences in human capital are a key determinant of wages, and therefore of differences in people's incomes.

LO 16.7 Describe the similarities and differences between the markets for land and capital and the market for labor.

The markets for land and capital are similar to markets for labor, with the major difference being that land and capital can be purchased as well as rented. The rental price is what a producer pays to use a factor for a certain period or task; the purchase price is what a producer pays to gain permanent ownership. The word *capital* is often used loosely to refer to financial capital as well as physical capital. When people invest money in the stock market or a company, they are using financial capital to purchase a share of the company's physical capital.

LO 16.8 Identify two reasons why a wage might rise above the market equilibrium, and describe their effect on the labor market.

There are two common reasons for a wage to rise above the market equilibrium: minimum wages and efficiency wages. A minimum wage is a price floor on the price of labor. In an efficient labor market, a price floor causes excess supply and unemployment. An efficiency wage is an above-market equilibrium wage that an employer voluntarily pays to employees to increase their productivity.

LO 16.9 Describe several causes of imperfectly competitive labor markets and their effect on workers and employers.

Just as the markets for goods and services are not always perfectly competitive, neither are labor markets. When a labor market has only one employer but many workers, the employer is called a monopsonist. A monopsonist has the market power to push wages below market equilibrium. Workers can also gain market power, by banding together to make joint labor supply decisions and push their wages above equilibrium. Through regulations, government can also impose costs on labor markets.

Review Questions

1. Consider the factors of production that go into a fast-food restaurant. Give an example of land, labor, and capital. **[LO 16.1]**

2. Suppose an auto manufacturer has one factory in the United States and one in Mexico. The auto manufacturer produces the same number of cars and the same models in each factory but hires more workers in Mexico than in the United States. Give an explanation for the discrepancy in the amount of labor hired in each location. **[LO 16.1]**

3. Suppose you run a flower-delivery business and employ college students to drive the vans and make deliveries. You are considering hiring an additional worker. What information would you need to know to decide whether doing so would increase or decrease your profit? **[LO 16.2]**

4. Christina runs an IT consulting firm in a competitive market. She recently determined that hiring an additional consultant would mean that she would be able to serve five more clients per week. Assuming her goal is to maximize her profits, explain why Christina did not hire another consultant. **[LO 16.2]**

5. Suppose your retired grandmother has complained of boredom and is considering taking a part-time job. Use the concept of opportunity cost to advise your grandmother how to decide whether to take the job. **[LO 16.3]**

6. Jackie and Samia are both nurses at the same hospital. Jackie and Samia have the same duties, experience, and performance reviews. Give an example that explains why Samia makes more than Jackie for the same job. **[LO 16.3]**

7. Suppose BMW runs a great ad campaign that increases demand and drives up the price of BMWs. What do you expect will happen to the demand for the labor in auto-manufacturing plants? Explain how the equilibrium price and quantity of labor will change. **[LO 16.4]**

8. Suppose a cafe owner wants to switch to automatic espresso machines instead of paying baristas to pack the coffee grounds by hand. The machines are twice as effective as a human; the fixed cost per machine equals the yearly wage of one employee.

Explain how the equilibrium price and quantity of labor will change. **[LO 16.4]**

9. Leo runs a bicycle repair shop. He recently examined information on wage and employment levels and noted that he employs the same number of workers today that he employed in 2009. However, wages (controlling for inflation) increased quite substantially between 2009 and 2013. Assume the supply of labor remained constant over this time period. Give two possible explanations for why Leo's workers are paid more in 2013. **[LO 16.5]**

10. Consider a labor market that traditionally discriminates against hiring women. Suppose a new law effectively prohibits this practice. What would you expect to happen to the wages of men in this industry? **[LO 16.5]**

11. Suppose your friend wants to become a doctor. Describe some of the human capital required to achieve this goal. **[LO 16.6]**

12. Madison has a full-time job, but she is considering going back to school for a master's degree. Describe how Madison might decide whether or not to continue her education. **[LO 16.6]**

13. Ariel is shopping for a space to open a new restaurant. She has two options in her target neighborhood. One space is available for lease and the other for purchase. How would you advise Ariel to think through her choice of restaurant location? What factors should she consider? **[LO 16.7]**

14. Suppose you have inherited a few acres of land from a relative and you are considering what to do with your inheritance. A farmer with land next to yours offers to buy your acres so he can expand his grazing area. How will you decide whether to sell your land to the farmer? What factors should you consider? **[LO 16.7]**

15. Large telecom companies like AT&T routinely send repair technicians to customers' homes. Although they are skilled laborers, they must usually train on the job, so it takes some time for them to reach a high standard of quality. In addition, their work cannot be constantly supervised. Explain why an efficiency wage could help telecom companies to increase the productivity of repair techs. **[LO 16.8]**

16. The Coalition of Immokalee Workers (CIW) claims that the going wage for farm labor is exploitative. The CIW supports a minimum wage for farm workers. Explain how the minimum wage would affect a farm's hiring decision. Are farm workers better off under this policy? **[LO 16.8]**

17. Suppose a new law passes requiring farms to provide health benefits to farm labor. Assume that workers value having health benefits. When the new law goes into effect, what will happen to the wage for farm labor at equilibrium? Now suppose farm workers place no value on health benefits. How does this affect your answer? **[LO 16.9]**

18. Suppose a group of high school friends work at the same fast-food restaurant. They all dislike the manager because she doesn't allow them to swap shifts with one another whenever someone has a big exam to study for or a date. One of the friends suggests that they all agree to walk out if the manager doesn't change her policy. Explain whether the manager will change her policy to avoid a walkout. **[LO 16.9]**

Problems and Applications

1. Recently, some college alumni started a moving service for students living on campus. They have three employees and are debating hiring a fourth. The hourly wage for an employee is $18 per hour. An average moving job takes three hours. The company currently does three moving jobs per week, but with one more employee, the company could manage five jobs per week. The company charges $80 for a moving job. **[LO 16.1, 16.2]**

   a. What would be the new employee's marginal product of labor?

   b. What is the value of that marginal product?

   c. Should the moving service hire a fourth worker?

2. Fresh Veggie is one of many small farms in Florida operating in a perfectly competitive market. Farm labor is also perfectly competitive, and Fresh Veggie can hire as many workers as it wants for $20 a day. The daily productivity of a tomato picker is given in Table 16P-1. If a bushel of tomatoes sells for $5, how many workers will Fresh Veggie hire? **[LO 16.1, 16.2]**

3. Dustin's labor supply curve is graphed in Figure 16P-1. **[LO 16.3]**

   a. Consider a wage increase from $5 to $6. For Dustin, does the price effect or income effect dominate his labor supply decision?

   b. Consider a wage increase from $7 to $8. For Dustin, does the price effect or income effect dominate his labor supply decision?

TABLE 16P-1

Labor	Bushels of tomatoes	MP of Labor	VMPL
0	0	—	—
1	12		
2	22		
3	30		
4	35		
5	38		
6	40		

TABLE 16P-2

Hourly wage ($)	Hours
8	10
9	14
10	18
11	22
12	26
13	30
14	34
15	38
16	42

FIGURE 16P-1

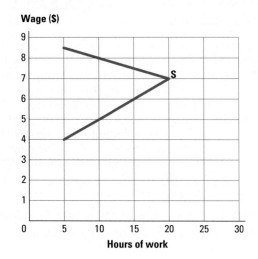

TABLE 16P-3

Wage ($)	Quantity supplied	Quantity demanded
3	2,000	5,000
4	3,000	4,500
5	4,000	4,000
6	5,000	3,500
7	6,000	3,000
8	7,000	2,500
9	8,000	2,000

4. Sasha has 60 hours a week she can work or have leisure. Wages are $8/hour. **[LO 16.3]**
   a. Graph Sasha's budget constraint for income and leisure.
   b. Suppose wages increase to $10/hour. Graph Sasha's new budget constraint.
   c. When wages increase from $8/hour to $10/hour, Sasha's leisure time decreases from 20 hours to 15 hours. Does her labor supply curve slope upward or downward over this wage increase?

5. Suppose you run a business that specializes in producing graphic T-shirts, using labor as an input. Based on Table 16P-2, graph the labor supply and demand curves and identify the market equilibrium wage and quantity. **[LO 16.4]**

6. Based on Table 16P-3, indicate what would happen in this labor market at various wage rates by selecting one of the three choices shown for each item. **[LO 16.4]**
   a. At $8/hour: excess labor supply; excess labor demand; or equilibrium.
   b. At $3/hour: excess labor supply; excess labor demand; or equilibrium.
   c. At $5/hour: excess labor supply; excess labor demand; or equilibrium.

7. Identify which way the labor supply curve would shift under the following scenarios. **[LO 16.5]**
   a. A country experiences a huge influx of immigrants who are skilled in the textile industry.
   b. Wages increase in an industry that requires similar job skills.

FIGURE 16P-2

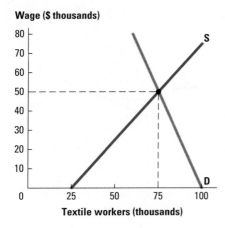

Wage ($ thousands) — vertical axis: 80, 70, 60, 50, 40, 30, 20, 10, 0
Horizontal axis — **Textile workers (thousands):** 25, 50, 75, 100
Curves labeled S and D.

FIGURE 16P-3

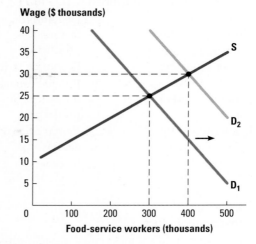

Wage ($ thousands) — vertical axis: 40, 35, 30, 25, 20, 15, 10, 5, 0
Horizontal axis — **Food-service workers (thousands):** 100, 200, 300, 400, 500
Curves labeled S, D_2, D_1.

c. New machines require additional maintenance over time, so that the marginal productivity of labor rises.

8. Figure 16P-2 shows the supply and demand for labor in the textile industry. In each of the following scenarios, graph any shift in the supply or demand curve and state whether the resulting equilibrium wage and quantity *increase* or *decrease*. **[LO 16.5]**

a. What is the original equilibrium?

b. Immigration and layoffs from other jobs increase the population of textile workers, shifting the supply curve to the right by 15,000 workers at any given wage.

c. A new technology for making self-printed T-shirts reduces the marginal product of labor for textile workers, shifting the demand curve to the left by 10,000 workers at any given wage.

9. Suppose that fast-food chains start using healthier ingredients, increasing the demand for fast food and therefore for food-service workers, as shown in Figure 16P-3. **[LO 16.6]**

a. What are the new equilibrium wage and quantity of labor in the fast-food industry?

b. Assume that the skills required of a sales clerk at a retail store are similar to those required of workers at a fast-food restaurant. If workers are completely indifferent between fast-food jobs and retail-sales jobs, what will be the wages for sales clerks?

10. Suppose a town's largest employers are its auto manufacturing plant and its airplane manufacturing plant. Airplane manufacturing jobs require

familiarity with a technology that is not currently used in auto manufacturing. Assume workers are indifferent between the two types of manufacturing work. **[LO 16.6]**

a. All else equal, which plant will pay its workers more?

b. Suppose the auto industry adopts the same technology used by airplane manufacturers and trains its current workers in this technology. What will happen to the pay differential between auto manufacturing and airplane manufacturing work?

11. Figure 16P-4 shows a local labor market for landscapers. What is the value of economic rent in this labor market? **[LO 16.7]**

FIGURE 16P-4

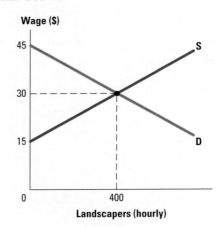

Wage ($) — vertical axis: 45, 30, 15, 0
Horizontal axis — **Landscapers (hourly):** 400
Curves labeled S and D.

12. Match the following aspects of factor markets with the corresponding characteristics. **[LO 16.7]**

    a. analogous to producer surplus

    b. affected by an asset's long-run productivity

    c. interest paid on loans

    d. determined by ownership of factors of production

    e. determined by the value of marginal product

    ____ Demand for factors of production

    ____ Economic rent

    ____ Purchase markets for factors of production

    ____ Rental price of capital

    ____ Income

13. Figure 16P-5 shows a local labor market. What is the quantity supplied and quantity demanded when the minimum wage is: **[LO 16.8]**

    a. At equilibrium?

    b. $15,000?

    c. $20,000?

14. The market for grocery-store baggers is a competitive labor market, as shown in Figure 16P-6. Suppose a new federal law raises the minimum wage to $10 per hour. **[LO 16.8]**

    a. What is the equilibrium wage rate prior to the law being enacted?

    b. What are total labor earnings at the equilibrium wage?

    c. How much labor is being hired at the minimum wage?

    d. What are total labor earnings with enactment of the minimum wage?

FIGURE 16P-5

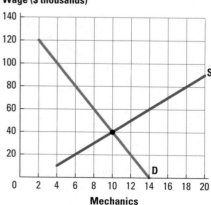

Wage ($ thousands)

Mechanics

FIGURE 16P-6

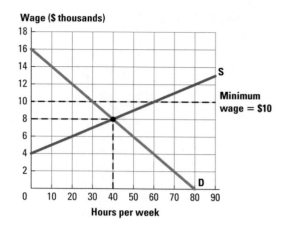

15. Imagine that, faced with budget shortfalls, a government changes its current policy of granting tax credits based on family size to a flat rate tax credit for a family with one or more children. **[LO 16.9]**

    a. Over time, what will happen to the average age in the population?

    b. Over time, what will happen to the size of the workforce?

16. In each scenario, will wages rise above the market equilibrium or fall below it? **[LO 16.9]**

    a. All but one of the factories in a town go out of business.

    b. All the software engineers in Silicon Valley organize into a union and go on strike.

    c. A major grocery store chain buys out all the other stores in the city.

Chapter Endnote

1. http://www.gallup.com/poll/147206/stock-market-investments-lowest-1999.aspx.

Chapter Sources

http://espn.go.com/mlb/player/_/id/4574/albert-pujols

http://www.bls.gov/oes/current/oes452092.htm

http://www.bls.gov/oes/current/oes272021.htm

http://www.ers.usda.gov/Briefing/LaborAnd Education/FarmLabor.htm

http://www.nytimes.com/2006/09/22/washington/22growers.html?_r=1&scp=1&sq=Pickers%20 Are%20Few,%20and%20Growers%20Blame%20 Congress&st=cse

http://www.aflcio.org/aboutus/thisistheaflcio/convention/2005/upload/fastfacts.pdf

International Trade

LEARNING OBJECTIVES

LO 17.1   Define comparative advantage and list some root causes of comparative advantage on a national level.

LO 17.2   Determine whether a country will become a net-importer or net-exporter of a good when it moves from autarky to free trade.

LO 17.3   Calculate the change in surplus and the distribution of benefits within a market when a country opens up to trade.

LO 17.4   Explain the effect of a tariff on quantity, price, and the distribution of surplus.

LO 17.5   Explain the effect of an import quota on quantity, price, and the distribution of surplus.

LO 17.6   Describe the effects of trade on the factor distribution of income.

LO 17.7   Discuss the challenges of establishing environmental or labor standards in international markets.

MADE IN LESOTHO

Around the year 2000, a tiny country in southern Africa called Lesotho suddenly developed a flourishing business making T-shirts and jeans for companies including Walmart, Old Navy, Levi Strauss, and Kmart. Lesotho is home to around 2 million citizens—smaller than the city of Houston, Texas. It doesn't grow cotton, as you might expect from a country with a T-shirt and jeans industry. In fact, it doesn't grow much of anything; the mountainous country's lowest point is 4,593 feet above sea level. Common ways of earning a living in Lesotho include herding goats and working in diamond mines. It's a difficult place to get goods into or out of: It's landlocked, meaning it has no seaport, and it also lacks a major airport. All in all, Lesotho seems like a strange place in which to suddenly find a garment-export industry. Stranger yet, many of the factories that sprang up were owned by firms based in Taiwan.

Why did Taiwanese businesses go to Lesotho to make clothing to be sold thousands of miles away in the United States? What changed in 2000 that caused this unexpected trade pattern to flourish?

In this chapter, we pick up on the story told in Chapter 2 of how clothing production has moved around the world over the last 200 years, following the path of cheap labor. When we left the story, China was the world's largest clothing maker, and many consumers in the United States were wearing shirts made in Chinese factories. China's success in making clothing—as well as Lesotho's sudden emergence as a garment manufacturer—is made possible only by a crucial fact: Americans can buy clothing made in China and Lesotho. That seems obvious, but the ability to buy goods from across the world is a relatively new development. Before the vast improvements in transportation over the last century, it was hard to reach far-off trading partners, let alone bring large quantities of goods back home.

Modern transportation and communication technology has made international trade much easier. But trade has also been shaped by a complex web of international agreements. For example, for most of the last 40 years, international trade in textiles and clothing was strictly regulated. The Multifibre Arrangement (MFA)—actually a whole group of separate treaties between individual countries—set limits on how much of what type of clothing could be traded between which countries, often on a level of detail that seems ridiculous in retrospect. How many pairs of cotton socks were Chinese firms allowed to sell to American consumers? How many wool sweaters? The MFA had an answer, and it was not "as many cotton socks and wools sweaters as Americans want to buy." In other words, there was some trade in clothing between the United States and China, but it was not unrestricted *free* trade. Similar restrictions applied to most of the major clothing-producing countries in the world.

At the same time, the United States made other treaties that exempted some countries from the limits set by the Multifibre Arrangement. Free-trade agreements with Mexico and Central American countries trumped the restrictions on clothing trade. So did the African Growth and Opportunity Act (AGOA) of 2000, which granted preferential

trading-partner status to some very poor countries in Africa—including Lesotho. Taiwanese clothing companies quickly figured out that the MFA meant they couldn't sell T-shirts and jeans to America if they made them in factories in Taiwan, but they *could* do so under AGOA if they built factories in Lesotho. So they did.

This garbled combination of trade policies didn't last long. By 2005, the restrictions set by the Multifibre Arrangement had been gradually phased out, freeing up trade in clothing and textiles. What effect did it have on consumers? How about the effect on workers in Asia and the United States—and in tiny Lesotho? As we'll see later in the chapter, that was good news for Asian suppliers and bad news for Lesotho.

In this chapter, we'll see how trade affects prices, workers, and consumers in different countries. We'll also see how trade provides enormous benefits to some countries and industries, but creates losers too. For a business owner, navigating this web successfully can be the difference between riches and bankruptcy. As workers and consumers, the wages we get and the prices we pay are deeply affected by trade, sometimes in ways that are hard to see at first.

Why Trade? A Review

Before we consider the reasons that trade between most countries isn't free, let's briefly review why countries would want to trade in the first place. We can draw on some basic economics concepts from Chapter 2 to predict where different goods will be made when markets function smoothly and what the advantages of trade will be.

Comparative advantage

LO 17.1 Define comparative advantage and list some root causes of comparative advantage on a national level.

The U.S. imports clothing from all over Asia, and especially from the People's Republic of China. What does that fact tell us? Most obviously, it tells us that both Chinese firms and American consumers have something to gain from this trade. As we know, voluntary exchanges generate surplus, leaving both participants better off than they were before. This is as true when firms or countries trade as it is when individuals do.

It also tells us that China must have some kind of advantage over the U.S. when it comes to producing clothes, or the U.S. would produce its own. What kind of advantage? It might mean that Chinese firms are simply more productive than those in the U.S. If that were true, we would say that China has an *absolute* advantage at clothing production. *Absolute advantage* is the ability to produce more of a good than others with a given amount of resources—for instance, to produce more T-shirts with the same number of workers.

But remember (from Chapter 2) that absolute advantage does not determine who produces what; *comparative advantage* does. *Comparative advantage* is the ability to produce a good or service at a lower opportunity cost than others can. The fact that companies in China sell clothing to the U.S. doesn't necessarily tell us that China is more productive at making clothes, but it definitely tells us that China's opportunity cost of making a shirt is lower than that of the United States. (For a review of absolute versus comparative advantage, look back at the section that starts on page 34.)

Gains from trade

If U.S. workers are at least as productive as Chinese workers at making shirts, why do U.S. firms import shirts made in China? Simply put, *both* countries can gain when each specializes in producing the good for which it has a comparative advantage. The two can then trade to get the combination of goods that people in each country want to consume. The increase in welfare in both countries that results from specialization and trade is called, straightforwardly enough, the *gains from trade.*

To see the gains from trade in action, let's compare total production and consumption with and without trade, as shown in Table 17-1. We've made up numbers to keep the example simple, but they capture the spirit of the real situation. For simplicity, we'll assume, as we did in Chapter 2, that only two goods are produced by the U.S. and China: wheat and T-shirts. Without trade, each country has to produce the combination of wheat and shirts that its people actually want to consume. Let's suppose that in the U.S., this means 300 million shirts and 1 billion bushels of wheat. In China, it means 1 billion shirts and 2 billion bushels of wheat. Total global production is 1.3 billion shirts and 3 billion bushels of wheat.

When trade is possible, each country can produce the goods that it has a comparative advantage at producing, rather than the exact combination of goods its consumers want. In our simple story, that means the U.S. will specialize in growing wheat, while China specializes in making shirts. The result is that global production is higher, and both countries can consume more than they were able to before. Under the free-trade scenario, the U.S. makes 3.5 billion bushels of wheat and China makes 2 billion T-shirts. There are 700 million more shirts and 500 million more bushels to go around than there were before, so the two countries can split this bonus in a way that makes both better off. Notice that in Table 17-1, both countries have higher consumption of both goods after specialization and trade. (To review the calculation of production specialization, look back at Chapter 2, especially Table 2-1.)

TABLE 17-1 Hypothetical global production and consumption with and without trade

	Country	Wheat produced (billions)	T-shirts produced (billions)	Wheat consumed (billions)	T-shirts consumed (billions)
Without trade	United States	1	0.3	1	0.3
	China	2	1	2	1
	Total	**3**	**1.3**	**3**	**1.3**
With trade	United States	3.5	0	1.1	0.8
	China	0	2	2.4	1.2
	Total	**3.5**	**2**	**3.5**	**2**

The roots of comparative advantage

The media often describe countries trading as national entities, just as we have done above with the U.S. and China. You might get the impression that trade requires governments to get together, employ an economic superplanner to crunch the numbers, and agree on who is going to specialize in what. But that's not the case at all. The reality is that the day-to-day business of trade is carried out almost entirely by firms and individuals, not by governments.

How does a factory in Atlanta, Georgia, know what its comparative advantage is relative to a factory in Beijing? This is a case of the "invisible hand" at work, but that doesn't mean that the right decision about what to produce and who to trade with happens *automatically*. If you own a factory, it's up to you to research the cost of inputs such as labor and raw materials, and the sale prices of different goods you could produce, and calculate the most profitable option. Get it right, and you'll make profits. Get it wrong, and you'll go out of business. Meanwhile, factory owners in Beijing and everywhere else in the world are all doing the same kind of research and calculations. When everyone *responds* to the profit motives they face as individual producers, they gravitate toward producing the products in which they have a comparative advantage, and the gains from trade fall into place.

Let's get a little more concrete. We discussed in the previous chapter how the prices of *factors of production* are determined. For instance, you might want to hire workers to sew shirts in your factory in Georgia, but those workers can also choose to supply their labor to a company that makes car parts. If the workers are more productive at making car parts than shirts, the car-parts factory will be willing to offer them a higher wage. This decreases the supply of labor for making shirts, which, in turn, pushes up the wage for shirt-makers. Now suppose that workers in Beijing don't have such good alternatives to shirt-making. They are willing to work in a shirt factory for lower wages, so firms in Beijing have a lower cost of producing shirts, which in turn makes them willing to offer shirts at a lower price on the world market.

In this way, the price of each factor of production incorporates the opportunity cost of using that factor to produce other goods. When you consider the prices of all the factors of production for shirts, and the price you could get for shirts on the world market, you conclude that your factory won't be able to break even selling shirts at this lower price. This is the market telling you that your factory in Georgia doesn't have a comparative advantage at producing shirts, and you should make something else instead. To put it another way, only a firm with a comparative advantage at producing shirts—that is, the lowest opportunity cost of production—will be able to make shirts profitably. Simply by responding to the prices of inputs and outputs and choosing to produce the good that earns it the highest profits, each firm ends up producing the good in which it has a comparative advantage.

So far, so good. But what *causes* firms in one country to have a lower opportunity cost of production for sewing shirts versus making car parts versus programming computers or anything else? Economists look to several national characteristics that affect the cost of producing goods in a particular country: natural resources and climate, endowment of factors of production, and technology.

Natural resources and climate. Why does Hawaii have a comparative advantage over Russia in growing pineapples? There's a simple reason—it's warm in Hawaii and often cold in Russia. Diversity in climate and natural resources is an important determinant of comparative advantage. Certain parts of California and France, for instance, have a complex combination of soil and weather that allows them to grow grapes that make world-class wine. Climate and geography may also affect the costs of transporting goods to other places once they are produced. For instance, a country with great seaports will be able to trade different goods than a landlocked country far from major consumer markets, such as Lesotho.

Factor endowment. The relative abundance of different factors of production makes some countries better suited to produce certain goods. For instance, a country with a lot of land relative to its population, such as New Zealand or Argentina, may have a comparative advantage in *land-intensive* activities such as grazing cattle or sheep. A country with plenty of capital and little land, such as Hong Kong or Japan, might do well with more *capital-intensive* activities such as producing high-tech electronics, providing financial services, or biomedical research.

Factor endowment helps to explain the story we told in Chapter 2 about how clothing production has moved around the world over the last few centuries, following the path of cheap labor from country to country. Clothing manufacturing is labor-intensive, requiring relatively little capital or technology. As workforces became more educated in countries that were early leaders in the textile industry, cheap labor became less abundant relative to skilled labor and capital, so comparative advantage shifted toward countries with more cheap labor relative to the other factors of production.

Technology. Lastly, technology can have an effect on comparative advantage. Over time, technology tends to spread from country to country, equalizing opportunity costs. However, at any given time, technology or production processes developed in a particular country may give that country a temporary comparative advantage. We saw in Chapter 2 that the invention of the power loom initially gave Great Britain an advantage at clothing production, but the new technology quickly spread to the United States, erasing that advantage.

Incomplete specialization

In our analysis of international trade we have talked about comparative advantage at the country level. But you have probably noticed that not everyone in a country has the same job. Not all Americans grow wheat, not all Chinese make shirts, not all New Zealanders graze sheep, and so on. If there are big gains to be had from specialization and trade, *why doesn't every country produce just one good?*

The answer has two parts. First, no national economy is a perfectly free market, and neither is trade between national economies. As we will discuss later in the chapter, specialization is often limited by trade agreements, which are dependent on noneconomic considerations such as national security, tradition, and not-so-rational politicking. Those restrictions and political concerns put limits on how much specialization we can expect.

PART 4 ■ Firm Decisions

Second, even if trade was perfectly free, nations would not specialize completely, because within each country there are differences in the natural resources, climate, and relative factor endowment of different areas. For example, it makes sense to produce wine in California, but not in Alaska; the opportunity cost of making cars may be low in Alabama but high in downtown Manhattan; land is fertile for growing wheat in much of Iowa, but not in much of Nevada, and so on. We can talk in general about China having a comparative advantage in producing shirts and the U.S. in growing wheat; but in a super-fertile wheat-growing region of China, the opportunity cost of growing wheat is lower than making shirts. It would make sense for China to grow wheat in that region, and import from the U.S. the rest of the wheat it needs.

✓ CONCEPT CHECK

- ❏ What is the difference between absolute and comparative advantage? Which one determines what goods countries specialize in producing? [LO 17.1]
- ❏ What are the major characteristics that determine comparative advantage? [LO 17.1]

From Autarky to Free Trade

Free trade between countries maximizes surplus, producing benefits for both parties, just as free exchanges between individual buyers and sellers do. But simply saying "the United States gains from trade" glosses over the fact that the United States consists of many different industries, firms, and individual people. In reality, some of these will gain and some will lose from trade, although the *total gains* will be higher than *total losses*. In order to understand the effects of trade on a more detailed level, and to see who exactly gains in what way, we need to dig deeper.

Let's start by imagining a world without any trade at all. We call an economy that is self-contained and does not engage in any trade with outsiders an **autarky**.

Suppose that the U.S. economy is an autarky, meaning it is impossible to import or export anything. **Imports** are goods and services that are produced in other countries and consumed domestically. **Exports** are goods and services that are produced domestically and consumed in other countries. Under autarky, nothing produced outside the country is sold inside, and nothing produced inside the country is sold outside.

What would the market for shirts in the United States look like without any trade? We can describe the domestic market with the same supply and demand curves that we've used in previous chapters. The supply curve shown in Figure 17-1 includes only *domestic* clothing manufacturers, and the demand curve includes only *domestic* consumers. This situation without any trade allows us to determine the price and quantity of shirts sold in the country by finding the intersection of the supply and demand curves, just as we've done all along. U.S. consumers and producers will buy and sell 300 million shirts per year at a price of $25.

Becoming a net-importer

LO 17.2 Determine whether a country will become a net-importer or net-exporter of a good when it moves from autarky to free trade.

LO 17.3 Calculate the change in surplus and the distribution of benefits within a market when a country opens up to trade.

Even though the United States isn't trading with other countries in this scenario, let's suppose that all other countries have free trade in clothing. This means that outside the

autarky an economy that is self-contained and does not engage in trade with outsiders

imports goods and services that are produced in other countries and consumed domestically

exports goods and services that are produced domestically and consumed in other countries

FIGURE 17-1

Domestic supply and demand for shirts in an autarky

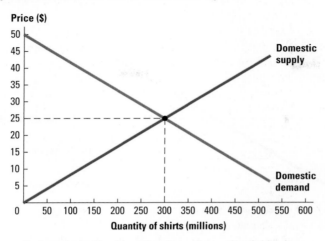

Under autarky, the domestic price and quantity of shirts is determined by the intersection of the domestic supply and domestic demand curves.

U.S., shirts are being bought and sold at a *world price,* which is not necessarily the same as the U.S. price. In fact, let's say that the world price of shirts is only $15.

POTENTIALLY CONFUSING

In reality, there is not a *single* world price for shirts. A shirt costs less in rural Mexico than it does in New York City, for a variety of reasons. However, the idea of a world price in an international market with free trade is a useful simplification that lets us describe a complicated situation. It's analogous to the market price in any other sort of market with free exchanges—any seller who tries to sell at a higher price will simply lose all of his customers to other sellers. If you are a U.S. company trying to sell your product, you can usefully think of the world price as the amount you could get for it by exporting to a wholesaler outside of the U.S.

What happens in our autarky example if the U.S. government decides to free up trade in clothing? The domestic price of shirts is $25, the world price is $15, and all of a sudden, shirts can be freely traded across U.S. borders. Now, U.S. consumers have no reason to pay more than $15 for a domestically produced shirt; they will simply import a shirt from abroad instead. The market price for shirts within the U.S. therefore falls to $15. At the lower price of $15, more U.S. buyers want to buy shirts. However, fewer U.S. producers are willing to produce shirts given the lower price. Figure 17-2 illustrates the interaction between domestic supply and demand and the world price. The lower price has pushed the quantity demanded up and the quantity supplied down. The gap between them is made up by shirts being imported from abroad.

Note that the domestic supply and demand curves themselves have not shifted. Trade doesn't affect the quantity that consumers want to buy at any given price, or the quantity that domestic producers are willing to sell at any given price. It does, however, allow consumers to buy at a price where domestic demand doesn't equal domestic supply. Of course, total quantity supplied still has to equal total quantity demanded at the equilibrium price—it's just that part of that supply can come from international producers.

FIGURE 17-2

Becoming a net-importer

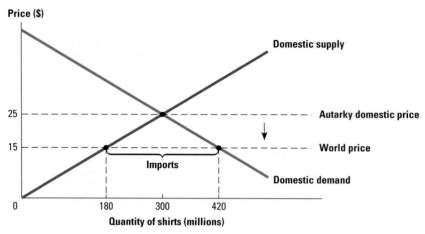

When a country opens its market to trade and the *world price is lower than the domestic price*, the domestic price will fall to meet the world price. At the lower price, domestic quantity demanded increases, but domestic quantity supplied decreases. Imports will make up the difference between the quantities domestically supplied and demanded at the world price.

In the new free-trade equilibrium, U.S. consumers buy 420 million shirts, U.S. producers sell 180 million shirts, and 240 million shirts are imported from abroad, all at a price of $15. The U.S. has now become a net-importer of shirts.

How does this trade affect the welfare of U.S. shirt buyers and manufacturers? Who gains from free trade, and who loses? Figure 17-3 shows how consumer and producer surplus in the market for shirts change when the U.S. goes from autarky to free trade in clothing. Panel A shows consumer and producer surplus in the domestic market under autarky. Panel B shows what happens after trade is possible. Notice that areas A, B, and D are surplus for somebody, both before and after trade: Area A is consumer surplus in both scenarios; area D is producer surplus in both scenarios; and area B represents surplus that was enjoyed by U.S. producers before trade, and is now enjoyed by U.S. consumers.

Area C, however, is new surplus that arises as trade enables consumers to buy more shirts at the lower world price. Overall, free trade increases *total* surplus by area C. We can say that the United States has gained from trade as a whole, because the surplus gained by shirt buyers is larger than the surplus lost to shirt producers. But that doesn't mean everyone in the U.S. is better off. Shirt consumers have gained a lot from trade, but shirt producers have lost out.

Becoming a net-exporter

Do producers always lose and consumers always win with free trade? Only when the world price is *lower* than the domestic price. The opposite happens when the world price is *higher* than the domestic price. Let's look at what happens when the United States opens itself up to international trade in a good where the world price is higher—say, wheat.

Figure 17-4 shows the domestic supply and demand curves for wheat in the U.S. As with shirts, before trade restrictions are lifted, we can find the domestic price and

FIGURE 17-3
Welfare effects of becoming a net-importer

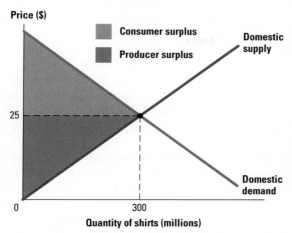

(A) Surplus under autarky

Under autarky, consumers receive the gold shaded area as surplus, while producers receive the area shaded in blue.

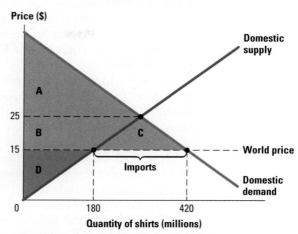

(B) Surplus after trade

When a country opens up to trade and becomes a net-importer of shirts, consumer surplus in the shirt market increases, while producer surplus decreases. In panel B, consumer surplus increases by the area B + C. Producer surplus decreases by the area B. Total surplus now equals A + B + C + D. The net increase in surplus is area C.

FIGURE 17-4
Becoming a net-exporter

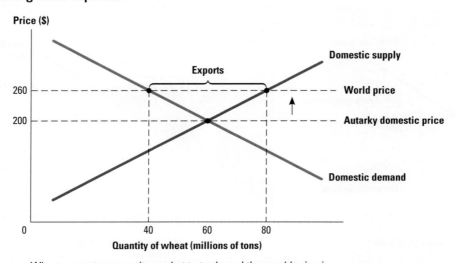

When a country opens its market to trade and the *world price is higher than the domestic price*, the domestic price will rise to meet the world price. At the higher price, domestic quantity supplied increases, but domestic quantity demanded decreases. Excess supply is exported to make up the difference between the quantities domestically supplied and demanded at the world price.

quantity of wheat at the intersection of the supply and demand curves. U.S. consumers buy 60 million tons of wheat at a price of $200 per ton. But in the rest of the world, a ton of wheat sells for $260 per ton. How will U.S. wheat producers *respond* to this difference in prices when trade opens up? Because they can sell as much wheat as they want to foreign consumers at $260, they have no incentive to sell it at a lower price in the U.S. Therefore, if U.S. consumers want to buy wheat, they will have to pay $260, too.

At the world price of $260 per ton, U.S. farmers are willing to produce more wheat—80 million tons. However, given the higher price, U.S. consumers demand a smaller quantity, only 40 million tons. The gap between the two—40 million tons—is sold outside the country. In this new equilibrium, the price of wheat is higher and the U.S. has become a net-exporter of wheat.

How does becoming a net-exporter of wheat affect the welfare of U.S. consumers and producers? Figure 17-5 shows surplus in the wheat market under autarky (panel A) and under free trade (panel B). Again, note that areas A, B, C, E, and F were surplus for somebody both before and after trade: Area A is consumer surplus in both scenarios; area E + F is producer surplus in both scenarios; and area B + C represents surplus that was enjoyed by U.S. consumers before trade and is now enjoyed by U.S. producers. Area D is additional surplus created by trade, which is gained by producers because trade enables them to sell more wheat at a higher price.

On net, total surplus increases by the area of D, so the post-trade equilibrium is more efficient than the pre-trade equilibrium. The U.S. as a whole is better off. But not everyone in the U.S. is better off: wheat producers have gained, but consumers have lost out.

FIGURE 17-5
Welfare effects of becoming a net-exporter

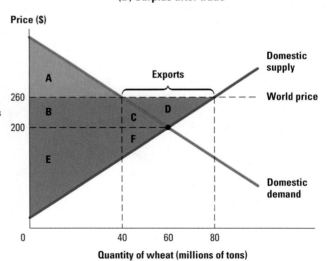

Without trade, consumers receive the gold shaded triangle in surplus, while producers get the area shaded in blue.

When a country opens up to trade and becomes a net-exporter of wheat, consumer surplus in the wheat market decreases, while producer surplus increases. In panel B, producer surplus increases by the area B + C + D. Consumer surplus decreases by the area B + C. Total surplus now equals A + B + C + D + E + F. The net increase in surplus is area D.

Big economy, small economy

If you were paying very close attention in Chapter 3 when we discussed the external factors that determine demand and supply, you might have wondered about our analysis of moving from autarky to trade. An increase in the number of buyers is one of the external factors that can move a demand curve to the right. So, you might ask, wouldn't free trade cause an increase in the world demand for shirts, as U.S. consumers join the world market, pushing the world price up? So wouldn't free trade cause an increase in the world supply of wheat as U.S. wheat farmers join the world market, pushing the world price down?

These are good questions, and the answer is: It depends how big the U.S. is relative to the total size of the world market. What do we mean by "big" in this context? To use the terminology of competitive markets, we assumed in our examples above that the U.S. is a *price taker* in the world market—the decisions of its citizens about what quantity to produce or consume have no effect on the world price. Remember that buyers and sellers are *price takers* if they are too small, relative to the total size of the market, to have enough market power to influence the price.

In other words, for the U.S. to be a price taker in the global market for some good, the quantity it produces and consumes must be very small relative to the total amount of that good bought and sold worldwide. In some markets, the U.S. is probably small enough to be considered a price taker. Consider for instance, the market for lychee—a tasty fruit that is very popular in Asia. Not many people eat lychee in the U.S., and almost nobody grows lychee. Imagine that the U.S. government had banned the import and export of lychee, and then decided to end the ban and allow international trade. Would it have much effect on the world price of lychee? Probably not, because the quantity of lychee produced and consumed in the U.S. is very small compared to the total quantity sold globally.

In a lot of markets, however, the U.S. is definitely a big economy. (In fact, in overall terms, it is the biggest economy in the world.) If the U.S. decided to stop trading shirts or wheat, this decision almost certainly *would* affect the world price. Why? Because the quantity of these goods that the U.S. produces and consumes is *not* negligible relative to the total quantity sold worldwide.

This means we need to add a level of nuance to the analysis. Figure 17-6 shows supply and demand in the *world* market for shirts. (Watch out not to confuse the world-market supply and demand curves with the domestic-market supply and demand curves, shown in Figures 17-1, 17-2, and 17-3.) When the U.S. moves from autarky to free trade, the world demand curve shifts to the right because U.S. shirt consumers have entered the market. (The world supply curve also moves a bit to the right, because U.S. shirt producers have also entered the world market.) To find the new equilibrium in the world market, we need to see where the new supply and demand curves intersect. On net, because demand has increased by more than supply, we can see that the effect of the U.S. joining the market is that the world price of shirts increases from $15 to $17.

What does this mean for U.S. shirt producers and consumers? Figure 17-7 shows what happens in this more realistic situation, when the U.S. decision to move from autarky to free trade increases the world price. The bottom line is the same as before: The price of shirts in the U.S. goes down, and the country as a whole is better off, but U.S. shirt producers lose out. Compared to the picture in Figure 17-3, though, we can see that the quantity imported is slightly smaller than it would be if the U.S. were a price taker on the world market. The overall gain in surplus for the U.S. is smaller, and U.S. shirt producers are hurt a bit less.

Now that we've added this nuance to the analysis, we can see that the U.S. move from autarky to free trade also affects shirt producers and consumers outside the U.S.

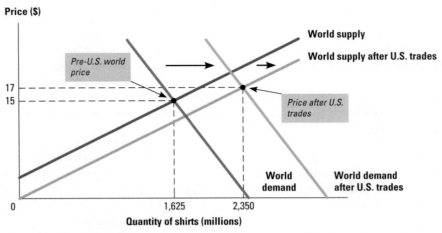

FIGURE 17-6
Impact of a big economy on the world price

Price ($)

Pre-U.S. world price

17
15

World supply

World supply after U.S. trades

Price after U.S. trades

World demand

World demand after U.S. trades

0   1,625   2,350

Quantity of shirts (millions)

When a large economy such as the U.S. enters the world market for shirts, it will influence both world supply and demand for that good. Because the U.S. is a net-importer of shirts at the world price, the shift in world demand is greater than the shift in world supply. The result is an increase in both world price and quantity of shirts.

FIGURE 17-7
From autarky to trade in a big economy

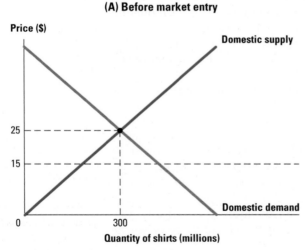

(A) Before market entry

Price ($)

Domestic supply

25

15

Domestic demand

0   300

Quantity of shirts (millions)

Under autarky, the United States produces 300 million T-shirts at a price of $25

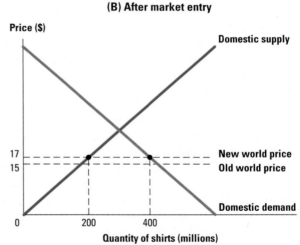

(B) After market entry

Price ($)

Domestic supply

17
15

New world price
Old world price

Domestic demand

0   200   400

Quantity of shirts (millions)

If the U.S. enters the world market as a large economy, it pushes the world price up from $15 to $17. The U.S. domestic price still drops relative to autarky, but by less than it would have if the U.S. was a price taker with no effect on the world market.

Because the U.S. entry into the world market has increased the price of shirts, consumers in the rest of the world have to pay $17 instead of $15 for their shirts, reducing the surplus they enjoy. Foreign shirt producers, on the other hand, enjoy higher surplus due to the higher price and greater quantity they sell. If we were to perform the same analysis for wheat, we would find that the effect of the U.S. entry into the world market would be to reduce the world price of wheat—good news for foreign wheat consumers, and bad news for foreign wheat producers.

✓ CONCEPT CHECK

❏ What is autarky? **[LO 17.2]**

❏ If the domestic price of a good is below the world price when it opens up to trade, will it become a net-importer or net-exporter of that good? **[LO 17.2]**

❏ When a country becomes a net-exporter of a good, what happens to domestic producer surplus? **[LO 17.3]**

Restrictions on Trade

Even from our simple analysis so far, we can see how proposals to impose or lift restrictions on trade will be viewed very differently by different groups of people. A proposal for the U.S. to move from autarky to free trade would be opposed by U.S. shirt producers and foreign wheat farmers, but welcomed by U.S. wheat farmers and foreign shirt producers. Americans who eat a lot of wheat-based food wouldn't like it, nor would foreign shirt-buyers. But Americans who buy lots of shirts would be happy, as would wheat-loving foreigners.

The big debates about international trade get more complicated because the questions are rarely about whether to completely forbid trade or to completely open it up to free global exchange. Instead, significant quantities of goods and services flow between countries, but much of it is heavily regulated. Understanding how prices and quantities will be affected by trade, and who wins and who loses, requires understanding trade restrictions.

Why restrict trade?

We saw in the previous section that trade is efficiency-enhancing—increasing total surplus regardless of whether the country becomes a net-importer or net-exporter of a particular good. Yet all countries restrict trade to some extent, and some restrict it quite heavily. Given that trade increases total welfare, why would anyone want to restrict it?

While some trade restrictions are based on global politics (as we'll discuss in the next section), much of the rationale has to do with protecting those who lose surplus, or are perceived to lose surplus, as a result of free trade. For this reason, laws limiting trade are often referred to as *trade protection,* and a preference for policies that place limits on trade is called **protectionism**. In contrast, policies and actions that reduce trade restrictions and promote free trade are often referred to as **trade liberalization**. In this section, we'll examine two common tools for restricting international trade, tariffs and quotas, and see how they affect the distribution of surplus within a country.

protectionism a preference for policies that limit trade

trade liberalization policies and actions that reduce trade restrictions

Tariffs

LO 17.4 Explain the effect of a tariff on quantity, price, and the distribution of surplus.

A **tariff** is a tax that applies only to imported goods. Just like any other tax, a tariff causes deadweight loss and is inefficient. It also raises public funds, but that is not usually its aim. Typically, the most important goal of a tariff is to protect the interests of domestic producers.

In 2002, for example, the United States imposed a tariff of up to 30 percent on the sale price of imported steel for a three-year period. The rationale behind the tariff

tariff a tax on imported goods

was explicitly to benefit the domestic steel industry. When President George W. Bush announced the new tariff, he described it as:

> ... temporary safeguards to help give America's steel industry and its workers the chance to adapt to the large influx of foreign steel. This relief will help steel workers, communities that depend on steel, and the steel industry adjust without harming our economy.[1]

Did the steel tariff accomplish this goal? Let's take a look. The price of a ton of steel in early 2002 was around $250. With a 30 percent tariff, foreign firms selling steel in the U.S. had to pay $75 to the government for the privilege of importing. How should we expect foreign steel producers to *respond* to this new cost? They will no longer sell steel in the U.S. for any price lower than $325 per ton—which, after paying the $75 in taxes, comes out to the same thing as the world price of $250. Why should they sell for less than that amount, when they can sell as much as they want for $250 per ton in other countries?

How will domestic steel producers *respond?* Assuming that $325 is still lower than the domestic price that would prevail under autarky, they have no reason to sell for less than $325 either, even though they are not subject to the tariff.

The tariff thus has exactly the same effect on the U.S. steel market as an increase in the world price to $325 per ton, as shown in Figure 17-8. The new, higher price pushes domestic producers up along the supply curve. They are still not willing to produce as much as consumers want to buy at that price, but they are willing to produce more than they were at a price of $250 per ton. The difference between the quantity supplied and the quantity demanded is still made up by imports, but that difference is smaller than it was before the tariff.

As a result of the tariff, domestic steel producers enjoy an increase in surplus. That, after all, was what President Bush said he wanted it to achieve. Their gain in surplus

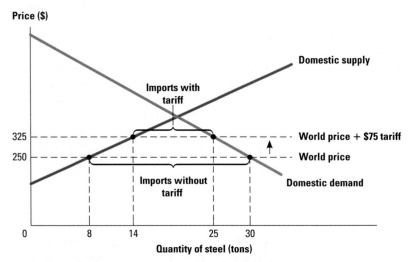

FIGURE 17-8

Effect of a tariff on imported steel

The world price before the tariff is $250. With a $75 tariff, the effective world price increases to $325. The higher price increases domestic supply, while it decreases domestic demand. As a result, the quantity of imports also decreases.

FIGURE 17-9

Domestic welfare effects of a tariff

(A) Surplus without a tariff

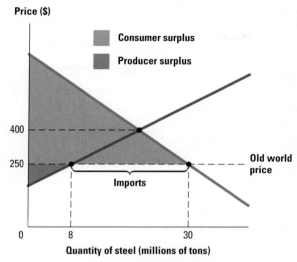

Without a tariff the world price is $250. Consumers demand 30 million tons of steel and domestic producers are willing to sell 8 million tons.

(B) Surplus with a tariff

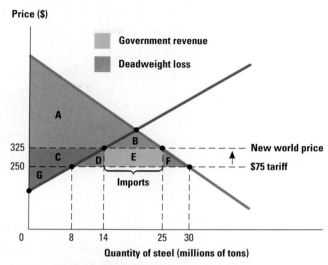

The tariff increases producer surplus by area C, and decreases consumer surplus by area C + D + E + F. Area E is the government revenue from the imposed tariff, while area D + F is the deadweight loss. Note that the loss of consumer surplus is greater than the sum of producer surplus and government revenue gains.

from selling a larger quantity at a higher price is shown in area C of Figure 17-9. Notice that this comes at the expense of a loss in surplus for domestic buyers of steel, such as the U.S. auto and construction industries. Those domestic steel consumers lose the surplus represented by area C to producers, but also lose areas D, E, and F. Part of that loss in consumer surplus is converted into revenue for the government, which collects tariff payments on imports—shown as area E. But the rest of the lost consumer surplus—areas D and F—becomes deadweight loss. In other words, the combined benefits that the tariff brings to steel producers and the U.S. government are outweighed by the loss in surplus suffered by domestic steel consumers.

We can see, then, that the steel tariff did not exactly achieve its goal of helping the domestic steel industry "without harming our economy." In the end, was it the right decision to impose the tariff? That depends on how highly you value the benefit to the U.S. steel-production industry versus the loss to steel-consumers like the auto and construction industries.

In any case, the steel tariff didn't last long. In 2003, the World Trade Organization ruled that the tariffs were illegal, and President Bush withdrew them. We'll say more about the role of the World Trade Organization later in the chapter.

Quotas

LO 17.5 Explain the effect of an import quota on quantity, price, and the distribution of surplus.

The Multifibre Arrangement (MFA), which regulated trade of clothing items from the 1970s to 2005, used another type of trade restriction—the quota. An import **quota** is a limit on the amount of a particular good that can be imported. Under the MFA, different

quota (imports)
a limit on the amount of a particular good that can be imported

FIGURE 17-10

Domestic welfare effects of a quota

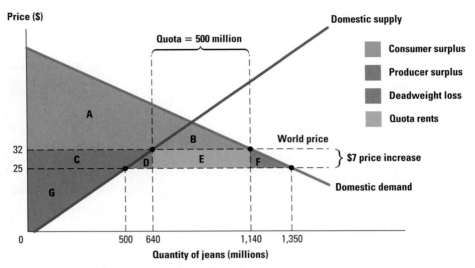

At the pre-quota price of $25, the gap between domestic demand (1,350 million) and supply (500 million) is met by an imported quantity of 850 million jeans. With an import quota of 500 million jeans, imports can't make up the full gap, pushing the domestic world price up to $32. As a result, producer surplus increases by area C, and consumer surplus decreases by area C + D + E + F. Area E is the quota rent gained by whoever holds the rights to import, while area D + F is the deadweight loss.

countries were subject to different quotas for different kinds of clothing goods. For instance, China could sell only so many cotton shirts in the United States, Pakistan could sell only so many, and Bangladesh, and so on.

Let's start with a simple example of a quota: a cap on the total number of pairs of blue jeans that can be imported into the United States. (For now, don't worry about how this quota is allocated between countries that produce jeans—we'll come back to that in a moment.) Figure 17-10 shows that under free trade, at the world price of $25 per pair, domestic jeans producers are willing to supply 500 million pairs of jeans. At that price, American consumers demand 1,350 million pairs of jeans. The difference—850 million pairs of jeans—is imported. But what happens if a quota is imposed, limiting the total number of imported jeans to 500 million? The domestic price of jeans has to rise from $25 per pair to $32 per pair in order to shrink the gap between domestic supply and domestic demand down to the 500 million limit imposed by the quota.

Notice that the effect of the quota is very similar to the effect of a tariff. The price within the U.S. increases over the world price. As a result, domestic demand decreases, domestic supply increases, and the quantity of imports falls. Domestic producers gain surplus from selling a higher quantity at a higher price; domestic consumers lose even more surplus from buying a lower quantity at a higher price, resulting in deadweight loss (areas D and F).

However, there is an important distinction between the impact of tariffs and quotas: *who benefits* from the difference between the value of jeans in the U.S. and their value on the world market. Under a tariff, the U.S. government collects tax revenue equal to the quantity of imports multiplied by the difference between the domestic price and the world price. Under a quota, this value goes to whoever holds the rights to import. For instance, if the U.S. government gives the rights to import jeans to the government of Bangladesh, Bangladesh can then choose to sell those rights or hand them out to favored firms. Thus, the value of tax revenue under a tariff turns into profits earned by foreign firms or governments under a quota, called **quota rents**. Who will be granted the right to import how much of what goods into which countries is among the thorny issues trade negotiators grapple with when deciding on the details of trade treaties.

quota rents profits earned by foreign firms or governments under a quota

Selective exemptions from quotas and tariffs. Sometimes, wealthy countries may try to help poorer countries by agreeing to exempt them from quotas. Remember from the beginning of the chapter that tiny Lesotho was one of the countries exempted from most of the quotas and tariffs on clothing imported into the United States, under a policy called the African Growth and Opportunity Act (AGOA). Should we expect this approach to succeed in doing good for Lesotho?

Lesotho has a higher opportunity cost of producing blue jeans than big clothing manufacturers such as China and Bangladesh. (We know this because if it weren't true, Lesotho would have been producing and exporting clothing even before AGOA.) If there were no quotas, we would not expect Lesotho to produce any jeans at all. However, as we have seen, the effect of quotas is to drive up prices. The quotas in the Multifibre Arrangement drove up prices so much that the benefits of making jeans in Lesotho started to outweigh the opportunity cost. Companies in Taiwan were not allowed to export as many jeans to the U.S. from Taiwan, so they started to build factories in Lesotho, from which they could export as many jeans as they liked. Quotas were bad for U.S. consumers and Taiwanese producers, but great for manufacturers and workers in countries such as Lesotho that were suddenly able to compete on the world market due to their preferential trade status.

The flip-side of this story is that when the U.S. began to peel back its trade restrictions on clothing, Lesotho once again faced competition from big, low-cost producers in Asia. By the time the Multifibre Arrangement was phased out in 2005, almost 70 percent of Lesotho's economy was based on exported clothing and textiles, so the country as a whole took a big hit from falling prices and rising competition. Moving away from the Multifibre Arrangement toward free trade was efficient, and increased total surplus in the world as a whole. It was great news for U.S. consumers and Taiwanese producers, for a start. But it was not universally beneficial. Trade policies—whether free trade or restricted—always generate both winners and losers, and one of the losers in this case was Lesotho.

✓ CONCEPT CHECK

❑ How does a tariff on an imported good affect surplus for domestic producers of that good? **[LO 17.4]**

❑ How does a quota on an imported good affect surplus for domestic consumers of that good? **[LO 17.5]**

❑ In what way are tariff revenues and quota rents similar? **[LO 17.5]**

Trade Agreements

Now that we understand what happens when a closed economy opens up to trade, and what happens when a tariff or quota is imposed or lifted, we can talk more about why these things happen. We've touched on reasons why U.S. politicians might want to protect domestic steel producers by imposing tariffs, or help impoverished African economies by exempting them from quotas. In this section, we'll dig deeper into how such decisions often are motivated by political and moral ideas, and see how economic analysis can be harnessed to understand their implications.

International labor and capital

LO 17.6 Describe the effects of trade on the factor distribution of income.

Political battles between free-traders and protectionists have always been fierce, and they continue to be so today. In the United States, protectionists accuse free-traders of shipping overseas the jobs of hard-working Americans. Free-traders accuse protectionists of giving handouts to big corporations at the expense of American consumers. Why are voters and politicians unable to agree on what is best?

Although the country as a whole gains from liberalizing trade, we've seen that certain segments of the population will lose out. As a general rule, free trade increases demand for factors of production that are domestically abundant, and it increases the supply of factors that are domestically scarce. In other words, it acts to equalize the supply of and demand for factors of production across countries, which in turn causes factor prices (such as wages) to converge across countries. The result is that the owners of domestically scarce factors of production lose due to increased competition, and the owners of domestically abundant factors gain from increased demand.

As we discussed in the previous chapter, people earn income from ownership of the factors of production. Changes in factor prices as a result of international trade have a big effect on the distribution of income within a country. Consider two examples of how trade has tipped the balance between owners of scarce and abundant factors of production: Bangladesh and the United States.

Bangladesh is a very small country in terms of land area, but a big one in terms of population: Imagine an area the size of Illinois or Iowa with a population equal to half of the entire United States. In the days before there was much international trade, land owners in Bangladesh benefited greatly from their control over that scarce resource, using cheap labor that was in plentiful supply. In other words, land was scarce in relation to labor. As the country became more and more connected to international markets through trade, textile firms seeking cheap labor moved in. Bangladeshis began to earn enough from textile work to be able to import food from countries where land is less scarce. As a result, the price of labor has risen, and the price of land has fallen. The relative incomes of the owners of labor and land have changed accordingly.

In the United States, a more subtle change in the factor distribution of income has taken place. With its tech-savvy, highly educated population, the U.S. has a relative

The rapid growth of exports from countries like China and Bangladesh opens new opportunities—and some new debates.

abundance of high-skilled labor—scientists, financial managers, engineers, and so on. In comparison to other countries, it doesn't have so many low-skilled workers. When the country didn't engage in much trade, this was good for the low-skilled workers. They represented a scarce resource relative to high-skilled workers, which drove up the wages of low-skilled workers. In the 1950s, for instance, the United States was a great place to be a factory worker. As trade has increased astronomically in recent decades, however, the balance has tipped. Many economists believe that this change explains part of the increase in income inequality that has occurred in the U.S. in recent decades. High-skilled workers

against the Castro regime. The Cuban American National Foundation goes so far as to argue that lifting the embargo "would be tantamount to sentencing the Cuban people to the continuation of the deprivation of economic, civil and human freedoms."

Opponents argue that the embargo has failed to motivate any change in the Cuban government since 1960. They believe that free trade and travel would nurture closer relationships between Cubans and Americans, which might be a more effective political tool than the embargo. They also emphasize that the economic costs of the embargo are not limited to Cuba: The U.S. Chamber of Commerce estimates that the embargo costs the U.S. economy $1.2 billion per year.

In recent years, parts of the embargo have been relaxed. Since 2000, the U.S. has allowed sale of agricultural goods and medicine for humanitarian purposes. In 2009, the U.S. loosened restrictions on Cuban-Americans who want to travel or send money back to Cuba, and Cuba was allowed to re-enter the Organization of American States.

What do you think?

1. An embargo is designed to put pressure on a foreign government by causing hardship to its citizens. How should the future value of achieving political objectives be weighed against the cost of current hardship for citizens?
2. Is the embargo against Cuba an effective way for the U.S. to pursue its foreign policy objectives?

Source: http://www.canf.org/issues/a-new-course-for-u.s.-cuba-policy/.

✓ CONCEPT CHECK

❒ What happens to the price of domestically scarce factors of production when a country opens up to trade? What happens to the price of domestically abundant factors of production? **[LO 17.6]**

❒ What does the WTO do? **[LO 17.6]**

❒ What is the purpose of an embargo? **[LO 17.7]**

Conclusion

The chapter has taken a close look at one of the most powerful economic insights: There can be big gains from specialization and exchange. This is true for countries as well as individual people and companies.

Even though the total gains from trade are usually positive on a national level, the distribution of those gains to different people and industries matters a lot in the real world. There are usually winners and losers from trade, especially in the short run. The hope is that opening up to trade eventually makes everyone better off, but getting to that point requires responsive political solutions.

Trade restrictions such as tariffs and quotas are used in varying degrees by every country in the world to protect some groups and industries from international competition. Some domestic policies, such as environmental and labor standards, can also affect trade.

Because trade takes place across countries, the role of public policy in shaping international trade is more obvious than in most of the domestic topics we've covered so far. In upcoming chapters, we'll tackle other ways that public policy drives the economy, on both the domestic and international levels.

◄ Mobile Window on the World—Scan this code with your smartphone to find more applications of the chapter content. (Need a barcode reader? Try ScanLife, available in your app store.)

Visit your mobile app store and download ► the Karlan and Morduch Study Econ app.

Key Terms

Summary

LO 17.1 Define comparative advantage and list some root causes of comparative advantage on a national level.

Comparative advantage is the ability to produce a good or service at a lower opportunity cost than others can. Absolute advantage is the ability to produce more of a good than others can with a given amount of resources. It is comparative advantage, rather than absolute advantage, that determines which countries produce which goods for trade.

The most efficient economic arrangement is one in which each country specializes in the good for which it has a comparative advantage and trades with others. Characteristics such as climate, natural resources, factor endowment, and technology determine which goods and services a country will have a comparative advantage at producing. Because features like climate, population, and technology are not uniform throughout an entire country, incomplete specialization, in which a country produces some of many different kinds of goods, can also be efficient.

LO 17.2 Determine whether a country will become a net-importer or net-exporter of a good when it moves from autarky to free trade.

When a country moves from autarky (a self-contained economy that does not trade with others) to trade, the difference between the world price and the domestic price of a good determines whether the country becomes a net-importer or net-exporter. If the world price is lower than the domestic price, the domestic price will drop when the country opens to trade. In that case, domestic supply will no longer be sufficient to meet domestic demand at the lower price. Imported goods will make up the difference, and the country will become a net-importer. If the world price is higher than the domestic price, the domestic price will rise when the country opens up to trade. Domestic supply will outstrip domestic demand at the higher price, and the country will export the excess supply, becoming a net-exporter.

LO 17.3 Calculate the change in surplus and the distribution of benefits within a market when a country opens up to trade.

When markets function well, total surplus increases when a country opens up to trade. The domestic distribution of surplus depends on whether the country becomes a net-importer or net-exporter of the good being traded. In net-importing countries, consumers gain surplus from buying a larger quantity at a lower price; producers lose surplus from selling less at a lower price. When a country becomes a net-exporter, consumers lose surplus from buying a smaller quantity at a higher price; producers gain surplus. In both cases, total surplus increases, making trade more efficient than autarky.

LO 17.4 Explain the effect of a tariff on quantity, price, and the distribution of surplus.

In order to raise public funds and redistribute surplus toward domestic producers, governments use import tariffs. A tariff is a tax on imports, and like any tax, it causes inefficiency and deadweight loss. A tariff raises the domestic price of a good, causing a reduction in the quantity demanded, an increase in the quantity supplied domestically, and a reduction in the quantity imported. Domestic producers will enjoy an increase in surplus as a result of selling more at a higher price, and government will receive tax revenue. However, domestic consumers lose surplus as a result of buying less at a higher price, and total surplus decreases.

LO 17.5 Explain the effect of an import quota on quantity, price, and the distribution of surplus.

Import quotas limit the amount of a particular good that can be imported. The effect of the quota on domestic price and quantity is similar to the effect of a tariff: Domestic price increases, quantity sold decreases, and the quantity imported decreases. Domestic producers gain surplus from selling at a higher price; domestic consumers lose surplus from buying a lower quantity at a higher price. Some surplus goes to whoever holds the rights to import, called quota rents.

LO 17.6 Describe the effects of trade on the factor distribution of income.

International trade equalizes the supply and demand of factors of production across countries. In general, trade increases demand for factors that are domestically abundant, and it increases the supply of factors that are domestically scarce. As a result, the price of domestically scarce factors will typically drop due to increased foreign competition, and the owners of these factors lose surplus. In contrast, the price of domestically abundant factors increases due to increased demand, and owners will gain surplus.

LO 17.7 Discuss the challenges of establishing environmental or labor standards in international markets.

Each country has its own set of laws and policies governing the economy. These regulations vary among countries, which can be a source of friction when economic activity takes place across national boundaries. Policy-makers and consumers approach the problem of inconsistent standards in several ways, ranging from explicit laws about imports to voluntary purchasing decisions by consumers.

Review Questions

1. Why might a country that is more productive in producing wheat than its trading partners end up importing wheat? **[LO 17.1]**

2. Imagine two nations with similar landmasses and levels of wealth that do not specialize in the same industries. What characteristics might drive differences in their comparative advantages? **[LO 17.1]**

3. Producing socks is labor-intensive, while producing satellites is capital-intensive. If India has abundant labor, and the U.S. has abundant capital, which good will the U.S. export? Is trade beneficial to textile laborers in the U.S.? **[LO 17.2]**

4. Suppose Egypt wants to open its trade borders to the world market for natural gas. What will determine whether Egypt becomes a net-exporter or net-importer of natural gas? If Egypt becomes a net-exporter, will domestic supply be equal to, less than, or greater than domestic demand? **[LO 17.2]**

5. If Argentina becomes a net-exporter of beef after trade barriers are removed, how does total welfare in Argentina change compared with autarky? Are Argentine cattle ranchers better or worse off? What about Argentine consumers? **[LO 17.3]**

6. Suppose a country opens its trade borders and becomes a net-exporter of beef. Is it better for domestic consumers of beef if the country is a large player on the world market or a small player? **[LO 17.3]**

7. Suppose Mexico wants to protect its domestic automobile industry from U.S. and Japanese competition. How will a tariff on imported cars help it to accomplish this task? How does the tariff affect domestic producer and consumer surplus? **[LO 17.4]**

8. Refer to Figure 17-9. Explain why area D is a deadweight loss. What about area F? **[LO 17.4]**

9. Imagine Mexico is considering using an import quota rather than a tariff to protect its domestic automobile industry. How does the outcome differ from that of a tariff? **[LO 17.5]**

10. Explain how lifting an import quota on other countries will affect an exporting country that had been exempted from the quota restriction. **[LO 17.5]**

11. Labor is relatively abundant in Mexico compared with arable land. Explain who wins and who loses in Mexico as a result of the North American Free Trade Agreement (NAFTA), which liberalized trade between the U.S., Canada, and Mexico. **[LO 17.6]**

12. If capital is domestically scarce in a country, do you expect owners of capital in that country to be free-traders or protectionists? Why? **[LO 17.6]**

13. Suppose Great Britain wants to take a stance on labor standards for imports. The prime minister imposes a blanket standard that requires all imports to meet certain labor standards. Who will benefit from this policy? What are the drawbacks for Great Britain and countries that export to Great Britain? **[LO 17.7]**

14. Suppose the U.S. imposes a trade embargo on North Korea in order to exert political pressure on the government. Consider how the embargo will affect U.S. producers. Under what conditions would they support the embargo? Why might they oppose it? **[LO 17.7]**

Problems and Applications

1. If a country has relatively abundant unskilled labor, with scarce land and capital, it is more likely to have a comparative advantage in which of the following industries? Check all that apply. **[LO 17.1]**
   a. Food service.
   b. Textiles.
   c. Agriculture.
   d. Financial services.

2. Suppose Ghana discovers it has lost its comparative advantage in the production of maize. Which of the following could explain the loss of comparative advantage? Check all that apply. [LO 17.1]

   a. Maize-processing technology developed in Ghana spreads to other maize-producing countries.
   b. Decline in global demand for maize.
   c. Immigration of cheap labor into Ghana.
   d. Growth of low-skill service jobs in Ghana.

3. Calculate the following values using Figure 17P-1, which shows domestic supply and demand for steel in the United States under autarky. [LO 17.2]

   a. What is the equilibrium price and quantity of steel under autarky?
   b. Suppose the post-trade domestic quantity supplied is 150 million. What is the domestic quantity demanded and the new world price?
   c. Is the U.S. a net-exporter or net-importer of steel?
   d. What quantity of steel is imported/exported?

4. Table 17P-1 shows the domestic supply and demand schedule for rice in Thailand. [LO 17.2]

   a. In autarky, what is the domestic quantity supplied and price?
   b. The world price of rice is $1.25 per kilogram. If Thailand opens up to trade in rice, what will be the new domestic price of rice? (*Hint:* You can assume Thailand is a small producer of rice relative to the world market.)
   c. What quantity of rice will be supplied by domestic producers?

TABLE 17P-1

Price of rice ($/kg)	Quantity demanded (millions of kg)	Quantity supplied (millions of kg)
3.50	2,100	3,300
3.25	2,150	3,200
3.00	2,200	3,100
2.75	2,250	3,000
2.50	2,300	2,900
1.25	2,350	2,800
1.00	2,400	2,700
0.75	2,450	2,600
0.50	2,500	2,500
0.25	2,550	2,400

   d. What quantity of rice will be demanded by domestic consumers?
   e. How much rice will Thailand import or export?

5. Guatemala represents a small part of the world poultry market. Based on Figure 17P-2, answer the following. [LO 17.3]

   a. Calculate producer and consumer surplus in autarky.
   b. Assume that the world price of poultry is $0.30/kg. If Guatemala opens to trade, what is the domestic quantity consumed and produced? What is the quantity of imports?
   c. Calculate the post-trade producer and consumer surplus. Who is better off after trade?

FIGURE 17P-1

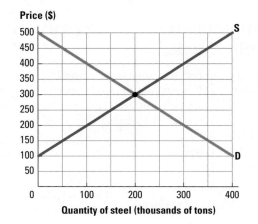

Quantity of steel (thousands of tons)

FIGURE 17P-2

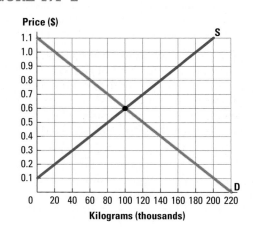

Kilograms (thousands)

6. Guatemala represents a small part of the world poultry market, and is fully open to trade. Suppose a $0.10/kg tariff is imposed on poultry imports. Based on Figure 17P-2 (above), answer the following. **[LO 17.3, 17.4]**

   a. What is the quantity of poultry consumed and produced in Guatemala under the tariff? What is the quantity of imports?

   b. Now suppose the tariff is eliminated and instead the world price of chicken feed increases significantly. This causes the world price of poultry to rise from $0.30/kg to $0.40kg. What is the quantity of poultry now bought and sold in Guatemala? What is the quantity of imports?

   c. Compare the efficiency of the two situations. Calculate the deadweight loss under the tariff. Calculate the deadweight loss resulting from the higher price of chicken feed.

7. The United States wheat market is shown in Figure 17P-3. Suppose the U.S. wants to protect its wheat industry by imposing a tariff of $1/bushel on foreign wheat, which currently sells at world price $4/bushel. **[LO 17.4]**

   a. Graph consumer and producer surplus after the $1/bushel tariff is imposed.

   b. How much revenue does the U.S. government collect from the tariff?

   c. Graph the deadweight loss associated with the tariff.

8. The United States wheat market is shown in Figure 17P-3 (above). **[LO 17.5]**

   a. How many bushels of wheat should be allowed under an import quota in order to increase the domestic price from $4 to $5 per bushel?

   b. Graph the domestic producer surplus increase as a result of this quota?

   c. Graph the deadweight loss that results from this quota.

9. Suppose a country imposes a tariff on coffee imports. Using the diagram of supply and demand in Figure 17P-4, identify the correct shaded areas as follows. **[LO 17.3, 17.4, 17.5]**

   a. In autarky, which area(s) comprise domestic consumer surplus? Which area(s) comprise domestic producer surplus?

   b. When the country opens up to trade, which area(s) do consumers gain as surplus? Which area(s) do producers lose?

   c. After trade, if an import tariff is imposed, which area(s) do domestic producers gain as surplus? Which do domestic consumers lose?

   d. With the tariff, which area is government revenue?

   e. Which area(s) represent deadweight loss as a result of the tariff?

   f. If the country uses an import quota instead of a tariff, what is the quota quantity if the quota price is $7?

10. Suppose a country where capital is scarce and most of industry is labor-intensive with low-skilled labor moves from autarky to free trade. Which of the following do you expect to happen? Check all that apply. **[LO 17.6]**

    a. Owners of capital become wealthier.

    b. Wages for labor increase.

    c. Income disparity between workers and owners of capital increases.

FIGURE 17P-3

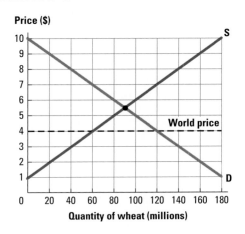

Quantity of wheat (millions)

FIGURE 17P-4

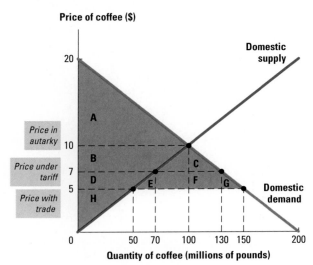

Quantity of coffee (millions of pounds)

425

11. Suppose two countries are considering a new agricultural trade agreement with each other. Country A has abundant low-skill labor and scarce land. Country B has abundant arable land but little population. In which country do land owners support a trade agreement? In which country do workers support a trade agreement? **[LO 17.6]**

12. Suppose a country has abundant capital but scarce labor. Which group would be more harmed by a trade embargo: owners of capital or laborers? **[LO 17.6, 7.7]**

13. Which of the following policies is likely to cause more pollution displacement: imposing environmental standards on domestic production or a blanket environmental standard on all imports? **[LO 17.7]**

Chapter Endnote

1. http://georgewbush-whitehouse.archives.gov /news/releases/2002/03/20020305-6.html.

Chapter Sources

http://www.economist.com/node/9516043? story_id=9516043

http://www.fas.org/sgp/crs/misc/RL32333.pdf

http://www.telegraph.co.uk/news/worldnews /europe/france/4306018/France-targets-Coca-Cola-in-escalating-cheese-wars.html

Part Five

Public Economics

The six chapters in Part 5 will introduce you to ...

how microeconomics helps solve important policy problems, including questions about technological innovation, the environment, inequality, and social security.

Until now, our analysis has focused on buyers and sellers in a particular market, but sometimes others have a stake in the outcomes. Everyone bears the cost when a polluting factory emits smoke that contributes to climate change. Or, to take a positive example, your classmates benefit when you get a flu shot that helps prevent the spread of flu on campus. Chapter 18 deals with these kinds of costs and benefits, which are known as *externalities.* Externalities cause some goods and services to be overdemanded ("too much") or underprovided ("too little"), relative to what would be optimal for society.

Chapter 19 describes two special types of goods that are underprovided or overdemanded in free markets: public goods and common resource goods. Public goods like national defense tend to be underprovided if left to the free market. Common resources suffer from the opposite problem: Individuals or firms will tend to use more of a common resource than is optimal socially. Overfishing in a lake is a classic example: Everyone would be better off if each person fished less in order to protect the long-term viability of the fish stock, but no individual has an incentive to cut back. We'll discuss how taxes, subsidies, and quotas can be used to get incentives right.

Few people love paying taxes, but most accept that taxes generate the revenue required by governments to build parks and highways, hire teachers and police officers, and provide other basic services for citizens. Chapter 20 describes the role of taxes, the burden they place on taxpayers, and how some types of taxes can target certain problems better than others.

Chapter 21 analyzes facts and policies related to poverty and inequality. We examine why some families are poorer and some are richer, and describe what new research suggests about reducing income gaps. At the end of the chapter, we look at insights from economics into the problem of discrimination.

No matter what the particular topic is, making policy choices involves both economics and politics. With that in mind, Chapter 22 looks at the political system through an economic lens. We show how economic analysis provides insight into fundamental political questions like why people vote, how politicians become corrupt, and how the president can influence the economy.

Chapter 23 describes a new set of ideas that are shaping policy discussions. The idea of "choice architecture" builds on the simple insight that how you frame a choice can shape the decision that's made. We show how policy-makers are using "nudges" designed to help people achieve goals like saving for retirement and conserving energy.

Together, these chapters show how microeconomics can be used to solve problems, big and small.

Externalities

Chapter 18

LEARNING OBJECTIVES

LO 18.1   Explain how external costs and benefits affect the trade-offs faced by economic decision makers.

LO 18.2   Calculate the effect of a negative externality on market price and quantity, and measure the resulting change in surplus.

LO 18.3   Calculate the effect of a positive externality on market price and quantity, and measure the resulting change in surplus.

LO 18.4   Describe how individuals could reach a private solution to an externality, and explain why this doesn't always occur.

LO 18.5   Show how a tax or subsidy can be used to counteract an externality, and discuss the pros and cons of such a solution.

LO 18.6   Show how quantity regulations can be used to counteract an externality, and discuss the pros and cons of such a solution.

LO 18.7   Show how tradable allowances can be used to counteract an externality, and discuss the pros and cons of such a solution.

• •

THE COSTS OF CAR CULTURE

California is a car culture. The country's first motel—or "motor hotel"—opened in California in 1925 as a stopover on the drive between Los Angeles and San Francisco, and the idea spread across the country. Los Angeles–based comedian Jay Leno is an extreme example of how much Californians love their vehicles: Leno owns about 100 cars, including 25 Corvettes.

But all of that driving has a downside as well. Los Angeles is notorious for its gridlocked freeways full of commuters. It's also one of the smoggiest cities in the country. If you're stuck in traffic, you won't need much persuading that the presence of all those other cars on the road is imposing a cost on you. (Of course, *your* presence on the road is also contributing to congestion that imposes a cost on everyone else.) Likewise, if you're an L.A. resident breathing in exhaust fumes every day, you're paying a price for the city's car culture.

In previous chapters, we saw that when people make individual decisions to maximize their own utility, competitive markets are typically efficient, maximizing total surplus through the magic of the invisible hand. That is true when the only people whose surplus we have to consider are buyers and sellers in the market. In many cases, that's a fair assumption. There are some situations, however—such as driving on congested highways—in which one person's decision has real implications for others.

429

In this chapter, we'll look at transactions that affect people other than the buyers and sellers directly involved. We'll see that in these cases, markets no longer work efficiently. That is, markets fail to maximize total surplus when individual choices impose costs or benefits on others.

We'll also look at some ways in which we can try to correct these market failures and restore efficiency. California's gasoline taxes—about 50 cents per gallon, the second highest of any state—are one example. As we will see, such taxes are partly an attempt to force drivers to consider the costs they impose on others when they get behind the wheel. Although there is much debate over the right way to design policies to control congestion and pollution, most economists agree that this is a case where government can be part of the solution. In this chapter, we'll see how taxes and other regulations can actually *increase* efficiency in the presence of externalities, by changing prices to reflect the true cost of individuals' decisions.

What Are Externalities?

Think about the decision to drive a car. Although you probably don't make a conscious calculation every time you sit in the driver's seat, there is an underlying *trade-off* that you consider, at least subconsciously. On the one hand, you have the benefit of driving: getting from one place to another quickly and easily. On the other hand, you have the costs of driving: paying for gasoline and some wear and tear on the car, and maybe also toll fees and the cost of parking at your destination.

Now let's consider another type of cost that you might not think about. Every mile you drive burns gasoline, which emits pollutants into the air. If you're the only one on the road, the costs are negligible, but they add up when there are lots of drivers. The pollutants have two kinds of costs, one local and one global. Locally, if pollution levels get high, they can create regional smog and health problems.

Globally, the cost of burning gas comes from the production of carbon dioxide. Carbon dioxide is a greenhouse gas, which traps heat from the sun in the atmosphere and contributes to global warming, the gradual warming of the earth's atmosphere. Rising temperatures contribute to higher sea levels and melting of glaciers and ice caps, as well as changed precipitation patterns around the world.[1] Although global temperatures have fluctuated throughout history, most scientists today agree that human production of greenhouse gases contributes to global warming.

Do you consider these costs every time you weigh whether to go somewhere in your car? We don't know many people who do. The pollution caused by burning gasoline is an *externality* associated with driving, because it imposes costs on people other than the driver. But let's say that drivers did take into account these kinds of costs, on top of the costs to themselves. Then their cost-benefit trade-offs would shift slightly, and they would, on net, drive a bit less. This suggests that the existence of the externality is causing people to drive more than is optimal from the perspective of society as a whole. The impact of externalities is a common problem in economics. The case of vehicle emissions is one in which millions of small externalities every day can add up to create big concerns.

External costs and benefits

LO 18.1 Explain how external costs and benefits affect the trade-offs faced by economic decision makers.

To think clearly about externalities, we'll need to introduce some new terminology. When we talk about costs such as gasoline, wear and tear on a car, road tolls, and parking fees, we're talking about costs borne by a driver herself. In general, we call costs that fall directly on an economic decision maker **private costs**. The cost of pollution is not a private cost, because individual drivers don't personally bear all—or even most—of the costs of the pollution they produce. Pollution, or any other cost that is imposed without compensation on someone other than the person who caused it, is an **external cost**.

When we add private costs to external costs, we call the sum **social cost**. (Why not "total cost"? Because total cost is a term used to describe costs of production. Also, the term social cost helps make it clear that we are thinking about this idea from society's perspective.) For example, suppose you decide to host a noisy party. The *private costs* might include food, drink, and any cleanup costs the next day. The *external costs* would include annoyance felt by neighbors who can't sleep or study because of the noise your party is creating. The *social cost* would be the sum of these two types of costs.

Externalities are not all bad news, though. There are lots of situations in which a person's behavior helps, rather than hurts, others. Imagine that you have decided to tidy up your messy front yard and paint your house. Clearly, you benefit from this decision: You have the aesthetic pleasure of a tidy yard and a prettier house, and the value of your property increases. These are benefits that accrue directly to the decision maker, called—as you might have guessed—**private benefits**. But your neighbors, too, benefit from your decision to fix up your house. They get the pleasure of living in a nicer-looking neighborhood, and the value of their properties may also increase a bit—all at no cost to them. A benefit that accrues without compensation to someone other than the person who caused it is called an **external benefit**.

When we add private benefits and external benefits together, the result is called **social benefit**. To take another example, suppose you decide to get vaccinated against the flu and to wash your hands frequently. The private benefit is that you are less likely to get the flu. The external benefit is that you are less likely to transmit the flu to other people. The social benefit is the sum of these two effects—the overall reduction in likelihood of the flu spreading, both to yourself and to others.

External costs and external benefits are collectively referred to as **externalities**. We typically call an external cost a *negative externality* and an external benefit a *positive externality*. Externalities are an incredibly important concept in economics. They are one of the most common causes of market failure. From this point on, we will use the terms learned in this section to distinguish between choices that are optimal from the perspective of an *individual decision maker,* and choices that are optimal from the perspective of *society as a whole.*

The size of the external cost or benefit caused by a particular action may vary based on location, timing, quantity, or many other factors. For instance, driving during the middle of the day in the summer usually contributes more to smog than driving at night or driving during winter (because sunlight is a key ingredient in the formation of smog). Painting the one derelict house in a nice neighborhood is likely to boost neighbors' property values more than painting one house in a neighborhood full of run-down homes. However, for the sake of simplicity, in this chapter we mostly assume that externalities involve a *constant, predictable* external cost or benefit.

Finally, there is one special type of externality that doesn't neatly fit into the categories we just laid out. A **network externality** is the effect that an additional user of a good

---

private cost a cost that falls directly on an economic decision maker

external cost a cost imposed without compensation on someone other than the person who caused it

social cost the entire cost of a decision, including both private costs and any external costs

private benefit a benefit that accrues directly to the decision maker

external benefit a benefit that accrues without compensation to someone other than the person who caused it

social benefit the entire benefits of a decision, including both private benefits and external benefits

externality a cost or benefit imposed without compensation on someone other than the person who caused it

network externality the effect that an additional user of a good or participant in an activity has on the value of that good or activity for others

or participant in an activity has on the value of that good or activity for others. Network externalities imply that people can help or harm others simply by virtue of their participation in a group.

Network externalities can be positive or negative. We've already described one example of a negative network externality—driving in L.A. rush hour. Every additional person who decides to use the L.A. road network imposes a *negative network externality* on other road users. You may have also experienced negative network externalities on wireless Internet networks, when each additional user draws down bandwidth, slowing the connection for other users.

Positive network externalities are frequently associated with technology, especially communication technology. An important historical example is the telephone. Telephones, like most communication devices, are useful only if other people have them too. When very few people had telephones, having one let you contact only a limited number of people. The more common telephones became, the more people they allowed you to contact, and the more useful they got. Each person who joined the telephone network made telephones more useful for everyone else—a positive network externality.

Social-media networks are a more recent example. The more people who belong to a service such as Facebook, LinkedIn, or Twitter, the higher the benefits of joining. To flip it around: Everyone who joins one of these services makes it more useful for everyone else. The effect of positive network externalities can be so powerful that it may even mean that social networking services like Facebook are effectively natural monopolies. Once they reach a critical mass of users, it becomes extremely hard for competitors to gain a foothold in the market, because users want to be in whatever network everyone else is in.

Negative externalities and the problem of "too much"

LO 18.2 Calculate the effect of a negative externality on market price and quantity, and measure the resulting change in surplus.

Because air pollution is an external cost, the costs of driving look smaller from the perspective of an individual driver than they actually are from the perspective of society as a whole. Because drivers don't take the external cost into account, they will decide to drive more than they would if they themselves had to bear the full cost of driving (which mostly includes the cost caused by any pollution).

Why is that a problem? It means people drive "too much"—that is, more than they would if they faced the social costs of their actions. Where there are externalities, the free market no longer allocates resources in a way that maximizes total surplus for society as a whole. To understand *why* this is the case, let's take a closer look at supply and demand in the market for gasoline in California.

Imagine that gas sales in California are completely unregulated (no gas taxes, no emissions standards, and so on). At any given price, as in any other market, a certain number of drivers decide that the private benefits of buying a gallon of gas outweigh the private cost. This is represented by the demand curve in panel A of Figure 18-1, which shows California drivers' demand for gasoline.

How do we quantify the *external costs* of a gallon of gas? It's not easy to put a dollar figure on all of the diffuse effects of air pollution around the world. Essentially, the question boils down to this: How much would people who are affected by pollution be willing to pay to avoid it? Or, to put it another way, how much would you have to pay the people who are affected by pollution to persuade them to accept it? Suppose that we estimate the cost of pollution at about $1 per gallon. The social cost of gas, therefore, is the market price plus the $1 external cost of pollution.

FIGURE 18-1

Internalizing a negative externality reduces demand

(A) Market with private costs only

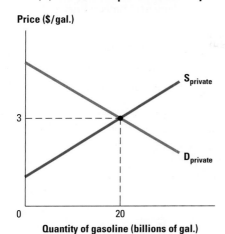

Without any regulation, the gasoline market reaches equilibrium based on private costs and benefits.

(B) Market with social costs

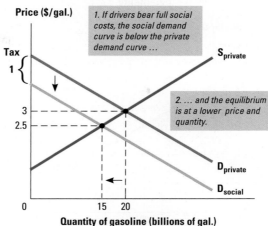

1. If drivers bear full social costs, the social demand curve is below the private demand curve ...

2. ... and the equilibrium is at a lower price and quantity.

If drivers are forced to take the external costs of pollution into account, the new demand curve for gasoline would be below the demand curve based on private costs alone. The market will reach equilibrium at a lower price and quantity, based on social costs and benefits.

The problem is that when drivers decide how much gas to buy, they take only the private cost into account. If they had to pay the higher social cost for each gallon, the cost-benefit trade-off would look less favorable, and they would choose to buy less gas. We represent this by drawing another demand curve below the original, shifted down by the amount of the external cost, as shown in panel B. This "social" demand curve reflects the trade-offs that drivers would consider if external costs were factored into their decision making. Drivers demand a smaller quantity at any given market price, because they know that the final price they will end up paying is actually the market price plus the additional $1 per gallon to cover external costs.

How can drivers be forced to consider external costs, and thus operate on the social demand curve? The most straightforward option is to implement a gasoline tax.[2] With a $1 tax per gallon, drivers literally pay the market price plus the external cost, represented by the social demand curve. When a gas tax is introduced, the equilibrium point moves down along the supply curve to its intersection with the social demand curve, resulting in a lower price-quantity combination. Note that although the market price is lower in this new equilibrium, the cost per gallon that is actually paid by drivers is higher, once the tax is included. The end result is that a lower quantity of gas is purchased. The example demonstrates a very important conclusion: *If drivers had to pay the full cost of gas, including the external cost of pollution, they would choose to buy less of it.*

In our discussion of taxes in Chapter 6, we said that the effect of a tax is always to reduce surplus. When there are external costs, however, a tax can increase surplus, making the market more efficient. What is the difference? The answer is that a tax does reduce the surplus enjoyed by *buyers and sellers of gas.*

To see why, look at Figure 18-2. Panel A shows consumer and producer surplus in an unregulated market in which drivers pay only the private cost of gas. The red-cross-hatched area shows the loss of surplus suffered by people who breathe polluted air. That represents the external cost per gallon ($1) times the number of gallons consumed, which is

FIGURE 18-2

Markets fail to maximize total surplus in the presence of externalities

(A) Surplus under a negative externality

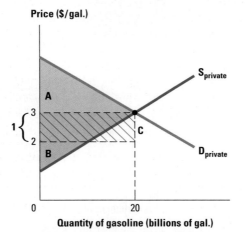

Price ($/gal.)

Quantity of gasoline (billions of gal.)

Under a negative externality, the surplus lost to those outside the market due to the external cost (in this case, pollution) is subtracted from consumer and producer surplus.

(B) Surplus when a negative externality is internalized

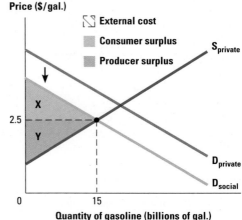

Price ($/gal.)

Quantity of gasoline (billions of gal.)

If the externality is internalized, consumer and producer surplus in the gasoline market are both lower. However, the external cost imposed on people who suffer from pollution has disappeared.

20 billion. Panel B shows what would happen if drivers were somehow forced to pay $1 to pollution sufferers every time they put a gallon of gas in the tank. Consumer and producer surplus have clearly shrunk, but now we no longer have to subtract the loss of surplus of people who breathe dirty air.

What has happened to *total surplus*—that is, the surplus not only of market participants, but of society as a whole? Let's crunch the numbers. First, we have to add consumer and producer surplus in the unregulated market and then subtract the loss of surplus to others. Based on panel A of Figure 18-2, we see that the total surplus in the presence of a negative externality is calculated as:

Equation 18-1 Total surplus in presence of a negative externality

$$\text{Total surplus} = \text{Consumer surplus} + \text{Producer surplus} - \text{External cost}$$
$$= \quad A \quad + \quad B \quad - \quad C$$
$$= \quad \$20\text{ billion} \quad + \quad \$20\text{ billion} \quad - \quad \$20\text{ billion}$$
$$= \quad \$20\text{ billion}$$

When drivers have to pay the social cost of gas—that is, when the pollution externality has been "internalized" into drivers' decisions—calculating total surplus is straightforward. Adding consumer and producer surplus together based on panel B of Figure 18-2, we find that total surplus is:

Equation 18-2 Total surplus when a negative externality is internalized

$$\text{Total surplus} = \text{Consumer surplus} + \text{Producer surplus}$$
$$= \quad X \quad + \quad Y$$
$$= \quad \$11.25\text{ billion} \quad + \quad \$11.25\text{ billion}$$
$$= \quad \$22.5\text{ billion}$$

In the end, we see that total surplus is $2.5 billion lower ($22.5 billion − $20 billion) when drivers consider only their private costs than it is when the cost of pollution is internalized into drivers' decisions. We can confirm graphically that a negative externality always reduces surplus, using Figure 18-3. The blue area is surplus lost by consumers and producers of gas when the externality is internalized ($20 billion). It reflects both the cost of paying the $1 per gallon tax, and the fact that fewer gallons are now bought and sold. The red-cross-hatched area is surplus gained by others in society when they receive the $1 per gallon that drivers pay for the external cost of pollution ($20 billion). The blue and yellow areas added together have the same total area as the red-cross-hatched box (because they have the same height and the same width). Thus, the yellow area represents the difference between red and blue—surplus gained minus surplus lost. The net gain in surplus is worth $2.5 billion.

Who gains and who loses? Consumer surplus falls because drivers buy fewer gallons of gas and pay a higher cost for driving; producer surplus falls because producers sell a smaller quantity of gas. So, who benefits from internalizing the externality? Other people—those not involved in this market as buyers or sellers. By reducing the quantity of gasoline consumed, the external cost on these other people has been decreased. Efficiency increases by shifting the external cost from those not involved in the market to those involved.

We've analyzed the problem of negative externalities by looking at the demand curve. We could just as easily apply the same analysis to the supply side. For example, think about companies that extract crude oil and refine it into gas before it is sold to motorists. The extraction and refining process itself causes some pollution, even before any cars hit the road. If these companies had to pay the *social cost* of production, rather than just the *private cost*, the "social" supply curve would be above the original market supply curve, as oil companies would want to supply less at any given price. This would reduce the equilibrium quantity, just as in our analysis above.

FIGURE 18-3

Internalizing a negative externality increases total surplus

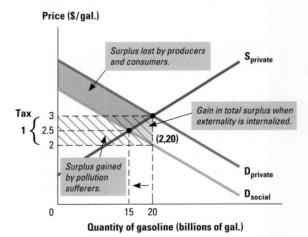

The surplus gained by those outside the market due to the reduction in pollution is greater than the surplus lost by consumers and producers in the market for gasoline when the negative externality is internalized.

Positive externalities and the problem of "too little"

LO 18.3 Calculate the effect of a positive externality on market price and quantity, and measure the resulting change in surplus.

It is tempting to think that a positive externality must be a good thing. A negative externality decreases surplus, so a positive externality must do the opposite, right? Sadly, that is not the case. A positive externality also pushes quantity away from the efficient equilibrium level, reducing total surplus.

Consider the decision to paint the outside of your house. A homeowner will paint her house if the private benefits (such as increased property value, a nicer-looking home) outweigh the private costs (such as the time and money required to paint the house or pay someone else to do it). But this personal decision doesn't take into account benefits that accrue to neighbors, who also enjoy increased property values and a tidier-looking neighborhood. As a result, houses get painted "too little"—that is, less than the amount that would maximize total surplus, once we also consider the surplus of people other than the homeowner and house painter.

Although the external benefits of house painting probably vary a lot, let's make a rough estimate. Suppose that the external benefits are worth $500 per paint job. In other words, $500 is the combined amount your neighbors would be willing to pay to *avoid* having your shabby-looking house lowering the tone of the neighborhood. Let's imagine that somehow it were possible to turn the external benefit into private benefit—by some magic, every time a homeowner paints her house, $500 is transferred from her neighbors' bank accounts into her own. If this happened, her trade-off would look different: The benefits of painting would increase, and the costs would stay the same. How would she *respond* to this change? Again, we can represent the difference between the private trade-off and the social trade-off (including the external benefit) by adding a new demand curve. At any given market price, homeowners will behave as if the price were reduced by the amount of the external benefit. We can represent this by adding the new demand curve $500 above the original demand curve, as shown in Figure 18-4. This causes the equilibrium point to move up along the supply curve, to a higher price-quantity combination.

Maintaining the outside of one's house creates both private benefits for the homeowner and external, social benefits for the neighborhood.

Just as forcing drivers to account for external costs looks much like the effect of a tax, forcing homeowners who paint their houses to account for external benefits looks much like the effect of a subsidy. That's not surprising: The process we imagined for the positive externality to be internalized is, effectively, that neighbors would be subsidizing your paint job by $500.

Didn't we learn in Chapter 6 that a subsidy reduces surplus in a well-functioning market? Yes, we did—but the existence of a positive externality tells us that a market is *not* well-functioning. In a market with no externalities, private costs and benefits are the same as social costs and benefits, so the market equilibrium maximizes total surplus. In this case, the private benefits of house painting understate the social benefits. The subsidy that the neighbors pay actually makes this a well-functioning market. Without the subsidy, we would see fewer homes painted than would be socially optimal.

Analyzing the effect of a positive externality on surplus is essentially the reverse of analyzing a negative externality. To find total surplus in the presence of a positive externality, we calculate consumer and producer surplus under the lower equilibrium price and quantity; we then *add* the value of the external benefit to those outside the market. Equation 18-3 and panel A of Figure 18-5 show the calculation of total surplus in the presence of a positive externality.

FIGURE 18-4

Internalizing a positive externality increases demand

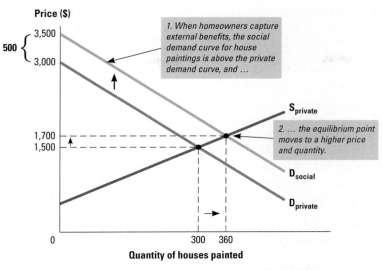

If homeowners are able to capture the external benefits of painting a house, a new demand curve is added above the old one and the market reaches an equilibrium with a higher quantity based on social costs and benefits.

FIGURE 18-5

A positive externality causes inefficiency

(A) Surplus under a positive externality

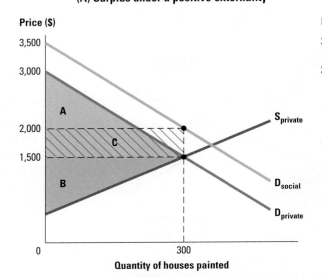

With a positive externality, the external benefits gained by those outside the market (represented by box "C") are added to consumer and producer surplus.

(B) Surplus when a positive externality is internalized

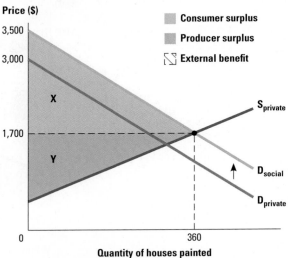

When the positive externality is internalized, total surplus increases. Producer and consumer surplus increase because the quantity of houses painted increases, which outweighs the loss of free external benefits to neighbors.

Equation 18-3 Total surplus in the presence of a positive externality

Total surplus = Consumer surplus + Producer surplus + External benefit

=	A	+	B	+	C	
=	$225,000	+	$150,000	+	$150,000	
=	$525,000					

If it were possible for this positive externality to be "internalized" by somehow transferring $500 from neighbors to homeowners who paint their houses, the number of mutually beneficial trades would increase. This increases producer and consumer surplus, as shown in panel B of Figure 18-5. On the other hand, the neighbors no longer enjoy any surplus: They are still getting $500 worth of benefits from the newly painted house, but now they are being forced to pay $500 rather than getting them for free. To find total surplus in the house-painting market when the positive externality is internalized, we simply add consumer and producer surplus based on the new equilibrium point.

Equation 18-4 Total surplus when a positive surplus is internalized

Total surplus = Consumer surplus + Producer surplus

=	X	+	Y	
=	$324,000	+	$216,000	
=	$540,000			

Total surplus is $15,000 higher when the positive externality is internalized. In other words, the positive externality caused inefficiency and reduced total surplus by $15,000. We can confirm graphically that a positive externality always reduces surplus, in Figure 18-6.

FIGURE 18-6

Internalizing a positive externality always increases total surplus

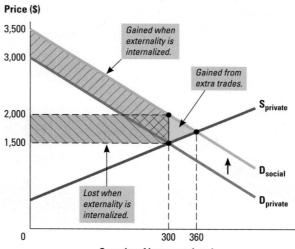

When a positive externality is internalized, the external benefits (the red area) become consumer surplus (the blue area). As both of these areas are the same size, this swap doesn't cause a net change in surplus. On top of this, though, internalizing the externality causes more trades to take place, which increases both producer and consumer surplus (the light green area).

The surplus gained by consumers who would have painted their houses anyway but now capture the external benefit (the blue box) is exactly equal to the surplus that was enjoyed by people outside the market before it was internalized (the red box). (*Hint:* The boxes aren't the same shape, but they have the same height, equal to the external benefit, and the same width, equal to the quantity consumed under the externality.)

These gains and losses exactly cancel each other out. They represent a direct transfer from those outside the market to those inside it. However, the change in the demand curve also causes an increase in quantity. This means that some people who wouldn't have painted their houses at all under the externality now do so, and consumers and producers gain additional surplus from the increased number of trades (the green triangle). Thus, the total gains in surplus from internalizing the externality outweigh the losses.

It is also possible to internalize the same positive externality by applying a subsidy to the supply side of the market. Think about a professional house painter who always collected $500 in tips from neighbors every time he did a job. If he was able in this way to reap the *social benefit* of supplying house-painting services, rather than just the *private benefit*, the entire supply curve would be higher, as he would be willing to paint more houses at any given price. This would increase the equilibrium quantity of houses painted, just as in our analysis above.

✓ CONCEPT CHECK

❏ What is the difference between a positive and negative externality? **[LO 18.1]**

❏ How is a network externality different from other externalities? **[LO 18.1]**

❏ How does a negative externality caused by consumers affect the demand curve? How does this change the equilibrium price and quantity relative to the same market in which the externality is internalized? **[LO 18.2]**

❏ How does a negative externality caused by producers affect the supply curve? How does this change the equilibrium price and quantity relative to the same market in which the externality is internalized? **[LO 18.2]**

❏ How does a positive externality change equilibrium price and quantity, relative to the same market without the externality? **[LO 18.3]**

❏ Does an externality cause total surplus to increase or decrease? **[LO 18.2, 18.3]**

Dealing with Externalities

We've learned that externalities lower total surplus, but that it is possible to address this problem by transforming external costs and benefits into private ones. By taking money from drivers and giving it to pollution sufferers, or forcing neighbors to subsidize the painting of shabby houses, efficiency can be restored. If it's possible to eliminate the problems created by externalities, why do they persist?

We will see in this section that solving the externality problems is often easier to describe than to implement. External costs and benefits can be diffuse, complex, and hard to control. Solutions must try to ensure that economic decision makers experience costs and benefits that are *equal in value* to the true social costs and benefits of their choices. If everyone affected has to be involved in the process, that could mean coordinating across millions—or even billions—of people. This is a tricky problem to solve, even for the smartest of policy-makers.

We will also see that there can be a tension between efficiency and fairness in finding solutions to externalities. Saying a market works *efficiently* means only that it maximizes surplus. It doesn't say anything at all about the *distribution* of that surplus. Some technically sound solutions might seem unfair (like rewarding people for *not* polluting, rather than taxing people who pollute), and thus might not get very far in the political arena.

Before we look at how governments try to solve these problems, let's first consider whether governments need to get involved at all. Under certain circumstances, private individuals may be able to deal with externalities, restoring efficiency to the market on their own.

Private remedies

LO 18.4 Describe how individuals could reach a private solution to an externality, and explain why this doesn't always occur.

Suppose a friend is enjoying her lunch, but her tuna sandwich is giving off a really strong smell. She would be causing a negative externality by eating the tuna in front of you. What can you do? You could ask her to eat it later, but she might object. If you felt strongly enough, you could consider paying her to not eat the sandwich. In practice, that would probably seem weird, but in principle it's a legitimate option for eliminating the externality. After all, nothing stops people from dealing with externalities on their own, without involving governments or other organizations.

Economists usually reserve the term "market failure" for situations in which the actions of private individuals and firms are *insufficient to ensure efficient markets.* An influential economic theory sets out the circumstances under which people should be able to solve externality problems by themselves. The underlying reasoning is actually quite intuitive. The idea of the "invisible hand" tells us that individuals will pursue mutually beneficial trades with other individuals. No mutually beneficial trade should go unexploited, because someone always has something to gain from pursuing it. The result is that when we add up all of the actions of self-interested individuals, every opportunity to gain surplus has been exploited, and total surplus is maximized.

But we've just seen that an externality reduces surplus. Therefore—somewhere, somehow—there are mutually beneficial trades *waiting to be exploited.* For instance, the people who bear the cost of air pollution lose more surplus than is gained by drivers who don't have to pay for it. Here's a crazy idea: Why don't those who suffer from pollution *pay* drivers to drive less? Since there is surplus to be gained from decreasing the quantity of gas burned, a mutually beneficial trade exists. If a given reduction in driving would cause drivers to lose $9.4 billion in surplus and Californians to gain $10 billion in surplus, why don't Californians agree to pay drivers, say, $9.7 billion to drive less? Both groups will be better off. The quantity of driving—and, hence, of pollution—would fall to the efficient equilibrium level, and total surplus in society as a whole would be maximized.

Coase theorem the idea that even in the presence of an externality, individuals can reach an efficient equilibrium through private trades, assuming zero transaction costs

The idea that individuals can reach an efficient equilibrium through private trades, even in the presence of an externality, is called the **Coase theorem**, after economist Ronald Coase. However, there are a couple of key assumptions that must hold: People can make enforceable agreements (also known as contracts) to pay one another, and there are no transaction costs.

Often, these two assumptions do not hold true. Can you imagine the elaborate organization that would be required to bring together all 38 million citizens of California, get each of them to voluntarily pay the amount that avoiding pollution is worth to them personally, redistribute that money to drivers who agreed to drive less, and then monitor those drivers to make sure they actually followed through? Whew! There comes a point where the costs of coordination and enforcement are higher than the surplus lost to the externality, and it's not worth doing.

The example illustrates a second drawback of the Coase theorem. The private solution yields an *efficient* outcome—the surplus-maximizing quantity of gas is bought and sold. But the distribution of that surplus is very different from the solution we imagined earlier, in which the *drivers* had to pay other Californians $1 per gallon to compensate them for pollution. Instead, now the *citizens of California* have to pay drivers not to drive.

The citizens are still better off than they were under the externality, but nowhere near as well off as they would be if drivers had to pay for their own pollution.

Notice that either solution is efficient, but the assumptions about what is "fair," and who has the "rights" to do what, are different. In one case it's assumed that drivers have a right to pollute, and have to be paid not to. In the other case, it's assumed citizens have a right to live free of pollution and have to be paid to accept pollution. The Coase theorem reminds us that efficiency is all about maximizing total surplus. It says nothing about achieving a "fair" distribution of that surplus.

This reasoning explains why it is often more a question of politics, law, and philosophy than of economics to decide who pays whom to solve the market failure. Even when it would make people better off to pay someone else to do, or stop doing, something that affects them, they often feel that it is not "fair" to do so. The movie *Erin Brockovich* is based on the true story of a woman who discovers that a big company is polluting the groundwater in her community, allegedly causing high rates of cancer and other health conditions. She goes on a legal campaign to force the company to stop polluting and compensate the families. Can you imagine if Erin Brockovich instead organized her community under the Coase theorem to *pay the company* to stop polluting? We very much doubt that moviegoers would have found it such a heartwarming, feel-good story.

People usually care not only about reaching an efficient equilibrium, but also about how we get there and who benefits. If you go knocking on your neighbors' doors to explain positive externalities and propose that they contribute toward the cost of painting your house, you'll probably get doors slammed in your face. For a somewhat unlikely application of the Coase theorem, look at the From Another Angle box "Does no-fault divorce law increase the divorce rate?"

FROM ANOTHER ANGLE

Does no-fault divorce law increase the divorce rate?

In 1969, California became the first state in the country to legalize "no-fault" divorce. Prior to no-fault laws, a divorce could be granted only if a person showed that his or her spouse was "at fault" for committing some wrongdoing, such as adultery, abandonment, or abuse. If both partners wanted out, they could agree to lie in court, pretending that one of them was at fault. But if only one partner wanted out, he or she was stuck. Under no-fault divorce, either partner could obtain a divorce, without agreement or having to show evidence of wrongdoing.

Should we expect this change in the law to increase the divorce rate? At first glance, the answer might be yes: Before, it was extremely difficult to get divorced if your partner didn't agree; now, it is relatively easy. However, the Coase theorem gives us a different perspective. It predicts that the number of divorces will stay the same, but the distribution of surplus between marriage partners will change.

To see how this works, imagine a situation in which one partner wants to get divorced and the other doesn't. Under the old law, the partner who wanted the divorce would have to make concessions to persuade his or her spouse to lie in court—say, offering more alimony, or greater visitation rights to the children. The partner who wanted to stay married needed to offer no concessions at all.

Once no-fault divorce came in, this situation was reversed: The partner who wanted to stay married would have to offer something that would improve the value of the marriage to the partner who wanted out, maybe by offering to dramatically change behavior or make amends for a serious failing. The Coase theorem predicts that roughly the same number of couples will eventually agree to divorce or stay married under no-fault divorce law as before—but the partner who wanted out will now get the better end of the bargain. The partner who wants to keep the marriage together will make the concessions.

As it happens, divorce rates *didn't* go up much after no-fault laws. A short flurry of divorces was followed by a return to pre-no-fault levels. In this instance at least, the Coase theorem made the right prediction.

Source: J. Wolfers, "Did unilateral divorce laws raise divorce rates? A reconciliation and new results," *American Economic Review* 96, no. 5 (2006).

Taxes and subsidies

LO 18.5 Show how a tax or subsidy can be used to counteract an externality, and discuss the pros and cons of such a solution.

Because of the cost and difficulty of coordinating private solutions, people often turn to public policy for solutions to externalities. Earlier in the chapter, we described how the effect of forcing decision makers to consider social costs and benefits looked similar to the effects of taxes and subsidies, respectively. It's no surprise, then, that the most basic public policy remedy to an externality problem involves counterbalancing the externality with a tax or subsidy.

Countering a negative externality with a tax. Let's return to the problem of air pollution from driving. Earlier, we imagined solving the externality problem of air pollution in L.A. by taking $1 from drivers every time they used a gallon of gas, and using that money to compensate sufferers from pollution. In fact, many governments around the world do use taxes to force drivers to consider social costs. Oregon was the first U.S. state to implement a gas tax, in 1909, and the federal government has taxed gas since the 1930s. While the motive for government taxation of gasoline also included raising general revenues to pay for roads, these taxes also counteract the negative externalities of driving.

Pigovian tax a tax meant to counterbalance a negative externality

A tax meant to counter the effect of a negative externality is called a **Pigovian tax**, after an economist named Arthur Pigou. Other Pigovian taxes include the "sin taxes" on alcohol and cigarettes as well as carbon taxes. As panel A of Figure 18-7 shows, the effect of a negative externality is that the demand curve $D_{private}$ is higher than it would be if consumers had to account for social costs D_{social}. The effect of a Pigovian tax—like any tax—is to increase the effective price that is paid for a good. This creates a new demand curve below the original, as shown in panel B of Figure 18-7. If the demand curve is pushed down just far enough, it will move the equilibrium quantity to the efficient level—that is, the level at which the market maximizes total surplus.

It would be equally valid to represent the effect of a Pigovian tax as adding a new supply curve above the original. It depends on whether the tax is levied on consumers or producers, but the ultimate effect is the same: increasing price and reducing quantity to the efficient level.

However, Pigovian taxes are not a perfect solution to externalities. There are two problems. The first is setting the tax at the right level. As we have seen, it is not always easy to put a dollar-and-cents value on external costs. In our example, we estimated the external cost associated with burning a gallon of gas to be $1, so we would choose an optimal Pigovian tax of $1 per gallon. If our estimate is wrong and the external cost is higher, then the tax is set too low. In that case, the market will move closer to the efficient equilibrium, but remain somewhat inefficient. If our estimate is too high, then the tax is set too high, and the market will overshoot—the new equilibrium quantity will be inefficient because it is too low, rather than too high.

Second, while taxes are effective at transferring surplus away from consumers and producers and toward the government, there is no guarantee that the government can or will then do anything to help the people who are bearing the external cost. The revenue collected from a Pigovian tax is sometimes used as compensation, but often it is not. It might seem "fair" for California gas taxes to be used to build centers for treating

FIGURE 18-7

A tax counteracts the effect of a negative externality

(A) The effect of a negative externality

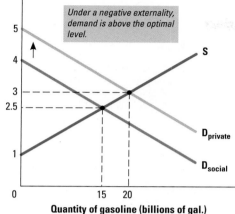

Under a negative externality, demand is above the optimal level.

(B) The effect of a Pigovian tax

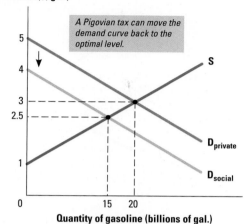

A Pigovian tax can move the demand curve back to the optimal level.

Under a negative externality, the demand curve ($D_{private}$) is above the level of demand that society as a whole would prefer (D_{social}). The difference between the curves is the external cost. From society's perspective, decision makers who are concerned only with their own private preferences will demand a quantity that is higher than the efficient level.

A Pigovian tax counteracts a negative externality. If the tax is set equal to the value of the external cost, the two cancel out, and the tax brings quantity back down to the efficient level.

people suffering from breathing disorders. But, whether or not the revenue is redistributed to pollution sufferers in this way, the tax still maximizes total surplus *in society as a whole*, by moving the gas market to the efficient equilibrium. Remember, the *distribution* of surplus is an entirely separate question from maximizing total surplus.

Capturing a positive externality with a subsidy. Just as a tax can counterbalance an external cost, a subsidy can help consumers or producers capture the benefits of positive externalities. If the government calculates that painting houses creates $500 worth of external benefits for neighbors, it might offer $500 subsidies to people who want to paint their houses. As shown in Figure 18-8 this subsidy would add a new demand curve above the original and move the market to its efficient equilibrium.

Remember that, as with a Pigovian tax, using a subsidy to increase efficiency does not necessarily equal fairness. Such a subsidy would maximize total surplus in society. But the *distribution* of that surplus depends on where the government gets the money to pay for the subsidies. It might seem more "fair" if the subsidies were paid for out of property taxes, as property owners have the most to gain from pretty neighborhoods, but total surplus would still be maximized if the money was collected from general taxation.

Public policies that use subsidies to solve externality problems are sometimes less noticeable than taxes, but are extremely widespread and important if you know where to look. One example that's a lot less trivial than painting houses is education. If parents had to pay to send their children to school, many might decide the trade-off wasn't worth it. Yet educating children has all sorts of external benefits: With education, children are more likely to become economically productive members of society and engaged citizens. That's why most governments offer public schools, which subsidize the cost of education.

You may also have seen how universities often subsidize small services in the campus community. Examples include free immunization shots to keep students from passing

FIGURE 18-8

A subsidy counteracts the effect of a positive externality

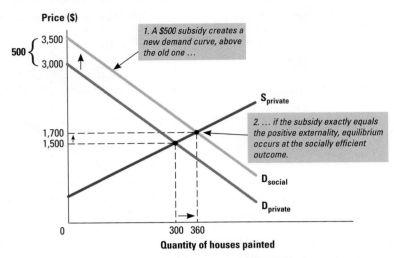

If the government decides to give a $500 subsidy to people who paint their house, a new demand curve is added above the original one. If this subsidy exactly equals the external benefit of painting houses, equilibrium occurs at the socially efficient outcome.

the flu around, and antivirus software to keep viruses and malware out of the university computer network. In both of these cases, the thinking is that if it were left entirely to the market, students would consume "too little" of these goods or services. That is, fewer students would pay for immunizations or antivirus software than the amount that would maximize total surplus on the campus as a whole.

As with taxes, solving a positive externality through subsidies requires quantifying the external cost or benefit accurately. If the subsidy is set too low—say, a $50 subsidy for painting your house—then the number of houses painted will remain inefficiently low. If the subsidy is set too high—say, a $5,000 subsidy—then total surplus will not be maximized either, because the increase in social benefits from the additional house painting will be less than the cost of the subsidy.

Quotas and regulations

LO 18.6 Show how quantity regulations can be used to counteract an externality, and discuss the pros and cons of such a solution.

If we know the socially optimal quantity of something—for instance, how much pollution we are willing to tolerate—why not simply regulate quantity rather than taxing? California could calculate the efficient quantity of gas, and limit each citizen's gas purchases to his or her share of that amount. In terms of controlling the amount of pollution, this approach would achieve the same end result as a tax.

However, perhaps surprisingly, limiting total consumption to the efficient quantity *does not* make the market efficient. The real magic of the invisible hand in a market is not just that it drives price and quantity to the efficient level, but that it does so by allocating resources to those with the greatest willingness to pay for them. Maximizing surplus depends not only on how much gas is bought and sold, but also on who buys and sells it. A tax allows the market to sort itself out in this way; a quota does not.

To see why limiting each driver to a gas quota is inefficient while a Pigovian tax is not, let's shrink the market for gas down to two L.A. drivers. Driver A owns a large, gas-thirsty Range Rover and drives to work every day. Driver B owns a Prius hybrid and walks to work, but likes to take trips to California's national parks on weekends. At a price of $3 a gallon, it just so happens that both drivers buy 60 gallons per month. But because these drivers have different preferences and reasons for driving, and different cars with different gas mileage, their individual demand for gas looks different.

Figure 18-9 shows the net benefit that each driver gets from an additional unit of gas—in other words, the difference between the marginal benefit and marginal cost of buying that gallon. For instance, if the price of gas is $3 a gallon, the Prius driver would be willing to pay up to $3.80 for the 20th gallon, and therefore derives a net benefit of $0.80 from buying it. The Range Rover driver has a willingness to pay of $4.33 for the 20th gallon, and therefore derives a net benefit of $1.33.

Under normal circumstances, both drivers would buy gas up to the point where the net benefit of the next gallon is zero (i.e., where marginal cost equals marginal benefit), equal to 60 gallons per month. Panel A of Figure 18-9 shows what happens to these drivers if a quota limits them each to 20 gallons per month. At this quantity, both drivers would like to purchase more gas, but the Range Rover driver would be willing to pay up to $1.33 for the right to purchase another gallon, while the Prius driver would be willing to pay up to only $0.80.

In contrast, panel B of Figure 18-9 shows what happens to the two drivers under a gas tax. If the tax is equal to $1 per gallon, each driver will buy gas up to the point where the net benefit of buying another gallon is zero *including the cost of the tax.* In this case, with a $1 tax, that means the point at which the pre-tax benefit is $1. Under a tax, the two drivers buy different amounts of gas, and neither is left wanting to buy more.

Note that, under the tax, the total quantity of gas consumed by the two drivers is 40 gallons—the same as under the quota. However, we can show graphically, in Figure 18-10, that surplus is higher under the tax than under the quota. The quota brings the two drivers to the same combined quantity of gas consumption as the tax does, but

FIGURE 18-9

A quota is less efficient than a tax

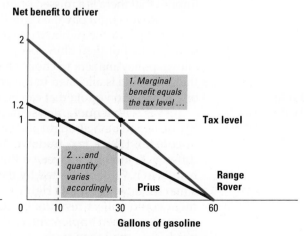

(A) Gasoline consumption under a quota

A quota forces both the drivers to reduce their individual consumption of gasoline to 20 gallons per week.

(B) Gasoline consumption under a tax

A tax causes both drivers to reduce their consumption of gasoline until their marginal benefit is equal to $1.
At this particular tax level, the total quantity of gasoline consumed by both drivers is the same as under the quota.

FIGURE 18-10
A Pigovian tax maximizes surplus; a quota does not

(A) Surplus under a quota
(B) Surplus under a tax

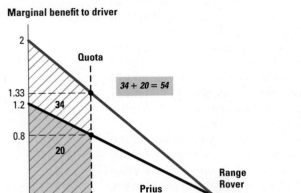
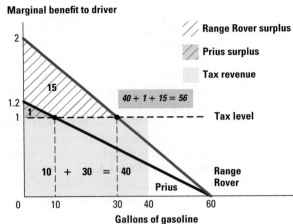

A quota forces both drivers to reduce their gasoline consumption equally even though they have different marginal benefits from consuming gasoline.

With a tax, both drivers receive less surplus from consuming gasoline as they are paying an extra $1 per gallon. But the fact that they can consume up to the point where marginal benefit is zero means that, together with tax revenue, total surplus is higher than under a quota.

does it inefficiently. Calculating the surplus of the drivers under the quota, we find that together they earn a surplus of 54 with a quota compared to surplus of 56 with a tax.

Tradable allowances

LO 18.7 Show how tradable allowances can be used to counteract an externality, and discuss the pros and cons of such a solution.

You may have spotted an obvious way to improve the quota system described above. The fact that the two drivers have a different willingness to pay for the next gallon of gas implies that there is a missed opportunity for a mutually beneficial trade: The driver of the Range Rover could pay the Prius driver some amount more than $0.80 and less than $1.33 in exchange for the rights to one more gallon, and both would end up better off. Why not set a quota, but then allow people to buy and sell their quota allowances? This solution allows policy-makers to choose a quantity rather than set a tax rate, while still ensuring that the quota is allocated to the people with the highest willingness to pay. A production or consumption quota that can be bought and sold is called a **tradable allowance**.

tradable allowance a production or consumption quota that can be bought and sold

Just as with a quota, a system of tradable allowances will result in the efficient quantity of a good being bought and sold (as long as the total quota is set at the right quantity, of course). Like a tax, tradable allowances maximize surplus. There is one important difference, though, between a Pigovian tax and a tradable allowance: The Pigovian tax results in revenue collected by the government, whereas the tradable allowance creates a market in which quota rights are bought and sold among private parties. The government could collect revenue by selling the initial quotas, but in cases where such programs have been implemented, they are more usually allocated for free to consumers or producers, who then trade among themselves.

For more on the recent policy debate over whether to institute a carbon tax or a system of tradable carbon allowances in the United States, read the Real Life box "The fight over cap-and-trade legislation."

REAL LIFE

The fight over cap-and-trade legislation

Pollution and greenhouse gases can be reduced by simple steps such as car-pooling and replacing incandescent light bulbs with energy-efficient ones. But, scientists argue, reductions of the scale that would be needed to slow climate change require more dramatic steps. In order to stabilize global temperatures at 3.5 degrees above pre-industrial levels, carbon in the atmosphere would have to fall to 50 to 85 percent of year-2000 levels.[3] The big target is reductions in the emissions from the burning of fossil fuels by factories and drivers.

In practical terms, this reduction could be accomplished in two major ways. The first, a tax on carbon, is the method favored by many economists. Most proposals put to Congress in 2009 called for a "starter" flat-tax amount—generally around $15 per ton of carbon released into the atmosphere. Every year thereafter, the carbon tax would increase by $10, up to a final tax amount of about $100 per ton. Lester Brown, director of the Earth Policy Institute, says that a tax of that magnitude wouldn't go nearly far enough to fight global warming. Instead, he recommends a much larger tax, which starts at $20 per ton and would increase all the way to $240 per ton. Economists argue that these taxes should be applied "upstream," meaning that rather than sending factories and drivers a bill based on how much carbon they released in a year, the tax would be applied when fossil fuels are produced or imported. (A $15 per ton tax would equate to about 4 cents per gallon of gas, for example.) This tax would cause the quantity of fossil fuels demanded to drop. With factories, businesses, and everyday drivers consuming less fossil fuel, carbon-dioxide emissions would drop as well. The government would collect any revenue generated by the tax.

The alternative solution is to create a market for carbon allowances—often called "cap-and-trade" because it would set a cap on the total amount of carbon emissions but allow businesses to trade their allowances. In 2009, the Waxman-Markey climate change bill proposed cap-and-trade as a way to reach the ambitious goal of cutting carbon emissions by 86 percent by 2050, measured against 2005 levels.

How would it achieve that goal? First, it would set a cap—the maximum amount of carbon emissions to be allowed over the course of a year. In the early years, this limit would be set very close to the current level of carbon emissions. Over time, the cap would be reduced until the desired goal is met.

Then comes the "trade" part: Firms would be given permits to emit a certain amount of carbon, which they can trade or sell. "Clean" firms that are able to achieve low carbon emissions at low cost can sell their permits to companies that find it harder or more expensive to reduce their emissions. If many firms find it expensive to decrease their emissions, demand for carbon permits would go up, and the price of the permits will increase. As new, clean technologies are invented and adopted, the cost of reducing emissions would go down, causing reductions in the demand for and price of carbon permits.

Cap-and-trade programs can be designed so the permits are auctioned off to firms at the beginning of the program; the revenue from the auction goes to the government. In the Waxman-Markey bill, however, over 85 percent of the carbon allowances were to be given away to firms for free. Since these permits are highly valuable, those who were lucky enough to receive the permits would essentially be getting a windfall profit, courtesy of the government.

Putting aside the question of who collects revenue, economists usually will tell you that the two proposed solutions actually produce quite similar outcomes. Both impose a cost on consumers, as they raise the cost of producing goods, driving up prices that consumers pay. Food, for example, has to be transported from farms to stores by trucks and boats that emit carbon, which means that higher carbon prices also increase the price of food at the supermarket. Critics worry that the higher prices could slow the economy and increase unemployment.

Of course, economists are not the people with the final say over public policy. After barely surviving a vote in the House of Representatives, the Waxman-Markey legislation died in the Senate in 2009 and was never implemented. (A carbon tax doesn't exist yet either.) However, in 2011 California introduced the nation's first state-administered cap-and-trade program of carbon emissions. Starting in 2013, many Californian industries face an enforceable cap on the amount of carbon they can emit.

Sources: http://www.time.com/time/health/article/0,8599,1700189,00.html; http://www.carbontax.org/progress/carbon-tax-bills/; http://www.arb.ca.gov/cc/capandtrade/capandtrade.htm.

Targeting externalities with public policy

When economists propose taxes or tradable allowances as a way to tackle externalities, they try to propose taxes based on the externality itself, rather than on the action that generates it. In this chapter, we've talked a lot about gas taxes, which are targeted at a good that generates pollution, rather than at pollution itself. Ideally, environmental policy would target the end product—carbon emissions—directly. That way, the policy would apply to all the thousands of different activities that generate an external cost through carbon emissions, from raising livestock, to operating a power plant, to lighting a wood fire in a fireplace. However, measuring emissions from all these different sources is extremely difficult, logistically speaking. Taxing gasoline, rather than pollution, is a second-best solution; the first-best solution may simply be unattainable.

Because of the difficulty of measuring pollution directly, many policies do target individual goods and processes. For instance, cars are generally required to have catalytic converters, a specific technology that reduces emissions of nitrous oxides, carbon monoxide, and unburnt hydrocarbons. Local governments often subsidize energy-saving light bulbs or recycling, or they ban wood fires during smoggy times of the year or when dry conditions make fires especially dangerous. The downside of targeting individual activities is that it risks misaligning the incentives that consumers and producers face with the goal of minimizing the externality.

For example, in 1975 the U.S. government imposed fuel-efficiency standards on cars, called the *CAFE standards.* The goal was to reduce pollution. But the regulations were designed in such a way that "light trucks" were subject to looser standards. The result? Auto manufacturers started producing cars that were big and heavy enough to be classed as a "light truck," and didn't have to meet the standards for cars. Average fuel efficiency of cars actually fell rather than increased.

A policy that directly targets pollution encourages the development of cleaner technology and processes, and doesn't give clever companies the chance to find ways around it. In fact, consumers and producers have an incentive to find new ways of doing things that *don't* generate pollution. This allows them to avoid having to pay for a tax or the rights to an allowance, aligning their incentives with the end goal of the policy. Since it is very difficult to monitor private citizens' carbon footprint, and relatively easy to monitor the pollution caused by large factories, the idea of a carbon tax or a tradable carbon allowance makes more sense on a corporate level than a personal one.

✓ CONCEPT CHECK

❐ What conditions are required in order for people to be able to privately solve externalities under the Coase theorem? **[LO 18.4]**

❐ Are subsidies used to account for positive or negative externalities? **[LO 18.5]**

- Which is a more efficient way of correcting a negative externality—a quota or a tax? **[LO 18.6]**
- What is the difference between a normal quota and a tradable quota? Which is more efficient, and why? **[LO 18.7]**

Conclusion

Typically, we rely on the invisible hand of markets to maximize total surplus by allocating the right quantity of goods to the right people. But what happens when one person's choices impose costs or benefits on others? Free-market outcomes can be less than ideal, and result in too much or too little of the good or activity in question.

As the examples in this chapter show, positive or negative externalities are a common part of economic life. They're the context for discussions of issues like climate change, pollution, blighted neighborhoods, and education policy. Sometimes, individuals can find private solutions, by paying others to do, or to not do, things that affect them. However, the difficulty of coordinating or enforcing these private agreements often overwhelms the benefits.

In these cases, we've seen that government policies like taxes and subsidies can actually *increase* efficiency, even though we typically think of them as creating distortions. This is because taxes and subsidies can counterbalance an externality by forcing buyers or sellers to take the value of the external cost or benefit into account. At first glance, quotas look like a simple way to counter the "too much" problem of negative externalities, but they fail to maximize surplus unless people are allowed to buy and sell the quotas.

In the "Public Goods and Common Resources" chapter, we'll examine other challenges that are closely related to the idea of externalities. When goods are collectively owned, individuals have limited incentive to take into account the impact of their actions on the publicly held resources. As we are about to see, the resulting market failures and corresponding policy solutions look very similar to those we've discussed in this chapter.

 ◀ Mobile Window on the World—Scan this code with your smartphone to find more applications of the chapter content. (Need a barcode reader? Try ScanLife, available in your app store.)

Visit your mobile app store and download ▶ the Karlan and Morduch Study Econ app.

 Study Econ | McGraw Hill

Key Terms

private cost, p. 431

external cost, p. 431

social cost, p. 431

private benefit, p. 431

external benefit, p. 431

social benefit, p. 431

externality, p. 431

network externality, p. 431

Coase theorem, p. 440

Pigovian tax, p. 442

tradable allowance, p. 446

Summary

LO 18.1 Explain how external costs and benefits affect the trade-offs faced by economic decision makers.

Any cost that is imposed without compensation on someone other than the person who caused it is an *external cost*. A benefit that accrues without compensation to someone other than the person who caused it is called an *external benefit*. External costs and benefits are collectively referred to as *externalities*, and we call the former *negative externalities* and the latter *positive externalities*. Costs and benefits that fall directly on an economic decision maker are *private costs/benefits*, while the total cost of the decision including any externalities is referred to as the *social cost*.

LO 18.2 Calculate the effect of a negative externality on market price and quantity, and measure the resulting change in surplus.

A negative externality makes the private cost of a decision lower than the social cost, which causes the individuals who bear only the private cost to demand or supply an inefficiently high quantity at any given price. In the presence of a negative externality, the market equilibrium yields a higher quantity than the efficient level, failing to maximize total surplus. The market price is too low relative to the social cost. The loss of surplus falls on those outside the market who bear the external cost of the decision.

LO 18.3 Calculate the effect of a positive externality on market price and quantity, and measure the resulting change in surplus.

A positive externality makes the private benefit of a decision lower than the social benefit, which causes individuals who enjoy only the private benefit to demand or supply an inefficiently low quantity at any given price. In the presence of a positive externality, the market equilibrium yields a lower quantity than the efficient level, failing to maximize total surplus. The market price is too high relative to social benefit. The loss of surplus falls on those outside the market who would gain from a larger quantity transacted.

LO 18.4 Describe how individuals could reach a private solution to an externality, and explain why this doesn't always occur.

The idea that individuals reach an efficient equilibrium through private trades, even in the presence of an externality, is called the *Coase theorem*. Because an externality fails to maximize surplus, in theory, everyone could be made better off if those who are burdened with external cost or benefits pay others to buy or sell the efficient quantity. The theorem assumes, however, that people can make enforceable agreements and that there are no costs involved in the transaction.

LO 18.5 Show how a tax or subsidy can be used to counteract an externality, and discuss the pros and cons of such a solution.

A tax meant to counterbalance the effect of a negative externality is known as a *Pigovian tax*. In order to exactly counterbalance a negative externality, policy-makers want to set the tax equal to the value of the external cost, thus reducing the equilibrium quantity. Similarly, a subsidy can counterbalance a

positive externality by moving the equilibrium to a higher quantity. When the tax or subsidy is set at the right level, the externality is exactly counterbalanced, and the market becomes efficient.

LO 18.6 Show how quantity regulations can be used to counteract an externality, and discuss the pros and cons of such a solution.

Setting a quota to counteract inefficiently high consumption due to a negative externality can bring quantity down to the efficient level, but it does not actually maximize surplus. Maximizing surplus and achieving efficiency depend not only on how much of a good is bought and sold, but also on who buys and sells it.

LO 18.7 Show how tradable allowances can be used to counteract an externality, and discuss the pros and cons of such a solution.

A production or consumption quota that can be bought and sold is called a *tradable allowance*. Just as with a quota, a system of tradable allowances will result in the efficient quantity of a good being bought and sold, as long as the total number of allowances is set at the right quantity. Like a tax, however, tradable allowances maximize surplus by allocating sales to those with the highest willingness to pay. The government can collect revenue by selling the initial quotas, but more often, they are allocated for free to consumers or producers, who then trade among themselves.

Review Questions

1. Describe an externality not listed in the chapter. Is it positive or negative? Who is the economic decision maker, and who bears the external cost or benefit? **[LO 18.1]**

2. Consider the decision to adopt a dog. Describe a private cost, a private benefit, an external cost, and an external benefit that result from your decision to adopt a dog. **[LO 18.1]**

3. What are the private costs and benefits associated with smoking cigarettes? What are the external costs? If smokers paid the social cost of cigarettes, what would happen to demand? **[LO 18.2]**

4. When U.S. farmers in the Southwest irrigate their land, salt in the ground soil leaks into the Colorado River. The Colorado River has become so salty that Mexican farmers further down the river cannot irrigate their own land, and Mexican crops have been devastated. Explain why this situation constitutes a negative externality, how it leads to too

much irrigation, and what it would mean for U.S. farmers to internalize the externality. **[LO 18.2]**

5. If education has private benefits to an individual as well as external benefits to society, explain why a less-than-optimal amount of education occurs. **[LO 18.3]**

6. Hand washing has external health benefits, helping prevent the spread of communicable diseases. If a program were somehow devised so that people got paid a small reward every time they washed their hands, how would it affect the number of people who are sick at any given time? **[LO 18.3]**

7. Jimi loves turning up his electric guitar amp all the way, but his next-door neighbor hates listening to him. How might Jimi and his neighbor reach a private solution to their problem? Describe potential problems that might make it hard for a private solution to occur. **[LO 18.4]**

8. Felix and Oscar are roommates. Oscar is messy, and Felix is planning to move out unless they can come to an agreement. For the roommates to reach a private solution, does it matter whether Oscar compensates Felix for being messy or Felix pays Oscar to clean up? **[LO 18.4]**

9. Suppose that you are an economic-policy advisor. Environmental groups are pressuring you to implement the highest-possible carbon tax, while industry groups are pressuring you to implement no carbon tax at all. Both argue that their position makes more sense economically. Explain to them what the most-efficient tax level will be, and why there are costs to setting the tax too high or too low. **[LO 18.5]**

10. In what circumstances will a tax make a market less efficient? In what circumstances will a tax make a market more efficient? **[LO 18.5]**

11. The city of Seattle limits each household to one can of free garbage collection per week. There are fees for any extra garbage collected from the curb. Is this policy the most efficient way of reducing waste? Why or why not? **[LO 18.6]**

12. Suppose an environmental impact study shows that the coral reef near Port Douglas, Australia, can sustain 20 scuba diving tours per week. Discuss the pros and cons of setting a quota of 20 dive tours per week. **[LO 18.6]**

13. The city of Seattle limits each household to one can of free garbage collection per week. There are fees for any extra garbage collected from the curb. Suppose that a neighborhood group in Seattle organizes a group of families so that those who plan to go over their one-can garbage quota can find

households that are under their quota and pay them to put out the extra trash. Does this change the efficiency of the policy? **[LO 18.7]**

14. Suppose the government is considering two policies to limit factory air pollution: taxing producers, or providing each producer with an allotment of permits they may trade with other producers. If both policies lead to the same amount of pollution reduction, why might producers prefer the tradable-permit option? **[LO 18.7]**

Problems and Applications

1. State whether each of the following primarily causes an external cost or an external benefit. **[LO 18.1]**
   a. Fishing at a popular lakeside vacation spot.
   b. Buying a fax machine.
   c. Conducting research to find an AIDS vaccine.
   d. Occupying a seat on a bench in a crowded park.
   e. Littering.
   f. Spaying or neutering your pet.

2. You are considering whether to enter a holiday lights display contest that pays $1,000 to the winner. State whether each of the following constitutes private costs, private benefits, external costs, or external benefits. Check all that apply. **[LO 18.1]**
   a. Increased traffic congestion and difficulty parking on your street.
   b. Increased electric bill from the holiday lights.
   c. Winning the holiday lights display contest.

3. The weekly supply and demand for packs of cigarettes in the U.S is given in Figure 18P-1. **[LO 18.2]**
   a. Suppose cigarette smoking causes a $6/pack external cost on nonsmokers. Draw the demand curve that would exist if the externality associated with smoking were internalized by consumers.
   b. How many packs of cigarettes are consumed per week?
   c. What is the efficient number of cigarette packs?
   d. What would be the total gain in surplus if this externality could be internalized?

4. Figure 18P-2 shows the marginal private benefit to a U.S. farmer for irrigating his land. It costs $100 per acre to irrigate the land.
   Each acre of land irrigation generates a gallon of salty runoff that winds up in the Colorado

FIGURE 18P-1

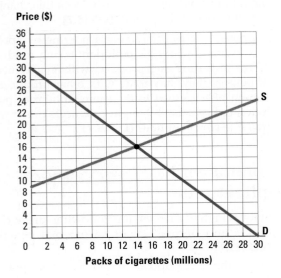

Price ($)

Packs of cigarettes (millions)

FIGURE 18P-2

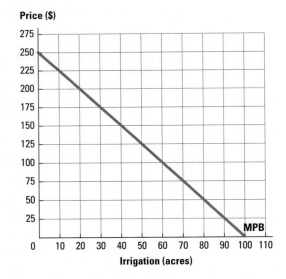

Price ($)

Irrigation (acres)

River. It costs $50 per gallon to desalinate the river water so Mexican farmers can irrigate their crops. **[LO 18.2]**

a. Draw the marginal private cost of irrigation on the graph.

b. Draw the marginal social cost of irrigation on the graph.

c. How many acres will the U.S. farmer irrigate?

d. What is the efficient level of irrigation?

e. What would be the total gain in surplus if this externality could be internalized?

5. Figure 18P-3 shows supply and demand for planting trees, based on private costs and benefits. Trees sequester carbon, meaning that they help counteract pollutants that contribute to climate change. **[LO 18.3]**

   a. Suppose that the carbon sequestration that results from planting a tree is worth $4. Graph the supply curve for tree planting based on the social benefits of trees.

   b. How many trees will be planted?

   c. What is the socially optimal quantity?

   d. How much surplus is lost when suppliers are unable to capture the $4 external benefit they provide from planting trees?

6. Figure 18P-4 shows supply and demand for first-aid training, based on private costs and benefits. **[LO 18.3]**

   a. Suppose that the external benefit from first-aid training is worth $6. Graph the demand curve for first-aid training based on the social benefits.

   b. How many hours of first-aid training will occur?

   c. What is the socially optimal quantity of first-aid training?

   d. How much surplus is lost when consumers are unable to capture the $6 external benefit they provide from first-aid training?

7. Your neighbor never mows her lawn. You don't have any legal right to force her to mow, but the mess in her front yard is making your neighborhood unsightly and reducing the value of your house. The reduction in the value of your house is $5,000, and the value of her time to mow the lawn

FIGURE 18P-3

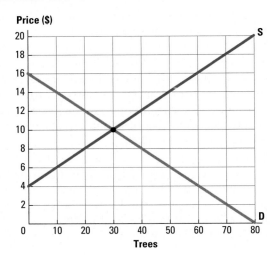

Price ($)

Trees

FIGURE 18P-4

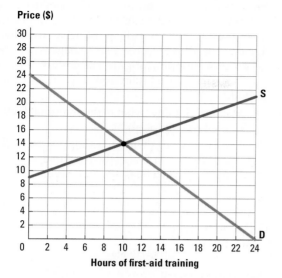

Price ($) vs Hours of first-aid training

FIGURE 18P-5

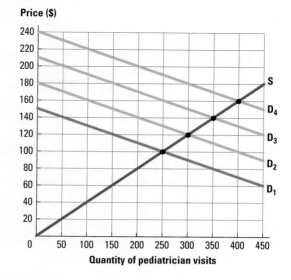

Price ($) vs Quantity of pediatrician visits

once a week is $1,000. Suppose you offer her a deal in which you pay her $3,000 to mow. How does this deal affect surplus? **[LO 18.4]**

a. The deal increases only your surplus.

b. The deal increases only your neighbor's surplus.

c. The deal increases both your surplus and your neighbor's.

d. The deal increases your surplus but decreases your neighbor's.

e. The deal increases your neighbor's surplus but decreases yours.

f. The deal does not affect surplus.

8. Johnston Forest in Rhode Island has a cave that houses thousands of fruit bats. Bat droppings are highly acidic and have ruined the paint on many cars. The flying radius of the Johnston Forest bats encompasses two towns, Johnston and Foster. The residents of Johnston collectively value bat removal at $400,000. Foster residents collectively value bat removal at $500,000. Pest control experts estimate that the cost of bat removal would be $450,000. Which of the following scenarios would lead to removal of the bats? Check all that apply. **[LO 18.4]**

a. Foster pays Johnston $50,000 to contribute to bat removal.

b. Foster and Johnston evenly split the cost of bat removal.

c. Johnston contributes nothing toward bat removal.

9. The local government has decided that because children's health has large external benefits, it will offer a subsidy to help families pay for visits to the pediatrician. However, the government isn't sure at what level to set the subsidy. Figure 18P-5 shows the current demand curve for pediatricians' visits (D_1), and three alternative subsidies, represented by curves D_2, D_3, and D_4. **[LO 18.5]**

a. Assume that the correct level of subsidy is D_3. Compared to the efficient outcome, graph the loss in total surplus that would result from subsidies D_2 and D_4.

b. What is the socially optimal level of pediatrician visits?

10. Figure 18P-6 shows the daily market for water-skiing permits on El Dorado Lake. Suppose each

FIGURE 18P-6

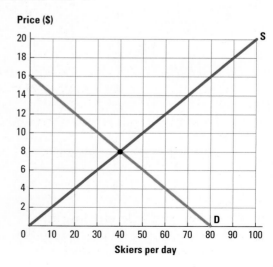

Price ($) vs Skiers per day

skier (each permit) causes $4 of damage to the lake. **[LO 18.5]**

a. Calculate the loss of surplus if there is no government intervention in this market.

b. Suppose the government imposes a $12 tax on suppliers of ski permits. Compared to no intervention, what is the net surplus gain or loss from this tax?

c. What is the socially optimal level of water skiing?

11. Suppose certain fireworks are legal in a residential area on the Fourth of July. The fireworks have been approved for safety, but they do cause noise pollution so their use must be limited. Jenny and Salo like to purchase fireworks for their families; Table 18P-1 shows the net marginal benefit that Jenny and Salo gain from each firework they purchase. **[LO 18.6]**

a. If a quota of 30 fireworks per person is imposed, what is the marginal benefit of the last firework for each?

b. What is the amount of tax that will achieve the same total number of fireworks to be purchased between Jenny and Salo? How many fireworks will each purchase under this tax?

c. Under a tax, what is the net marginal benefit of the last firework for each after the tax is subtracted?

12. Many municipalities are concerned about the environmental impact of plastic bags, which often end up as litter, clogging drains and hanging from tree branches. A town is considering whether to impose a tax on plastic bags to be collected at the store, or a per person quota. Cindy and Carl are two average citizens who both use plastic bags when they go grocery shopping. Figure 18P-7 shows the net marginal benefit they gain from each bag they use. **[LO 18.6]**

a. Under the quota, what is the marginal benefit of the last bag for each?

b. How many bags will each shopper use under the tax? What is the marginal benefit of the last bag for each? What is

TABLE 18P-1

Net marginal benefit	Q Jenny	Q Salo
10	0	0
9	10	5
8	20	10
7	30	15
6	40	20
5	50	25
4	60	30
3	70	35
2	80	40
1	90	45
0	100	50

FIGURE 18P-7

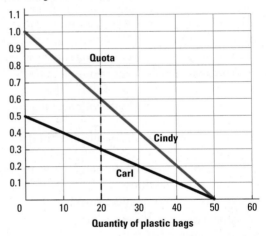

(A) Quota

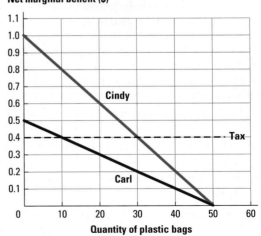

(B) Tax

TABLE 18P-2

Firm	Current carbon emissions (tons)	Cost of reducing emissions by 1 ton ($)
A	80	150
B	100	200
C	70	50

TABLE 18P-3

	Cost of reducing pollution by 1 unit ($)
Ferry line A	1,500
Ferry line B	2,500
Ferry line C	1,800

the marginal benefit of the last bag after subtracting the tax?

   c. Would you recommend that the town adopt a plastic-bag quota or tax?

13. Table 18P-2 shows current carbon emissions and the cost of reducing carbon emissions for three industrial firms. The government introduces a cap-and-trade policy to regulate carbon emissions. The total cap on emissions is 180 tons of carbon, and each firm receives an initial allocation of tradable permits for 60 tons of carbon emissions. **[LO 18.7]**

   a. Which firm(s) will buy emissions permits? How many will they buy and from whom?

   b. What is the minimum amount the selling firm must receive to break even?

14. There are three major ferry lines operating on the East River, each generating 100 units of pollution per year. The ferry lines face the costs of reducing pollution that are shown in Table 18P-3. **[LO 18.7]**

   a. The government has decided it wants to reduce pollution levels by 50 percent and requires each ferry line to cut its pollution in half. What is the cost of pollution reduction

for each ferry line, and what is the total cost of pollution reduction?

   b. Suppose the government decides to give each ferry line 50 tradable permits. Each permit allows a ferry line to produce one unit of pollution. Which ferry line will buy permits? How many permits will it buy and from whom?

   c. What is the total cost of pollution reduction under this system of tradable permits?

Chapter Endnotes

1. *Advancing the Science of Climate Change,* National Research Council (Washington, DC: The National Academies Press, 2010).

2. You can see that our graphical treatment of what happens when decision makers are forced to consider social costs looks very similar to our graphical treatment of the effect of a tax in Chapter 6. (See Figures 6-7 and 6-9.)

3. http://ntl.bts.gov/lib/32000/32700/32779/DOT_Climate_Change_Report_-_April_2010_-_Volume_1_and_2.pdf.

Public Goods and Common Resources

Chapter 19

LEARNING OBJECTIVES

LO 19.1   Define different types of goods in terms of rivalry and excludability.

LO 19.2   Describe the free-rider problem and its consequences.

LO 19.3   Describe the tragedy of the commons and its consequences.

LO 19.4   Explain how and when social norms can effectively solve problems with public goods or common resources.

LO 19.5   Describe how several types of government regulation can be used to solve problems with public goods or common resources.

LO 19.6   Explain how and when expansion of property rights can effectively solve problems with public goods or common resources.

A NEW TRAGEDY OF THE COMMONS

In 1910, there were roughly 300,000 rhinoceroses roaming the savannas of East Africa. A century later, there are no more than 2,000. A growing human population encroaching on the rhinos' habitat is part of the explanation, but the real cause of the rhinos' downfall has been its own value to hunters. In the early 1900s, thousands of big-game hunters traveled from Europe and America to shoot rhinos for sport, including U.S. president Theodore Roosevelt. These days, it's mostly illegal to hunt rhinos, but a flourishing illegal trade in ivory from rhino horns continues. In parts of Asia, ivory is an ingredient in traditional medicines and is worth more than its weight in gold. As a result, some species of rhino—such as the northern white—are on the verge of extinction.

Why are poachers killing rhinos so fast that they're becoming extinct? As soon as they become extinct, after all, that's the end of the profits for poachers. Wouldn't poachers want to carefully manage the rhino population, so that it can produce ivory for many years to come? The problem, as we'll see in this chapter, is that the rhinos don't "belong" to anyone in particular, so no one has an incentive to maintain their value. Instead, everyone wants to get in quickly and take what they can before the rhinos are gone.

The near-extinction of rhinos in East Africa isn't just a problem for biologists and nature-lovers; it's also an example of an important type of economic inefficiency. Not all goods are allocated efficiently by competitive markets, and in this chapter,

we'll discuss two major types of goods that are subject to market failure. The first category is *common resources* such as rhinos and other wildlife, which end up *over-consumed* and depleted. The second category is *public goods,* such as national defense, public health, roads, education and research, which end up *undersupplied.* In both cases, we'll see that the root of the problem is the difficulty of forcing people who consume the goods to pay for what they take. Both the problems this causes and the corresponding solutions are related to the concept of external costs and benefits we discussed in the previous chapter.

In the end, rhinos aren't doomed. Some policies for protecting common resources and providing public goods have proved to be extremely effective. As a result, the population of rhinos in South Africa has taken the opposite path from that in East Africa. Although in South Africa there were only about 20 remaining white rhinos in 1900, there are 20,000 today. What made this difference? Paradoxically, part of the solution was to encourage people to hunt rhinos—but only on their own private land. The government of South Africa also established well-protected national parks. In this chapter, we'll see why these and other examples of government action and thoughtfully designed public policies can go a long way toward allocating both public goods and common resources more efficiently.

Characteristics of Goods

LO 19.1 Define different types of goods in terms of rivalry and excludability.

excludable a characteristic of a good or service that allows owners to prevent its use by people who have not paid for it

rival in consumption (rival) the characteristic of a good for which one person's consumption prevents or decreases others' ability to consume it

private good a good that is both excludable and rival

What types of goods tend to go the way of the rhino, suffering from overuse? River water, but not orange juice. Fish in the sea, but not chickens on the farm. Computers at the public library, but not personal laptops. What is the common thread?

The first thing to notice is that river water, fish in the sea, and public-library computers are not usually owned by a private individual. Instead, they are held collectively by a community or country.

We can go further and specify two important characteristics that determine how goods are used and whether they are allocated efficiently by markets:

- When a good is **excludable**, it is possible for sellers to prevent its use by those who have not paid for it.
- When a good is **rival in consumption** (or just **rival**), one person's consumption prevents or decreases others' ability to consume it.

Most of the goods we've discussed in this book are **private goods**, which are *both* excludable and rival in consumption. Many goods, however, lack one or both of these characteristics. Before describing these types of goods, we'll explore the ideas of excludability and "rivalness" a bit further.

Excludable goods

Excludability matters because it allows owners to set an enforceable price on a good. If you can't prevent people from consuming something, then they have little reason to pay for using it.

For instance, street lights are a nonexcludable good. Once they are put up in a neighborhood, everyone who comes through gets the benefit, regardless of whether they've paid to put up the lights. How would you prevent the person who didn't pay from getting the benefit of the lamps? Have a police officer standing by to make him wear special dark sunglasses? Make him close his eyes? Wall off the neighborhood? Most of the time, it's hard to imagine that you could allow some people but not others to enjoy the benefit of street lights.

Excludability can be a matter of degree, though. Take roads: It is possible to make bridges, tunnels, and major highways excludable by setting up toll booths at every entrance, but for most roads this is not a practical option. You can't have a toll booth at the end of every driveway to make sure that people pay before getting onto the roads.

Rival-in-consumption goods

Rivalry has to do with whether or not a good is "used up" when someone consumes it. Rhino horns are a rival good. Once someone shoots a rhino and cuts off its horn, the next person to come along can't also use the rhino for that or for any other purpose. The same goes for many—in fact, most—other goods. When fish are caught by one fishing boat, they're not there to be caught by the next one. When one person buys a pair of jeans at the store, there is one fewer pair to be bought by future customers.

What types of goods are nonrival? Streetlights, which we just saw are nonexcludable, are also nonrival. Two people walking down a lit-up street are just as able to enjoy the light as one person. A song on the radio is nonrival—one person listening doesn't "use it up," preventing others from listening as well.

In general, knowledge and technology are nonrival, because once something has been thought up or invented, everyone can take advantage of it.

Often, rivalry is a matter of degree. Again, think of roads. A rarely used country road is probably not rival in consumption. If one more person drives on the road, it has a negligible effect on the ability of other drivers to use it. A heavily congested highway, however,

> Sunlight is a public good—both nonrival and nonexcludable.

PEANUTS © 1994 Peanuts Worldwide LLC. Dist. By UNIVERSAL UCLICK. Reprinted with permission. All rights reserved.

has elements of a rival good. Every car that gets on the highway increases the amount of traffic, slowing down other cars and reducing the value of the highway for other drivers.

Four categories of goods

Whether a good is excludable and rival in consumption has important implications for how it is allocated through a market system. By combining the concepts of excludability and rivalry, we can define four categories of goods, as shown in Figure 19-1.

- *Private goods* are goods that are both excludable and rival. They are usually allocated efficiently by competitive markets, as we've discussed throughout the book.
- **Public goods** are the opposite of private goods, as the name suggests; they are neither excludable nor rival.
- **Common resources** are not excludable but are rival.
- *Artificially scarce goods* are excludable, but not rival.

We won't discuss the economic issues surrounding artificially scarce goods in this chapter, because we have discussed them already in the chapters on monopoly and monopolistic competition. Essentially, the markets for artificially scarce goods function

public good a good that is neither excludable nor rival

common resource a good that is not excludable but is rival

FIGURE 19-1
Four types of goods

	Excludable	Nonexcludable
Rival	**Private goods** Plane tickets, pizza, minivans	**Common resources** Forests, fisheries, wildlife
Nonrival	**Artificially scarce goods** MP3s, pay-per-view movies, subscription-only websites	**Public goods** Open-source software, traffic lights, national defense

just like the markets for private goods, and it is the lack of close substitute for a good that makes it artificially scarce. This scarcity allows the sellers of these goods some power to charge a price above what is possible in a perfectly competitive market.

✓CONCEPT CHECK

- ❏ What does it mean for a good to be excludable? **[LO 19.1]**
- ❏ What does it mean for a good to be rival in consumption? **[LO 19.1]**
- ❏ What is the difference between public goods and common resources? **[LO 19.1]**

The Problems with Public Goods and Common Resources

Markets work well for allocating private goods efficiently, but not always so well for allocating public goods and common resources. The reason is that the price charged by competitive firms charge does not capture the true costs and benefits of consumption. In this way, the problems with public goods and common resources are closely tied to the problems of externalities discussed in the previous chapter.

Here we discuss two particular types of problems associated with public goods and common resources, respectively: the free-rider problem and the tragedy of the commons.

The free-rider problem

LO 19.2 Describe the free-rider problem and its consequences.

Think about a public bus. It costs something to run the bus along its route—to pay the driver, buy gasoline, make repairs, and so on. To support these costs, the bus driver charges riders a fare as they enter the bus. But suppose someone decides he doesn't want to pay the fare, and slips in the back door when the driver's not looking? This person gets to ride the bus for free. In fact, we might even call him a "free rider."

If this free rider is alone, then no great harm is done. He takes up a seat on the bus, but doesn't fundamentally detract anything from others. Also, there are still enough paying riders to cover the cost of operating the bus.

However, imagine a bus with a back door that is always open. Riders can choose to get on through the front door and pay the fare, but they can also simply choose the back door and not pay anything. Under these circumstances, we'll likely see a lot of free riders. As more people choose to ride for free, the city will have less revenue to cover the costs of operating buses. If too many people ride for free, the city will no longer be able to afford to run as many buses as before. The reduced bus services don't reflect reduced demand or a lower value to riders, though. There are still enough people riding the bus to justify and pay for the cost of the system, but no individual person has an incentive to voluntarily pay the fare.

In technical terms, the **free-rider problem** we've just described is caused by nonexcludability leading to undersupply of a public good. When a good is not easily excludable, what people pay for it will not necessarily reflect the real value they place on it. After all, even if you value the bus ride highly and would willingly pay for a ticket if you had to, you might still hop on for free if presented the chance, right? The problem is that when this happens, the good will be undersupplied compared to the efficient quantity.

free-rider problem a problem that occurs when the nonexcludability of a public good leads to undersupply

Note that the free-rider problem *does not* have to do with whether nonpaying riders are taking up seats on the bus. Imagine a bus that could fit an infinite number of riders: Seats would not be in short supply, but not enough riders would pay the fare to cover the cost of running the bus. Even J. K. Rowling's Knight Bus, which can defy the laws of physics, charges Harry Potter 11 sickles to ride.

Since public goods are, by definition, nonexcludable, the free-rider problem is a common one. Public transportation is the classic example for which the problem is named, but there are many other cases in which people metaphorically "ride" for free. All sorts of services end up undersupplied as a result. Imagine a public bathroom with a sign reading, "Please clean the sink when you're finished." How many people would do that? Surely not everyone, even if everyone places some value on having a clean public bathroom. Or suppose if, after a big snowfall, everyone was expected to get a shovel and clear part of the road. If everyone pitched in, the road would get cleared in no time. But this is not usually what happens. If given the opportunity, people will free-ride; they will walk out of the bathroom without cleaning up, and they will choose not to go outside to shovel the road.

One way to think about the free-rider problem is that free riders enjoy positive externalities from others' choices to pay for bus rides, clean public bathrooms, or shoveled roads. As we saw in the "Externalities" chapter, when positive externalities exist, the equilibrium quantity of the good or service is less than the level that would maximize total surplus in society as a whole. The result is that public transportation, clean public bathrooms, and clear roads after a snowstorm are *undersupplied* if left solely to the market.

As we'll see in more depth later in the chapter, this undersupply problem can be solved in a variety of ways—from making the good or service more excludable (such as the pay-per-use public toilets found in some big cities) to the government making somebody responsible for the provision of a certain quantity of the good or service (such as municipal snow plowing on public roads).

Some important public goods are more abstract than buses or bathrooms. Health, cleanliness, general knowledge, and safety are all public goods that have a huge impact on everyday life. Consider an example from public health. If 99 percent of the population is vaccinated against a disease—such as polio or smallpox—the remaining 1 percent can probably remain unvaccinated without fear of getting sick. But if everyone tried to be a free rider by remaining unvaccinated, the risk of disease would quickly increase. It's not possible to exclude the unvaccinated from the benefits of living around others who are vaccinated. When there are too many free riders and an undersupply of vaccination, the result is that everyone is more likely to get sick. Similarly, an army, police force, or "neighborhood watch" are all ways of providing public safety. It is not possible to easily exclude free-riding residents who don't contribute from enjoying the benefits.

One of the most abstract public goods is general knowledge or information. For a case in which the free-rider problems surrounding these public goods seem to have been overcome to everyone's benefit, look at the From Another Angle box "Why does Wikipedia work?"

FROM ANOTHER ANGLE

Why does Wikipedia work?

In 2001, Jimmy Wales and Larry Sanger launched Wikipedia, a free online encyclopedia generated entirely by voluntary contributions from users. Contributors are unpaid and unsupervised. Anyone can edit Wikipedia, and anyone can choose to read articles without making a contribution. In other words, Wikipedia is a classic public good: nonexcludable, because anyone can use it for free; and nonrival, because generally speaking, one person reading a web page doesn't diminish others' ability to do so.

Given what we know about public goods, it's easy to think of ways that Wikipedia might have failed. At best, we might expect articles to be undersupplied. After all, how many people will want to spend their time writing encyclopedia articles for free? At worst, we can imagine contributors filling Wikipedia with self-serving or misleading information. Stephen Colbert, host of the satiric news-commentary show *The Colbert Report,* was once banned from Wikipedia for asking his viewers to edit the page on elephants to say that their population had tripled in three months. Colbert's point, of course, was that "facts" on Wikipedia are sometimes subject to the whims and biases of contributors.

In Wikipedia's early days, it seemed as if these predictions might cripple the project. Articles were short, riddled with errors, and much more likely to be about *Star Trek* than Friedrich Nietzsche. Ten years later, however, Wikipedia had 3.5 million articles—seven times the number in the *Encyclopedia Britannica.* A spot-check of 45 articles on general science topics found that Wikipedia is just as accurate as traditional peer-reviewed encyclopedias. How does Wikipedia overcome the problems of undersupply and misuse that generally plague public goods?

To rephrase the question: What sort of benefits could outweigh the costs of time and effort involved in editing Wikipedia? When asked directly in a survey, the vast majority of contributors listed altruistic-sounding reasons, such as: to "fix an error" or "contribute to the share of knowledge." Only 2 percent of all contributors listed fame or recognition as a motivation for editing. We might be somewhat skeptical about this modesty, though. After all, many contributors register a user name and page that provides a history of their edits for others to view.

Whatever the exact motivation of contributors, Wikipedia is designed in a way that is conducive to overcoming the challenges it faces as a public good: Since the costs of contributing are relatively low (just click "edit," type the changes, and click "submit"), it is easy to correct abuses. As a result, fewer than 5,000 dedicated editors (those who make over 100 edits a month) in the English version at last count do a remarkably good job of correcting incidences of vandalism and misuse. In addition, the project capitalizes on the idea that sharing knowledge is good for society. This motivates users to contribute and police one another on their own.

As Wikipedia and other free, open-source resources become more prominent, economists are adapting their ideas about the provision of public goods, and the motivations that drive people to contribute to them.

Sources: Denise Anthony et al., "Reputation and reliability in collective goods: The case of the online encyclopedia Wikipedia," *Rationality and Society* 21, no. 3 (2009), pp. 283–306; http://upload.wikimedi.org/wikipedia/foundation /a/a7/Wikipedia_General_Survey-Overview_0.3.9.pdf; http://stats.wikimedia.org/EN/TablesPageViewsMonthly .htm.http://stats.wikimedia.org/EN/TablesWikipediansEditsGt5.htm.

The tragedy of the commons

LO 19.3 Describe the tragedy of the commons and its consequences.

As we have seen, rhinos are not a public good, because they are rival—if someone shoots a rhino, it is definitely *not* there for the next person to enjoy. Usually, when you consume a rival good, you have to compensate the person who owns it. When you want to eat chicken, you pay the grocery store, or the restaurant, or the chicken farmer. But historically, before land was divided into private pieces, when you hunted a wild animal such as a rhino or buffalo or elephant, you didn't have to pay anyone. No one owned the wildlife, so no one could force you to pay. In other words, wildlife was typically rival, but also nonexcludable—a common resource.

How can we characterize demand for a common resource? Nonexcludability causes people to demand a higher quantity than they would if they had to pay for what they consumed. Because a common resource is also rival, it gets "used up" every time someone accesses it. This combination of inefficiently high demand and dwindling quantity leads to what is often called the **tragedy of the commons**—the depletion of a common resource due to individually rational but collectively inefficient overconsumption. Notice that whereas the free-rider problem is triggered by nonexcludability alone, the tragedy of the commons arises from the combination of rivalry and nonexcludability.

How can equilibrium quantity be both individually rational and collectively inefficient? To start with the *individually rational* part of the equation, think about the consumption decision from the perspective of a rhino hunter: On the benefit side, he gets the high value of rhino ivory on the black market. On the cost side, he faces the cost of hunting equipment, the time spent hunting rhinos, and the risk of getting in trouble with the law. But he does not have to pay anyone for the rhino horn he takes. As a result, hunters will hunt more than they would if they had to pay someone for the rhino horn.

Why is this *collectively inefficient*? Because we don't typically think of rhinos as having market value, it may be difficult to see that unrestricted hunting does not maximize total surplus. However, using a common resource imposes a negative externality on others: When the rhino population is depleted through poaching, the people of East Africa lose a key part of the local ecosystem. Anyone who wants to go on safari to see rhinos will lose surplus, as will local communities that get a boost from safari tourism. Lastly, if rhinos go extinct, there is a loss to the world's biodiversity.

Applying the reasoning we used in the previous chapter, if rhino hunters could be forced to consider the external costs of their activities, their demand curve would shift downward. The equilibrium quantity of rhinos poached would fall to the efficient level—the level that would maximize surplus in society as a whole.

tragedy of the commons the depletion of a common resource due to individually rational but collectively inefficient overconsumption

✓ CONCEPT CHECK

❑ How does the free-rider problem affect the supply of public goods? What is the resulting effect on equilibrium quantity? **[LO 19.2]**

❑ How does the tragedy of the commons affect the demand for common resources? What is the resulting effect on equilibrium quantity? **[LO 19.3]**

Dealing with Public Goods and Common Resources

We've seen that problems with undersupply of public goods and overdemand for common resources lead to an inefficient quantity of production and consumption. In other words, both types of goods are subject to market failures. There are many possible solutions, which generally fall under three categories: social norms, government regulation and provision, and private property rights.

In some cases, society tries to get people to act in the interest of society by shifting social norms. For example, campaigns to embarrass litterers, or to shame those who try to sneak on the back of the bus, may change people's opinions on what is individually optimal. In other cases, the government tries to fix the market failure through regulation or direct provision. Such approaches attempt to adjust the quantity of a good that is produced or consumed by either restricting private production (if a good is overproduced) or expanding production (if a good is underproduced).

Finally, some solutions involve creating property rights that turn a nonexcludable good into an excludable one. As with government regulation and provision, such approaches attempt to solve the market failure by converting social costs to private costs. Thus, when individuals act optimally, the socially optimal outcome is achieved.

As we discuss each solution, think about how it changes the *trade-off* between costs and benefits that people face when supplying or consuming a public good or common resource. We'll see that the range of solutions to these two problems is related to externalities.

Social norms

LO 19.4 Explain how and when social norms can effectively solve problems with public goods or common resources.

Dirty public spaces arise because littering is easy. Littering saves you the trouble of finding a garbage can, and is very unlikely to incur any real punishment or cost, so there is little incentive to take into account the negative externality imposed on others. In spite of this potential problem, lots of public spaces manage to stay clean and pleasant and relatively free of litter. How does this happen?

Sometimes, especially in big cities, public spaces stay clean because the government pays janitors or public works employees to clean them. But there are many public spaces, especially in close-knit neighborhoods, that stay clean through a simpler mechanism: the expectations and potential disapproval of the community. If you don't litter, we're guessing that it's *not* primarily because you're afraid of being caught and fined by the police, but simply because you've learned that it's not a *nice* thing to do.

As we have seen, both the free-rider problem and the tragedy of the commons are problems of *trade-offs*—people are able to enjoy the benefits of something without paying the corresponding costs. Strong social norms can help rebalance the trade-off by imposing "costs" on people who litter, sneak through the back door of the bus, fail to do their bit of snow shoveling, and so on. Remember, costs don't have to be financial. Social disapproval or guilt or conflict with those in your community can also be costs.

As you would expect, social disapproval carries a higher cost in places where you know the people around you, care about their opinions, and expect to interact with them again in the future. For example, we might expect social norms to be more effective at deterring free riders on a small-town bus system than on the subway in New York City.

Some specific "design principles" make informal, community-based solutions to public goods and common-resource problems more effective. These principles include: clear distinctions between who is and is not allowed to access the resource; the participation of resource users in setting the rules for use; and the ability of users to monitor one another.

Elinor Ostrom won the 2009 Nobel Prize in economics for her research showing that unregulated, commonly held property is frequently managed better than standard theory would lead us to expect, due to strong local organizations and social norms.

Beginning with the observation that groundwater was managed by informal associations in southern California, she moved on to studying other cases where resource management didn't fit neatly into either the market or the government realms, from irrigation systems in Nepal to Maasai pastureland in Kenya. In her research, Ostrom showed that social norms can sometimes be powerful enough for commonly held property to be managed extremely well.[1]

Bans, quotas, and government provision

LO 19.5 Describe how several types of government regulation can be used to solve problems with public goods or common resources.

What happens when informal institutions and rules are not enough? The management of public goods and common resources is one case in which government intervention can be productive and efficiency enhancing. The reason for this is simple: Often, government bodies have the power to impose limits on how much of a resource is consumed or to make up for inadequate supply, when individuals and informal associations do not. Within that broad justification, however, there are many different ways that governments can intervene, such as direct management of a resource and provision of a public good. We will consider three: bans, quotas, and government provision.

Bans and quotas. When thinking through some of the examples we've discussed, you might feel that we are missing the most obvious solution to the nonexcludability problem. Have a problem with keeping public spaces clean? Make littering illegal. Worried about rhinos and other endangered species becoming extinct? Make hunting them illegal, or impose a quota on how many rhinos each poacher is legally allowed to hunt.

Of course, littering usually is illegal, and bans or quotas apply to hunters in many countries. Yet the problems persist, so clearly this is not a perfect solution. To see why, we have to understand that making something illegal is simply one way of changing the *trade-offs* that people face, by creating costs for breaking the ban or exceeding the quotas. The cost that rule-breakers expect to face depends both on the punishment associated with rule breaking *and* on the likelihood of being caught and punished. If the punishment is not severe, or the likelihood of getting caught is low, the cost may not be high enough to change the trade-off.

Bans and quotas therefore often fail in situations where it is difficult or costly for authorities to monitor and punish rule-breakers. For instance, the United States and other wealthy countries tend to have relatively well-funded, well-policed national parks and conservation areas, which effectively protect endangered species. More than 90 percent of species listed as endangered in the United States have increased or stabilized populations since being declared endangered.[2]

In contrast, poorer countries find it much more difficult to enforce laws against poaching and habitat destruction. Most governments in East Africa, for instance, typically lack the funds to hire enough park rangers, build enough fences, and take other measures needed to fully protect wildlife. Bans on poaching rhinos thus have limited impact.

In contrast, South Africa has several large and well-managed national parks that protect rhinos and elephants effectively. As a result, the ban on hunting rhinos has proved to be effective. In countries that have the resources to enforce them, bans or quotas that limit the use of common resources are straightforward public-policy approaches to solving the problem of overuse. Especially when the optimal quantity of consumption is zero—for instance, with an endangered species on the brink of extinction—it may be the best approach.

In conservation, tough moral and practical questions come into play. In particular, policy-makers argue over both the principle and the pragmatism of setting total bans on use of endangered species and habitats versus allowing people to earn money from limited use. For a deeper consideration of these questions, read the What Do You Think? box "Should conservationists be principled or pragmatic?"

WHAT DO YOU THINK?

Should conservationists be principled or pragmatic?

Can you put a dollar value on the existence of tigers? How about elephants? How about the Devil's Hole pupfish, a tiny fish less than one-inch long that is native to a single pool in a limestone cavern in Death Valley National Park in California? What about unique habitats such as the Grand Canyon or the Amazon rainforest? How much would you be willing to pay to preserve these natural wonders?

Some conservationists argue, on principle, against efforts to place a monetary value on the existence of beautiful, unique creatures and landscapes. Such things are beyond value, they argue, and even trying to put a price tag on them demeans and undermines conservation efforts.

Other conservationists feel that putting a price on endangered land and animals is the only practical way to save them in the long run. When something has no monetary value, they argue, no one has an incentive to protect and sustain it. Saying that something is "beyond" financial value sounds great, but functionally, they argue, it is the same as saying that it has *zero* financial value.

Those who take the latter approach promote programs that allow people to earn money from controlled use of endangered resources. These pragmatists favor use of private incentives to improve excludability and conservation. They point out that locals often face a steep opportunity cost of conserving land or endangered species by forgoing hunting, farming, or logging.

A prime example of this pragmatic strategy is ecotourism. It offers locals an alternative way to earn money by showing interesting flora or fauna to travelers, and gives them an incentive to conserve natural areas.

In a related strategy, some nonprofit groups in the United States are paying ranchers and other landowners to set aside parts of their land. These agreements—known as *easements*—allow landowners to enter voluntarily into legal contracts that restrict what they can do with their land. For instance, a conservation group might pay someone who owns sensitive marshland in a suburban area to agree not to build on that land. The owner earns money from leaving the land undeveloped. Similar ideas are being tried in East Africa, either directly paying locals to maintain endangered plants or habitats, or giving them the rights to earn money through tourism or controlled hunting or harvesting.

Even conservationists who believe it is possible to put a price on conservation, though, sometimes criticize such pragmatic approaches. Their concerns relate to difficulties in monitoring and enforcement. The U.S. may have a well-functioning legal system, but many endangered species and landscapes are located in countries that do not. When there is a lack of effective monitoring mechanisms, it can be difficult to distinguish legitimate activities from illegitimate activities. An outright ban may therefore be easier to enforce.

What do you think?

1. Should we try to put a dollar value on the existence of endangered species? If so, how could we go about calculating it?
2. If the existence of a place or species is a public good, how could we get individuals to contribute the real value they put on it, rather than free riding?
3. Is it always better to hold a hard line and stick to a pure preservation, zero-use approach to avoiding the tragedy of the commons? Or are there situations in which limited-use approaches are more likely to succeed?

Government provision. Bans and quotas are applied to common-resource problems, to reduce the inefficiency created by overuse. To combat the undersupply of public goods, the more typical regulatory solution is for the government to step in and provide it directly. In the United States and many other wealthy countries, we see government provision of public goods everywhere: in transportation systems, education and research, parks, safety, and much more.

Well-intentioned people can argue about when it makes sense for government to provide these services directly and when it should contract with a private company to provide them or force individuals to pay a private provider. Whichever method a government chooses to supply a public good, two common issues arise: First, what is the right amount of the public good to supply? Second, who will pay for it?

In a functioning market, people will buy a good up to the point where the marginal benefit they enjoy from the last unit is equal to the marginal cost of that unit. If the marginal benefit were greater than the cost, they could increase their utility by buying more. If the cost were greater than the marginal benefit, they could increase their utility by buying less. This same analysis applies to public goods: If the government is supplying a public good, such as road maintenance, *the efficient quantity is the one at which the marginal social benefit equals the cost.*

Local governments usually repair roads. Why doesn't the private sector do it instead?

What is the marginal social benefit? Each individual who uses the road network gains some marginal benefit from increased road maintenance (more potholes filled, more frequent repaving). When roads are in good repair, everyone who uses them enjoys the benefits. Therefore, the marginal social benefit is actually the sum of the marginal benefit gained by each individual user. The government should calculate the cost of increased road maintenance, add up the marginal benefit to every user, and supply the quantity of road maintenance at which the two are equal.

Unfortunately, this cost-benefit analysis is simpler in theory than it is in practice. How can the government find out the true value that each citizen places on an additional unit of road maintenance? You might think one way would be to simply ask everyone how much they value well-maintained roads. Unfortunately, each individual has an incentive to overstate the marginal benefit he will receive, because he expects the government to pay for it. Since no individual driver pays the cost, each might as well petition for perfectly maintained roads. This is another example of individually rational behavior being socially inefficient.

In reality, governments try to conduct a cost-benefit analysis when deciding how much of a public good to supply, whether it is road maintenance, schools, the army, or cancer research. This means making a best guess at what the marginal social benefit of an additional unit will be. Sometimes economic research can help with this problem. It can, for example, attempt to quantify the diffuse benefits that people get from better schools or reduced disease or safer neighborhoods. But we usually have to accept that our best guess will be an imperfect one.

The second issue is figuring out how to pay for government provision of public goods. Determining who will pay depends in part on how easy it is to exclude people who don't pay. In some cases, it is possible to make the good excludable using the power of the government to monitor use and enforce payments among those who actually use them. Examples are the tolls that drivers pay to use toll roads, the fares that riders pay on buses and trains, and the tuition that students pay at public universities.

In other cases, it is either difficult or undesirable to charge user fees. For services that are "used" by almost all citizens—sewer systems, police and fire protection, and military defense—it may be more costly to try to exclude nonusers than it is worth. Instead, these services are usually funded through general tax revenue, usually in a way that is not directly connected to the services themselves, as we'll see in the chapter on "Taxation and Public Spending."

If the environmental policy challenges raised in this chapter interest you, you might want to learn more about a field of economics described in the Where Can It Take You? box "Environmental economics"

WHERE CAN IT TAKE YOU?
Environmental economics

The problems associated with common resources are at the center of environmental conservation, whether it's saving the rhino or the rainforest or slowing global warming. If you're intrigued by these challenges, you may be happy to know that there is a whole field dedicated to the study of the economics of the environment. *To learn more about this field, continue reading by scanning the QR code near the end of the chapter or by going online.*

Property rights

LO 19.6 Explain how and when expansion of property rights can effectively solve problems with public goods or common resources.

Public goods and common resources are not allocated efficiently by markets, but private goods are. Wouldn't the most convenient solution be to turn everything into a private good? In some cases, the answer is, yes!

The classic case of turning a common resource into a private good is the one that gave the "tragedy of the commons" problem its name. Hundreds of years ago, most villages in Europe and America had town "commons"—open, grassy areas in the middle of town that were used by everyone and owned by no one. Farmers could graze their livestock on the common. You know the end of this story: The town common was a common resource, and each farmer had an incentive to graze more and more animals, with no incentive to limit his own usage in order to preserve the value of the common for everyone. The grazing land was ruined, and everyone was left worse off.

In the end, the solution to this original tragedy of the commons was surprisingly simple. The first step was to institute rules about who got to graze where and when. The ultimate step was to break up the town commons into private lots, so that people had to graze their livestock on their own land. In New England, many towns still have a small "green," which is the descendant of the town common, but you are unlikely to see sheep or cows grazing there. When each farmer had to bear all the costs and all the benefits of his choices about how many animals to graze, each made the most efficient decision for his own land. Privatization solved the nonexcludability problem.

The idea of turning the commons into private property has many modern applications. The patent system, for example, is an example of turning a common resource—knowledge—into private property. As we saw with the example of Pfizer's drug Lipitor in the "Costs of Production" chapter, the idea behind intellectual property rights is to assure corporations that others will not be able to free-ride on their innovations. Such protection increases their incentives to undertake research that will create new knowledge.

There are also more literal modern applications. One policy credited with contributing to rhinos' recovery in South Africa allowed farmers to own wild animals on their land. Landowners are eligible for tax breaks if they keep and protect endangered species (such as rhinos). They also can earn money by selling the animals or admitting tourists to see them. This law essentially "privatizes" rhinos and other large animals like elephants, allowing individuals to capture the benefits of protecting them. This gives people an incentive to keep out poachers and increase the population of rhinos.

Increasingly, many governments are taking this sort of combined public-private approach to wildlife and other resource management. The privatization aspect helps introduce excludability and assign responsibility for costs and benefits; the public aspect helps counteract remaining externalities.

Assigning property rights over common resources is often far from simple. Especially in cases in which many people are already using a resource, it can be very difficult to decide who owns what. Not surprisingly, no one wants to be the person who has to reduce her consumption. However, some obvious mistakes can be avoided. For a case that illustrates some mistakes in the management of a very important common resource, see the Real Life box "Why the Colorado River no longer reaches the ocean"

REAL LIFE
Why the Colorado River no longer reaches the ocean

The mighty Colorado River once carved out the Grand Canyon. Now, it barely trickles into Mexico, and vanishes altogether before even reaching the Gulf of California. The reason? As the river passes through five U.S. states and six dams, vast amounts of water get diverted to grow thirsty crops in arid dusty fields and to supply drinking water to the booming cities in the Southwest. *For the full story, continue reading by scanning the QR code near the end of the chapter or by going online.*

Tradable allowances. One common way that governments can institute private property rights is through the use of tradable allowances or permits. Remember that quotas can control total quantity, but they don't necessarily allocate supplies in the most efficient way. They can result in undesirable side-effects, such as damaging extraction methods or rushes to get as much of a resource as possible before hitting the quota.

The method of using tradable allowances works the same way for solving a common-resource problem as it does for solving an externality problem. A cap is set on the total quantity of the resource that can be used, and shares of that total are allocated to individuals or firms. After the initial allocation, people can buy and sell their shares. Trading ensures that the resource is allocated to those with the highest willingness to pay, while still limiting overall quantity to an efficient level. The people who own shares now have private property rights—and an incentive, as owners, to make sure that the common resource does not get overused.

This may sound familiar. In the "Externalities" chapter, we discussed tradable allowances and permits as a way to tackle negative externalities. Since the depletion of common resources imposes a negative externality, tradable permits are also useful in allocating common resources.

The use of tradable permits is part of an ongoing battle to protect the world's fisheries from overuse. The story of how these allowances have been used in the United States is told in the Real Life box "North American fisheries learn from failure."

REAL LIFE

North American fisheries learn from failure

Visitors to Maine in the 1600s gave accounts of cod so plentiful the fish could be scooped out of the sea in baskets. The incredible bounty of the Grand Banks and Georges Bank fisheries supported coastal communities from Newfoundland to Massachusetts for hundreds of years. But in the mid-twentieth century, fishing technology began to change dramatically. Small fishing vessels gave way to huge ships that could carry 8 million pounds of fish and drag nets large enough to ensnare a jumbo jet. These technologies allowed fish to be harvested faster than ever before—at rates much faster than the fish could reproduce.

Since cod were a valuable and unregulated common resource, free for the taking, there was an incentive to catch as many cod as possible before they disappeared. That approach made sense for individuals, but not for the fishing community as a whole. It's individually rational but collectively inefficient. Authorities tried to solve the problem by instituting a quota, but they made two errors. First, worried that sharp reductions in the amount of cod that could be harvested would hurt the small towns whose economies relied on fishing, regulators set the quota far too high.

Second, the quota covered the total catch rather than individual fishing operations. That meant each fisherman still had an incentive to catch as many fish as possible as quickly as possible, before the total quota was met. The result was an annual "fishing derby," in which boats stuffed with gear had only a few days to pull in their catch for the whole year. Fishermen got injured, and the sudden glut of cod that hit fish houses in the days after the derby meant that fishermen received low prices for their catch.

None of these plans worked, and so the Canadian government placed a *total* ban on all fishing in the Grand Banks. As a result, 20,000 people lost their jobs. The economies of small towns all along the coast suffered.

Fortunately, younger fisheries in North America have learned from the disaster that occurred on the Grand Banks. In 1995, the harvest of Pacific halibut was put under an Individual Fishing Quota program—a tradable allowance system. Under it and many programs like it (often called "catch-shares"), a limit is set on the total catch and a share of that total is given to an individual fisherman, community, or fishing association. Every year, regulators adjust the total allowable catch. They allocate shares accordingly, with a goal to carefully manage the fish population.

Catch-shares allow permit holders to fish whenever and however they find most convenient and profitable. Most importantly, the shares are completely transferable and can be freely bought and sold. This feature creates a market for permits, which ensures that fishers harvest an environmentally sustainable quantity in the most efficient manner. This system should sound familiar: It's exactly the same as a cap-and-trade approach to carbon emissions.

Based on the success of early catch-shares programs, all U.S. Pacific Ocean fisheries adopted the practice in 2008. The success of these efforts stands in stark contrast to the overall health of the world's fisheries. Scientists estimate that if current practices continue, by 2048 we may have few commercially viable fisheries.

Sources: http://www.edf.org/page.cfm?tagID=3332; http://www.nefsc.noaa.gov/history/stories/groundfish/grndfsh1.html; http://hmapcoml.org/publications/.

✓ CONCEPT CHECK

❏ How can social norms change the trade-offs faced by potential free riders? **[LO 19.4]**

❏ Why is a tradable quota more efficient than a traditional quota? **[LO 19.5]**

❏ How can turning a common resource into private property solve the tragedy of the commons? **[LO 19.6]**

Conclusion

Public goods and common resources are an important source of market failure. Generally speaking, unregulated public goods will encounter the free-rider problem, in which nonexcludability leads to undersupply. On the other hand, unregulated common-resource goods will fall prey to the tragedy of the commons, which occurs when nonexcludability and rivalry combine to cause overconsumption and depletion of the resource.

These challenges can be overcome through a variety of solutions. In some cases, strong social norms or local organizations can improve excludability and increase the cost of free riding or overconsumption enough to avoid market failure. In other cases, government can step in, enforcing bans or quotas to limit the use of a common resource. Sometimes, it makes sense for government to simply provide a public good to counteract undersupply.

In general, limits on use work only when they are backed by sufficiently strong monitoring and enforcement. In places where this is not the case, privatization or combined public-private solutions can harness individual incentives to manage use and improve excludability. In the next chapter, we'll look into the practical details of how governments fund the provision of public goods and other services.

◄ Mobile Window on the World—Scan this code with your smartphone to find more applications of the chapter content. (Need a barcode reader? Try ScanLife, available in your app store.)

Visit your mobile app store and download ► the Karlan and Morduch Study Econ app.

Key Terms

excludable, p. 458

rival in consumption (rival), p. 458

private good, p. 458

public good, p. 459

common resource, p. 459

free-rider problem, p. 461

tragedy of the commons, p. 463

Summary

LO 19.1 Define different types of goods in terms of rivalry and excludability.

When a good is *excludable,* those who haven't paid for it can be prevented from using it. When a good is *rival,* one person's consumption prevents or decreases others' ability to consume it. Most of the goods discussed in this book are private goods, which are both excludable and rival. Public goods are the opposite of private goods: They are neither excludable nor rival. Common resources are rival, but not excludable. Artificially scarce goods are excludable, but not rival.

LO 19.2 Describe the free-rider problem and its consequences.

The free-rider problem is caused by nonexcludability leading to undersupply of a public good. When a good is not easily excludable, individuals have no incentive to pay for it. Therefore, supplying a public good involves a significant positive externality to free riders who receive the benefits without paying for them. The positive externality causes the supply curve to shift leftward, and moves the equilibrium quantity to an inefficiently low level.

LO 19.3 Describe the tragedy of the commons and its consequences.

A tragedy of the commons is the depletion of a common resource due to individually rational but collectively inefficient overconsumption. The ability to access the benefits of a common resource without paying any costs increases demand. Because the resource is rival in consumption, it imposes a negative externality on those whose ability to consume the resource is reduced. The negative externality shifts the demand curve upward, and moves the equilibrium quantity to an inefficiently high level.

LO 19.4 Explain how and when social norms can effectively solve problems with public goods or common resources.

Strong social norms can help rebalance the trade-offs involved in consuming public goods or common resources, by imposing social costs on those who break the "rules" of good behavior. Imposing costs of free riding or overconsumption can help bring the quantity consumed closer to the efficient level.

LO 19.5 Describe how several types of government regulation can be used to solve problems with public goods or common resources.

Often, government bodies have the power to solve the nonexcludability problem, while individuals do not. Banning or limiting use of common resources is a straightforward public-policy approach to solving the problem of overuse. However, such bans and limits often fail in situations where it is difficult or costly for authorities to monitor and punish rule breakers, and it is not necessarily efficient. Tradable allowances are a way of making quotas efficient by creating a market for the rights to consume a common resource, ensuring that it is allocated to those with the highest willingness to pay. In some circumstances, it makes sense for the government to supply a public good and fund service provision, through either user fees or a general tax on the population.

LO 19.6 Explain how and when expansion of property rights can effectively solve problems with public goods or common resources.

Sometimes the best way to solve the tragedy of the commons is to convert a common resource into a private good. Privatization works when it is possible to divide up a resource and make it excludable by giving a private owner control over its use. The owner has the right incentives to ensure an efficient level of use—bearing all of the costs and reaping all of the benefits. Privatization can be difficult, though, in cases where it is not possible to divide a resource or when it is not clear how to do so in a fair way. It can also be combined with public-policy approaches, such as privatizing a resource and also subsidizing it to counteract remaining externalities.

Review Questions

1. Popular software can cost thousands of dollars even though the marginal cost of producing another copy on CD or via download is near zero. What kind of good are these programs? **[LO 19.1]**

2. Suppose a popular band decides to hold a free concert in its hometown. Admission is available on a first-come, first-served basis. Is the concert a public good? **[LO 19.1]**

3. A talented musician plays for tips on the street, but never seems to make very much money. Explain why his tip jar is never very full. **[LO 19.2]**

4. Suppose a community garden in your neighborhood has both individually owned plots and a large, common plot. If soil and sunlight conditions are the same everywhere in the garden, explain why tomatoes grown in individually owned plots are so much better than tomatoes grown in the common plot. **[LO 19.2]**

5. Aquifers are underground sources of clean water that stretch over thousands of square miles. People who own land over the aquifer are free to take as much as they want. What is likely to happen to water supplies in an aquifer? Is this efficient? **[LO 19.3]**

6. Which do you expect to be more sustainable: grazing on public land or grazing on privately owned pastures? Why? **[LO 19.3]**

7. Even though many school zones don't have much traffic and aren't regularly monitored by the police for speed, most drivers are very careful to drive at or below speed limits when near schools. Why might this be the case even in the absence of strong government intervention? **[LO 19.4]**

8. Consider a fundraising campaign for your school's library. What is the free-rider problem in this situation? How might publically listing the names of donors to the library fund affect this problem? **[LO 19.4]**

9. The government of India has made killing Bengal tigers illegal, but poaching of the endangered animal continues. List some possible reasons that the ban hasn't been very successful, and suggest an alternative approach. **[LO 19.5]**

10. Why is it difficult for private markets to provide the optimal quantity of a public good? Why is it difficult for government to provide the optimal quantity of a public good? **[LO 19.5]**

11. The U.S. government is concerned about the huge numbers of people converging on Yellowstone Park every year. Government officials are worried that the park might be getting overused and the natural beauty will be ruined as a result. Suppose someone suggests dividing the park into private lots and selling it to individuals. How might this solution address the tragedy of the commons that is occurring? **[LO 19.6]**

12. Consider a proposal to privatize street lighting. Would this be feasible? Why or why not? Does street lighting suffer from a tragedy of the commons problem? **[LO 19.6]**

Problems and Applications

1. Identify whether each of the following goods is usually excludable or nonexcludable. **[LO 19.1]**
   a. AM/FM radio.
   b. A round of golf on a course.
   c. Street art.
   d. A museum exhibition.
   e. Toll roads.

2. Identify whether each of the following goods is rival or nonrival. **[LO 19.1]**
   a. Cable TV.
   b. A pair of jeans.
   c. Street signs.
   d. Attending a baseball game.

3. Consider community safety or defense, meaning freedom from crime and threats, to answer the following questions. **[LO 19.2]**
   a. What sort of good is community safety?
   b. If you lived in a place with no government-funded police force, would you expect community safety to be *oversupplied* or *undersupplied*?
   c. Suppose that some neighbors get together and organize a block watch group. What term do economists use to describe someone who lives in the neighborhood but chooses not to volunteer as part of the block watch?

4. From the list below, which of the following do you expect to suffer from a free-rider problem? Check all that apply. **[LO 19.2]**
   a. Pay-what-you-can yoga classes.
   b. Unlimited yoga classes with monthly membership dues.
   c. Fundraiser for public television.
   d. Neighborhood park cleanup day.
   e. Housecleaning business operating in your neighborhood.
   f. Suggested museum-admission donation.

5. In much of the United States and Canada, logging takes place in both privately owned and government-owned forests. **[LO 19.3]**
   a. Are privately owned forests excludable? Are they rival? What type of good are they?
   b. Suppose that anyone is legally allowed to enter a government-owned forest and start logging. What type of good are these forests?
   c. Do you expect the rate of logging in government-owned forests to be faster, slower, or equal to the efficient level?

6. Suppose that the government decides to start regulating use of its forests, charging anyone who wants to log. Which of the following ways of calculating the price to charge for each acre will lead to an efficient quantity of logging? **[LO 19.3]**
   a. The sum of the marginal social value of each acre to all logging companies.
   b. The average price citizens say they would be willing to pay for an acre.
   c. The external cost that logging an acre imposes on all citizens.

7. Which of the following subway announcements are attempts to establish or enforce a social norm? **[LO 19.4]**
   a. "Loud music and phone conversations are discourteous to fellow riders. Please keep the noise down."
   b. "If you see something, say something."
   c. "Please watch your step as you exit. Be careful of the gap between the train and the platform edge."
   d. "Please be patient and allow others to exit the train before you attempt to enter."
   e. "The train is being held at the station due to traffic ahead. We apologize for the inconvenience."

8. Would you expect tourists or locals to be more likely to give up their seat on a bus to an elderly person? **[LO 19.4]**

9. Determine whether each of the following policy interventions is designed to increase supply or decrease demand for a public good or common resource. **[LO 19.5]**
   a. A city government increases the frequency of street sweeping.
   b. London begins charging a toll to all vehicles that drive within the city limits.
   c. A gated community passes a bylaw requiring all homeowners to mow their lawns once a week during the summer.
   d. The National Park Service increases the cost of a pass to enter the Everglades.

10. Consider the following government-provided goods. Which of these goods necessarily require funding via general taxation (as opposed to direct user fees)? **[LO 19.5]**
    a. Street lights.
    b. A park.
    c. A fireworks display.
    d. Public radio.
    e. A library.

11. Public-opinion polls in a small city have revealed that citizens want more resources spent on public safety, an annual fireworks display, and more community swimming pools. Which of these three citizen requests could be privatized by assigning property rights? **[LO 19.6]**

12. For each of the following examples, state which of these approaches is being taken to manage a common resource or supply a public good: social norms, quota, tradable allowance, government provision, or property rights. **[LO 19.4, 19.5, 19.6]**

    a. A nonprofit organization spray-paints signs on storm drains reminding everyone that it "drains to the ocean" with a picture of a fish.

    b. A city starts a free program that collects recyclable glass, paper, and plastic from residents' doorsteps.

    c. In England, municipal-waste authorities are given a percentage of an overall limit that can be put in the landfill each year. These percentages can be traded among municipalities.

    d. American bison, which once roamed freely across the Great Plains, are now raised on ranches for commercial purposes.

Chapter Endnotes

1. Elinor Ostrom, *Governing the Commons: The Evolution of Institutions for Common Action* (New York: Cambridge University Press, 1990).

2. http://esasuccess.org/report_2012.html#.UA8e_WHOwro.

Chapter Sources

http://wwf.panda.org/what_we_do/where_we_work/project/projects/index.cfm?uProjectID=ZA0032&source=ge

http://www.economist.com/node/16941705?story_id=16941705

http://www.nature.org/aboutus/howwework/conservationmethods/privatelands/conservationeasements/about/easementaction.html

http://nobelprize.org/nobel_prizes/economics/laureates/2009/ostrom_lecture.pdf

Taxation and the Public Budget

HAPPY TO PAY TAXES?

Lawn signs are a common sight during election season. With bright colors and catchy slogans, they try to draw the attention of passersby to the name of a favored political candidate. In 2003, however, a new and rather unusual type of sign appeared on the lawns of some Minnesota voters. In place of a politician's name, the bright orange signs simply read, "Happy to pay for a better Minnesota."

The governor of Minnesota had been elected on a campaign promise to balance the state budget without raising taxes. Yet, the Minnesota couple behind the "happy to pay" campaign told reporters that they weren't promoting any particular candidate or party. They simply wanted to share their opinion that a tax increase was not necessarily a bad thing. In their view, a tax increase would allow Minnesota to have a balanced budget *and* maintain public services.

The "happy to pay" campaign raised eyebrows because it bucked the usual trend of voters demanding lower taxes. Sometimes, as with the "Tea Party" movement that swept U.S. politics in 2009–2010, voters demand cuts in *both* government programs and taxes. Other voters express a desire for functional roads, good schools, and other services, while also wanting lower taxes. Governments can, and often do, borrow money, rather than raise taxes, to pay for public spending. But the borrowed money comes due eventually. Sooner or later, somehow or other, government will always need to collect tax revenues to pay for what it spends.

Each time you vote, whether for your mayor or a national candidate, you're likely to face choices between candidates with different views on taxes. In this chapter we describe general principles of taxation and spending that can help you disentangle the debates. In earlier chapters we saw that when externalities exist, taxes can correct market failures, and thus increase total surplus. But we also saw that when markets are already efficient, taxes reduce total surplus. Here we investigate the effects of a variety of taxes: how much money they raise, how much inefficiency they cause, and who bears the burden. We'll explore arguments for and against each kind of taxation, and give you the tools to weigh the issues and make informed choices when casting your vote.

Why Tax?

LO 20.1 Describe the major public policy goals of taxation.

Taxpayers often dread April 15th—the day when federal taxes are due. Unlike the "happy to pay" tax supporters in Minnesota, many citizens grumble about the bite that taxes take out of their paychecks. Some even take to the streets in protest, as members of the Tea Party did in hundreds of rallies around the country on April 15, 2010. Why do voters continue to support governments that tax them? What's the gain that balances the pain? We saw in earlier chapters that taxes do two things: raise revenue and change the behavior of buyers and sellers.

- **Raising revenue:** The most obvious use of taxes is to raise public revenue. This revenue allows governments to provide goods and services to citizens, from national defense to highway building. Many tax-funded programs, such as public schools and roads, are intended to increase surplus and stimulate economic growth. Others are intended to provide basic human needs such as food, health care, or housing to people in need. People may disagree about which services should be funded through tax dollars, but most agree that at least some services are necessary.
- **Changing behavior:** Taxes change behavior because they alter the incentives faced by market participants. Taxes drive a wedge between the price paid by buyers and the price received by sellers, resulting in a lower equilibrium quantity of the good or service being consumed. In some cases, this effect on incentives is just a side effect of a tax designed to raise revenue; in others, it is the explicit purpose of the policy. Taxes on alcohol, tobacco, and gasoline are examples of policies designed partly to reduce demand.

Figure 20-1 summarizes these two effects of taxes.

We saw in the "Externalities" chapter that when a market involves negative externalities, such as air pollution, the effect of a tax can be to *increase* total surplus in society as a whole by moving the market to a lower equilibrium quantity.

However, we also saw in the "Government Intervention" chapter that when implemented in an already-efficient market, a tax causes *deadweight loss*. Deadweight loss is usually considered a *cost of taxation*. Sometimes, though, even when markets are functioning efficiently, governments use taxes to discourage certain purchases. For a discussion of whether such taxes increase or decrease total surplus, see the From Another Angle box, "Love the sinner, love the sin tax."

FIGURE 20-1

A tax raises revenue and changes behavior

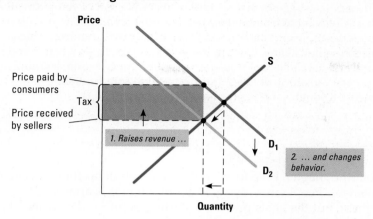

A tax shrinks the market, moving equilibrium to a lower quantity and driving a wedge between the price paid by buyers and the price received by sellers. A tax also raises revenue, equal to the tax rate multiplied by the quantity traded under the new equilibrium.

FROM ANOTHER ANGLE

Love the sinner, love the sin tax

Any teacher, preacher, parent, or politician will tell you that people don't always know what's best for them. However, economists usually start from the premise that what people *do* tells us what maximizes their utility—hence the concept of revealed preference we saw in the "Consumer Behavior" chapter. For instance, if smokers choose to smoke and drinkers choose to drink, that tells us something about their true preferences.

Despite this, many people advocate for taxes on alcohol and tobacco. To make the point, these policies are sometimes called "sin taxes."

The potential motivations behind sin taxes are numerous. One is to combat negative externalities: There are the costs to others associated with breathing secondhand smoke and encountering drunk drivers on the road. Some voters support sin taxes simply because they disapprove of smoking and drinking. Advocates for sin taxes often believe that reducing smoking or drinking through taxes accomplishes a moral goal.

Economists add another layer to the analysis. They argue that we should also take into account the well-being of smokers and drinkers—and not in the direction you might think. Even if a community is better off with less tobacco and alcohol use, smokers and drinkers are made worse off by having to pay more in taxes. The right policy then depends on the relative size of the cost to smokers and drinkers versus the size of the benefit to the broader community.

However, the rise of behavioral economics has brought a more nuanced perspective to the economic analysis of sin taxes. Smoking and drinking are not like other economic activities. Some people want to stop smoking and drinking (or at least cut back), but have a tough time following through, due to problems with self-control or addiction. Under these circumstances, revealed preference doesn't tell the whole story about what people really want. That's why new research on cigarette taxes suggests that economics *can* explain how, under certain circumstances, a sin tax could make "sinners" better off as well.

Economists Jonathan Gruber and Sendhil Mullainathan looked at how the self-reported happiness of people in the U.S. and Canada changed as cigarette taxes rose.

They found that increases in cigarette taxes actually made people who were likely to smoke happier.

Why? The research suggests that sin taxes can act as a sort of commitment device for people who truly want to change their behavior but have problems with self-control. Making cigarettes more expensive provides a disincentive to smoke, which helps motivate people struggling against temptation. As economists gain a better understanding of behavioral and psychological responses to public policy, we are learning more about the nuances and versatility of taxes. It turns out that some of the people who thought that they'd lose through sin taxes turn out to be winners.

Source: Jonathan Gruber and Sendhil Mullainathan, "Do cigarette taxes make smokers happier?" *Advances in Economic Policy and Analysis* 5, issue 1 (2005).

Throughout the chapter, keep in mind the two goals of taxation: raising revenue and changing behavior. People may disagree about when it is appropriate to use taxes to accomplish them, but the goals provide a starting point for discussion about the costs and benefits of taxation.

Even when people have agreed on a goal, some types of taxes may be more effective than others in achieving it. In this chapter, we will evaluate the effects and side effects of different methods of taxation. As a voter, you can combine this factual understanding of taxes with your moral or political beliefs about which public services should be funded and what types of behavior ought to be discouraged.

✓ CONCEPT CHECK

- ❏ Does a tax increase or decrease the quantity of the taxed good that is consumed? **[LO 20.1]**
- ❏ Why does a tax in an efficient market decrease total surplus, while a tax in a market with a negative externality increases total surplus? **[LO 20.1]**

Principles of Taxation

If you live in the United States, your state constitution (unless you live in Vermont) requires that the state budget be balanced. So, if your governor has ambitious ideas to improve the state, keep in mind that the legislature and governor almost surely have to raise fees or taxes to make it happen. Even if your governor is working to reduce taxes, he or she has to decide which kinds of taxes to cut and how fast. The economic question is how to tax in a way that keeps the economy healthiest.

Not all taxes are alike, and there are different ways to design a tax to raise a certain amount of revenue. In this section, we focus on understanding how to analyze the impact of different types of taxes. Three concepts are particularly useful in evaluating the costs and benefits of alternative types of taxes: *efficiency, revenue,* and *incidence.* We'll discuss each of these concepts as a framework for evaluating the costs and benefits of a particular tax.

Efficiency: How much (extra) will the tax cost?

LO 20.2 Explain how deadweight loss and administrative costs contribute to the inefficiency of a tax.

When considering the costs and benefits of a tax, it is tempting to assume that the cost is the amount that taxpayers have to pay, and the benefit is whatever services are provided using those funds. However, we know from the analysis of taxes in earlier chapters that it's not quite that simple. Taxes cause changes in economic behavior, potentially shifting supply and demand away from their optimal levels, and we need to take that into account. In addition, collecting taxes takes up resources in itself.

Just because a tax creates inefficiency does not necessarily mean that the tax is bad. While the tax itself may create an inefficiency, the revenue it generates may be used to fix another one. The net effect is specific to each tax and to each use of government proceeds from the tax. Here we will discuss two types of inefficiencies that taxes can create.

The first kind of inefficiency we consider is one we have described already: *deadweight loss*. This is the difference between the loss of surplus to taxpayers and the tax revenue collected. The second form of inefficiency is *administrative burden,* which represents the effort to collect and manage revenue. We'll discuss these two costs and how to calculate their size.

Deadweight loss. Remember from the "Government Intervention" chapter that a tax in an efficient market decreases total surplus. This loss of surplus is called **deadweight loss**. It occurs because the quantity of a good that is bought and sold is below the market equilibrium quantity.

It's important to distinguish deadweight loss from the total amount of surplus lost to those in the market as the result of a tax. The surplus that is lost to buyers and sellers but converted into tax revenue is not considered a cost, because the tax revenue funds public services. Those services provide surplus to citizens who benefit from them. Sometimes these are the same people who paid the taxes, and sometimes not. The value of that surplus may be transferred to someone else through government policies, but it is not lost.

In contrast, deadweight loss is value that simply *disappears* as the result of a tax. Neither buyers nor sellers nor recipients of government services benefit from it. It is lost altogether.

Let's briefly review how to calculate the value of deadweight loss that results from a tax in an efficient market—say, the market for jeans. Suppose that the market equilibrium for jeans is 4 million pairs at a price of $50 per pair. For the sake of simplicity, let's imagine that the sales tax on clothes is a flat dollar amount (rather than a percent of the sale price). Figure 20-2 demonstrates the effect of a $20 per pair tax on jeans. (We'll admit that's a pretty large tax, but it helps clarify the example.)

What happens? The tax causes the demand curve to shift down by the amount of the tax. The reason: The effective price paid by consumers is now $20 higher at any given market price. The tax drives a wedge between the price received by sellers (the market price, i.e., $40) and the price paid by buyers (the market price plus the $20 tax, i.e., $60). The shift in the demand curve causes the equilibrium point to slide down the supply curve to a lower market price and a lower quantity. Under the tax, 1 million fewer pairs of jeans are sold. The consumer and producer surplus that is no longer generated by those sales is deadweight loss.

How much deadweight loss a tax causes depends on how *responsive* buyers and sellers are to a price change. In other words, the size of deadweight loss is determined by the price elasticity of supply and demand. The more price-elastic the demand or supply curve, the larger the drop in equilibrium quantity caused by a given increase in price, and the larger deadweight loss will be. Figure 20-3 shows graphically that the area of the triangle representing deadweight loss is larger in a market with higher price elasticity of demand, given a tax of the same size. This leads to a general principle of taxation: Deadweight loss is minimized when a tax is levied on something for which people are not likely to change their behavior much in response to a price change.

deadweight loss
a loss of total surplus that occurs because the quantity of a good that is bought and sold is below the market equilibrium quantity

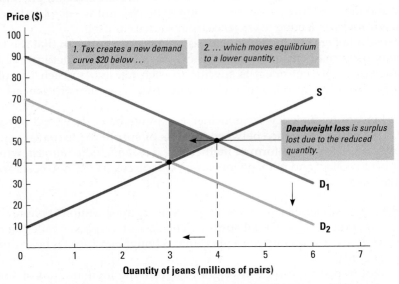

FIGURE 20-2

A tax causes deadweight loss

1. Tax creates a new demand curve $20 below ...

2. ... which moves equilibrium to a lower quantity.

S

Deadweight loss *is surplus lost due to the reduced quantity.*

D₁

D₂

Price ($) — vertical axis: 10, 20, 30, 40, 50, 60, 70, 80, 90, 100

Quantity of jeans (millions of pairs) — horizontal axis: 0, 1, 2, 3, 4, 5, 6, 7

A tax of $20 on jeans adds a new demand curve, sliding the equilibrium point along the supply curve from 4 million to 3 million pairs. The surplus lost to people who would have bought and sold those 1 million pairs of jeans but no longer do so under the tax is deadweight loss.

It is worth bearing in mind that this discussion also applies to the markets for factors of production. In general, a tax discourages people from engaging in whatever behavior is taxed. For example, a tax on income discourages people from working extra hours. How much inefficiency is caused by income tax, and how much revenue is raised by it, depends on how price-sensitive people are. In other words, how much will workers reduce the quantity of labor they supply in response to a tax on wages? (Not surprisingly, policy-makers are particularly interested in the answer to this question.)

If deadweight loss is minimized when we tax activities that people will continue to do anyway, why not push this idea to its logical conclusion and simply tax people for existing? This idea—of taxing everyone the same amount, regardless of their economic behavior—is called a **lump-sum tax**, or **head tax**. To understand why a lump-sum tax is very efficient, think about *how taxpayers will respond* to the tax. If everyone is required to pay $1,000 to the government each year no matter what they do, or how much they earn, or what they buy, there is no incentive to change behavior. If our only goal in implementing a tax was to maximize efficiency and minimize deadweight loss, a head tax might be the way to go. But while head taxes may be highly efficient, many people do not think it's fair to have everyone, both rich and poor, pay the exact same dollar amount in taxes. It also reduces the total amount of revenue that can be raised, because the size of the tax is limited by the poorest citizens' ability to pay. For these reasons, we rarely see lump-sum taxes.

Administrative burden. Administering and collecting taxes carries costs, whether the market is efficient or inefficient. Someone has to create procedures for collecting revenues, enforcing tax payments, and handling the collected funds. These logistical

lump-sum tax (head tax) a tax that charges the same amount to each taxpayer, regardless of their economic behavior or circumstances

FIGURE 20-3

Deadweight loss increases with price elasticity

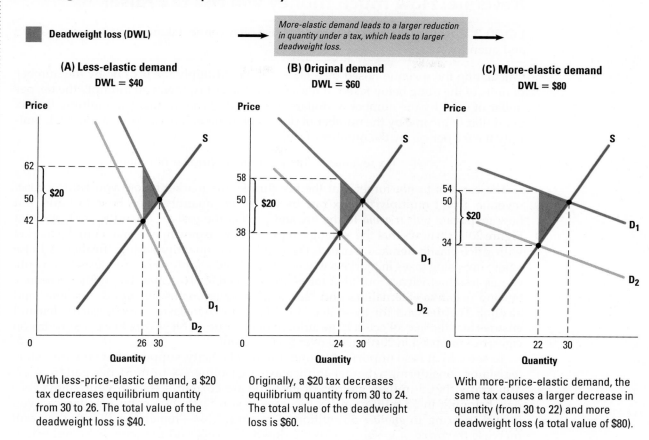

■ Deadweight loss (DWL)

More-elastic demand leads to a larger reduction in quantity under a tax, which leads to larger deadweight loss.

(A) Less-elastic demand
DWL = $40

(B) Original demand
DWL = $60

(C) More-elastic demand
DWL = $80

With less-price-elastic demand, a $20 tax decreases equilibrium quantity from 30 to 26. The total value of the deadweight loss is $40.

Originally, a $20 tax decreases equilibrium quantity from 30 to 24. The total value of the deadweight loss is $60.

With more-price-elastic demand, the same tax causes a larger decrease in quantity (from 30 to 22) and more deadweight loss (a total value of $80).

costs associated with implementing a tax are called the **administrative burden**. It includes the time and money spent by the government agencies that track and follow up on tax bills. It also includes taxpayers' time and expense of filing their returns and hiring accountants and lawyers to give them tax advice. For instance, in 2012 the federal government spent $13.3 billion to run the Internal Revenue Service (IRS), the government agency tasked with collecting around $2.5 trillion (or $2,500 billion) in tax revenue.

In general, the more complex the tax, the higher the administrative burden will be. Consider, for instance, the difference between the federal income tax and a local sales tax. The federal income tax requires people to fill out pages and pages of forms, calculate types of income from different sources, and account for deductions and exclusions. Record-keeping takes time and sometimes involves hiring an accountant or tax preparer. On the government side, the income tax involves an entire government agency devoted to calculating and processing tax returns, and tracking down people who fail to pay. In contrast, a sales tax, while certainly not costless, is much easier to process. Merchants calculate and collect the tax with each purchase, and they send this tax revenue to the local government. The sales tax doesn't require as much extra time or effort to process. If maximizing efficiency was our only goal, simpler taxes would certainly trump more complicated ones.

administrative burden the logistical costs associated with implementing a tax

Revenue: How much money will the tax raise?

LO 20.3 Calculate the effect of a tax increase on revenue, taking into account price and quantity effects.

Calculating the revenue raised by a tax is simple: Multiply the tax rate by the number of units of the thing being taxed. If it's a general sales tax, then you multiply the tax per dollar of sales by the number of dollars in sales. If it's an income tax, multiply the tax per dollar of income by the number of dollars of income. If it's a tax on a toll road, multiply the fee per car by the number of cars.

$$\text{Tax revenue} = \text{Tax per unit} \times \text{Number of units}$$

The catch is to not forget that the tax shrinks the market before you get to collect revenue. Don't multiply the tax rate by the *pre-tax* quantity—you have to figure out how taxpayers will *respond* to the tax and predict the *post-tax* quantity. Look again at Figure 20-3. It shows that the rectangle representing tax revenue is smaller in the market with price-elastic demand because the equilibrium quantity shrinks further. All else equal, imposing taxes in markets where demand and supply are price-inelastic not only causes less inefficiency but also raises more revenue. This may be another reason—beyond negative externalities and "sin"—why governments like to tax cigarettes and alcohol: The demand for these goods is highly price-inelastic. This inelastic demand ensures that the tax collects a large amount of revenue. In New York State, a $1.60 tax on cigarettes imposed in 2010 raised over $500 million.

To see why it is so important to understand elasticity, suppose that you are a state legislator considering whether to increase a gasoline tax from $1 per gallon to $2. You know that 5 million gallons of gasoline are currently sold in your state every day, bringing in $5 million in tax revenue. If you raise the tax by a dollar, can you expect to bring in *another* $5 million of revenue? No—remember that the tax will increase the price of gasoline, driving down demand, and reducing the equilibrium quantity bought and sold. In an extreme case, the net effect of a tax rise could even be to *reduce* total tax revenue. For example, if the tax increase reduces the equilibrium quantity to 2 million gallons, your $2 gas tax would bring in only $4 million in revenue.

In other words, we have to consider two opposing effects of a tax increase. Raising taxes means that the government gets more revenue per units sold—the *price effect*. But the higher tax rate causes fewer units to be sold—the *quantity effect*. This idea, shown in Figure 20-4, is parallel to the discussion in the "Elasticity" chapter of the relationship between price elasticity and revenue for a private firm.

We can generalize this point to see that raising taxes has diminishing returns to revenue, as shown in Figure 20-5. As tax rates get higher, we can expect revenue to increase at a slower and slower rate as the quantity effect catches up with the price effect. At some point, taxes can get so high that the quantity effect dominates, and raising taxes reduces total revenue. The point at which the revenue-maximizing tax level is reached depends on the elasticity of supply and demand: The more elastic, the quicker the revenue-maximizing point will be reached.

After the revenue-maximizing point, *lowering* taxes *increases* total revenue. The graph shown in Figure 20-5 is sometimes referred to as the *Laffer curve*, after economics professor Arthur Laffer. As an advisor to President Ronald Reagan in the 1980s, Laffer argued that U.S. tax rates had become so high (especially on the wealthiest Americans who paid 70 percent of their income in taxes in 1980) that Reagan could achieve a politician's dream: He could lower tax rates and simultaneously increase government revenue. Reagan took this advice and signed large-scale tax cuts into law in 1981.

FIGURE 20-4

Raising taxes has both price and quantity effects on revenue

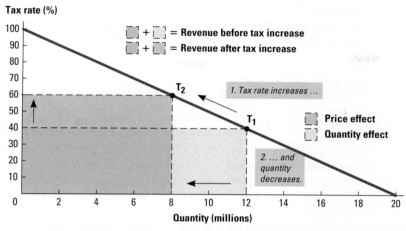

An increase in the tax rate increases the amount of revenue earned per unit, but the higher "price" of taxes means that quantity decreases. The net effect on revenue depends on whether the quantity effect outweighs the price effect.

The idea that people change their behavior in response to taxes is uncontroversial among economists, but the question about how much and in what ways they change their behavior is the subject of much research. Most of that research suggests that the elasticity of the labor supply with respect to taxes is very low for most people. In contrast to Laffer's prediction, people hardly increase the amount they work when tax rates fall. However, research shows that people do rearrange their income from different sources to reduce their tax burden, especially higher-income people who face the highest tax rates. In the end, we can't say for sure at what point the Laffer curve reaches its maximum. Estimates range from 40 percent to near 80 percent. This may seem high, but

FIGURE 20-5

Raising taxes first increases and then decreases revenue In the beginning, raising the tax rate increases revenue. After a certain point, further increases in the tax rate decrease the amount of revenue collected. At this point, maximum revenue is collected.

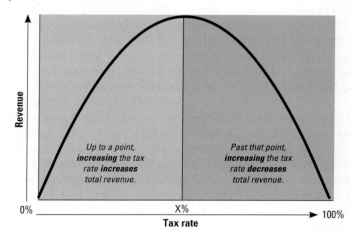

remember, this is the tax rate that maximizes the government's revenues, not the level that is "best" for the economy.

As we'll discuss later in the chapter, knowing the price and quantity effects of taxation is critical when weighing political arguments about who should be taxed and by how much.

Incidence: Who ultimately pays the tax?

LO 20.4 Identify proportional, progressive, and regressive taxes.

We have seen that a head tax would theoretically be more efficient than other types of taxes. That's because a head tax is levied equally on everyone, no matter how much they earn or what they buy. As a result, a head tax won't distort economic behavior, and thus it minimizes deadweight loss. So, why don't governments simply collect all of their tax revenue using a head tax?

Let's use some real numbers to draw a rough sketch of what a head-tax-only system would look like in the United States. Say the goal is to collect $2.345 trillion in taxes—which was the approximate federal tax revenue in 2010. With around 155 million taxpayers in the country, a head tax would have to be about $13,000 per taxpayer. Given that roughly one in five American households earns less than $20,000, the head tax would be a very big percentage of many people's income. For some, it could be more than their total income.

The larger lesson here is that policy-makers—and taxpayers, of course—are concerned not only with what a tax does, but also with who pays it. In the "Government Intervention" chapter, we introduced the idea of incidence as the relative burden of an excise tax on buyers versus sellers. We can now generalize the concept of **incidence** to describe who bears the burden of any sort of tax. This means not just buyers and sellers, but also old people or young people, rich people or poor people, and so on.

In the chapter on "Government Intervention," we also described an important insight that's not immediately obvious. We observed that the burden a tax places on buyers versus sellers is independent of which side is charged for the tax. This idea says that the *statutory* incidence of the tax (i.e., who is legally obligated to pay the tax to the government) has no effect on the *economic* incidence of the tax (i.e., who actually loses surplus as a result of the tax). Instead, the side of the market that is more inelastic—the side that responds less to changes in prices—will bear more of the tax burden. This means that policy-makers do not have much power in shifting the tax burden between buyers and sellers.

The distinction between statutory and economic incidence is important. For instance, the statutory incidence of a sales tax may fall entirely on consumers, since they're the ones actually paying the tax at the cash register. But if consumers respond by buying less, the tax will clearly also affect the stores where they shop. If the stores respond by reducing prices, the stores are effectively sharing part of the tax burden. The economic incidence of the tax thus falls in part on the stores, even though they don't literally pay the tax.

Similarly, an income tax that employees are legally obliged to pay will also affect the corporations that employ them: If the tax reduces employees' willingness to supply labor at any given price level, corporations may choose to raise wages in response. The higher wages could lead corporations to reduce the dividends they pay to shareholders or to increase the prices charged to customers, a loss of surplus. In short, the people who pay the tax can be very different from those who ultimately feel the pinch.

Behavioral economists are adding another layer to our understanding, and they have started to discover ways in which statutory incidence *can* actually affect people's

incidence
a description of who bears the burden of a tax

behavior: See the Real Life box, "Who really pays the sales tax?" for a discussion of how an understanding of behavioral responses to taxes can affect our analysis of taxes.

REAL LIFE

Who really pays the sales tax?

Forty-five of the 50 states charge a sales tax on consumer goods. How this tax is incorporated into prices varies from state to state and store to store. *To the see the economic effects of this difference in policy, continue reading by scanning the QR code near the end of the chapter or by going online.*

We generally assume that policy-makers do not have the power to redistribute the tax burden between consumers and producers. But they *do* have the ability to affect the relative economic incidence of the tax burden on the rich and the poor. Economists and policy-makers classify taxes in one of three categories: proportional, regressive, or progressive.

A tax that is **proportional** takes the same *percentage* of income (as opposed to the same dollar amount) from all taxpayers. In other words, people are taxed *in proportion* to their income. In a political context, a proportional income tax is sometimes called a "flat tax." Under a 25 percent flat tax on income, for instance, someone with an income of $20,000 would pay the same *proportion* of his or her income as someone with an income of $200,000. This means the absolute amount paid by each would be $5,000 versus $50,000, as shown in Figure 20-6.

The current income tax in the United States is not a proportional tax. Instead, it is **progressive**. A tax is considered progressive if people with low incomes owe not only a smaller absolute amount, but also a smaller *percentage* of their income than high-income people. The U.S. personal income tax has different "brackets" for people with different levels of income; the percentage of income owed increases with each bracket. Figure 20-6 also shows an example of a progressive income tax: The person earning $20,000 pays 20 percent taxes (an absolute amount of $4,000); the person earning $200,000 pays 30 percent (an absolute amount of $60,000).

The final category of tax incidence is **regressive**. A regressive tax is levied in such a way that low-income taxpayers pay a greater proportion of their income toward taxes than do high-income taxpayers. Most countries avoid explicitly regressive income taxes. That is, they structure their tax systems so that people in lower brackets do not pay a higher percentage of income in taxes. However, other taxes can still be regressive. The lump-sum tax is an example, as shown in Figure 20-6. If both taxpayers must pay the same absolute tax of $13,000, that amount equates to a much higher proportion of the poorer taxpayer's income—65 percent compared to only 6.5 percent for the high earner.

As we consider different types of taxes, it is important to keep in mind the relationship between efficiency and incidence. For example, some politicians propose replacing all income taxes with a single sales tax. The beauty of the idea is that it would be much simpler and more efficient than the current system. On the other hand, it would be regressive: On average, people with lower incomes spend a higher proportion of their income, rather than saving or investing it. Thus, a higher proportion of their income is affected by a sales tax. In contrast, an income tax system like the one currently in place is more progressive, but is also probably less efficient due to the higher administrative burden and incentive effect on richer households.

proportional/flat tax a tax that takes the same percentage of income from all taxpayers

progressive tax a tax that charges low-income people a smaller percentage of their income than high-income people

regressive tax a tax that charges low-income people a larger percentage of their income than it charges high-income people

FIGURE 20-6

Proportional, progressive, and regressive taxes Under a proportional tax, everyone pays the same percentage of their income in taxes. With a progressive tax, lower incomes are taxed less as both a percentage of their incomes and in total amount paid. A regressive tax charges the poor a higher percentage of their income than the rich, even though everyone is taxed the same dollar amount.

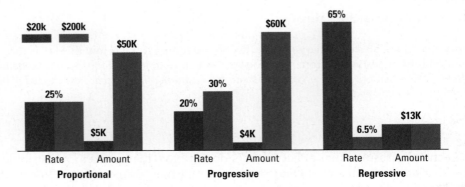

We can see some of the challenges faced by politicians and economists as they try to find taxes that are fair and efficient and that raise enough money. Finding a tax system that pleases everyone is seldom possible. As a voter you can expect to have to weigh both *positive* judgments about the efficiency of a proposed tax and *normative* judgments about the "fairness" of its incidence.

✓ CONCEPT CHECK

- ❏ Which is likely to be more efficient: a tax on a good with highly price-elastic demand or a tax on a good with inelastic demand? **[LO 20.2]**
- ❏ What is the difference between the price effect and the quantity effect of a tax increase on tax revenue? **[LO 20.3]**
- ❏ Is a tax that charges $100 to every citizen for garbage collection regressive, proportional, or progressive? **[LO 20.4]**

A Taxonomy of Taxes

LO 20.5 Describe the sources of tax revenue in the United States, and discuss the role played by different types of taxes.

So far, we've mentioned several types of taxes without going into much detail on how and why they are levied. In this section, we'll explain the important features of different kinds of taxes. We'll focus on the revenue, efficiency, and incidence of each tax.

Let's start first with an overview of U.S. government tax revenue. The federal government calculates taxes by *fiscal year,* which begins in October of one calendar year and runs through September of the following year. In fiscal year 2010 (that is, October 2009 through September 2010), the federal government collected $2.345 trillion in revenue.

Where does all this tax money come from? Figure 20-7 lists the various categories of taxes and the percentage of total tax revenue that they contribute. Over 90 percent of tax revenue comes from three sources: Contributing nearly equal shares of more than

FIGURE 20-7

Federal tax receipts in the United States The U.S. government earns most of its revenue from individual income taxes and social insurance and retirement contributions. The vast majority of social insurance and retirement contributions come from Medicare and Social Security payments.

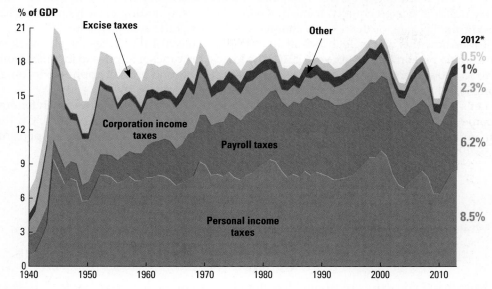

*Represents an estimate.

Source: GPO, Historical Tables, 2.3. http://www.gpo.gov/fdsys/search/pagedetails.action?granuleId=&packageId=BUDGET-2011-TAB&fromBrowse=true.

40 percent each are the personal income tax and payroll taxes. In third place, with less than 10 percent, is the corporate income tax. In this section, we'll discuss each of these three major federal taxes, as well as other, smaller ones. Because state-level taxes vary a lot, we'll focus mainly on federal taxes. (In many states, sales taxes provide the most revenue, followed by a personal income tax if the state has one.)

Personal income tax

An **income tax** is exactly what it sounds like: a tax charged on the earnings of individuals and corporations. The largest source of income for most people is wages earned at work. Other sources may include income from interest in savings accounts, rental income from properties you own, investment income, or even lottery and game-show winnings.

In the United States, the federal government withholds federal income tax from your paycheck based on your *expected* annual income. (You'll see later that income from certain sources is subject to additional or lower taxes.) Many states also withhold a state income tax. When you file taxes at the end of the year, you report your *actual* earnings. If they are lower than the expected earnings, the government returns some of the taxes it withheld. In that case, you get a tax refund. If actual earnings are higher than expected earnings, you have to write a check to the government for the additional money you owe. This makes collecting the taxes easier, because it does not require that people remember to put the money aside. Imagine if the government didn't withhold money for taxes, and people forgot to put money aside for their eventual tax bill. April 15th would come around and many would find themselves unable to pay their tax bill.

income tax a tax charged on the earnings of individuals and corporations

The higher your income, the higher your income tax "bracket." Each bracket is taxed at a different tax rate, and those in higher tax brackets pay a higher percentage of their income. The relationship between tax rates and brackets is somewhat complicated—not every dollar is treated equally. Instead, the tax rate corresponding to each tax bracket is a **marginal tax rate**, or the tax rate charged on the last dollar a taxpayer earns.

marginal tax rate the tax rate charged on the last dollar a taxpayer earns

To see how this works, let's look at an example. Table 20-1 illustrates the tax brackets for a single person for the tax year 2011. The lowest tax bracket applies to incomes from $0 to $8,700 and has a marginal rate of 10 percent. The second bracket applies to incomes from $8,701 to $35,350 and has a marginal rate of 15 percent.

Let's say that you are a single person who earned $30,000 in 2010. How much federal income tax would you owe? On the first $8,700, you owe 10 percent, or $870. On the remaining income over $8,700 ($30,000 − $8,700 = $21,300), you owe 15 percent, or $3,195:

$$\begin{aligned} \$\,8{,}700 \times 10\% &= \$\ \ \ 870 \\ +\ 21{,}300 \times 15\% &= \underline{\ \ \ 3{,}195} \\ \text{Total tax} &= \$\,4{,}065 \end{aligned}$$

While your marginal tax rate is 15 percent, your average tax rate is 13.55 percent:

$$\frac{\$\,4{,}065}{\$30{,}000} = 13.55\%$$

Note that if you earn any amount less than $8,700, your average tax rate is 10 percent. Once you earn above that amount, the more you earn, the higher your average tax rate will be. In other words, the American individual income tax is *progressive:* The more people earn, the higher the percentage of their total income they pay.

Economists debate the extent to which income taxes discourage people from supplying their labor. One argument in favor of a progressive income tax rests on the idea that the supply of labor becomes more price-inelastic as people earn more. In other words, high earners tend to be highly educated people in jobs they like for reasons beyond the paycheck. They tend to be motivated by enjoyment of their work and the social status of their positions, not just the salary. If this is the case, we could expect that increasing the marginal tax rates on high earners would not cause them to work significantly fewer hours. Thus, progressive tax rates should bring in tax revenue without causing much deadweight loss. Note that this is a *positive* argument about the efficiency of progressive income tax rates (not a *normative* or philosophical one).

Many complicating factors can make the amount you owe in income taxes different from what would be suggested by your tax bracket alone. For instance, people who live in a household with a spouse or dependent children or disabled relatives will be charged

TABLE 20-1

U.S. personal income tax brackets in 2011

Source: IRS Rev. Proc. 2011-52, p. 7, http://www.irs.gov/pub/irs-drop/rp-11-52.pdf.

Single Tax Bracket ($)	Marginal Tax Rate (%)
0–8,700	10
8,701–35,350	15
35,351–85,650	25
85,651–178,650	28
178,651–388,350	33
388,351+	35

less for the same level of income. Certain types of expenses, such as charitable donations, college tuition, and business expenses can be "deducted" from your taxable income. In reality, therefore, you might earn $30,000, but your *adjusted (or taxable) income* would probably be lower than that.

Although the personal income tax doesn't generally distinguish between income from different sources, there is one important exception: capital gains. People often buy real estate, shares on the stock market, or other financial assets as investments. They hope, eventually, to earn a "return" by selling those capital assets at a higher price in the future. While they own these assets, they may earn income from them—dividends on shares, or rent on real estate—that is taxed as normal income. However, the profit earned by buying investments and selling them at a higher price is called a *capital gain.* Capital gains are taxed separately from other types of income, under the appropriately named **capital gains tax**.

Taxes on capital gains in the United States are somewhat complicated and the subject of much debate. The relevant fact, however, is that income from capital gains is taxed at a lower rate than most other income. Congress lowered the tax on long-term capital gains in 2003, and the tax rate was raised in 2013. The intent of the lower rate was to give individuals and corporations greater incentives to invest in capital, and by doing so, to encourage entrepreneurship. Critics contend that because higher-income people earn more through capital gains, the benefits of this tax cut go mostly to the wealthy.

The tax law has special provisions meant to reward some kinds of investment. For instance, assets that are owned for longer than one year are taxed at a lower rate than those held for a short time. Also, the sale of a house that was used as a primary residence is taxed at a lower rate than other real estate.

capital gains tax
a tax on income earned by buying investments and selling them at a higher price

Payroll tax

In the United States, part of your income is taxed in a way that is based strictly on your wages and not income earned in other ways. Because it is deducted directly from your paycheck, it is called a **payroll tax**. Payroll taxes are used to pay for Social Security and Medicare.

In the United States, payroll taxes are charged to both employees and employers, with the total tax bill split down the middle. The employee's portion shows up on your paystub as *FICA withholding* (FICA stands for Federal Insurance Contribution Act). Your employer withholds that amount and sends it to the federal government on your behalf. Employers pay their half directly to the government at the same time. (Of course, you know that statutory incidence is not the same as economic incidence. The evidence suggests that most of the burden of payroll tax ultimately falls on employees, in the form of lower wages.) If you are self-employed, you pay both parts of the tax (the employee and the employer parts). As Figure 20-7 showed, FICA makes up a huge portion of federal government revenue.

payroll tax a tax on the wages paid to an employee

The payroll tax in the United States is different from the personal income tax in several critical ways. First, it is charged only on "earned" income, such as wages or income from self-employment. Thus, it excludes other sources of income such as investments or gifts. Second, for the year 2013 all wage earners are charged at the same rate of 6.2 percent of earnings up to $113,700 for Social Security and 1.45 percent for Medicare.[1]

The most important difference is that the U.S. payroll tax is tied directly to specific government programs. Income taxes go into general government revenue, to be allocated through the public budget. FICA is a direct contribution to Social Security and Medicare, programs that provide income and medical benefits to retired people. Since people who pay FICA during their working years are eligible for Social Security and Medicare benefits when they retire, the payroll tax is sort of like forced saving for retirement.

However, the connection between what you pay and what you get is indirect. The government doesn't just hold your money until you retire and then pay it back to you. Instead, the Social Security system is based on a pay-as-you-go model, under which people who are currently working pay taxes which are then spent to provide benefits for people who are currently retired. The benefits that the elderly receive are determined through a complex formula based on earnings (and therefore FICA tax payments) during their working years. When you retire, your benefits will be paid for by the next generation. As the number of retired people relative to the number of working people grows, this system has run into problems, which we discuss later in the chapter.

FICA is usually considered a regressive tax. As we have seen, people who make more than $110,100 pay a lower percentage of their total earnings the more they earn. This is not inherent to the nature of a payroll tax. One could design a payroll tax that has no cap, or one that charges higher marginal rates for people with higher wages.

There is a second reason for considering the payroll tax to be regressive: It taxes only income earned through wages, and not income from other sources, such as interest payments or investments. Because people with higher overall income also tend to receive a higher percentage of it from these other sources, they end up paying less in payroll taxes as a percentage of their total income. However, the benefits people receive from Social Security are progressive: Those who had higher income during their working years receive higher benefits in absolute dollar amounts, but lower benefits as a percentage of their earnings.

Corporate income tax

Like individuals, corporations also pay taxes, the most prominent of which is the corporate income tax. In the United States, the corporate income tax is progressive: Smaller corporations pay a lower percentage of their income. The federal corporate income tax starts out at a rate of 15 percent for the smallest companies. It tops out at a marginal rate of 35 percent for companies with income over $18 million. Most states, although not all, also charge a corporate income tax; most top out with the highest bracket somewhere between 6 and 10 percent.

Although it is corporations who are legally responsible for paying the corporate income tax, the burden of the tax could be borne in varying degrees by shareholders (through lower dividends), employees (through lower wages), or customers (through higher prices).

Other taxes

sales tax a tax that is charged on the value of a good or service being purchased

excise tax a sales tax on a specific good or service

Even if you've yet to pay income tax, it's a safe bet that you have often paid sales tax. **Sales tax** is charged based on the value of a good or service being purchased. Many states have a general sales tax, but exempt certain classes of items considered to be necessities, such as food or clothing. Often, states also charge separate sales taxes, called **excise taxes**, targeted at specific goods, such as gasoline or cigarettes.

In the United States, there is no federal sales tax, but sales taxes are a major source of revenue for state governments. In fact, in 2009 sales taxes made up almost half of state tax revenue, with about two-thirds of that generated by general sales taxes and one-third by excise taxes on goods such as alcohol, insurance premiums, gasoline, and cigarettes. This average conceals wide variation across states. For instance, California's sales tax is over 8 percent, while states such as Montana, New Hampshire, and Oregon have no sales tax at all.

For many people, a house is the most valuable item they own. **Property tax** is a tax on the estimated value of a home, or any property owned by a taxpayer. Property taxes are an important source of revenue for local governments in many parts of the country. For instance, property taxes often fund public schools. The local taxing authority assesses property values every few years, and charges a fraction of the value as the tax. (Property taxes are not collected at the federal or state levels in the United States.)

The categories we've just discussed cover the major types of taxes and bring in the majority of federal and state government revenue. There are also many minor taxes, which make up only a small part of the federal budget but sometimes pack an outsized political punch. These include taxes on certain types of imports, taxes on large financial gifts (unless they are donations to a recognized nonprofit group), and taxes on money and assets that are left to heirs when you die. This last tax—the *estate tax*, also sometimes known as the inheritance or "death" tax—has been a particularly divisive issue in recent years. Read up on it in the What Do You Think? box, "Death, taxes, and 'death taxes.'"

property tax a tax on the estimated value of a home or other property

WHAT DO YOU THINK?

Death, taxes, and "death taxes"

Taxes are the subject of many heated political arguments. In this chapter, we've focused primarily on facts about taxes and how to analyze them. But although people frequently disagree about the correct answers to *positive* analyses of taxes, debates over taxation are just as often driven by underlying *normative* disagreements. One of the most politically divisive arguments over U.S. tax policy has centered on the estate tax. This tax is charged when a person dies and passes money or assets on to his or her heirs. Opponents of the estate tax sometimes refer to it as the "death tax."

Here's how the estate tax works: After a person dies, his or her estate is valued, and the value determines the tax rate. No tax is due if the value of the estate is less than a certain sum—$5.25 million in 2013. For estates worth more than that, marginal rates start at 10 percent and increase to 40 percent. There are exemptions for widows and widowers and for people in specific circumstances, such as inheriting family-owned farms. Only a very small number of wealthy people pay the tax at all. Estimates by the American Bar Association, for example, suggest that the tax affected less than one-half of one percent of people who died in 2011.

So, why the big fuss about a tax that affects only a tiny minority of Americans? One possibility is confusion caused by the success of its opponents in popularizing the term "death tax." After all, everyone dies, so you might assume that everyone must be subject to a "death tax," right? There is, in fact, some evidence that such confusion exists: One survey found that almost half of the voters surveyed wrongly thought that the estate tax applied to "most" American families. If it were popularly referred to as, say, the "inherited-wealth tax" instead, such popular confusion might be reduced.

Beyond this possibility, the estate tax hits a nerve, as it addresses underlying political and moral disagreements over the role of taxes in redistributing wealth. Opponents argue that people should have a right to do what they want with their money. That includes saving it and passing it on to their children. The estate tax, some argue, is an unfair double tax. First people are taxed when they earn their income, and then they're taxed again when they give it away at the end of life. (Of course, if the estate tax is a double tax, then we are all being taxed four or five times already: Payroll taxes, income taxes, sales taxes, excise taxes, and property taxes all cut into our earnings at some point.)

Supporters of the estate tax, including the billionaire Warren Buffett, counter that it's healthier for the economy and society to give each generation incentives to work their way up on their own merits, rather than living off inherited wealth.

What do you think?

1. Which of the arguments—for or against the estate tax—do you find more convincing? Should there be any limits on people's ability to pass down wealth across generations?
2. If you were in charge, what, if anything, would you change about the estate tax? Would you abolish it? Would you make it even more progressive by increasing the marginal rates or lowering the exemptions?

Sources: http://www.nytimes.com/2010/12/18/your-money/taxes/18wealth.html; http://www.irs.gov/businesses/small/article/0,,id=98968,00.html; http://home.gwu.edu/~jsides/estatetax.pdf.

✓ CONCEPT CHECK

❑ Why is there a difference between the marginal tax rate associated with an income tax bracket and the average tax rate that people in that bracket end up paying? **[LO 20.5]**

❑ Why is FICA a regressive tax? **[LO 20.5]**

❑ What is the difference between a general sales tax and an excise tax? **[LO 20.5]**

The Public Budget

LO 20.6 Discuss the important features of the public budget and the relationship between revenues and expenditures.

The U.S. federal government collected $2.3 trillion in revenue in 2012. That's a big sum of money—so big, that it's a bit difficult to visualize what it means in real terms. There are a number of ways to consider tax revenue that make it easier to grasp. In our flat-tax thought experiment earlier in the chapter, we estimated total tax revenue as an average amount paid per taxpayer (approximately $13,000).

Another, more common approach is to look at tax revenue in comparison to the size of the total economy. The gross domestic product (GDP) is one way to measure the size of a country's economy. Total federal tax revenue in the United States for 2012 was approximately 16 percent of the country's GDP.

Comparing the quantity of tax revenue collected in other countries to tax receipts in the United States is another way to better understand the quantity of taxes collected by the federal government. As Figure 20-8 shows, low-income countries tend to collect less in taxes as a percentage of GDP. High-income countries, especially those with extensive government-provided social benefits, tend to collect taxes that represent a greater share of their GDP. (The United States is an extreme exception to this rule.) Norway, for example, collects taxes equal to more than 50 percent of its GDP. In contrast, the taxes collected by the government of Uganda represent only 14 percent of the country's total GDP.

Expenditures

The relationship between public revenues and public spending is messy. On one hand, spending eventually has to be covered by revenues. Even the government can't go on forever spending more than it earns. On the other hand, most public spending is not

FIGURE 20-8

Taxes around the world Looking at tax revenue as a percentage of GDP is one way to compare taxes across countries. Wealthy countries that provide many social services to their citizens tend to collect a greater share of GDP in taxes in order to pay for those services. (Data for the United States excludes contributions for Social Security and similar social programs. If these data were included, the U.S. figure would rise to about 22 percent of GDP.)

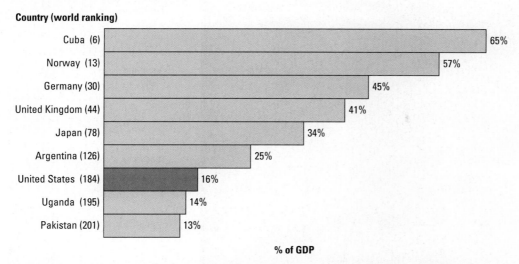

Country (world ranking)

Country	% of GDP
Cuba (6)	65%
Norway (13)	57%
Germany (30)	45%
United Kingdom (44)	41%
Japan (78)	34%
Argentina (126)	25%
United States (184)	16%
Uganda (195)	14%
Pakistan (201)	13%

% of GDP

Source: Estimated percentage of 2012 GDP, for 215 countries: www.cia.gov/library/publications/the-world-factbook/fields/2221.

tied directly to government revenue, let alone to particular taxes. Revenue collected at a certain time or place can be stockpiled or moved around to pay for expenditures in a different time or place. Or, more commonly, governments borrow against future revenues to finance expenditures today.

Figure 20-9 shows how the U.S. government spends tax revenues. In recent years, health expenditures represent the largest category of outlays. Social Security is the largest percentage of government spending for a standalone program. This program is funded by proceeds from the payroll tax and provides income to people aged 65 years and older. National defense represents the third-largest category of government expenditures. The fourth-largest category of expenditure includes programs to support people with low income, such as welfare, public and subsidized housing, and food stamps.

One interesting feature of federal government spending in the United States is that little of it is **discretionary**. Discretionary spending involves public expenditures that have to be approved each year, such as the military, public construction and road building, and scientific and medical research.

In contrast, the vast majority of federal expenditures are nondiscretionary, going toward programs for which spending is mandated and regulated by permanent laws. Social Security, Medicare, and welfare programs are all examples of **entitlement spending**. Under these spending programs, people are "entitled" to benefits by virtue of age, income, or some other factor. Spending on entitlement programs automatically rises and falls with the number of people who are eligible according to the legal criteria. Therefore, expenditures on these programs cannot be decreased without changing the eligibility requirements and benefits set in the laws on which the programs are based.

You may be surprised by some of the things that are *not* included in Figure 20-9. Many of the public services that touch people's daily lives in the most noticeable

discretionary spending public expenditures that have to be approved each year

entitlement spending public expenditure that "entitles" people to benefits by virtue of age, income, or some other factor

FIGURE 20-9

Federal government spending in the United States The allocation of the U.S. budget has shifted in response to national events. In World War II, defense took priority. In recent years, as the U.S. population ages, health and social security have risen.

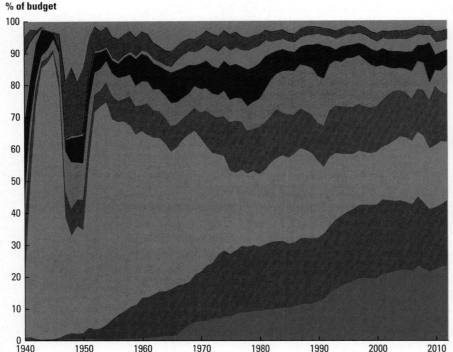

% of budget

Function	% of budget (2012)
Other	2.7
Veterans affairs	3.3
Education and social services	3.1
Physical resources	4.7
Net interest	9.1
Income security	15.0
National defense	18.2
Social Security	20.5
Health expenditures	23.4

Source: Budget of the United States FY 2012, http://www.gpo.gov/fdsys/pkg/BUDGET-2012-TAB/pdf/BUDGET-2012-TAB.pdf.

ways are funded by state and local budgets. For instance, public education is largely (although not entirely) supported at the state and local level. Services such as police and fire protection, motor vehicle registration, and garbage collection also come out of state or local budgets. Many of the most visible federally funded services—such as subsidized student loans and national parks—actually make up a very small proportion of the federal budget.

Balancing the budget

budget deficit
the amount of money a government spends beyond the revenue it brings in

budget surplus
the amount of revenue a government brings in beyond what it spends

In many years, the federal government spends more than it brings in. When a government spends more than it earns in revenue, we say that it has a **budget deficit**. When it earns more than it spends, we say it has a **budget surplus**. Deficits and surpluses are commonly calculated as a percentage of national GDP. So, if the federal government brings in $2.1 trillion in tax revenues and spends $3.5 trillion, the budget deficit in absolute terms is $1.4 trillion; that amount is usually stated as a deficit of 10 percent of GDP ($1.4 trillion ÷ U.S. GDP of $14 trillion). Historically, the United States has gone back and forth between surplus and deficit, as shown in Figure 20-10.

You may notice that there have been a lot more deficits than surpluses in recent years. Many people are concerned about the growing public budget deficit—for the same reasons you'd be worried about a family sinking deeper and deeper into debt.

FIGURE 20-10

Surpluses and deficits in recent U.S. history For most of the past three decades, the U.S. government has run a budget deficit. Although deficits have not been correlated with recession historically, the most recent large budget deficit occurred during a deep recession.

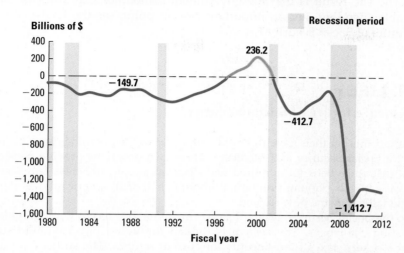

Source: Economic Report of the President, http://www.gpoaccess.gov/eop/tables10.html table B78; and NBER, http://www.nber.org/cycles/cyclesmain.html.

Debts have to be paid at some point, and the longer you stay in debt, the more you owe in interest. For this reason, some people favor balanced budget laws, which require the government to spend no more than it owes in any given year. In fact, most state governments have a balanced budget requirement of some sort, although some are stricter than others.

On the surface, balancing the budget seems like an unarguably great idea. It forces policy-makers to adopt responsible spending policies that prevent the government from doing into debt over the long run. So *why don't all governments balance the budget every year?*

In practice, it can be difficult to balance a public budget every year. Even with the best planning, it is unlikely that revenues will exactly equal planned expenditures in any given year. For instance, think about what happens during an unexpected economic downturn. If people lose their jobs and companies earn lower profits, the government gets less individual and corporate income tax revenue than it was expecting. It also may collect less sales tax revenue as people cut back on purchases. At the same time, it has to increase its spending on entitlement programs as people's incomes decrease and more qualify for unemployment benefits or food stamps. This means that balancing the budget in a year when the economy is doing poorly would require deep cuts in discretionary spending. Some economists argue that, by contrast, discretionary public spending should be *increased* during a downturn, to help stimulate the economy back to growth.

For these reasons, many economists argue that governments shouldn't try to balance the budget every year. Instead, they advocate that public budgets be balanced *over the business cycle.* In brief, the idea is that governments should run surpluses when the economy is doing well, and deficits when the economy is doing poorly—striking a balance in the long run. In other words, they should behave like a responsible family that saves up when times are good so they can spend down their savings when times are bad.

Sounds sensible, right? Unfortunately, policy-makers are under just as much pressure from voters and lobbyists to spend when the economy is doing well as when it's doing poorly. The result is that the government sometimes gets stuck in patterns of unsustainable spending. For an important case in point, see the Real Life box, "The insecure future of Social Security."

REAL LIFE

The insecure future of Social Security

Most Americans get their paychecks only after part of their earnings have been taxed to pay for Social Security and Medicare. These two programs provide pension and medical insurance benefits to retired and disabled people and their families. Social Security is a hugely popular program. Without it, half of all Americans over the age of 65 would fall below the poverty line.

So far, the Social Security system has worked well, but recent demographic shifts are creating challenges. The system is funded through a pay-as-you-go strategy: Current workers' taxes fund benefits for current retirees. The strategy works well when there are a lot of people of working age relative to the number of retirees. The trouble is that over the last half-century, Americans began to live much longer and have fewer children. As a result, the number of working-age people relative to retired people has decreased. In 1950, there were 16 workers for every retiree. By 2035, there will be only two.

This means that Social Security has to support more and more retirees with tax revenue from fewer and fewer workers. As Figure 20-11 shows, the outlay for Social Security is projected to increase over the coming decades, while the revenues stay steady. Figure 20-11 also shows that in past decades, revenues have exceeded outlays. The good news is that this money is being saved up in the Social Security Trust Fund. The bad news is that this fund is projected to run dry by 2037—well before most of today's college students reach retirement age.

Many proposals have been floated to fix the Social Security problem. Some solutions focus on reining in spending by making retirement benefits less generous—for example, by raising the retirement age. With that change, people would work and pay into the system for longer. Raising the retirement age by two years, as was done by Congress in 2011, is projected to save the system an average of $30,000 per worker.

Other proposed solutions focus on increasing tax revenues. As it stands, the social security payroll tax only applies to earnings up to $106,800. Anything you earn beyond that cap isn't taxed. So one idea is to eliminate the cap, which would effectively increase the payroll taxes paid by high-income workers. Another option would be to increase the rate of payroll taxes that fund Social Security for all workers (currently 12.8 percent of earnings, split between employers and employees).

Because Social Security is an entitlement program, with benefits defined and mandated by law, making changes requires action by Congress. Neither raising taxes nor dropping benefits is popular with constituents, so legislators have been slow to act. This no doubt will remain a hot debate for years to come.

Sources: http://www.ssa.gov/pressoffice/basicfact.htm; http://www.msnbc.msn.com/id/41293592/ns/politics-more_politics/; http://www.cbo.gov/doc.cfm?index=11943&zzz=41347; http://www.gallup.com/poll/141611/americans-look-wealthy-help-save-social-security.aspx.

FIGURE 20-11

The future of Social Security Presently, the revenue stream for Social Security is greater than the outlays paid in benefits. Funds can be withdrawn from the Social Security Trust to make up the difference between revenue and outlays for several more decades, but the trust fund is projected to run out in 2037.

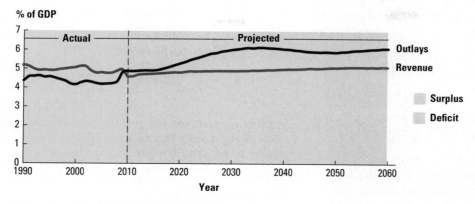

Source: Congressional Budget Office, http://www.cbo.gov/publication/41644.

✓ CONCEPT CHECK

❒ What is the difference among discretionary, nondiscretionary, and entitlement spending in the public budget? **[LO 20.6]**

❒ Why is maintaining a balanced budget every year more difficult than it might seem at first? **[LO 20.6]**

Conclusion

The fine points of tax law are complex, but the basics are fairly straightforward. The ideas and evidence in this chapter show what's at stake in political debates. Understanding the implications of taxes can also help you make better personal financial choices.

When it comes to taxes, economists focus on trade-offs between revenue, efficiency, and incidence. In other words, we're concerned with how much money is raised, how costly it is to raise it, and who ultimately shoulders the burden. We've seen why governments need to balance revenues and expenditures in the long run, but also why they might not want to do so in the short run.

Public support for taxation depends on whether citizens like how governments spend their tax dollars. If voters think that governments misuse money or spend too much, they'll want to reduce taxes. When voters think that governments are helping to create stronger communities and better opportunities for citizens, they won't mind the tax bite as much. We'll dig deeper into some of these questions in the next chapter, as we address issues around poverty, inequality, and the uses of public funds.

Key Terms

Summary

LO 20.1 Describe the major public policy goals of taxation.

The most important goal of taxation is to raise public revenue. This allows governments to provide goods and services such as education, highways, and national defense. A second use of taxation is to change the behavior of market participants by driving a wedge between the prices faced by buyers and sellers. This function of a tax can counterbalance a negative externality, bringing consumption down to an efficient level. Taxes may also be used to discourage specific behaviors, such as smoking or drinking, for reasons that are not necessarily related to negative externalities.

LO 20.2 Explain how deadweight loss and administrative costs contribute to the inefficiency of a tax.

There are two sources of inefficiency associated with taxation: administrative burden and deadweight loss. Administrative burden includes the time and money spent by the government to collect and monitor tax payments, as well as the time and money spent by individuals on filing tax returns or hiring accountants. Deadweight loss is the reduction in total surplus that results for the decrease in the number of trades that occur due to the tax.

LO 20.3 Calculate the effect of a tax increase on revenue, taking into account price and quantity effects.

Two forces are at play in the relationship between tax rates and revenue. Raising taxes means that the government gets more revenue per units sold, which increases total revenue. But the shrinking effect of a higher tax rate causes fewer units to be sold, which decreases total revenue. In other words, a change in the tax rate has both a *price effect* (the government collects more tax for every unit) and a *quantity effect* (the government collects taxes on fewer units). Raising taxes has diminishing returns to revenue, because the quantity effect gradually overtakes the price effect. At some point, taxes can be so high that the price effect dominates, and raising taxes actually reduces total revenue.

LO 20.4 Identify proportional, progressive, and regressive taxes.

Incidence describes who bears the burden of paying a tax. Incidence can describe whether the tax burden falls on buyers or sellers but also on how much is paid by the rich versus the poor. *Proportional* taxes take the same percentage of income from everyone. *Progressive* taxes take a higher percentage of income from those with higher income. *Regressive* taxes do the opposite, charging a higher percentage of income to those with lower income. The economic incidence of the tax describes who ultimately bears the burden of the tax and is not necessarily the same as the statutory incidence of the tax, which describes who is legally obligated to pay it.

LO 20.5 Describe the sources of tax revenue in the United States, and discuss the role played by different types of taxes.

The vast majority of tax revenue the U.S. collects comes from personal income and payroll taxes; a significant minority comes from the corporate income tax.

Personal income taxes are charged on income from all sources, with increasing marginal rates for higher income levels. Payroll taxes are charged at a flat rate on earned income, and are tied directly to Social Security and Medicare expenditures. The personal income tax and corporate income tax are progressive; the payroll tax is generally considered to be regressive. In contrast to the federal government, many state governments bring in most of their revenue through general sales and excise taxes.

LO 20.6 Discuss the important features of the public budget and the relationship between revenues and expenditures.

The U.S. takes in tax revenue equal to about 15 percent of its GDP. However, spending is not tied directly to government revenue. Revenue collected at a certain time and place can pay for expenditures in a different time or place, and the federal government can and does borrow money to pay for current expenses. The majority of federal government spending goes to nondiscretionary budget items. These include entitlement programs like Social Security and Medicare, for which benefits are mandated by law. Both tax revenue and spending fluctuate from year to year as the economy goes up and down, resulting in budget deficits or surpluses.

Review Questions

1. Both a payroll tax and an excise tax on alcohol raise revenue and, respectively, shrink the markets for labor and alcohol. Although both have some functions in common, governments may have different goals when levying them. What goals do you think motivate a payroll tax? What goals motivate an alcohol tax? **[LO 20.1]**

2. The demand for cigarettes, which create negative externalities through secondhand smoke, is often relatively inelastic. That is, when the price of cigarettes changes, the quantity demanded changes by a smaller portion. Using this fact, explain to what extent you think a tax on cigarettes would fulfill each of the goals of taxation. **[LO 20.1]**

3. Which would you expect to be less efficient, a flat tax on all income or a property tax (charged based on the assessed value of real estate)? Explain why, in terms of both deadweight loss and administrative costs. **[LO 20.2]**

4. A local government is considering ways to raise taxes to pay for making sidewalks. One prominent citizen suggests taxing people based on how much they walk on the sidewalk, measured in yards each day. Explain why, despite its apparent fairness, this tax is likely very inefficient. **[LO 20.2]**

5. In an election debate, two candidates for governor are debating about whether to raise the general sales tax from 5 to 7 percent. One argues that this would increase tax revenues, enabling the state to maintain essential services. The other argues that the tax would hurt retailers and consumers, and would actually slow down the economy so much that it would decrease tax revenues too. Restate these candidates' positions in economic terminology, and explain what assumptions they must be making in order to justify their different positions, in terms of price and quantity effects. **[LO 20.3]**

6. Explain, with reference to the price and quantity effects, why all else equal, taxing several goods at a modest rate is better than taxing one good at a very high rate. **[LO 20.3]**

7. People with low income spend more, as a share of their overall income, on food and clothing than wealthier people. As a result, they tend to spend a higher proportion of their income relative to people with high income. Given this trend, explain how a general sales tax of 8 percent could be regressive. Now, suppose that food and children's clothing are exempted from the sales tax. Is this likely to make the tax more or less regressive? **[LO 20.4]**

8. Suppose you turn on the television to find an ad by a local politician accusing car dealers of making too much money off consumers. As a remedy for this abuse, the official proposes to tax the dealers at a higher rate and reward car buyers with the proceeds of the tax. Drawing on the idea of economic incidence and administrative cost, explain why this tax may not benefit consumers after all. **[LO 20.4]**

9. Your friend Edgar has just finished his first year working full-time, and comes home beaming with an envelope from the IRS, which has sent him a check for $650 after he sent in his tax forms. Explain to Edgar why this does not mean that he didn't pay taxes. **[LO 20.5]**

10. Explain why most people's marginal tax rate is higher than their average tax rate. Is a system in which average tax rates are higher than marginal tax rates regressive, proportional, or progressive? **[LO 20.5]**

11. A challenger presidential candidate vows to cut entitlement spending by 20 percent in the first few weeks that he is in office. Why is it unlikely the candidate could achieve this reduction? **[LO 20.6]**

12. When the federal government borrows money, it can fund higher expenditures in the short term, but incurs a debt that accrues interest and has to be paid off in the long term. What does this imply about the trade-off between current and future taxes? How might this trade-off change if the overall size of the economy grows over time? **[LO 20.6]**

Problems and Applications

1. Consider each of the following tax policies. Decide for each whether the primary public policy goal is most likely raising revenue or changing behavior (with or without a market failure). **[LO 20.1]**

   a. Income tax.

   b. Cigarette tax.

c. Gas tax.

d. Payroll tax.

e. Toll road.

f. Income tax exemption for charity donations.

2. Governments throughout history have levied some very interesting taxes (http://azweird.com/history/weirdest_taxes_in_history-731.html). Each of the following taxes changed citizens' behavior. Determine whether it's likely that the tax also addressed a market failure. **[LO 20.1]**

a. *The Hat Tax:* Adopted by the British Government, requiring every hat to bear a stamp on the inside showing it was legal.

b. *The "Flatulence Tax":* Proposed, but ultimately not adopted, in New Zealand to help reduce methane emissions from livestock.

c. *The Window Tax:* Levied by English King William III on the number of windows in a house, which tended to be more numerous in wealthier homes.

d. *The Cowardice Tax:* Introduced in medieval England and applied to people who refused to defend the country at request of the king.

3. Suppose the government wants to levy a new excise tax. For each of the following goods, determine whether you would expect an excise tax to result in high or low deadweight loss. **[LO 20.2]**

a. Alcohol.

b. Milk.

c. Diamonds.

d. Tropical vacations.

e. Socks.

4. Table 20P-1 shows supply and demand in the market for sub sandwiches in Wheretown, where the local government wants to raise revenue via a $1 tax on all sandwiches, collected from sandwich shops. **[LO 20.2]**

a. Graph supply and demand. Before and after the tax: What is the equilibrium quantity? What price is paid by consumers? What price is received by suppliers?

b. Calculate consumer and producer surplus before and after the tax.

c. How much tax revenue does Wheretown receive?

d. How much deadweight loss is caused by the tax?

e. Suppose it costs Wheretown $35 to collect the tax revenue from sub shops. In the end, how much revenue from the sub tax is actually available to spend on public services?

TABLE 20P-1

Price of sub sandwich ($)	Quantity demanded	Quantity supplied
8.00	0	100
7.50	10	90
7.00	20	80
6.50	30	70
6.00	40	60
5.50	50	50
5.00	60	40
4.50	70	30
4.00	80	20
3.50	90	10
3.00	100	0
2.50	110	0
2.00	120	0

5. Figure 20P-1 shows a hypothetical market for gasoline. **[LO 20.3]**

a. Suppose an excise tax of $1.50 per gallon is levied on gasoline. What price will consumers pay? What price will sellers receive?

b. How much government revenue will result from the tax?

FIGURE 20P-1

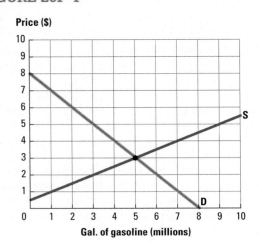

c. Suppose the tax is raised to $3 per gallon. How much additional revenue will this raise compared to the $1.50 tax?

d. Would raising the tax further to $4.50 per gallon increase or decrease tax revenue?

6. In each of the following examples, determine whether the price effect or the quantity effect dominates when the tax is applied. **[LO 20.3]**

a. The government raises taxes on the 10 million iPods sold each year from $10 per iPod to $20 per iPod. The new equilibrium quantity is 9 million iPods.

b. In response to concerns about chewing gum in schools, the government raises the tax on packs of gum from 20 cents per pack to 30 cents per pack. Before the tax increase, 50 million packs were sold each year. After the tax increase, 40 million packs are sold each year.

c. Worried that Americans are addicted to coffee, the government raises the 5-cent tax on a cup of coffee to 10 cents. Before the tax increase, 10 billion cups were sold each year. Afterward, 5 billion cups are sold each year.

7. Determine whether each of the following taxes is proportional, regressive, or progressive. **[LO 20.4]**

a. An income tax of 25 percent on income from all sources.

b. An income tax with three brackets and corresponding marginal tax rates: 10 percent for income up to $50,000; 20 percent for income up to $100,000; and 30 percent for income over $100,000.

c. A fee of $500 per year for municipal services, charged to everyone who lives within the city limits.

d. A capital gains tax that charges a flat rate of 40 percent, but only on capital gains over $1 million.

e. A payroll tax of 10 percent on income under $200,000.

8. Table 20P-2 shows an income tax schedule for the imaginary country of Independence. Connor is a citizen of Independence who earns $95,000 per year at his job. Assume Connor is not eligible for any deductions or exemptions. **[LO 20.4, 20.5]**

a. How much does Connor pay in income tax?

b. What is Connor's marginal tax rate? What is his overall tax rate?

c. Connor isn't crazy about his job and wants to move to a job in a related industry that pays

TABLE 20P-2

Taxable income ($)	Marginal tax rate (%)
0–5,000	5
5,001–15,000	7
15,001–30,000	9
30,001–50,000	11
50,001–75,000	13
75,001–100,000	15
100,001–130,000	20
130,001–175,000	21
175,001+	22

$100,000. How much will Connor have to pay in taxes in the new job?

d. Is the income tax in Independence regressive, proportional, or progressive?

9. Evangeline is a citizen of Independence, whose income and expenditures are shown in Table 20P-3. Table 20P-2 (above) shows Independence's personal income tax schedule. In answering the following questions, you may assume the following. **[LO 20.5]**

(1) All income other than capital gains falls under the personal income tax.

(2) Deductible expenses are subtracted from income before income tax is calculated.

(3) Charitable donations and money paid in payroll taxes are tax-deductible.

(4) Payroll tax is 5 percent of earned income up to $50,000.

(5) Capital gains tax is 3 percent on capital gains over $10,000.

(6) Sales tax is 6 percent.

TABLE 20P-3

Category	Amount ($)
Income earned in wages	90,000
Income from capital gains	20,000
Spending on consumer goods subject to sales tax	10,000
Spending on charitable donations	3,000

a. How much does Evangeline pay in payroll taxes?

b. How much does Evangeline pay in capital gains taxes?

c. What is Evangeline's adjusted income subject to the personal income tax? How much does she pay in personal income tax?

d. How much does Evangeline pay in sales taxes?

e. How much does Evangeline pay in taxes, in total? What percentage of her income does this represent?

10. Table 20P-4 shows an economy's GDP, current expenditures, and tax revenue for 2013–2016. **[LO 20.6]**

a. Complete the table by filling in the prior-year debt for each year listed.

b. For each year, is this economy experiencing a budget surplus or budget deficit?

c. Debt is what percentage of GDP in 2013?

d. Between 2013 and 2016, by what percentage has GDP changed? By what percentage

has the debt changed? Is debt as a percentage of GDP growing, constant, or shrinking between 2013 and 2016?

11. Table 20P-5 shows an economy's GDP, population, debt, and GDP per capita for 2013 and 2014. **[LO 20.6]**

a. Complete the table by filling in the debt per capita for both years.

b. What is the percentage change from 2013 to 2014 in each of the following? (i) GDP. (ii) Population. (iii) Debt. (iv) GDP per capita. (v) Debt per capita.

c. Which is growing faster—GDP per capita or debt per capita? Why?

Chapter Endnote

1. Beginning in 2013, an additional Medicare tax of 0.9 percent applies for individual wages of more than $200,000 ($250,000 for married couples filing jointly).

Chapter Sources

http://news.minnesota.publicradio.org/features/2003/04/28_helmsm_happytopay/

http://www.irs.gov/pub/irs-drop/rp-09-50.pdf

http://www.irs.gov/taxstats/article/0,,id=171961,00.html

http://www.nytimes.com/2010/02/07/us/politics/08palin.html

http://economix.blogs.nytimes.com/2010/08/25/the-costs-of-war/ Economic Report of the President

http://www.gpoaccess.gov/eop/tables10.html, Table B81

http://www.taxfoundation.org/taxdata/show/245.html

TABLE 20P-4

Year	GDP ($)	Prior-year debt ($)	Current expenditures ($)	Tax revenue ($)
2013	8,500	5,100	1,200	950
2014	8,650		1,400	1,525
2015	9,000		1,800	1,500
2016	9,200		2,100	1,600

TABLE 20P-5

Year	GDP (millions of $)	Population (millions)	Debt (millions of $)	GDP per capita ($)	Debt per capita ($)
2013	10,675,000	305.0	7,472,500	35,000	
2014	10,995,250	311.1	7,920,850	35,343	

Poverty, Inequality, and Discrimination

Chapter 21

LEARNING OBJECTIVES

LO 21.1   Discuss the difference between relative and absolute measures of poverty.

LO 21.2   Explain and interpret different methods of measuring income inequality.

LO 21.3   Describe how income mobility differs from income equality.

LO 21.4   Identify the public policies that are used to reduce poverty and inequality.

LO 21.5   Explain the trade-off between equity and efficiency in poverty-reduction policy.

LO 21.6   Explain why demographic differences in income or wages do not necessarily imply discrimination.

STRIKING IT RICHER

How rich is super-rich? In 1915—the era of the Rockefellers, Vanderbilts, and Carnegies, whose names are synonymous with extraordinary wealth—people worried that the wealthiest 1 percent of the population held 15 percent of the nation's income. Today, the richest 1 percent holds *20 percent* of the income—and, the richest 10 percent together earns nearly half (48 percent). To be part of the richest 1 percent in 2010, your family had to earn over $352,000. That's roughly what an average Wall Street worker in New York City took home in 2012; it's $100,000 more than the typical surgeon earns, and seven times the average salary of elementary school teachers.[1]

While the rich have gotten richer, the poor have gotten richer too. Fifty years ago, almost a quarter of Americans lived in poverty. Over just a few decades, the national poverty rate fell by half. How can poverty be falling and inequality be rising at the same time? The answer is that the poor have gotten richer, but the rich have gotten richer at an even faster rate. Economic growth has increased incomes throughout the population, but a disproportionate amount has stayed with the wealthy. Economist Emmanuel Saez, who has studied millions of U.S. tax returns, finds that between 1993 and 2010, the incomes of the richest 1 percent grew by 58 percent. The other 99 percent saw incomes grow by just 6.4 percent on average, and some incomes were flat or falling.[2]

Internationally, the picture looks similar. Hundreds of millions of people have been lifted out of poverty by economic growth in recent decades, but global inequality is also high. A lot of this has to do with differences between countries: Being born into a poorer family in the United States places you at about the same income level as the upper class in India or China.

Does inequality matter? The more equal a society is, the more that everyone will gain when the economy improves. But it doesn't necessarily follow that the most equal society is the best society, or even that it provides the most resources for its disadvantaged members. One view is that inequality gives people an incentive to work hard and take risks. In that view, work and risk-taking creates jobs and contributes to economic growth that can benefit everyone, including the poorest.

Thinking about the "right" level of inequality is one of the hardest economic questions we face. Does success at the top trickle down to benefit the poor? To what extent do taxes and programs that equalize income also create a disincentive for hard work and entrepreneurship?

In this chapter, we will explore tough issues surrounding poverty and inequality—how they can be measured, how they affect people's lives and choices, and how governments design public policy in response. What can economics say about these big questions? We'll show examples of how innovative economic problem solving has provided new approaches to fighting poverty. We will also explore the economics of discrimination, an issue that is tied to longstanding patterns of poverty and inequality in many countries.

As we weigh ideas and evidence in this chapter, we ask you to remember the distinction between positive and normative analysis. We will use positive analysis to understand what poverty, inequality, and discrimination look like and how they affect the economy. That's a separate question from the big normative issue: Should governments try to reduce poverty, inequality, and discrimination in the name of social justice and fairness?

Even in the United States, where the financial sector is much more developed, it can be difficult for people without collateral or with bad credit histories to get loans. Sometimes these potential borrowers are genuinely risky or have bad investment ideas. But even someone with a low-risk, profitable opportunity will have trouble getting a loan if they don't have the collateral or the credit history to back it up. As a result, credit constraints can limit the ability of talented but poor individuals to make profitable investments that will help them climb up the income ladder. Credit constraints are one reason why a lack of human capital isn't a simple problem to fix. A talented kid may not be able to borrow money to invest in education or internships, even if those opportunities would more than pay for themselves later in life in the form of better jobs and higher wages.

Poverty in the community. In some places in the world, there are opportunities to earn more money and live in greater comfort, even if they may be difficult to come by. In others, these opportunities may not exist, at least not for the majority of the population. What is it like to live in a society where a third or a half of the population is poor and most of the people you know struggle to find jobs?

Consider the difference, for instance, between having trouble paying your electric bill and living in a place where there is no electrical grid, even if you could afford it. Or, what would it be like to search for a job in a place where very few formal jobs exist? What if you lived in a country where even if you had a good business idea, it takes two years and a fortune in bribes to get a business permit? This is the case in many developing countries around the world.

Even in wealthy countries, communitywide poverty creates problems beyond those faced by individuals. In these communities, transportation may be limited, jobs scarce, and schools below average. When most of the region is poor, it's hard for local governments to raise money through taxes; that makes it harder in turn for the region as a whole to invest in infrastructure, jobs, and schools. Long-term solutions to poverty must, then, involve ways to grow the economy and expand the range of opportunities available to the population.

✓ CONCEPT CHECK

- ❑ What is the difference between an absolute and a relative poverty threshold? **[LO 21.1]**
- ❑ What is the international poverty line most commonly used, and why is it adjusted for purchasing power parity? **[LO 21.1]**
- ❑ What is a credit constraint, and how is it an example of a poverty trap? **[LO 21.1]**

Inequality

Poverty in the United States has decreased over the last few decades. However, income inequality has increased, mostly as a result of gains by the rich.

Does inequality matter? Some argue that overall economic growth is more important than the distribution of income. Those who hold this view note that if everyone is getting richer, the relative speed of these gains isn't as important. Others care about inequality for its own sake, believing that it is fundamentally unjust for some people to have so much when others have so little. The degree of inequality can be an important factor that signals or causes other things going on in the economy, such as the incentive people at the top have to work hard or the resources available to people at the bottom to invest in human capital.

In this section, we'll discuss how inequality can be measured and how it can relate to economic growth and stability. We'll also see some evidence of how unequal different countries actually are and how easy or difficult it is to go from being poor to rich or vice versa.

Measuring inequality

LO 21.2 Explain and interpret different methods of measuring income inequality.

Imagine that we could line up every adult in the United States in order of the amount of income they earn. We make their heights proportional to their incomes: People with average income are of average height, and the more money someone makes, the taller he or she is. Now, we ask them all to march down Main Street in that order, over the course of one hour. As bystanders watching this parade, what would we see?

The first marchers would be invisible, with their heads underground. These are people who own businesses that are losing money. Then, we would see tiny people walking by, only inches high. These people earn very small amounts of money; they may be unemployed or on a small fixed income. As we pass the half-hour mark, halfway through the parade, the people going by are still only waist-high. These marchers in the middle represent minimum-wage workers, retail sales people, unskilled clerical workers, and the like. Even as skilled tradespeople and office workers start to stroll by, they are still below average size. Finally, at about 40 minutes, the people going by are of average adult height. In the parade's last 10 minutes, we start to see giants, more than 10-feet tall. These are specialist doctors, lawyers, scientists, and so on. Then, corporate executives go by, hundreds of feet tall. Next come movie stars and professional athletes, thousands of feet tall. In the last seconds of the parade, some of the richest people in the country go by (hello, Mark Zuckerberg, Bill Gates, and Warren Buffett), with their heads towering several *miles* above the ground.

This parade—first imagined by economist Jan Pen—is a visual representation of the income distribution in the United States.[4] It uses the marchers' heights as an analogy that allows us to see the relative income of people throughout the population. The parade image emphasizes some notable features of the income distribution. People of average height and income don't show up until well after halfway through the parade. The rich are *really* rich, compared not only with the poorest but even with highly paid professionals.

However visually striking the parade analogy may be, economists need more precise ways of summarizing the income distribution. The simplest method divides those marchers into five equally sized groups. In a country of just over 300 million people, the approximate population of the United States, the first group is the 60 million poorest people, the second group is the next 60 million, and so on, until the fifth group is the 60 million richest people. Since we have divided the country into five groups, we call each one a *quintile,* or 20 percent of the population.

We can use our quintiles to organize several different types of statistics that describe income inequality. Table 21-3 shows these statistics for the United States. First, we could find the average income within each quintile (column 2). Second, we could add up everyone's income, and find out what percentage of income earned in the whole country is earned by people within each quintile. If income were distributed completely equally—that is, if every person in the country made the same amount of money—each quintile representing 20 percent of the population would also earn 20 percent of the income.

Income is not distributed perfectly equally anywhere in the world, though. Thus, we always see that the top quintiles earn a disproportionately high share of income (more than 20 percent) and the lower quintiles earn a disproportionately low share (less than

Quintile	Average pre-tax income ($)	Share of pre-tax income (%)
Lowest 20 percent	18,400	4.0
Second 20 percent	42,500	8.4
Third 20 percent	64,500	13.1
Fourth 20 percent	94,100	19.3
Highest 20 percent	264,700	55.9
Top 1 percent	1,873,000	19.4

TABLE 21-3

Income distribution by quintile

The United States does not have an equally distributed income. The gap between the average incomes of the richest 20 percent and the poorest 20 percent is over $180,000. The richest 20 percent hold over half of the income earned in the United States, while the top 1 percent earn nearly a fifth of pre-tax income.

Source: http://www.cbo.gov/publications/collections/tax/2010/AverageFedTaxRates2007.pdf.

20 percent). In the United States the top 20 percent earns over 50 percent of total income, while the poorest 20 percent earns only 3.3 percent of total income.

We can also summarize income inequality visually, using a graph called the **Lorenz curve**. The Lorenz curve maps the percentage of the population against the cumulative percentage of income earned by those people. It shows the cumulative percentage of the population on the y-axis, and the cumulative percentage of income those people earn on the x-axis.

The best way to understand the Lorenz curve is to see that if every person earned the exact same amount, the curve would be a straight line with a slope of 1, as shown in panel A of Figure 21-3. That is, 20 percent of the population would earn 20 percent of the income, and 73 percent of the population would earn 73 percent of the income, and so on. However, if income is unequally distributed, the Lorenz curve will be bowed out in a U-shape: The poorest 1 percent of people will earn less than 1 percent of income, and the richest 1 percent will earn more than 1 percent of the income, as shown in panel B.

The Lorenz curve allows us to calculate a final and even more concise inequality metric—the **Gini coefficient**. The Gini coefficient describes inequality by putting a single number on the shape of the Lorenz curve. Specifically, the Gini coefficient is equal to the area between the Lorenz curve and the line of perfect equality (area A in Figure 21-4) divided by the total area under the line of perfect equality (area A plus area B in the figure). This calculation gives us a single number to describe income inequality.

If everyone earned the same amount and the income distribution were perfectly equal, the Gini coefficient would be zero: The Lorenz curve would *be* the line of perfect equality, and so the area between them would be 0. If one person earned all of the income and no one else earned anything, the Gini coefficient would be 1. In reality, the distribution is always somewhere between these extremes. The closer the Gini coefficient is to 1, the more unequal the income distribution.

Lorenz curve
a graphic representation of income distribution that maps percentage of the population against cumulative percentage of income earned by those people

Gini coefficient
a single-number measure of income inequality; ranges from 0 to 1, with higher numbers meaning greater inequality

Inequality in the U.S. and around the world

Now that we have some tools for measuring inequality, what can we say about how income distribution differs between countries and over time?

Most countries in the world have Gini coefficients ranging from 0.25 to 0.60. As you can see in Figure 21-5, there are significant geographic clusters. Most of Europe has relatively low inequality. Much of Latin America and southern Africa has relatively high inequality.

The global pattern of inequality has been changing in recent decades. Inequality *between* countries, in terms of differences in their average national incomes, has been decreasing; economic growth has lifted billions of people out of poverty, especially in China and India. Nonetheless, the poorest 5 percent of people in the United States are still richer on average than 70 percent of the rest of the world. Inequality

FIGURE 21-3
The Lorenz curve

(A) Perfectly equal income distribution

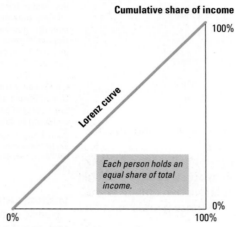

With a perfectly equal income distribution, each extra 1 percent of the population earns another 1 percent of income. In that case, the Lorenz curve forms at a 45-degree angle.

(B) Unequal income distribution

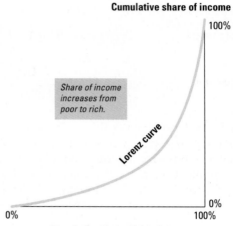

When income is not distributed equally, each extra percent of poorer segments of the population earn less than 1 percent of the total income. Among the richer part of the population, each extra 1 percent of the population adds more than 1 percent of their income. This distribution gives the Lorenz curve a concave shape.

FIGURE 21-4
The Gini coefficient

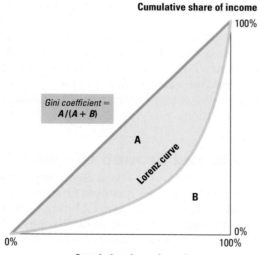

The Gini coefficient is calculated by measuring the area between the line of perfect equality and the Lorenz curve. This is represented by $A/(A+B)$. The greater the inequality, the deeper the U-shape in the Lorenz curve. The greater the area of A, the higher the Gini coefficient.

FIGURE 21-5

Gini coefficients around the world The Gini coefficient is one way to measure inequality. Countries in Western Europe generally have low Gini coefficients and less income inequality. Countries in South America and southern Africa have much higher Gini coefficients.

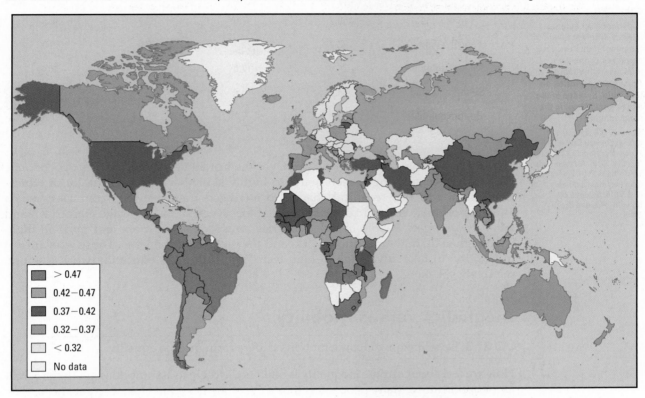

Source: Data from Human Development Report 2010, Human development statistical tables, http://hdr.undp.org/en/media/HDR_2010_EN_Tables_reprint.pdf. Map created through StatPlanet, www.statsilk.com/software/statplanet.

within countries has largely been on the rise. This is true both for rich countries and poor ones, for countries with large amounts of growth and those that are barely growing at all.

Gini coefficients in China have risen significantly since the 1980s, as the country has experienced strong economic growth. In India and other Asian countries, though, which have experienced similar amounts of growth, income inequality has not changed much at all: Gini coefficients are essentially the same as they were three decades ago. To paint a more specific picture of inequality within a sample of countries, Table 21-4 shows income distribution, measured in quintiles, in four countries. Here we can see how the United States compares with Sweden (a rich European country), Uganda (a poor African country), and Brazil (a middle-income Latin American country). Uganda's income *distribution* is the one the most similar to the United States, although of course the total *amount* of income being distributed is much lower. *Average income* in Sweden is much closer to that in the United States. But the distribution of that income is very different, with nearly three times as much held by those in the bottom quintile in Sweden.

What causes such big differences in income distribution between countries? One factor is the extent to which governments redistribute income through the public budget. In many European countries, for instance, taxes on the rich are higher than in the United States; public services and income support to the poor are also higher. The result is that the after-tax income distribution is more equal than the income distribution before taxes were paid and public services provided.

Economists also attribute a large part of the increase in inequality within countries like the United States to something called *skill-biased technical change*. That's a mouthful,

TABLE 21-4

Income distribution comparison, four countries

The amount of income held by different levels of the population in various countries is one way to measure inequality. Among the countries on this table, Sweden is the most equal; Brazil is the most unequal.

Sources: U.S. data: U.S. Census Bureau Current Population Report: Consumer Income (2010). All other data: World Bank WDI. Figures are from the latest available data (U.S. 2010, Sweden 2000, Uganda 2009, and Brazil 2009).

	% of total national income			
	United States	**Sweden**	**Uganda**	**Brazil**
Top quintile	50.2	37.0	50.7	58.6
Fourth quintile	23.4	22.7	20.0	19.0
Middle quintile	14.6	17.6	13.8	12.4
Second quintile	8.5	14.0	9.64	7.13
Bottom quintile	3.3	9.1	5.84	2.85

but what it means is straightforward: Over the last 50 years, the benefits of economic growth have increasingly been going to highly skilled workers with a lot of education. Then, add this technical change to increased trade between countries (which allows more manual and rote jobs to be done overseas in low-wage countries), and what do you get? People in rich countries are specializing more and more in high-tech, high-skill, high-education work, and they reap huge benefits. Those who are not in position to take advantage of high-tech, high-skill, high-education work lose out, relatively speaking.

Inequality versus mobility

LO 21.3 Describe how income mobility differs from income equality.

How we feel about income inequality is often tied closely to assumptions about the equality of opportunity. Many people feel that if everyone has a fair chance to get ahead, then the fact that some people do get ahead and some don't matters less. One way to consider the relationship between inequality and opportunities is to look at **income mobility**—the ability to improve one's economic circumstances over time. Measuring income mobility tells us how likely one is to end up rich if one starts out poor, or vice versa.

A standard way to measure mobility is to compare people's income to their parents' income. The idea is that if opportunities are truly equal, it should not matter much if your parents are rich or poor. Just as with poverty, we can measure income mobility in both absolute and relative terms. In absolute terms, we can look at whether a person's income is higher than her parents'. In relative terms, we can look at whether a person's income places her higher up in the income distribution than her parents. Both measures are important.

The United States has had high absolute mobility in the last century. This is not surprising considering it has had relatively high economic growth. Until recently, every generation has, on average, earned more and lived longer than their parents. In relative terms, however, the United States has much less income mobility. Almost half of those whose fathers were in the lowest income bracket end up in the lowest bracket themselves, and fewer than 1 in 10 make the "rags to riches" jump to the highest quintile. (In contrast, "perfect" income mobility would imply that 1 in 5 people with fathers in the lowest bracket should end up in each quintile.) On the other end of the distribution, it takes an average of six generations for the benefits of being born into a wealthy family to disappear. In other words, we have to go back six generations before your ancestors' place in the income distribution ceases to have any predictive power for what your own will be. In contrast, in Norway it takes only three generations. Figure 21-6 shows how relative mobility in the United States stacks up against a selection of other wealthy countries.

income mobility
the ability to improve one's economic circumstances over time

FIGURE 21-6

Income mobility in rich countries This mobility measure shows the amount of intergenerational income elasticity (the relationship between parents' and children's incomes) for countries relative to the United States. Canada is, for example, 2.5 times more mobile than the United States. On the whole, Scandinavian countries and Canada have a high level of economic mobility; the United States and United Kingdom do not.

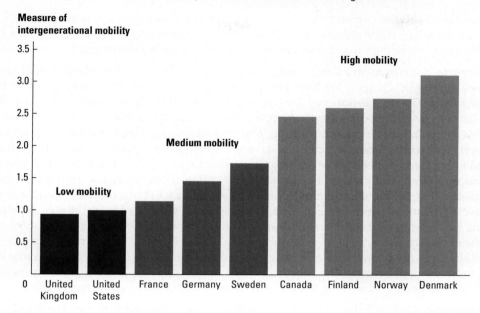

Sources: http://www.economicmobility.org/assets/pdfs/EMP%20American%20Dream%20Report.pdf; http://www.economicmobility.org/assets/pdfs/EMP_InternationalComparisons_ChapterIII.pdf.

✓ CONCEPT CHECK

❏ What variables are on the *x*- and *y*-axes when we graph the Lorenz curve? **[LO 21.2]**

❏ What does it mean if a country's Gini coefficient is 0? What does it mean if the Gini coefficient is 1? **[LO 21.2]**

❏ What is income mobility? **[LO 21.3]**

Policies to Reduce Poverty and Inequality

Most governments, in both rich and poor countries, aim to limit poverty and inequality to some extent. Yet views differ about how to do so. It's also a difficult and controversial area of policy-making. Some people feel that taking from the rich to give to the poor is justice and others feel that it's theft. Some focus on equalizing opportunities rather than outcomes. Others focus on creating a safety net for people who lose their jobs or get sick. Even when people agree on policy goals, they may disagree about how to design the best policies to accomplish those goals. In this section, we'll discuss both motivations and design issues surrounding poverty-fighting policies.

Public policy goals

Before we talk about the "how" of policy-making, we have to talk about what policy-makers are trying to accomplish. Why might it be desirable to reduce poverty or inequality? Some people cite humanitarian reasons—concern for others suffering from hunger or homelessness. Some focus on the harm to the economy and social disadvantages that may result when much of the population lacks of access to quality education, health care, and basic services like banking. Still others take a strictly pragmatic approach—a country with too much poverty or glaring inequalities is prone to violence, political unrest, or economic instability.

We can distinguish among three different types of public policy approaches related to poverty and inequality: economic development, safety nets, and redistribution. Knowing which goals are being pursued has important implications for designing public policies.

Economic development. Often, policy-makers look for investments that will spur future economic growth. We can group these policies under the category *economic development:* The goal is not only the immediate effect of the policy on poverty but also the growth it will produce for the entire economy. Common examples include public investments in education, job training, and infrastructure. These policies help reduce poverty indirectly, through increased economic growth and opportunities in the future.

Many of these policies serve dual goals—providing services in the short run and contributing to long-run growth. For instance, education is considered an important good in itself. Most people want their children to have access to education for its own sake. However, from the perspective of the government, it is also a tool for economic development: Better-educated children grow up to be more productive workers who contribute to the economy and who are less likely to be poor and unemployed. Similarly, a plan to revitalize the downtown area of a struggling city may have dual goals: It may make living there more pleasant in the short run. The hope is also that it will attract businesses and new residents, improving the city's economy and reducing poverty in the long run.

Safety nets. Earlier in the chapter, we looked at the difference between transient and chronic poverty. Most people go through hard times at some point in their lives—an illness, a death in the family, the loss of a job, and so on. For those living close to the edge of poverty, one bad event can be enough to tip the scales.

Many policies are designed to protect against the temporary hard times that can lead to transient poverty. We can broadly categorize these as **social insurance** programs. Under these programs, people pay into a common pool and are in turn eligible to draw on benefits under certain circumstances. Important examples in the United States include unemployment insurance, Social Security, and Medicare.

social insurance government programs under which people pay into a common pool and are eligible to draw on benefits under certain circumstances

Such programs are referred to as "social insurance" because they share important characteristics with private insurance programs, pooling risks across a large population. (For a more general discussion of insurance, turn back to the "Time and Uncertainty" chapter.) Unemployment insurance, for example, pools risk across the labor force. Since a large majority of people in the labor force have a job and pay taxes, the system is able to provide benefits for the minority who lose their jobs. The same is true for Social Security and Medicare, but the risks in these programs are spread across time. In both programs, benefits are provided by younger workers, who pay into the system under the promise that they'll get benefits when they retire.

One difference from private insurance programs is that social insurance programs usually serve everyone who meets baseline eligibility requirements. For instance, people who paid payroll taxes during their working years can draw on Social Security and Medicare when they retire or suffer a disability; those who live longer or have higher health care costs don't have to pay higher premiums in order to receive benefits.

Redistribution. Some policies explicitly seek to redistribute resources with the aim of alleviating the effects of poverty or income inequality. For instance, homeless shelters and food banks don't have much to do with long-run economic development. Instead, they are meant to provide comfort and security to people who face an immediate lack of food and shelter. Similarly, government-subsidized housing, food stamps, Medicaid (health insurance for low-income households), and many other programs offer resources to the poor over the long term. Most people see the primary purpose of these programs as using resources from society's wealthier members to ensure a basic minimum standard of living for its poorer members.

The welfare state

The term "welfare state" describes the idea that government has a responsibility to promote the economic well-being of its citizens. The basics of the welfare state in the United States started as part of the New Deal legislation that responded to the Great Depression in the 1930s. The government rolled out a variety of programs, including Social Security and the Civilian Conservation Corps, which were intended to help the growing number of poor and unemployed workers. From those beginnings, the United States created a variety of programs to help guarantee a minimum standard of living for all. These programs range from food stamps that help the poor buy food, to Head Start, an early-childhood education program. In this section, we discuss some of the more important economic welfare policies and whether they promote economic development, social insurance, or redistribution goals.

Progressive taxation. Governments can address poverty and inequality both through how public money is spent and how people are taxed. The design of the U.S. federal income tax system is *progressive,* which means that the government charges lower tax rates to those with lower incomes. This design has the effect of reducing income inequality: Those with high income tend to pay a larger proportion of their income as taxes than those with low income. The result is that the after-tax gap between rich and poor is smaller than the pre-tax gap.

As discussed in the "Taxation and Public Spending" chapter, other types of taxation—such as sales and payroll taxes—can be *regressive.* The overall burden of federal taxation in the U.S., though, is progressive. One tax policy, the Earned Income Tax Credit (EITC), has a particularly large effect on the poor. The EITC is exactly what it sounds like: Those with low income are eligible for a tax credit, proportional to the amount of income they earn and the size of their families. The more the family earns, the higher the credit, which is then subtracted from the amount of federal tax owed. For those with very low incomes, the credit may be larger than the amount owed in taxes, in which case the balance is paid to the family as a tax "refund." The EITC is a way to encourage work while still providing income support to families with very low income.

Income support. Government programs that give money to the poor are commonly referred to as "welfare." In fact, there is no single program in the United States called "welfare." Rather, the term *welfare* is used to refer broadly to the various income-support programs for the poor run by each state.

In 1996, Congress passed a law that greatly changed the role of the federal government in providing welfare. Until then, the federal government administered a program called Aid to Families with Dependent Children (AFDC). As the name suggests, this program gave money to poor households with children. To be eligible, the children had to be "deprived of parental support" in some way, usually having a single or divorced parent. Each state set the level of income at which families of different sizes were eligible, as well as the amount of benefits received. Anyone who met the eligibility criteria was entitled to benefits. Under the program, each state received unlimited reimbursement from the federal government to cover the cost.

We can think of AFDC as an "unconditional" cash-transfer program; it provided financial support to any eligible person, without any restrictions on how the money could be used. In

conditional cash transfer a program in which financial support is given only to people who engage in certain actions

contrast, the program that replaced AFDC in 1996—called Temporary Assistance to Needy Families—is a **conditional cash transfer** program. Under this program, financial support is given only to people who engage in certain actions. The exact requirements vary from state to state. Generally, welfare recipients are eligible for benefits for a maximum of five years, must start working within two years of joining the program, and must work a minimum number of hours per week. These conditions have shifted the nature of welfare away from a redistribution program toward a social insurance program. They are designed to help people through temporary hard times rather than provide long-term income support.

Conditional cash transfer programs are an increasingly popular antipoverty strategy, both inside and outside the United States. Often, the conditions attached to financial transfers require recipients to invest in health and education for their children. Such conditional cash transfer programs combine redistributive goals with economic-development goals. To learn more about programs that promote investment in human capital, look at the From Another Angle box "Paying people to help themselves."

FROM ANOTHER ANGLE

Paying people to help themselves

What might happen if you got paid to do well in school? We imagine you might put in a few extra hours on the next term paper. This reasoning was the force behind the creation of a program in which New York City gave cash rewards to students with high test scores. This program, part of a larger effort called *Opportunity NYC*, is an example of a conditional cash transfer program (called CCTs for short). CCTs offer benefits in exchange for actions that the government views as beneficial, such as going to school or a health clinic more often.

CCT programs operate throughout the world. In Mexico, the *Opportunidades* (formerly *Progresa*) program pays poor families to make sure their children attend school and visit the doctor regularly. In Brazil, the *Bolsa Familia* program gives mothers money as long as their children are vaccinated and have a school attendance rate above 85 percent. *To learn more about CCT programs and whether they accomplish their goals, continue reading by scanning the QR code near the end of the chapter or by going online.*

Source: http://web.worldbank.org/WBSITE/EXTERNAL/TOPICS/EXTSOCIALPROTECTION/EXTSAFETYNETSANDTRANSFERS/0,,contentMDK:20615138~menuPK:282766~pagePK:148956~piPK:216618~theSitePK:282761,00.html.

in-kind transfer a program that provides specific goods or services, rather than cash, directly to needy recipients

In-kind transfers. In contrast to cash-transfer programs, many government programs involve **in-kind transfers**. These programs provide goods or services, rather than cash, directly to needy individuals or households. In the United States, common in-kind transfers include public housing, free school lunches, and the medical treatment benefits provided by Medicaid. Often, in-kind transfers take the form of vouchers that are redeemable only for certain items. For example, the Supplemental Nutrition Assistance Program (formerly known as the Food Stamp Program) sends vouchers to families that can be used to purchase only approved food items.

In-kind transfer programs are, by design, more restrictive than cash-transfer programs. When a poor household receives income support, it can use the money to buy whatever goods and services it wishes. When that same household receives an in-kind transfer, the choice of how to spend the money has already been made. If we believe that people make considered choices to maximize their own well-being, then in-kind transfers are inefficient. After all, cash provides recipients with the flexibility to choose the goods that will do them the most good. Why might a government prefer in-kind transfers? One reason is that it prevents recipients from spending cash on luxury items or on socially disapproved goods such as alcohol or drugs.

Social insurance. Social-insurance programs are designed to help people weather temporary bad periods, but they also help people survive old age, disability, or other long-term conditions. As we noted above, in these programs, the government plays a role similar to that of a private insurance company: It collects contributions from working people in a common pool, defines the circumstances under which people are eligible to draw benefits, and administers and monitors the allocation of those benefits.

In the United States, the largest social insurance programs are:

- *Social Security,* which provides pensions to retired and disabled people.
- *Medicare,* which provides medical insurance to retired and disabled people.
- *Unemployment insurance,* which gives short-term income support to the unemployed.

Disability and unemployment benefits are examples of social insurance in a straight-forward sense. If you lose your job, or have an injury or medical condition that prevents you from working, the government will step in to provide a small stipend to help cover everyday living expenses.

Retirement benefits are less like private insurance (which is generally used to protect against unexpected events) and more like a collective saving program. Nevertheless, because there is an uncertainty about the circumstances the elderly face—when they will retire, what medical problems they will face, how high the cost of living will be, and how long they will need to live on retirement income—retirement benefits are widely seen as an example of social insurance. They play an important role in reducing poverty among the elderly, as we showed earlier in the chapter.

Trade-offs between equity and efficiency

LO 21.5 Explain the trade-off between equity and efficiency in poverty-reduction policy.

Public welfare programs can be costly and have to be paid for by taxes. As we saw in the chapter on "Taxation and Public Spending," higher taxes usually mean larger dead-weight loss. Pursuing equity (that is, greater income equality) thus means accepting some inefficiency due to increased taxation.

Welfare programs themselves can also distort choices and create inefficiencies. Some government programs that aim to reduce poverty are universal, meaning that everyone qualifies regardless of whether or not they are poor. Public schools are one example. Many programs, however, are **means-tested:** They define eligibility for benefits based on recipients' income. The goal of means-testing is to target resources toward those who need them the most. Often, means-testing is more complex than a simple eligible/not-eligible distinction. For instance, under the Earned Income Tax Credit described earlier, the size of the credit at first increases with earned income at very low income levels and then begins to decrease as income rises past the poverty line. The thinking is that a family with income *just* under the poverty threshold requires less support to access basic goods and services than a family very far below the line.

means-tested the characteristic of a program that defines eligibility for benefits based on recipients' income

Unfortunately, means-testing can create perverse incentives. Imagine a simple means-test: If your income is under the poverty line, you are eligible for a cash transfer of $5,000 per year, but if your income is over the poverty line, you are not. Now imagine you are working part-time and living just under the poverty line. Your boss offers you the opportunity to pick up an extra five hours of work each week. If you accept, your income will increase by $3,000 over the course of the year, pushing you over the poverty line. As a result, you will lose your government transfer of $5,000. On net, you will end up $2,000 poorer. How would you respond to this situation? Would you accept the extra hours? Unless there is some sort of extra benefit we're not considering (gaining experience or favor with your boss that will improve your job opportunities down the road, for example), most people would say no to longer hours for lower income.

It is possible to fix this sort of perverse incentive by designing more nuanced means-tests. For instance, a program could phase out benefits as income increases (like the EITC) rather than use a strict cutoff. That way, there will be no point at which a large amount of benefits are lost from a small increase in income. In general, the more narrowly targeted support is to those with low income, the greater the potential inefficiency caused. These examples show why economists often see a trade-off between equity and efficiency in poverty policy.

This is not to say that poverty policy is always inefficient. Some policies, like those that alleviate credit constraints, can improve both equity and efficiency. In this case, a market failure is being solved, so there is no trade-off. But, understanding the potential for trade-offs and unintended consequences is an important consideration when designing poverty policy.

✓ CONCEPT CHECK

- ❑ What is social insurance? **[LO 21.4]**
- ❑ What's the difference between a conditional and an unconditional cash-transfer program? **[LO 21.4]**
- ❑ What is means-testing? **[LO 21.5]**

Discrimination

You may be wondering why we're discussing discrimination in this chapter. In many ways it's a separate topic from poverty and income inequality. Not everyone who is poor is discriminated against, or vice versa. We chose to discuss these topics in the same chapter because, historically, they have often gone hand in hand. It's important to understand when discrimination, poverty, and inequality are connected, when they are not, and how to tell the difference.

discrimination
making choices by using generalizations based on people's observable characteristics like race, gender, and age

Economists think about **discrimination** as the practice of making choices using generalizations based on observable characteristics like race, gender, or age. But people can also discriminate based on ethnic origin, appearance, sexual orientation, what type of music you listen to, or any other observable characteristic that allows them to generalize about what type of person you might be. In the "Information" chapter, we said that discrimination can be a useful tool for making decisions when we don't have access to full information. In common language, however, when people say "discrimination," they usually mean "unfair or illegal discrimination."

Economists recognize that *statistical discrimination*—making a choice based on the difference in average characteristics between two groups—can sometimes be rational. For instance, imagine that an employer has to make a quick decision on which of two candidates to employ, a younger candidate versus an older one. She decides to hire the younger one as she believes that the younger candidate would be healthier and miss work less frequently. When forced to make a decision without full information, the employer is making a rational guess based on her knowledge of the average differences between middle-aged people and young people. It's an understandable strategy if she doesn't have good information about the health of the two candidates as individuals; but that doesn't make it fair or efficient for society. Society loses when talented individuals who face discrimination are discouraged from acquiring the skills, education, and positions that they otherwise might get. In short, statistical discrimination can be rational for an individual employer, but that doesn't necessarily make it right, socially efficient, or even legal.

Measuring discrimination in the labor market

LO 21.6 Explain why demographic differences in income or wages do not necessarily imply discrimination.

There's little doubt that discrimination has played a major role in U.S. history. Does it still matter today? It's surprisingly hard to say how big an effect discrimination now has on people's economic opportunities and success.

We can start to answer this question by looking at the outcomes achieved by people in different demographic groups. Table 21-5 shows that average income for adults still varies widely across gender and racial groups. It's possible that these differences are due to discrimination in the labor market, but there are also plenty of other possible explanations. For instance, on average, white men have higher educational qualifications than people in other groups. To the extent that being more educated is a signal or a cause of higher productivity as a worker, this could explain higher wages. Similarly, women are more likely than men to choose to leave the labor force when they have children, and therefore have less work experience on average.

We should be careful about confusing *correlation* with *causation*. In this case, income is *correlated* with race and gender. That doesn't necessarily mean that discrimination based on race and gender is *causing* the difference in wages. To draw on a concept from all the way back in Chapter 1, it's possible that *omitted variables* are causing the correlation. These other factors, which are related to both earnings and race or gender but which we are not observing, could include education, work experience, and choice of occupation.

It's also important to remember that we don't know what might be causing differences in those other factors. Suppose that a large part of the difference in wages between men and women can be explained by differences in occupational choice. For instance, men are more likely to be doctors, and women are more likely to be nurses. Since doctors earn more on average than nurses, this contributes to the difference in earnings between men and women. This doesn't tell us *why* women are more likely to be nurses—maybe it's a response to social pressures, or a need for flexibility in work hours, or maybe it has to do with differences in how girls and boys are brought up. These explanations may also be partly a function of a kind of discrimination.

To read about an innovative way researchers tested one of the factors that could be causing a discrepancy in wages in the labor market, read the Real Life box "Are Emily and Greg more employable than Lakisha and Jamal?"

TABLE 21-5 Income by race and gender in the United States

Median personal income distribution varies by race and gender in the United States.

Group	Female ($)	Male ($)
Asian	36,267	23,612
White	34,047	20,947
All	32,137	20,831
Black	23,203	19,700
Hispanic	22,233	16,269

Source: U.S. Census Bureau Current Population Survey, Table P2: Race and Hispanic Origin of People by Mean Income and Sex, http://www.census.gov/hhes/www/income/data/historical/people/.

REAL LIFE

Are Emily and Greg more employable than Lakisha and Jamal?

Many companies go out of their way to advertise their support for diversity in the workplace or to note they are an "equal opportunity employer." Title VII of the Civil Rights Act of 1964 made it unlawful to discriminate on the basis of race, color, religion, gender, or national origin when hiring employees. Yet in spite of the good intentions of many companies and legal prohibitions against racial discrimination in the workplace, people of different races still have very different rates of employment and levels of earnings. How much of this, if any, is due to lingering discrimination by employers?

To answer this question, economists Marianne Bertrand and Sendhil Mullainathan conducted a study to test for racial discrimination in the job-application process. They created resumes for fictitious applicants, and sent them out in response to help-wanted ads. Some resumes represented a fake applicant with a "white-sounding" name, such as Emily Walsh or Greg Baker. Others were given traditionally black names like Lakisha Washington or Jamal Jones. Aside from the difference in names, the actual qualifications and job experience were the same on average across "white" and "black" resumes.

The researchers found that white names—with otherwise-identical qualifications—were 50 percent more likely to receive callbacks in response to a job application. On average, Emily and Greg had to send out 10 resumes in order to receive a response from an employer. Lakisha and Jamal had to send out 15.

Furthermore, resumes with black names got less benefit from increased qualifications. An "Emily" resume with more education or job experience got 27 percent more callbacks than an "Emily" with a lower-quality resume. In contrast, resumes with black names and higher qualifications got only 8 percent more callbacks than those with lower qualifications. In other words, black applicants received fewer rewards in their job search for the same increase in accomplishments. From the perspective of real young people of different races, this gap presents very different incentives to invest time and money in education and skill-building.

Sources: http://www.eeoc.gov/laws/statutes/titlevii.cfm; Title VII of the 1964 Civil Rights Act; http://www.economics.harvard.edu/faculty/mullainathan/files/emilygreg.pdf.

Do free markets reduce discrimination?

How does the idea of discrimination fit into a model of efficient, well-functioning markets? Under some conditions, markets may help to eliminate discrimination. For instance, imagine a shop owner who has a unique prejudice against people over six feet tall. He refuses to hire tall employees or to serve tall customers. Since no one else in the market has this strange bias against tall people, the shop owner's competitors will take advantage of his discrimination: They will hire good workers who happen to be tall and will get business from the customers he refuses to serve. If the market is competitive, the discriminatory shop owner will get pushed out of the market; his competitors will benefit from his inefficient choices.

Under other circumstances, however, discrimination can be consistent with an efficient market. For much of the twentieth century, for instance, shopkeepers who discriminated against black customers were the norm rather than the exception. As long as their competitors and their white customers agreed with and supported this discrimination, it was unfortunately often in their interest to maintain it. For instance, a shopkeeper in the 1940s who allowed black people to sit at the same counter as white people risked losing business from prejudiced white customers. In situations where businesses discriminate in response to the preferences of consumers, discrimination is consistent with efficient markets (which, of course, doesn't make it morally right or acceptable).

Long-term effects of discrimination

Even though the passage of the Civil Rights Act in 1964 made many forms of discrimination illegal, it couldn't undo the effects of discrimination that took place in earlier decades. Discrimination can have long-lasting effects on people and markets, even after the active discrimination itself ends.

We noted earlier that differences in educational attainment explain part of the difference in earnings between racial groups. We have to ask ourselves: Why do people of different races have more or less education on average? Although there are many complicated social, cultural, and economic reasons, some part of it is certainly the lingering result of discrimination decades ago.

On the most basic level, a black person who was born in the United States in the 1940s probably completed most of her education in segregated schools. But, the lingering effects of historical discrimination can affect new generations, even if they didn't grow up under discriminatory policies. One important example is segregated communities. Earlier in the chapter, we discussed the idea that people's chances in life are affected by the human capital of those around them. Imagine that, at one time, people of a certain race, national origin, or religion experienced discrimination that made it harder for them to get a good education or acquire job experience or productive skills. Even after that active discrimination ends, imagine that they still tend to cluster together in neighborhoods. The kids who grow up in these neighborhoods are surrounded by adults who have low education or job experience, affecting the development of the kids' human capital. This is one reason often put forward for "affirmative action" programs that ensure people of other races gain access in college admissions or hiring decisions, as described in the What Do You Think? box "Affirmative action in college admissions."

WHAT DO YOU THINK?

Affirmative action in college admissions

In 1961, President John F. Kennedy required government contractors to "take affirmative action to ensure that applicants are employed [. . .] without regard to their race, creed, color, or national origin." That original use of the term "affirmative action" meant taking steps to avoid racial discrimination. Over time, the term evolved to refer to the general practice of giving preference to members of underrepresented groups.

One of the most hotly debated areas of affirmative-action policy is in university admissions. Since the 1970s, many universities have practiced "positive discrimination" to increase the number of women and racial minorities they admit. Early on, many of these policies took the form of specific racial quotas, such as reserving 15 percent of available spots for nonwhite students. The Supreme Court ruled quotas unconstitutional (in the 1978 case *Regents of the University of California v. Bakke*), but allowed less-explicit forms of racial affirmative action. In a hard-fought case involving the University of Michigan (*Gratz v. Bollinger* in 2003), the Court ruled that considering race as a "plus" in a multifactor admissions decision is acceptable if it helps achieve diversity among students. However, the Court noted that it viewed this as a short-term solution that would be unnecessary in 25 years.

Proponents of affirmative action in university admissions commonly base their support on one of two ideas: First, having a diverse student body is inherently valuable and serves educational purposes. Second, "positive discrimination" is a temporary measure to counteract the lingering, intergenerational effects of historical "negative discrimination."

Opponents often argue that there is no such thing as "positive" discrimination." They feel that preference on the basis of race is simply wrong, regardless of who is harmed or helped by it and that two wrongs don't make a right. Still others argue that if affirmative action is intended to address historical disadvantages, it should take a wider view than race. For example, has the son of a poor white coal miner or the son of a wealthy black neurosurgeon been more disadvantaged by his family background?

What do you think?

1. In what ways, if any, do you think that students applying to U.S. colleges today might be affected by past racial and gender discrimination? Think about human capital investments, social networks, and economic mobility.
2. If some students are adversely affected by historical discrimination, are college admissions an effective way to correct that disadvantage before graduates enter the labor market? How should we think about the benefits and costs of such a policy, including the opportunity cost? Can actions be taken to counter these disadvantages elsewhere in society or the economy?

✓ CONCEPT CHECK

☐ How do economists define discrimination? **[LO 21.6]**

☐ Why don't differences in income between demographic groups necessarily imply discrimination? **[LO 21.6]**

Conclusion

Understanding the roots of poverty, inequality, and discrimination matters for economists and policy-makers alike. From an intellectual perspective, these topics push us to understand how markets and institutions really work. They also take us below the surface of statistics such as average income and GDP to understand who gets how much and why. From the perspective of a policy-maker or a concerned citizen, they may raise challenging economic and social issues. What does a fair society look like? How much poverty is acceptable? Does equality of opportunity matter more than the distribution of income itself?

We've seen in this chapter that even the measurement of poverty, inequality, mobility, and discrimination can be tricky. We have to decide whether we care more about absolute or relative measures, adjust for differences across regions, and pick out the causal factors we care about. In the next chapter, we turn to the question of how these and other policy issues are dealt with in the political world. We'll see that arriving at policy choices is even more complicated than simply finding the facts and establishing goals. The workings of the political system itself have a huge influence on the shape of the economic policies that are created.

 ◄ Mobile Window on the World—Scan this code with your smartphone to find more applications of the chapter content. (Need a barcode reader? Try ScanLife, available in your app store.)

Visit your mobile app store and download ► the Karlan and Morduch Study Econ app.

Key Terms

absolute poverty line, p. 505

relative poverty line, p. 506

poverty rate, p. 506

purchasing power parity (PPP) index, p. 508

human capital, p. 511

poverty trap, p. 512

credit constraint, p. 512

Lorenz curve, p. 515

Gini coefficient, p. 515

income mobility, p. 518

social insurance, p. 520

conditional cash transfer, p. 522

in-kind transfer, p. 522

means-tested, p. 523

discrimination, p. 524

Summary

LO 21.1 Discuss the difference between relative and absolute measures of poverty.

An absolute poverty line defines poverty as income below a certain amount. The poverty line is fixed at a certain dollar amount at a given point in time; it is usually set based on the cost of certain essential goods. In contrast, a relative poverty line defines poverty in terms of the income of the rest of the population. The official U.S. poverty line is an absolute amount based on the price of food in the 1960s; poverty rates in the U.S. have fluctuated between 10 and 15 percent of the population in recent decades.

The most commonly used international poverty measure is also an absolute poverty line, $1.25 per person per day at purchasing power parity. According to this metric, roughly one-quarter of the world's population lives in poverty.

Absolute poverty lines measure people's access to concrete goods and services; relative poverty lines do a better job of capturing the importance of economic conditions relative to those of others.

LO 21.2 Explain and interpret different methods of measuring income inequality.

Income inequality is commonly summarized by measuring the average income in each quintile of the population, or the percentage of total income held by people in each quintile. We can also represent income inequality using a graph called the Lorenz curve. It maps the cumulative percent of the population against the cumulative percent of income those people earn. The Gini coefficient summarizes inequality in a single number by dividing the area between the Lorenz curve and the line of perfect equality by the total area under the line of perfect equality.

LO 21.3 Describe how income mobility differs from income equality.

Income mobility is the ability to improve your economic circumstances over time. Measuring income mobility in a country tells us how likely you are to end up rich if you start out poor, or vice versa. We can measure income mobility in both absolute and relative terms. In absolute terms, we can look at whether a person's income is higher than her parents'. In relative terms, we can look at whether person's income places her higher up in the income distribution than her parents.

LO 21.4 Identify the public policies that are used to reduce poverty and inequality.

Four main policies are used to reduce poverty and inequality. Progressive taxation reduces inequality, as it taxes the rich at a higher rate than the poor, narrowing the gap between these two groups. Income support comes in two forms, conditional cash transfers and direct cash transfers. In both, families receive cash from the government. In-kind transfers give goods and services (most commonly, food stamps and housing vouchers) to the poor instead of cash. Social insurance programs, including Social Security and Medicare, pool risks across the population by providing income support and health care, respectively, for the elderly.

LO 21.5 Explain the trade-off between equity and efficiency in poverty-reduction policy.

Means-tested programs define eligibility for benefits based on recipients' income. Often, means-testing involves not just a simple eligible/not-eligible distinction, but also a determination of how much recipients are eligible to receive. However, anytime benefits decrease as income increases, the motivation to earn additional income is reduced. There is no way to prevent everyone from falling through the cracks without loss of efficiency. Thus, economists see a trade-off between equity and efficiency in poverty policy. Trade-offs are also created due to the inefficiencies created by taxes levied to pay for anti-poverty programs.

LO 21.6 Explain why demographic differences in income or wages do not necessarily imply discrimination.

Income for adults varies widely by race and gender in the United States. These differences could be the result of discrimination in the labor market. They also could be the result of other factors that are related to both earnings and race or gender, such as education, work experience, and choice of occupation. It is difficult to distinguish the causal effect of discrimination from these other unobserved factors.

Under some conditions, markets may help to eliminate discrimination. When consumer preferences are not in agreement with the discrimination (or when the discrimination is irrelevant to consumers' preferences), markets will cause those who discriminate to lose profitable opportunities. However, when consumer preferences support discrimination, discrimination and efficient markets can coexist.

Review Questions

1. In season three of the TV show "The West Wing," the federal government considers redefining the national poverty measure in a way that would classify an additional 4 million people as poor. The president worries that his administration will be criticized for leading the country into greater poverty. Explain whether this change would have reflected a shift in an absolute measure of poverty, a relative measure of poverty, or whether it cannot be known. Finally, explain why all else equal, the president is not responsible for causing greater poverty. **[LO 21.1]**

2. Poverty in Decilia is measured relatively, with people in the bottom 10 percent of the income distribution being defined as poor. Suppose a politician in Decilia promises to halve the poverty rate in five years. Explain why this could never be achieved given the poverty statistic Decilia uses. Propose an alternative measure of poverty that would allow the politician to achieve that goal. **[LO 21.1]**

3. Is it possible for two countries to have the same Gini coefficient but different distributions of income? Explain how you came to your conclusion. **[LO 21.2]**

4. Explain why it's possible for income inequality to decrease globally while increasing in every country at the same time. **[LO 21.2]**

5. In which of the following countries is income mobility likely higher? Explain your answer. **[LO 21.3]**
   a. A country with a poverty rate of 25 percent, of which 80 percent represents chronic poverty.
   b. A country with a poverty rate of 30 percent, of which 20 percent represents chronic poverty.

6. Suppose there is an economy where 80 percent of people earn more than their parents and 40 percent end up in a different income quintile than their parents. What measure of the income distribution does the first statistic tell you about? What about the second? **[LO 21.3]**

7. In March 2010, President Barack Obama signed into law the Patient Protection and Affordable Care Act, which required insurance companies to accept patients with preexisting conditions. Classify this provision into one of the approaches to alleviating poverty discussed in the chapter and explain your reasoning. **[LO 21.4]**

8. If unconditional cash transfers have the same effect as conditional cash transfers, which one allows the government to alleviate poverty more effectively? In answering the question, draw on your knowledge of administrative costs. **[LO 21.4]**

9. John Rawls is a philosopher famous for his "maximin" principle, which states that society should maximize the position of the people with the minimum amount of goods, and not focus only on the level of inequality. For instance, Rawls would favor a society in which the bottom 10 percent earn $30,000 per year and the top 10 percent earn $2 million over a society in which the bottom 10 percent earn $28,000 per year and the top 10 percent earn $40,000 per year. Drawing on the trade-off between equity and efficiency, explain whether Rawls would favor (a) redistribution that limits growth but creates equality or (b) economic development that encourages growth but creates inequality. **[LO 21.5]**

10. Your professor has decided that, from now on, students who receive less than a 60 percent grade on any exam will be eligible to go to a review session. If they attend the session, they will receive an extra 10 percent on their grade. You see a problem with this policy, and instead propose to your professor that people who go to the review session should receive 50 percent of the difference between their grade and 60 percent. Explain why this situation represents a trade-off between equity and efficiency. **[LO 21.5]**

11. Is it possible that even though men make more than women in a particular industry, there could be gender discrimination *against* men in that industry? If no, explain why not. If yes, explain why and give an example. **[LO 21.6]**

12. For each of the scenarios below, determine whether you think it is likely that an employer could be discriminating against a person because of his or her age. Explain why or why not. **[LO 21.6]**
    a. A young lawyer who just finished work on a multimillion-dollar development deal downtown is hired by an economic development firm in lieu of an older lawyer who works on litigation.
    b. A large retail outlet hires an 80-year-old woman to greet customers instead of a 30-year-old woman who has been greeting customers in other stores for a decade.
    c. The owner of a local, hip smoothie bar in a university town just fired a graduate student who had worked at the bar for three years and instead hired a college sophomore.

13. Jackie Robinson broke baseball's color barrier in 1947, which precipitated integration in all major league teams after 12 years. Explain why the market might have acted to eliminate discrimination in this example. **[LO 21.6]**

14. Some economists have studied the effects of "lookism," or discrimination based on how attractive a person is. Give an example of a case in which the market might encourage lookism and an example of a case in which the market might combat lookism. **[LO 21.6]**

Problems and Applications

1. Table 21P-1 shows a data set that contains the income of 20 households, each with a household size of four people. **[LO 21.1]**
   a. What percent of these households are below the national poverty line of $18,250 for a household of four people?
   b. What is the average income of the bottom 20 percent of the households?
   c. Which poverty measurement (the national one, or the bottom quintile) gives a higher poverty rate?

2. Table 21P-2 shows the incomes of 10 households in two different years, 2020 and 2021. Assume that the government is considering two different measures of poverty, an absolute level of below

TABLE 21P-1

Income of households 1–10 ($)	Income of households 11–20 ($)
30,000	10,000
11,000	41,000
88,000	21,500
17,000	78,000
21,000	25,000
75,000	13,000
24,000	103,000
81,000	149,000
52,000	76,000
44,000	27,000

TABLE 21P-2

Household	Income in 2020 ($)	Income in 2021 ($)
1	20,000	20,050
2	8,000	9,000
3	13,000	13,000
4	33,000	34,000
5	2,000	2,500
6	7,500	8,000
7	9,050	10,100
8	80,000	85,000
9	40,000	42,000
10	3,000	3,100

$10,000 and a relative measure of being in the bottom 40 percent of income earners. **[LO 21.1]**
   a. What is the poverty rate using the *absolute* measure of poverty in 2020? In 2021? Does it go up, down, or stay the same between the two years?
   b. What is the poverty rate using the *relative* measure of poverty in 2020? In 2021? Does it go up, down, or stay the same between the two years?
   c. Which yields a higher rate, the absolute measure of poverty or the relative measure of poverty in 2020? In 2021?
   d. Now assume that the government decides to index the poverty rate to inflation. Suppose inflation was 5 percent from 2020 to 2021. Now what is the poverty rate according to the absolute measure in 2021? Is it higher than the relative rate in 2021?

3. Using the data for income distribution found in Table 21-4 (page 604), determine the following. **[LO 21.2]**
   a. Does Sweden or Brazil have a higher Gini coefficient?
   b. From the bottom quintile to the middle quintile, is the Lorenz curve for Brazil above or below Sweden's?

4. Look at the various measures of poverty in 2009 for several countries in Table 21P-3. (The data are provided by the World Bank.) **[LO 21.2]**
   a. Rank the countries from the country with the highest inequality to the lowest using

TABLE 21P-3

Country	Gini coefficient	% of income held by bottom 10%	% of income held by top 10%
Argentina	46.13	1.24	33.29
Chile	52.06	1.53	42.77
El Salvador	48.33	1.03	37.00
Honduras	56.95	0.43	42.4
Panama	52.03	1.26	40.49
Paraguay	51.04	1.01	38.95
Uganda	44.3	2.35	36.1

the Gini coefficient. (Higher Gini coefficients represent higher inequality.)

b. Rank the countries from the country with the highest inequality to the lowest using the ratio of the top decile to the bottom decile.

c. Rank the countries from the country with the highest inequality to the lowest inequality using the share of total income held by the top 10 percent.

5. Determine whether each of the scenarios is possible. [LO 21.3]

a. A poverty rate based on a relative measure is high, income mobility is low, and there is perfect income equality.

b. A poverty rate based on an absolute measure is high, income mobility is zero, and there is perfect income equality.

c. A poverty rate based on an absolute measure is high, income mobility is high, and there is high income equality.

d. There is no poverty based on a relative measure, income mobility is high, and there is perfect income equality.

6. The left column of Table 21P-4 shows the income data for 10 people at age 40. The right column shows the income for one of their children at the same age (adjusted for inflation). [LO 21.3]

a. How many people in the second generation are in a higher income quintile than their parents?

b. How many people in the second generation are in a lower income quintile than their parents?

c. How many people are in the highest income quintile who had parents who were in the lowest quintile?

7. Classify the following social policies based on the approach taken to alleviating poverty: economic development, safety nets, or redistribution. [LO 21.4]

a. The government of Zimbabwe reorganizes property rights, giving traditionally marginalized black Zimbabweans access to land owned by white Zimbabweans.

b. As part of a package called the GI Bill, the United States offered to pay the college tuition of newly returned veterans of World War II.

c. The government of Chile privatizes its social security system. The new system sets up private accounts that require contributions of at least 10 percent of income. This money is

TABLE 21P-4

Income for 1st generation (at age 40) ($)	Income for 2nd generation (at age 40) ($)
800	2,225
9,120	2,105
12,830	1,380
1,275	1,140
6,260	10,200
1,600	11,880
4,150	1,250
2,200	15,000
975	420
3,590	5,630

invested by private actors and then returned to each person at retirement.

8. Imagine a person who makes $400 per week working 40 hours per week for 50 weeks of the year. She is currently eligible for a welfare program, available to people with income below $21,000, that gives her $800 a year. No such program is available to people with income above $21,000 per year. Her boss offers her a promotion that would increase her wage by 25 cents per hour. **[LO 21.4]**

   a. What is her total income before the promotion?

   b. What is her total income if she accepts the promotion?

   c. Should she accept the promotion if she wants to have higher income?

9. President Joe Nositall just published a report for his country, laying out various scenarios for the economy in the next year. Table 21P-5 shows his report, with various levels of GDP growth, income equality, and tax rates. **[LO 21.5]**

   a. Rank the scenarios from the most equal to the most unequal income distribution (defined as the average income of the top decile of earners divided by the average income of the bottom decile of earners).

   b. Rank each scenario in terms of the level of GDP growth between 2010 and 2011.

   c. Between which scenarios is there no trade-off between GDP growth and income equality?

10. Which of the following are means-tested programs? **[LO 21.5]**

   a. A local public university starts to give financial aid to individuals who score above the 98th percentile on the SAT.

   b. The United Kingdom decides to start giving out pension benefits based on individuals' prior amount of savings.

   c. A government decides to give tax credits to anyone who purchases computers made domestically.

   d. Canada begins to pay half of the cost of public transportation for people who do not own a car.

11. Table 21P-6 shows hypothetical salaries for four pairs of men and women who share the same position. It also shows the average increase in income associated with having certain qualities as a worker; assume these represent the only qualities that are relevant for doing the job well. Using these averages, determine for each pair whether there is gender discrimination. If so, say who it is against and how large the gap is in dollar terms. **[LO 21.6]**

12. Working women in the United States earn only three-quarters of what men earn. Consider each of the following explanations for this statistic, and say whether each *could be true* or *must not be true* in order to explain this fact. **[LO 21.6]**

   a. Women choose lower-paying professions (e.g., becoming a nurse rather than a doctor).

   b. Women are discriminated against when being considered for promotions or raises.

   c. Women are more educated and have more work experience than men, on average.

   d. Women are discriminated against in the hiring process.

   e. Women benefit from affirmative action in the hiring process.

13. Are the workings of the free market likely to encourage or discourage discrimination in the following examples? **[LO 21.6]**

   a. The musical director of a symphony orchestra that records but never performs in front of an audience refuses to hire female musicians.

   b. In apartheid South Africa (where racial discrimination was legal and popular among

TABLE 21P-5

Scenario	GDP in 2010 (trillions of $)	Average tax rate (%)	Average total income for the bottom 10% of earners ($)	Average total income for the top 10% of earners ($)	GDP in 2011 (trillions of $)
A	14.1	16	25,000	100,000	14.6
B	13.0	40	35,000	80,000	13.2
C	16.5	30	27,000	90,000	17.2
D	18.0	45	40,000	95,000	18.1

TABLE 21P-6

Industry-average compensation	Gender	Years of schooling $1,000 per year of schooling	Years of experience $2,000 per year of experience	Salary ($) A base salary of $50,000
A	Male	5	10	75,000
	Female	3	8	69,000
B	Male	0	5	60,000
	Female	2	7	70,000
C	Male	3	5	63,000
	Female	3	7	63,000

white voters for many decades), a white business owner refuses to hire black candidates to work in management positions dealing with white customers.

c. In a Martian culture in which blue hair is considered the most beautiful, a Martian modeling agency preferentially hires blue-haired models.

14. Consider Table 21P-7, which shows several different types of goods sold in a hypothetical town. Imagine a new competitor enters who refuses to discriminate between locals and foreigners in hiring employees. Determine whether the new competitor will do well in the town, given market conditions. [LO 21.6]

TABLE 21P-7

Good	% of customers who will buy the good only from companies that hire only locals	% of stores that hire only local employees
Pajama pants	50	70
Bow ties	70	50
Yo-yos	10	5

Chapter Endnotes

1. Report on earnings on Wall Street: http://www.osc.state.ny.us/press/releases/oct12/100912.htm. Survey on salaries in America by occupation (Bureau of Labor Statistics, U.S. Department of Labor: http://www.bls.gov/oes/current/oes_nat.htm. Accessed October 2012.

2. Data on the income of the top 1 percent is from Emmanuel Saez, "Striking It Richer: The Evolution of Top Incomes in the United States (Updated with 2009 and 2010 estimates)," University of California, Berkeley, March 2, 2012, http://elsa.berkeley.edu/~saez/saez-UStopincomes-2010.pdf.

3. Data are from Shaohua Chen and Martin Ravallion, "An update to the World Bank's estimates of consumption poverty in the developing world," Development Research Group, World Bank (03-01-12). Available at http://siteresources.worldbank.org/INTPOVCALNET/Resources/Global_Poverty_Update_2012_02-29-12.pdf.

4. http://www.theatlantic.com/magazine/archive/2006/09/the-height-of-inequality/5089/.

Chapter Sources

http://www.census.gov/prod/2010pubs/p60-238.pdf

http://www.nber.org/aginghealth/summer04/w10466.html

http://www.bea.gov/national/index.htm#gdp

http://www.irp.wisc.edu/publications/focus/pdfs/foc262g.pdf

http://www.princeton.edu/~deaton/downloads/presidential%20address%2019january%202010%20all.pdf

http://www.economicmobility.org/assets/pdfs/EMP%20American%20Dream%20Report.pdf

http://www.economicmobility.org/assets/pdfs/EMP_InternationalComparisons_ChapterIII.pdf

http://www.census.gov/prod/2011pubs/p70-123.pdf

http://web.worldbank.org/WBSITE/EXTERNAL/EXTDEC/EXTRESEARCH/0,,contentMDK:21882162~pagePK:64165401~piPK:64165026~theSitePK:469382,00.html

Political Choices

LEARNING OBJECTIVES

LO 22.1   Explain the predictions and assumptions of the median-voter theorem.

LO 22.2   List the characteristics of an "ideal" voting system, and assess which criteria are met by real systems.

LO 22.3   Discuss problems with the idea of the "rational voter," and explain the idea of rational ignorance.

LO 22.4   Explain the persistence of policies that provide concentrated benefits to a few while imposing diffuse costs on the majority.

LO 22.5   Explain why corruption and rent-seeking can persist in a democratic system.

GLOBAL WARMING HOT POTATO

Since the turn of the 21st century, debate over climate change has been a fixture of American politics. Scientists and economists have been drawn into this debate to provide their expert opinions on the factual questions involved. Economists aren't well suited to weigh in on the earth-science side of the issue, but the question of how to tackle negative externalities is a familiar economic problem.

Two economic solutions to counter the externalities associated with carbon emissions have been widely debated. The first is a carbon tax levied on businesses, which provides an incentive to reduce emissions. The second approach is a "cap-and-trade" policy that grants businesses the right to emit a certain amount of carbon, and then allows them to buy or sell those allowances as needed. Both policies would reduce the total quantity of pollution by raising the price of burning carbon-based fuels.

However, both proposals died in Congress. Why? It is possible for reasonable and informed people to disagree about the merits of a carbon tax versus a cap-and-trade policy, and indeed, the necessity of either. But the failure of the proposals appeared to have little to do with science, and a lot to do with old-fashioned politics.

Most economists, regardless of political philosophy, believe that a carbon tax is a simpler and more transparent and efficient solution than cap-and-trade. But many policy-makers viewed backing any sort of "tax" as political suicide. Some policy-makers and electric companies instead favored a cap-and-trade proposal that granted companies some free carbon allowances. In the end, however, politicians rejected even the cap-and-trade proposal, worried that the resulting increase in consumer heating and gas prices would anger voters.

Chapter 22

In the previous few chapters, we've seen how government action can correct market failures and increase total surplus. The fight over a carbon tax versus cap-and-trade is just one illustration of how difficult it can be to translate economic theory into government action. Students of economics, therefore, have an interest in understanding how policy is formed through the political process. Economics is, after all, the study of how resources are managed, and governments play a major role in resource allocation.

The most basic economic model for understanding electoral politics starts from standard assumptions of economics—that people are rational and fully informed. The model assumes that voters have preferences regarding policy, have full information about candidates, and vote for the one whose policy platform most nearly resembles their preferences. Once those candidates are in office, they simply implement the platforms on which they were elected. In this way, rational voters directly determine the shape of public policy.

You may have noticed, however, that the real world is much more complicated. Voters are not necessarily well informed; politicians often pursue their own interests rather than those of voters; and small groups with large stakes in a policy proposal (such as electric companies in the case of a carbon tax) can have a big influence on the outcome.

To help account for these real-world observations, in this chapter we'll build an economic model of political choices. We'll talk about why it's not so simple to arrive at policy conclusions by just adding up the votes. We'll question the assumptions that voters are rational and informed, and that they vote according to their preferences. We'll look at post-election policy choices, and talk about why voter preferences won't necessarily translate directly into policy. Finally, we'll see how political structure affects policy outcomes, and will zoom in on some specific features of the U.S. political structure which affect the national economy.

The Economics of Elections

To start, imagine that the typical voter has clear opinions on a broad range of policy issues and knows the positions held by every candidate in every election. (To assess the realism of this assumption, take a quick quiz: Do you know your senators' and representative's positions on the death penalty or taxes? Very few of us, sometimes including politicians themselves, can actually answer questions like these with confidence.) Even if these assumptions held true, how do you think that elections would play out? We'll start by thinking about a simplified model, and then get more realistic in two important ways.

Stick to the middle: Median-voter theorem

LO 22.1 Explain the predictions and assumptions of the median-voter theorem.

Does it ever seem to you that political candidates in the United States seem to agree more often than they disagree? That even though they might stake out different positions in debates, in fact candidates tend to converge on similar policy ideas? If so, a basic theory of political decision making in economics can help explain why.

Imagine a one-dimensional policy question, such as how much money to spend on the military. Now, suppose that all voters have a preference along this one dimension (more spending or less spending on the military). Each person will vote for the politician whose policy platform is closer to his or her own preferences. To simplify the math, let's also imagine there are only seven voters. (You can think of each of the seven as representing one-seventh of all the real voters.) In this simple model, how should two candidates running for election choose their policy positions?

Suppose the two candidates start by saying what they really think. One candidate, Mr. Dove, advocates relatively low military spending. As shown in panel A of Figure 22-1, his position is between the third and fourth voter. The other candidate, Ms. Hawk, favors very high military spending. The result? Ms. Hawk will get only two of the seven votes; the other five voters are closer to Mr. Dove's position.

Suppose you were employed by Ms. Hawk's campaign. What would you advise? If she moves her position to the left (in other words, lowering proposed military spending), she can steal voters #4 and #5 from Mr. Dove and win the election, as panel B shows. How can Mr. Dove *respond* to this strategy to regain the lead? He can move right, recapturing the vote of voter #4, as shown in panel C.

If we take this electoral game to its logical conclusion, the only way for either candidate to maximize votes is to take the exact same position as voter #4—the median, or middle, voter. If either candidate moves away from this position, he or she loses the middle voter and thus loses the election. So, regardless of what they really think, if they want to maximize their chances of winning, we would expect both candidates to end up advocating the *exact same position.*

This simple model is called the **median-voter theorem**. It suggests that politicians maximize their votes by taking the policy position preferred by the median voter, under certain conditions. The conditions are:

- There is a single, one-dimensional policy question (such as more or less spending).
- Voters always vote for the candidate whose position is closest to their own.
- There are only two candidates.
- A candidate wins by majority vote.

median-voter theorem a model stating that under certain conditions, politicians maximize their votes by taking the policy position preferred by the median voter

FIGURE 22-1

Candidates win by catering to the median voter

(A) An extreme position loses the election: Seven voters are ranked on a one-dimensional scale. Each voter votes for the candidate who is closest to his own preferences. Opinion polls show that, by taking an extreme position, Candidate B is set to attract the votes of only two out of seven voters.

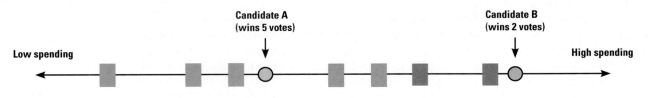

(B) Moving to the center wins more votes: Candidate B looks at the polls and decides to moderate her position. New opinion polls show she will now win the election with four votes, against three for Candidate A.

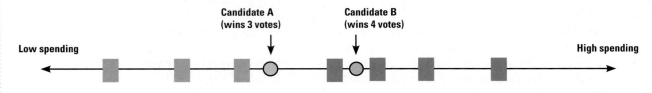

(C) Candidates end up catering to the median voter: Candidate A now looks at the opinion polls and decides to moderate his position, too. By moving closer to the median voter, he now wins 4-3. This process of moderating positions continues until both candidates are advocating the position held by the median voter.

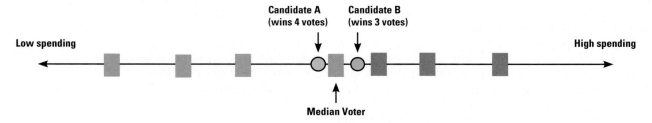

Note that under this model, the chosen policy will be the one preferred by the *median* voter, rather than the average voter or the largest number of voters. We can imagine a situation, for instance, in which three voters want zero spending on the military, three voters want to spend 50 percent of the budget, and only one wants to spend 20 percent. Median-voter theorem says that military spending will end up being 20 percent of the budget (which is the middle ground), even though only one voter actually preferred that solution.

Of course, real elections aren't this simple. Many policy issues are not one-dimensional. (You may care about the level of military spending but also how that money gets spent—for example, whether on fighter jets versus higher salaries for the troops.) Also, voters usually care about more than just one policy issue. Nonetheless, the median-voter theorem offers a powerful explanation for the observation that candidates in a two-party system often take similar policy positions, regardless of their political party. It also casts light on why we often see presidential candidates change their positions over the course of a campaign. They may advocate relatively extreme positions during party primary elections, and then adopt more moderate positions in the general election. (In the primary, the goal is to appeal to the median *of voters in their own party*. In the general election, they want to appeal to the median *of all voters*.)

The elusive perfect voting system

LO 22.2 List the characteristics of an "ideal" voting system, and assess which criteria are met by real systems.

Now, let's get more realistic. What happens if voters care about more than one policy (say, military policy and the budget deficit), or if they have more than two candidates to consider? Once voting becomes more complicated, the way in which votes are cast becomes important.

How do we take the preferences of all voters and add them up in a fair and consistent way, so that the opinion held by the most voters carries the day? Imagine that voters were directly voting on the issues, rather than for a candidate. In his book *Social Choice and Individual Values,* economist Kenneth Arrow proposed four criteria for an "ideal" voting system:

1. **Unanimity.** If everyone in the group prefers option X to option Y, then X beats Y. In other words, if every voter would rather spend more on education than on national parks, then the ideal voting system would be structured so that education spending wins.

2. **No dictator.** There is no person who has the power to single-handedly enact his or her own preferences. A voting system would not be ideal if someone has the power to put all funds into national parks, even if most would rather spend the money on schools.

3. **Transitivity.** If option X beats Y, and Y beats Z, then transitivity says that X also beats Z. In other words, if voters would rather spend on schools than parks, and they would rather spend on parks than alternative energy, then any voting system that could result in alternative energy winning out over schools would not be considered ideal.

4. **Independence of irrelevant alternatives.** If a group is voting on option X versus option Y, this decision should not depend on any information or preference about another unconnected option, Z. In other words, whether or not spending on alternative energy also happens to be an option shouldn't affect whether voters prefer spending on schools versus parks.

These all sound reasonable enough. You might think it should be straightforward enough to create a voting system that meets these four criteria. To see why it isn't, let's look at how a couple of existing voting systems measure up.

First-past-the-post. In most elections in the United States (and in many other countries) the voting system is simple: All candidates go up against each other at once; each voter can choose one and only one of them; and the candidate who receives the most votes wins. This voting system is often referred to as *first-past-the-post,* or *plurality voting.*

First-past-the-post has merits, notably simplicity. Voters have to think about only one thing—which candidate is their favorite—and then check the box next to that candidate's name. But plurality voting is not an ideal system: It fails the "independence of irrelevant alternatives" criterion, also known as the "third-party problem." In most national elections in the United States, the major candidates represent the two major parties: the Republican Party and the Democratic Party. Every once in a while, which of them wins depends on whether an additional candidate from a minor "third party" is also on the ballot.

Consider the 2000 presidential election between Governor George W. Bush and Vice President Al Gore. Consumer advocate Ralph Nader also ran, as the candidate of the Green Party. In total, Nader received less than 3 percent of the vote, yet many commentators believe Nader's presence on the ballot swung the election for Bush over Gore in a tight race.

FIGURE 22-2

The third-party-candidate problem

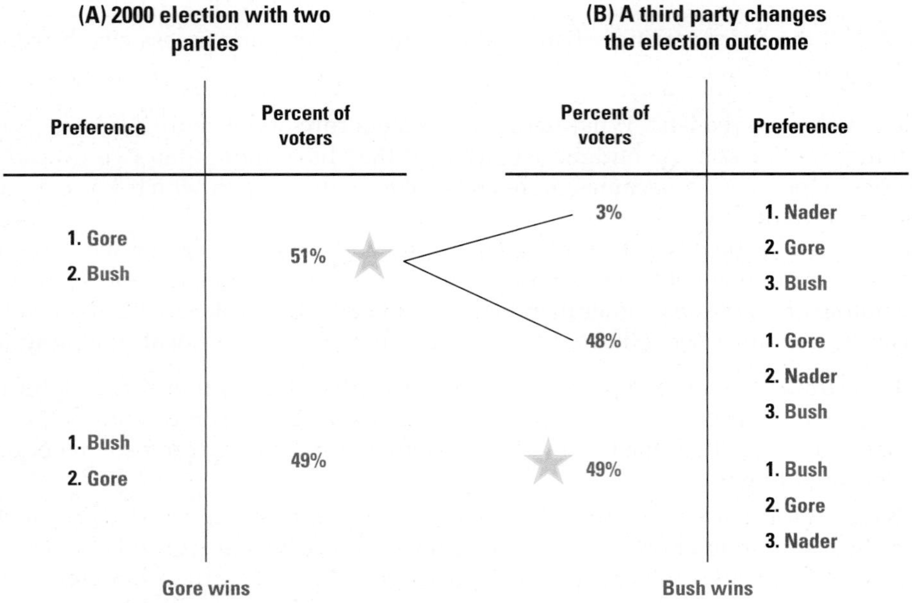

(A) 2000 election with two parties		(B) A third party changes the election outcome	
Preference	**Percent of voters**	**Percent of voters**	**Preference**
1. Gore 2. Bush	51% ⭐	3%	1. Nader 2. Gore 3. Bush
		48%	1. Gore 2. Nader 3. Bush
1. Bush 2. Gore	49%	⭐ 49%	1. Bush 2. Gore 3. Nader

Gore wins

With only two parties in the election, Gore is the first preference of a larger share of voters than Bush. This means that Gore wins the election.

Bush wins

If Nader enters the race, some of the people who previously voted for Gore switch their votes. Although voters' preferences between Gore and Bush are the same, Bush now is the first preference of the largest share of voters, and wins the election.

It turned out that the election hinged on the workings of the Electoral College system, and Florida was the deciding state in that election: Whoever won the popular vote in Florida won the presidency. Panel A of Figure 22-2 shows a theoretical distribution of voters' preferences between the two major-party candidates in Florida. If the choice were between only these two, our theoretical figures show that Gore would win Florida and the election 51 percent to 49 percent.

What happens when we add Nader into the mix, in panel B? Notice that Nader's presence doesn't change any voters' preferences between Bush and Gore. Any Floridian who wanted Bush over Gore or vice versa still feels the same way. But because in this example the 3 percent of voters who now vote for Nader would have favored Gore, the effect is that Bush now wins Florida, and the election, by 49 percent to 48 percent. The addition of an "irrelevant alternative"—Nader—flips the outcome of the election. Plurality voting fails one of the ideal voting-system criteria.

Condorcet paradox. How might we avoid the third-party problem? One possible answer could be to use a system called *pair-wise majority voting*. It gets its name because options are taken in pairs, and the majority vote wins. When all options have been put to a "head-to-head" match between a pair of opponents, you might expect the most popular option to win. Likewise, we might expect the best tennis player to win a tournament consisting of a series of head-to-head matches.

To see how this might work, imagine that in the 2000 election voters had first been asked to choose between Bush and Nader. It turns out that more voters would prefer Bush to be president, so Bush wins round one. He then goes on to face Gore in round

FIGURE 22-3

Condorcet voting paradox

(A) Preferences of 3 city council members

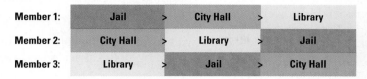

This table shows the ordered preferences of three city council members who are choosing among three different projects on which to spend the city's construction budget.

Member 1:	Jail	>	City Hall	>	Library
Member 2:	City Hall	>	Library	>	Jail
Member 3:	Library	>	Jail	>	City Hall

(B) Election outcomes depend on the order in which options are considered

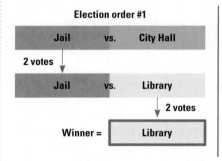
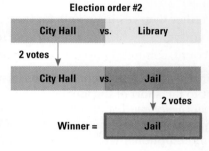
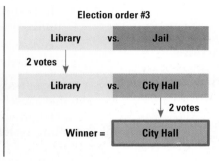

When pairs of the three construction options are considered in different orders, the ultimate outcome of the vote changes. This chart shows that any of the three buildings can be chosen depending on the order of votes. As a result, the person who "sets the agenda" by choosing the order in which options are considered has the power to affect the outcome.

two. More voters prefer Gore, so Gore becomes president. This result holds true regardless of the order of the vote. Gore would defeat both Bush and Nader in any round in which they were pitted against each other.

However, it turns out that this system fails another of our criteria—transitivity. To see why, imagine a city council with three members, voting on how to spend the city's construction budget for public buildings. The council has three choices: a new jail, a new city hall, or a new library. Each council member has his or her own order of preference, as shown in panel A of Figure 22-3.

If the council members took a simple vote, the result would be a three-way tie. Suppose that they decide to use pair-wise majority voting to narrow their choices. They decide to vote first on the jail versus the city hall. As shown in panel B of Figure 22-3, the jail wins this matchup, with two votes to one for the city hall. As the winner of the first round, the jail goes up against the library, and loses. Therefore, the council decides to build the library. Tie broken, right?

Not so fast. What if the council changed the order in which they voted on each pair? For instance, suppose they vote on the city hall versus the library first, and then the library versus the jail. In this case, the jail beats the library, and ends up as the overall winner. In fact, if they started with library versus jail, and then jail versus city hall, the city hall would win. In other words, it's possible for any of the three building plans to be chosen, depending on the order in which they vote on the pairs. Even though each individual's preferences are transitive, this method of aggregating the group's preferences is not transitive. (Remember that transitivity means that if an option X is preferred to another option Y, and Y to a third option Z, then X must be preferred to Z.) This is called the **Condorcet paradox**.

Condorcet paradox a situation in which the preferences of each individual member of a group are transitive, but the collective preferences of the group are not

When voting systems fall short of the ideal by violating the principle of transitivity, the power to set the agenda is sometimes crucial in shaping the final outcomes. The person who decides on the order in which issues are brought to a vote for the city council, for example, wields considerable power.

Arrow's impossibility theorem. We've looked at two ways of holding elections. There are many more possible systems, devised over the years by political scientists, social scientists, and economists. Here are several, for example:

- Variations on first-past-the-post, such as holding a runoff between the top two candidates.
- "Instant-runoff" systems, in which voters rank all of the candidates by *order* of preference rather than casting a vote for their single most preferred candidate.
- "Approval voting," in which voters can vote for multiple candidates.
- The Borda count, commonly used to rank sports teams in national polls.

We won't go into detail about each. Each has its merits, but each also has some problem that causes it to fall short of the ideal.

In fact, in *Social Choice and Individual Values,* economist Kenneth Arrow proved that no voting system can aggregate the preferences of voters (assuming they are choosing among three or more options) while meeting all of the criteria described at the beginning of this section. This idea is called **Arrow's impossibility theorem**. Although the proof of Arrow's theorem is well beyond the scope of this book, his takeaway message is worth remembering: No voting process is perfect.

Arrow's impossibility theorem a theorem showing that no voting system can aggregate the preferences of voters over three or more options while satisfying the criteria of an ideal voting system

Political participation and the myth of the "rational voter"

LO 22.3 Discuss problems with the idea of the "rational voter," and define the idea of rational ignorance.

So far, we've assumed that voters are rational and fully informed. What if they're not?

Politicians do not behave as if they believe most voters are influenced only by policy issues. Instead, politicians often use tactics that have little to do with policy positions—handshaking, baby-kissing, mudslinging, eating food at state fairs, and so on. Research demonstrates that elections can be swayed by factors other than the rational policy considerations of well-informed voters. See the Real Life box "Face value—May the best-looking politician win" for more about these factors.

REAL LIFE

Face value—May the best-looking politician win

The opening debate of the 1960 election was the first presidential debate ever to be aired on television. Before then, debates had been broadcast only on radio. One of the candidates, Senator John F. Kennedy, understood the difference. He arrived looking tanned, fresh, and well rested. His opponent, Vice President Richard Nixon, did not. Nixon was out campaigning until just hours before the debate. He arrived tired and unshaven, refused the attention of make-up artists, and went on the air looking pale, sweaty, and sporting a five o'clock shadow. Supposedly, his own mother called him after the debate to ask if he was sick.

This dramatic difference in appearance had a remarkable influence on voters: Those who had watched the debate on television overwhelmingly reported that Kennedy had won the debate. Those who listened on the radio—and therefore, only heard the candidates but didn't see them—thought Nixon carried the day. The television opinion won out, and shortly after the debates, John F. Kennedy pulled ahead in polling and eventually won the election.

If voters were rational and based their voting decisions purely on the policy statements of the candidates, these results would be hard to explain. No one seriously thought that Nixon was too sick to function as president; nor is a tan usually considered to be a meaningful indicator of political ability. But looks are an important part of electoral politics.

This finding has been backed up by formal studies around the world. In a study of Australian elections, attractive candidates consistently did about 1.5 to 2 percent better in the vote than plainer-looking competitors. Studies of Finnish national elections and German state-level elections found similar results.

Why does physical appearance influence voters? One explanation is the *halo effect*. The halo effect is a psychological bias in which the perception of one trait in a person is influenced by the perception of their other traits. This means, for instance, that voters might assume that more-attractive candidates are also more intelligent or more competent.

Research has found appearance to be more influential in "low information" elections, in which voters know little about the candidates. The halo effect fades as voters gain more substantive information about the person they are evaluating.

Sources: http://people.anu.edu.au/andrew.leigh/pdf/BeautifulPoliticians.pdf; http://webscript.princeton.edu/~tlab/wp-content/publications/Todorov_Science2005.pdf; http://www.ifo.de/portal/page/portal/DocBase_Content/WP/WP-CESifo_Working_Papers/wp-cesifo-2007/wp-cesifo-2007-05/cesifo1_wp2002.pdf.

Let's not be too hard on voters for not being fully informed. After all, it takes time to learn about the issues and the candidates, and that time could be spent doing something else. The trade-off may simply not be worth it. Economists call this idea **rational ignorance**. It means choosing to remain ignorant when the opportunity costs of gathering information outweigh the benefits. We saw in the "Public Goods and Common Resources" chapter that what is individually rational is not necessarily socially optimal. If we think of good governance as a public good created by well-informed voters, we can predict that it will be undersupplied.

rational ignorance choosing to remain ignorant when the opportunity costs of gathering information outweigh the benefits

Even voting *itself* is not costless. The time you spend getting to a polling place, waiting in line, and marking your ballot could be spent on other things. What are the benefits of voting that outweigh these opportunity costs? The most obvious answer is to influence the outcome of the election and have your preferences represented in government. However, the odds of one vote actually making the difference in any given election are extremely low. In all of the U.S. congressional elections in the past 100 years, only one has been decided by one vote. In over 40,000 elections for state legislators, with 1 billion votes cast, only seven have been decided by a single vote. In the end, only 1 out of 100,000 votes cast in U.S. elections was pivotal in changing the outcome of an election. In other words, your vote has a 99.999 percent chance of being pointless. Would a rational person find a better use for his time?

Research has shown that voters are, indeed, more likely to turn out in elections with small electorates and when the election is likely to be very competitive. These results suggest that the likelihood of casting a pivotal vote may influence the choice to show up to vote. However, by looking at voting only in terms of time costs and likelihood of casting the pivotal ballot, we may be missing the point. Perhaps voters gain "expressive benefits" from voting. In other words, they get utility from participating in a civic event, regardless of whether their votes are likely to be decisive. Alternatively, voters may altruistically decide to contribute to the democratic process by voting, even when it is not personally beneficial to do so.

Another theory suggests that people may vote partly in response to social pressure to "do their duty" as citizens. For example, when Switzerland—which has famously high levels of voting—started allowing people to mail in their ballots rather than go to a polling place, voting decreased in small towns. On the face of it, this is a baffling result. Mail-in ballots, after all, represent a significant reduction in the time costs associated with voting. One explanation is that people in small Swiss communities went out to vote because they wanted to be seen to be carrying out their civic duty. Once voting wasn't visible to the rest of the community, people had less incentive to do it at all.

✓ CONCEPT CHECK

- ❏ Can the median-voter theorem be applied to multidimensional policy questions? **[LO 22.1]**
- ❏ What does it mean for a voting system to satisfy the independence of irrelevant alternatives? **[LO 22.2]**
- ❏ Why might it be rational for voters to remain uninformed? **[LO 22.3]**

The Economics of Policy-Making

Now that we've looked at who gets elected, we'll turn to how policies get made. In this section we'll see why a minority of voters who feel strongly about an issue can often win out over a larger group with a different opinion. We'll also look at how the interests and incentives of policy-makers help predict their behavior.

Diffuse costs, concentrated benefits

LO 22.4 Explain the persistence of policies that provide concentrated benefits to a few while imposing diffuse costs on the majority.

In the "Public Goods and Common Resources" chapter, we saw that markets won't necessarily allocate public goods like national parks and police protection efficiently. The problem is that people are often reluctant to voluntarily pay for goods and services that provide benefits for everyone, even for those who don't pay. This is the "free-rider" problem, and it happens when people think, "Why pay if I don't have to?" If enough people think like that, valuable goods and services are under-supplied because everyone hopes that someone else will pay for them.

The same idea can apply to political advocacy and engagement. Inefficiencies can happen when people think, "Why get personally involved if I can spare myself the hassle but still benefit from the solutions that others create?" The problem is that the best ideas might not win out if lots of people fail to lend their support.

collective-action problem a situation in which a group of people stands to gain from an action that it is not rational for any of the members to undertake individually

We refer to situations in which individuals need to act collectively to reach solutions that will make everyone better off as **collective-action problems**. In these situations, a group of people stand to gain from an action that is not rational for any of the members to undertake individually.

However, engaging in collective action has costs. It takes time and money to organize a group or a campaign and to get the attention of lots of busy people. As a rule, the larger the group that needs to be organized, the more difficult and costly it is to coordinate successful collective action. Even if the total benefit to coordinating is big, each individual member may stand to gain only a small amount.

Combining these two ideas, we find that organizing larger groups often involves higher costs and lower benefits per person. The likelihood of successful collective action can therefore be lower for large groups. This leads to an interesting prediction: If two groups disagree about a policy, a smaller group that experiences higher benefits per person can be the one more likely to get its way.

Imagine, for instance, there is a national park where private companies run tour buses. Many people who visit the park find the tour buses to be disruptive and also harmful to the wildlife. Some organize a campaign to tighten regulations on tours in the park. Alarmed by this proposal, the tour-bus companies work together to contest the proposed new regulations. Whichever group is more effective in organizing and influencing the opinion of park management will get its way.

We can imagine that there are only a few owners of tour-bus companies. It will be easy for them to coordinate. We can also imagine that each one gains a lot from unrestricted use of the park. Thus, they will all be willing to devote a lot of resources to fighting the proposals. Even if restricting bus use would deliver higher *total* benefits to the many people who visit the park occasionally, those benefits are much lower per person. The park visitors may be willing to sign a petition or write an e-mail; but most will not feel strongly enough to fight as determinedly as the tour-bus operators. The benefits of pro-bus policy are *concentrated* for tour-bus company owners. The costs of anti-bus policy are *diffuse* for private park users. From this difference, we can predict that the tour-bus owners will likely get their way.

The theory that groups with concentrated benefits tend to win out in policy battles over those with diffuse costs has many applications. Economists use it to explain the persistence of policies that don't appear to be in the interest of the majority of voters. For instance, observers are sometimes puzzled by the staying power of large farm subsidies and trade protections for agricultural goods. These policies push up the costs of food and taxes for the majority of voters. Why don't voters elect officials who will end these policies?

One theory is that the typical voter experiences only small costs—a few extra cents in the price of milk and sugar, a few dollars in taxes. At the same time, a small number of commercial farms and agricultural businesses experience high benefits. The members of the small group find it easier and individually worthwhile to organize themselves for lobbying and public relations efforts to capture those large benefits. Organizing a whole nation of voters for a comparable effort to fight the small increase in the price of groceries would be extremely difficult.

Corruption and rent-seeking

LO 22.5 Explain why corruption and rent-seeking can persist in a democratic system.

An economic analysis of politics needs to account for the fact that policy-makers have their own interests, biases, and priorities. In other words, they have their own *wants and constraints*. Of course, we would like to think that all policy-makers *want* to do what their best judgment tells them is in the public good. But some may, instead, *want* to promote their own personal gain, or that of their friends and family. In that case, they will be constrained only by the capacity of their opponents and of watchdog organizations to find out what they are doing and make voters care about it. At its extreme, the use of the powers of government by public officials to achieve personal gains is *corruption*.

More generally, government can create waste and inefficiency by contributing to **rent-seeking**. Rent-seeking is the act of pursuing privileges that increase the surplus

rent-seeking the act of pursuing privileges that increase the surplus of a person or group without increasing total surplus of a person or group without increasing total surplus. Often, this activity involves lobbying by groups that receive exclusive benefits or contracts to keep others from getting access; on the flip side, it can involve lobbying by those who don't yet have access to such benefits, but want to have it. Some lobbying shapes trade regulations—say, domestic-steel producers trying to keep imports out. Others shape licensing policy—for instance, protecting doctors who want to strictly limit who gets to call themselves a doctor. Big campaign contributions usually come alongside the lobbying efforts, all in an attempt to get extra clout for groups that benefit from particular regulations and licenses. Such rent-seeking and lobbying are perfectly legal, but can be wasteful.

Why doesn't the process of electing officials prevent rent-seeking and corruption? If a politician starts making policies that hurt his constituents or promote himself at their expense, why doesn't he get kicked out of office by angry voters in the next election? Why don't corrupt bureaucrats always get fired? The reality is that it is costly to acquire information about what public officials are and should be doing. What voter has time to study public expenditures looking for corrupt behavior? How many voters care enough to analyze whether a particular firm wins a government contract because it is the most qualified or because it is owned by the mayor's buddy?

Of course, political opponents have every incentive to dig up dirt on incumbents before an election, and to inform voters about anything bad they find. But such revelations can get lost in the noise of campaigning. Also, voters might not be sure that the opponents will end up being more trustworthy than the incumbents. The news media—blogs, television, radio, newspapers—can play an important role in uncovering corruption. But even in a relatively free society, the media may face mixed incentives: Reporters rely to some extent on public officials' willingness to give them information about what's happening in government. If reporters blow the whistle on minor offenses, they may suddenly find that their sources are no longer so friendly.

Bureaucratic capture is a specific avenue through which corruption and rent-seeking can occur. This involves filling government positions with people who have close ties to the group they are supposed to regulate. Of course, there are sensible reasons for appointing people with practical experience in a certain area of policy. But having close ties between regulators and those they are regulating can introduce biases or personal sympathies. In the aftermath of the 2008 financial crisis, for instance, some questioned the effectiveness of the Securities and Exchange Commission (SEC)'s supervision of capital markets. Critics accused the SEC of failing to enforce regulations that might have mitigated the crisis. They say this was because the SEC was staffed by people with close ties to the financial industry.

Corruption goes one step further than the types of rent-seeking described above. Since it is illegal, corruption is by nature hidden. As a result, it can be difficult to find out how much of it really goes on, and what methods are most effective at reducing it. This is why attempts to reform government actions believed to be corrupt center on transparency. The more the public knows about the actions of government, the theory goes, the more they will be able to see and oust corrupt actions and politicians. The issues surrounding corruption may go beyond transparency, though. In the Real Life box "Monitoring corruption in Indonesia," we discuss a unique attempt at measuring and reducing corruption.

REAL LIFE

Monitoring corruption in Indonesia

For decades, Indonesia was ruled by Suharto, a dictator who presided over an incredibly corrupt political regime. Transparency International, an international watchdog organization, cited Suharto as the most corrupt ruler of the 20th century. Even though he was overthrown in 1998, a deep tradition of corruption still exists in Indonesia at all levels of government. As the world's fourth most populous country seeks to improve its democratic system and tackle poverty, ensuring that government uses public funds for their intended purpose is a pressing question.

The Kecamatan Development Program (KDP) is a large public works program in Indonesia. It provides money to rural villages, which then decide how to spend the money. Often, villages choose to pave dirt roads, but road-building projects are regarded as especially prone to corruption. How might misuse of funds be minimized so that villages can put every dollar to productive use? One possibility is to make projects subject to audits by government officials. Another is to force local planners to account for their spending at open community meetings. Which, if either, method will more successfully reduce corruption?

Economist Ben Olken attempted to answer this question. His idea was to get an objective estimate of what a road-paving project *should* cost. He then would compare that cost to what was actually spent. The comparison would give him a reasonable measure of the degree of waste and corruption. Olken employed a team of engineers to estimate the true cost of paving a road in different villages. Then, he randomly selected villages that were building roads to receive different types of project oversight: Some were told they would be audited; others participated in efforts to increase involvement in community meetings; and others had no oversight.

Olken found that over a quarter of funds went missing, but that telling villages that they would be subject to a government audit reduced missing amounts by almost a third. Since the audits cost less than the average reduction in missing funds, Olken found that the effort of auditing every single project would be cost effective.

Increasing community involvement, on the other hand, had less effect on corruption. The program *was* successful at getting more villagers to attend community meetings. But more involvement had no average impact on overall levels of missing funds. There was one specific and interesting exception. The only area of spending where misuse of funds was reduced by increased community involvement was labor costs. This was a factor that villagers, as the people being employed to work on roads, had the most direct interest in controlling. Otherwise, citizens appeared to have little leverage over their leaders to make them toe the line.

Sources: Ben Olken (2007), "Monitoring Corruption: Evidence from a Field Experiment in Indonesia," *Journal of Political Economy* 115 (2): 200–249; http://news.bbc.co.uk/2/hi/3567745.stm; http://www.nytimes.com/2008/01/28/world/asia/28suharto.html?pagewanted=1.

The system matters: How political structure affects outcomes

During the eighteenth century, the Polish legislature used the *liberum veto* (Latin for "I freely forbid"). At any time, a member of parliament had the right to shout *Nie pozwala!* ("I do not allow"). This move forced an end to the current session and voided any legislation that had been passed. The intent was to make sure that there was complete consensus about new laws.

As you might expect, the system instead often led to chaos. Eventually, foreign powers took advantage of this system and bribed Polish legislators to oppose unwanted legislation with a cry of *Nie pozwala*, grinding the Polish political system to a halt. Not surprisingly, the *liberum veto* went out of fashion. Still, the lesson remains relevant: The rules of the game can have a big effect on outcomes.

There are too many aspects of political structure to discuss all of them here. (We'll leave that to political science professors.) There are, though, three worth singling out. These three have a particularly big impact on how voters' preferences are translated into policy choices.

Number of political parties. The first is the number of viable political parties. Few countries—with the exception of single-party dictatorships—have explicit requirements about the number of parties. In general, first-past-the-post voting, like that used in the U.S., leads to a two-party system. Since candidates have to obtain a plurality of votes to win an election, a third party could consistently win 20 percent of the votes and still win zero elections. As a result, if smaller parties want to have a say in policy-making, they have an incentive to consolidate with larger ones. Doing so will increase their chance of gaining enough vote share to win elections and have a say in policy-making.

In contrast, many countries use a *proportional-representation* system. In such systems, a party that receives 20 percent of the votes nationwide will receive about 20 percent of the seats in the legislature. Under such a system, small parties can carve out niches. From these, they are able to influence policy-making by forming coalitions with others after being elected.

Compared to proportional-representation systems, two-party systems are thought to lead to more centrist politics. (Remember the median-voter theorem.) In addition, since both parties have to represent large portions of the population, they sometimes lead to unwieldy combinations of policies within one platform. For instance, supporters of lower government spending often vote Republican, but these voters may have a wide range of opinions about social issues. As a result, people with different policy preferences may have to make compromises when voting. (If, for instance, you support both low taxes and gay marriage, you might have to decide which of those issues is more important to you when choosing which party will get your vote.)

Proportional-representation systems, on the other hand, are thought to bring more diverse views into the policy process, and offer a wider variety of platforms among which voters can choose. One criticism of this system, however, is that small extremist parties can wield disproportionate power. When a big party doesn't get an outright majority, it has to ask small parties to join with it in a governing coalition in order to form a majority. In bargaining for political support, the smaller party will often insist that some of its policies be enacted, even if those policies don't represent the preferences of most people.

Term limits. A second feature of political structure that's worth mentioning is *term limits.* Term limits prevent officials from holding office for longer than a certain amount of time. For instance, U.S. presidents can't hold office for more than two consecutive terms. These laws are typically thought to discourage corruption by ensuring that one person isn't allowed to hold onto power for too long.

However, some have speculated that the opposite might be true under certain circumstances. Politicians who know they will be out of office at the end of their term, regardless of their behavior, have less of an incentive for good behavior.

In Brazil, for example, mayors are limited to two terms. While first-term mayors who are up for reelection have an interest to stay relatively clean, mayors who know they will be out of office at the end of their term regardless of their behavior have less of an incentive to do so. A recent study by two economists found that misappropriation of funds was 27 percent lower among mayors who had to face reelection than among second-termers. If this is right, then getting rid of term limits could reduce losses due to corruption by $160 million, equal to about half of the amount spent on *Bolsa Familia,* Brazil's largest social program to help poor families.

Increased enfranchisement. The final important part of political structure comes from *enfranchisement,* or who has the right to vote. In the past, voting systems in most countries required that you be both male and hold property in order to vote. Historically, controlling who was able to vote was an important tool for those wanted to keep other groups out of power, especially women, ethnic and religious minorities, and the poor. Even when the right to vote is universal, poll taxes, literacy requirements, or other such

3. Three friends are trying to decide where to go to dinner. There are four restaurants nearby: Thai, Italian, Tex-Mex, and sushi. Assume the friends have the following preferences: **[LO 22.2]**

   Gabe: Thai > Italian > Sushi > Tex-Mex

   Arnold: Italian > Tex-Mex > Sushi > Thai

   Julie: Sushi > Tex-Mex > Thai > Italian

   a. The friends decide to hold a majority vote that pits the Thai place against the Italian; the winner of that vote against the Tex-Mex; and then the next winner against the sushi. Which restaurant do they end up going to?
   b. If they vote on sushi versus Tex-Mex, the winner against Italian, and then the winner against Thai, which restaurant will they choose?
   c. Which of the criteria for an ideal voting system is violated in this example?

4. In a runoff election, if no candidate receives a majority of votes in the first round of voting, the top two candidates face each other in a second round. Let's say that people voting on Candidates A, B, C, and D in a runoff election have the following preferences. **[LO 22.2]**

   12 voters: A > B > C > D

   8 voters: C > B > D > A

   10 voters: D > B > C > A

   4 voters: B > D > A > C

   a. Does anyone receive an outright majority in the first round? If so, which candidate? If not, which two candidates move on to the second round, and which of them wins?
   b. Suppose Candidate A drops out of the race. Does any candidate now receive an outright majority in the first round? If so, which candidate? If not, which two candidates move on to the second round, and which of them wins?
   c. Does this situation violate the independence of irrelevant alternatives?

5. According to the rational voter theory, will the following increase or decrease voter turnout? **[LO 22.3]**
   a. Electronic voting machines make the process of casting a ballot faster and less complicated.
   b. 24-hour news networks emphasize how close they expect the election to be, with only a few thousand votes deciding the outcome.

   c. The number of polling stations increases.
   d. Pollsters predict a landslide victory for the incumbent candidate a few days before the election.

6. Determine whether each of the following represents rational ignorance. **[LO 22.3]**
   a. Doug doesn't know the return on his retirement account in the last quarter or the types of investments that comprise the account.
   b. Sally doesn't know about a new provision in nuclear energy regulation, which is decided by a national panel overseen by nuclear physicists.
   c. Jim doesn't know whether to support new requirements for licensing among city contractors.
   d. Tom doesn't know the average price of a parking ticket, despite parking on the street every day.

7. For each of the following, state who benefits and who bears the costs, and whether the costs and benefits are concentrated or diffuse. Based on this assessment, predict which side is likely to get its way. **[LO 22.4]**
   a. A rubber producer lobbies the government to prohibit the import of cheaper foreign rubber, driving up the cost of consumer goods.
   b. The government increases federal gas taxes by 1 cent per gallon to finance building high-speed train routes between major East Coast cities.

8. For each of the following conditions, determine whether a collective-action problem exists. **[LO 22.4]**
   a. Diffuse benefits, diffuse costs.
   b. Diffuse benefits, concentrated costs.
   c. Concentrated benefits, diffuse costs.
   d. Concentrated benefits, concentrated costs.

9. Decide which of these labels best fits each of the following situations: rent-seeking, corruption, or bureaucratic capture. (If more than one is potentially applicable, pick the one that is the most narrowly tailored to the scenario.) **[LO 22.5]**
   a. A contract manager at a government department is bribed to ensure that his friend's company gets a construction contract even though it was not the lowest bidder.
   b. A senior-citizens group lobbies the city government to spend more on special public-transit shuttles for the elderly.

c. The president appoints a former head of an investment bank to the Securities and Exchange Commission (which oversees capital markets and enforces financial regulations).

d. The head of a local teachers' union offers support to a political candidate in exchange for her promise to spend more of the state budget on teacher salaries.

10. Determine whether each of the following shifts is likely to increase or decrease the prevalence of rent-seeking. **[LO 22.5]**

a. The spread of smartphones enables more widespread access to information.

b. Judges strike down a law that forces politicians to report when they receive a gift worth over $500.

c. Congress passes a law requiring lobbyists to spend at least two years in another unrelated position before getting hired in government to regulate the industries they were advocating for as lobbyists.

Chapter Sources

http://www.washingtonpost.com/wp-dyn/content/article/2007/03/31/AR2007033101040.html

http://grad.econ.ubc.ca/fujiwara/jmp.pdf

http://www.fec.gov/pubrec/fe2008/2008presgeresults.pdf

http://www.nytimes.com/2005/11/06/magazine/06freak.html?pagewanted=1

http://www.econ.upf.edu/~funk/papers/Signalling_Manuscript.pdf

http://citeseerx.ist.psu.edu/viewdoc/download?doi=10.1.1.65.3703&rep=rep1&type=pdf

http://press-pubs.uchicago.edu/founders/documents/v1ch13s7.html

http://www.econ.berkeley.edu/~ffinan/Finan_Termlimits.pdf

http://www.britannica.com/EBchecked/topic/339388/liberum-veto

http://www.economist.com/blogs/freeexchange/2011/09/climate-policy

Public Policy and Choice Architecture

Chapter

23

LEARNING OBJECTIVES

LO 23.1 Define choice architecture, and explain how nudges can influence individual decision making.

LO 23.2 List and explain several ways in which human decision making does not conform to the model of full information and rational choices.

LO 23.3 Explain how demand for commitment devices can be rational.

LO 23.4 Describe how default rules affect people's choices and the implications for policy.

LO 23.5 Describe how framing affects the way people process information and its implications for policy.

SAVING MORE FOR TOMORROW

Many Americans save little for retirement outside of the "forced" savings of contributions to Social Security paid through payroll taxes. Taken alone, this fact isn't necessarily puzzling; maybe most people don't want to save more than that. What makes it strange, though, is that most Americans *say* that they want to be saving more.

If people want to save more, why don't they just do it? Typically, economists assume that people make rational, purposeful decisions about saving. They save up when income is high and spend down savings when income is low or gone, such as in retirement. Based on the idea of revealed preference, economists infer that whatever choices people are making must be "right" for them and their situations in life. If someone occasionally doesn't save as much as planned one month, we assume that he or she will simply adjust to put a little more in the bank in the future. Over the long term, we expect to see people's actions matching up with their intentions.

But suppose that some people are consistently making mistakes by letting current temptations get in the way of long-term saving goals. They're not just miscalculating for a month here and there, but are saving much less than they'd like to over years and years. They may find themselves with less than they want to have in the bank to support their kids' education or to live on in retirement. Can anything be done, in their moments of reflection and planning, to help them make decisions that they would feel better about? Economists Shlomo Benartzi and Richard Thaler designed a program to help people overcome their own limitations and save more.

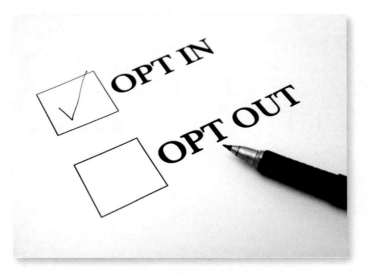

This approach, called Save More Tomorrow (or SMarT™), offers employees the option to commit a fraction of future pay raises to a tax-free retirement savings account. Benartzi and Thaler realized that most of us dislike the feeling of giving up what we already have—such as having to accept a cut in our current pay in order to save more. By tying increases in saving to *future* pay raises, SMarT helps people save without feeling they are "giving up" something in order to save more. (To be as flexible as possible, the program allows people to change their minds later on and, if desired, back out of their saving commitments, if they want, and lower their savings rate back down.)

If people are already making optimal choices about saving, then a program like SMarT will have no effect. But it turns out that people who participated in SMarT almost quadrupled their savings rate over a few years. That rate went from 3.5 percent of income to 13.6 percent. This increase suggests that people really *were* saving less than they wanted to, but needed a little nudge to get them on track. SMarT is designed to help employees overcome at least two different types of mental barriers to saving.

First, SMarT takes advantage of a *status-quo bias:* We often are reluctant to make active decisions to change something, even if it is fairly easy to do so. SMarT makes it so that *no action* leads to an increase in future savings. If you want to change your mind, you can do so easily, but it turns out that making saving the default option makes people more likely to go through with it.

Second, SMarT takes advantage of the fact that many people are unwilling to forgo current consumption to save now, but *are* willing to cut back future consumption to save for the even farther-off future. Why? Saving more right now means giving up things that are immediately tempting to us. Saving later doesn't feel as painful right now, so we are more willing to agree to do it.

The SMarT program shows that simply changing the way we present options can affect people's behavior and help them overcome mental biases and avoid regret. Thaler and his collaborator Cass Sunstein have come up with a term for this idea: choice architecture. When we think critically about how to design the environment in which people make choices, we are engaging in *choice architecture.* In their book *Nudge: Improving Decisions About Health, Wealth, and Happiness,* Thaler and Sunstein promote the idea that the structure of policies and products affects the outcomes of individuals' decisions. They argue that it is possible to design policies and products in a way that gently "nudges" people toward choices that will make them happier in the long run. Thaler and Sunstein don't want to dictate what people should do. Instead, they want to make it easier to make better choices, while leaving people free to make those choices themselves.

In this chapter, we'll describe how choice architecture works. We'll start by describing some of the psychological biases that can shape economic choices. Then we'll explore how policy-makers, private companies, and choice architects of all sorts are putting the ideas into action to help guide people toward decisions that they say they want to make.

Choice Architecture and Nudges

Sometimes people do things that they themselves would agree are not the right decisions. They might say they want to save money, but never get around to opening a savings account. They might agree that they'd be better off dieting, but they keep eating junk food.

We first approached this idea in the "Behavioral Economics" chapter. Here, we'll apply some of the insights of behavioral economics to see how policy-makers can design products and policies that nudge people toward making better decisions.

Why nudge?

LO 23.1 Define choice architecture, and explain how nudges can influence individual decision making.

A growing pile of evidence indicates that people's decisions can be influenced by how options are presented to them. **Choice architecture**—the organization of the context and process in which people make decisions—can alter actual decisions and thus the ultimate outcomes. Choice architecture focuses on such factors as the timing of choices and how different options are described.

choice architecture the organization of the context and process in which people make decisions

"Choice architects" are people who are in a position to shape the decision-making environment. Because they can influence the outcomes of people's choices, we have to ask how they ought to exercise this influence. As Uncle Ben told Peter Parker (aka Spiderman), "with great power comes great responsibility." Some might say choice architects should aim to use their power as lightly as possible, by being "neutral."

On closer inspection, though, it's not clear what a neutral policy means in most situations. For instance, research shows that supermarket shoppers are more likely to purchase items placed in noticeable locations, such as at eye level on the shelf. No matter how you arrange things, some products are going to be located at eye level and others aren't. There's no such thing as "neutral" shelving. But we *can* make a choice about which items end up at eye level. This is where the power of choice architecture comes into play.

If policy can't be neutral, what should it be? For the supermarket manager, the answer is easy enough. He wants to put at eye-level items that will maximize profits. What if the choice architect has goals in mind other than maximizing profit? In that case, the decision is a tougher one: Should choice architects aim to encourage choices that *they* think will be better for society? Or should they try to push people toward things that people themselves would agree are better for them? In this chapter, we focus mainly on describing *how* policy can influence people's decisions. We leave open the question of the appropriate use of these tools.

Thaler and Sunstein use the term **nudge** to describe an implementation of choice architecture that alters people's behavior in a deliberate and predictable way without changing economic incentives much. In other words, a nudge is a gentle push in a particular direction, but anyone who wants to go in a different direction is still able to do so. The SMarT program, for example, nudges people toward higher savings, but people still have the freedom to change their minds and lower their savings rate. In the grocery store, placing an item at eye-level nudges shoppers toward selecting it, but they can still choose items from higher or lower shelves instead.

nudge an implementation of choice architecture that alters people's behavior in a deliberate and predictable way without changing economic incentives much

Nudges can sometimes accomplish public policy goals in a less expensive and coercive way than more traditional methods. Why set tough quotas, crank up taxes, or make something illegal if you can nudge people in the socially desired direction? Below, we'll see numerous examples of successful, cost-effective nudges. These help people make the choices that they would actually prefer to make for themselves. Most importantly, unlike strict rules, they still preserve freedom of choice for others who don't want to go in the direction they're being nudged in. Read the Real Life box "Committing to fertilizer" for one example of a nudge from the developing world.

REAL LIFE
Committing to fertilizer

In Western Kenya, many people make a living by growing crops. However, the soil is very poor. As a result, these subsistence farmers typically earn the equivalent of a dollar a day. By applying small amounts of fertilizer to the top of the soil, farmers can increase their harvest by 48 percent. The return on this investment is well worth the cost of the fertilizer, and farmers are well aware of these benefits. But still, 55 percent of farmers in this region have never used fertilizer. Why?

There's an obvious answer: Maybe the farmers can't afford it. This explanation has led to a traditional policy response: huge subsidies on fertilizer. Zambia, another East African country, dedicates 2 percent of its entire public budget to such subsidies.

However, economists Esther Duflo, Michael Kremer, and Jonathan Robinson wondered if there might be another explanation. When they asked the farmers, most said that they *intended* to use fertilizer, and that they earned enough at harvest time to be able to afford it. But when the time came to plant their crops, money was tight again, so they decided to forgo it. Much like people who intend to save more for retirement but find it hard to consume less now to do so, Kenyan farmers had trouble saving after the harvest to pay for fertilizer at planting time.

In response to this problem, the three economists created a nudge to help farmers follow through on their intention to use fertilizer. The nudge worked by offering farmers the chance to buy fertilizer at different times during the year. Field workers sold vouchers that let farmers pay in months when they had surpluses, with a guarantee that fertilizer would be delivered to them at the next planting season.

Sure enough, when the workers visited farmers shortly after a harvest, fertilizer purchases increased by 60 percent. The fertilizer vouchers enabled the farmers to *commit* to use fertilizer by paying for it when they had money available. Of course they could have saved the money for those three months, but without the commitment, that often didn't happen.

The evidence suggests that timing was everything. When farmers were allowed to pay for the vouchers just a few days later—as opposed to having to pay during the initial sales visit—the percentage of those who purchased fertilizer fell by over half. Farmers who were offered vouchers later in the off-season were also much less likely to buy fertilizer—even when the price was reduced by 50 percent.

The findings suggest an alternative to expensive government subsidies to increase fertilizer usage. More broadly, they also show that choice architecture—in this case, altering the *timing* of the farmers' decision about fertilizer purchases—can make a real difference even to people who are among the poorest in the world. The farmers already knew it was in their best interests to buy fertilizer. All they needed was a nudge.

Sources: Esther Duflo, Michael Kremer, and Jonathan Robinson. 2011. "Nudging Farmers to Use Fertilizer: Theory and Experimental Evidence from Kenya." *American Economic Review,* 101(6): 2350–90. DOI:10.1257/aer.101.6.2350

What is a "bad" choice?

When we talk about a "mistake" or a "bad choice" in this chapter, we're not imposing our own views about the merits of a choice in question. Instead, we're defining "mistake" from the perspective of the person doing the choosing. A mistake is a choice that the chooser later regrets.

It's worth a short side trip to consider how economists think about good and bad choices. Economics allows for the idea that people have diverse preferences. As a result, it's difficult to say what constitutes a good choice for others. For some, the frustration of sticking to a diet is worth the weight loss. For others, it might not be. As a rule, economics assumes that people weigh trade-offs and make choices that maximize their utility. In a traditional economic view (as seen in the idea of *revealed preference* described in the "Consumer Behavior" chapter), there is no such thing as a "bad" choice. That's because we assume, by definition, that people choose what is best for themselves.

Consider a person who runs up huge debts by taking out expensive loans. A psychologist might conclude that he must be a compulsive shopper with a self-control problem. But economists usually start with the assumption that his decision can be explained by his preferences. If he has a strong preference for current consumption, for example, then he is rationally maximizing his utility by taking on heavy future repayment obligations to buy more stuff now.

This traditional economic approach is at the core of this book for good reason. For one thing, it's based on a reasonable simplifying assumption: People do tend to *try* to act in their own self-interest. It also gives people the benefit of the doubt that they often know what's best for themselves, at least better than others do. However, studying behavioral economics, choice architecture, and nudges allows us to integrate some lessons from psychology into this core economic approach. That we can go beyond the simplifying assumption that people *always* make the choices that are best for themselves.

However, this leaves us in a tough spot. When people make choices that look funny to others, is it simply because they have different preferences? Or are they actually making mistakes? A behavioral economics approach suggests that it could be either. Who gets to decide what constitutes a "bad" choice? Neighbors? Parents? Policy-makers? How and when should their opinions be put into action? Answering these questions could take up entire textbooks by itself, and we don't attempt to address them here. Instead, we use "bad choice" and "mistake" only when the decision makers *themselves* would later agree that they have made a bad choice or mistake.

Mistakes people make

LO 23.2 List and explain several ways in which human decision making does not conform to the model of full information and rational choices.

Once we accept that people try to maximize their well-being but sometimes make mistakes, we start to find that those mistakes happen in common and predictable ways. Here, we consider some important categories of biases in human decision making. In the next section, we'll see more examples of how choice architects can put these insights to work.

Temptation. In the "Behavioral Economics" chapter, we talked about how people struggle with temptation and procrastination. How can we as economists and policy-makers understand people who say they want one thing—to save money, or stay on a diet, or quit smoking—but then do something else? Our economic model described temptation as sort of split-personality problem: We have one set of preferences about what to do today and another about what to do in the future.

We use the term **time inconsistency** to describe a situation in which we change our minds about what we want simply because of the timing of the decision. People's preferences about the present are inconsistent with their preferences about the future, simply because the future choices are more distant. Note that it's not time inconsistency if your preferences are different because the circumstances are different in some important

time inconsistency
a situation in which we change our minds about what we want simply because of the timing of the decision

way. For instance, if you want to eat junk food now because you're on vacation and you will start a diet next week when the vacation is over, that's not inconsistent. Time inconsistency is when you want to start your diet one week from today, but when that time comes, you want to start it in another week, and so on. In this case, your preferences changed simply because time passes. As we saw in the chapter-opening story, inconsistency is one of the common biases that the SMarT program helps to tackle.

Limited processing power. We learned in the chapter on "Political Choices" why it can be rational to choose to not be fully informed about a political issue. You would probably do a bit of comparative shopping before buying a new computer, but few people become world experts on computing technology. Is it possible that you're making the wrong decision about which machine is best for you? Sure. But is it really worth spending a whole year researching computers in order to be more sure that you're picking the exactly right model? Probably not. Think about all of the other things you could be doing during that year that are worth more to you than the risk of having a less-than-ideal computer.

Sometimes, though, our ignorance isn't so carefully considered, and the consequences of bad choices are big. We might simply get overwhelmed by the complicated information involved in a choice. For example, the question of how much you should be saving at any given time in your life to achieve a comfortable retirement is challenging to answer, even for economics professors. Psychological research shows that choices that involve processing lots of complicated information are, unsurprisingly, likely to turn out worse than those involving simple information.

Practice can make perfect, even when making hard decisions. But unfortunately, lots of important choices in life don't come with practice rounds. Familiar choices—like what to eat for dinner—are easy. They are easier than choices that we make only infrequently, such as choosing between different types of surgery or how to invest retirement funds. In part, this is because we have all eaten enough dinners to understand the utility we are likely to get from different choices. We're more likely to make mistakes with situations we face infrequently, such as how to invest our retirement funds, how different types of surgery are likely to affect us five years down the road, or which college we should go to.

This is especially true when it's not clear how to translate available information into something personally meaningful. When deciding which college to go to, you may have been bombarded with statistics and stories—average SAT scores, how many students graduate on time, professor-to-student ratios, and so on. This information was useful to you only insofar as you could translate it into a prediction for how enjoyable and productive your life as a student at that college would be. This problem gets even worse in situations where you're not sure what will ultimately matter to you. If you've never been to college before, how can you know whether you care about how big your classes will be?

Reluctance to change. People go with the flow. They tend to stick with the current situation over other options, even when it is cheap to switch. Economists call this **status-quo bias**. It is one of the common mistakes we saw in the chapter-opening story about SMarT.

In the arena of decision making, status-quo bias means that the "'default'" option—the one that will automatically take place if the chooser fails to make an active decision—has a lot of power. For an example of status-quo bias at work, consider what happens when you sign up for a free trial of an online product. Most of the time, if you don't go back and cancel, you'll be signed up for the full program automatically at the end of the free trial. Many of us plan to cancel, but then just forget and end up paying for something we didn't really want.

status-quo bias the tendency to stick with the current situation over other options, even when it is cheap to switch

An interesting twist on status-quo bias is the **endowment effect**. This is the tendency to place a higher value on something you already own simply because you own it. In a well-known experiment, psychologist Daniel Kahneman and economists Jack Knetsch and Richard Thaler doled out plain coffee mugs to one group of people. They then asked another group that didn't get mugs how much they'd be willing to pay to get one. (Everyone could see the mug and assess its quality.) They also asked students with mugs how much they'd have to be paid to give up their mugs. If the students had similar tastes on average (which is reasonable to assume, given that they were randomly split into groups), we'd expect that the values for the mugs would be roughly the same. But in the experiment, students who had been given mugs placed a higher value on them than students who hadn't—more than twice as much, in fact.

The endowment effect is related to **loss aversion**, a general tendency for people to put more effort into avoiding losses than achieving gains. Loss aversion is not to be confused with *risk aversion,* which we described in the chapter on "Time and Uncertainty." Risk aversion is about preferring certain outcomes over uncertain ones. Instead, the insight behind loss aversion is that people will typically put out more effort to avoid losing $100 than they would to gain $100.

Framing matters. Choice architects know that whether something *feels* like a loss or gain often depends on how it is *framed.* For instance, suppose you are a shopkeeper who charges a slightly higher price for credit-card transactions than for cash purchases. We could describe this in two ways: as a "discount" for paying in cash, or as a "fee" for paying with a credit card. Evidence shows that people care more about avoiding a fee than they care about getting a discount. So as a shopkeeper you can expect a greater tilt toward cash-paying when you advertise a "credit-card fee" than if you advertise an equivalent "discount" for paying cash.

There are many other situations in which people respond to the way choices are framed, even when that framing does not change the substance of the options available to them. Imagine you're deciding which of two universities to attend. University A sends you a brochure saying, "Within three months after graduation, 80 percent of our students have found jobs!" University B's brochure says, "Three months after graduation, 20 percent of our students have failed to find jobs." Which school do you want to choose?

As we're sure you noticed, universities A and B actually have identical job-placement rates—but university A clearly has a better public relations department. On a purely rational level, a reader should see that 80 percent of graduates from both schools have jobs and 20 percent don't. But our subconscious processing system interprets the information differently. We respond better to the positive framing (emphasizing the successful graduates) than to the negative (emphasizing the failures).

endowment effect the tendency of people to place more value on something simply because they own it

loss aversion the tendency for people to put more effort into avoiding losses than achieving gains

✓ CONCEPT CHECK

❒ Does a nudge force people to make a better choice? **[LO 23.1]**
❒ Explain how time inconsistency accounts for procrastination. **[LO 23.2]**
❒ What is the endowment effect? **[LO 23.2]**

Tools of Choice Architecture

In this section we explore techniques that choice architects use to structure the decisions that people face. Remember that we're discussing methods—not necessarily endorsing the outcomes.

Commitment devices

LO 23.3 Explain how demand for commitment devices can be rational.

In a simple world, we usually assume that having more options is a good thing. Typically, there is no cost to ignoring options you don't like. So, in the best-case scenario, you gain new, good options; in the worst-case scenario, you ignore all the new, bad options and are in the exact same spot you were before.

However, understanding time inconsistency shows us why someone might rationally want to limit her own options. Assume you want to start a diet in a week, but you know that your future self will be tempted to keep putting off the diet. You don't quite trust yourself to make the right choice. So, you might want to take actions now to make sure there won't be any junk food in the house next week. By limiting your food options, you make it harder for your future self to make bad choices.

In the "Behavioral Economics" chapter we saw some examples of tools that allow people to voluntarily restrict later choices so they can make better decisions in the future: setting personal deadlines for long-term assignments, signing up for a savings account that requires regular deposits, or installing a browser extension that limits your access to time-sink websites.

commitment device a mechanism that allows people to voluntarily restrict their choices in order to make it easier to stick to plans

These voluntary mechanisms are **commitment devices**. They allow people to voluntarily restrict their choices in order to make it easier to stick to plans. Some commitment devices are completely informal—such as not buying junk food this week so that you won't have ready access to it next week when you intend to start your diet. Other commitment devices are formal policies and products. For instance, salaried workers can sign up to have their employers automatically deduct pension contributions from future paychecks.

Commitment devices are an example of using choice architecture to help people overcome temptation. Some commitment devices have strong commitments that are hard to get out of, and some have weak commitments that are easier to change. Neither is inherently better than the other. Rather, specific people and situations call for different types of commitment. SMarT is a weak commitment device; it commits you to a savings plan, but it's easy to reverse the decision later. One way of seeing the economic insight is to think about commitment devices as methods to increase the price of your vices or lower the price of your virtues.

Information campaigns and disclosure rules

Because choices are hard and people have limited processing capacity, we often rely on rules of thumb. Rules of thumb help us translate complicated information into a simpler and more familiar framework. A rule of thumb is an example of a **heuristic**—a mental shortcut that helps us make decisions. Some such rules of thumb can be entirely personal. For example, one person we know always goes with the spicier option when facing unknown food choices in a new restaurant. However, researchers have found there are several common heuristics that many people use to make choices.

heuristic a mental shortcut for making decisions

One popular heuristic is *anchoring*—estimating unknown quantities by starting from a known "anchor" point. Suppose you were asked to estimate the cost of a flight from Omaha to New Orleans for Thanksgiving vacation. You might start by thinking of a figure you happen to know that is somewhat related—say, the cost of a flight from Chicago to Houston. You then would do something to that figure—say, add a bit, because you're not sure how far apart Omaha and New Orleans actually are, and you know that flights are generally more expensive around Thanksgiving. It's a rough way of making a guess, but you'll probably be closer than someone who has no idea what any plane tickets cost, and so has no anchor point.

However, research shows that people also tend to latch onto any nearby number as an anchor point, without even realizing it. Suppose we asked, "Guess how much an Omaha to New Orleans flight costs. Is it more than $200?" You might think, "Surely it's got to be more than that . . . say, $300?" But if we asked, "Guess how much an Omaha to New Orleans flight costs. Is it less than $600?" you might think, "Gee, that does sound like a lot. . . . Is it $500, perhaps?" The question hasn't changed, but suggesting an anchor has changed your guess.

Anchoring can bias choices in some predictable ways. Think of how charities solicit donations. Nonprofits often send fundraising requests in the mail, with suggestions of amounts to contribute. People who get a solicitation with boxes suggesting donations of $50, $100, or $500 will tend to give more than if the boxes suggested $1, $5, or $10—even though the donor is also given the option to write in any amount they want instead of checking a box. A clever choice architect at a charitable organization can nudge people to give more simply by suggesting different amounts on a web page or a mail flyer. (Of course, there is a balance to be struck. If you set the anchor points too high, you risk scaring people away from donating at all.)

Choice architects can also affect the choices that people make by nudging them toward the use of specific choices in particular situations. For example, the Environmental Protection Agency (EPA) has for decades required car manufacturers to use a standard-format sticker disclosing the city and highway gas mileage of each car model. However, the average person may not be able to translate gas mileage into facts that really matter to them: How much might I spend on gas each year? How much gas will I need to drive 100 miles? Recognizing the importance of translating this into helpful information, the EPA has updated the formatting of the stickers to try to help people make better choices.

New formatting of EPA stickers (bottom sticker) gives estimated annual fuel costs to nudge consumers toward vehicles that have better fuel efficiency.

Can presenting information differently also help people stay out of debt? In the 2007–2009 recession, for example, many families got into trouble from having run up too much debt on their credit cards. The federal government already required lenders to disclose detailed information about fees, interest rates, and so on. But many people do not read in detail, or do not understand, the lengthy sections of small print on the credit-card application and monthly statements. Recognizing this problem, Congress passed the Credit Card Accountability, Responsibility, and Disclosure Act (CARD Act), which went into effect in 2010. It requires credit-card bills to state the interest rate and other terms of the card, and also to translate that information in ways that customers will understand. For example, all credit-card bills are now required to tell you how long it will take to pay off the full balance if you only pay the minimum amount. They also must tell you how much you would have to pay each month to pay off your balance within three years.

Even more than credit-card companies, "payday lenders" are often accused of not providing the information that would help their clients make informed choices about whether to use their services. Payday lenders provide high-fee, high-interest, short-term loans meant to help people pay for expenses until their next paycheck arrives. If these loans aren't paid off quickly, the costs add up fast. Recently, researchers have tried to figure out whether borrowers really understand what they're getting into when they take out payday loans. To find out what happened, see the Real Life box "Is payday lending predatory?"

REAL LIFE

Is payday lending predatory?

You've run out of money, and it's only halfway through the month. What can you do? You can visit a "payday lender" who will give you a cash loan that you are supposed to repay when payday rolls around in a couple of weeks.

Payday lenders commonly charge fees on the order of $15 for every $100 borrowed. If you think $15 doesn't sound like a lot of money, you may be falling prey to a psychological bias known as the *peanuts effect*—the tendency to discount small sums, even when they are large *relative* to the total amount in question. In fact, that $15 fee translates into an annual interest rate of about 400 percent APR, about twenty times a typical credit-card rate. The fact that payday lenders charge such high rates has led some critics to conclude that uninformed borrowers are being suckered into making poor financial decisions. *For more about whether payday borrowers are making an irrational choice, continue reading by scanning the QR code near the end of the chapter or by going online.*

Default rules

LO 23.4 Describe how default rules affect people's choices and the implications for policy.

Earlier, we noted that people tend to stick with the current or starting option in many choice situations. Even if they're completely free to change things, they often don't. If your employer starts you off with a basic retirement plan, for example, you're more likely to stick with it than you would be to choose it yourself from a whole set of options. We call this starting option a **default rule**; it defines what will automatically occur if someone fails to make an active decision otherwise.

default rule a rule defining what will automatically occur if a chooser fails to make an active decision otherwise

For example, many workers have retirement savings accounts called 401k accounts; some employers offer to match their employees' contributions to the accounts. Commonly, companies will add an amount equal to half of what an employee adds, up to some percent of their salary. It's usually a good deal: The matching contribution from the company is "free money," and you can defer paying taxes on it until you withdraw from the account. However, signing up for a 401k retirement account usually requires filling out paperwork, and a large fraction of people who are eligible for such a plan simply fail to enroll. In many cases, the default is "no contribution," and lots of people stick with this default.

Choice architects suggest a simple solution: Change the default option so that all new employees are automatically enrolled. Those who don't want to put money into a 401k account can still opt out, and those who do want to won't have to both filling out forms.

The idea of changing behavior by changing default rules has been applied in unexpected places. For an example, see the Real Life box "Who doesn't want to be an organ donor?"

REAL LIFE

Who doesn't want to be an organ donor?

Over 110,000 people in the United States are currently waiting to receive a donated organ, like a healthy kidney or lung. Many transplants do take place (about 30,000 each year), but over 9,000 people die each year while waiting for an organ. On the face of things, it's hard to see why there is such a mismatch between supply and demand. The vast majority of Americans say they support organ donation. Since many people die with healthy organs every year, the supply of organs for transplants should be plentiful. But it's not.

A big part of the reason lies in how people are asked about organ donation. The rules governing organ donation differ from state to state. In most cases, when people receive or renew their driver's licenses, they are asked if they would like to be a donor. In other words, people have to actively opt-in to being an organ donor; the default is to *not* be a donor. The result is that only 37 percent of adults are registered donors, in contrast to the 90 percent who say they support organ donation.

Some policy-makers have suggested a different system. Why not simply require people who *don't* want to be organ donors to opt out? This system, often called *presumed consent*, sets donation as the default option. Countries with an opt-out system have a startlingly higher rate of organ donation. Germany has an opt-in system, and only about 12 percent of its population registers to donate. Contrast that rate with its neighbor Austria, which has an opt-out system and where 99 percent of the population is registered to donate. In Belgium, kidney donation doubled within three years after presumed-consent legislation passed.

Researchers have found similar results in studies in the United States. They divided people into two groups. Each group was told to imagine they had moved to a different state and needed to make a decision about whether to be an organ donor. For one group, the default was to be a donor. Over 80 percent of people in this group stayed with the default. In the other, the default was to not be an organ donor. Only 50 percent stayed with that default. A simple change of the default rule was enough to cause a 30 percentage point difference in the number of (hypothetical) registered donors.

Even without changing the default rule, subtle differences in the way people are asked about organ donation are correlated with big differences in outcomes. In the states with the highest donation rates (60 to 80 percent), at the time when you receive or renew your driver's license, employees of the Department of Motor Vehicles are required to ask whether you want to be an organ donor. In the states with the lowest rates (such as Michigan, with a 23 percent donation rate), applicants have to volunteer that they want to be an organ donor, or find a checkbox deep in the driver's license renewal forms. When it comes to figuring out who wants to be an organ donor, the answer depends on how you ask the question.

Sources: http://www.econlib.org/library/Columns/y2009/Tabarroklifesaving.html; http://optn.transplant.hrsa.gov/; http://nudges.org/2010/10/10/how-required-choice-for-organ-donation-actually-works-in-practice/; http://www.dangoldstein.com/papers/DefaultsScience.pdf; http://www.hks.harvard.edu/fs/aabadie/pconsent.pdf.

Framing choices

LO 23.5 Describe how framing affects the way people process information and its implications for policy.

We have seen already in this chapter some examples of how the *framing* of choices can affect people's decisions. In fact, marketers in private companies knew this long before behavioral economists came along and started talking about "nudges" and "choice architecture." As we saw in the "Monopolistic Competition and Oligopoly" chapter, advertisers know that *framing* a product matters: Associating the product with young, beautiful people partying on a tropical island will cause more people to buy it, even if the product has nothing to do with being young, beautiful, or on a tropical island. The ways that framing can be used to influence people's choices are diverse. We'll focus on two that are particularly relevant for public policy-makers: social norms and loss aversion.

If you were a policy-maker in charge of persuading people to pay their taxes, how would you go about it? You could run a campaign informing them about fines for non-payment, but it turns out there's an even more powerful way to persuade them: Inform them that almost everyone else pays their taxes. Researchers have found that when you frame choices in terms of *social norms*—that is, what others do—people tend to go along with the majority. Most of us don't like to feel that we are outliers.

Pressure to conform to social norms can be a double-edged sword for choice architects, though. If you were charged with increasing voter turnout among the young, you might want to raise awareness of the problem by talking about how "only about 20 percent of young people voted in the last election." Unfortunately, this approach might actually make the problem worse. Hearing this, young people may conclude, "So it's no big deal if I don't vote—no one else is doing it either."

Some creative researchers wrestled with a similar problem as they tried to harness the power of social norms to reduce home-energy consumption. The results, described in the From Another Angle box "Turn down the AC for a smiley face," might surprise you.

FROM ANOTHER ANGLE
Turn down the AC for a smiley face

Americans spend a lot on energy to heat and cool their homes. This isn't necessarily a "bad" choice. Still, many people say they want to use less energy, and energy companies have tried many techniques to encourage them to follow through. They may increase prices during periods of peak energy use, or ask people to commit to reducing their consumption. One study found that simply asking people to set goals for their own energy use caused a reduction of 4 to 7.5 percent. Providing people with feedback on how well they did increased the reduction to 12 percent.

A group of researchers wondered if there might be an easier, cheaper way. What if we harnessed the power of social norms to frame people's choice about how high to crank up the air conditioning? What if we simply tell people if they're using more electricity than their neighbors?

One such experiment was conducted in San Marco, California. Hundreds of households received notices telling them how much energy they had consumed in the last two weeks relative to the average energy consumption in their neighborhood. Sure enough, in response to this information, households that had been consuming more than average reduced their usage. Unfortunately, though, households that discovered they had been consuming less than average actually *increased* their usage! In other words, both high- and low-use consumers moved toward the middle, an outcome that researchers refer to as the "boomerang effect." Maybe customers who discovered they were low-use felt able to indulge themselves a bit more by turning up the AC. Or maybe people simply like to do whatever everyone else is doing, for better or worse.

This was a head-scratcher. How could the energy company nudge high-use customers to use less electricity, without inadvertently also nudging low-use customers to use more? The answer turned out to be very, very easy: The researchers added a smiley face to the notice for households consuming less than average. It added a frowny face for households consuming more than average. The reduction by high-use customers increased, and the boomerang effect among low-use customers disappeared.

While people's most basic impulse is to be average, you can overcome that impulse. You just have to find a way of signaling to them that it's good to be better than average.

Sources: Hunt Allcott, "Social norms and energy conservation," *Journal of Public Economics* (2011), DOI:10.1016/j.jpubeco.2011.03.003; P. W. Schultz, J. Nolan, R. Cialdini, N. Goldstein, and V. Griskevicius, "The constructive, destructive, and reconstructive power of social norms," *Psychological Science* 18 (2007), 429–434.

We have already seen a couple of examples of how choice architects can use the idea of loss aversion: the SMarT program's tying of saving to future pay raises, and the difference between a "cash discount" and a "credit-card fee." Sometimes, what constitutes a loss versus a gain depends on your perspective. A study of law schools and student debt found that the combination of framing and loss aversion is so potent, it can change perceptions of gain versus loss even for major life choices like what career to choose after you get your degree. For details, see the Real Life box "Scholarships, debt forgiveness, and public service."

REAL LIFE

Scholarships, debt forgiveness, and public service

Perhaps you've heard this story before: A young, optimistic law-school graduate wants to use her newly minted degree to save the earth or provide legal services for the poor. But when she finds that the lifestyle of an environmental lawyer or public defender involves living in a tiny cramped apartment and eating brown-bag lunches, she heads to a higher-paying private firm serving corporate clients.

Don't be too hard on her, though. She may simply be worried about paying off her debt. In a nationwide survey of law students, 66 percent said they wouldn't consider a low-paying "public-interest" job due to the need to pay off their debt from law school. To encourage more of their graduates to take public-interest jobs, some law schools offer "income-contingent loan repayment assistance" programs. That is a fancy way of saying that the school promises to help pay off the loans of anyone who goes into a public-interest job after graduation.

New York University Law School experimented with an interesting twist, to see how framing would affect these career decisions. *To learn more, continue reading by scanning the QR code near the end of the chapter or by going online.*

✓ CONCEPT CHECK

❏ What is a heuristic? **[LO 23.3]**
❏ Why does status-quo bias imply that default rules are important? **[LO 23.4]**
❏ How do choice architects use social norms to frame choices? **[LO 23.5]**

Conclusion

Advertisers know that sales depend on more than delivering an appealing economic proposition. Clinching the deal often depends on hitting the right psychological buttons. Recently economists have also started bringing psychology into their problem-solving approach, and it's delivering practical ways to help people make choices that they are less likely to regret.

Choices are often influenced by the way that options are presented. Almost any presentation subtly pushes people toward one option or another, so it's difficult for choice frameworks to be truly neutral. In this chapter, we described how "choice architects can present options in a way that helps people overcome biases and voluntarily make choices they are happier with.

We've walked through some of the tools that choice architects can use to "nudge" people toward better decisions. Often, these nudges are simple and inexpensive: changing the wording or increasing the clarity of information provided to people; redefining default options; or offering people ways to commit to a desired course of action. Used thoughtfully, nudges can help companies earn more profit, and can help policy-makers achieve economic and social goals. One of the most striking lessons from behavioral economics is that small changes in choice architecture can sometimes lead to big changes in behavior.

 ◄ Mobile Window on the World—Scan this code with your smartphone to find more applications of the chapter content. (Need a barcode reader? Try ScanLife, available in your app store.)

Visit your mobile app store and download ► the Karlan and Morduch Study Econ app.

Key Terms

choice architecture, p. 557

nudge, p. 557

time inconsistency, p. 559

status-quo bias, p. 560

endowment effect, p. 561

loss aversion, p. 561

commitment device, p. 562

heuristic, p. 562

default rule, p. 564

Summary

LO 23.1 Define choice architecture, and explain how nudges can influence individual decision making.

Choice architecture is the design of the environment in which people make decisions. It matters because evidence shows that people's decisions are influenced by the way in which options are presented to them. Although the idea that people are rational utility-maximizers is a useful simplifying assumption, we know that people also make mistakes in their efforts to increase their own well-being. They choose options that they themselves would agree were not the right ones to pick. A nudge is an aspect of choice architecture that affects people's behavior without coercing them or fundamentally changing the economic incentives they face. Nudges can be used to help people bypass their own shortcomings to make better choices.

LO 23.2 List and explain several ways in which human decision making does not conform to the model of full information and rational choices.

People make mistakes in some common and predictable ways. Time inconsistency—a situation when we change our minds about what we want simply because of the timing of the decision—helps us explain procrastination and temptation. People also have limited ability to process information. They are more likely to make mistakes when the decisions they face are complicated, unfamiliar, or for which the relationship

between available information and the outcomes that actually matter is unclear.

In general, people have trouble with change, tending to prefer the status quo, avoiding losses, and ascribing more value to things they own than things they don't. Finally, decisions are influenced by the way in which options are presented, including minor details like phrasing.

LO 23.3 Explain how demand for commitment devices can be rational.

Commitment devices are strategies and tools that allow people to commit to make good choices in the future by voluntarily restricting their own options. If a person is aware of her own time inconsistency, she might prefer to have fewer options to choose from (or to make bad options more expensive); these strategies might help reduce the chance that she'll give in to temptation in the future. As a result, allowing people to voluntarily opt-in to a commitment device can actually help them increase their own well-being.

LO 23.4 Describe how default rules affect people's choices and the implications for policy.

People tend to stick with what they're given—whether that is a mug or a default option for investing their retirement funds. This fact means that default rules in products and policies, which define the option that will automatically occur if someone fails to make an active decision, have a power to influence people's choices. Default rules can nudge people toward particular outcomes.

LO 23.5 Describe how framing affects the way people process information and its implications for policy.

People respond to the way in which the choices are framed, even when that framing does not change the substance of the options available to them. Choice architects can encourage people to make certain choices through the context or way in which they present information. For instance, people are more likely to do something if they think everyone around them is also doing it; giving people information on how they compare to their peers can encourage or discourage behaviors.

Review Questions

1. Is instituting a $200 fine for anyone caught littering a nudge? Why or why not? **[LO 23.1]**

2. Suppose two parents present their 16-year-old with a list of the cars that they will allow him to buy. If the parents decide to add another vehicle to the list, is that affecting the choice architecture for their son? Why or why not? **[LO 23.1]**

3. Suppose you have plans to save 5 percent of your salary next year. Then your company goes bankrupt, your pay gets slashed by 30 percent, and you end up not saving at all. Is this an example of time inconsistency? Why or why not? **[LO 23.2]**

4. With his first paycheck, Steve decides to buy a car. After spending hours researching the many specifications each car has—from gas mileage to horsepower—he decides to give up trying to find the perfect car based on these metrics and buys the best-looking one on the first lot he visits. Explain one aspect of bounded rationality discussed in the text that this example exhibits. **[LO 23.2]**

5. At the website stickK.com (started by one of the authors of this book), you can sign up for a contract in which you promise to meet certain weight-loss targets each week, and forfeit money that you put up as stakes if you fail to meet those targets. Describe why a rational person might be willing to pay money if he does not lose weight, and how this constitutes a commitment strategy. **[LO 23.3]**

6. One contributor to the rational demand for commitment devices is the time-inconsistency problem. Explain how limited processing capacity might also contribute to the demand. **[LO 23.3]**

7. Many online subscription services have "automatic renewal" policies, in which they will automatically bill you for another year's subscription when your current one runs out. Why is this default rule a savvy business strategy on the part of the online company? **[LO 23.4]**

8. Explain the psychological bias that causes people's decisions to be affected by default rules or the endowment effect. **[LO 23.4]**

9. Imagine a public service announcement on television that is intended to scare kids away from using drugs. A big focus of the PSA is that a *lot* of teens are already on drugs. The directors of the PSA intend this statement to emphasize the size of the problem. Explain why this strategy for framing the anti-drugs message to teenagers could backfire. **[LO 23.5]**

10. Suppose you're trying to get your friends to go to dinner with you. Would it be wiser to frame the decision as costing only $5 more than the food they'd make for themselves, or that it will cost $5 less than every other restaurant around town? **[LO 23.5]**

Problems and Applications

1. In each of the following scenarios, determine whether the change in people's behavior is the result of a nudge or a substantive change in economic incentives. **[LO 23.1]**

   a. A country with a low birth rate decides to offer free public child care for kids under the age of five.

   b. A nonprofit organization runs a highly publicized campaign offering teenage girls a very small symbolic reward (say, $5) for each week that they stay in school, come to support group meetings, and avoid pregnancy.

   c. A country with a rapidly growing population levies steep fines on any family that has more than two children.

   d. A government agency runs an ad on television informing women about low-cost birth-control options.

2. Determine whether each of the following changes represents a shift in the choice architecture of a decision. [LO 23.1]

   a. After presenting the dessert menu to patrons, the waiter at a restaurant mentions that there's an additional option for dessert not on the menu.

   b. A restaurant presents dessert menus to patrons before they have eaten.

   c. A waiter shows patrons a menu without prices.

   d. A waiter asks patrons whether they would like to order more fries after telling the couple that the plate of fries is very small.

3. Label each of the following examples as a case of *time inconsistency, limited processing capacity, status-quo bias,* or *framing.* [LO 23.2]

   a. A person buys a nice bottle of wine for $50 and leaves it in the pantry for 20 years. At that point, the wine has aged and the value has appreciated to $250. Although he would never be willing to buy a bottle of the same wine for $250, the person plans to drink his old bottle rather than sell it.

   b. Every night, a person sets her alarm for 7 a.m. the next morning, and every morning, she hits the snooze button at least four times.

   c. People who are told the survival rate for a surgical procedure are more likely to undergo it than people who are told the death rate (even though the death rate is actually the same in both cases).

4. Determine whether each of the following represents loss aversion. [LO 23.2]

   a. Nearing retirement, an investor chooses investments with lower return and lower risk, because she wants to make sure she has a certain amount of money available in five years.

   b. A gambler refuses to play a game in which if heads shows up after a coin toss he will win $40, but if tails shows up he will lose $50.

   c. Offered a brand-new blanket that is twice as comfortable and cute as her old one—the only two criteria she cares about in a blanket—a toddler refuses to give up her old blanket.

   The following information applies to Problems 5, 6, and 7: Clocky™ is an alarm clock that rolls off your bedside table and runs away when you hit the snooze button. When the alarm goes off again,

Clocky will be hiding somewhere on the opposite side of your bedroom, so that you are forced to get out of bed to turn off the alarm.

5. Clocky is a commitment device to help overcome time inconsistency. Which of the following are the time periods over which someone might have inconsistent preferences and need Clocky's help? [LO 23.3]

   a. Between the time the person hits the snooze button and the time the alarm goes off again.

   b. Between the time the person sets the alarm the previous night and the time the alarm goes off.

   c. Between the time the person actually gets out of bed one morning and the time he sets his alarm for the next morning.

6. Which of the following are relevant areas of preference inconsistency that Clocky is able to help? [LO 23.3]

   a. The optimal volume for an alarm.

   b. What time to go to bed at night.

   c. What time to wake up in the morning.

   d. Whether an alarm should be placed on the bedside table or across the room.

7. How much should someone with time-inconsistent preferences be willing to pay for Clocky? [LO 23.3]

   a. Nothing, because a regular alarm will work just as well.

   b. Something, because Clocky increases his utility by getting him up at the right time.

   c. You'd have to pay him to use Clocky, because his utility is decreased by having to get out of bed and search around to shut off the alarm.

8. Which of the following is not a strictly rational reason for someone to be interested in a commitment device? [LO 23.3]

   a. The device can eliminate the time-inconsistency problem.

   b. By making the decision to restrict choices now, the person saves future effort in deciding among more, but undesirable, choices.

   c. Restricting choice now eliminates the possibility of considering other, potentially better choices that can't be foreseen right now.

   d. The device helps the person make the choice that she wants to make right now, but might not make in the future.

9. Which of the following are true statements about default rules? (You can choose more than one.) **[LO 23.4]**

  a. Defaults have staying power because opting out of them is typically very costly, requiring people to hire lawyers or prove to authorities that they have sufficient reason for choosing another option.

  b. The more difficult it is to opt out of the default option, the more likely people are to stick with it.

  c. One reason default options might have staying power is that people often equate "default option" with "recommended option."

  d. Default rules work to influence choices only if people are aware of the default option.

10. In which of the following examples would we see the influence of a default option? (You can choose more than one.) **[LO 23.4]**

  a. A doctor recommends continuing treatment, but the ultimate decision of whether to continue treatment is left up to the patient.

  b. A website automatically checks the option "share my activity with my friends on Facebook" when users sign up.

  c. Pets from an animal shelter are automatically spayed or neutered unless the owner would prefer them not to be.

  d. A mobile phone user has to enter a choice at start-up between installing a special feature or not. The user is informed that most people choose to install the special feature.

11. A group of people is offered two scenarios and asked which they would prefer: (A) a 3 percent wage decrease in a world with no inflation, or (B) a 3 percent wage increase in a world with 6 percent inflation. **[LO 23.5]**

  a. What is the increase or decrease in the real wage in option A? What about in option B?

  b. Knowing what you know about framing and loss aversion, which option do you expect more people to prefer?

  c. In light of your answer to b, if you were an employer trying to cut real labor costs, would you prefer to have some inflation or no inflation in the economy?

12. Choose the statement that people are more likely to choose based on the framing of the choice. **[LO 23.5]**

  a. Stock investment:
    i. Invest in a stock with low uncertainty of return.
    ii. Invest in a stock with high certainty of return.

  b. Car purchase:
    i. Buy a car that costs $20,000, which is $5,000 cheaper than the next level for that maker.
    ii. Buy a car that costs $20,000, which is $5,000 more expensive than the lower level for that maker.

  c. Movie choice:
    i. Go to the movie that 100 out of 150 people give a five-star rating.
    ii. Go to the move that 50 out of 150 people give less than a five-star rating.

  d. Choice of college class:
    i. Take a class in which 50 percent of students get an A.
    ii. Take a class in which 50 percent of students don't get an A.

Chapter Sources

Cass Sunstein and Richard Thaler, *Nudge* (New Haven: Yale University Press, 2008)

http://www.anderson.ucla.edu/faculty/shlomo.benartzi/smartjpe226.pdf

http://kgt.bme.hu/targyak/hagyomanyos/BMEGT30SZ84/irod/thaler_khaneman_knetsch_coase_theorem.pdf

http://bucks.blogs.nytimes.com/2010/02/22/what-the-credit-card-act-means-for-you/

http://ca.lifehacker.com/5780575/limit-visits-to-time+wasting-web-sites-and-give-your-willpower-a-break

Gilded Age, 170
immigration timeline, 381
income by race and gender, 525
income mobility, 519
income tax brackets in 2011, 488
labor laws, 391
largest social insurance programs, 523
nation of immigrants, 380
number of firms and employees, 255
number of workers, 37
population under poverty line, 506
poverty line and family size, 506
poverty line basis, 505–506
poverty rate over time, 507
quintiles of income, 515, 518
size relative to world market, 409–411
sources of immigration, 381
United States Chamber of Commerce, 421
United States Postal Service, 325
United States Supreme Court
Gratz v. Bollinger, 527
Regents of the University of California vs. *Bakke*, 527
Unit-elastic demand, 84, **85**
Unit-elastic supply, 91
Universal Music Group, 337, 351–357
market share, 339
University of North Carolina, 386
Used car market
lemons problem, 222
solution to lemons problem, 226–227
Utility, 157
and altruism, 172–173
basic idea of, 155–160
in decision making, 157–158
decision making based on, 153
and frames of reference, 170–171
in gift-giving, 154–155
indifference curves for, 178A
measuring, 158–159
and reciprocity, 173–174
and revealed preference, 158–160
and society, 169–174
sources of, 169
and status, 169–171
Veblen goods, 168
Utility function, 160
consumption bundles in, 178A
Utility maximization, 429, 477
with constraints, 162–165
and income change, 178I
and price changes, 178I–178J
rational, 157–158, 180
and selfishness, 171

V

Value; *see also* Expected value
created by markets, 110
creation by voluntary exchange, 98–100
determination of, 11
lost by taxation, 479
and price, 105–106
total surplus, 109
Value of the marginal product, 369
and demand curve for labor, 370–371
and demand for land, 384
and labor demand, 379
and number of workers hired, 370
Value over time
compounding, 240–241
interest rates, 239–240

present value calculation, 241–242
time preferences, 238–239
time value of money, 254A–254C
Vanderbilt family, 503
Variable cost curve, 267–269
Variable costs, 260; *see also* Average variable costs
description, 272
as explicit costs, 261
in perfect competition, 292
Variables
dependent, 46D
and direction of slope, 98A
graphs of one, 46A–46C
graphs of two, 46C–46F
independent, 46D
linear relationship, 76A
omitted, 14, 15
and slope, 46G–46J
Veblen, Thorstein, 170
Veblen goods, 168
Verizon Communications, 339
Vertical splits, 326
Voluntary exchange, 98–100
Voting system, ideal
Arrow's impossibility theorem, 542
and Condorcet paradox, 540–542
criteria for, 539
first-past-the-post, 539–540
pair-wise majority voting, 541–542
third-party problem, 542
Vouchers, 558

W

Wages
effect of increase in labor supply, 372–375
efficiency wage, 388–389
equilibrium, 375–376
minimum wage, 387–389
price of labor, 369
and profit-maximizing quantity of labor, 370
and social value, 386–387
and unions, 390
Waldfogel, Joel, 154
Wales, Jimmy, 462
Walfers, J., 442
Walmart, 273–274, 313, 384, 399
Wants, 5–6, 157
and choices, 155
of firms, 284
and gains from trade, 39
and information asymmetry, 221–222
in labor demand, 369
of monopoly, 314
of policy makers, 545
in production possibilities frontier, 27
and willingness to pay or sell, 101
Warner Music Group, 337, 351–354
market share, 339
Wealth of Nations (Smith), 42
Websites, top five for news, 46B
Welfare costs
of monopolistic competition, 345–346
of monopoly, 321–323
Welfare effects
of import quotas, 414
from net-exporters, 408
from net-importers, 407
of price ceilings, 128
of price floors, 132
Welfare reform legislation, 522

Welfare state
Bolsa Familia, Brazil, 548–549
conditional cash transfer programs, 522
definition, 521
income support, 521–522
in-kind-transfers, 522
means-tested programs, 523–524
progressive taxes to support, 521
social insurance, 520, 523
Wendy's, 339
West, Kanye, 337, 338
Wikipedia, 462
Willingness to pay/buy, 53, **100–101**
to avoid pollution, 432
and demand curve, 101–102
factors affecting, 78
versus haggling or bluffing, 104–105
and indifference points, 105
for Internet, 105–106
and price discrimination, 328–329
by tourists, 331
Willingness to sell, 59, **101**
versus haggling or bluffing, 104–105
and supply curve, 103–105
Witness Protection Program, 201
Wonder, Stevie, 337
Workers; *see also* Employees
cost of providing labor, 379
effect of taxes on, 480
labor supply decisions, 371–375
levels and types of human capital, 511
low-skilled vs. high-skilled, 416–417
market power from unions
response to higher wages, 373–375
and social value, 386–387
World Bank, 510
World Database of Happiness, 158–159
World market, 409–411
World price
effect of big economy on, 410–411
effect of quotas, 414
effect of steel tariff on, 412
higher than domestic price, 406–408
lower than domestic price, 405
World Trade Center attack of 2001, 55
World Trade Organization, 417
ruling on steel tariff, 413
Wright, G., 76

X

X-axis, 46C–46D
X-coordinates, 46D

Y

Yahoo!, 46A–46B
Yale University, 219–220
Y-axis, 46C–46D
Y-coordinates, 46D
Yellowstone National Park, 88–89
Yen, H., 254
Y-intercept, 76A
Yunus, Muhammad, 3–4, 6, 9, 10–11, 12, 322

Z

Zambia, 558
Zero economic profit, in perfectly competitive markets, 297
Zero profit, 343–344
Zero-sum game, 109
Zinman, Jonathan, 347
Zuckerberg, Mark, 514

Study Econ Mobile App

> *Have you ever wished there was a fun way to learn **key terms** and **concepts**?*

> *Do you need more help understanding **math**?*

> *Would you like to be more **efficient when studying** for exams?*

The Study Econ mobile app was built with the student in mind. You are on the go, and your study tools should be, too!

McGraw-Hill is proud to offer a new mobile study app for students learning economics from Karlan and Morduch's *Microeconomics*. The Study Econ app that accompanies your textbook will allow you to study on the go…whether you're waiting for a class to start, sitting on a bus, or just lounging on the couch.

Features of the Study Econ mobile app include:

- Flashcards of every key term and definition from the textbook, and are customizable by chapters.
- Basic math review for those pesky formulas we sometimes forget. For example, how do you calculate a percent increase? Not sure? Well, it's in the app!
- Customizable self-quizzes that allow for more practice and feedback.
- Explanation of potentially confusing topics to help you avoid common mistakes.
- Chapter summaries for an easy and quick review of a chapter's main concepts.

Visit your mobile app store and try Study Econ today! Search "Study Econ" and download Karlan and Morduch's *Microeconomics* mobile app.